D0348264

From the publishers of:

ELIE HALEVY A History of the English People in the Nineteenth Century

PIETER GEYL The Revolt of the Netherlands; The Netherlands in the Seventeenth Century

J. J. JUSSERAND English Wayfaring Life in the Middle Ages

JOHN FORTESCUE Wellington

J. WIGHT DUFF A Literary History of Rome

A HISTORY OF ENGLAND

A HISTORY OF
ENGLAND

PART ONE
From Prehistory to the Close of the Middle Ages
JOHN THORN
HEADMASTER OF REPTON SCHOOL

PART TWO
To the Accession of the Hanoverians
ROGER LOCKYER
LECTURER IN HISTORY AT GOLDSMITH'S COLLEGE IN THE
UNIVERSITY OF LONDON

PART THREE
To the Close of the Second World War
DAVID SMITH
HISTORY MASTER AT THE MANCHESTER GRAMMAR SCHOOL

LONDON
ERNEST BENN LIMITED

First published 1961 by Ernest Benn Limited
Bouverie House · Fleet Street · London · EC4
English Language Book Society edition 1963
First edition in this form 1964
© John Thorn · Roger Lockyer · David Smith
Printed in Great Britain

Foreword

THE AIM of this History of England is to tell an old story in as direct a manner as possible – not too difficult for the younger reader, not too elementary for the older one. We hope at the same time to have shown some of the ways in which the work of twentieth-century historians has modified the verdicts of such old friends as J. R. Green's *History*, and *Little Arthur's England* – those classics on which an older generation based its judgments of the past. There is no such thing, of course, as a final verdict. New evidence, or a shift of emphasis, forces us constantly to change our attitude. So also does the world around us. Fifty years ago the history of England was still the story of

> A land of settled government
> A land of just and old renown
> Where Freedom slowly broadens down
> From precedent to precedent.

This is, in its way, as good a summary of English development as any. It reflects the pride and confidence of Englishmen at the time – their pride in the examples of political and industrial development which this country had set before the world, and their confidence that this progress would continue and extend its unmixed blessings to every people in the world. A later age questions this simple view. We know that progress has not been uniform; that other political ideas have seized the imagination of the world; that the Industrial Revolution has produced social and political problems to be set against its advantages and to test the validity of cherished political rights. We have not lost our pride in the English achievement, but we take perhaps a less heroic view of it. To the older historians Montfort, Cromwell and Gladstone were the obvious heroes – men who had advanced the cause of liberty by identifying themselves with the voice of the people and leading the struggle against tyranny at home or abroad. They remain heroes for us. But we are less inclined to draw them in

7

simple blacks and whites. Was Montfort really a good House of Commons man? Is there nothing to be said for the Stuarts? And – in many ways the most important qualification of all – who were the 'People' of England whom these leaders were leading?

We do not claim to have answered all these questions, but we have at least been aware of them.

John Thorn
Roger Lockyer
David Smith

Contents

9

List of Maps

List of Tables

PART ONE

FROM PREHISTORY TO THE CLOSE OF
THE MIDDLE AGES

CHAPTER I

Britain Before the Romans

ABOUT the year 5000 B.C., the narrow belt of marshy land linking
the north-west of Europe with a peninsula beyond it sank
beneath the sea. The waters of what we now call the English
Channel and the North Sea joined together, and Britain became
an island.

The human population of the new island at that time was a few
hundreds, who lived by hunting with the rudely fashioned tools
they had laboriously chipped from the softer stones about them.
They lived in an age of slowly changing climate, as very gradually
the dry winds from the north and east were giving place to the
moisture-laden air from the Atlantic Ocean which in Britain still
prevails today. And as the climate changed, so did the vegetation
which surrounded these early inhabitants. Their remote ancestors
had roamed through grassland and pines rather like the modern
steppes of Russia and had hunted with ease and comfortable
excitement. But now, instead of the pine and the hazel woodland,
the increasing rainfall had brought dense, dank forests of alder
and oak springing from a tangled undergrowth, the haunt of wild
boar, wolf, and brown bear, dangerous and scarcely penetrable to
man. Food was now more difficult to get. Life was harder, and
possible only on the chalk downs and limestone hills whose soils

could not support the great mass of forest that now covered the lower ground.

But at the very time that this separation of Britain from the Continent was taking place, a revolution was occurring thousands of miles away in the Near East which was to change for ever the life of man. He was learning not merely to hunt and kill for his food, but to keep the animals who provided it in captivity, to feed them so that they could feed him. He was learning, too, to gather the seed of the grasses he found he could eat and scatter them about him to grow into the food he desired. He was learning, in short, to be a farmer.

Men with this momentous new knowledge did not cross the still widening-waters between Europe and Britain until about 2300 B.C. And when they came they had still to keep to the chalky and sandy soils where trees were few and where with their clumsy tools they could turn the ground over for their seeds to grow. So the area they settled on was very limited. They made their landings wherever there was a beach which seemed to lead to such sparsely wooded hills or up the rivers which wound among them. And once in the hills they walked along the ridges until they came to unoccupied ground, there to make their homes. Now it happens that there are many such chalk ridges in southern England – the South and North Downs, which join in Hampshire; the downs of Dorset; the Chiltern Hills which link up with the heights of East Anglia. At Salisbury Plain they all met in a spacious plateau. So it is not surprising that Salisbury Plain became the first notable centre of population in Britain, and even today signs of its importance to primitive man can be seen in its numerous small humps or mounds which are the burial places of Britain's first farmers. A modern farmer scorns its light soils and willingly gives it up to the training and manoeuvres of armies, for he has the equipment to dig the heavy, richer soils which were barred to early man.

These first settlers on the chalk ridges were men to whom the sea was a natural barrier. They crossed it only if they had to, if they needed fresh space in which to live; and they crossed it where it was narrowest and where they would not lose sight of land. But there were others for whom it held fewer terrors, men living along the coasts of Spain or Brittany. When they crossed, it was where

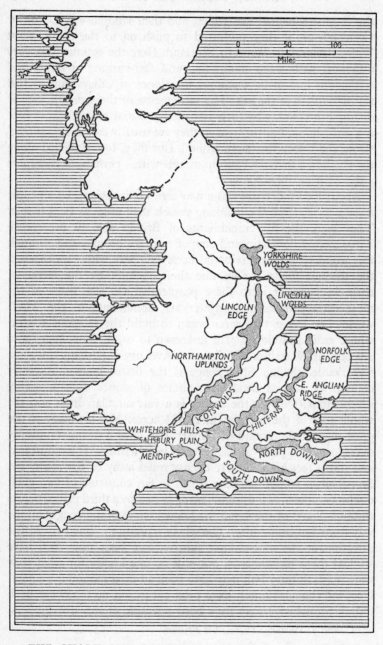

THE CHALK AND LIMESTONE UPLANDS OF BRITAIN

the English Channel was wider, and their landfall was Devon or Cornwall, or, if they preferred to push on to the north, West Wales, Ireland, or Western Scotland. Here the country was very different, with steep mountains and fast-rushing streams, and settlement had to be made on the slopes of valleys approached through inlets of the sea. The settlements of these people can be distinguished today by their remarkable burial places, whose roof is a great stone. For this reason they are usually called 'megalithic' (from the Greek for 'large stone'). But they, too, travelled along the chalk to Salisbury Plain to mingle with – perhaps to dominate – the existing inhabitants.

About 1900 B.C. there was a new series of invasions, by a people known to us, from the drinking vessels they used, as Beaker folk. They were the first inhabitants of Britain able to use metal. They melted down tin and copper to make bronze, and through this wonderful discovery could hack their way with axes through the thickest forests or subdue their enemies by the terror of their weapons. It is to these people that we owe some of the most extraordinary and mysterious monuments in the whole world. For it was they who began to build the religious centres whose exact function is still unknown to us, at Stonehenge and Avebury in Wiltshire. Of the two, Avebury is perhaps the most remarkable, though Stonehenge is the better known. Avebury consists of several concentric circles of stones each weighing several tons. Outside the stones is a vast circular ditch and the whole area of the monument is 28½ acres. Not far away is the great man-made mound of Silbury Hill, 'like a steamed pudding dished up for a giant' as has recently been written.[1] It is a hundred and thirty feet high. Nearly twenty miles away to the south lies Stonehenge, which before it began to fall consisted of two great circles of stones, two uprights being joined by a third placed across the top. Some of the stones we know to have been brought all the way from Pembrokeshire. The whole structure is lined up in the direction of the midsummer sunrise. For years now men have studied these monuments, but still no one knows for what they were used. Silbury Hill may have been a burial mound for a great king, but though tunnels have been cut into it no tomb has been found. Stonehenge may have been a temple of sun-worshippers,

[1] C. and J. Hawkes: *Prehistoric Britain*.

but of the nature of the worship we know nothing, nor why great stones had to be brought to it over the sea and rough country from the mountains of western Wales. Avebury may have been first and foremost a huge fortification. But why these vast stones? All we can say for certain about these places is that the men who built them were highly organized, intelligent, and driven to their labours by some tremendous force. At Stonehenge they were even subtle enough to make the stones wider at the top than at the bottom to prevent the illusion of foreshortening which we get if we look up at a building from the ground.

Stonehenge, like a medieval cathedral, was not the work of a single generation. It has been estimated that additions were made to it for some 500 years. But of one thing we can be certain. Its building had nothing whatever to do with the Druids, for they were a group of priests who had probably been in Britain only a few years when the Romans first came in 55 B.C.

After the invasions of the Beaker people, who must have come in considerable numbers and in many separate waves, the pace of immigration slowed. Between 1500 and 1000 B.C. Britain had few newcomers – though about 1450 a small group of intelligent and more knowledgeable people spread into Wessex and dominated the existing population. They brought more refined techniques of metalwork and made the last additions to Stonehenge, additions which show that they had come from lands where architecture – the planning of buildings – had been developed. Perhaps their original home was in the eastern Mediterranean – even it may be in the city of Mycenae in Greece where the slow, halting birth was beginning of one of the great civilizations of the world. There is one small piece of evidence at Stonehenge, discovered not many years ago, which supports this strange possibility. On some of the great stones there can be faintly traced the carving of bronze axe heads and of a dagger. Of this particular type of dagger there is no other carving known north of the Alps. But on one of the gravestones at Mycenae there is a carving of a warrior driving a chariot. In his hand he clutches a dagger. Except for one small detail it is exactly the same as that on the great stone on the Wiltshire downs. Throughout her long history Britain has had countless gifts from the great civilizations of the Mediterranean. It may be that this, on our most famous prehistoric monument, is the first.

It was about the year 900 B.C. that a large westward movement of races on the European continent, a movement at whose causes we can only guess, produced another invasion of Britain, by a people who are the first to have left to this island something more than material remains. These were the Celts, and they spoke a language of which the native tongues of Ireland, Wales and the highlands of Scotland are direct descendants. At first they came in small groups; but about 750 B.C. a big wave arrived who were to transform again the primitive agriculture of Britain. For they were people who had developed new ways of growing the cereal crops which were their chief source of food. Instead of the slow inefficient hoe, they used a plough drawn by two oxen and controlled from the back by a man. It was an elementary plough, which merely cut up top soil, and it could still do nothing with the heavy clays of the valleys. But it enabled its users to work definite fields and to grow enough for a steadily increasing population. Some of these field systems can still be seen today in Sussex and Hampshire or on Salisbury Plain.

The Celtic invasions continued for many centuries. About 500 B.C., some Celts arrived who brought knowledge of the use of iron to Britain – nearly a thousand years after its discovery in Asia Minor; and a hundred years after that came more groups who did more than merely use iron as tools and household vessels – they fashioned it into works of art which are still among the wonders of the world. We possess hand mirrors, shields, and fragments of swords which show a marvellous combination of exact drawing and fantastic imagination, in the interweaving of snake-like curves to make a complicated but symmetrical pattern. Some of these objects are in gold and studded with precious stones. Yet with all this love of creation went, in the Celts, a fierce fighting spirit. Their entry to Britain did not go unresisted, and much of their settlement was made only by pushing other peoples back by force to the highland areas of north and west Britain. They fought, too, among themselves, tribe with tribe, and, showing the need they must have felt for strong defences, they began to build the complicated hill forts whose remains can still be seen all over Britain. It was probably for protection that some of them chose not to live on dry land but to build houses on stilts above the waters of lake or marsh. Near Glastonbury in Somerset a whole village of such lake-dwellers has been excavated. It had over sixty huts of wattles, mud, and reeds; its inhabitants had on their doorstep a plentiful supply of wildfowl and fish and could while away their time with games of dice. Their currency was in iron bars, which they used not only for gambling but for trading in tin from Cornwall, lead from the Mendip Hills, or iron from the Forest of Dean. They were a thriving, prosperous, and creative community.

We know the names of many of these Celtic tribes, since it was they who first encountered the Romans when in 55 B.C. they made their first raid into Britain. The Parisii, for example, who gave their name to the capital of France, came up eastern England and settled in the East Riding of Yorkshire. To East Anglia came tribes whom the Romans knew as Iceni and whose queen, Boadicea (or Boudicca), was to lead the first big revolt against the Roman people. These peoples came from Gaul, like so many before them, and many came because behind them were new peoples pressing westward – the Germans. These Germans were one day to invade Britain themselves, and in a way to continue their slow inexorable pressure on the Celts. They were prevented from doing so now, however, by the power of the growing Roman Republic. It was in 58 B.C. that Julius Caesar struck out from the south-east corner of Gaul (which the Romans called 'provincia' – the province – and is now called Provence) determined to conquer the whole of it. Within three years he was on the Channel coast and looking across to the chalk cliffs of Britain to which so many of his enemies had gone. In 55 B.C. he determined to cross the Channel and see for himself how far his conquest could be extended. His first raid met heavy resistance, but in the following year, with a larger force, he came again, perhaps merely to punish and to exact tribute, perhaps in the hope of making a new colony. But the weather and the fierceness of the Celtic tribesmen was too much for him. He retired to the continent and was swept into a struggle for power among his own countrymen.

It was nearly a hundred years before the Romans came to Britain again, but in that time Britain was far from isolated. A new group of tribes, Celtic but with German blood in them, had begun to cross before Caesar came and now invaded in larger groups. These were the various tribes of the Belgae, settled before in northern

Gaul and the Low Countries. Like the Romans, they were resisted, but they nevertheless built up a group of petty kingdoms in the south-east of the country. In their ways of life they were more advanced than the older Celts. They used a heavy plough, with which at last the heavier soils of Britain's valleys could be tamed. They could make their pottery on the fast-spinning potter's wheel. And they had learned the use of coin, so much easier to handle than the iron bars of earlier Celts. They were masters, too, in the art of fortification, as can be seen at Maiden Castle in Dorset with its complicated pattern of ditch and earthen wall. Those tribes they did not conquer they nevertheless influenced, and one such, the Trinovantes, began to build on the site of what is now Colchester the first communal settlement in Britain which can be called a town – Camulodunum. Here ruled Cunobelin, the Cymbeline of Shakespeare's play and perhaps the Old King Cole of the nursery rhyme, trading freely with the Roman world, striking coins in his own image, and on the northern banks of the Thames setting up a trading station which one day would grow into the great city of London. He died in A.D. 41. Two years later came the mighty invasion of the Roman Emperor, Claudius.

With the coming of the Romans the pre-history of Britain ends and its history begins. For history, strictly speaking, is the knowledge of the past we gain from written records. All our scanty knowledge of the times before Caesar's invasions is gained, not from the written word, but from the study of material remains excavated by the archaeologist. It is a study of recent birth. A hundred years ago we knew little more about the inhabitants of Britain before the Romans than what Caesar himself told us. They were generally lumped together as Ancient Britons, wild men frighteningly painted with woad, magnificent drivers of war-chariots, urged on by fanatical Druid priests whose religion demanded perpetual human sacrifice enacted on the altar stone of Stonehenge.

The true picture, revealed by archaeology, is very different. But its pattern is strangely similar to what was to come after. From the very earliest times to the coming of the Normans in 1066, Britain was subjected to continual invasion from the continent of Europe. Its fertility and climate made it a desirable prize for westward-moving people for thousands of years. And each new wave of invaders found inhabitants already there and pushed them out of the gentle lowland zone into the highlands to the north and west, while other more occasional raiders entered the highlands direct from the sea. So the inhabitants of Britain were a rich and remarkable mixture, varying greatly in their race and ways of life. Only after the last great invasion, by William the Conqueror, could the process begin of creating a single people sharing one language and a common tradition and then themselves moving outwards to bring it to the rest of the world.

CHAPTER 2

Roman Britain

'IT WAS now near the end of the summer, and winter sets in early in those parts . . . Nevertheless Caesar made active preparations for an expedition to Britain, because he knew that in almost all the Gallic campaigns the Gauls had received reinforcements from the Britons. Even if there was not time for a campaign that season, he thought it would be of great advantage to him merely to visit the island, to see what its inhabitants were like, and to get to know the lie of the land, the harbours and the landing-places.'[1] The words are Caesar's own, as he describes what led him to make his first expedition to Britain in 55 B.C. His army was back in Gaul before the end of September, but he had seen enough to gauge the fighting qualities of the British tribes. His preparations for a second expedition were consequently far more elaborate, and in 54 B.C. he launched it. He gives no clue in his writings about the ultimate aim of this second crossing, but though it penetrated the country north of the Thames it, like the first, was back in Gaul before the end of September. It may be that conquest was not Caesar's aim. It may be that he was satisfied with the hostages and the favourable treaties he had won from the tribes of south-east Britain; for it was the common Roman custom to secure a frontier by making the tribes beyond it the allies or clients of Rome. In any case, developments in Rome itself took Caesar hundreds of miles from the Channel coast and he never returned. Civil wars rocked the Empire, and when order was restored by Augustus Rome's need was to consolidate the possessions she had rather than to add to them a remote and mysterious island in the far north-west.

But a further attempt was inevitable sooner or later. In A.D. 40 Cunobelin, king of the Trinovantes at Colchester, expelled his

[1] Caesar *De Bello Gallico*, trans. S. A. Handford.

son from his kingdom. The son went to Rome to appeal to the
Emperor Gaius Caligula for protection and to offer the submission
of the Trinovantes. Caligula was already mounting an expedition
on the coast of Gaul, but it never left Boulogne, since Caligula,
who was probably mad and certainly unpopular, had other things
to think about – including, it is said, making his horse a consul.
But his successor, Claudius, took up the idea of invasion more
seriously. He was a bookish, rather nervous, but able man who
clearly desired to perform some action that would increase his
prestige. He had legions to spare. Britain was known to be rich
in minerals. The British coastal tribes had for a long time been
raiding the continent and harbouring wanted rebels from Gaul.
And current notions of geography placed Ireland midway between
south-west England and Spain so that its capture would, the
Romans thought, open up a useful line of communication round
the outside of Gaul.

To the Roman legions, however, the idea of this new conquest
was not attractive and they refused for some weeks to embark.
The Britons soon heard of this and naturally thought that the
fiasco of Caligula's invasion attempt was going to be repeated.
They sent their army home and left the coast virtually undefended.
When, therefore, the Roman force of four legions, totalling perhaps
40,000 men, landed in the summer of A.D. 43, there were few
Britons to oppose them. Kent was rapidly conquered, a British
army was defeated in a stern two-day battle on the Medway, and
Claudius himself joined the legions when they paused on the
Thames. Soon Cunobelin's former capital at Colchester was in
Roman hands and the Emperor was able to receive the submission
of eleven kings, and also to order the laying out of a new city and
the building of a temple to himself as god, before returning to
Rome to enjoy his triumph and continue the studies that were
his first love.

By the year A.D. 50 the Roman legions securely held all the
country to the south and east of the Severn and Trent and were
already pressing beyond them. In the year 61 they had reached
north Wales and were striking at the isle of Anglesey and the
centre of the Druid cult, taking it with massacre after viewing
with fear and horror the wild fanaticism of the Celtic priesthood.
But in that same year the Romans had to face a sudden and

appalling danger when the East Anglian tribe of the Iceni rose
to avenge the scourging of their queen Boudicca and the dis-
honouring of her daughters. 'The Britons,' wrote the Roman
historian Tacitus, 'make no distinction of sex in their leaders.' But
they could have found no male leader fiercer than this redoubtable
woman. 'They hunted down the Roman troops in their scattered
posts,' wrote Tacitus, 'stormed the forts and assaulted the colony
[Colchester] itself, in which they saw their slavery focused.' They
tore down the great symbol of Roman mastery, the temple to
Claudius, and marched on the growing trading centre of London.
Excavators in the city still come across the ash to which Boudicca's
warriors reduced the town and the skeletons of those she massacred. Retribution inevitably followed, though the queen herself
took poison to escape execution. But henceforth Roman rule was
more lenient, under a milder governor, sent – strangely enough it
may seem – by the Emperor Nero.

The Romans had, by the year 75, increased their area of occupation as far as York and Chester in the north, Caerleon and
Wroxeter on the Welsh border, and Exeter in the west. And in
77 the greatest of all Roman governors, Agricola, arrived in the
island. His military achievements were impressive, for he conquered Wales and pushed north well into the Scottish highlands,
building a line of forts across the narrowest part of England, from
the Tyne to the Eden, along the line of the future Roman wall.
He also tried to 'romanize' the native peoples, to make them
adopt Roman dress and customs, to encourage them to live in
towns and enjoy the luxuries to which Romans were accustomed.
But civilization is not adopted by cleanliness and good tailoring.
As Agricola's son-in-law, Tacitus, scornfully wrote: 'In place of a
distaste for the Latin language came a passion to command it. In
the same way, our national dress came into favour and the toga
was everywhere to be seen. And so the Britons were gradually led
on to the amenities that make vice agreeable – arcades, baths,
and sumptuous banquets. They spoke of such novelties as
"civilization" when really they were only a feature of enslave-
ment.'[1]

Nevertheless, behind the turbulent military frontier where the
four legions kept watch, the Britons were beginning to enjoy a

[1] Tacitus: *Agricola*, trans. H. Mattingly.

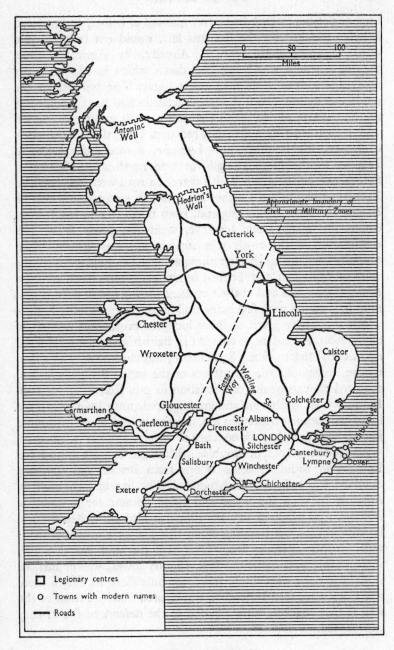

ROMAN BRITAIN

time of prosperity they had never guessed at before, and material benefits which, after the Romans left, would not be met again until the nineteenth century. Already, by Agricola's time, the road system was being laid down which is still an easily recognizable feature of road maps today. The purpose of the roads was military, and, though Colchester had been intended as the first centre of the island's government, it was from London with its better position that they radiated. From the Kentish ports of Dover, Richborough, and Lympne, a road led straight to London. From there, Watling Street went north-west to Wroxeter, the fortress on the north Welsh march; a road went due north to York; another led to Colchester; a fourth swept south-west to Exeter. Running across England, from north-east to south-west, connecting many roads together, went the Fosse Way. The engineering of the roads was superb and the surface, when properly kept, better than anything achieved in England until the work of Macadam and Telford in the early nineteenth century. Along these roads and at their crossings many towns were beginning to grow up with fine stone buildings, often centrally heated, which must have given to those lucky or prosperous enough to enjoy them, a standard of comfort in British winters not achieved again until modern times. Such luxury was enjoyed only by a few, by the Roman officials themselves or the native Britons who had acquired enough wealth or education to gain Roman citizenship. But improved agriculture and growing trade must have helped the lot of the humbler tribesmen too, unless, through crime or capture in war, he had sunk to the bondage of slavery.

About the year 100, troubles within the Empire forced the Romans to withdraw some troops from Britain and southern Scotland was temporarily abandoned. The line of forts built by Agricola between the Tyne and Eden became for a time the frontier. And when, in 123, the Emperor Hadrian visited Britain, he commanded the building along this line of a great defensive wall, seventy-six miles long. Over half the wall was of stone, some sixteen feet high; the rest, slightly lower, was of turf. In front of it was a wide ditch, and every mile along its length there was a defensive fort. Vegetation was cleared from the front of the wall so that attackers were exposed to the defenders' fire as they approached.

Twenty years after the building of Hadrian's wall, however, the frontier was again pushed northward, and another, less elaborate, turf wall was built from the Forth to the Clyde. For fifty years this wall was garrisoned, but in the year 190 a civil war broke out in the Empire, the first of many which for Britain were to have similar effects. There was no law of succession to the imperial throne, and it is therefore not surprising that the death of an emperor should frequently lead to violent disputes. Sometimes these disputes were confined to the capital itself, but often they involved the whole Roman world, as local generals with the devoted support of their own legions were acclaimed in their own provinces and led their troops towards Rome to make their claim good by the show or the use of force. Every such conflict brought a weakening of frontiers, and every weakening of a frontier brought attacks by the tribes outside, jealous of the life and wealth within and eager for opportunities of plunder. In the year 193, one Albinus, a general stationed in Britain, led his legions across the Channel to fight for his claim, denuding the Forth-Clyde wall of troops. The Caledonian tribesmen, now often called 'Picts', broke through at once, overran the Scottish lowlands, and reached Hadrian's wall, now wide open and undefended.

It was Septimius Severus, Albinus's successful rival for the imperial throne, who came to restore the situation. The Pictish tribesmen were driven back, but no attempt was made to win back the lost lands of the Scottish lowlands. Hadrian's Wall was rebuilt and its defences made stronger, but henceforth it remained as the true Roman frontier. Scotland was never penetrated again, and it remained unconquered by the south until the campaigns of Oliver Cromwell over fifteen hundred years later.

The work of Septimius Severus in the first decade of the third century inaugurated the most peaceful and splendid period of Roman Britain. For although at this time the Rhine and Danube frontiers of the Empire came under strong and constant pressure from the German tribes beyond them, Britain lay secure behind her wall and its outlying forts. This was the great century of villa life, and a time of extensive rebuilding in the towns.

The Roman villa was not merely a dwelling-house. It was often the centre of a complete economic unit, where slaves and freemen worked on the land or in what amounted to small industries. In some there are signs of metal work, in others of cloth making, in others of the tanning of hides. The villa owners were sometimes retired Roman soldiers or administrators, but more often they were native Britons who had adopted completely the ways of life and outlook of their conquerors, decorating their walls and floors with pictures from Greek and Roman myths or the works of Virgil and Ovid. The villas varied in size, but as in later centuries new generations of owners added new wings and new refinements – baths, verandas, fountains, ornamental courtyards, or outbuildings to house dependent workers – so they grew to the size of small palaces.

Towards the end of this third century, however, a new danger to this settled life of country and town began to appear, a danger which eventually was to engulf and stamp it out for ever. From the North Sea coasts of Germany, just to the east of the Roman Gallic frontier, came small groups of raiders, stealing up the river estuaries or landing on the sandy shores, plundering, and slipping away. They were the Saxons. Such a menace had they become by about 290, that a line of forts was built along the coast, from Norfolk to the Isle of Wight, and a special officer, called the Count of the Saxon Shore, was appointed to deal with them. At the same time, raiders from Ireland and Scotland began to appear on the west coasts. It was impossible for more troops to be sent from Rome, for all along the imperial frontier the menace of invasion was increasing, and unified control was so difficult that the Emperor Constantine, after founding in 330 the great new capital in the east which bore his name, appointed a special co-Emperor to deal with the dangerous situation in the West. In the face of these threats along its lengthy frontier, it is surprising that the Roman Empire lasted in the West as long as it did. That it survived until 410 is largely due to the continual flow of barbarians who came into its frontiers not to destroy it but to enjoy and preserve its blessings. But this influx of barbarian soldiers seeking careers rather than conquests had its own dangers, for civil wars between rival provincial armies became even more frequent. In 367, one such conflict caused yet another exodus of the Roman legions in Britain, and it was a signal for a combined attack by Saxons and Picts which broke through Hadrian's Wall and penetrated deeply into regions free from such violence for cen-

turies. Once more, the intervention of an efficient soldier, Theodosius, shored up the cracking defences; but it was the beginning
of the end. In the year 410, the western emperor, Honorius, a son
of Theodosius, sent a message to the Britons informing them that
henceforth they must protect themselves. In the year he wrote,
Rome itself was sacked by Alaric, the king of the Visi-Goths, and,
shortly after, the Roman legions left. The great wall crumbled.
The forts of the Saxon shore were destroyed one by one. And
Roman Britain slowly died.

Exactly what the Romans left to Britain after these three and a
half centuries of occupation cannot be measured. Their roads are
an obvious legacy, even today. Their towns, though they slowly
fell to ruin under the new invasions, remained as sites for new
and greater cities. Their language all but perished, leaving only a
few words among the Celtic tribesmen who were pushed into the
northern and western extremities of the island. But, most important, they left their religion. Christianity had been made the
official religion of the Empire early in the fourth century, by
Constantine, and though Roman paganism did not lose its hold
over the Romano-Britons, the new faith spread so deeply among
the population that it was carried by them wherever they were
driven by the Saxon invaders. The story of Roman Britain can
well end with one of its greatest gifts to subsequent ages, the work
of St. Patrick.

Patrick was born some time at the end of the fourth century, the
son of an educated Romano-British official. At the age of sixteen,
he was carried off from his parents' farm somewhere in western
Britain by a band of Irish raiders. He was taken, a prisoner, to
the North of Ireland and for six years he tended the herds of his
masters. He had been born a Christian, and having escaped from
his Irish captivity and fled to Gaul he determined that one day he
would go back to his former captors and bring them to his faith.
One night he had a dream. He seemed to see a man whose name
was Victorious, who bore in his hand a bunch of letters. One of
them he gave to Patrick. It was from the Irish. 'I imagined,'
wrote Patrick later, 'that I heard in my mind the voice of those
who were near the wood of Fochlad, which is near the western
sea. And thus they cried: "We pray thee, holy youth, to come and
walk again among us as before." '

So, after more years of study, Patrick returned to Ireland, and from then until he died in 461 he worked among its people, organizing among them a Church whose members one day were to journey back to Britain, bringing again the faith of the last Romans to the new heathens who had come from Europe.

CHAPTER 3

The Coming of the English

WITH the departure of the Roman legions, the Dark Age descends on Britain. It was dark for those who lived in it, but above all it is dark for the historian, who now must rely on the testimony, not of civilized memoir writers, but of storytellers, for whom a story was worth telling for its drama and glory rather than its truth. One of these writers, a Welshman called Nennius, was quite honest about his methods. 'I have made,' he said, writing about A.D. 800, 'a heap of all I have found.' And what he had found was a mass of legend, tribal saga, and accidentally preserved fact. He lumped it together and called it the *History of the Britons*. The effect is much as we would get if we asked a man who had never looked at history since his schooldays to jot down what he remembered of it.

Nennius put his book together two or three hundred years after the events it describes, though he used fragments of much earlier writing. There is, however, one writer who lived during this Dark Age after the Roman departure. He was a British monk called Gildas. Some time about A.D. 547 he wrote a long, angry sermon to his fellow Britons, telling them that the horrors and woes they were now enduring at the feet of the pagan invader were the fault of their own sin, of the idleness and luxury they enjoyed or sought, of the wars they waged among themselves. It is not a history book at all. But it is a sign of our ignorance of these centuries that we have to weigh every sentence Gildas wrote.

Nennius and Gildas were Britons. What they described was a defeat. But the Angles and Saxons who came to make this island their own had their own versions of the story. For them it was a story of triumph. We are lucky here, for one of the Saxon writers was a genius who knew quite well when a story was true, when it was probably true, and when it was only a tradition. This man, the Venerable Bede, wrote his *Ecclesiastical History of the English Nation* about 732 in a monastery on the banks of the Tyne. He had, of course, many of the difficulties of a modern historian when he came to finding out what actually happened. In fact, for many pages, reluctantly and with his own suspicions, he was forced to copy out large pieces of Gildas.

A century and a half after Bede, in the reign of King Alfred, the Anglo-Saxon Chronicle was begun. It was to recount the deeds of the Anglo-Saxon peoples from their first landings onwards and then be kept up to date. But this chronicle, great and unique though it is, has its own difficulties. Its dates are unreliable. Enthusiastic monks would enter the numbers of the years in a column on the left of their page before the events were inserted. Then, when an entry spread over several lines, the column of years would have to be changed or rubbed out. There is scarcely a page of the chronicle without such corrections, some of them difficult to disentangle. Also, like most men of their time, the Anglo-Saxons never decided on what day of what month a year actually began.

Happily, we do not have to rely these days solely on these scraps of written record about this dark time when the Roman legions had gone. There is archaeology; and there is the evidence of place names. But both have severe limitations. Anglo-Saxon building in this early period, unlike Roman, was not of the kind to endure. Houses were of timber, wattles, or mud – long ago perished. Fortifications were seldom more permanent, though here and there some great rampart like the Wansdyke – which stretches from the hills near Newbury almost to the Severn and for much of its length is still visible – provides both answers and more puzzles. (It is still not certain whom it was to defend, and from what.) Most of the evidence for the archaeologist lies, as it does for pre-Roman Britain, in burial grounds; and here the modern investigators suffers from the clumsy zeal of the Victorians, who sometimes seem to have attacked the sites like a soldier frenziedly digging a slit-trench. And one can anyway find out only a little of a people from the way they bury their dead.

Place names, too, sometimes produce as many questions as they do positive clues. Some are easy – the Roman ones for example.

Most people know that the Latin *castra* becomes -chester, -cester, or something like it. But is Chichester really named after Cissa, the son of Aelle, whom the chronicle tells us founded the kingdom of the South Saxons? We shall never know.

Recently, historians have found one particular kind of place-name especially interesting. It is a name connected closely with the fifth century, where other evidence is most scanty. There are numbers of places ending in *-ing* or *-ings*. Now we know that the Anglo-Saxons, when they added the word *-ingas* to the name of a leader, meant to denote his followers. Hastings, for example, or *Haestingas* as it was, meant the place occupied by the followers of Haesta. There is a widely held theory that wherever we find such names they show a place that was settled by the invaders very early in the invasion period, when they were coming in small groups and remaining under local leaders. And indeed the area covered by such names is, with some exceptions, the area where we most frequently find pagan burials, along the river valleys and coasts of southern and eastern England. We can probably learn more of the early progress of the Anglo-Saxons from this than from all the written evidence there is.

Still, the picture is faint. Here and there a small detail is sharp where a larger outline is scarcely to be seen. But it seems that after the legions left, about the year 410, the same year that Rome herself was sacked by Alaric the Goth, petty rivalries and feuds broke out all over Britain, so that she lay feeble before any outside threat that appeared. At first, the most dangerous enemies were the Picts and the Welsh, living beyond or inside the old military area of the Romans. They had already broken in, in 367, when the intervention of the great Theodosius had repulsed them. Now they swarmed in again, and the Britons were powerless to hold them for long, intent as they were on their own local quarrels and ambitions. The central government collapsed. Local chieftains seized power, held it, were toppled. One such, abler or more ruthless than the rest, called by Gildas a 'proud tyrant', by Nennius 'Vortigern', decided to use the old Roman technique of employing foreign mercenaries. He appealed across the sea to the peoples living along the north-west German coast, peoples who already, for many years, had been raiding the eastern coasts of

Britain. So came to Britain, in eager answer to the call, the leaders whom Bede calls Hengist and Horsa. The date was about 450.

The newcomers were not content to be mercenaries. After giving Vortigern effective aid against his enemies, they turned on him. In the words of the Anglo-Saxon Chronicle: 'In this year [455] Hengist and Horsa fought against Vortigern the kiug at a place which is called Aegelsthrep [Aylesford in Kent]; his brother Horsa being there slain, Hengist took command, and Aesc his son.' And Bede claimed that a monument was set up to the dead Horsa which could still be seen in his day.

From now on, the Angles and Saxons came not to rob and plunder, but to stay. As previous invaders had found, the eastern parts of Britain, with long deep estuaries of slow-flowing rivers, were very vulnerable. It is along the banks of these rivers that the earliest settlements are found. But the progress was gradual. There is no sudden single invasion of a large army, as with the Romans in A.D. 43, the Danish Great Army in 865, or the Normans in 1066. Instead, small groups filtered inland at suitable points, and the familiar English kingdoms were formed later, not by the design of men, but through the natural boundaries of the land itself.

Bede thought the invaders came from three great nations in Germany – Saxons, Angles, and Jutes. 'From the Jutes,' he wrote, 'are descended the people in Kent, and of the Isle of Wight, and those also in the province of the West Saxons who are to this day called Jutes, seated opposite to the Isle of Wight. From the Saxons . . . came the East Saxons, the South Saxons, and the West Saxons. From the Angles . . . are descended the East Angles, the Midland Angles, Mercians, and all the race of the Northumbrians, that is of those nations that dwell on the north side of the river Humber, and the other nations of the English.' Bede was such a careful writer that it is dangerous to disbelieve him, but today people think he had made it too simple, and that the races were far more mixed in their settlement here. And it is certain that when St. Augustine set foot in Kent in 597, Angles and Saxons, in spite of the names of their kingdoms, thought of themselves as one great race, to which they were already giving the name of 'English'.

Whatever the quarrels of the Britons in the years that followed the departure of the Romans, the new threat gave them, for a time, a new and vital unity. Though the angry Gildas was to find plenty of objects for his abuse among his countrymen it is certain that for the hundred years between 450 and 550 their resistance was strong and well-organized. Such a magnificent rampart as the Wansdyke could only have been built by a large and disciplined labour force. Bede gives the name of one British leader: 'Ambrosius Aurelius, a modest man, who alone by chance of the Roman nation had survived the storm, in which his parents, who were of the royal race, had perished. Under him, the Britons revived, and offering battle to their conquerors by the help of God came off victorious.' But the most famous name is that of Arthur.

'Some time after the death of Hengist,' says Nennius, 'Arthur was wont to fight against them [the Saxons] in those days along with the kings of the Britons, but he himself was the leader of the battles.

'The first battle was at the mouth of the river which is called Glein. The second, third, fourth, and fifth on another river which is called Dubglass and is in the region of Linnius. The sixth is on the river which is called Bassas. The seventh was a battle in the wood of Celidon . . . The eighth was the battle at Castellum Guinnion, in which Arthur carried the image of St. Mary ever Virgin on his shoulders, and the pagans were put to flight on that day and there was great slaughter of them through the power of our Lord Jesus Christ, and through the power of St. Mary the Virgin, His Mother. The ninth battle was fought at the City of the Legion. The tenth battle was fought on the shore of the river that is called Tribuit. The eleventh battle occurred on the mountain which is called Agned.

'The twelfth was the battle on Mount Badon, in which there fell together in one day nine hundred and sixty men in one onset of Arthur, and no one laid them low save himself alone.

'And in all the battles he remained victor.'

It is an impressive list. But we cannot say for certain where a single one of these battles was fought, not even the last, which was clearly a great and decisive victory and which is mentioned by other writers. They have clearly come from Nennius's heap, some of them perhaps from his imagination. However, it is safe to say that this Arthur was an able and successful general, probably

working with a mobile cavalry force preserving some of the
traditions of Roman discipline. The Battle of Mount Badon must
have occurred about 500, and after it, for half a century, the pagan
invaders were forced to pause and give the Britons respite.

After the death of Arthur at the hand of one of his own people
his fame grew slowly but surely among the Britons and Welsh.
But his real personality was submerged in legend. It was said that
he was carried to the magic isle of Avalon and that one day he
would come again to lead his people to victory. He lived, said the
various legends, in Cornwall; or in Snowdonia; or in Anglesey; or
in Scotland. As the centuries rolled on he became the property of
all western Europe, but particularly of France, where in the twelfth
century he became the ideal king of fashionable chivalry. In this
form his story returned to England, to be written down by a
scapegrace knight in prison during the Wars of the Roses, Sir
Thomas Malory. And King Henry VII of the Welsh house of
Tudor, dreaming of a new unity for all Britain, called his short-
lived eldest son, Arthur, Prince of Wales.

Under such men as Ambrosius and Arthur the traditions of
Roman Britain survived for perhaps a century or a century and a
half after the legions had gone. But it was only a respite. Unable,
after Mount Badon, to advance quickly, the invaders settled down
and consolidated their strength before moving on. By the time of
Augustine's mission the Anglo-Saxons were masters of all but
the northern and western fringes of England. And from the confusion of those years had grown a number of kingdoms in which
the pagan invaders ruled all the scattered Britons who had not
died or fled before them.

More than anything it was geography that made these kingdoms.
In the south-east, Kent, then more than now a peninsula, cut off
from Sussex by forest and by Romney Marsh, was the old conquered land of Hengist. The impenetrable forest of the Weald
cut off the kingdom of the South Saxons – Sussex – from the
north, as marsh cut it off from the east. Beyond it, to the west,
the West Saxons had, from their original centre in the upper
Thames, driven the Britons to the wild moors of Devon. The
swamps and heavy clays of Essex had prevented the settlement
there of a large population, but the East Saxons had pushed up
the Thames, overcome the Middle Saxons and the old Roman

Londinium, and crossed the river to take in the 'southern district' whose name is preserved in the county of Surrey.

To the north of the East Saxons lived the East Anglians, divided from the beginning into the North Folk and the South Folk and partly divided by the fenlands from their western neighbours. These were the men of Mercia, too busy trying to dig the heavy local clay to turn much to military adventure. The swift-flowing Humber divided them from the northerners whom Bede first called Northumbrians and whose kingdom crossed the crumbling Roman wall and the present Scottish border to reach the Firth of Forth.

Beyond these kingdoms, and a few smaller ones wedged in among them, the Celtic tribes maintained their independence – in Wales; west of the Pennines in Strathclyde; in northern Scotland; in Devon and Cornwall. Among some of these tribes much of the Roman heritage lived on, and particularly that last gift of the Romans to Britain – Christianity. The heathen idols of the Saxons had virtually extinguished Christianity in the areas of their conquests. But in Cornwall and Devon, in Wales, and above all in Ireland, it flourished and grew, through the work of some of the greatest saints of Christendom. In the year 563, Columba, one of the noblest sons of the Irish Church, sailed with twelve disciples from Ireland to the small island of Iona off the west coast of Scotland, there to found a community whose fame and influence were to spread far in the north and to help bring Christianity to the Saxons.

But this Celtic Church was cut off from events on the continent of Europe. It had developed in its own way after the Romans' going. It was withdrawn, austere, neglectful of the practical organization given it by Patrick. It was more by the compelling power of individuals than by controlled planning that its victories were won. Though it made many converts among the northern Anglo-Saxons, the new conquest of Britain – the conquest of its soul – was, like an earlier one, planned and guided in Rome. It was in the year of Columba's death, in 597, that Augustine and his monks set foot nervously on the shores of the kingdom of Kent.

These years between the going of the Roman legions and the coming of the Roman monks had seen a slow but complete revolution in our island. First, the population had changed. The old peoples of Roman tradition were expelled to the west or reduced to near serfdom. The language of the new peoples was to the Romans harsh and barbaric. It preserved in England little or nothing of Latin or Celtic. And the land was re-named. A handful of towns kept signs of their Roman foundation, but only in a few field names and rivers can we detect the Celtic tongue. The towns themselves crumbled away, many, like Silchester, never to be occupied again, others, like London or Canterbury, unheard of for a century and a half. In very few Roman towns can it now be proved that habitation continued. The great villas, centres of government and economic life, lay ruined. Christian churches were turned to the use of the Saxon gods, Tiw, Woden, and Thunor. The network of roads was used still, but unrepaired they changed to muddy tracks, running dead straight from one derelict city to another.

Yet from the ruin and decay the new England was emerging, and from the settlement of the German invaders to this day we can trace the continuous development of features already marked when Augustine landed. Little inroad yet had been made on the vast forests and swamps which had so limited the course of the invasion. But already the shire boundaries of today were being traced. The tradition of English kingship and the development of English law had begun. And the primitive mouthings of the Angles and Saxons, so laughable to cultured Roman ears, were slowly turning to the language of a literature that in the two centuries before the battle of Hastings was to be the finest of its time in Europe. As we travel about England today we see little of Roman Britain but the roads. But all around us, in village, in law court, in government, lies the imprint of the Anglo-Saxons.

CHAPTER 4

The Conversion and the Early English Kingdoms to 886

IN THE year 596, the Bishop of Rome, Gregory the Great, sent a small mission to convert the English to the religion of Christ. Its leader was the provost of the Roman monastery of St. Andrew, and in the spring of this year he set out across the Alps with a party of monks. But he did not get very far. Somewhere in Southern Gaul the little party was overwhelmed by dread of what might lie in this remote island and returned to Rome to ask for release. Gregory, who some fifteen years before had himself set out for Britain only to be recalled by some business in Rome, restored their courage and sent them off again. This time they went on, crossed the Channel, and early in 597 landed on the Isle of Thanet, in the territory of King Ethelbert of Kent.

So Augustine came to Britain, nervous and hesitant, to bring her back to the faith she had first learned of the Romans. There were still a few Christians scattered among the pagan Anglo-Saxons. Ethelbert's own wife, a princess of the Frankish royal house, was a Christian and was permitted to practise her religion in private. But the roots of paganism were deep, and the few Christians there were had little inclination to carry their faith to others. Ethelbert welcomed Augustine warmly enough and gave him an old ruined building in Canterbury which was said to have been a church under the Romans. And before the year was out Ethelbert himself was converted.

Augustine died before 609 and his own achievement was not perhaps very great, but he lived to be made the first Archbishop of Canterbury and to see the consecration of two other bishops, one of London and one of Rochester. Even this moderate success was not maintained, however, and within a few years of his death new rulers of Kent and Essex had taken many of their people back to the old heathen ways.

The next step was in the north. A daughter of Ethelbert married the king of Northumbria, Edwin, and took with her one of Augustine's old companions, a monk called Paulinus. Within two years he had succeeded in convincing Edwin of the truth of the new faith, and in 627 Edwin was baptized in a chapel in York. Many of his subjects followed his example. But again there were setbacks. In 632, in battle against a coalition of Welsh and English at Hatfield Chase, Edwin was slain. Paulinus and all but one of his company fled to Kent. The Northumbrians, after his sudden departure, might have returned to paganism as easily as they had left it, but within a year a new mission had reached them, this time from the north, and with it their new king, Oswald.

It came from Columba's island of Iona, and was led by the austere and humble Aidan. It made its headquarters on the isle of Lindisfarne, or Holy Island as it is sometimes called, connected at low tide to the Northumbrian coast by a causeway. Aidan was made bishop of Lindisfarne, and in twenty years he and his followers had re-established Christianity in the north.

The community of Lindisfarne, like their mother community at Iona, lived in gaunt simplicity, caring nothing for the material things of this world, building only rough churches of timber and thatch. But their fame spread far, and from this northern centre went out a missionary wave which reached as far south as Essex, since the hasty flight of the first Bishop of London bereft of spiritual leadership. Among the still heathen Mercians, too, the work of conversion went on, and their king was baptized in 653 by Aidan's successor.

So England was gripped by a kind of spiritual pincer, one arm Celtic, the other Roman. The Celts had perhaps the greater saints and the fiercer energy. But their organization was primitive. It was typical of them that their northern headquarters should be an island monastery. Their bishops roamed at large, untied to any geographical area, baptizing, preaching, and passing on, leaving no firm foundation for work to continue. In their ways they were cut off from the main stream of Christianity on the Continent.

One of the most important differences between the two Churches was over the date of the greatest festival of the Christian Church,

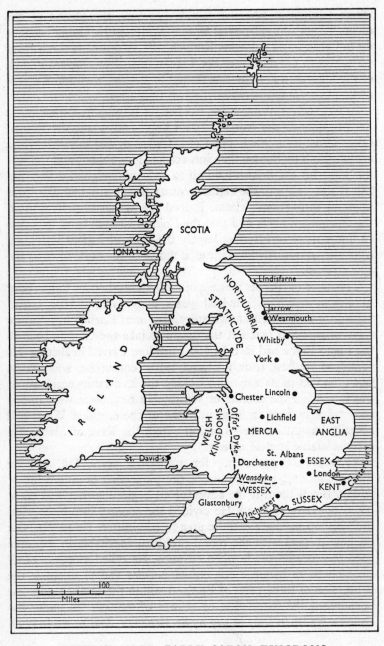

BRITISH ISLES: EARLY SAXON KINGDOMS

which follows, as had the Jewish Passover, the phases of the moon. Easter was celebrated by one Northumbrian king, brought up in Celtic ways, while his Kentish wife, educated in the Roman ways, was in the middle of her Lenten fast. If an efficient branch of the Church was to be established in Britain, then some agreement was essential between the two traditions.

In 663 such agreement was reached, at Whitby in Yorkshire, in the presence of the Northumbrian king; and it was the Roman cause which triumphed. The Celtic leaders agreed to correct their arithmetic. The Roman date was accepted for Easter, and the way was clear for the British Church to become one great enterprise. But it was well into the eighth century before any real unity was imposed throughout Britain. Indeed the Welsh Church resisted the change until 768, and that the English Church became united so much more rapidly was largely the work of a great statesman from the eastern Mediterranean, a native of the same town as the apostle Paul.

Theodore of Tarsus was appointed Archbishop of Canterbury in Rome, nearly a hundred years after Gregory the Great, according to the well-known story, had seen English boys in the slave market and first felt the desire to take the Church back to the island Rome had lost. In 669 Theodore arrived in Britain. He found, as we have seen, a Church full of enthusiasm and energy, but muddled in its aims and lacking the leadership necessary to put into effect the decrees of Whitby. In fact, there were in 669 only three bishops in England. One of these, called Wine, had actually bought his see – London – from the King of Mercia for a considerable sum of money.

Theodore was archbishop for twenty-one years. The work he did sounds dull, perhaps, beside the pioneering of Augustine or Aidan. But without it the adventurous beginning they had made could not have endured. He divided the country into bishoprics, each bishop having a definite area to administer. He gave advice on how to deal with the moral problems inevitable in a people used to centuries-old heathen customs. He called meetings of all his bishops to hammer out united policies and to organize the conversion of those parts of England still in the heathen grip. He encouraged the foundation or reform of monasteries under the Rule drawn up in Italy in 529 by St. Benedict. And he made small beginnings at forming districts into parishes under a resident priest – though it remained for a long time the custom for priests to wander from village to village preaching in the open air or celebrating the Communion in improvised sheds. In a way it is true to say that the English Church was founded, as a unit, not by Augustine, not by the Celtic saints, but by this remarkable man from the Levant. He is not the least of our debts to the Near East. In him the dream of Gregory the Great in the Roman slave market at last came true.

In Theodore's day, then, the English Church could at times work as one body, and its leaders could meet together in synod and talk over their problems. But among the English kings there was no such unity. The result of the Anglo-Saxon invasions had been the destruction of the single-minded administration of the Romans, and in its stead had grown up higgledy-piggledy a number of kingdoms whose boundaries and powers were constantly shifting. Now one, now another of these kingdoms would assert itself over others, usually by battle, and from time to time a single king would earn for himself the title of Bretwalda – or overlord.

In the seventh century, the century of Whitby and Theodore, the greatest power lay in Northumbria. Aidan could not have worked so freely without the support of the Northumbrian royal house, and this support was given, too, to a magnificent flowering of art and learning that made northern England famous throughout western Europe. Some of the sculpture of the time can still be seen, rough-hewn but of great power. So can the wonderfully intricate Lindisfarne Gospels, made on the island about 700 and now in the British Museum. And in the first years of the eighth century Bede was writing his numerous books: commentaries on scripture, scientific studies, instructions on methods of dating the years, and above all his history. He was the greatest scholar of his age; yet it is unlikely that he ever travelled beyond the borders of Northumbria. He was famous, too, as a teacher; and it is not surprising that when, later in the century, Charlemagne was searching for a tutor at his palace school, he should have chosen a Northumbrian, Alcuin of York. From Northumbria, too, went one of the most influential of all English missionaries, St. Willibrord, who carried Anglo-Saxon Christianity to the Frisians of north Germany in 695. A remarkable change had come over the barbaric tribes who, not many generations before, had wrenched northern England from the weak grasp of the Romano-Britons.

Northumbria's greatness in learning continued well into the eighth century. But her political influence in England dwindled before the rising power of the midland kingdom of Mercia. In the eighth century, Northumbria had a dozen kings, most of whom met violent deaths. From 716 to 795, Mercia had two: Aethelbald, and – from 757 to 796 – Offa the Great, ablest of all Anglo-Saxon kings before Alfred.

Offa was the first man to call himself 'King of the English' and 'King of the whole land of England'. And this was no empty claim. His fame stood so high on the Continent that Charlemagne, the Frankish king who was himself to claim the title of Emperor of the Romans, treated him as a near equal and joined their families together by marriage. Offa's power is shown, too, in the great defence work he built against the Welsh, parts of which can still be seen. Offa's Dyke, as it is called, stretched from the Dee to the Bristol Channel. It could only have been built by a king who had at his command wealth and human labour not known since the departure of the Romans – except perhaps briefly in the mysterious days of Arthur. The Pope thought him sufficiently important to send a special mission in 786 for the first time since the mission of Augustine. English coinage until long after the Norman Conquest was based on Offa's silver penny, though the word 'penny' itself is probably derived from the name of an earlier, heathen, Mercian king – Penda. And, lastly, the history of the English coronation ceremony as a religious rite begins with the hallowing, in 787, before the great king's death, of Offa's son, Egbert.

After Offa's death in 796, power shifted south again. But three years before it an event occurred whose consequence was yet another revolution in the character of English history.

In the Anglo-Saxon Chronicle, under the year 793, are written these words: 'In this year, terrible portents appeared over Northumbria, and miserably frightened the inhabitants. These were exceptional whirlwinds and flashes of lightning, and fiery dragons were seen flying in the air. And soon followed a great famine, and after that in the same year the harrying of the heathen miserably destroyed God's church in Lindisfarne by robbery and slaughter.' The next year, the monastery of Jarrow, where Bede had worked in peace, was similarly ravaged. The year after that it was the turn of Iona. So the Scandinavians enter the history of Britain, with the sack of three of her most sacred shrines.

The Scandinavian peoples have left a permanent mark on the story of Europe. Across the plains of Russia, as far south as Constantinople, went Swedish warriors and traders, making native peoples subject to them. Along the southern Baltic coast, pushing up river estuaries, probing the islands of Frisia, went the Danes. And these, with the Norwegians, crossed the North Sea to northern France, to England, Scotland, and Ireland, to the islands between Scotland and Iceland, to Greenland, perhaps to the American continent. They came first as mere pirates, looting, burning, carrying plunder to their homeland; then as warlike traders; finally as settlers, bringing to the arts of government and agriculture the same vigour and skill they had shown as seamen and robbers. Later still, having absorbed the ways of those they had conquered, they appeared as military adventurers under the Christian banner, with William of Normandy in 1066, or with Bohemond and Tancred to the Holy Land in the First Crusade. They have been accused of greed, of ruthlessness, of appalling cruelty, but seldom of sloth. To Anglo-Saxon England they brought terror and brutality at first, so that the chronicle speaks of them with dread. But later they made a vital contribution to the strange hybrid that is the English nation.

In the first instance, they came to Britain along two routes. The Norwegians crossed from their native fjords south-westerly to the similar coastlines of north Scotland, founding there and in Ireland in the early ninth century powerful and aggressive kingdoms. The Danes made the shorter crossing to the Northumbrian and East Anglian coasts, or crept along the coasts of narrower seas to descend on southern England.

The raid on Lindisfarne in 793 yielded fine booty, and reports of it brought fresh raids in the following years to other places of whose wealth the raiders had heard. And there must have been a multitude of further raids of which we have no record until, in 835, there is the first certain evidence of a group remaining for the winter, in the Isle of Sheppey.

For nearly three centuries before these raids England had lived free from the fear of foreign invasion. That Aidan had founded his monastery in the exposed isle of Lindisfarne is proof of the security the Northumbrians felt from continental attack. But as the eighth century drew to its close this security vanished. The raiders came to an almost defenceless land, to kingdoms accustomed only to fighting each other. The power of Offa's Mercia, which dwindled after his death, was finally crushed in 825 by the south-western kingdom of Wessex at Ellendun, near Swindon in Wiltshire. And when, in 865, the Danes made their first attack in great force, there was in all northern and eastern England no power that could withstand them.

The Danish 'Great Army' – as an Englishman of the time called it – landed in 865 somewhere in East Anglia. In the course of fifteen years it took possession of most of eastern England, showing as it did so a wonderful discipline and power of united action. It made first for York, which was taken in November 866, just at the moment when an independent army of Norwegians from the Hebrides was attacking Dumbarton, the capital of Scottish Strathclyde. The Northumbrians could do little. In a few months, this ancient kingdom, with its marvellous achievements in art, learning, and the religious life, virtually ceased to exist.

In 869, the Great Army was again in East Anglia. At Thetford, the first English king to earn the title of martyr was slaughtered by them. He was Edmund, King of East Anglia. His name is perpetuated in the monastery and town of Bury St. Edmunds.

From the East Anglian plains, the Army marched to the Thames valley, making a base at Reading in 870. But now at last it received a check. For the kingdom whose leader half a century before had smashed the power of Mercia, and which slowly since then had been building up its strength, was ready and waiting for the inevitable assault. When the Danes left their base at Reading for the open country of the Berkshire downs – then called Ashdown – they met the army of Wessex in a battle that lasted all the day long. As night descended the Danes fled to Reading. Five years after landing, they had at last met their match. They had met the kingdom they were never to defeat. They had met, too, the man who, by sheer will and military skill was to bring them to terms and to Christian baptism – Alfred the Great, fighting now as brother to the king but in the year afterwards to be king himself.

The battle of Ashdown showed that the Great Army could be defeated in the open. But it did little to lessen its strength. For five years it kept away from Wessex. Part of it ranged over Mercia, bringing its eastern half under Danish control but never conquering the rest. In Yorkshire, Lincolnshire, and East Anglia another part continued to settle, preferring for a while the plough to the sword. But in 875 a more active section attacked Wessex again, this time by a different route. Instead of striking up the Thames valley they made for the south coast by Poole Harbour. But now the ships bringing their supports were scattered off Swanage in a storm. Fearing open battle with the new king, Alfred, the remaining Danes made hurried terms and slipped away. Wessex was saved again.

Alfred, however, was not left in peace for long. Early in 878, a part of the Army, under Guthrum, again descended on Wessex, this time from Gloucester. For some reason this third attack caused a panic among the West Saxons. Many fled, and more submitted; and while Alfred and a small band of followers hid in the Somerset marshes at Athelney, the Danes encamped at Chippenham.

Slowly, Alfred gathered strength for a last effort. Off the Devon coast a Danish naval force was defeated, and when, in the early summer, Alfred emerged from his forests and marshes to the open chalklands of Salisbury Plain, men flocked to him from Wiltshire and Hampshire. Fifteen miles south of Chippenham, at Ethandun – the modern Edington – he brought Guthrum to battle and won an overwhelming victory, pursuing the Danes to their fortress at Chippenham and forcing them to make terms. Guthrum agreed to receive baptism and to leave Wessex for good. The tide had turned. But for the courage of Alfred, all England might have become a Danish colony.

Eight years after Ethandun, with Guthrum and his followers withdrawn to East Anglia, Alfred was strong enough to occupy London and to make a new treaty with his old enemy. Map 4 shows how the area controlled by the Danes, later called the Danelaw, was defined in this year, 886. But such a settlement could scarcely last. Alfred had defeated one Danish army under one leader. But there were others bound by no settlement, and still more on the opposite side of the Channel ready to join in any expedition that might bring land and profit. So the last years of Alfred's life – he died in 899 – were far from quiet, and he gained no more striking victories. His success lay more in the fact that he held his own and that he was able to organize his people for the defence of it. He built ships to harry the Danes and fortresses to deter them. He divided his *fyrd* – or conscript army – into two halves, so that one could always be on the watch while the other was working the land. By such methods he was just able to keep what, by his treaty with Guthrum, was his by right. It was left to his son and grandson, both soldiers of genius, to turn this holding action into a magnificently successful counter-attack.

Alfred's labours then had two important results. The Danes were held, and eventually made to accept the West Saxon king as their overlord. But, in addition, the West Saxon resistance to the invader was to make the Wessex kings true kings of England. Gone were the days of the petty rival kingdoms, the days of bitter enmity between Northumbria and Mercia, Mercia and Wessex. Though the differences between the peoples of the old kingdoms did not disappear, the opportunity was at hand to mould from their ruin a single kingdom; and the Wessex kings of the tenth century took this opportunity. After the Danish invasions of 865 had spent their force there were no more kings of Northumbria, of East Anglia, of Kent, or of Mercia, though it would be a long time before the peoples of these lands could feel themselves to be, above all else, English.

More had gone than the old kingdoms. The sack of Lindisfarne had been a sign of the aggressive paganism of the early Danes. Wherever Danes went they attacked churches and monasteries, not so much through hatred of Christianity as for the wealth the shrines contained. The glories of the Anglo-Saxon church were brought low. Monasteries were desolate and ruined, their rule of life forgotten, the clergy disheartened and few, schools abandoned. The military task of subduing the invaders was heavy enough, but that of restoring the civilizing influence of the Church with its treasures of learning was heavier still. Had Alfred been just a soldier his fame would be wide. But not for this alone was he called Great. He saw the deeper needs of his people. To his courage and skill was added a vision of an educated nation, conscious of its history, able to write and read the language it spoke, worshipping God with knowledge as well as devotion. The small band of fugitives behind the ramparts of Athelney had been fighting for more than the safety of their bodies.

BERNICIA

STRATHCLYDE

York ● ●Stamford Bridge
KINGDOM OF YORK

D
A
N
GYNEDD   Chester ● DANISH   ● Lincoln
E
POWYS   Nottingham●   L   ● Elmham
Derby●   A   Stamford●
Repton●   W   KINGDOM   Norwich●
Leicester●   OF
WALES   Lichfield●   EAST Bury
Tamworth●   ● St.Edmunds
ANGLIA
ENGLISH MERCIA

Chippenham
Ashdown   LONDON●
Bristol   ✕   Sheppey
Wedmore●   Reading●   Rochester●
Glastonbury●   Eddington●   Kingston   ●Dover
Athelney● WESSEX   Canterbury
Sherborne● Winchester●   Chichester   ●Pevensey
Crediton●   Selsey
Exeter● Dorchester●
CORNWALL   ●Swanage

0   50   100
Miles

Danish and Norwegian held land in 900

BRITAIN IN THE TENTH CENTURY

CHAPTER 5

The Supremacy of Wessex and the Second Danish Invasions
886-1016

WHEN, in about the year 894, Alfred produced his own translation of Pope Gregory the Great's 'Pastoral Care', he described in a preface the state in which he found the English Church at his accession. 'When I began to rule,' he wrote, 'there were very few men on this side of the Humber who could understand their Mass books or even translate a letter from Latin into English; and I think not many beyond the Humber. So few were there that I cannot even call to mind a single one south of the Thames.' It was this state of affairs that he felt himself called to remedy, even in the midst of constant campaigns against the Danes.

His plan was simple and practical. There were no books in his native language, so, first of all, translations must be made from the Latin and Englishmen taught to read them. But since Latin was the language of the Church and the second tongue of all men of learning, Latin must be taught to all who would need it, so that the great monastic libraries which had survived the fire of the Northmen could be used again.

Slowly and painfully, in the years that followed his treaty with Guthrum, the king himself learned Latin. By about 894 he felt himself able to begin his own translations. With the help of scholars, some from Mercia, some from abroad, Alfred turned into the Anglo-Saxon – or, as it is sometimes called, the Old English – tongue, five of the most widely read works of his day, freely adding any comment he thought might aid his countrymen. The translations are often inaccurate, but that a busy man of action should attempt them at all places Alfred, in the stature and scope of his mind, above any sovereign from that day to this.

He had time only for a tentative beginning in the educating and civilizing of his people, and it is probable that when he died the results of his work had not spread far beyond his own court. But what he had begun went on, and the great revival in the English Church during the reign of his great-grandson, Edgar, would have been impossible without his pioneering work. In Alfred's reign, too, was begun the Anglo-Saxon Chronicle, without which we would know almost nothing of the English history of this time. Nowhere else in Europe was a native tongue being used for extensive writing. Everywhere, if men wrote, it was in a Latin that would have made a Roman writhe.

Monastic life in England, after the Danish invasions, had almost ceased. The noble abbeys of the time of Bede were crumbling ruins inhabited by a few men and women living a life far removed from that intended by St. Benedict. Alfred could do nothing himself towards restoring their earlier vitality. His one attempt to found a religious community for men, in his fortress isle of Athelney, was a failure. The monks imported from abroad quarrelled incessantly with their German abbot and two of them tried to kill him. For the time being, it seemed, the desire for the remote solitude of the monk's life was dead in England. It would take another generation to restore it.

Alfred was succeeded, after his death in 899, by a line of able and energetic kings whose achievement it was to conquer the Danes in England and push the limit of their control far to the north. Edward the Elder, Alfred's son, who reigned until 924, spent almost all his adult life in warfare for Wessex. He had fought with skill in his father's later campaigns and, when king himself, showed that he was a strategist of genius. He was fortunate in having as his faithful ally his own sister, Ethelfleda, who had married one of the great lords of Mercia and who made sure that the remnant of old Mercia still in the hands of the English made common cause against the Danes. So, while Ethelfleda kept the Danes busy by harassing them along the Watling Street frontier, Edward moved north into the east midlands. Then, in 917, in a general assault, they were able to bring all England south of a line from the Mersey to the Humber under their control – and this included areas, like Lincolnshire and East Anglia, where the Danes were settled most thickly. It was far from a wholesale conquest, and Edward did as much by a mere show of power as he did by actual fighting. But the Danes were disunited and lacked leaders of the quality of those who had brought the Great Army such prestige. For the most part, Edward was content with their submission. Given this, he interfered little with their life and laws. These they preserved until after the Norman Conquest.

Edward's son and successor, the strikingly handsome Athelstan, who earned the Irish tribute 'the pillar of the dignity of the western world', was as fine and successful a soldier as his father. To keep his kingdom secure, he had to press his frontier further forward into the lands to the north of the Humber, about whose history at this time we know so little.

The old Northumbrian kingdom had been destroyed after the Great Army's occupation of York in 866, and since then it had been a prey to enemies on all sides. From the north, the Scots had come down from the Forth–Clyde line to somewhere near the modern Border; and the kings of Strathclyde had bitten into the north-western corner of the old kingdom. But most dangerous of all were the attacks from the Norwegians who had been settling throughout the ninth century on the islands and coasts of west Scotland and Ireland. Edward had already encountered these new raiders when they landed on the Wirral peninsula between Mersey and Dee; but it was left to Athelstan to break up the kingdom they were trying to found in York. A period of cut-and-thrust warfare ended in 937 when Athelstan met the combined forces of Norwegians, Scots, and the men of Strathclyde at Brunanburh.

The field

Grew dark with the blood of men, after the sun,
That glorious luminary, God's bright candle,
Rose high in the morning above the horizon,
Until the noble being of the Lord Eternal
Sank to its rest. There lay many a warrior
Of the men of the North, torn by spears,
Shot o'er the shield; likewise many a Scot
Sated with battle, lay lifeless.
All through the day the West Saxons in troops
Pressed on in pursuit of the foe,

Fiercely, with swords sharpened on grindstone,
They cut down the fugitives as they fled.[1]

So ran the poem which was written into the chronicle for the year. Where Brunanburh is we do not know; but its memory has lived in this song of victory. 'Life long glory, in battle won, with edges of swords, at Brunanburh.'

Athelstan's fame was not confined to Britain. He was the first English king since Offa of Mercia to enter into continuous relations with continental powers. And this is hardly surprising. His victory at Brunanburh is the climax of a triumphant era for the kings of Wessex. From the dark days in Athelney, the West Saxon kings fought battle after battle to bring them at last a united kingdom whose boundaries are roughly those of England today. And though in the reigns of Athelstan's successors the kingdom was again attacked, it kept its power. In the title given to Athelstan's nephew, Edgar 'the Peaceable', is seen the measure of the achievement of this remarkable dynasty.

This Edgar came to the throne in 959, twenty years after the death of Athelstan. In those intervening years three kings reigned. Two, Edmund and Edred, were soldiers of skill who fought doggedly to keep what their brother Athelstan had gained. The third, Edwig, was less successful and has been given a bad name by contemporary writers. His greatest crime seems to have been that he quarrelled with Dunstan, then Bishop of London, after leaving the solemnities of his coronation for the company of some women. But his reign was short, and when his younger brother Edgar succeeded, Dunstan was recalled from what proved to be a fruitful exile on the Continent and was made Archbishop of Canterbury. He and Edgar were then responsible for directing one of the most important reform movements the English Church has ever known.

For some time now the Church on the Continent had been in the grip of a movement of reform which was to have widespread results on the whole of society. One of its original centres was the monastery of Cluny, in eastern France. Founded in 910, it was vowed to the living of a purer and richer monastic life with a strict but elaborate form of St. Benedict's rule. From Cluny, other

[1] The translation is that of G. N. Garmonsway in the Everyman Library.

new monasteries were founded with the same ideals, and another movement was spreading from the Rhine valley.

In the middle of the tenth century, English churchmen came into contact with the new ideals. Dunstan, before his quarrel with King Edwig, had been an important figure at court and had tried with limited success to reform the life at Glastonbury. His exile he spent at one of the reformed monasteries, at Ghent in Flanders. And he was not the only influential Englishman abroad at this time. From the north of England, Oswald, whom Edgar was to make Bishop of Worcester, paid a visit to a monastery on the Loire which had been founded from Cluny.

When these men and their companions returned to England they found in Edgar a young man devoted above all else to one ambition – rebuilding the crumbled abbeys of England and peopling them again with monks vowed for life to poverty, chastity, and obedience. So the enterprise began. All over southern England, on land granted by the king or given, often unwillingly, by his lords, the reconstruction started. Men of impure life were driven out of the abbey buildings with their women. One of Dunstan's pupils, Ethelwold, made Bishop of Winchester, went through its two monasteries like a purifying fire. Continental artists, glaziers, builders, and musicians were invited over to give their assistance to the material part of the work. Within a decade, at Glastonbury, Winchester, Canterbury, Abingdon, Worcester, and a score of others, the strict rule was once more observed. And now – so different from the unhappy days of Athelney – there seemed to be no shortage of native recruits.

A monastic revival like this inevitably meant a revival of education. Here Alfred's work could find its full fruition. Translations into Anglo-Saxon continued. Latin works were copied. Boys were taught to sing the chant and to read. Though of the buildings of these monasteries little trace remains – since they were replaced with sturdier work by the Normans – we still have many manuscripts of the time to show us the skill of these Englishmen. Simplicity in script and nobility in illustration go together to give some idea of the confidence of these tenth-century reformers. And working together, supervising it all, were Edgar and Dunstan, an example, unhappily rare in medieval England, of king and archbishop in perfect harmony.

The part of the tenth century spanned by the reign of Edgar, from 959 to 975, is the high point of Anglo-Saxon history. We have no record of Edgar's taking the field of battle. But there is an old tradition that in the year 973 he was rowed across the river Dee by six kings. By this act of humility they seemed to symbolize his lordship over them. They came from Scotland and from Wales, and their action followed a splendid ceremony in Bath Abbey, where, on Whitsunday, 973, fourteen years after his accession, Edgar was solemnly crowned and anointed. From this ceremony we can trace a direct line of development to the coronation in Westminster Abbey in 1953 of Queen Elizabeth II – nearly a thousand years later.

An eye-witness account of the ceremony makes it clear that more important than the placing of the crown on Edgar's head was the anointing with holy oil, the part of the rite in which God himself conferred on the king some special quality which set him apart from other men for ever. And it is probably not coincidence that in this year Edgar reached the age of thirty, at which, by the law of the Church, a man could be ordained priest. To Edgar, to Dunstan, and to the multitude who watched, the similarity in the ceremony must have been manifest. When, in 1066, the Duke of Normandy was crowned and anointed in Westminster Abbey, he became heir to a power greater than any he had wielded in Normandy and of a totally different kind. To be king of the English, however one had come by the honour, was to possess a supernatural power that God gave to no one else.

The reign of Edgar the Peaceable was one of comparative order. But in 975, in his thirty-third year, he died. As the chronicler wrote: 'Edgar, of Angles king, chose him another light, beauteous and winsome, and left this frail, this perishable life . . . and then his child succeeded to the kingdom, a babe ungrown, prince of earls, whose name was Edward.' That autumn a comet appeared, and the following year a great famine, 'and very many troubles over the Angles' race'.

The monks who wrote this chronicle must indeed have felt an age had gone. For within three years the young Edward was brutally murdered at the gate of Corfe Castle in Dorset. 'To the Angle race was no worse deed than this since they first sought Britain.' The murderer seems to have been Edward's stepmother,

Edgar's second wife, who evidently wanted the throne for her own ten-year-old son, Ethelred. Whatever the reason for the deed, it is clear that the death of Edgar had brought widespread disorder in the land, showing how much depended on the sheer personality of the king. With this disorder came a reaction against Edgar's and Dunstan's monastic movement. Many lords had been forced to give land and money to the monasteries against their will, and Edgar's death brought a good chance to take them back. It was not only greed that prompted them. Many must have felt that too much of the kingdom's best land was coming under church ownership and perhaps becoming less productive. But all our records of the time are the work of monks, and they could see nothing but villainy and violence.

The new king, Ethelred, as he grew up, gave little sign of the ability needed to pull his kingdom together. He was nicknamed by a punster, 'Aethelraed Unraed', a phrase meaning literally 'Noble-Counsel No-Counsel'. But the modern word 'Unready' describes him as well. He was unready, as were most Englishmen, for the new terrors that were now to descend on the land.

In 980, new Danish raiders began to appear on the English coasts. At first they were merely pirates, as unwanted in Denmark as in England. But soon organized bodies of professional armies were coming, commanded by the Kings of Denmark themselves. Instead of the toughness and skill which Alfred had shown a hundred years before, inefficiency, treachery, and stupidity now met the invaders. In 1010 a chronicler at Abingdon wrote: 'When the enemy was to the east our own army kept to the west, and when the enemy was to the south then was our army kept to the north . . . At last there was not a leader who was willing to assemble an army, but each fled as best he could.'

Here and there resistance was firmer than this writer suggests. In 991, for example, at Maldon in Essex, Byrthnoth the local ealdorman, with unpractical chivalry, allowed a party of raiders to cross a narrow causeway so that they could fight him on level terms. He fell in the battle with a group of his thegns who preferred death at his side to the ignominious flight more typical of the times. To the raiders this was just an incident. To us it is more, for the battle was described in a magnificent Anglo-Saxon poem.

The eventual result of these new and relentless attacks, and of the uncertain resistance they met, was the establishing on the throne of England of a Danish warrior, Canute. Of Ethelred, who died in 1016 while Canute's fleet was on its way to an assault on London, the best the chronicler can find to say is this: 'He held his kingdom with great toil and difficulty, while his life lasted.' His failure was not all his fault. For these were degenerate days for the English, such as often follow times of greatness. The opposition Edgar's firmness had aroused turned in the time of his sons to disobedience and the pursuit of petty ambition. Ethelred was not the man to check it, nor the greater threat that came from abroad.

For a year after Ethelred's death his famous son, Edmund Ironside, gallantly defended the honour of the West Saxon house, but at Ashingdon, in Essex, half his army having deserted, he was routed and became a fugitive. His fame was such that Canute was forced to come to terms with him. But the divided kingdom these terms would have produced was not inflicted on the English. In November, 1016, he suddenly died. By early next year, all England had accepted the Danish Canute as king.

CHAPTER 6

Anglo-Saxon Society

'IN THE name of the Holy Trinity I promise three things to the Christian people subject to me. First, that God's Church and all Christian people of my dominions shall keep true peace. Second, that I forbid to all ranks robbery and all injustice. Third, that I promise in all judgments justice and mercy.' So ran the oath which King Ethelred the Unready swore at his coronation. He did not of course keep it – and scarcely tried. But it shows what was expected of an Anglo-Saxon king: to give the Church and people peace and order, justice and mercy. For this he was chosen, and for this he was crowned and set apart from his fellows. All his subjects, whoever might be their own local lord, owed direct allegiance to him and to his officers, were bound to appear at his courts and to fight in his army. As a contemporary of King Ethelred's wrote: 'After he is consecrated king, he has authority over the people, and they cannot shake his yoke off their necks.' When the king wrote out an order and put his seal upon it – in a document called a 'writ' – all men must obey; and this custom of making writs gave the Anglo-Saxon kings a power beyond that held by most rulers of the day.

Yet this power was severely limited. It was limited first by the law, the age-old custom of the Angles and Saxons which the king was expected to interpret and enforce but not to change. And if he did change it – which some kings did – he usually so worded his changes that they looked like old laws adapted to new circumstances. When Wessex conquered the whole of England her king let local customs stand as they were. King Edgar, drawing up his legal code, said 'It is my will that among the Danes such good laws shall be valid as they themselves decide'; and even William the Conqueror let them stand. It was wisdom not weakness. The inhabitants of England would behave better under laws they knew.

The king's power was limited, too, by his Council – the Witanagemot or Council of Wise Men. No king could govern successfully if he rejected the advice of this council too often, though kings who were great soldiers, like Alfred, Edward the Elder, or Athelstan, had enough prestige to make the Witan follow *them*. No one came to the Witan by right. The king called whom he wished; but if he was wise he would call the people who mattered, the churchmen and landowners who could best see the decisions were carried out. When the king died, the Witan elected his successor, for there was no strict law of hereditary succession in England until many centuries after the Norman Conquest. But the successor would normally be a member of the royal family, usually the one most fitted to rule – for England never sank to that pitiable condition where a weak king is elected so that he can be dominated by a powerful aristocracy. Men wanted peace; and in times of natural disorder, when tempers flared more easily than now, when human life was considered cheap, when argument easily turned to violence, peace could only be enforced by the strong and by the threat of brutal punishment.

Archbishop Wulfstan when he drew up laws for Ethelred and Canute wrote: 'Christian men shall not be condemned for all too little; but one shall decide on lenient punishments for the benefit of the people, and not destroy for a little matter God's own handi-work which he bought at a great price.' But hanging remained the usual punishment for theft, treachery to a lord, and arson, as well as murder; and Wulfstan includes the loss of a limb as a 'lenient' punishment. We should not expect, however, that in days when there was no organized police force and when most criminals remained uncaught, punishment could be anything but severe. Even when a criminal was caught, it was still difficult to determine his guilt. Men still used the 'ordeal', which was a direct appeal to God to tell them the truth by seeing what happened when a man was thrown into holy water or swallowed consecrated bread.

For offences of violence against men who were not the king's officers, the Anglo-Saxons used the system of the 'wergild' or 'man-price'. The origins of this lay deep in the primitive past of the German peoples, when what held men together were primarily ties of family, when an outrage committed by one family on another had to be revenged and might lead to long and bloody vendettas. The payment of a sum of money to the injured family developed as a way of stopping these blood feuds, and soon the courts were fixing the amounts of wergilds and enforcing the payment of them by the guilty. Wergilds varied in size with a man's level in society. According to one document, the king's wergild was fifteen times that of a thegn, but normally an offence against the king would be regarded as a breach of his 'peace' and thus an offence against the whole people. The king's peace extended to all his household and to all his property, and to break it was to be guilty of something far worse than the injuring of an ordinary man. Much later, when Henry II, in the twelfth century, was trying to bring more cases under the jurisdiction of his own courts, he found it very useful merely to extend the king's peace. And to this day certain offences are known as 'breaches of the peace'. English law has a history which goes back to the days before the Angles and Saxons ever crossed the North Sea to this island.

The 'thegns', who were the order of men next in importance to the king and his family, and whose wergild was fifteen times less than his, were originally the king's personal companions in battle. He rewarded them with grants of land or the privilege of living in his own household. To begin with, the rank was not hereditary, but by the time of King Edgar the rank of thegn was being handed down from father to son as a part of the dead man's inheritance. Yet the status of 'thegn' did not depend on land or wealth. After the Norman Conquest, when as we shall see, what is called 'feudalism' came to England, a man's rank in society depended on how he held his land, whether directly from the king or not. But among the Anglo-Saxons this was not so. Some thegns were great landholders, members of the witan or perhaps in charge of whole shires. Others were merely small farmers. When constant war ceased, men were beginning to become thegns otherwise than by fighting beside the king. One document says: 'If a churl prospered, so that he had fully five hundred hides of land [about six hundred acres] of his own, a church and a kitchen, a bell-house and a castle-gate and a special office in the king's hall, then he was henceforth worthy of the rank of thegn.' But he could also gain this rank by crossing the sea three times in his own ship.

Below the rank of thegn was the churl. Later on, this word

became a term of abuse; but in Anglo-Saxon times it denoted a
free man who had about a hide of land of his own and farmed it.
In the Middle Ages the distinction between 'free' and 'unfree' was
vital. A free man could use the courts to defend his right and was
not bound to the soil. An unfree man – and for centuries after the
Norman Conquest most Englishmen were unfree – could not use
the king's courts and could not move at will in the country. In the
the play *1066 and All That*, in the scene of the signing of Magna
Carta of 1215, as the Charter is read so a chorus of barons shouts:
'Except the Common People'. And it is true that seemingly liberal
laws which began 'No free man . . .' were, until perhaps the end of
the fourteenth century, deliberately omitting most of the
population.

So the churl was free – at least technically. But as the Anglo-
Saxon period drew to its close his freedom was often slipping away.
Many churls, to gain protection, had been 'commending' themselves to powerful neighbours, accepting them as 'lords' in return
for the safety they could give. The Normans, who reduced most
churls to the status of 'villein', were probably not making them
much worse off than before.

In many parts of England the churl's hide was already being
farmed in a way that was to last for many centuries – in huge open
fields. Many villages began as clearings in the forest, and as the
trees were cut down so the fields grew around the small groups of
houses. In some parts of England, notably the Midlands, it became
usual to have three such fields, and crops rotated among them so
that each field lay fallow once in three years. A man's holding
would not be all in one piece but in a series of strips, so that each
man had his fair share of good and bad soil. Each new encroach-
ment into the forest would be fairly divided up. It was not an
economical way of farming. It was expensive on land and on
labour. But few people in this age farmed for a surplus. A village
would produce only for its own needs. When, in later centuries,
men began to think of farming for profit, and perhaps found more
profit in sheep than in grain, then the strips would disappear to be
replaced by enclosed areas under single ownership. But the Anglo-
Saxons knew nothing of this 'enclosing'. Even in parts of the
country where strip farming on the three-field system was rare –
in the Danelaw for example, or in Kent, where concentrated

small holdings were the rule – the chief object of farming was to provide for the farmer's family.

Any surplus there was would go to the towns, which the Anglo-Saxons slowly rebuilt after their ruin in the invasions. Many of these towns, like London, Colchester, or Lincoln, were on old Roman sites, usefully placed on the still existing Roman roads. But others were new. Bristol was beginning its life as a port. So was Dunwich, in Suffolk, today submerged under the encroaching sea. Other towns had grown from fortifications. The Danish Army had settled round certain Midland forts – Derby, Nottingham, or Stamford – which grew from places of security into centres of trade. The size of most of these towns was little more than that of a large village today, and less than a tenth of the country's population lived within their walls. But most of them had a great future to come and already were beginning to trade in those commodities which one day would bring them prosperity; and London was already attracting merchants from the continent who could be sure of finding there samples of everything that England could produce and buyers for anything they could bring. London was not yet, in any sense, a 'capital' city – for the king's government was wherever the king might be, and his treasure was usually kept in Winchester or Glastonbury behind the walls of a monastery – but it was again, as it had become under the Romans, the greatest of English towns in population and in wealth.

Many towns were centres of what were called 'shires'. The shire was originally a Wessex institution, but it had spread with the spread of West Saxon conquest. The borders of most English counties of today are still the same as they were in the tenth century, and many take their names from the towns which were their centres – Wiltshire from Wilton, Somerset from Somerton, Cheshire from Chester. Over each shire was the king's representative. In the tenth century this was the ealdorman, but by the Conquest his place had been taken by the shire-reeve (or sheriff), who sat in the shire court, saw to the collection of taxes and was responsible for the raising of the *fyrd*. When the Normans came they found a tradition of local government ready for their command. Sheriff and shire court were retained and, though much altered in function, they still stand as evidence of the wisdom of the Anglo-Saxons.

King Edgar's chief adviser throughout his reign had been Dunstan, his Archbishop of Canterbury. We have no record of the extent of the advice Dunstan gave, but he and his fellow bishops were by far the best educated men in the England of their day and churchmen were, through most of the Middle Ages, the natural advisers of kings. It is not easy for twentieth-century man to appreciate the hold that the Church and its officers had on so much of the nation's life in those days. Even the most evil-living of men believed that there was not an action that went unmarked by God and would not be used in the terrible judgment that awaited all men, from kings to slaves. The Church was not just a place where men went to worship on Sundays, or went for baptism, marriage and burial. As kings were constantly advised by bishops so all men lived all their lives under the protecting hand of the Church. They paid taxes to bishops, priests and monks. They fasted in Lent at its command. They traded under its watchful eye. They took its oaths in court and underwent its ordeals to prove their innocence. They believed that every disease, every accident, every death was a sign from God of His will over them. The biographer of Dunstan shows how every decision the saint took was a response to a message of God. A falling rock that just missed him was a sign that he must give up a journey. Diseases were signs that a man's way of life must be changed. And the only perfect, Christ-like life, men believed, could be lived in that complete surrender of the selfish will which the life of a monk demanded. The great monastic revival under Edgar was one of many in the Middle Ages and cannot be explained merely as a desire to escape the uncertain and violent life of the villages and towns. Some idea of the way men heard the call to the cloister can be gained from this passage in a twelfth century life of a Northern abbot, Ailred of Rievaulx. The writer tells how Ailred first heard the call to this life of complete surrender:

'Now he had to pass long the edge of the hill overlooking its valley [of Rievaulx] where a road led down to the gate of the monastery, and when he reached the spot, still aflame with the heat of the Holy Spirit . . . he asked one of his servants, whom he called his friend, if he would like to go down to the abbey and learn something more than he had seen the day before . . . So they went down to the monastery of Rievaulx . . . There was no more dissembling for him, now that his duty had been made clear. He divided all his goods, he abandoned everything he had. He kept beside him only the one man of his company who wanted to stay. As he owned to me afterwards, the four days of waiting where he was were like a thousand years, so great was his longing and haste to be taken to the novices' cell.'[1]

Such descriptions do not explain the power that directed these men, but no one will understand the Middle Ages who cannot, for a moment, see how, amid all the cruelty, the massacres, the mutilations, the famine, the injustice of lords, a man's life could be changed in an instant by a call such as this.

---

[1] Walter Daniel: *The Life of Ailred of Rievaulx*, trans. Sir Maurice Powicke.

CHAPTER 7

From Canute to Hastings

1016-1066

THE REIGN of Canute, from 1016 to 1035, was the last period of
stable government granted to England before the Norman
Conquest. Canute was no mere barbarian chieftain. He was a
remarkable man. For some years in his reign he ruled a larger
block of territory than any medieval king of England. In 1019,
after he had been three years king of England, he succeeded his
brother as king of Denmark; and in 1028 he seized by war and
trickery the throne of Norway, and with it dominion over Greenland, Shetland, Orkney, the Hebrides, and the Isle of Man. Had
he been the father of a line of able rulers, England might have been
for centuries a part of the Scandinavian world, and our language,
literature, art, and customs very different from those we know. But
with his death his empire melted away, and England was drawn
irrevocably into another, richer world. Moreover, by the very
vastness and diversity of his empire, Canute helped to leave England
at his death as weak and disunited as he found it.

No empire of the Middle Ages could be kept together without the
constant journeyings of its ruler across it. Canute was away from
England for long spells on four occasions in the score of years he
reigned. He had to fight for his inheritance in Denmark, to defend
himself against the Swedes, and to gain his precarious hold on the
Norwegian throne. He also visited Rome in 1027 for the coronation
of the Emperor, Conrad.

He had therefore to delegate his powers in England. So he
grouped the Anglo-Saxon shires in blocks, setting over them
'earls', who replaced the ealdormen of the centuries before. Three
of these earls were to play great and conflicting parts in subsequent
English politics: Godwin, who was made Earl of Wessex; Leofric,

who was given Mercia; and Siward – Earl of Northumbria, who plays a dramatic, if unhistorical, part in Shakespeare's *Macbeth*. Godwin and Leofric were native-born Englishmen, and Canute had no desire to replace native lords or native customs if he could avoid it. Indeed, soon after his accession, in a council at Oxford, he publicly re-affirmed the code of Edgar which allowed English and Danes to follow their own laws. And there is no record of any English rebellion in his reign. People seem to have recognized that whatever his legal claim to the throne he was a man to keep the peace and give justice. As such they respected him.

With enemies and rivals to the throne he could be ruthless. The old West Saxon line had not died out with Edmund Ironside. Over in Normandy, Ethelred's son, Edward, was growing to manhood, pious and unworldly, but a possible centre of opposition. Edmund Ironside's own sons were summarily dispatched to the remote kingdom of Hungary. And Canute kept about him a devoted bodyguard of picked troops, called his 'housecarls', ready at all times to defend his person.

It was probably to avoid other dangers to his throne that Canute put away his first wife, Aelfgyfu, and married Ethelred's widow, Emma. As the church had never recognized Canute's first marriage, this strange arrangement was allowed. Outwardly at least, Canute kept the church in great respect. Born a heathen, he had been baptized before coming to England, and as king he showed great interest in church affairs. He endowed at Bury St Edmund's a monastery which was to become one of the richest in the land, its patron saint being the king slain in the first Danish invasions. He had the bones of Alphege, the Archbishop of Canterbury martyred by the Danes in 1012, enshrined with great solemnity in Canterbury cathedral. The chroniclers of the English church remembered Canute as a righteous protector, but of his real sincerity we cannot be certain. Like many kings of his age he saw in the organization of the church and the education of its officers a sturdy prop to the throne. In Scandinavia, his religious reputation is low. By Norwegians he is remembered as the enemy of their patron saint, St Olaf, a rival for the throne.

Canute died in Shaftesbury in 1035, at the age of forty-one. He was buried beside the West Saxon kings at Winchester. Four

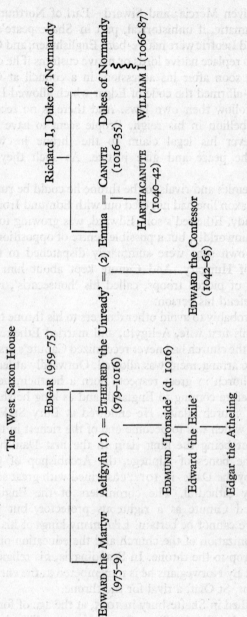

TABLE I. *English Kings before the Norman Conquest*

The West Saxon House

King HAROLD HAREFOOT (1035-40) was son of Canute by an earlier marriage.

hundred years later his body was found, the crown still on its head. But for thirty years after his death England lay in uncertainty, surrounded by enemies and by watchful claimants to a disputed throne.

Canute's sons did him no credit, and it was not at first obvious which of them should take his place. Harthacanute, his son by his second wife, Emma, was in Denmark when his father died, fending off the new king of Norway. In his absence the throne fell to his half-brother, Harold Harefoot, son of Aelfgyfu. When he died in 1040, Harthacanute was invited to England. But his reign too was short. Two years after his arrival he died – 'as he stood in his drink', said the outspoken chronicler. Neither king had had time or inclination to rule like his father, and before Harthacanute's body was in its grave the old West Saxon line had been restored with the acclamation in London of Edward, known to history as the Confessor.

One of the most significant marriages in English history had taken place in 1001, when Ethelred the Unready had married Emma – that same Emma who was later to marry Canute – the daughter of Richard I, Duke of Normandy. The only son of the marriage to grow to manhood was Edward, later given by the Church the title of 'Confessor'. All through the reigns of the Danish kings Edward had remained in Normandy, so that when he came to accept his inheritance in England he came as a stranger, Norman in speech, and in friends, Norman in feeling, half Norman in blood.

The area of northern France later to be called Normandy had suffered in the age of Alfred the same experience of Scandinavian raid and invasion as Britain. In 910, a weak king of France had indeed been forced to grant territory to the leading Northman, Rollo, much as had the kings of Wessex. As these Northmen – or Normans – settled down they lost much of their Viking identity, though little of their Viking energy. In language and custom they became French, and their dukes regarded themselves as the fellows and equals of the other powerful dukes and counts who owed, but seldom gave, obedience to the French king. They accepted Christianity quickly and showed themselves more zealous than any other continental people in the reformation of the Church. By the time of Edward the Confessor's sojourn there their abbeys were becoming renowned in Europe for purity of life and learning. And in the art of building they rapidly became masters.

But as they multiplied, land became short and their younger sons aggressive. As their ancestors had been adventurers at sea so they turned to adventure on land. Parties of them rode away from Normandy to high deeds on the southern coasts of Europe, in the Roman Empire of the East, in Sicily, and in the Holy Land. But the eyes of their duke, William, who, though illegitimate, succeeded his father in 1035, were most often turned to England.

The Norman friends and connections of Edward the Confessor were hardly likely to be popular among the English and Danish warrior lords whom Canute had raised up. Particularly were they disliked by the ambitious Earl of Wessex, who had played a scheming part in the feuds and rivalries of Canute's wives and sons. Godwin was probably no worse than most of the magnates of the day, but seeing the weak and unworldly Edward ascend the throne he determined to be the power behind it. Along with his own rivals, Leofric of Mercia and Siward of Northumbria, he was present at Edward's Easter coronation at Winchester in 1043, and he had soon placed himself in a dominating position by arranging the marriage of his daughter, Edith, to the king. But Edward can have had little love for his new father-in-law, and in 1051 an event occurred which gave the king a chance to free himself from his continual and watchful presence.

What exactly happened in that year we do not know, but it began with a brawl at Dover between the visiting Count of Boulogne and some citizens of the port. To soften the anger of his foreign guest, who felt himself grievously insulted by the scuffle, Edward ordered Godwin to punish Dover with fire and sword. Godwin, whose lands by now stretched from Cornwall to Thanet, curtly refused and raised an army to help make his point. But this time the earl had overreached himself. As his army approached Gloucester, where the king was, he heard that Edward was being reinforced by Leofric and Siward. A full-scale battle seemed imminent, and Godwin, thinking he would probably lose it, agreed to terms. Within a month he and his large brood of truculent sons were in exile, and his daughter, the queen, enclosed in a Wiltshire nunnery, her goods in the keeping of the relieved and triumphant king.

With Godwin temporarily away, Edward felt free to call over his old Norman friends, giving them generous gifts of lands and church offices. He had much at his disposal, for Godwin and his sons possessed nearly half England. And a more important guest came over, the Duke of Normandy himself. Edward, with no direct heir of his own body, had apparently determined that William would succeed him. The monastic ideals which Edward held so dear were most purely practised in Normandy, and for this reason more than any other William seemed to Edward the only possible choice. After a brief stay, William departed, in the knowledge that the throne of England might one day be his. He was not a man to let slip a prize like that.

It was, however, this very influx of Normans to positions of power that enabled Godwin and his family to return. Godwin had been methodically collecting a fleet just as Edward, equally methodically, had been disbanding one. In the midsummer of 1052, he sailed from Flanders and began to harry the south coast, meeting there another squadron which his son Harold had brought from his exile in Ireland. Together, and with a further strengthening from Kentish supporters, Godwin and his son sailed up the Thames. This time it was Edward's turn to make terms. At a meeting of the Witan outside London Godwin rebutted all the charges against him and the king gave way. All Godwin's lands were restored. Normans were turned out of what they had so recently won. The queen returned from her Wiltshire retreat to continue her bullying of the king. But Godwin had only a few months to enjoy his victory. In April 1053, he died, his inheritance and much of his political role passing to his eldest surviving son, Harold.

So nearly half Edward's reign had passed, in trouble and alarums. The rest of it brought, in England at least, somewhat more peace. But beyond England's borders and coasts dark threats remained. The kings of Norway, for example, regarded themselves as proper heirs to the whole of Canute's dominions. William of Normandy, his influence gone at Edward's court, waited impatiently for the death of the ageing king, seeing as he waited a growing barrier to his inheritance in the able and energetic Harold, who would hardly give up the throne without a fight. And in Wales, Gruffydd ap Llewellyn, ambitious king of Gwynedd and Powys – roughly, Wales's northern half – was uniting the whole country and threatening to cross the Severn.

It was against Gruffydd that Harold first showed his military skill and began that climb which made him for a few months in 1066 king of England. Gruffydd had powerful allies – a treacherous son of Leofric of Mercia and a Norwegian fleet. But in 1062 Harold struck quickly and deeply into Wales and drove Gruffydd into flight. And in the following year he harried the Welsh court so effectively that in desperation Gruffydd's followers murdered their leader to buy peace. To the king in London Harold brought the Welshman's severed head, while Wales, once more split into small provinces, vowed, not for the last time, eternal loyalty to England.

In 1063, Harold's fame was at its height. And Edward now took little interest in politics. For him the real crown of his life's work was the great abbey he was building some miles to the west of London at Westminster. As he sickened, the problem of his successor grew more acute. In 1052, he had promised the crown to William. But there was a member of the old West Saxon house still living, the grandson of Edmund Ironside and the Confessor's own great-nephew – Edgar the Atheling. But this Edgar was a child, and in times of peril it was unlikely that the English would permit him to succeed. More and more it seemed that Harold, who had proved himself so capable of defending the land, would be chosen when the old king died.

Harold, however, had put himself in a difficult position. Some time in 1065, he had been sent on a mission by Edward to the continent and had unluckily landed on Norman territory and been taken before William. According to the Bayeux Tapestry, which vividly paints the tale of these years, he joined William in some local military adventure and took an oath of fidelity to the Norman duke. Exactly what this oath was we cannot tell, but the Normans later claimed that it made all his later conduct that of an oath-breaker and a man who could morally claim the allegiance of none.

From the autumn of 1065 to the October day of Hastings events in England moved rapidly. The Northumbrians suddenly rose against their earl, now Harold's brother Tostig, plunging the north into confusion. Edward fell gravely ill. He was too weak to attend the consecration of Westminster Abbey at the end of the year, and on 5 January 1066 he died. By unanimous decision of the Witan in London, Harold was chosen king. Hearing it, William began his preparations for invasion.

That William and not Harold won at Hastings was largely due to luck. But luck often rides with great commanders. It so happened that William's own usually hostile neighbours, in Anjou, Flanders and Paris, were for the moment eclipsed, and the whole French coast from Brittany to the mouth of the Scheldt was either his or manned by his allies. Volunteers, eager to join so renowned a warrior, flocked to him from France and from the southern Norman lands, in the firm hope of estates and loot. From the pope came moral support, for William was to fight not only against an oath-breaker but against an Archbishop of Canterbury – Stigand – who was considered in Rome to have been wrongfully elected. To William's waiting army was sent the banner of St Peter.

Harold, with a united country behind him, might yet have been equal to this threat. But his luck was as bad as William's was good. Had he had but one enemy to face, there might have been a Norman invasion without a Norman conquest, for Harold had concentrated on the south coast more troops than William could have brought by sea. But there were other foes, just as much to be feared. Harold had been forced, for the sake of peace, to support the Northumbrians in their action against his brother, Tostig, and now Tostig was in exile seeking ways of revenge. In Norway, the king, Harold Hardrada, still claiming the full inheritance of Canute, was preparing a great maritime expedition against England. He was a warrior to be reckoned with, fearless, ruthless, experienced from days spent commanding the Emperor's guard in Constantinople. If he were to land in Northumbria, where Harold's hold was light, he might easily recreate, in more formidable form, the old Norwegian Kingdom of York.

During the spring of 1066, Harold reckoned that the Norman menace was the greater. While William slowly built up his invasion force, Harold summoned and grouped the English *fyrd* and kept his housecarls in continuous training. In May, his defences were tested when Tostig, with an improvised mercenary fleet, began to harry the south coast. Harold chased him away, but Tostig then sailed up the east coast and put into the Humber estuary. There he was confronted by Edwin, Earl of Mercia, of the house of Leofric, and his men were sent scurrying back to their ships to try again further north. But Edwin's brother, Morcar, stopped a further landing in Yorkshire. Temporarily foiled, Tostig sailed to Scotland, where England's enemies were usually made welcome, and there remained for the summer in close touch with the king of Norway.

For Harold Godwinson, patiently patrolling with his channel fleet, all this was little more than a nuisance. What mattered to him might come any time – a shift in the wind from east to south that would bring the Duke of Normandy. By mid-August the Normans were ready. But the wind blew steadily from between north and east and William's invading force lay idle. By early September, Harold's men were so restless, so impatient for action or for home and harvest that he was forced to disband the *fyrd* and lay up his fleet. The Channel lay open to William, and in a westerly breeze he edged nearer his goal, sailing from near Le Havre to the mouth of the river Somme.

Then, suddenly, to Harold, came the news of Hardrada's landing with more than 300 ships on the Yorkshire coast and of his advance to the city of York. There was no time to be lost. The wind still blew in the faces of the Normans. The Channel was empty. Harold turned with his housecarls to the north. There Hardrada had already met the Earls Edwin and Morcar at Fulford forcing them, after an indecisive and expensive battle, to make terms. And now he placed himself astride the river Derwent at the road junction of Stamford Bridge. On 25 September, after a forced march up the old Roman road, Harold came upon him. By the end of that day the Norwegians were shattered, their king and Harold's brother Tostig dead on the field. Of the 300 ships in which they had come they needed only twenty-four to take their remnant back to Norway. Vowing never to threaten England again, they sailed away to the north-east in a gentle southerly breeze.

But this same wind that took the Norwegians brought the Duke of Normandy.

It was two days after Stamford Bridge that William sailed with his mixed host of adventurers, six or seven thousand of them, under the Papal banner. Of Harold's doings in the north they knew nothing. They expected to have to face him as soon as they landed; and when their duke's own ship parted from them in the freshening wind they must have wished themselves back in the safety of their estuary. But Harold was 250 miles from Sussex with his half-manned fleet helplessly landlocked in the Thames. On the 28th William, safely united with his men, landed at Pevensey.

After fortifying Pevensey he moved on to Hastings. The news of Harold's absence and its cause brought new confidence. Indeed he could not have known, as he waited at Hastings which Harold he would meet.

It was 1 October when Harold of England, resting at York, heard of William's landing. Sending out orders for all available troops to meet him in London he left on the 3rd for the south. One of the most astounding marches in history brought him to the Thames in eight days, and by the 13th he was in sight of the Normans, his army tired and depleted, his fresh reinforcements few. In sheer numbers he probably surpassed his enemy, but the Normans had been resting for over a fortnight and were sure of victory. While Harold's men feasted in a last desperate hour of gaiety, the Normans, their own chroniclers assure us, turned the night into a vigil of prayer.

14 October decided the future of England; but until late in the day the battle could have swung either way. From their shield wall on a hill to the north the English flung back attack after attack with showers of arrows, spears, or stones, or with the great two-handed axe of the housecarls that cut through the Norman mail like boxwood. In their elation at the wavering of the Norman cavalry, however, the English rushed down from their hill, unable to forgo the joy of pursuit. But at this point William himself rallied his faltering men who turned ferociously to throw the pursuers back. About the English now there was a fatal wildness, but the Normans had the discipline still to repeat their withdrawal and once more bring the English down from their height. As they streamed down from there into the trap, Harold lay dead from a chance arrow, two of his brothers with him. Hearing it, the English crumpled. The day was lost. England had been successfully invaded for the last time.

CHAPTER 8

The Norman Conquest
1066-1087

WILLIAM did not rest long on the laurels of Hastings. The immediate pursuit over, he returned to the field of victory to feast amid the corpses and to command the siting of an abbey dedicated to St Martin and later known as Battle. Then he began the process that was to turn the defeat of an army into the conquest of a people.

The first goal must obviously be London. But to approach it William had to march right round the Kentish coast avoiding the dense oak forest of the Weald. On his way, he punished the men of Romney for a chance skirmish with his men, set in hand the fortification of Dover, and for a month delayed in Canterbury, the spiritual centre of England. A march up the southern bank of the Thames then brought him to Southwark; but, deciding that the storming of London Bridge would be too rash, he struck out in a wide arc to the west of the city laying waste the country as he went. Crossing the Thames at Wallingford, he turned back towards the city and at Berkhampstead received the submission of its now terrified citizens. At first, the Londoners had thought of resistance and had nominated Edgar Atheling, Edmund Ironside's grandson, as king, but the ruthless, destructive progress of the Normans soon made them change their mind. Led by Stigand, the archbishop whose deposition William had promised to effect, they came out to make their peace and to offer him what he had long ago determined to have, the crown of England. So on Christmas Day, 1066, before the high altar of the Confessor's church at Westminster, William was made king, while outside the church, the Norman guards, mistaking the congregation's cry of agreement for the yells of assassination, set fire to houses in sudden panic.

The England that stretched before William had changed little from that which Edgar the Peaceable had governed a century before. Less than a million and a half people were scattered unevenly over a land in which forest still predominated. About five million acres were under the plough – less than half that in our own day – and all but a tenth of the population were countrymen, scratching an uncertain living from great open fields and meadows spread round villages and hamlets. Except for the small number of slaves this country population was still free in law, but, as we have seen, the status of the churl had by 1066 undoubtedly declined; many were having to work for their lords in order to keep their right to their plots of land. The villagers were still responsible for law and order in their districts and had to attend a few times a year at the local hundred courts where the king's sheriff or bailiff would preside. And all men were liable to military service in the *fyrd*.

Towns had been slowly but steadily growing. London's population had by now reached about 20,000. But only York, Norwich and Lincoln had more than 5,000 inhabitants, with Oxford, Thetford, Ipswich and Gloucester close behind. Trade was sporadic rather than regular, most of it local and conducted by barter, though overseas commerce and the use of money were increasing. Already those gilds which were to be so prominent a part of medieval town life had come to birth and were beginning to regulate the merchants and craftsmen of the towns.

There was, by modern standards, little sense of national unity in the England that faced William. There was much more than in France, whose king's power outside his own small domain around Paris was almost nil. There was more than in Germany, whose dukes still wrestled ceaselessly for power. But the inhabitant of the England of 1066 was far more conscious of being a man of Sussex or of Mercia, than of being an Englishman; and it is probable that when William was crowned many men in the remoter spots had not even heard that he had landed. A man's duty to his king was certainly keenly felt, but his duty to his immediate lord was stronger simply because he was nearer. Customs and laws varied in different parts of the land. It would have been foolish for any king to try to root them out or to weld them into one iron system.

That the new king was a foreigner, then, was of little account. Among recent kings, Canute and his sons had been Danes, Edward a Norman in all but blood, and Harold the son of a man of obscure birth. This may help to explain why William, after Hastings, met no grand national uprising. For the most part men accepted him, with little enthusiasm, with some resentment, but only here and there, under some local warrior leader, with armed resistance. To his new subjects William's policy, like most things in his character, was simple and direct. Where men were loyal he was generous and humane. Where they fought him, he was ruthless and without pity.

So confident was he at first that in March 1067, after a brief progress in the south and the raising of a few castles, he returned to Normandy. He left to govern in his stead a mixed council of Normans and Englishmen, headed by his companion in arms, William FitzOsbern, now made Earl of Hereford, and his own half-brother, Odo, the fighting Bishop of Bayeux, whom he made Earl of Kent. But his confidence was premature. At the end of the year he returned to find turmoil, with the flag of rebellion raised in many corners of the land, the people furious at the harsh rule and taxes of the Norman barons. Luckily for him, the risings could be dealt with separately and had no central organization. Three years William spent in crushing them – at Exeter, in the Midlands, in Yorkshire, along the Welsh border. The most terrible, in its threat and its consequences, was the rising in Northumbria, aided as it was by a Danish fleet and marked at its beginning by the slaughter of a Norman expeditionary force.

It was this northern rising which finally prompted William to give up his policy of firmness mixed with conciliation, of co-operation where it was possible with the native aristocracy, and made him turn to terrorism. He determined that an example would be made, an example so frightful that the English would be cowed for ever into obedience. It took the hideous form of a devastation of the north, so complete, so thorough, that it was many years before the region began to recover. Not only did he burn the crops and slaughter the cattle, as he had in some earlier marches. He turned a thousand square miles into a desert, littered with the charred remains of dwellings, the bodies and limbs of men, the fragments of those farm tools wherein lay the only hope of quick revival. Even Norman writers speak of it with horror. The compilers of the great Domesday survey fifteen years later can only describe parts of the north country with the stark, vivid word: 'waste'. Between York and Durham there was left not one inhabited

place. But on such ruin and starvation William built at last a
stable throne.

The gruesome work was finished by 1070. Soon of all the English
rebels only one, the most famous, still held out, in the swamps of
the Isle of Ely. But with the downfall of this stronghold Hereward
the Wake moved out of history and into the timeless legends of his
people.

So William's early experiment of joint Anglo-Norman rule
came to an end. Along with the killing had gone a large-scale removal of the old English landed families. Not only do English names
vanish from William's council but they go from local records of
landowners. By the end of the reign only one sizeable estate in ten
was held by an Englishman. The rest were in the hands of
William's men.

With the change of men came a change in custom of far-reaching
consequence.

It was as a military conqueror that William came. It was as a
military conqueror that he remained. Above all else he was concerned with military security. And that meant for him two things:
the building and garrisoning of castles; and the constant supply of
mounted troops. The castles he began building as soon as he
arrived, the first being at Pevensey and the second at Hastings.
A castle began as a simple strong-point made up of a mound surrounded by a wooden stockade and a ditch. If more strength was
needed and if time permitted a stone keep would be built and the
weakest point of the stockade, its entrance, re-inforced by a stone
gatehouse. Such castles were not merely defensive but were bases
from which occupying troops could hold down the countryside.
By the end of the century not a single large town in England was
without one.

Of William's forces the core was the armoured knight, now
virtually supreme in European warfare and to remain so until the
arrival of the long bow. Before 1066, the armoured knight who
fought on horseback with lance and broadsword was unknown in
England, where men would ride to the field but dismount to fight.
William, however, on settling his leading comrades on the
conquered land, naturally demanded from them what he had been
wont to receive in Normandy, the provision when needed of
knights for his army. He demanded it not only from his military

lieutenants but from the bishops and abbots he appointed as well. Only on such conditions was land granted, and when an area was so granted it was called in Norman-French a *fief* and in Latin a *feudum*. From this term *feudum* historians many centuries later coined the word 'feudalism' to describe a society where land was normally held in this way, and it can be safely used to describe post-Conquest England.

The man who held land from the king on these terms, who was called a tenant-in-chief, in order to be able to provide the necessary knights, must himself grant away portions of it to the knights themselves; for the proper upkeep of horses and arms – both expensive commodities in those days – needed both wealth and a secure holding of land. So society became in a sense a great pyramid, with the king at its summit, his tenants-in-chief below him and their tenants below that. Such had been the arrangement in Normandy and thus it was repeated in England. Yet it was in England not quite so simple. Outside this pyramid altogether, the King of Norman England, because he wore the crown of the Anglo-Saxons, held every man to a special loyalty, called 'fealty', which soared above any lesser allegiance and prevented England from falling into the welter of private war which inevitably attended feudalism on the continent. William demanded from his English subjects an obedience he would not have dreamed of giving to his own continental lord, the king of France.

To the low-born Englishman, the Conquest then meant first a change of lord. For the old thegn was substituted the new knight. It was usually a change for the worse. Before the Conquest the freeborn churl had, it is true, been becoming less and less free. But now he was classed, along with many who were once his inferiors, as a *villanus* or villein – a wide term which, though it once meant merely 'countryman', was soon describing anyone who was bound to the soil, bound to work for his lord, a member of an estate called a *manor*, who could often obtain freedom or better conditions only by running away. And beside the old courts to which he was accustomed, there grew up the court of the manor, meeting more frequently, before which he could be summoned for offences against his lord and over whose proceedings he had little influence.

Another Norman innovation made the life of a peasant still worse. 'The forest', said a writer in the twelfth century, 'has its

own laws, based, it is said, not on the Common Law of the realm
but on the arbitrary law of the king . . . In the forests are the secret
places of the kings and their chief delight. For here they come,
laying aside their cares, now and then, to hunt as a rest and
recreation. It is there that they can put from them the anxious
turmoil of the court and take a little breath in the free air of nature.
And that is why forest offenders are punished only at the king's
pleasure.' Hunting was indeed the chief leisure occupation of the
Norman kings, and great tracts of England's wood and moorland
were set aside for them, where a peasant discovered killing game
was subject to savage mutilation or even death. The most famous
of these areas was the so-called New Forest, but all over the land
the sacred preserves were to be found. Most of Essex was one, as
were the Derbyshire peaks, the famous Sherwood Forest, and
great expanses of the midlands. In such places villagers suddenly
found that one of their chief sources of food was theirs only at
their extreme peril, and from the sentence of the forest court there
was no appeal. Not until the end of the twelfth century did the
prohibited areas stop growing, and it is probable that to most
Englishmen the Charter of the Forest of 1217 brought far more
good than the better-known Magna Carta of two years before.

In the pursuit of their open-air pleasures and in the punitive
devastation of rebellious lands, the Norman kings showed themselves at their most savage and tyrannical. But it cannot be denied
that in general they brought to England strong and beneficial
government in an age when the absence of it was the inevitable
signal for worse misery. Those were days when a people judged
their king by the order he brought. Of the Conqueror an English
chronicler said: 'Among other things must not be forgotten the
good peace he made in this land; so that a man of any account
might go over his kingdom unhurt with his bosom full of gold'.
After the weakness of the Confessor this was something worth
having. The stern castle and the forbidden forest meant that there
was on the throne a king who meant to be obeyed, not only by the
conquered but by the conquerors themselves. 'The king was very
dignified', wrote the same chronicler. 'Thrice he wore his crown
each year, as oft as he was in England. At Easter he wore it in
Winchester, at Whitsun in Westminster, at Christmas in Gloucester. And then were with him all the rich men over all England:

archbishops and bishops; abbots and earls, thegns and knights. So very stern was he and hot, that no man durst do anything against his will.'

These ceremonial crown-wearing occasions were the meetings of the Great Council of the realm, which had replaced the old Saxon Witan. It contained all those who held land direct from the king, his tenants-in-chief. But most of his governing was done through a smaller body of advisers, a few great barons and permanent royal officials who would travel about with him through his kingdom when he exercised the powers he had inherited from the Confessor, demanding from each man the obedience due from all to the king. The cream of William's army was the feudal knight; but like his predecessors he still demanded both the service of the *fyrd* and the general tax of Danegeld, first levied in panic on his people by the ineffective Ethelred. The cause of it was gone. There were no longer invading Danes to be bribed into good behaviour. But the Conqueror found in it a source of income wider and steadier than any he had known in his homeland. Moreover, without the powers left him by the Saxon kings he could hardly have set on foot the remarkable survey of his kingdom's resources which he began in 1086.

This Domesday survey, as it is called, has no parallel in Europe. Its results, in the Domesday Book now kept in the Public Record Office in London, are a mine of information to the historian as they must have been to the Norman kings, and they are a sign too of the immense efficiency of the king's clerks. As the surveyors toured the country they made a minute inquiry into the resources of every plot of land. Who held it in the days of King Edward? they asked. Who holds it now? What is it worth? Into the book the answers were carefully copied and gave the king as complete a picture as it was possible for him to get of the wealth and estates of his subjects. It can never cease to amaze us that the leader of a few thousand adventurers should, in twenty years, have established a power so great that, as a reluctant admirer wrote: 'there was not a hide in England that he knew not who had it, or what it was worth, and afterwards set it down in his book. It is shameful to tell,' added the writer wryly, 'though he thought it no shame to do it'. Such prying efficiency was not popular with the easy-going English. But they had to suffer it.

They also had to endure a reorganization of their church. Not so long ago, historians used to think that the Anglo-Saxon church had by 1066 sunk from its greatness under Dunstan to a state of illiteracy and sloth, that its clerical morals were abysmal, and that it was under the control of a laity who ran it like successful racketeers. Thus the Normans, went the theory, brought to it new light and fresh vitality. We think rather differently today. It is true that the burst of zeal which Edgar and Dunstan encouraged and controlled in the tenth century had mostly spent itself; that there was some inefficiency and slackness; that too many priests, in defiance of the law of the church, had taken wives and were treating their livings as hereditary; that too few had enough education to guide the souls under their care. But this state of things was probably no worse than in most European churches of the day. We know the names of many saintly English clergy at the time. For holiness of life there was no Norman bishop to equal Wulfstan of Worcester. In the arts of illumination and line drawing the Normans had almost everything to learn.

But one reform the Anglo-Saxon church most certainly needed, and that was reorganization. Its dioceses – areas controlled by a bishop – were haphazardly arranged, having grown with the old Saxon kingdoms. Some sprawled across many shires. In many the bishop's seat – or 'cathedral' – was sited miles from a town or centre of communication. It was not even clear who was head of the Church, the Archbishop of Canterbury or of York. Canterbury had no authority beyond the Humber, and the holder of the office, Stigand, had been rejected by the pope. The Archbishop of York ruled with little reference to anyone over a province of indefinite extent. In the monasteries there were, in spite of the reforms of Dunstan, too many different customs and an uncertain method of outside inspection; and true it is that many of them were regarded by the family of their founder as his personal property with the abbot as his nominee.

Into this church of assorted holiness and looseness, discipline and laxity, there came, in 1070, as Stigand's successor, a scholarly Italian monk. He was abbot of the Conqueror's own foundation at Caen and had been prior – that is to say, second in command – of the more famous Norman abbey of Bec. Before this, he had had a legal training in Italy, possibly in his birthplace of Pavia. His name was Lanfranc, and William had possibly intended from the beginning of his enterprise that he should be appointed to the see of Canterbury. For Lanfranc, as for his successor Anselm, the promotion brought no thought of joy or excitement. He had found peace in the cloister and had no desire for the bustle and anxieties of church government and politics. Yet he became one of the most illustrious of all Canterbury's archbishops, effecting in twenty years a complete overhaul of the administration of the English church.

First, he made sure that as Archbishop of Canterbury he would in fact and in law be its head. From the new Norman Archishop of York he demanded and at length reluctantly received a profession of obedience, making it permanent by the use of documents which, probably unknown to Lanfranc, were in fact forgeries. York was left with a province which began at the Humber and stretched far into Scotland. But even there his rule was liable to be challenged by Scotland's king or by the princely and independent minded bishops of Durham. Yet the act was final. Quarrels there would be; but henceforward the Archbishop of Canterbury was Primate of All England.

With these new powers and with the close support of William, Lanfranc set about his task of reorganization. The remoter cathedrals were moved to centres of communication: from Selsey to Chichester, Sherborne to Salisbury, Dorchester-on-Thames to Lincoln. Their bishops were called, as in Theodore's day, to frequent synods, and whenever there was a vacancy it was promptly filled with a Norman from Lanfranc's own circle of enthusiasts. But the archbishop was no ecclesiastical bulldozer. He knew that his church must be an English church, that only if its members were loyal could it be strong. So over the age-old question of the clergy's wives he moved cautiously. Those married already, he said, might keep their wives, but newly ordained priests must be single and remain so. Nor did he make any wholesale removal of English bishops and abbots. Only those who had never been properly consecrated were removed. The rest were left until God created a vacancy.

Inevitably, there was some bitterness. Local saints and their relics, long precious to the English, were sometimes laughable to the Normans who refused to pay them any reverence. And not all

Normans had Lanfranc's moderation. The new Norman abbot of
Glastonbury, most ancient of English houses, was so eager to
impose Norman chants on the conservative monks that he lost his
temper at their obstinacy and ordered his soldiers into the abbey to
change their tunes at the point of the arrow. Two monks were
killed and a dozen wounded. The new abbot was exiled, but
William Rufus, typically, let him buy himself back into his job
again.

The English chronicler called Lanfranc 'the father and consolation of monks'. He was always ready with advice and advisers.
Most of his abbots did in fact bring new ideas and new life and
helped to bring the English into contact with continental reforms,
of which they had had little since the days of Dunstan.

He worked so closely with the king that William saw no danger
to his throne in giving the church jurisdiction over its own affairs.
In 1072, he ordered that no ecclesiastical case must be heard in the
shire or hundred courts but must be taken to the bishop, who
would judge it according to church law. So a separation was made
which a hundred years later was to bring a new martyr to Canterbury and which was a cause of smouldering conflict between
church and king until Henry VIII, who neatly abolished the
quarrel between the two courts by becoming the head of both of
them.

Strong churchman though he was, Lanfranc was no supporter of
the increasing claims being made at this time by the pope to
govern the whole church more completely. Lanfranc had been
brought up at a time when the papacy was weak and ineffective,
when reform could only be accomplished by enthusiasts on the
spot. So he saw no wrong in William's insistence that the pope
should exercise no authority in England without royal permission.
To the claim of Pope Gregory VII that the land converted by the
pope's own messenger, St Augustine, belonged to the pope by
right William the Conqueror sent a short, stern answer. There is
no evidence that Lanfranc opposed it.

Today, when the old monasteries are dead and the bonds of
Rome broken seemingly for ever, we still have about us a permanent memorial of the Normans. They were magnificent builders.
Their changes and reforms were symbolized in massive stone walls
which in fortress and church began to arise within a few years of

Hastings. The Norman building was built to last. The stone roof vault, replacing the inflammable wood, could then only be borne by thick walls and broad pillars, and even where from the outside an English cathedral seems the work of a later age it will often be found to have only an elaborate disguise clothing a skeleton of Norman foundations and columns. The new building techniques can be seen at their best at Durham, where the great cathedral on its rock above the river Wear still reminds us of how the Normans dominated England. Durham was not begun until after the Conqueror's death, but work began on a new cathedral at Canterbury soon after Lanfranc's arrival and in seven years was completed. Lincoln was begun in 1072; Old Sarum, on the hill above the present town of Salisbury, a few years later; St Albans, Rochester, Ely, Winchester, and Worcester, all before 1087. On the field of Hastings the new abbey of Battle was soon finished, and scores of parish churches sprang up everywhere.

The prime mover in it all, William I of England, died in 1087, as his Domesday survey neared completion. A year before, at Salisbury, he had held a council at which he demanded from all the more important tenants of his own tenants a solemn oath of fealty. Here 'they bowed themselves before him, and became his men, and swore that they would against all other men be faithful to him'. It was a fitting end to his reign, more fitting by far than his actual death, which came in the midst of a campaign against his own feudal lord, the king of France. As he rode through the burning town of Mantes falling brands caused his horse to stumble, and William suffered an internal injury which was mortal. He died in September on the hills above his old capital of Rouen with a few to attend him. As life left his body, those few stripped him of his clothes and ornaments and rode away.

CHAPTER 9

The Sons of the Conqueror

1087-1135

WILLIAM THE CONQUEROR left three sons. None of them was attractive, and they spent much of their lives fighting one another for the dead king's inheritance.

The most pleasant was the eldest, Robert, called from the shortness of his legs, Curthose. To him, with some reluctance, the Conqueror left his homeland, the Duchy of Normandy. A dumpy, jovial little figure, he was affable and lazy, kind but easily led, brave in the moment of battle but preferring the well-loaded dining-table. Of the arts of government he knew and cared little. He was spasmodically ambitious and vaguely felt he ought to be king of England. But he gave little help to those who tried to realize his ambitions for him.

England, the Conqueror gave to his second son, the stocky, burly, bad-tempered William Rufus. He was in many ways the opposite of Robert. He was energetic and practical, preferring to win what he wanted by diplomacy – which usually meant bribery – rather than by war. He could be wildly generous and relentlessly grasping by turns. Military adventurers from all western Europe flocked to his court at the news of his generosity, while the English people complained bitterly of his weighty taxation. He was totally irreligious, though the master of much of his youth was Lanfranc, and he regarded the Church as a useful additional treasury. Just as Robert was Duke of Normandy and felt he should be King of England, Rufus was King of England and wanted Normandy. But unlike Robert he usually got what he wanted.

The youngest son, Henry, was left landless by his father. Instead he was given five thousand pounds of silver which he characteristically weighed on receipt. A later age called him

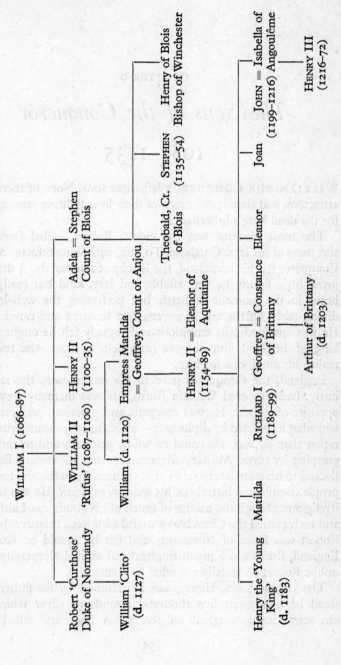

TABLE II. *The Norman and Early Plantagenet Kings*

WILLIAM I (1066–87)

- Robert 'Curthose' Duke of Normandy
  - William 'Clito' (d. 1127)
- WILLIAM II 'Rufus' (1087–1100)
- HENRY I (1100–35)
  - William (d. 1120)
  - Empress Matilda = Geoffrey, Count of Anjou
    - HENRY II (1154–89) = Eleanor of Aquitaine
      - Henry the 'Young King' (d. 1183)
      - RICHARD I (1189–99)
      - Geoffrey = Constance of Brittany
        - Arthur of Brittany (d. 1203)
      - Matilda
      - Eleanor
      - Joan
      - JOHN (1199–1216) = Isabella of Angoulême
        - HENRY III (1216–72)
- Adela = Stephen Count of Blois
  - Theobald, Ct. of Blois
  - STEPHEN (1135–54)
  - Henry of Blois Bishop of Winchester

Beauclerk, or 'fine scholar', but it is not clear why. He was intelligent, certainly, and when he was king he patronized a few men of learning. But like most contemporary rulers, he could not write and could read only haltingly. He had most of Rufus's bad qualities and none of Robert's good ones. He was dominated by greed for money. His private life was scandalous. To religion he gave only lip service, choosing his chaplain for his speed in saying mass. Yet he had some of the marks of a statesman, and as King Henry I of England did much to bring good, if stern, government. His motive, no doubt, was personal gain, but this was an age when a selfish and brutal king could bring to his people better conditions than a pleasant easy-going ruler.

This was demonstrated in Normandy soon after the Conqueror's death, by Robert, its new duke. Under the Conqueror the restless duchy had lain quiet through fear and through the expectations of loot which loyal service to the duke might give. But that the Conqueror's government was based on little more than force and terror was amply proved on his death, when his garrisons, placed carefully in baronial castles, were removed, suppressed, or won over by the castle owners, and when any semblance of general order vanished from the countryside. All Robert did was to accept the situation, occasionally winning support by a gift or by a cession of lands for cash. The landless Henry, for example, was given much of the west of the duchy in exchange for some of his precious silver; but this did not satisfy him for long.

The weakness of Normandy gave great satisfaction to its neighbours. The Conqueror had made it the most powerful duchy in France but by doing so had made bitter enemies. To the south of Normandy lay the county of Anjou, ruled by a family as ruthless in ambition as the Normans. Between Normandy and Anjou lay a small, rich tract of land called Maine, annexed by William in 1063, constantly in rebellion against him, now opportunely seized by Fulk, count of Anjou. To the south east of Normandy, round the growing city of Paris, was the domain land of the King of France, now the almost immovably fat Philip I, ready to support any cause which might weaken the duchy and preserve from it the small county in between them, the Véxin. It had been in a campaign for the Véxin that the Conqueror had died, and now it was firmly held by Philip. To the west of Normandy was Brittany, a wild land looking much like Cornwall and peopled largely by men of Celtic descent, difficult to control at any time, now vaguely subject to Normandy but a fruitful field for Normandy's enemies. Finally, to Normandy's east was Flanders, already beginning her climb to her medieval supremacy in the cloth trade. Flanders and Normandy were bitter enemies. Only a temporary lull in their quarrels had made possible the Conqueror's English expedition and for the rest of his reign they gave him continual trouble.

A history of England cannot leave out these complicated continental relations. For one of the main results of the Conquest was to bring England into close connexion with them. The Norman kings were Normans first and foremost and in their quarrels with their neighbours inevitably involved the English. And the Normans were to be followed shortly as English kings by the family of Anjou, called Plantagenet, so that the area of English interest was pushed still farther south – with Henry Plantagenet's marriage as far as the Pyrenees.

It is fairly clear that Rufus, on rushing from his father's bedside to collect the royal treasure at Winchester and the crown at Westminster, had determined that Robert should not hold Normandy for long. But he was at first challenged in his own part of the inheritance. In apparent support of Robert's claim to England, the English Normans rose in large numbers, led by the ambitious and unpriestly Odo, Bishop of Bayeux. But Rufus was equal to the situation. He besieged Odo at Pevensey, then at Rochester, and banished him to Normandy. The rebellion quickly collapsed. Robert had given it no military support and Rufus had found strength in his native English subjects, who now saw in their king a friend against the grasping and bellicose barons who were their masters. It was a new twist. The Conqueror's chief fear was the native English. His barons had been given power to hold them down. But now the situation was reversed. It is a startling demonstration of how under the new kings the old Anglo-Saxon tradition of monarchy had endured. Not for the last time did the people of England join their king, whom personally they disliked, against his overmighty subjects. The great Tudors were to build their power on the same alliance.

The following year, 1089, saw the death of Lanfranc, whose last months could hardly have been happy as he watched the disintegration of so much the Conqueror had so painfully constructed. For Rufus his death was a double pleasure. It meant the removal of an annoying restraint on his actions; and it brought, till he chose to find a successor, the revenues of the archbishopric to himself. He had no intention of looking for a successor too diligently. He needed money, for in 1090, he was bribing Norman barons on the lower Somme away from their allegiance to Robert; and in 1091 he landed in Normandy himself, forcing Robert, weakened by desertions, to make terms and to promise to join in an enterprise to dislodge Henry from what he had bought with his silver. Henry shut himself up in the Benedictine priory of Mont St Michel, and the brothers amused themselves and their followers with jousts on the sands around the islands. It was hardly serious warfare, but Rufus thought Robert was carrying chivalry too far when he let Henry's men out to get water. Soon Henry gave in, and the three brothers, in a rare moment of amity, went off together to fight the Scots, who were making one of their usual forays across the border. The Conqueror had himself had trouble from them and had built the New Castle on the Tyne to deter them. And now Rufus, with great practical sense, having pushed the invaders back, built a stronghold at Carlisle and brought peasants from the south to settle in the newly won territory. But precise border there was yet none, and much blood would be wasted before the two kingdoms would agree on one.

The brothers' concord did not last long. Robert returned to his disorderly duchy, Henry to the remains of his holdings. In 1093 Rufus fell ill and thinking himself at the point of death decided he must fill the see of Canterbury. There was only one obvious candidate, the present abbot of Bec, the saintly and humane philosopher Anselm. Like Lanfranc he was an Italian. Like Lanfranc, too, he had no desire for the job. He had to be dragged protesting to Rufus's bedside and the pastoral staff forced into his fingers. But, as soon as he recovered, the king's spiritual ardour disappeared and he was locked in quarrels with Anselm which lasted for the rest of his reign. When, in 1097, the archbishop left the kingdom to consult with the pope that Rufus had refused even to recognize, his goods were seized and he never saw Rufus again.

In 1094, Rufus made another attempt on Normandy but he was recalled by further rebellions in England, rebellions which he put down with utmost savagery. But in 1096 the duchy fell, as it were, into his lap. For Robert, weary with the drain on his energies and money of constant fighting – even though occasionally supported by Philip of France who 'belching from daily excess came hicupping to war' – had heard the call to take the cross. In 1095 Pope Urban II, at the Council of Clermont in central France, had awakened both the conscience and the greed of the west with his call to aid the persecuted Christians in the Holy Land, and had followed the call with a preaching tour through France. In Robert the call awakened his latent chivalry and stoked up his dying love of adventure. He sold Normandy to Rufus for 10,000 marks, and departed with a company that contained no Englishmen.

Rufus's rule in Normandy was very different from Robert's. Normandy was soon reduced to the same unwilling obedience as England, the day of unbridled brigandage for a time being past. With a subdued Normandy at his feet Rufus was ready for further aggression and lost little time in attacking the disputed territories of the Véxin and Maine. In the Véxin his only achievement was the taking of Gisors, where he built a castle later famous in the bloody annals of Anglo-French war. Maine he took, but his hold was precarious and after his death it slipped back to Anjou.

Over Rufus's death, clouds of mystery still hang. In August 1100, while hunting in the New Forest near Brockenhurst, he was struck by an arrow from the bow of an attendant Norman knight, Walter Tirel. He died almost at once, and his body lay where it had fallen till some peasants threw it on a cart and took it to Winchester, where it still lies. Many theories have been advanced to account for the killing: that it was a sacrificial murder in a strange but widely distributed religious sect of which Rufus was a member, that it was a plain accident, or that it was a deliberate plot engineered by Henry. We shall never know the answer; but Henry waited for no mourning. Losing no time he rode to Winchester and seized the royal treasury, and three days later was crowned in Westminster. If the killing was not his work, then it was a very convenient accident.

Henry I may have been unpleasant, with his greed, his cruelty, his unnumbered illegitimate children, but he was one of the medieval kings whose work, whatever the motives behind it, was both constructive and lasting. Normandy was his first love, and

desire to possess it ruled his early years as king, but he showed
wisdom and statesmanship in his dealing with the English he
despised. And this was shown by two acts to which he gave
calculated publicity, his issue of a coronation charter and his
marriage. 'I abolish,' his charter said, 'all the evil customs with
which the realm of England has been unjustly oppressed,' and he
went on to enumerate them in some detail. The best of kings could
not have kept all the promises, and Henry broke most of them. But
at his death he gained grudging tributes from a people who clearly
respected a harsh king who did justice more than a kind king who
did none. His marriage, too, found a narrow way to their hearts. It
was to the daughter of the late King of Scotland and his English
queen Margaret, and with it Henry united the Normans with the
old West Saxon line. It was a tragedy for him that his careful
building of a dynasty should have been swept away with the death
of the only son of the marriage in the *White Ship* in 1120.

Also to gain security and popularity, Henry threw Rufus's chief
agent of oppressive taxation, Rannulf Flambard, into prison, and
recalled Anselm from his patient and scholarly exile. But all this
did little to placate the Norman barons. The history of Rufus's
reign was repeated as within a few months of his accession a series
of rebellions broke out, with Robert – now returned in fame and
triumph from captured Jerusalem – once more its focus, and
Rannulf Flambard, escaped from the Tower, its adroit organizer.
This time Robert came over to England in person, confident that
his journey to Westminster would be little more than a parade.
But just as the English *fyrd* had checked Odo of Bayeux at Rochester, so now they turned out in company with loyal Norman barons
in such numbers that Robert was forced to sue for terms. By the
Treaty of Alton in 1101 he agreed to return to Normandy as its
duke with an annuity and leave England to Henry.

Normandy sank again to its former chaos, now made worse by
the presence of the brutal Robert of Bellême, banished by Henry
from his English lands and venting his spleen on the Norman
peasants. With men such as him Robert Curthose had to make
friends if he was to hold the little he had, and while he hung fear-
fully on, Henry with crafty diplomacy prepared his counter attack.
In 1106, with a predominantly English force, he crowned his
invasions of Normandy with a crushing victory over Robert at

Tinchebray. It was 28 September. The coincidence did not
escape the great chronicler William of Malmesbury. 'It was the
same day on which, forty years before, William had just landed at
Hastings and it was doubtless by the wise dispensation of God that
Normandy should be subject to England on the same day that the
Norman power had arrived to subjugate that kingdom.' Robert's
days of adventure were over. He died in 1134 in Cardiff, after
twenty-eight years of comfortable confinement, much of it spent
in learning Welsh.

Robert left a son, William Clito, and it was not long before the
new and more enterprising King of France, Louis VI, was trying
to use him as a means to oust Henry from his newly won duchy.
For the rest of his reign Henry knew little peace. The conquest
of Normandy brought him, as other French possessions brought
his successors, little but trouble, endless journeyings and expense.
He was a match for it, as some of those who followed him were not.
His diplomatic skill was remarkable and his tentacles stretched
into Germany, where he was able to give his daughter Matilda in
marriage to the Emperor Henry V. He was able to exploit too the
suspicion which a stronger French monarchy sometimes aroused
in neighbouring fiefs. But when he died at the age of sixty-six,
unusually advanced for those days, he left a situation, at home and
abroad, fraught with danger and instability. His heir had been
drowned in 1120, and though his English barons had unwillingly
accepted the now widowed Matilda as his successor in 1128 no one
could tell whether in fact they would be content to be ruled by a
queen. The second marriage of Matilda to Geoffrey of Anjou, of the
family traditionally hostile to the Normans, though a triumphant
piece of work, was unpopular in both Normandy and England,
and improved but little the chances of a peaceful succession. In
spite of his energy, in spite of the fact that he spent half of his time
in Normandy and most of that in strife, Henry's lasting achievements were among the people he despised, whose chronicler at
Peterborough said of him: 'A good man he was; and there was
great dread of him. No man dared do wrong with another in his
time.'

CHAPTER 10

Anglo-Norman Government and Church; Stephen 1135-1154

WILLIAM RUFUS and his brother Henry were above all men of greed. They had in England many who feared them, some who admired them, few who loved them. There are constant complaints by the chroniclers of the exactions of Rufus and his lieutenant Rannulf Flambard, and Henry's fierce taxation was, though put to better use, hated as much. Yet strangely enough England has good cause to be thankful that these men loved gold. Much good government came of it. The Norman kings had little use for abstract ideas like 'good government' or 'justice'. Their interest was in what they considered their rights. The power of the king was limited, by custom, by the difficulties of communication, by the lack of loyal and obedient underlings. It was a power far less than that wielded by a democratic government today. But kings were determined to make the most of it, and if possible increase it – because if they did so they would get more money. If the king could increase his power, he could collect more taxes. If he made the courts more efficient, he could collect more fines. And as it happened, in a society always ready to slip into anarchy or the rule of local war lords, if he did both these things he probably in the long run brought more security and more happiness.

The reign of Henry I shows this very well. In order to keep his treasury full he had first to see that the taxes to which the kings of England had a right – and they were many – did in fact reach him and did not disappear into the pockets of the collectors. The taxes were of two chief kinds: the old rights of the Anglo-Saxon kings like the *danegeld*; and the new ones that came with feudalism, levies that the king could make when his tenants succeeded to their fiefs, or married, or failed to obey a summons to war. The job of collecting most of them was given to that very useful Anglo-Saxon

99

official, the sheriff, whose powers the Normans vastly increased. The sheriffs, having collected them, had to bring them to the king and give a full account. If the king was in England, they had to appear before him in person. He sat at a great table spread with a green cloth, on which was placed a large chequer board. These were days when Roman numerals were still in use in Europe and few people knew how to add a column of figures on parchment. So it was all done with counters on the chequer board, and the office where it was done was called the Exchequer. No doubt the sheriffs could still cheat, but it was less easy when they were confronted with a little elementary arithmetic.

These sheriffs were seldom, however, the loyal servants the king would have wished for. Every active and efficient medieval king preferred to govern through men whose power depended on him, men whom he had raised. But such aims were not popular with the greater barons of the kingdom who felt that by their position as landholders with recognized authority in their own domains they should be the advisers the king heard. Much of English history in the Middle Ages is taken up with the struggle between kings and barons on this point, and neither side cared much which was better for the English people.

In Henry I's day many sheriffs were great barons, but whenever he could the king used his own officials, men who perhaps had begun a career in his own writing office or chancery. Such sheriffs of humbler origin had less temptation to use their office to erect little local kingdoms of their own. And the king probably found them better tax gatherers.

The exchequer and the sheriffs, then, helped the king's revenue. So did Henry's growing interference in the courts of law. To have the right of holding a court was a valued prize in the Middle Ages. It was very profitable. Most offences were punished by fines, and these went into the pocket of the men in whose name the court was held. Nowadays, all courts are crown courts, all judges and magistrates the crown's servants, but this has not always been so. In the England of Henry I most cases never reached a royal court, being dealt with by the lord of a manor, the officials of a borough, or by the agents of a great baron. Those which were royal were the court of the shire and the courts of the king's own Curia Regis in which he might sit himself or which might be called by one of his travelling justices. It would be to the advantage then of a king in love with money as well as anxious for order to get as much business as he could into his own court, or make it a 'plea of the crown'. And this was just what Henry I did – though he could only do it on a small scale. He saw that those who broke the 'King's peace' were punished by his own court; and a variety of serious offences – treason, murder, violent robbery among them – were by custom breakages of the king's peace. And more than that, he invited men who had been ejected from their lands to bring their complaints to him – usually for a stiff fee.

The power the king gained was power the barons lost, and only the forceful energy of Henry made these moves possible. With his death and with no certain successor to his throne the barons saw a golden chance of flinging off the chains that the king seemed to be putting on their ambitions. But while he lived they bore them.

One man, however, resisted Henry to the end. This was his Archbishop of Canterbury, Anselm. Anselm was born at Aosta, by the Great St. Bernard pass over the Alps, about 1034. He left a rich home early in life to join the hundreds of students who wandered through Europe at this time in search of knowledge at scattered cathedral schools. It was not long before he heard of the fame of the Norman abbey of Bec and of its great teacher, Lanfranc. And there he settled, taking the vows of a monk, and rising, while Lanfranc was at Canterbury, to be abbot. He was a warm-hearted, lovable man with a gift for friendship rare in that rough age. But in Europe he was best known as the greatest philosopher of his day, perhaps the greatest in the west since the classical age. When Lanfranc died in 1089 it seemed obvious to Englishmen that Anselm should succeed him in England, but Rufus did not seem to think Lanfranc needed any successor and, as we have seen, it was not till he felt himself about to die that he appointed Anselm. Anselm's reluctance to take the job was better founded than Lanfranc's, for he lacked Lanfranc's administrative skill and thorough statesmanship. He was a man of the cloister and the writing desk, whose loves were prayer, thought and friendship. But for all his open friendliness he had one massive quality, an unshakeable obstinacy in what to him were matters of principle, whether it were a principle of the monastic life or a principle about the Church's role in the world. His principles were to send him into exile twice and to bring about the first serious quarrel in England between king and archbishop, or, put another way, between Church and State.

The Church's role in the world – about this men have argued for centuries, and still do. In the lifetime of Anselm a change had been coming over the Church's own view of it so marked that it can be called a revolution. In the days of Edgar the Peaceable the inspiration for the monastic reform of the English Church had largely come from Cluny, the monastery in eastern France where, from 910 on, a stricter and more elaborate form of St Benedict's rule was being practised. But the influence of Cluny in Western Europe was far wider than this. Men of Cluny or men influenced by Cluny were elected to high offices in the Church, even to the papacy itself. And with the help of the German kings who had followed Charlemagne in calling themselves Emperors, they had been trying to lift the papacy out of the rut into which it had sunk, where it was at the mercy of prominent Roman families. The greatest of the popes who burned with the desire to reform it was Gregory VII, who became pope in 1075. It was not coincidence that he took the name Gregory, for in the days of Gregory the Great the papacy had had the moral leadership of Europe. Gregory VII was determined to regain that position. When Cluny had been founded it had been granted freedom from any kind of control by laymen, and now Gregory VII, whom Cluny had deeply influenced, was to strive for the same idea for the whole Church. He saw the Church as a divine society, whose humblest priests were set apart from other men by the power granted them of administering the sacraments, of dispensing the goodness or grace of God to sinful men. Only through priests could men be saved from eternal punishment. It was therefore absurd that the Church anywhere should be controlled by laymen, that laymen, for example, should have the power to appoint priests to livings, or bishops to their sees. The pope was Christ's vicar – or representative – on earth and thus greater than any king, greater even than the emperor.

Such views were not new in Europe, but it was new to have them held so firmly and so widely as they were at the end of the eleventh century. They stirred up opposition from the kings of Europe, and indeed from churchmen too. They met with little support, for example, from Lanfranc and none from the Conqueror. But in 1095 there began a movement in Europe which to many seemed to confirm them. In that year the pope, Urban II, at a Council of clergy in Clermont, in central France, preached the Crusade. Dwelling at length on the sufferings of Christian peoples in the Holy Land, for centuries under the domination of the Moslems, he urged his hearers to take up arms and march to their aid. The result was astounding. Urban had perhaps expected a small expeditionary force. What occurred was a mass migration, of men from all levels of society from ignorant peasants with the haziest ideas of Jerusalem's whereabouts to great princes bent on no more than the conquest of land. And in so far as the movement had a commander at all it was the Bishop of Le Puy, specially appointed by the pope. So it seemed for a time as though in truth the pope was the ruler of Europe, that at his bidding men would lay down their smaller loyalties for their loyalty to the Church.

This new spirit in the Church was shown, too, in a new monastic movement. Some men, at the beginning of the twelfth century, had come to think that the rule of St Benedict, as practised in most of the houses of the Black Monks, was too lax, that the monasteries were still too close to the world. At Cîteaux, in Eastern France, a new order was forming, largely under the influence of an Englishman – Stephen Harding – vowed to greater extremes of austerity. These monks – Cistercians as they were called – spread their ideas rapidly over western Europe. They spent more time in solitary prayer. They lived not in common dormitories but in separate cells, seldom speaking. Their buildings were as simple as they could make them, without ornament, without stained glass. In England – at Fountains, Rievaulx or Tintern the ruins of their building can still be seen, grand and stark in valleys that were the loneliest they could find.

Such was the Church of Anselm's day, confident that it could overcome the world, that kings could not stand against it, that they were its protectors but also its servants. And the gentle, saintly Anselm, to his own monks of Bec the mildest of men, thus had the strength to stand up to the fierce, tempestuous bullying of Rufus and the avaricious cunning of Henry I.

He became Archbishop in 1093. Within a few weeks he was quarrelling with Rufus, who for his own political purposes wanted to avoid recognizing Urban II as pope. Other quarrels followed and in 1097 Anselm decided to leave England to seek advice in Rome, and he remained abroad till Rufus's death. Henry I recalled him, wanting as far as possible to show himself to the English people as an improvement on his brother, but Anselm returned only to more conflicts. And now the dispute was one which was becoming familiar in Europe, a dispute made inevitable by Gregory VII's view of the Church.

It will be remembered that the Conqueror had demanded from the bishops and abbots, as from his lay barons, the full obligations of a feudal vassal, the provision of knights, by virtue of the lands which the Church held in such great quantities. These obligations the churchmen were in general prepared to discharge, but the question now arose whether a bishop was first a pastor – a spiritual father of a flock – or whether he was first a feudal lord, part of the military arrangements of the kingdom. The dispute centred on the ceremony at which bishops were given their sees. Should a bishop first be consecrated, given his spiritual power, and then do homage to his king for his lands? Or should he do homage first? There was more in it than merely the right order to take an agenda at a committee meeting, for in an illiterate age the details of ceremonies were powerful symbols. Men would see in the order of a ceremony the priorities of human life. It was therefore a principle to Anselm that the consecration should be first in time as it was first before God. In the same way it was a principle to the king that he should have as his bishops men who could rule a fief for the general security of the kingdom.

The result was a deadlock, and Anselm, now an old man, once more went abroad, in 1103. After some years of fierce argument by letter and by legates a compromise was reached, in which the king's powers as feudal lord were hardly touched but were to be exercised more tactfully. Bishops were to be elected by their cathedral or monastic 'chapters' but under the eye of the king. They had to do homage before their consecration but the king no longer gave them the token of their office, the ring and staff. This arrangement changed little throughout the Middle Ages, and indeed today, in the Church of England, cathedral chapters merely elect the government's nominee for a bishopric. Anselm gave ground at the end because the pope himself had given ground, finding it impossible to break the will of every king in Europe and preferring perhaps that his bishops should have their sees and some of their principles rather than all their principles and no see.

So Henry I was the effective ruler of the English Church, acknowledging the pope's authority only when he wanted to, appointing his own bishops and abbots much as he did his sheriffs and justices. But in the strict logic of the Church's law he was nothing more than his humblest villein, a sinful man in desperate need of the grace that only a priest could pass to him from God. The uneasy compromise of Anselm and the king might at any time be shattered by a churchman who chose to stand on the letter of his law or a king who turned in fury to force.

Henry's death in 1135 was a disaster for the English. Twice had the English barons vowed allegiance to Empress Matilda in Henry's lifetime, but he knew as well as they that the oath meant little. A woman had never ruled in England. Matilda's husband, Geoffrey of Anjou, was of a family loathed by the Norman barons. Her son Henry had developed little more than his strong will, being but two years old. Henry I died in Normandy, campaigning again to preserve the peace of the uneasy duchy now endangered by his son-in-law Geoffrey, making a premature attempt to grasp his wife's inheritance. Matilda was with her husband, and hearing of her father's death she did nothing to make sure of her English inheritance. Perhaps she felt it was secure. Perhaps she felt, like her husband, that it was more important to get Normandy first. Anyway, she stayed where she was, on the Norman border of Anjou. And within three weeks, at Westminster, the crown of England had been placed on the head of another – Stephen of Blois.

Stephen of Blois was a favourite nephew of the dead king, a son of Henry's sister Adela who had married the ruler of the small county of Blois to the east of Anjou. Stephen was a gentle, courteous man, a warrior of some renown, popular among his fellow barons. Hearing of Henry's death he had wasted little time in slipping across the channel from France and persuading the English Church and barons that it would be to their advantage to renounce their oath to Matilda and make him king, using the pretext that England needed a male sovereign. At first, indeed, it seemed as though the decision of the English was right. London took to Stephen. He looked like a soldier and a king and had no reputation for cruelty or treachery. But before long it was clear that whatever the personal merits of Stephen the land and people could only suffer by his coming. His conception of kingship was very different from the Normans'. He was used to conditions in France, where the king was but 'first among equals' who ruled by making bargains and laying sieges. Had there been no rival for the throne Stephen's reign would have been lawless. He was always prepared to make concessions to gain a temporary advantage, as a schoolmaster might keep order by giving out sweets. He showed plenty of energy when he had to turn from bribery to war, but it seldom lasted. He began sieges with a will but could never be bothered to finish them. He could fight a battle but not plan a campaign. For the barons who had chafed under Henry, such a king was a golden opportunity. 'A mild man, soft and good,' wrote a chronicler. 'But he did no justice.'

Stephen's power, then, was little enough. But Matilda was not prepared to let him enjoy it, either in England or Normandy. In 1139, in company with her half-brother, Henry's bastard son Robert of Gloucester, she landed in Sussex to claim the allegiance she had once been given. The civil war that followed was long and dreary, a war of few decisive battles and many sieges. For the English people it was a time of untold misery, for they had to endure not only a straight fight for the throne but the local wars, raids, robberies, and burnings in which the baronage began freely to indulge. In the fenland, Geoffrey de Mandeville held a whole district in terror of his thugs and his dungeons. For him the war of succession meant a constant changing of sides for a higher price each time, as it did for many other barons. Soon England was littered with small hastily built castles, the abode of rival gangs. To the chronicler of Peterborough, living near Geoffrey de Mandeville, it seemed in truth that 'Christ and his saints slept'.

Gradually, however, Stephen gained the upper hand. In 1147 Matilda's chief supporter, Robert of Gloucester, died, and a year later she left the country to join her husband, who had achieved his own private ambition of conquering Normandy for the Anjou cause. He ruled it not in his own name, but in the name of his eldest son, Henry. In 1151 Geoffrey of Anjou died and this son

added to his dukedom of Normandy the county of Anjou, thus
uniting in his person the two age-old rival titles. A year after
that he further added to his power with a marriage to the cast-off
wife of the French King, Eleanor of Aquitaine. His power now
stretched from the Channel to the Pyrenees. In 1153, with a small
but efficient force and a quite definite purpose, he crossed the
Channel. He intended to be King of England.

CHAPTER 11

Henry II
1154-1189

HENRY 'PLANTAGENET' had visited England twice already in his mother's cause, once in 1147, when he was only fourteen, in an expedition which had given Stephen little trouble, and again two years later when he had tried to enlist the support of the King of Scotland. But now, in 1153, he came as a mature man of action prepared to renew the war that his mother had given up. Success was easy and needed little fighting, for Stephen was ageing and since the death of his own eldest son had lost interest in his family's future. At Winchester in November 1153 he came to terms with the young Henry, agreeing to let him help in the government till his own death, which came within a year in October 1154.

With Henry II's accession there was once more a masterful man on the throne of England. He came from a family whose origins were popularly supposed to go back to the Devil, a family which by ruthless statecraft had grown from a minor position on the river Loire to be rulers of a sizeable French fief and which now, in Henry and his wife, dominated an empire a thousand miles in length. Henry was restless, self-willed, and short-tempered; not tall but sturdy and immensely strong. He needed little sleep, avoided luxuries, liked the intelligent talk of scholars whom he encouraged to stay at his court. He made friends easily through his charm but lost them as easily through his rages. He loved power and a full treasury, like his grandfather Henry I. He hated disorder, inefficiency and a dishonest servant. After the 'nineteen winters' of Stephen's reign he had the qualities England needed.

Stephen's reign had proved how much still depended on the personality of the king. Henry I's carefully ordered kingdom, with his presence removed, had soon sunk into confusion. There were

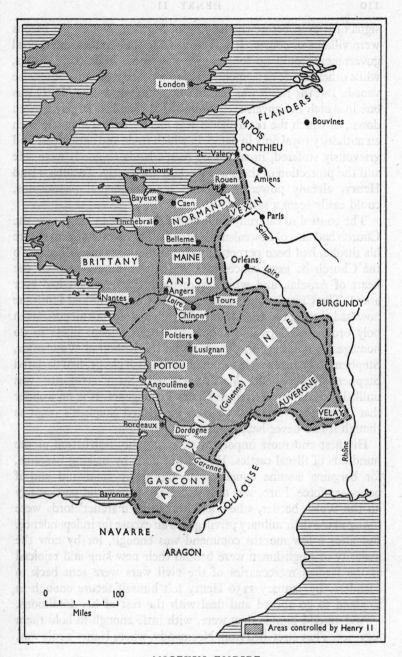

London

FLANDERS

ARTOIS

Bouvines

St. Valery   PONTHIEU

Cherbourg   Rouen   Amiens

Bayeux   Caen   VEXIN

Tinchebrai   NORMANDY   Paris

Seine

Belleme   Orléans

MAINE   Loire   BURGUNDY

BRITTANY

ANJOU

Nantes   Angers

Loire   Tours

Chinon

Poitiers

Lusignan

POITOU

Angoulême   AUVERGNE

(Guienne)   VELAY

Bordeaux   Dordogne

Garonne   Rhône

GASCONY

Bayonne   TOULOUSE

NAVARRE

ARAGON

0   100
Miles

Areas controlled by Henry II

ANGEVIN EMPIRE

signs of it even before the landing of Matilda. Not all the barons were villains of course. It was to provide the security the central government could no longer give that some built their castles, while others made agreements to keep a peace that must otherwise vanish. But the result was that the England which met Henry was one in which the government from the throne had largely broken down, in which the royal sheriff was merely a local magnate with an authority royal only in name, in which trade and agriculture had grievously suffered, in which no man's lands or goods were safe and the protection of the law uncertain and costly. To such a land Henry, already powerful through his continental possessions, could easily seem a saviour.

The control so carefully built up by the Norman kings over the Church had also been weakened. Stephen, in his attempts to secure his throne, had been perpetually bargaining with his subjects. To the Church he gave concessions which would have rejoiced the heart of Anselm, and which were more than Anselm had ever asked. The Church courts created by the Conqueror and Lanfranc now had the right to try not only Church matters but all persons in holy orders. Bishops and abbots had been seldom made to do homage. At one stage in the civil wars the Bishop of Winchester, Stephen's own brother, in a council of English clergy, had declared Stephen deposed and Matilda elected. Such arrogance was unlikely to commend itself to Henry Plantagenet. It is no wonder that in his early acts and charters he treated Stephen's reign as though it had never happened.

His first and most important task was the destruction of the hundreds of illegal castles. He did not do it by making bargains, for bargains assume equality. He did it by command and if necessary force. Force was only necessary at first and particularly on the Welsh border, where as always the 'marcher' lords were trying to use their military privileges as an excuse for independence. But after a few months command was enough, for by now the majority of Englishmen were behind their new king and rejoiced as the lawless mercenaries of the civil wars were sent back to Flanders. By January 1156 Henry felt himself secure enough in England to go abroad and deal with the rest of his dominions.

And an odd jumble they were, with little enough to hold them together. They stretched from Normandy, where Henry's rule was, thanks to the work of his father and grandfather, firm and comparatively untroubled, through his own Anjou to Aquitaine, a wild lawless region where he ruled only as Eleanor's husband. To this and to his British lands historians sometimes give the name: 'Angevin Empire'. But it is a misleading phrase. There was no one central government, no one set of laws, no common language. In each territory Henry ruled under a different title. Some he held as a vassal of the king of France. But though the word 'empire' is misleading, Henry had much about him which a later age would have called 'imperialist'. He wanted to do more than hold his possessions. He wanted to increase them.

In the British Isles he was successful. Among the consequences of Stephen's weakness had been the inroads made into English territory by the Scots and the Welsh. Stephen had defeated the Scottish king at the Battle of the Standard in 1138, but he had done nothing to follow up his victory and by the end of his reign the Scottish king held Northumberland and Cumberland. But William the Lion, king of Scotland, fell into Henry's hands in 1174 and by the Treaty of Falaise agreed to become Henry's vassal and to hold Scotland as a fief from him. From the Welsh, Henry won back the lands they had taken from Stephen but he never succeeded in invading the country. He had his lordship formally acknowledged and built a line of castles along the frontier, and Wales gave him little trouble.

He looked beyond Wales, however, to Ireland. This land had been isolated from Britain and the Continent by the Viking invasions of the ninth and tenth centuries and was now ruled by six kings of little power perpetually immersed in petty squabbles. Its Church too was cut off and developing in its own ways remote from Roman control. In 1170, a party of Norman adventurers from Wales answered a call for help from the king of Leinster, whose throne had been seized by a rival; and when the leading Norman, Richard Strongbow, Earl of Pembroke, had himself installed as king of Leinster, Henry thought it time to intervene himself. He crossed to Ireland in 1171 and in a six-month stay forced the submission of scores of Irish kings and princes. And for his expedition he had the backing of the pope, anxious to bring the Irish Church again into the Roman fold. But when Henry left he had done little to give peace to the Irish. He gave tham better government than they were used to, perhaps, but he left them the prey to other tyrants than their native tyrants. He had added Ireland to England's dominions and the notorious 'Irish problem' to English cares.

On the Continent his imperialism was less successful. Here at first his chief weapon was not military but matrimonial. Eleanor dutifully provided him with eight children. One, Geoffrey, he married to the heiress of Brittany, over which wild area he thus had some control. Another he married to the king of France's daughter. A daughter he married to one of the great princes of Germany; another to the king of Castile, in Spain, a third to the king of Sicily. But his ambitions on the Continent were checked first by the disobedience of his own sons, who had enough of his own ambitions not to wish to be merely his tools; and second by the accession to the throne of France in 1180 of a king as wily, intelligent, self-seeking and energetic as himself – Philip Augustus.

In England, Henry did not stop short at restoring what his grandfather had achieved. Had he done that he would have been remarkable enough. He went much further and thus has a place among the very greatest of our kings. Henry I had striven to increase royal power, as by so doing he increased his own wealth. Henry II had the same need for money and nearly the same love of it. But he had a greater vision. He had seen in the lives of his predecessors the limitations of feudalism, of a state whose order depended on the continual activity of the king himself, without which only the private agreements between lords and vassals, barons and fellow barons could prevent chaos. For Henry II something more was needed, and the fact that his son Richard, when he succeeded him, could spend most of his reign in the Holy Land and yet leave England in comparative peace showed that something more had been found.

Henry's way was first to do as his grandfather had done and increase the power of the royal courts and of the justice they dispensed. His idea was not to force people to come to the courts with their complaints but to prove to them that it would be to their advantage if they did. In 1166 he told his people that any free man who had been wrongfully dispossessed of his land could bring his case to a special court, called the Assize of Novel Disseisin, where it would be heard before royal justices who, because they were probably not local men, would decide the case fairly on the evidence; and the evidence they heard would be that of a panel of local men telling the truth on their solemn oath. Other, similar, courts followed, all designed to bring the name and power of the king into the disputes of his subjects. His subjects might not always be pleased. To some it was wanton interference in matters best settled quietly by bribery or roughly by arms. But to most it was a boon, and made it seem that the king was in truth the protector of all his subjects, regardless of their wealth and their strength.

Henry was showing them too that he could protect them from violence other than the seizing of land. In the same year that the Assize of Novel Disseisin first sat, 1166, Henry from his hunting lodge at Clarendon, near Salisbury, ordered that in every hundred and village in the land, when the justices or sheriffs were visiting, men should come forward and state on oath whom they believed to be murderers, robbers, or harbourers of them. Suspected criminals must undergo the ordeal by water. Thrown into a pool of water blessed by a priest, they were judged guilty if they floated, innocent if they sank. But those who sank, if they did not drown, were still made to leave the country within eight days as men of evil reputation with their neighbours. This measure is called the Assize of Clarendon, and shows an early use of a kind of jury – not a modern jury which declares an accused innocent or guilty, for that was still being left to God – but a group of men on oath helping the king's justices to root out evil.

What Henry was doing was this. He was saying to his subjects: 'You already have a multitude of courts: of the manor, of the borough, of the hundred. But they are not all my courts and will not all give you the best law. But I have a better law, better because it has all my authority behind it. I will give it to you to redress your grievances, and I will bring it to you if you break my peace.' With this policy in mind it was natural that he would want to bring *all* his subjects under the power of his law. But one important group of them were outside it and had been since the days of Stephen – the churchmen. It was possibly to help bring them inside that in 1161 he appointed to be Archbishop of Canterbury, his friend, chancellor, and chief adviser, Thomas Becket.

Thomas Becket was a Londoner of Norman stock, who, like

many ambitious townsmen of the day, had sought a career in the Church. He went during Stephen's reign into the household of Theobald, the Archbishop of Canterbury; and Theobald, recognizing his remarkable gifts, commended him to Henry. Before long Henry had made him his chancellor (chief of his writing office) and the two became great friends. Becket accompanied the king on most of his expeditions abroad and it seemed to Henry as if they were of one mind. With Becket on the throne of Canterbury the story of the Conqueror and Lanfranc might well be enacted again.

But within a year of the appointment Henry soon realized he had miscalculated. Becket the archbishop was not Becket the chancellor. On receiving the honours and dignities of his new office Becket began to be as single-minded in it as he had been in the king's household. As chancellor he had had the mind of the king. Now he must have the mind of the Church, of the divine society whose least officer was greater than the greatest layman. He became as obstinate as Anselm, but without Anselm's charm or sweetness of character. And he was defending more than Anselm. He was defending what the Church had won only very recently in the troubled reign of Stephen, the right to try and punish all its officers in its own courts, in the courts set apart by the Conqueror to deal with ecclesiastical matters not ecclesiastical men. Had the Church's officers been only its bishops and priests all might have been well, but in those days 'holy orders' of a sort could be conferred on young students, on men of small education and little maturity, men as likely to misbehave as any laymen. But to Becket all such were 'clerks', and liable only to the justice of the Church, a justice with little coercive power.

Henry had a tidy mind. But he also had a strong will. Rejecting compromise or some vague form of words that might have satisfied both parties, he insisted at Clarendon in 1164 in drawing up a series of 'Constitutions' which laid down in detail the rights of the king over the English Church, including the right to try 'criminous clerks' in his own courts. In a moment of strange weakness Becket agreed to them, but after a few months he revoked his agreement. Henry was furious. Summoning him to a council at Northampton he accused Becket wildly of dishonesty while chancellor. Becket met the abuse and taunts with dignified silence, but that same night he fled to France.

There followed years of propaganda war. The king, with most of the English bishops behind him, put the constitutions into effect. Becket's reply was to threaten with excommunication – or cutting off from the Church – all who obeyed the king. The crisis came when Henry had his son crowned by the Archbishop of York in 1170, to which Becket's reply was to ask a worried and rather muddled pope to suspend all religious services in the land.

Faced with such a prospect Henry arranged a meeting with the archbishop and a cold, formal reconciliation took place. But it meant very little and both men knew it. When Becket crossed to England, after six years' exile, he brought not peace but a challenge. On Christmas Day, 1170, from the pulpit of his own cathedral in Canterbury, he pronounced the excommunication of all who had assisted at the prince's coronation. And four days later he was dead.

He was murdered by four knights by the altar of the cathedral. How far Henry himself was responsible for the deed will never be known. Perhaps he only gave the knights a hint of what, in the face of this new insult, would please him. But in his rages reason fled. The order might well have been his. In any case, in the eyes of the shocked world the blame was his alone. Four years later he did public penance at the scene of the murder and paid for an expedition to the Holy Land. Becket had won his point, and the crown of a martyr. His shrine quickly became a place of pilgrimage, a symbol of how even kings could be opposed, till Henry VIII had it razed to the ground.

Though the murder of Becket shocked western Europe, Henry for the most part found the English people pliant to his will. Their memories of Stephen's reign were harrowing enough for them to approve his strength and his purpose. And England was for Henry the easiest of his great dominions to govern. Of his thirty-five years' reign he spent only fifteen there. For the other twenty he was striving to keep the peace in his continental territories, to preserve them from invasion by the French king or from the fierce ambition of his own sons.

Eleanor of Aquitaine, a beautiful, intelligent, but forceful woman, was not the ideal wife for Henry. For some years they were happy together while she bore him eight children, but after a time they drifted apart, he finding more pleasure in the company of mistresses, she in the cultured conversation and love poets of her

sunny Aquitaine. As her sons grew to manhood they became
ambitious, not for dignity but for power. And power Henry
refused to give them. Titles he dispensed generously, but the
emptiness of these served only to make his sons more resentful. In
1174 a serious rebellion broke out, with Henry's eldest son 'the
young king' as he was called, aided by his second and Eleanor's
favourite, Richard, holding castles in disobedience in France, with
Eleanor herself approving in the background and the French king
seizing his chance of cracking open this empire that reduced him to
such lowly impotence. The rebellion spread to England, where a
few barons, angry at Henry's attacks upon their powers and joined
by the opportunist king of Scotland, raised armies against him.
But Henry did not lose his head. The danger was widespread but
disorganized. The bulk of the English stood by him. The rebels
south of the channel had no policy and little common interest.
Within a year the rising had collapsed and the Scottish king was a
prisoner at Falaise in Normandy.

The years after the abortive rebellion saw Henry at the height
of his power. His public penance for the Becket murder had been
well received. In England, by the Assize of Northampton of 1176,
he extended the jury procedure of Clarendon to cover arson and
forgery and made the punishments more severe. By the Assize of
Arms of 1181 he revived the old *fyrd*, compelling able-bodied men
of all classes to have weapons ready to use in his service. His sons
continued their insidious plotting but were as much a danger to one
another as to him. Only in 1183 did they break into violence again
when the 'young king' Henry – 'a prodigy of unfaith, a lovely
palace of sin' – and his brother Geoffrey, attacked Richard, now
made Duke of Aquitaine. The attractive but worthless young
Henry luckily died in the same year thus ending the episode. But
the last five years of Henry II were yet to be full of battle, treachery
and tragedy.

In 1180 a youth of fifteen came to the throne of France, Philip
II, to whom historians have rightly given the name of Augustus.
He was unpleasant, with little charm or humanity, but of remarkable ability. From the beginning he set himself the task of breaking
the Angevin power which stretched from the north to the south of
his kingdom of France and which if unchallenged would ruin any
hope of making France what England now was, a real kingdom.

The area ruled by the French king was still little more than the
Ile de France, stretching from a little north of Paris to the river
Loire at Orleans. Such was the eventual success of Philip that to
Frenchmen he seems the equivalent of Alfred and Henry II
together. From the year of his accession onwards he cleverly used
the sons and enemies of Henry to give him no peace, using particularly the hatred Richard was now feeling for his younger
brother John, Henry's favourite, whom Henry was planning to be
next king of England. Richard did homage to Philip for his lands
and promised to join him in a concerted enterprise against the old
king.

A Welsh writer, Giraldus Cambrensis, has described how
Henry II explained a painting he had had made in his palace at
Winchester. It showed an eagle, with a brood of five eaglets. Four
pecked at the parent's vitals. The fifth waited poised to peck out
the eyes. 'The four eaglets,' said the king, 'are my four sons who do
not cease to persecute me even to my death. The youngest of them,
whom I now embrace with such affection, will in the end insult me
more dangerously than any.' His prophecy came terribly true.
As Philip and Richard reduced castle after castle in Anjou and
Touraine, Henry's strength gave way. As he lay dying in his
favourite castle of Chinon he heard that John had joined the rebels.
In despair he submitted to the terms of his enemies. He died on
6th July, 1189.

Henry II was one of the greatest kings of England. He had ruled
dominions more powerful and nearly as wide as Canute's. He had
given the English strong government and peace. He was a man of
learning, of culture, of keen legal intelligence. But he was jealous
of his power, hot with fury when it was baulked. His will and his
jealousy had involved him in two immense tragedies, the murder
of his archbishop, the defection of his family. In the last resort,
his wisdom was at the mercy of his temper.

CHAPTER 12

The Sons of Henry II

1189-1215

IN THE autumn of 1187 news came to the kings of western Europe of a great disaster in the East. Almost the entire crusading army had been cut to pieces at the Battle of Hattin, Jerusalem conquered with so much blood in 1099 had been lost, and with it the most sacred relic in all christendom, the Holy Cross. The remaining crusaders, except those in the north at Antioch and Tripoli, were bottled up in the coastal town of Tyre. The man who had wrought this disaster was the brilliant, chivalrous and humane Moslem leader, Saladin.

For the Christian west the news was an appalling shock. The capture of Jerusalem nearly a century before had been hailed as a triumph for God and his Church, though more recent failures – like the Second Crusade – had sobered the wildest enthusiasm and led many to think that Christians were too proud, quarrelsome, and greedy to deserve what had been won. And now this greater disaster was seen as a judgment of God on a kingdom whose rulers had shown so little charity and wisdom, who had weakened their cause with perpetual bickering. For it was a divided kingdom that Saladin had overwhelmed, an example of the worst side of feudalism, a kingdom whose richest lord had been suspected of treachery, whose lesser lords often preferred Moslems to their fellow Christians.

But in the west the crusading ideal was still potent. Within a short time of hearing the news the three greatest western rulers had taken crusading vows: Frederick Barbarossa, the German emperor; Philip Augustus, King of France; and Henry II. The last of these was an old man. He could hardly have expected to perform his vows, and his wars with France and his own sons held him till his death.

His eldest surviving son, however, who succeeded him as King of England, was in the prime of youth, and had every intention of fulfilling his vow. Richard I of England, known before long as Cœur de Lion, was a man of thirty-three, of magnificent physique, tall, golden haired and handsome. Though his first love in life was war, he was far from being a grandiose thug. Of all Henry's sons he had been closest to his mother, and he shared her love of poetry and the stories of romance. He was as greedy as other Angevins but could show the ostentatious generosity that made reputations. He had little sense of responsibility and thought little of the larger objects of his wars, but he had a flair both for strategy and tactics at a time when warfare was too often merely a mixture of dreary siege and occasional tests of brute force in the open field. His personal courage was superb, his political wisdom small. He was ten years king of England, but was there only for two stays of a few months.

Paying his father's body brief respect – kneeling beside it, it was said, for long enough to say the Lord's Prayer – Richard sailed from France for his first visit to England as king, a visit which lasted four months and gave him time to be crowned and to make temporary arrangements for the government of the country. He then returned to Normandy. He finally set out for the Holy Land in the summer of 1190, but in spite of his military ardour there was little haste in his journey. He spent a winter in Sicily enjoying the unwilling hospitality of his sister and brother-in-law; and then continuing east he paused to conquer Cyprus – which henceforward became a useful crusader base. For some of the journey Philip Augustus was his companion, as they had planned a joint expedition. But though they had a healthy respect for one another they had no love and they disagreed almost every time they met. Philip was the opposite of Richard. He had no taste for the expensive and unpractical adventure that crusading provided. His business was in France, his object the expulsion of the Angevins. He went to the Holy Land because public opinion seemed to demand it and he came back as soon as he could. After the capture of the port of Acre in July 1191 he left the Holy Land for good, giving Richard a promise that he would not attack his French possessions till Richard, too, came back.

Richard, however, remained, to cover himself in glory. His goal was Jerusalem and the return of the Cross. He achieved neither, but in a pitched battle at Arsuf he routed Saladin's army, charging at the head of his knights and somehow controlling them in their precipitate fury. He then marched on Jaffa, rebuilt its fortifications, and demanded from Saladin the cession of both Jerusalem and the Cross. Saladin proudly refused and desultory fighting went on for another year till Richard, seeing the impossibility of his task and the growing weakness of his army, decided the time had come to patch up terms and depart. He left Palestine in 1192, with a promise from Saladin that Jerusalem would be open to Christian pilgrims and with his conquests on the coast confirmed to the Crusaders. Though less than he had aimed for it was a brilliant achievement.

It was 1194 before Richard reached England. Crossing Europe in disguise he fell into the hands of the Emperor Henry VI whom he had insulted at Acre, and was kept prisoner for a year. He was released only on the payment of a huge ransom and the promise – which of course was not kept – to become the Emperor's vassal. But again Richard's visit to England was short. He longed for another Crusade, but for four and a half years he was kept in France by the relentless attacks of his French overlord, Philip Augustus, who had already broken his promise and begun to nibble away at the long, vulnerable frontier of the Angevin Empire.

The England Richard so seldom visited was meanwhile showing the full effects of his father's remarkable creative energy. What is perhaps more extraordinary for that violent age was the mere fact that the land remained calm and untroubled by private or civil war for the nine years of Richard's absence. It showed that order no longer depended on the king's presence or the threat of it. There was always the possibility of conspiracy and defiance, particularly from the north or the Welsh marches, and there were still limits to what royal government could do; but what had grown up in England since the death of Stephen was something like a tradition of order. There were enough people who saw the value of it and there were institutions – like the itinerant justices and the royal courts – capable of enforcing it. There were also the beginnings of what we would call a civil service – a body of educated officials, seldom of noble origin, who could run their departments and use the king's name without his continual interference. The work and influence of the Exchequer, for example, grew year by year. It even had its own court which in the king's name could try those who cheated the king's revenue. And all this could happen with the king two or three months' journey away in the Holy Land.

English society itself was changing. The great barons, already losing some of their powers and privileges, were ceasing to be the only people in England, apart from king and Church, who really mattered. Towns were growing in number, population, and wealth and were being granted charters from the king which gave them freedom from the control of feudal lords, freedom to regulate their trade and raise tolls. Such an arrangement was to the king's advantage, for charters had to be bought and the newly freed towns were regarded as part of the king's personal domain and thus liable to his direct tax called a *tallage*. There was an old German saying that 'Town air makes free' and into the towns came many fugitive villeins to work as artisans or perhaps eventually to set up as master craftsmen or merchants. But the town's freedom was both limited and jealously guarded. Both merchants and craftsmen were organized into guilds which protected their interests and attacked non-members who tried to steal their custom. They regulated prices, kept up standards of work, dispensed charity to bereaved families, prayed for the souls of their dead. Initially, when protection was vital, their influence undoubtedly benefited town activities but as time went on their jealous grasp of privileges probably acted as a curb on expanding trade.

The feudal nobility, losing influence at court and in towns, were losing it too in the countryside. Here the cause lay in the slowly changing nature of warfare. Campaigns now were longer and more distant, and kings found it more convenient to rely on a professional army of mercenaries than on short service feudal levies or knights. The mounted knight was still the most potent weapon of war but by the end of the twelfth century fewer knights went to war as a feudal duty to a lord, more as professional soldiers. So at home the knight, settled on his land after the Conquest in return for service, was becoming more of a country gentleman, thinking of the welfare and profits of his land rather than of his armour and war horse. He was able, too, to pay a sum of money to the king in the place of his military service. This was called shield money or scutage. It had been used as early as the reign of Henry I but now was becoming far more common.

But we must not exaggerate these changes. The castle still stood dominating the countryside, a symbol of the military power that was still the ultimate arbiter in England. Private war could still occur in the more remote areas. The manor house was still built for security rather than comfort. Military service was still demanded and given. And not all the increases in royal power were accepted, for many were abused. The time was coming when the power which had challenged the feudal baron – knocked down his castle, summoned him to justice, taxed him, persuaded men to by-pass his courts – would itself be challenged and forced to yield.

A king was still expected, above all, to be successful in war. Cœur de Lion would have had more trouble had his military glory been dimmed. But as it was he showed in his years of war with the French king the same skill as in the Holy Land. Knowing that Philip's most glittering prize would be Normandy, which would give him an outlet to the Channel, Richard built a castle of immense strength on a rock about the Seine, the Chateau Gaillard. From this bastion he prevented Philip from doing more than make small dents in the Norman frontier. But in 1199 Richard died. A stray arrow made a wound which festered. Childless, he was succeeded by his brother John.

Of Richard Cœur de Lion a recent historian has said: 'He was a bad son, a bad husband and a bad king but a gallant and splendid soldier'.[1] Personal glory he won and certainly deserved, but for the peace in England in his reign he had to thank his father and a few devoted ministers like Hubert Walter, Archbishop of Canterbury. He did nothing to further it himself. A Frenchman in speech and blood, his interest in England was limited to its soldiers and its taxes which others raised for him. John, on the other hand, who for centuries has been dubbed a 'bad king', had a far greater regard for the interests of his kingdom. He had the usual Angevin greed and hot temper – and slightly more of these than Richard – but he had distinct ability and with better luck might now be remem-

[1] Sir Steven Runciman. *A History of the Crusades, Vol. III.*

bered as a great, if unpleasant, king. His is a difficult character to plumb. At times he showed a capacity for quick decision and action worthy of his father. He was an efficient administrator of justice, taking a personal interest in its working and frequently sitting on the bench himself. He saw that the exchequer barons and the sheriffs scraped together every ounce of gold that was the crown's due. But in strange contrast to this he had periods when, to quote a chronicler, 'he minded nothing but feasting, luxury, and lying in bed till dinner time'. And then there was his cruelty, cold and pitiless, notorious in his own day. The court rolls tell us that once he was 'moved to compassion', but his treatment of his political prisoners seems to show a wanton delight in hurting or the technique of slow starvation.

Yet with more luck he could have been a successful king. Many medieval kings more successful had worse characters. But circumstances always seemed against him, making him more bitter, more revengeful, more furious in his rages. The continental position he inherited was hopeless. Richard's military skill, in both engineering and movement, had just kept Philip at bay, but the frontiers to be defended were long and Philip could work on interior lines of communication. In addition Philip had a useful catspaw in a pretender to the English throne. This was the young Arthur, son of John's elder brother Geoffrey, Count of Brittany. Rejected by the English as a claimant, he could yet find adherents in Anjou or Brittany, and Philip used him unscrupulously.

In the inevitable war which followed the death of Richard, John showed the paradox of his character. In 1202 he acted with magnificent speed to march eighty miles in two days to capture Arthur who was besieging the aged Eleanor of Aquitaine in the castle of Mirebeau in Poitou. With Arthur were captured 200 Poitevin lords, most of whom were sent to a short term of imprisonment. Arthur himself disappeared and was probably murdered by the king. But the result of this combined brilliance and brutality was a change of sides by many of John's supporters. Two great Norman castles fell to Philip while John did nothing. And as Philip closed his net John withdrew to England. In March 1204 the great stronghold of Chateau Gaillard fell, on the very day that John was dispatching his hounds and falcons to begin another hunting season in Normandy. John never went there again. In

June, Philip entered Rouen in triumph and the great duchy which had given England her kings was lost.

John did not bear its loss without a counter-offensive. Philip's growing power was alarming Europe and John showed great skill in building an alliance against him. But by now his English subjects were lukewarm. They had borne heavy taxation for years, for the crusade, for Richard's ransom, for the long French wars, taxation less willingly borne in failure. A thrust northward out of Poitou in 1206 failed for lack of strength, and by 1208 John was in the midst of another quarrel, this time with the pope – who by John's ill chance was the ablest ever to sit on the throne of St Peter – Innocent III.

It began with a dispute which at another time might have been settled quickly and amicably. On the death of Hubert Walter in 1205, the archbishopric of Canterbury became vacant. The prior and monks of Christ Church Canterbury announced the election of a candidate. With the advice of his bishops, John elected a second. The dispute being sent to Rome, Innocent announced the appointment of a third, a distinguished scholar, Stephen Langton. A lesser, weaker pope would probably have complied with the wishes of the king. But under Innocent, papal theory had developed so much that he was both claiming and practising an authority over kings beyond even Gregory VII's. He ordered John to accept Stephen.

John refused. Innocent's answer was to place England under an interdict. All services except baptism and confession of the dying were prohibited and church bells all over the land were silent. It was a condition for men of faith almost impossible to bear. But still John would not give way. He pillaged the property of the Church, collecting from it over £100,000. He was then, in 1209, excommunicated – placed outside the fellowship of men, no longer able to claim allegiance. Only two of his bishops remained in England. The people, their means of salvation cut off, grew restive. The King of France offered himself as a willing crusader against the now cursed king and prepared an invasion.

John saw that his only answer was to submit. He saw the truth of the words the pope had written him: 'We could more easily be killed than defeated'. But from his humiliation John emerged with new strength. Innocent had written: 'You cannot win except through defeat; but it will be a more glorious victory for you when, through defeat, you have become the victor, for you will be indisputably victorious when you are conquered not by man, but by God: to be conquered by God is glorious for man'. John promised to restore all he had stolen from the Church, to take Stephen as archbishop, to become the pope's feudal vassal, to pay him 1,000 marks a year for England and Ireland. But henceforward, in all his subsequent troubles, with Philip and with his own subjects, the pope was John's constant and unwearying supporter.

With new power, then, John resumed his fight to regain what he had lost, which by 1206 was Normandy, Anjou and Touraine. In 1213 he once more gathered together his anti-French coalition, including Flanders and the Emperor, Otto IV of Germany. Such an alliance was a terrible threat to Philip, but it turned out to be unwieldy, and on the dusty field of Bouvines in Flanders in 1214 Philip utterly crushed it. It was one of the decisive battles of European history. For Philip it meant the control of the Channel coast from Flanders to Brittany and a pre-eminent position for France in Europe. For John it meant a physical defeat to add to his moral defeat and a return from the Continent to face the anger and resentment of his people. But out of those defeats a new government and order were to be born for the English.

CHAPTER 13

A Struggle for Power

1215-1265

THE HEAVY taxation of John's French wars might have been for-
given and borne had he been successful. But from the loss of
Normandy in 1204, through the long years of interdict to the final
defeat at Bouvines, his enterprises met nothing but failure. To
sustain them he had taxed every class of the community to the
utmost, going beyond the great sums to which he was entitled, to
demand what had never been given before. He had abused his
feudal rights by indiscriminate fines; he had made the persecuted
Jews pay heavily for his protection; he had taxed the country's
increasing trade; his judicial efficiency had brought additional
profits from the courts; he had strictly and cruelly worked the
forest laws to his own advantage. Finally, having stopped scores of
time-honoured loopholes in its incidence, he levied a heavy
scutage for his campaigns of 1214.

This scutage was the immediate cause of the revolt which led to
Magna Carta. It began with the 'defiance' or 'faith-breaking' of a
small group of northern barons, who were quickly joined by others
who saw a long-awaited chance of creating trouble and winning
back what, from the times of Henry II, they had lost. The country's
interest was of little account to these men, and a sordid civil war
of the kind so common in Europe might easily have followed,
lasting for years, had not a group of men, advised by the archbishop, Stephen Langton, intervened both to moderate the rebels
and to persuade the king to come to terms. At Runnymede on
the Thames, on 15 June 1215, the terms were agreed to in a
document that because of its length was soon called the Great
Charter.

No-one at Runnymede could guess that the document they signed and witnessed was to become one of the most famous charters of government in the history of mankind and that it would be quoted, misquoted, discussed and misunderstood for centuries. For in truth it was only a little more than an agreement that a king who was personally disliked would not abuse the powers he rightfully possessed, and a warning that if he did he must face armed rebellion. The work of Henry II and his ministers was not undone. The courts they had set up were to continue, but it was to be made harder for John to interpret the laws so that they merely became a way of filling his money bags, a technique in which he had shown extraordinary ability. It was also made more difficult for him to try his subjects secretly or to imprison them without any trial at all. A few vaguely worded clauses were put in as a sop to the Church and the merchants – that the Church should be free and that trade should be unhampered – but no-one knew exactly what this meant, and anyway within a few months Pope Innocent III, with little understanding of England, told his now 'well-beloved son in Christ' that the charter was null and void, and threatened Stephen Langton with excommunication for supporting it.

It is possible that John intended, at least for a time, to keep to the Charter. But the barons did not trust him. Some of the northern extremists did not even wait for it to be signed but returned to fortify their castles and plunder the royal manors. War soon broke out again, war in which John showed skill, energy, and such success that the barons invited Philip Augustus's son Louis to come over with an army and remove for ever the line of Plantagenet from the throne. But in the midst of the struggle, having lost nearly all his movable possessions in the treacherous sands of the Wash, John died, leaving his troubled inheritance to a boy of nine. It was October 1216.

There followed one of the most surprising and remarkable periods in English history. For the first time since the Norman Conquest the king of England was a child. The whole of European history before and after was to show the acute danger in such a situation, even when the accession was quiet. And the young Henry III was succeeding in the middle of a civil war, with the country swarming with mercenaries and partly occupied by an able and ambitious foreign prince. Yet within little more than a year the country was quiet, Prince Louis had left, and a group of responsible barons and churchmen had set up a regency which was quickly respected and obeyed. That this should have happened reveals that the institution of hereditary monarchy was of intense power and that it was against John himself rather than his throne that men had risen.

In these tense months, too, the seemingly short-lived treaty of Runnymede was turned into a truly Great Charter. Reissued within a month of John's death, and again after the French prince had been persuaded to leave, it became a symbol of good government. The king was too young to govern himself, so the moderate barons, led by William the Marshal, promised to govern in his name and within the limitations of the Charter. The English people, who had had a brief taste of the horrors of civil war, were content; and though William the Marshal died in 1219 and those who followed him often struggled among themselves for power, the king's boyhood passed away in peace.

It is doubtful whether, without the Charter, this could have occurred. The Charter's signatories had been thinking primarily of their own quarrel with John. They had so little faith in his honesty that they had set down in writing the conditions on which they were prepared to let him govern them, and they had told him what they would do if he rejected these conditions. But the result was that here, for the first time in English history, was a document which stated in some detail what the king's most powerful subjects believed good government to be. 'No free man,' it stated, 'shall be taken, or imprisoned, or disseised, or outlawed, or exiled, or any wise destroyed . . . but by the lawful judgment of his peers or by the law of the land. To none will we sell, to none will we deny or delay, right or justice.' Whatever these words exactly meant in 1215, however they might be twisted into other meanings in the future, a principle had been stated which, for many centuries after, would not be altogether forgotten.

The reign of Henry III is the third longest in our history, Henry living till 1272, when he was sixty-five. It spanned a time of tremendous mental and spiritual activity all over Europe, and not least in this island. It was in 1218 that Richard Poor, Bishop of Salisbury, began to move his cathedral and turn from the bleak windy uplands of Old Sarum, dominated by its royal castle, down to the Avon Valley below. The new cathedral of Salisbury, begun in 1221, was finished in 1262. It shows the fruition of the changes in building style which had been going on in England all through the previous century, away from the stern and massive nobility of what we call the Norman style to the lighter higher Gothic with its thinner walls, its spacious windows, its more delicate carving. At Lincoln a quiet and lengthy rebuilding was begun in 1192 and continued into the middle of Henry III's reign. Its new choir is one of the glories of England. And the king himself, from 1245 on, directed the rebuilding of Westminster Abbey, shrine of his patron Edward the Confessor. He imported masons and sculptors from France for the work, and Westminster is still the most French of our greater churches, with its rose windows, its great height, its eastern apse and radiating chapels. Down in Somerset, English masons were carving the magnificent west front of Wells, with its rows of figures, then highly coloured, depicting the whole pyramid of the Church's life rising to its summit in God the Father. The sculpture is now grey, weathered, scarred by the fury of later reformers, but the great design can still be traced, a design showing forth the Church Triumphant. As St John the Divine had seen the 'New Jerusalem, coming down from heaven, prepared as a bride adorned for her husband', so at Wells the society of Heaven, the apostles, prophets, and angels, stand above the earthly society, pope, bishop, priest, deacon, monk, king, noble and knight. In the great purpose of God each has his place, in the Revelation of St John and in the stone revelation of Wells.

The new buildings, their sculpture and stained glass, are evidence of the new confidence in the Church's life. The enclosed monasteries were no longer in this century the most important or influential of the Church's institutions. The English bishops of Henry III's reign were remarkable administrators, builders, and educators, men of integrity and often of sanctity. But few of them had been monks. It was in 1221 that the first friars reached England from Europe, followers of St Dominic, highly trained in theology and the art of preaching. And three years later came the Franciscans, vowed to poverty and to work among the downtrodden and the diseased in the tradition of their great founder, Francis of Assisi. The friars were men under a rule as strict as that of many monasteries, but their work was not behind closed walls. It was on the roads with their crowds of vagabonds, in the streets of the new towns, in the new schools, and above all perhaps in the slowly evolving universities of Oxford and Cambridge.

In the later years of the twelfth century, groups of scholars had been gathering in the city of Oxford, living together in halls, attracted by the reputation of a few teachers. By 1230 there were probably about 1,300 students there and after the middle of the century the colleges which exist today were being founded and endowed as organized places of residence. At the same time, the more recently founded university in the small market town of Cambridge, staffed at first by exiles from Oxford and visitors from Paris, was developing on like lines. Both universities were controlled and directed by the Church and were the special interest of the kings of England, who saw them as a more effective training ground for royal administrators than the humbler *familiae* or households of the bishops. The monasteries kept their great libraries and their skill in manuscript illumination. But slowly they were losing their pupils and their prestige.

The first chancellor of the University of Oxford was Robert Grosseteste, who was Bishop of Lincoln from 1235 to 1253. He was one of the most remarkable men of his or any age. No Englishman since Alfred combined with a busy administrative life such a wide variety of interests, qualities, and skills. As Bishop of Lincoln he personally supervised the rebuilding of the cathedral and the pastoral work of a large diocese. Oxford he nursed through years of uncertainty and strife. He kept up a voluminous correspondence with the great men of his age in England and abroad. But to crown it all he was perhaps the first man in western Europe since classical times to attack some of the great problems in science by what is called the scientific method of observation and experiment. His work on the nature of light had an influence on Newton. He tried to plumb the mysteries of the rainbow. He recommended the use of magnifying lenses for bad sight. He urged a reform of the Julian calendar, already several days out – but for that England waited till 1752. He made records of comets. He rightly thought that heat was a form of motion in the particles of matter. Such was his position and reputation that he was never accused of heresy, but one of his pupils, the Franciscan Roger Bacon, a man of brilliant and inventive mind, sometimes called the founder of English philosophy, was to the ignorant public a wizard who raised spirits from the dead, and was twice imprisoned for his dangerous notions.

There were few in thirteenth-century England who could read the work of Grosseteste or Roger Bacon, fewer still who could understand it or appreciate its value. For most men the struggle merely to live was still hard and the surplus of food so small that a bad harvest could bring local or national disaster. The population was increasing. A million and a half in 1066, it had doubled by the end of the thirteenth century. There was now far more land under cultivation. The forests were shrinking. There were new towns too, like Salisbury, Portsmouth, or fortified boroughs of the Welsh Marches, and many of them were spaciously planned. There were few new industries. Most of England's exports were traditional ones encouraged by the Romans – iron, tin, lead and above all wool. In this century about eight million fleeces left England yearly, most of them for Flanders. The monasteries, declining in the power of their spiritual life, were among the greatest sheep farmers. The northern lands devastated by the Conqueror, re-colonized by the Cistercians, were crowned with the vast sheep runs which brought wealth to the austere air of Fountains or Rievaulx. And beside the growing wool trade the manufacture of cloth was increasing. In quantity, English cloth could not compete with the work of Flemish weavers, of Bruges or Ghent, but its quality was unsurpassed. The invention of the 'fulling mill', which used water power to put the finish on the cloth, was transferring the cloth industry from the towns of the east to the fast-running streams of the west and north, bringing centuries of prosperity to the Pennines or the Cotswolds. All over England the rising prosperity of the wool and cloth areas was shown in the crop of new parish churches which replaced the heavy, ill-lit buildings of Norman times. Like the new cathedrals, the smaller churches were higher and lighter, and often had room for far more people than the parish could provide. But in their size and splendour they were helps to prestige as well as worship.

Not all English exports were handled by native merchants. The great towns, and particularly London, had their communities of foreigners, between whom and the natives feeling often ran high. In London, the Baltic merchants of the Hanseatic League had a fortified enclosure, called the Steelyard, like a small colony. Italian bankers provided the credit facilities without which trade was cumbersome. It was becoming possible now by using a kind of rudimentary cheque, to go on trading missions without carrying loads of money. Without the presence in the capitals of Europe of representatives from the great Lombard banking firms this would have been impossible.

In the countryside too the use of coin was becoming commoner. Paying for a land-holding by service alone had never been universal. Money rents had been paid for centuries. But in the thirteenth century more and more villeins were turning the service they owed to their lord into rents, more and more work was being done by paid labourers. But such 'commutation', as it is called by historians, did not bring freedom. Lords were now writing down elaborate 'customs of the manor' which outlined the services due from tenants and in times of difficulty the services which had lapsed could always be revived. In the fourteenth century there was much distress and bitterness among those who had tasted freedom or watched it in others and found it snatched away.

Against this background of creation and change King John's only son, Henry III, grew to a manhood which was to have more than its share of troubles. The tottering Plantagenet throne had been made secure by the loyal group of barons and officials after John's death, but the time of the regency till Henry, at nineteen, declared himself of age, made an indelible mark on the government of England. Most of what Henry II had done to strengthen the king's power was retained. But among the many men who had kept the peace in Henry III's minority the feeling was growing that this power should properly be exercised with the co-operation and advice of the great men of the kingdom. The quarrels and bloodshed of Henry's long reign arose from the fact that he failed to see this and had not the political or military skill to win battles by himself.

Henry III was no fierce choleric tyrant like his father. He was intelligent, religious, and affectionate, a lover of beauty and craftsmanship, careful in dress, meticulous in ceremonial. He was determined to be a good son of the Church, to be the obedient vassal of the pope that John's surrender had made him. But he was determined, too, to be a real king, to choose his lieutenants from men he felt would be faithful to him, and to win back from the king of France what his father had lost.

After his victory at Bouvines in 1214 the French king Philip Augustus was diverted from any conquest of the remaining English possessions by the pope's call for a crusade against the Albigensian heretics of southern France. But two years after Bouvines, his son Louis was leading a party of French knights in England against King John. Philip Augustus died in 1223 having revolutionized the position of the French crown in Europe, and his son succeeded as Louis VIII. He immediately invaded Poitou, which along with Aquitaine was all that remained English in France. He overran it but was checked on the border of Aquitaine and died in 1226, leaving the throne to his twelve-year-old son, the future St. Louis. For the English it was a welcome breathing space and in 1230, Henry III, flushed with ambitions of reconquest, landed in Brittany, marched triumphantly south to Bordeaux and back again without having to do any serious fighting, fell ill, and returned to England having impressed no-one and achieved nothing – unless it was to reassure the Bordeaux wine shippers that their chief customer could still bring soldiers to France.

In 1236 Henry married the beautiful Eleanor of Provence, who brought with her a number of relations to the English court. Many received the king's favour, to the growing disgust of the native English barons. Then in 1238 Henry married his sister to a young French nobleman who had inherited the earldom of Leicester, Simon de Montfort. The barons, little knowing that Simon would one day be their leader, were further disgusted at this new favour to a foreigner. In 1242 Henry decided on a new military adventure aimed at the permanent recovery of Poitou. It was an expensive failure. The mood of the barons became more dangerous. Step by step they were being excluded from that share in the government which the Charter and the Regency had led them to expect and their places were filled with Henry's relations from Poitou or his wife's from Provence and Savoy. And the great offices of state passed from their possession. After 1241 there was no justiciar. After 1238 minor household officials of the king held the office of chancellor. And the Exchequer, round whose green baize cloth the greater barons watchfully sat, was losing its hold on the revenue as the king diverted more and more of his heavy war taxes into his own personal departments of the 'Wardrobe' and 'Chamber'. All this he had a perfect legal right to do; but unless he could prove to the barons that he was efficient and could be successful in war, he did it at his peril.

The barons seem to have made strong protests, but without a strong leader they made little impression. It was not long, however, before they had such a leader, in one of the very foreigners to whom they had at first objected but whom, through his tenure by hereditary right of the great earldom of Leicester they had slowly come to accept – Simon de Montfort.

Simon is one of the great men of English history. He had charm, political ability, and ideals beyond his mere selfish interest. He was honest, faithful to the Church, a friend of Bishop Grosseteste and the Franciscans. He came of a famous family of stern warriors and crusaders. But he was proud, unwilling to forget an insult, intolerant of weaker or more pliant men. And he came initially to lead the barons because of an intense personal quarrel with his brother in law, the king. In 1248, Henry, worried by the news of disturbances in Gascony (the southern part of Aquitaine) had sent Simon there as governor. To Simon the only remedy for the situation there was sternness, and when the Gascons complained to the king, Simon received instead of moral support a curt summons to appear in Westminster. Simon came, and his rule was vindicated, but he never forgave Henry for the insult.

Having made a new enemy of one who had once been his friend, Henry plunged more deeply into adventures beyond his resources. He was very conscious of being the pope's vassal, and in 1254 he agreed to help the pope in a wild scheme to remove German influence from Sicily. To finance the scheme he used the pope's permission to tax the English clergy and levied a heavy tax on the laymen as well.

The summer of 1256 was wet. The harvest failed. The next year there was serious famine and another harvest failed. In the early spring of 1258 frosts halted ploughing and decimated the flocks. The country seemed on the brink of an explosion while a frustrated pope threatened Henry with excommunication for failing to produce the promised money. In such an atmosphere, at last, the barons took up arms, demanded a Great Council, and drew up a programme of reform for the kingdom. Almost all the great lords of the kingdom were present, Earl Simon among them. Starvation was rife in England as yet another harvest failed. The royal treasury was almost empty. Henry could do nothing but surrender, agreeing to the reforms in exchange for 'supply', or taxes.

The reforms appeared in 1258 in a document later called the Provisions of Oxford. The abuse of power by royal sheriffs was to cease. The traditional offices of state were to be restored. The royal revenues were to be paid into the Exchequer. A baronial council of fifteen was to be set up to advise the king. A year later, by the Provisions of Westminster, the activities of baronial officials as well as baronial estates were to be watched as were the king's sheriffs.

It was a fine programme. But its success depended on unity among the reformers. Within a few years their unity was gone and they were quarrelling bitterly among themselves, some moving to side with the king, others angry that their own local tyrannies might be unveiled by the Provisions of Westminster. Seizing his chance and helped by his young son, Edward, Henry revoked the Provisions and made the pope annul them. In disgust, Earl Simon left England for France.

For a year or two Henry ruled as before, but no more successfully. Over-confident, he crossed to France in 1262 to discuss the question of Aquitaine with St. Louis and fell ill. While there he heard that Prince Llywelyn of Wales had launched an attack across the English border. The marcher lords called Earl Simon to their aid. Simon returned to stir up once more the old cause of reform. With the barons in arms again civil war seemed inevitable, but it was delayed while St. Louis was called in to arbitrate between the two sides. His prestige in the Christian world was enormous and in the so-called Mise of Amiens in 1264 he declared for the king. Kings, he said, had the right to choose whom they would as their ministers. Simon angrily rejected the decision, war followed, and at Lewes in Sussex the royal army was shattered by the barons, Henry and his son, Prince Edward, being captured.

There followed Simon's fifteen months of uncertain power as with the ageing Henry in his keeping, he tried to govern through a committee of three 'electors'. The barons were jealous of him, for they saw in his essential fairness little hope of more power for themselves. Most of Simons' support came from the clergy, the townsfolk, or the knights of the shire, to whom he had always been a symbol of justice, and to make the most of his support he called together with the Great Council, representatives of shires and boroughs in an assembly which was ultimately to develop into the House of Commons. Simon has been called the founder of the House – and not wrongly – but his calling of the burgesses and knights was for him the clutching at a straw. He went for money to the people who liked him. But his enemies were too strong. The Prince Edward escaped from captivity, raised an army from among those to whom, for one reason or another, Simon was dangerous – those who could not abide his attack on the king, those who wished for advancement under the heir to the throne, and those who thought his rule no more favourable to baronial interest than Henry's. Caught in a bend of the river Avon at Evesham, in August 1266, Simon's army was overwhelmed, he himself killed, his body cruelly dishonoured. But his memory, and much of his work, were to remain.

CHAPTER 14

The Early Years of Edward I

1265-1290

KING HENRY III was nearly sixty when Evesham was fought and for the rest of his reign he took little part in politics. Like his own patron Edward the Confessor it was the abbey at Westminster which possessed his mind. He could free himself from the cares of state the easier because his son, the real victor of Evesham, was already showing the wisdom and statesmanship which were to make him one of the greatest of all English kings. A lesser man than Edward would have branded Simon's ideas as well as his body with the mark of treachery and returned to the household government of Henry with chosen friends as advisers. But Edward had greater vision. He saw that, though misguided, Simon had shown the way to a government in which more of the people of England could participate but which preserved the necessary power of the king.

A year after Evesham, as the remnants of Simon's supporters surrendered at the earl's castle of Kenilworth, Edward put out a kind of manifesto of the principles by which he would abide. The king's authority would be restored, but unfair summary justice would cease. The liberties of the Church would be preserved. Magna Carta was confirmed, and Simon's tainted followers who had lost their lands were to be allowed to buy them back again. The treason was not to be forgotten but the divisions it had brought were to be healed. And by 1270 the kingdom was so quiet that Edward felt free to fulfil the vow his father had made long ago and take the Cross. For Henry the abbey, for Edward the Holy Land – these were what mattered above all in 1270, more than the cut and thrust of politics, more than the making of constitutions and the framing of laws. Medieval man saw himself first as struggling for his salvation before his God, and doing so not only in the loneliness of a room but in the great, ostentatious action of building or crusade.

Edward's crusade had little effect. He was horrified on reaching the East to find the remains of the kingdom of Jerusalem deep in corruption; fighting for little but its own material existence. He found that Venetian merchants were supplying the Sultan with war material and that the Genoese were running the Egyptian slave trade. He found that the Christian knights on the island of Cyprus had no desire to leave it and that their Mongol allies were too occupied in Central Asia to be of much help. After a few skirmishes, a truce, and a narrow escape from death at the hand of an assassin, Edward left in September 1272. In mid-November Henry III died and the absent Edward was quietly proclaimed king 'by hereditary right, by the will of the magnates, and by their oath of fealty'.

Edward did not hurry home. There seemed no need. He visited the pope, he tried to avenge the murder by one of Simon's sons of his cousin Henry of Almain, he took part in a great tournament at Chalons, he did homage to the French king in Paris for the lands he held of him, and he travelled south again into Gascony. It was August, 1274, before he landed at Dover – though all the time he had been in France he had through men and letters been keeping in contact with English affairs. His leisurely journey was no sign of a lazy mind.

Indeed Edward I can be rivalled in energy only by his great-grandfather, Henry II. He was a man of superb physique, formidable in personal combat, the most famous knight of Christendom. That in itself in those days brought great force to his commands as king. But he had as well a calculating, legalistic, organizing mind. Though he was hot tempered like all his race, his decisions were coldly, calmly taken. He was religious in a correct, unemotional way. He was a loving and faithful husband to his wife Eleanor of Castile. He was intolerant of inefficiency, muddle, and opposition. He knew the limitations of military conquest, was aware that battles won were useless without castles and law courts to prolong their effects. He knew that all government was impossible without adequate money and that the people to tax were the people who had it. He saw the value to a community of thriving trade and prosperous merchants. All this has placed him with

Alfred and Henry II among the greatest of our earlier kings. But
there was something inhuman about him. He seemed to see men
less as living souls, more as pieces to be used and controlled in a
game whose ultimate object was his own greatness. 'With all my
strength,' he said once to his archbishop, 'I will defend my right
that is known to all the world.'

His 'right'. It was his first task as king to discover exactly what
that was. In the England of those days there was not, as there is now,
one law, one authority from which all others took their source.
Society was a network of petty authorities, local laws – the
authority of lord over tenant, baron over knight, bishop over priest,
priest over layman; the law of the Marches, the custom of the
manor, the law of the boroughs, the law of the Church. Nowadays
all courts are the crown's courts. Then it was not so. And it was
difficult for a king to know exactly what his powers were. Edward
was determined to find out, and then to exercise his powers to the
full. So he began to send round the country commissioners who
asked of everyone who claimed any sort of legal right 'quo
warranto' – 'by what warrant' – they had it. If they could not
answer satisfactorily the king claimed the right for himself. He
began his inquiries in 1274 and continued them for over four years.

In this he was creating nothing new. He was rather trying to put
the clock back to a past when, he imagined, a king had more power
than himself. But he went beyond this. In a series of statutes, or
decrees of his Great Council, he tried to simplify the remarkable
complications which feudalism had grown. Over the centuries
since the Conquest it had lost its simple framework of king–tenant-
in-chief–subtenant. Land had been sold and re-sold. Men had
died without heirs. Marriages had joined fiefs together. Two men
might well be both lords and vassals of one another. One man
might be vassal to a score of different lords. Edward's attack on all
this is very technical and historians are still not certain exactly
what some of his statutes meant. But the general aim of them seems
to have been to ensure that the king should know who was really
responsible for what and therefore whom he could tax for what.

Many of the quarrels between kings and their subjects in the
thirteenth and fourteenth centuries were over this right of taxation.
A king was expected to govern efficiently, to preserve his honour
against his enemies, to be strong and win wars. But to do this he

must have money and service. The old feudal host, the knights giving freely of the forty days' service, had long been inadequate to fight wars. Professional armies were becoming essential. But professional armies had to be paid, and by Edward's reign it was obvious that the old feudal taxes – imposed when fiefs changed hands, when vassals married, when knights could not come in person to war – were not nearly enough in time of war, and barely enough in time of peace. Edward and his successors were almost always at war with someone – with Wales, with Scotland, or above all with France. So other money had to be found. There was no shortage of it in the kingdom. The Church grew continually richer; so did the towns; so did the county gentry who bred the vast flocks of sheep. There are two ways of getting money – by force and by agreement. Force was still useful but usually led to civil war. Agreement was more risky, since it could always be refused, but it gave to men who agreed a sense of sharing in the kingdom's business which made loyalty deeper and more likely. It was out of this need of the king for money that the English Parliament grew.

The word 'parliamentum' – which meant a talking-together – had been used for a long time in a general sense. But it had been used particularly of those solemn meetings of the Great Council when the king, his bishops, and his barons discussed the business of the realm, the ceremonies described by the Saxon Chronicler when King William 'thrice wore his crown each year'. Simon de Montfort, in his brief year of power, had summoned to such a meeting not only his supporters among the barons but the knights of the shires and the important men of the boroughs. He did it largely for the selfish reason that such men of the middle orders loved him more than the barons did. But the idea did not die with him. Edward used it in 1295, and again from time to time in his reign. And gradually these men came to be regarded not merely as individuals but as representatives of the communities (or *communes*) from which they came, empowered to give or withhold assent to the king's demands for money and also to bring before the king and his Great Council the grievances they wanted redressed. Their presence was not essential to a Parliament. King Edward I called many without them. But they came more and more frequently till in Edward III's reign they came to all the Parliaments he held and were beginning to be known from the 'communes' they

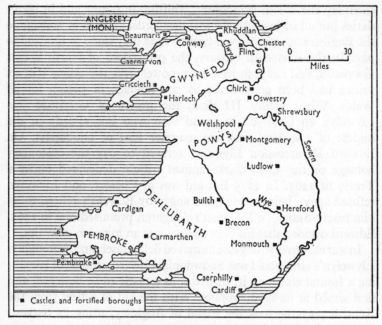

WALES IN THE TIME OF EDWARD I

represented, as the House of 'Commons'. Politics were not their province and advice to the king on how to govern was not welcomed, but with every decade that went by their grip on the royal purse strings became firmer and such a grip must inevitably mean, one day, political power.

In the earlier years of his reign Edward seldom quarrelled with his subjects, in Parliament or out. He had, like Henry II, the people's memory of troubles just endured to help him, and he had business to do with his neighbours which his subjects saw must be done. His first business was with Wales.

Wales had for long been in turmoil. The Saxons had penetrated there seldom, then only on brief punitive expeditions. William the Conquer had planted between Wales and himself extensive earldoms giving to their governors powers greater than he gave any of his other subjects. These marcher earls (earls of the Welsh 'march' or border) had extended their power westward and ruled a mixed population of Welsh and English with laws of their own. Beyond them lay the Welsh princedoms, shifting in power and in boundaries but all owing, like the marcher lords, an oath of homage to the English king which from time to time they came to England to pay. In the thirteenth century, the princedom of North Wales, Gwynedd, had come to have such power over the others that its prince had been accustomed to pay homage in person for all Wales. When Henry III died, the prince of Gwynedd was Llywelyn ap Gruffydd, a proud man who was already in the middle of a quarrel with the marcher Earl of Gloucester. On Edward I's accession Llywelyn refused to pay the customary homage or the 3,000 marks annual tribute demanded under a Treaty of 1267. In 1275 Edward was at Chester, and Llywelyn refused again, being made more angry by Edward's refusal to let him marry Simon de Montfort's daughter, promised him in 1265. Edward decided that his only answer was an invasion of Wales.

In war as in everything else he moved deliberately and thoroughly. Llywelyn's stronghold was Snowdonia. Edward, instead of launching a frontal attack on it, treated it as a castle to be besieged, and first aimed at its food supplies. With the aid of a fleet from the Kentish ports he took the island of Anglesey, using its harvest, destined for Llywelyn, for his own army. Within a few months Llywelyn had surrendered and was forced to give up his claim to rule any of Wales but Gwynedd. But Edward knew well that in such country a campaign ending in verbal promises of loyalty would be an expensive waste of time without the continual presence of military forces. And in those days that meant castles.

The castle had developed steadily from the simple stone keep of Norman times. Natural elaboration and the contact with the east which came from the crusades had turned castle-building into a complicated technique needing architects trained in the needs of warfare. Such an architect Edward happened to have in Master James of St. George, whom he had obtained from his kinsman Count Philip of Savoy. Master James's work can still be seen in Wales today, and in the years after Edward's expedition of 1277 great strongholds were built at Flint, Rhuddlan, Builth, and Aberystwyth. All began by using to the full the water and the contours that make natural defences. Fitted into these was, on the outside, a wide moat, on the river bank of which was a curtain wall about fifteen feet high, through the slits in which bowmen could

fire across the moat and down into it. There then came a space of
about thirty feet, called the outer ward, until the inner curtain
wall was reached. The height of this was more than twice that of
the outer wall, and from its top bowmen commanded the far side
of the moat and, should it be taken, the outer ward. At the corners
of the inner curtain were huge circular towers, over sixty feet in
height and forty in diameter. They jutted out from the line of the
wall so that from them cross-fire could be directed at those who
might try to scale it and, at longer range, at those attacking across
the moat. Inside this towered curtain wall was the inner ward,
with living quarters built against the wall itself. The diameter of
the whole, from moat to moat might be a quarter of a mile.

  Such structures were more than places of defence. They were
barracks, store places, and centres of government, and Edward
turned them into centres of trade as well, building towns outside
their walls and encouraging English merchants to go and live in
them. He certainly meant his power to last. But to the proud
Welsh this visible dominance was intolerable, especially when it
was accompanied by English justices with their strange, foreign
laws. In 1282 rebellion broke out again, when Llywelyn's brother
David besieged Flint and Rhuddlan and by his bold action spread
resistance through the whole principality. Once more Edward had
to raise an army. He used the same methods again, first suppressing the lower lands, isolating Snowdonia, and waiting patiently
for surrender. Llywelyn was killed. His brother David was hunted
down and hanged, and in 1284 at Rhuddlan, Edward issued a
statute which was to be his final plan for Wales. All Wales except
the old lands of the marcher lords were to be subject directly to
the English crown and to accept English justice. A new group of
castles was begun – Conway, Harlech, and Caernarvon. And
Edward hoped for peace. He had important business elsewhere.
The Welsh wars had been expensive. The massive castles had
used immense resources of stone and labour. The fleet and armies
had had to be paid. He was continually asking his Parliaments for
money. But Wales was still not entirely at peace. There was one
more great rising in 1294, while the king was about to leave for
Gascony. He moved his army from its embarkation ports with
great speed, tried for a quick victory, fell into mountain ambushes,
but finally won. It was the last spark. The Welsh did not rise

again for more than a century. And in 1301 Edward made his son, Edward, who had been born at Caernarvon, their prince. It was a good gesture, and helped to make the Welsh feel better disposed towards the gleaming white castles and strange laws by which they were governed. The conquest and settlement of Wales was one of the greatest successes of Edward's reign.

The particular needs of the campaign caused another nail to be driven into the coffin of the old feudal army. In the first place it required specialists – *ingeniatores* and *balistarii* to make and operate the great catapults necessary in sieges; *fossatores* or pioneers to cut a way through the dense forests for the armies; miners to bring down defensive walls; and above all the bowmen who were gradually building up an ascendancy against the heavy mounted knight. It was sometime near the end of Edward I's reign that the light bow was being replaced by the longbow with its greater range and hitting power. A longbowman took years to train. Muscles had to be developed to produce the great tension required on the string and to eliminate a wobbly aim. But the training which was to bear such fruit on the field of Crecy was beginning. The heavy armoured knights still rode to battle, but there were now in England only a few hundred of them, and they seldom appeared in force on the Welsh campaign. Many were 'bannerets', distinguished by the square banners they flew on the march, who commanded squadrons of paid troops – foot soldiers, bowmen, or lighter armed cavalry. In battle, the old undisciplined clash of armour was giving way to deliberate tactics, with archers and cavalry interspersed, timing their movements according to a set plan. And Edward had seen the vital importance, in land campaigns, of the command of the sea. In war as in so much else he showed himself a master.

In 1290, with Wales seeming peaceful and his English subjects contented, Edward announced his decision to go again on crusade. He had cherished the plan ever since his fruitless expedition of 1270, for he was a great king and the Cross was a great king's greatest task. He announced his decision in a Parliament in October. But within a month his plans were shattered. He was suddenly summoned to the bedside of his devoted wife, Eleanor of Castile, who after a long, slow fever, was on the point of death. Her loss was a bitter blow. 'My harp is tuned to mourning,' he

wrote to his bishops. She died near Lincoln, and Edward followed
her bier in its progress to Westminster, commanding that at every
stopping place a cross should be raised to the memory of her
'whom living I have dearly cherished and whom dead I shall not
cease to love'. But it was only the beginning of troubles. For at
the same time the news reached the king that the child Queen of
Scotland, the maid of Norway, destined to be the bride of Prince
Edward, had died in Orkney. Succession to the Scottish throne
was wide open. Only Edward had the authority and prestige to
settle it. Consumed with personal grief, he watched the kingdom
of Scotland split into furious rival factions. Setting aside his cross,
he spent a lonely Christmas and turned slowly towards the North.

CHAPTER 15

Scotland and Edward II

1290-1327

THIRTEENTH-CENTURY Scotland was a land of mixed race. Celts, Scandinavians, Angles and Saxons, Irish, Normans, Flemings, and many others, made up a population which in 1300 stood at about 400,000, of whom about half lived in the regions of the rivers Tay, Forth, and Clyde. The Norman conquerors of England, with their Breton and Fleming allies, had ventured in scores through the ancient kingdom of Northumbria to the wild lands beyond and, as in much of Europe, had lost little time in gaining local power over less intelligent or energetic residents. It is remarkable how many great Scottish families have sprung from this continental stock: the Stuarts, whose name comes from the office of Steward of Scotland which they held, came from the Breton family of FitzAlan; the Morays from Flanders; the Bruces from Normans who had settled in Yorkshire. There was a Scottish king and an English king, but the boundary of their realms was vague and many lords were liegemen of them both and would have been hard put to it, like many Gascons and Poitevins, to say to which nation they properly belonged. The Latin name 'Scotia' was applied only to the lands north of the Forth, beyond the limit of the old Northumbrian kingdom. South of the Forth lay Lothian, ruled by the Scottish king, but only as a fief from England, and terminating in a disputed border which ran roughly from Berwick to the English fortress at Carlisle.

It had long been the custom for Scottish kings to do homage to the kings of England, not for their realm as a whole but for the region of Lothian; but occasionally it had been said in the south

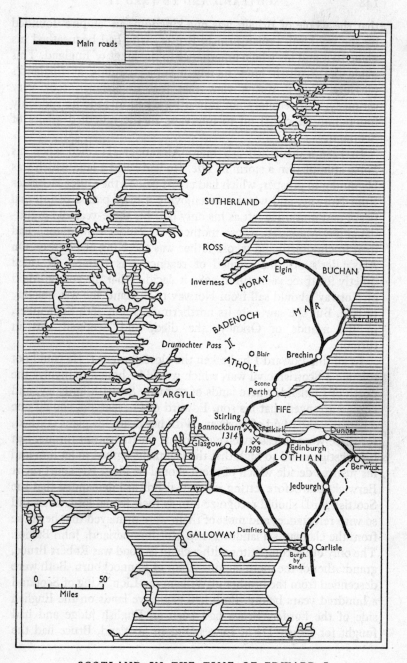

Map legend: Main roads

SUTHERLAND

ROSS

Inverness

MORAY Elgin BUCHAN

MA R

Aberdeen

BADENOCH

Drumochter Pass

O Blair

Brechin

ATHOLL

Scone
Perth

FIFE

ARGYLL

Stirling

Bannockburn
1314

Falkirk

Dunbar

Glasgow

1298

Edinburgh

LOTHIAN

Berwick

Ayr

Jedburgh

GALLOWAY

Dumfries

Carlisle

Burgh
by
Sands

0   50
Miles

SCOTLAND IN THE TIME OF EDWARD I

that the whole of Britain was one kingdom, an 'empire' founded by the mythical Trojan prince, Brutus, who had bequeathed his name to it and his whole inheritance to the kings of England. This made the Scottish king merely a subject, ruling at England's pleasure. But it was a view that few Englishman took very seriously, and certainly not Edward I when in 1290 he suddenly found himself called on to intervene in the muddled affairs of Scotland.

In 1286 a great Scottish king, Alexander III, died when his horse stumbled in a storm in Fife. He had ruled a land which was beginning to prosper, which had at last gained the Outer Hebrides from Norway, and which was enjoying a brief period of internal peace and unity. He left as his only heir his three-year-old granddaughter, Margaret, whose mother – Alexander's daughter – had died in childbirth and whose father was the King of Norway. On Alexander's death a council of regency was formed. It ruled quietly for three years till in 1289 it decided that the young 'Maid of Norway' should sail from Norway to the land she was one day to rule. But she saw only its northern cliffs. On 26th September, in the islands of Orkney, she died, and Scotland was in turmoil.

In all this Edward I had taken the closest interest. He could not tolerate a Scottish civil war, which would be bound to involve the north of England, where lands of so many Scottish lords lay, and he had arranged that his son, Edward of Caernarvon, should one day marry the Maid of Norway. With her death his plans crashed, for there were at least twelve claimants for the vacant throne. But his prestige stood so high that the claimants agreed to let him and his justices decide which of them should be king. His court sat at Berwick, but before letting it proceed Edward demanded that the Scottish lords should recognize him as their feudal lord. They did so with reluctance; and most of them were dismayed that he chose from the claimants a landowner in Northumberland, John Balliol. The only other competitor with a claim as good was Robert Bruce, grandfather of the more famous victor of Bannockburn. Both were descended from the brother of William the Lion, King of Scotland a hundred years before. Both had extensive lands on the English side of the border. Bruce had been an English judge and had fought for Henry III at Lewes. But in Scotland, Bruce had the greater following, and the coronation of Balliol on the famous stone at Scone on St. Andrew's Day, 1292, was received with little enthusiasm.

All might yet have been well. Edward I had given his judgment after immense pains. Scotland had a crowned king, John, unpopular but possibly capable of keeping the peace. But all was not well. Edward was not a man to let go rights when he thought them due to him, and in the midst of the judgment he had insisted that he was lord of Scotland – otherwise how could he make a judgment? Now he began to claim that his lordship really meant something more than a vague superiority, that it meant, for example, as it had in Wales, the right to hear appeals from Scottish courts, the right to summon even the king of Scotland to London. In Scotland resistance grew, and John Balliol – the 'lamb among wolves' – did not know whether to lead it or check it, unaware that he had the power to do neither. When in 1295, Edward, in the throes of troubles with France, demanded the feudal military service of the Scottish king, it was proudly refused, and the Scots made an alliance with the king of France, the constant threat of which was to be their most potent weapon against the English for four hundred years. The spring of 1296 saw Edward cross the border, determined not to conquer Scotland but to show her who was lord. He met little resistance as he marched slowly north and through the highlands to Elgin. On his way back he collected the coronation stone from Scone and the 'Black Rood' of St. Margaret from Edinburgh. The coronation stone was installed in the symbolic centre of English kingship, the Confessor's Chapel at Westminster. The Scottish problem seemed settled and King John had been shown just how insignificant he was. Edward went on preparing for greater deeds in France.

But the following year the Scots were in arms again, now led by William Wallace, a proud knight who threw his whole soul into the cause of independence. Edward being the other side of the Channel, an English army under Warenne was crushed at Stirling, and Wallace led his triumphant band to ravage northern England. Once more, in 1298, Edward collected an army. His 12,000 infantry, including 10,000 Welsh, and his 2,000 cavalry, half serving for pay, met the Scots at Falkirk in July, beat them after a hard fight, burned Perth and St. Andrews, and returned south. Perhaps this time the Scots had learned their lesson.

What Edward was slowly discovering, however, was that Scotland was not like Wales. In the first place it was much larger. Where Wales required a dozen great castles Scotland would have required three dozen, and the road to the highlands lay through a hundred and fifty miles of hilly lowlands. Secondly, it was a different shape. Wales had a long border from which it was nowhere more than a hundred miles to the coast. Llywelyn's mountain strongholds of Snowdon were only fifty miles from Chester and ten from the sea. But from Carlisle to Inverness is nearly three hundred, from Inverness to the north-west coast nearly half that again. Edward could win battles against the Scots, at immense cost and with, for those days, large armies. He could burn towns and hang traitors – as in 1305 Wallace was hanged. But he could not conquer Scotland.

His own people, too, were becoming restless. It was not only Scotland which was draining Edward's resources and making him tax his subjects more heavily. He was deeply involved in a struggle against the French king, who in 1294, following a sea battle off Brittany between English and French merchant fleets, had condemned Edward to lose his fief of Aquitaine. Edward had governed his French possessions with care and wisdom, building fortified boroughs and encouraging trade. He had no intention now of surrendering them. But he could only keep them by war. He made an alliance with the Count of Flanders, hoping to divert the French king from the south. He sent expeditions to Aquitaine. But it brought him little profit and from England much complaint. In 1297 he was forced by his assembled barons to issue a solemn confirmation of Magna Carta. Three years later he had to accept twenty 'Articles on the Charters' which made him promise to give up various methods of taxation which he felt to be within his sacred rights but over which his barons and knights felt they had no control.

Those last years of Edward's life were bitter and sad. The reign which had begun in unity and in the splendour of the tall prince returning from crusade, was ending in constant warfare and squabbles over money. Edward himself did not improve as he grew older. His wife's death in 1290 was a blow from which he never recovered. His eldest surviving son, Edward of Caernarvon, was turning out to be everything his father disliked. There had never been much warmth in Edward I, but now the last embers of it were fading. He travelled over his realm as a new century dawned, a tired, gloomy, ill-tempered man. The Scots he had defeated in 1298 were carrying on incessant wars with his officers and in 1303 he had to take his army north again for another ponderous parade through the Highlands. It seemed to settle things; and yet within two years of his leaving, the young Robert Bruce had been crowned king and was gathering round him all the elements in Scotland to fight for independence. Wearily, in 1306, Edward once more turned to the north. But he never crossed the border. Near Carlisle, on 7th July, 1307, after a long and painful illness, he died.

Edward of Caernarvon, who succeeded him, was his third son. No greater contrast between father and son could be imagined. The father was stern, purposeful, subordinating everything to the pursuit of his kingly rights, seldom in his later years indulging in the luxury of human feelings, treating men as machines, politics and war as his life purpose, doing little on impulse, feared but seldom loved, a great king but remote from his people. The young Edward II hated politics, the business of kingship, and the rough fighting-men of his father. At a time when the only pursuits considered manly were war, the tournament, and the chase, he liked rowing boats, swimming, acting plays, thatching and bricklaying. Nowadays such interests might be admired in a king. Then they were despised as base 'mechanic arts'. Hated and despised, too, was Edward's great friend, the Gascon knight Piers Gaveston, who had been exiled by Edward I and was, on the old king's death, immediately recalled to have honours showered upon him. Between him and the new king there was a strong bond of affection. On Edward II's side it was so strong that from the beginning of his reign he made it clear that he put Gaveston above all other men and above the kingdom itself. Where the old Edward had subordinated all to the business of ruling, the young Edward subordinated all to Piers Gaveston, and by so doing began a chain of events which ended in the appalling tragedy of Berkeley Castle twenty years later.

'Edward II,' a modern historian has written,[1] 'sat down to the

[1] N. Denholm Young, in his preface to the *Vita Edwardi Scundi* (Nelson).

game of kingship with a remarkably poor hand, and he played it very badly.' The hand was a kingdom oppressed by the severe taxation that followed wars with three countries; a kingdom for whose barons the death of Edward I was the lifting of a massive burden and the accession of his inadequate son an overdue piece of luck; a kingdom whose northern neighbour was ruled by a hostile and able king who was already harrying Northumberland; a kingdom whose overseas territories were perpetually threatened by the cruelly calculating Philip the Fair, the greatest French king since Philip Augustus.

Edward's method of playing such a hand was to raise a foreign adventurer to the highest office, to give him an earldom and English lands, to let him mock the great barons with insulting nicknames, and to barter the royal power and the royal rights that this Gaveston should be allowed to keep his state. So from 1307 to 1312 the struggles between Edward and his barons, which were inevitable anyway, centred round Gaveston. In 1308 Edward called him back from Ireland, where he had been a surprisingly successful Lord Lieutenant, and promised the barons that he would reform the royal government if only Gaveston could remain. Though happy at the idea of reform, the barons still refused to tolerate the upstart favourite and the king took him north to ravage Scotland in imitation of his father. But such military parades were expensive and Edward was forced to summon Parliament to raise money. He left Gaveston in a powerful Northumberland castle and drifted slowly towards the reckoning that awaited him in Westminster.

There he was presented with a collection of 'Ordinances'. His favourites were attacked for their evil counsel. They had led him, said the barons – who came to be called Ordainers – away from the true interests of his people, in a futile war with Scotland, into selling crown lands, into debts to foreign bankers. In future the king must govern with his true and natural advisers, the great barons of the realm. He must avoid tyrannical taxation. He must not leave the kingdom or make war without consent. He must not appoint ministers without baronial agreement. He must not interfere with the law of the realm. In short, he must do what no king before him had ever been forced to do. He must be the mere mouthpiece of his barons. But all Edward accepted, for in return

Gaveston was to be given a safe conduct to leave the country in peace.

Edward, however, had no intention of keeping the Ordinances. Gaveston disappeared for a few weeks – no-one knows where – only to reappear in time to keep Christmas with the king at Windsor. To the ordainers it was an open challenge and they took it. Gaveston was excommunicated by the Archbishop of Canterbury and the hunt began. Once more the king and his favourite had gone north, but at Scarborough Gaveston surrendered on a promise he would not be harmed, and was brought a prisoner to the south. The barons probably intended that he should be tried. But one night he was left with a few guards near the lands of Guy Beauchamp, Earl of Warwick, for whom in the days of gay liberty Gaveston had invented the name 'Black Dog of Arden'. The rest a chronicler can describe:

'When the Earl of Warwick learned all that was happening, he took a strong force, raised the whole countryside and secretly approached the place where he knew Piers to be. Coming to the village early one Saturday, he entered the gate of the courtyard and surrounded the chamber. Then the earl called out in a loud voice: "Get up, traitor, you are taken." When Piers heard this, seeing that the earl was there with a superior force and that his own guards did not resist, he dressed himself and came down. In this fashion Piers was taken and led forth not as an earl but as a thief . . . He whom Piers called Warwick the Dog has now bound Piers in chains.'[1]

He was put in prison, while his captors debated his fate. It did not take them long. Led by the king's cousin, Thomas of Lancaster, they ordered his immediate death. On Blacklow Hill by the town of Warwick he was executed by two Welshmen.

'Such Peter's end, who climbing up too high,
Crashed into nothingness from whence he came.'

And the chronicler added a moral. 'Let English courtiers beware lest, trusting in royal favour, they look down upon the barons. For they are a chief constituent of monarchy, and without them the

[1] *Vita Edwardi Secundi:* trans. N. Denholm Young.

king cannot attempt or accomplish anything of importance.' Of royal favourites Gaveston was the first but by no means the last to find such a fate and provoke such a moral.

Edward was powerless to do anything but grieve at Gaveston's death. He never forgave the murderers and waited many years in patience for his revenge, but for the time being he walked carefully, his sorrow slightly lessened by the birth in November 1312 of a son to his wife Isabella, daughter of the French king Philip the Fair. Between himself and the barons a peace was patched up, with some hollow apologies on both sides, most of the barons preferring such a peace to the extreme course Thomas of Lancaster desired. And in the midst of this short, muttering peace Scotland came again to claim the king's attention.

While Edward quarrelled with his barons in the south, English control in Scotland had shrunk to little more than a garrison in Stirling Castle, built on a steep-sided rock controlling the main road to the Highlands. Nearly all the rest was in the hands of Robert Bruce and his supporters, and parties of Scottish troopers made frequent forays over the border to add, in 1313, to the miseries of a bad harvest. It was clear that if Scotland were not to be lost altogether something must be done. Edward showed uncommon resolution. He ordered his barons to provide an army, collected troops of his own, and marched north with an army of impressive size. On 17 June 1314, he crossed the border and marched to the planned relief of Stirling.

A week after crossing the Tweed, on Midsummer Day, 1314, the English were crushingly defeated at Bannockburn. The English cavalry, making no impression on the squares of Scottish pikemen, fell back towards their own infantry, and in the confused melee which followed were thrust into suffocating death in marsh and stream. The remnant of the English fled, leaving the Scots to their plunder. Edward, refused entrance into his own castle, was chased to the coast at Dunbar, where a ship took him back to Berwick. 'O day of vengeance and disaster,' wailed the chronicler, 'day of utter loss and shame, evil and accursed day, not to be reckoned in our calendar.' Bannockburn was the greatest disaster to the arms of England since Hastings. It ensured the independence of Scotland for many centuries and the humiliation before his countrymen of the ill-starred English king.

Such a defeat in battle before a weaker nation made Edward helpless. He promised again to put the Ordinances into full effect and to do nothing without baronial consent. But the barons themselves had little unity, and many followed a middle course under the wise leadership of Aymer de Valence, Earl of Pembroke, while Thomas of Lancaster sulked in his castle of Pontefract. Edward accepted Pembroke's counsel for a time and there was peace, but he was beginning to find new and dangerous friends in the two Despensers, father and son. The elder, Hugh, had long been a supporter of the king. His son, also Hugh, was a lively companion and Edward's age. Neither was wicked; but both were ambitious and from the king's service hoped to build for their family a large earldom in the Marches of south Wales. It was their territorial ambitions which brought civil war again to England. Sent into exile by the jealous barons in 1321, they returned a year later. Lancaster put the north in arms against them, but the king was now supported by enough of Lancaster's enemies to raise a strong force against him. In March 1322 Lancaster's army was defeated at Boroughbridge in Yorkshire and with the delight of long-awaited vengeance Edward ordered his execution. So the man who ten years before had ordered the killing of Gaveston now 'mounted on some worthless mule' was led from his own castle of Pontefract and beheaded. It was part of the pattern of this unhappy reign. In fifteen years, from the high deeds of Edward I, England had slipped to this dreary play of spite and vendetta. Thomas of Lancaster had been proud and bitter but he was made more in the stamp of the elder Edward than that king's son. Now, by his people in the north, his faults were forgotten. Within weeks of his death he was venerated as a martyr, protector of the liberties of Church and State.

Boroughbridge and Pontefract were Edward II's greatest triumphs. For four years he uneasily enjoyed them, propped up in his state by the Despensers. But soon a new and worse danger threatened. In 1325 his queen, Isabella, took her young son to France, where it was arranged that the prince should do homage for the French lands to which he would one day succeed. Isabella had come now to hate her husband and the favourites by whom he was surrounded and while she was away she began to plot against him. She began a love affair with Roger Mortimer, a

Marcher landowner who had every reason to hate the land-grabbing Despensers; and in September 1326 they landed in Suffolk with a small force, publicly proclaiming that they had come for the Despensers' heads. Barons and knights flocked to them. A London mob rose in their name, murdering indiscriminately all they suspected of being the Despensers' friends. With his few remaining supporters Edward fled to the west, pursued by his implacable queen and her lover. The Despensers were caught and hanged. The king was declared deposed with no voice raised in his favour. He was imprisoned first at Kenilworth and then in a dungeon at Berkeley. And there he disappears from history.

He never left Berkeley alive and was almost certainly murdered there. But like his cousin, Thomas of Lancaster, he had power in his death. The canons of St. Augustine's, Bristol, were too frightened to take his body, but it was accepted by Benedictines of Gloucester, who ordered for it a splendid tomb and from the gifts of pilgrims built a new choir to house it. Tomb and choir are still there in delicate beauty, a strange memorial to a blood-stained reign.

CHAPTER 16

The Opening of the 100 Years' War

1327-1360

KING EDWARD III, who was to reign for fifty years and to launch the greatest international war western Europe had yet known, came to the throne of England at the age of fifteen as a mere piece in his mother's game of kidnapping and murder. Two years before, Queen Isabella had carried him off to France, ostensibly to pay homage to the French king for Aquitaine but in truth to help her fight the battle she was preparing against the husband she had come to hate. For two years he was with her on the Continent, a witness of her scandalous connexion with Mortimer. When her own French relations began to grow weary of her, she retired to the Low Countries and gave her son in marriage to the daughter of the Count of Hainault in return for an army of Hainaulters she could use in an invasion of England. And for three years after the crime at Berkeley the future victor of Crécy watched passively as Mortimer grew in power and arrogance in England and yet was forced by the Scots to the 'base peace' of Northampton when all for which Edward I had fought was returned to Robert Bruce, and the humiliation of Bannockburn made complete.

But it was unlikely that the English baronage, who had hated national disgrace as much as they had hated Edward II, would long put up with this new pawning of the kingdom, and in the autumn of 1330 a group of them plotted with the young king the fall of Isabella's lover. Bursting aside her plea to 'have pity on gentle Mortimer' they seized him at Nottingham Castle, tried him with the form of law but no pity in Westminster, and hanged him with the full horrors of a traitor's death. Her royal blood saved Isabella. The 'She-Wolf of France' was given an annuity and left in peace to read romances and collect relics. She died in the habit of a Franciscan nun, two years after her son's victory at Crécy.

Thus, three years after his accession, Edward III began truly to rule, and from the first he seemed resolved to blot out the memories of his father's ignoble reign. In an age that despised the eccentric he was entirely conventional. The creative skills of his father were not for him. His loves were the loves of the knightly class of his time, the chase, the tournament, and the noblest occupation of all – war. For hunting he had every chance in the great forests of his kingdom. In the mock warfare of the tournament he had been conspicuous from his boyhood. Once, with his young companions, he had dressed as a Tartar chieftain and challenged all the world in the lists at Cheapside. And for real war – scarcely more dangerous than the tournament – a golden opportunity soon came to him. He seized it with enthusiasm but little wisdom, crossing the Channel to begin the conflict which was to drag on for over a hundred years, to bring untold misery to England and France and to alter the course of their history for ever.

The loss of Normany in 1204 had left England still with the bulk of Henry II's old Angevin Empire; but, within a few years, of all that great tract of territories only the south-west province remained – the Duchy of Aquitaine (or Guienne) – which had come to Henry II through his wife. In 1259 the English had signed a treaty at Paris, which confirmed their possession of Aquitaine but made it clear that in so far as the king of England was Duke of Aquitaine he was the vassal of the king of France. Such a situation was not unusual in those days. It was an essential part of feudalism. But it held the seeds of endless squabbling. In the first place, the actual boundaries of the Duchy were vague. In the north there was the wide estuary of the Gironde, its banks crowded with the finest vineyards in the world. In the south were the Pyrenees. But to the east there was a maze of lands to which both kings at times laid claim. In the second place it was by no means clear what the overlordship of the king of France entailed. When kings of England reluctantly crossed the Channel to do homage for the Duchy they might, according to their interpretations, be going merely to a formal ceremony, or to vow themselves in truth the 'man' of the French king, bound to support

him against all his enemies – the chief of whom might well be the
king of England! And as for the inhabitants of Aquitaine themselves, they were most content with the master who taxed them
least and governed them lightest, provided they could sell the
wine and salt which their ships took up the coast to England. They
were deeply conscious of being Gascons or Bordelais, not at all
of being French.

Edward I, his attention concentrated on his own island, had
little time to give to his French possessions, though he governed
them wisely and well. The ambitious nibblings of the French
kings he countered by making alliances in the Low Countries,
but he avoided full-scale war. His son, too, avoided continental
trouble as much as he could. But the risk was always there, so long
as the French Kings continued to increase their power and their
ambitions. During these years the French frequently 'punished'
their Plantagenet vassals by confiscating the fief, but they usually
restored it again for a consideration and happily watched their
officials interfering in the duchy's affairs as an overlord's officials
had a legal right to do. They further annoyed the English by
supporting the Scots. In 1328, however, the Capetian family, who
had been France's kings for 400 years, were left without a direct
male heir with the death of Charles IV, and to many it seemed
that the next in line of succession was King Edward III, whose
mother, Isabella, was Charles IV's sister. French lawyers hurriedly
decided that the Crown could not be transmitted through a woman
and it was passed to Philip of Valois, the dead king's uncle, who
was crowned as Philip VI. But the Plantaganet claim remained,
a useful legal weapon for Edward to use.

By 1337, Edward decided that his 'rights' demanded action.
Aquitaine had been confiscated again. All of it but its coastal strip
was occupied by the French, and Philip was demanding the
payment of a fine due for the ending of the previous confiscation.
So Edward sent the Bishop of Lincoln to Paris bearing his official
defiance to 'Philip of Valois who calls himself King of France'. At
the same time he began to collect allies on the northern borders of
France. The 100 Years' War had begun.

It did not begin with a great battle or a strong invasion. It
began, as did many medieval wars, with a parade of arms and
fashion, together with the assumption of high-sounding titles. The

young Edward crossed to the low countries in the summer of 1337 and set about buying help for his enterprise. Various states on the lower Rhine joined him in exchange for gold or the promise of gold. The German Emperor, in the middle of a private quarrel with France, created him Vicar of the Empire, an imposing but largely meaningless title. And the Flemings, who bore the yoke of their French master unwillingly and were suffering from the cutting off of English wool exports, gave promise of support. Edward even had a new crown made and quartered the French fleur-de-lys on his shield all ready for his hoped-for coronation in Rheims. But of purposeful military operations there was little sign. Edward's allies were freer with their promises than their troops. The emissaries of the pope constantly intervened to save the peace. And Edward's slender resources soon melted away. He had to pawn his glorious new crown, and when in 1340 he returned to England, he had to leave behind his wife and children as security for his debts.

He found in England little enthusiasm for his cause and a Parliament restless at his constant devices for raising money. The Commons had since the death of Edward I been steadily growing in power. The conflicting parties in Edward II's time had carefully wooed them and growing trade had enriched them. They were in no mood to pay for policies which had no success to show. Edward's ministers in London, led by Archbishop Stratford, had been both unpopular and inefficient, and even a royal victory over the French fleet at Sluys on the Flemish coast – though it started Edward's extraordinary military reputation – did not altogether appease Parliament. In 1341 again Edward had to return home to face not only his tax payers but his own archbishop. Stratford, accused by the frustrated king of treason, began to imagine himself a second Becket and gathered such a sympathetic following that he had to be appeased. The king, in return for the subsidies he so badly needed, agreed to yet another confirmation of Magna Carta.

So far his fortunes had been uncertain. His financial difficulties had forced him into one of the many truces that filled the 100 Years' War. But in 1346, while Henry of Lancaster was campaigning successfully in Aquitaine, Edward landed with a small force in Normandy, scored some minor successes, and then turned

north-east towards Boulogne. His army reached the River Somme
in a state of exhaustion. His Flemish allies had been turned back
forty miles away. A large and fresh French army was watching
him, waiting its chance to attack. Edward took up a position with
his back protected by the wood of Crécy-en-Ponthieu and prayed
that somehow the enemy would hold off. Had he known better
his prayer might have been different. Had the French paused to
group their army and attacked the hungry and weary invaders
after a night's sleep they might have ended Edward's military
career for ever. But their cavalry was impatient. The English
seemed an easy prize, and with little thought the French swept
to the attack to the setting of an August sun. They rode down
their own crossbowmen whose slow deliberate fire had merely
used up all their arrows, and they ran straight into the fire of the
English longbows. 'And ever still the English shot where they
saw the thickest pass; the sharp arrows ran into the men at arms
and into their horses, and many fell, horse and men, among the
Genoese, and when they were down they could not rise again,
the press was so thick that one overthrew another.' Again and
again, with superb courage, the French knights charged, but
against the rain of arrows they were powerless. By nightfall it was
all over. Never before had there been such a victory of English
arms in Europe as on the field of Crécy.

Within a few days Edward was before Calais. While there he
learned that his other great enemies and France's allies, the Scots,
had been defeated at Neville's Cross. Before a year had passed the
great fortress of Calais was his, and to replace the expelled
inhabitants English colonists came in whose descendants held it
for England for over two hundred years.

Edward was a hero, to his people and to Europe. But like many
heroes he had been lucky. The English longbowmen had won
Crécy, with a skill learned in campaigns in Wales and Scotland
and handed down from father to son. But the French had made
it easy for them, presenting time after time the close-packed
colourful target that was the bowman's dream. Crécy and Calais
seemed to change the English. A war which had seemed a dour
necessity now for a while became a glory and a high adventure.
On St. George's Day, 1348, King Edward formally inaugurated
the Order of the Garter, a fellowship of king and twenty-five

knights, 'co-partners both in peace and war, assistant to one another in all serious and dangerous exploits, through the whole course of their lives to show fidelity and friendliness one towards another', as a later historian put it. Banished now it seemed were the days of civil violence, the memories of Blacklow Hill and Boroughbridge. King and baronage were bound together in the great enterprise of war and in his young son, Edward, the Black Prince, who had won knighthood at Crécy, Edward seemed to have found what to his ancestors had been so frequently denied, a worthy heir to his fame.

But war was not only romantic. It was profitable. Whatever the original motives of the French wars it was clear after Crécy that plunder and ransoms were its likely pickings, that participation in it could, for a younger son or an unsuccessful man of ambition, lead to fame and fortune. Already companies were being formed of freelance fighting men who slipped across the Channel to disguise their greed as patriotism in the rich countryside of France. Such 'free companies', as they were called, were to become the curse of France and, after their final expulsion, the blight of fifteenth-century England; but in the high days after Crécy, they offered a chance of adventure which, since the end of the Crusade, had been hard to find.

It was only a little over a year after the Garter festivities at Windsor, however, that there appeared among the coastal towns of Dorset a deadly and appalling disease, which from its effects, men called the Black Death. Long known in Asia it had been spreading quickly along the trade routes of Europe, carried in the fleas of the black rat. A high fever, a terrible thirst, lumps on the skin, a rapid and agonizing death – these were its manifestations. In the crowded insanitary cities of the Middle Ages it spread like fire. There was no cure. Most who caught it died. It reached London in November 1348, the North Country in the following year. How many it destroyed we shall never know. It came, not in a single violent burst, but in a series of outbreaks, some – like the first or that of 1361 – widespread, others local but just as lethal. It lasted in Britain till the eighteenth century. It has been estimated that by 1350 it had killed a fifth of the population and that by the end of the fourteenth century the population of England was little more than half that of the year of Crécy.

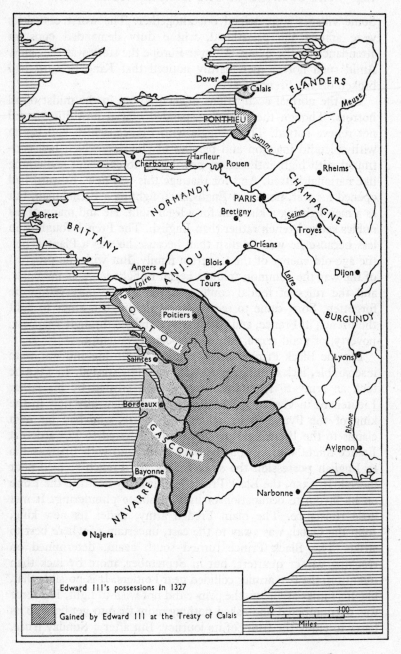

Dover
Calais
FLANDERS
PONTHIEU
Meuse
Somme
Cherbourg
Harfleur
Rouen
Rhelms
NORMANDY
PARIS
CHAMPAGNE
Bretigny
Seine
Brest
Troyes
BRITTANY
ANJOU
Orléans
Dijon
Angers
Blois
Loire
Tours
Loire
BURGUNDY
POITOU
Poitiers
Saintes
Lyons
Rhone
Bordeaux
GASCONY
Avignon
Bayonne
NAVARRE
Narbonne
Najera

Edward III's possessions in 1327

Gained by Edward III at the Treaty of Calais

0   100
Miles

FRANCE AT THE TREATY OF CALAIS, 1360

Some villages were wiped out altogether. The worst casualties were among the priesthood, whose duty demanded constant attendance on the dying. All over Europe the story was the same. Amid such horror men hardly noticed that King Edward had broken off his French war.

But the normal occupations of men go on, in the midst of all horrors. Though the plague suspended official hostilities it did not relieve hatred. The struggle with France, which had begun with splendid inaction and parades of chivalry, which had continued with high enthusiasm, now began to engender something like national hatred. And for that age this was new. Edward had opened his war, not as an Englishman fighting a Frenchman, but as a man fighting a kinsman for a legal right. He and many of his nobles spoke French rather than English. The French fought him less because he was English than because he was a Plantagenet, the age-old enemy of the Capetian family. But with the progress of the war the common soldiers began to fight more as nationals, and the rules of feudal conflict, never strictly observed, were forgotten. So it came to seem natural for English kings to fight the French in France, and whose who refrained through weakness, poverty, or good sense, earned abuse and contempt.

For the Black Prince, at any rate, to whom life and war were inseparable, lack of military activity was time wasted. In 1355 he took an army to Aquitaine, having been created by his father Lieutenant in Gascony. The English had a new ally now in the king of the Pyrenean Kingdom of Navarre, who had his own claims to the French throne and had suggested to Edward that France might well be split between them; and with Brittany too in English possession the situation for the French seemed poor indeed. In 1356, the Black Prince led his army north to the Loire on its favourite occupation of indiscriminate plundering. It met little resistance. The main French army, under its new king, John the Good, was away to the east, uncertain of where best to strike. The Black Prince turned south again, determined on reaching winter quarters, but in September, more by luck than intention, the two armies collided near Poitiers. It is possible that, like his father at Crécy, the prince did not wish to fight. His force was outnumbered and asked nothing more than to get back to its bases to enjoy the fruits of its journey. But after a Sunday truce, engineered by the emissaries of the pope, the French advanced to attack. In ten years they had learned few of the lessons of Crécy. Once more their cavalry were mown down as they were sent in by their chivalrous but foolish king. And they fared little better when they dismounted, for to the showers of the arrows they had no reply. Their own archers were far in the rear. When the day ended they were in full flight and their king was dining with the English prince, a prisoner.

It was a greater triumph than Crécy, but again the French blunders as much as the English skill had won it. And it brought Edward III little nearer his goal of the French crown. He treated John not as a usurper but as a rightful king, and he demanded for him a king's ransom. He simply did not have the resources to turn Poitiers into a conquest, even though the French, with the king of Navarre still to resist and peasants' risings setting the country aflame, had little with which to fight. The peace signed at Calais in 1360 was proof of English victory, since the Duchy of Aquitaine was enlarged and released from France's overlordship, Calais and some neighbouring land in the north were retained by the English, and King John's ransom was fixed at half a million pounds. But Edward renounced his claim to the French throne and faced, as so often, an empty treasury. With his son, he had won glory and astonished the world. But for all the money spent on arms and wavering allies he had little that was tangible to show and had ensured that for many decades the French war would be a burden to his people. For the French would hardly sit down and watch the enemy they now hated in arrogant possession of rich Aquitaine.

CHAPTER 17

Years of Decline
1360-1399

CRÉCY, Poitiers, and the Treaty of Calais – these were the steps
in the ladder which had made Edward III by 1360 the most
famous soldier and king in Europe. He was not a wise king or a
constructive statesman, and he is remembered for little but his
deeds in the warfare which was his first love. But his reign followed
years of weakness and disgrace, and his aggressive foreign policy
had fitted in with the mood of his greater subjects, so that the
barons ceased from the squabbles and rivalry which Edward II
had both endured and encouraged, and joined him loyally in
search of fame and profit. So in the middle years of his reign he
was one of the most popular of all England's kings. But in 1360
he was forty-eight years old, and every year saw his vigour and
activity decline. In 1361, a year when the Black Death once more
swept across Britain, his subjects noticed that he seemed to have
lost much of his interest in politics, coming to the Council more
seldom and listening abstractedly to political discussion. In 1364,
the year in which King John died in voluntary captivity after a
default in his ransom, Edward took as his mistress the grasping
Alice Perrers who preyed on his wealth and corrupted his will till
the end of his life. And while France began to recover under its
new and able king, Charles V, the government of England lost
direction and fell into the hands of a group of clerical ministers,
who had to keep their positions by their wits, who soon became
unpopular among the barons, and whose efficiency was most
obvious in the skill with which they gathered the taxes. Their
leader was William of Wykeham, who became Bishop of Winchester in 1367 and used much of his vast wealth to found a great
school at Winchester and the splendid New College at Oxford.

166

Had the heir to the throne been in England in these years, decline might have been arrested, but in 1362 the Black Prince had been invested with full powers as Duke of Aquitaine and there he kept a sumptuous and warlike court for which the Gascons had to pay. In the past they had welcomed English rule for the simple reason that it was lighter than French, but now they became restless as they paid for more and more English officials and for colourful military enterprises which brought them little profit. Though by the terms of the Treaty of Calais, Aquitaine was no longer ultimately subject to France, its inhabitants began to appeal with increasing frequency for the French to come and shake off their new tyrant. The Black Prince's campaign beyond the Pyrenees against a pro-French pretender to the throne of Castile, which culminated in the great victory of Najera in 1367, only increased their burdens and gave to the prince the slow, lingering fever which was soon to make him as inactive as his father. In 1371, too sick to leave his bed, he returned to England, leaving his Duchy open to the sudden thrusts of Charles V's pompous but intelligent captain, Bertrand du Guesclin. Within a year the Duchy was nearly back to its size before the war had begun, and the English control of Brittany – so vital a link in the communications with the south – had been lost by 1373.

With all the strength of 1360 now only a memory, the English barons had turned on the king's clerical council. Wykeham had been removed in 1371 with many of his fellow Bishops, while Edward III seldom left his hunting lodges and the protection of his wily mistress. The Black Prince was in no condition to fill the gap in national leadership. Attended by his devoted wife, he languished in his palace at Kennington and watched the strings of power pass to the hands of the eldest of his surviving brothers, John of Gaunt.

John, Duke of Lancaster, had been born at Ghent (or Gaunt) in 1340, the year of Sluys. He was Edward's second son, and from his birthplace was always known as John of Gaunt. In 1359, by the king's desire, he had married Blanche, heiress of the powerful and immensely wealthy Lancaster Duchy which Edward, remembering the trouble it had caused in his father's time, clearly wanted to bring back under royal control. His marriage made John of Gaunt the next most powerful man in England to the king and

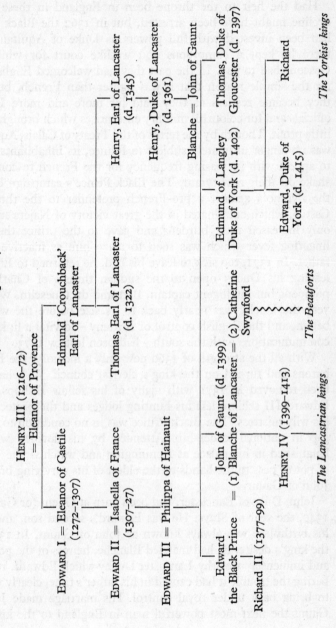

TABLE III. *The Later Plantagenets*
(much simplified)

the Black Prince, and the passing of both from active politics brought him suddenly in his early thirties to the head of affairs. In Shakespeare's *Richard II* he is made the symbol of noble patriotism as in his dying speech he speaks the lines:

> This royal throne of kings, this scepter'd isle,
> This earth of majesty, this seat of Mars,
> This other Eden, demi-Paradise,
> This fortress built by Nature for herself.
> Against infection and the hand of war. . . .

The real John of Gaunt never lived up to such august ideals. His second marriage to the Spanish princess, Constance of Castile, was to send him off on a purely selfish venture for the Castilian throne. He was a poor soldier. To preserve his power in England he built up a faction which ranged from Oxford heretics to London drapers. His Palace of the Savoy in the Strand was more sumptuous than the royal palaces. When rioting peasants burned it in 1381 they were expressing the fierce hatred in which he was often held. And yet, like Cardinal Richelieu in seventeenth-century France, almost all his love of power he used to preserve the prestige and rights of the throne, soon once more to be in peril. Even his Castilian ambitions could have harmed them little. On the English throne itself he had no designs. To it, as to his own friends, he was completely loyal.

After the removal of Wykeham, Gaunt dominated the Council, in the years when every month brought news of fresh reverses in France. Bertrand du Guesclin avoided the pitched battles which before had been so fatal, but he gave the English garrisons little respite. In 1375, a truce was arranged by Gaunt which brought military relief but little pleasure to the barons, who could make profit from war even when they were losing. In the following year an exasperated Parliament turned on all the royal officials, and particularly Gaunt, refusing further money till concessions were given. Gaunt had to give way, allowing this 'Good Parliament' as it was called, to imprison the king's ministers and to set up a committee to watch over the accounts. But an effort by the reformers to use the Black Prince as their patron was frustrated by his death that same year. The great prince's life, like Edward III's, had been devoted to war. He had been magnificent, generous, and cruel by turns. His tomb at Canterbury can fittingly be compared with Edward II's at Gloucester. That at Canterbury is simple, severe, hung with the grim tokens of war: the other is intricately ornamented, its figure soft, almost feminine in its beauty. Both are part of the complex pattern of the Plantagenet story.

Within a year, the Black Prince's death had been followed by that of his father, who since suffering a stroke had been slowly weakening in his palace at Sheen. Alice Perrers was faithful to his wealth if not to him. As he breathed his last, so she seized his jewels and fled with them. It was a sordid end to the conqueror of half of France, and it left the throne to the Black Prince's son, Richard II, who had been born at Bordeaux ten and a half years before. So once again the throne of England was occupied by a child. There must have been many abroad who thought that in the quarrels of warring faction Richard would be thrust rudely aside, his place taken by one of his many uncles, sons of Edward III. And indeed it might have been so had it not been for Gaunt, who from the very start of the new reign began a careful and deliberate campaign to build up what today would be called the 'image' of the king. At the time Gaunt was in the middle of a quarrel with the citizens of London and for years he and William of Wykeham had been sparring for power. But instead of taking advantage of his position as the new king's guardian he arranged two ceremonies at which it seemed that Richard was publicly ending both quarrels, and he followed them with the most splendid coronation London had ever seen, complete with a revised service which emphasized more strongly than ever the power which made kings a different order of humanity, chosen not by their people but by God through hereditary succession. Of this day a chronicler joyfully wrote: 'it was the long awaited day when peace and the laws of the land returned, exiled for long by the weakness of an old king and the greed of his servants'.

Richard was to grow up intelligent, sensitive, highly emotional, quite unstable, a man of fierce hatreds and deep loves. His childhood memories of this greatness and magnificence played their part in his eventual downfall, but four years after his coronation they served to aid both him and his class in the greatest social crisis of the Middle Ages, the moment when England came nearer than

at any time to the horrors of a violent revolution. This was the
Peasants' Revolt of 1381.

Some of the grievances which had built up among the working
classes of England will be described in the next chapter; but what
precipitated the rising itself was probably the 'poll tax' which was
imposed in 1381 in another effort to pay for the seemingly eternal
French war. This tax was to be borne by every person in the
kingdom, at one shilling a head, regardless of rank or wealth. It
was accompanied by the empty advice from the government that
in paying it the rich could help the poor. For the poorest peasants
a shilling was a large sum, but it was actually in the more prosperous parts of England, in Kent and East Anglia, that revolt was
fiercest, among peasants who were chafing less at grinding poverty
than at the legal bonds of villeinage. It began in Essex, where a
particularly greedy tax-collector was touring the countryside. It
soon spread to Kent, where a large company of peasants collected
and began to march on London, murdering and burning as they
went. In mid-June the men of Essex and the men of Kent, at
Mile End and on Blackheath, were threatening the city, while the
young king and his council took refuge behind the walls of the
Tower.

At this stage, Richard began to show that remarkable courage
which was to be the chief cause of the rising's failure. He set out
with his council to go down the Thames to Greenwich, and would
have landed but for the restraint of his advisers. Meanwhile, the
rebels crossed London Bridge and rushed into the city, opening
prisons, burning Gaunt's great palace at the Savoy, terrorizing all
who opposed them. From the Tower, Richard offered to meet
them and parley at Mile End. With only a handful of supporters
he rode out to the multitude, heard their demands – for the
handing over of 'traitors', the abolition of villeinage, and free
bargaining for wages. He agreed to consider them all and, having
quietened them a little, returned to the Tower. But still they would
not disperse and at Smithfield he met another group, angrier than
the first, led by the Kentish soldier, Wat Tyler, whose manner
was rough and insolent. There was a brawl. Tyler threatened the
king. He was struck down by the Lord Mayor. The mob seemed
about to tear the royal party to pieces. But with extraordinary
bravery in a fourteen-year-old boy Richard rode out to confront

them. 'Sirs,' he shouted, 'will you shoot your king? I am your captain. Follow me.' Saying it, he turned his horse towards the north, followed wonderingly by the mob. Soon after, they agreed to return to their homes, joyful in possession of a royal pardon but all the fight gone out of them.

The crisis had passed. But all over the south-eastern half of England for some days revolt went on. At St. Albans and Bury St. Edmunds the townsfolk rose against the monasteries. At Cambridge, the town paid off old scores against the university, sacking Corpus Christi College and the university church. But these outbreaks were soon suppressed and before the end of June the country was relatively quiet. The government had had a shock and Richard further proof of his own greatness. In the end the rebels got almost nothing of what they had demanded; but the reprisals of the government, possibly on the king's recommendation, were surprisingly mild.

For five years more, John of Gaunt remained in England as the king's chief counsellor, but early in 1386 he decided to go on his long-desired expedition to Spain and Portugal to collect the Crown which through his Castilian marriage he thought he deserved. Richard by now was of age and tiring of his uncle's tutelage but he soon showed how great was the loss of Gaunt's political experience.

One of the recurrent problems of the Middle Ages in England was: who was to advise the king and how much power was he to have? For a king who was successful in war the problem seldom arose, but for unsoldierly or inactive kings it was ever present. Most kings preferred the advice of their own friends or their own officials, men on whom they could rely, whose greatness depended directly and solely on the Crown. But such government left out the baronage, who felt that their lands and position gave them a right to advise. It left out, too, the members of Parliament, who by the fourteenth century held many strings of the royal purse and whom kings affronted at their peril. For having the wrong friends and taking the wrong advice, Henry III and Edward II had suffered. Now it was to be Richard's turn.

Already, before Gaunt departed, he had been turning for counsel to a few close friends – to Robert de Vere, to Simon Burley, his old tutor, to Robert Tresilian, a faithful lawer. Now a group of

barons, led by the king's uncle, Thomas of Woodstock, and the
Earl of Arundel, decided to end a situation which kept them from
power. They made Richard call a Parliament, and in 1387, before
an assembly mostly made up of their supporters, they accused the
king's friends of treason and incompetence. The following year, in
the well-named 'Merciless Parliament', they succeeded in having
Burley, Tresilian and many others of noble birth beheaded or
hanged. But, as so often, they had gone too far, and Richard,
though he had to move warily, was able to collect enough moderate
support to dismiss Thomas of Woodstock (now Earl of Gloucester) and Arundel from his Council in 1389, the year Gaunt returned
from his useless venture in Spain.

For Richard it had been a sharp lesson. But it was a lesson from
which he learned to look for strength, not wisdom. His uncle,
John of Gaunt, had carefully nursed him to be a great and splendid
king. The Peasants' Revolt had seemed to show him 'the divinity
that doth hedge a king'. The 'Merciless Parliament' had shown
him the fury of the jealous magnates. He decided that for a time
he must woo them, showing favour but only from on high. The
true way to popularity he spurned, for a renewal of all-out war
with France could bring only higher taxes and thus more aggressive Parliaments. His confidence in himself did not give him any
desire to emulate his father and grandfather in stern and ultimately futile conquest. So the barons, who saw the chance of
profit in France removed, took his favours grudgingly and bided
their time.

Among the great lords who at this time gave Richard this grudging support was the son of John of Gaunt, Henry Bolingbroke, a
tough, ambitious, warlike but conventional man. Also turning for a
time to Richard was Thomas Mowbray, soon to be Duke of
Norfolk. With the help of these two, Richard slowly built up his
strength and began perhaps to have those visions which were to
lead to his violent death, visions of an absolute monarchy, making
and breaking laws at will, untrammelled by Parliament, family, or
nobility. To this end he began to recruit support among the
knights and gentry and to collect from the loyal county of Cheshire
a personal bodyguard of archers wearing his own badge of the
White Hart, who would stand between him and all his enemies.

In 1394 a rebellion broke out in Ireland, since the days of

Henry II a turbulent English protectorate, and Richard crossed the sea to quell it. Two and a half centuries later King Charles I was to be accused of planning to employ an Irish army to hold down England. Men now seemed to fear the same of Richard as, instead of using resources in military repression, he made treaties with the rebel Irish chiefs and returned with all the air of having made a diplomatic triumph. In 1396 he concluded a truce with France, designed to last twenty-eight years, and sealed it with a marriage – his second – to the French princess, Isabel. Conscious now of sufficient strength, he struck in the next year at his old enemies – his uncle Gloucester and the Earl of Arundel, the leaders of the Merciless Parliament. Gloucester was banished to Calais where he soon died mysteriously but probably violently. Arundel was executed. In the same year Richard let it be known that he was seeking support among the German princes as a candidate for the throne of the Holy Roman Empire. To his illusions of grandeur there seemed no end.

But the last shreds of noble support in England now began to vanish. Bolingbroke and Norfolk quarrelled, were ordered to settle their difference in battle at Coventry, and then as they appeared in the lists in the autumn of 1398 were suddenly banished. Titles and favours were heaped on Richard's more faithful henchmen. The title of 'Duke', reserved till now for the royal family, was bestowed on the three great nobles who still supported him. But the land itself now had to endure a tyranny such as it had never known, while Richard began to show signs of madness. There were forced loans, imprisonments without trial, interference in elections. Had Richard been able to perpetuate his rule for the normal term of his life, the whole course of English history would have been different.

Chance, however, and his own folly intervened. Early in 1399, John of Gaunt died. He had been selfish, greedy, and vain, but Shakespeare was probably not far wrong when at the end of the dying speech already quoted, after the great hymn of praise to England, he made Gaunt say:

> This land of such dear souls, this dear dear land,
> Dear for her reputation through the world
> Is now leased out – I die pronouncing it –
> Like to a tenement, or pelting farm.

Richard spent no time mourning his dead uncle and one-time guardian. He seized his lands, setting aside the claim of the banished Henry Bolingbroke, and then set out on a further expedition to deal with the Irish chiefs, once more risen against their masters.

Bolingbroke meanwhile was in France. Setting out with a small force he landed at Ravenspur in Yorkshire in July, claiming he had come for nothing but his Lancaster inheritance. He was soon joined by the great northern families, the Percies and Nevilles who were naturally his rivals rather than his friends, and marched south against Richard's supporters, now rapidly deserting. Richard returned determined to crush what he felt must be a trivial invasion, to find that he had few friends and no army. Dejected and defeated, he gave himself up and was taken to the Tower of London, once his stronghold, now his prison. On the last day of September, 1399, he was, following the precedent of 1327, declared deposed. John of Gaunt had sought a crown overseas and never found it. Now his son, amid the acclamations of a relieved populace, was anointed as King Henry IV.

CHAPTER 18

The England of Chaucer and Wyclif

IN THE year following the fall of Richard II, when Henry IV was beginning to discover that it was easier to win a crown than keep it, Geoffrey Chaucer died in London, famous as a poet, trusted as a royal servant. He left unfinished his manuscript of *The Canterbury Tales*, a collection of stories told by a group of pilgrims as they journeyed to the shrine of St. Thomas Becket in Canterbury. The pilgrims form a magnificent cross-section of English society at the end of the fourteenth century. Only the very highest and the very lowest of the classes of men are without a representative in Chaucer's band, and in order to build up a picture of the England of that day one can do little better than begin with them as Chaucer described them, in his Prologue, assembling in the Tabard Inn in Southwark before their journey.

Chaucer wrote his poem in the midland dialect of English, and that itself is significant. The English language had been written down, it is true, in every century from the Norman Conquest to Chaucer's day, but by the educated and governing classes it had been spurned. They almost all spoke French, and it was in French or Latin that they preferred to read. No man without Latin was educated, no man without French would go far in public service. Yet all the time the English language developed. From despising it the governing classes had gradually come to learn it, to speak it, and to modify it. In 1362 Edward III, who himself preferred French speech, addressed his Parliament in English for the first time and ordered English to be used in the law courts. And the long war with France undoubtedly hastened the death of the old Anglo-Norman French which had once in the court of Normans and Plantagenets reigned supreme. Chaucer's English is very different from Anglo-Saxon. It contains many French words and phrases. But it has become a language rich in vocabulary, expressive, flexible, a language fit to be the vehicle of a great literature.

Among Chaucer's company is a Franklin, or freeman – a man, that is, who has loosed the bonds of villeinage as more and more Englishmen were doing in this century of change. He is prosperous, a figure in society:

> Without bake mete was nevere his house
> Of fish and flesh, and that so plenteous
> It snowed in his house of mete and drynke.[1]

Often he was called to represent his shire in Parliament, for a government short of money would naturally want to treat with those who had it. He would employ many labourers of his own and some of his land would be let out on an annual rent. He might well have bought his estate in the first place from some great landowner who was finding the farming of huge demesnes no longer profitable.

But though through the fourteenth century the unfree villeins were more and more loosing their bonds, they still made up the majority of the population. There were great differences in their wealth. Some were almost as prosperous as the Franklin but some still scratched out a wretched existence at the mercy of the vagaries of the weather and the whims of their lords. These would have suffered from the greed and ruthlessness of Chaucer's Reeve or manorial official. 'They were in dread of hym as of the death.' The shortage of labour that followed the Black Death put the villeins in a position where they could sell the work of their hands to the highest bidder, and wages rose in spite of Parliament's efforts in the Statute of Labourers in 1351 to check them by law. Such a situation led many lords to demand in full the unpaid services of their villeins which had perhaps for half a century not been given. No wonder the reeve, who had to enforce these demands, was so hated. In the Peasants' Revolt in 1381 the abolition of villeinage was a major demand. Many manorial officers were murdered and their records burned. But the law of supply and demand cannot be stopped by Parliament, and neither the Statute nor the Revolt did much to prevent the villeins of England slowly turning themselves

[1] Chaucer's spelling has been modified only where the original would be hard to understand.

into free hired labourers, often just as poor but now protected by courts which gave the free man a right to be heard.

Chaucer's Merchant was as prosperous as his Franklin.

> A marchant was ther, with a forked berd
> In motley, and high on horse he sat
> Upon his head a Flanderish bevere hat,
> His bootes clasped faire and fetisly. [neatly]

He was a solemn man, full of the greatness of his calling, his mind and his conversation seldom off his profits, but honest and worthy. He lived in a century which had seen many changes in his class. The export trade in raw wool which for centuries had been England's livelihood and whose importance was symbolized in the 'woolsack' on which the Chancellor sat in Parliament, was at last beginning to decline with the rise of the trade in cloth. At the beginning of the century England was still importing cloth, much of it made in Flanders from England's own wool, but by Chaucer's day only a few special luxury cloths were coming in. The rest was home made, and enough was made to send to all parts of the known world, more often than not in English ships.

For this change there were many reasons. Even before the 100 Years' War conditions in Flanders were sufficiently troubled to make it an uncertain market for raw wool. French influence there was strong, and the French discouraged English wool. When war began, the situation was made worse by Edward III's notion that wool could be used to the profit of the crown. He put a heavy duty on it. He impounded it so that he could sell it abroad himself. He instituted 'staple' towns, at home or abroad, through which all wool must pass. Only 'Merchants of the Staple' had the right to trade through the staple towns and they did their best to keep out interlopers. The result was that more wool stayed at home to be turned into cloth, and on the cloth trade the government as yet had laid no hands. But the rising cloth industry was differently distributed now. The invention of the fulling mill in the thirteenth century had taken the industry to the countryside, where fast-running water necessary to work the mill was to be found, to the Cotswolds or the Pennines. Many old cloth towns, like Lincoln, Leicester, or Stamford began to decline, though some were able to switch to some more thriving business.

Chaucer's Merchant may well have come from London. Changes in trade had only served to increase the power and splendour of the capital, though it was still small beside some continental cities, with a population of less than 70,000. It was a cosmopolitan city. The German merchants of the Hanse, unpopular rivals of the native traders, still had their great fortified steelyard. There were Flemish weavers, Italian bankers and goldsmiths. But the English were more and more ousting the foreigner from his preserves. When Italian banks broke, as they did when Edward III defaulted on his debt payments, the English took their places. No king or great lord could afford to ignore the City. Gaunt needed his faction there. Edward II's power waned as the Londoners deserted him. So did Richard II's. And if they were not struggling with their kings, the Londoners were squabbling with themselves – victuallers against drapers, masters against artisans. The Londoners opened the gates to the Kentish rebels in 1381, sacked Gaunt's palace, opened the prisons, beheaded an archbishop, broke into the Tower. It was a proud, fierce, and turbulent city, slowly reaching for the domination of all southern England, its wharves stacked with the incoming riches of Europe and the East.

London boasted already three grammar schools, at St. Pauls, St. Mary of the Arches, St. Martin's le Grand. But pre-eminent in English education was still the city and university of Oxford. Among Chaucer's company was a 'clerk', an Oxford student:

> A clerk ther was of Oxenford also
> That unto logyk hadde longe ygo.
> As leene was his hors as is a rake,
> And he was not right fat, I undertake,
> But looked hollow and thereto soberly.

He was lean and poor, like many of his fellow students, because he had as yet no ecclesiastical living, or benefice. Learning could bring advancement, but success had to be fought for, by cunning or by acquiring a rich patron. Though the Colleges which are the peculiar institution of Oxford and Cambridge were being founded apace in the fourteenth century through the generosity of the rich and the noble, the majority of students still lived in wretched lodgings, short of books, gaining most of their knowledge from lectures and their quickness of thought from the long and exacting debates, called 'disputations', success in which was necessary for the coveted degree of Master of Arts.

From Oxford and Cambridge many students went to London, to the 'Inns' of Court to study the law, outside the Church the most respected and profitable of professions. Chaucer's Man of Lawe had an excellent practice:

> Of fees and robes hadde he many a one

And he was already adept at making the law difficult for ordinary folk to understand.

Oxford, Cambridge, and the Inns of Court were the summit of fourteenth-century education. Most literate men climbed no further than the Song School described in the Prioress's Tale, where little was taught but

> to syngen and to rede
> As smale children doon in their childhede

And most of England's population could not achieve even that.

The Prioress is only one of many types of clergy and members of religious orders in Chaucer's band. Only a bishop is missing. There are a monk, a friar, a prioress, a nun, a pardoner, a summoner, a parson of a town parish. And only the last escapes Chaucer's criticism. Like many men of his age, Chaucer, himself a man of faith, found the general state of the Church corrupt, its officers careless of their trust and avaricious. The Pardoner hawks false relics about with the power of pardoning sins. He had Our Lady's veil, and part of the sail of St. Peter's fishing boat. 'He made,' says Chaucer tersely, 'the parson and the people his apes.' The Summoner, who liked garlic, onions, leeks, and plenty of red wine, had the job of summoning men to the Bishop's court to answer for their sins, and he made a good business out of it. The Friar was loved for being an easy man to confess to. The Monk was a great hunter. He owned greyhounds and would forget all his rule for a dish of roast swan.

Chaucer's purpose is entertainment; human folly and evil are generally more amusing than virtue, and of the former there was plenty to be found in the fourteenth-century Church. But there is, among the hypocrites and religious pedlars, the Parson of the

Town, whose portrait is filled in with loving care, a man who lived, as many did, in the image of the apostles:

> But Cristes Lore, and His apostles twelve
> He taught, but first He folwed it Hym-selve

It would therefore be wrong to judge the Church by its more entertaining hypocrites, but there were many men of the day, with objects more serious than Chaucer's, who were led from criticism of its faults to open rebellion.

In the thirteenth century, in the days of Innocent III who had placed the Interdict on England and brought John to heel, the prestige of the Papacy was enormous. But in the early fourteenth century the popes, weary of the unrest of Italy, had gone to live in Avignon in the south of France and came under the influence of the French king. To cover increasing expenses they continually demanded, from kings and clergy, heavier and more frequent taxes. Throughout the first half of the 100 Years War, they constantly intervened to restore peace, but in England their efforts were always interpreted as pro-French manoeuvres. They were claiming, too, a power over the offices of the Church which gave them the right to appoint or 'provide' men for many livings, from parish priests to bishops. In general they used this power discreetly, and it is probable that they often provided better men than would have the lay patrons. Nevertheless the practice of 'Provisions' was resented wherever it was used, and in England it was condemned by Parliamentary statute as being interference in what was ultimately the right of the king. Then, in 1378, the situation suddenly worsened. In 1370 the pope, Gregory XI, decided to move from Avignon back to the Papacy's ancient home, and when he died in 1378 the cardinals elected an Italian, Urban VI. Enraged, the French faction among the cardinals returned to France and elected a pope of their own. So now, there were two popes, one in Rome and one in Avignon, each declaring the other's election invalid. This was the beginning of the Great Schism, which was to last for thirty years. It not only destroyed much of the papacy's prestige but it also made worse the squabbles of European kings, who supported one pope because their enemies supported the other.

The Schism also increased the financial burdens of the clergy since each pope demanded a full income.

Many English clergy were well able to pay. For many were rich, holding many livings and collecting their incomes without discharging their responsibilities. Such clergy were dubbed contemptuously 'possessioners' and many were objects of the peasants' fury in 1381 – abbots, bishops, or university fellows. The Black Death caused more deaths among the clergy than among any other class, since the clergy's place was beside the sick and dying, in the very midst of infection. There were thus more empty livings to be possessed. Some were taken into the grasp of the possessioners; others were often filled by inferior men of little learning.

The 'possessioners' were not always parasites, living uselessly on the flesh of the land. Many were highly placed in the government, for government needed the educated; and though educated laymen – like Chaucer himself – were increasing in number, the prizes still went largely to the clerics. Many, too, used their riches for the benefit of both contemporaries and posterity. William of Wykeham's foundations at Oxford and Winchester set new standards in education. The rich glories of fourteenth-century architecture – at Exeter Cathedral, York Minster, or Canterbury – would have been impossible without the revenues of livings improperly filled. But criticism was growing. The state of the Papacy, the idleness of monks, the riches of a minority, the misuse of the confessional, the traffic in relics – all were targets for the critics, whose abuse was made stronger by nationalism encouraged by the war and by the growth of the English language. Chief among these critics was John Wyclif, an Oxford graduate who was born in 1320, twenty years before Chaucer, and who died three years after the Peasants' Revolt.

Of Wyclif's life we know few details. He was born, it seems, near Richmond in Yorkshire. He was an undergraduate at Balliol College Oxford, and spent most of his life at the University, in one college or another. He was ambitious, and was lucky in gaining the patronage of John of Gaunt, who found him useful in his own feud against the clerical ministers of Edward III – lucky not only because John of Gaunt was the most powerful man in the kingdom but because he was, in spite of his faults, loyal to his friends. And Wyclif needed such protection, for in a series of long and now rather tedious Latin works he attacked almost all the faults of the Church of his day. In 1376 he attacked the misuse of property by the clergy and stated that no-one had a right to wield power who did not live a good life. He singled out especially the 'Caesarean clergy' – as he called them – who left the cure of souls to run the king's government. The Great Schism of 1378 made him sceptical of the pope's claims to be Christ's representative on earth. Five years later he wrote that he welcomed the Schism as Christ's way of showing the emptiness of Papal authority. Monks, friars, the selling of pardons, the general ignorance of Holy Scripture – all were condemned. The clergy were told they should bow to kings as Christ bowed to Pilate. The official doctrine of the Mass was called in question, and Holy Scripture was erected as the only safe guide a man had, in all this corruption and wickedness, to salvation. There is scarcely an idea of Wyclif's which is not echoed a century and a half later, at the Reformation. His is the first full-scale attack from within the Church on all that the Church had come to believe about itself. Not unjustly has he been called the 'Morning Star of the Reformation'.

He was never called upon to face martyrdom. He was tried in a special court held by the Bishop of London, but he was well protected by his patrons and though forbidden to preach he was allowed to retire from Oxford to a country living at Lutterworth. In his works there is little warmth or passion; and he seems at times, in his early days, to be stating the views most likely to bring him advancement and power among the Lancastrian party. His books were too long and turgid to be read widely outside Oxford. It is doubtful if he did much to further the long-needed reform of the Church. Because he had attacked the Papacy and the Mass as institutions and not in their particular abuses, all his writing was declared false and evil, and much healthy criticism was branded as evil heresy.

Two things he left, however, to posterity – a group of devoted followers and a translation of the Bible into English. The followers, who were nicknamed Lollards – or babblers – went about preaching the more extreme of his views and may possibly have added one more ingredient to the Peasants' Revolt. Their growth led directly to the passing, for the first time in England, of a Parliamentary statute for the burning of heretics in 1401. The Lollards were never utterly stamped out. The English Reformation, when it came, owed some of its force to their continued if underground existence.

Wyclif's Bible, of which he himself wrote little, was the first version in English since Anglo-Saxon times. The medieval Church did not encourage the indiscriminate reading of Scripture, preferring to declare its truths through the mouths of instructed clergy lest it should be wrongly interpreted. Wyclif's Bible was condemned along with his other works. But it survived, a monument not only of the strength of his rebellion but of the new power of the English language. However different in intention, *The Canterbury Tales* and the English Bible stand together as evidence that in this fourteenth century an individual nation was slowly coming to birth.

CHAPTER 19

The Lancastrian Triumph

1399-1420

IN SHAKESPEARE'S *Richard II*, there is a scene in a London street where the fallen king, who had just surrendered the crown to his enemy, Henry Bolingbroke, is accosted by the head of the Percy family, Henry Earl of Northumberland.

'My lord,' says Northumberland, 'the mind of Bolingbroke is chang'd;
You must to Pomfret, not unto the Tower.'

Richard stops in his tracks. Brushing aside the order he points at the triumphant, gloating Percy:

'Northumberland, thou ladder wherewithal
The mounting Bolingbroke ascends my throne,
The time shall not be many hours of age
More than it is, ere foul sin gathering head
Shall break into corruption. Thou shalt think
Though he divide the realm and give thee half,
It is too little, helping him to all;
And he shall think that thou, which knowst the way
To plant unrightful kings, wilt know again,
Being ne'er so little urg'd, another way
To pluck him headlong from the usurp'd throne.'

Just as the dying Gaunt had prophesied the end of Richard's 'rash fierce blaze of riot', so now Richard himself is a prophet, foretelling the fatal instability of the Lancastrian throne.

Henry Bolingbroke was able to overturn Richard's tyranny because it had deprived Richard of almost all his friends. But his own friends were to prove no more constant. He had landed in

Yorkshire and had soon been joined by the leaders of the two great families which, with that of Lancaster itself, ruled the north – the Percies and the Nevilles, earls of Northumberland and Westmorland. Up in the northern marches, thinly populated, in constant terror of Scottish border raids, the king's power had always been fitful. Like the marcher lords of Wales, the Percies and Nevilles, forced to be continuously armed against England's enemies, ruled almost as petty kings. They were not to forget that they had put Bolingbroke where he was. It was a Neville who, later in the fifteenth century, was to get the title 'Kingmaker'. To either of the families it might well have been given earlier.

Henry IV's coronation was splendid and joyful – as Richard's had been – but whereas the deposition of Edward II had led to the crowning of the Prince of Wales and heir apparent, the fall of Richard had made way for a usurper. A better legal claimant was Edmund Mortimer who, through his mother, was descended from Lionel, Duke of Clarence, an elder son of Edward III than was John of Gaunt. In fact it was clear to everyone that Henry IV ruled through conquest, a conquest made possible by noble support, and no-one took seriously the story he put about that Edmund Crouchback, Earl of Lancaster, Henry's ancestor on his mother's side, had in fact been an elder son of Henry III than King Edward I. Such a claim would have invalidated all the English kings of the fourteenth century! Henry himself could scarcely have believed it. He made it because he was nervous.

And he had every reason for nervousness. In so far as his usurpation had any principle but revenge behind it, it was an attack on tyranny, on government by a king who was claiming unlimited power and governing through a clique of willing henchmen. The new king had to prove that his government would reject such abuses. He had to show his aristocratic supporters that they were what they had always claimed to be – his 'natural' counsellors. Richard had also raised unparliamentary taxes. So Henry had to be virtuous in this – and thus was perpetually short of money. Richard had believed in peace with France, for which the nobles had accused him of weakness. So Henry had to be warlike – and for this he had no money. And over his head all the time was the threat that what had happened to Richard could happen also to him.

Richard did not live long after his deposition. Plots to restore

him made it too dangerous to keep him alive; he was murdered in
Pontefract (or Pomfret) Castle, where, long before, Henry's
ancestor, Thomas of Lancaster, had been beheaded by Edward II.
It was given out, of course, that Richard had 'died in prison', and
his body was exhibited to prove it, but rumours began to circulate
that he was still alive and they were fostered by the Scots and the
French. In 1402 a Scottish army carried out one of its customary
invasions of northern England and was defeated at Homildon Hill
by the Percies, who preferred to the tale that Richard still lived the
useful truth that Henry had murdered him and that the murder
had been a crime. Henry had borrowed money from them and did
not look like repaying it, so they made common cause with a fiery
Welshman, Owen Glendower, and raised a rebellion, whose object
was the enthroning of Edmund Mortimer, Earl of March. So the
crown of the great Edward III seemed to be the plaything of the
nobility and the clouds of the Wars of the Roses were mounting on
the far horizon.

The Percies were defeated. Henry caught them at Shrewsbury
in 1403, Glendower having failed to meet them and the Earl of
Northumberland himself being conveniently sick at Bamburgh.
But the great Hotspur, Northumberland's son, 'the flower and
glory of Christendom', fell on the field, and his uncle the Earl of
Worcester was taken and executed.

Three years later Glendower and Northumberland were plotting
again, their venture blessed by the Archbishop of York, Richard
Scrope – a kinsman of the Percies. This revolt too was defeated by
Henry, and Northumberland's pickled head soon decorated a
tower on London Bridge. Glendower held out in Wales for some
years longer and provided useful military experience for Henry's
son, the Prince of Wales, but with his retreat to the mountains the
real danger was over, and for the rest of his reign Henry's greatest
worry was his own bad health. He died in 1413, having seen the
power of active government pass more and more into the hands of
his son. His usurpation had brought him little but vexation and
war. He had hoped for victories in France. He had vowed to lead
Christendom in another Crusade to the Holy Land. But all he saw
of Jerusalem was the Jerusalem Chamber in the Abbey of
Westminster where he died. 'Only God knows', he said on his
death bed, 'by what right I took the crown.'

Shakespeare's great cycle of historical plays was written to demonstrate, among other things, the consequences of the murder of Richard. Having broken into the hereditary succession, the Lancastrian kings had no title but their own strong arm. Should the arm weaken, revenge for the murdered Richard would be the war cry on the glib tongues of the rebels. That full-scale civil war did not come sooner was due to the military genius of Henry IV's son, whose arm was strong enough both to put down actual rebels and to enrol potential rebels in the golden enterprise of France.

To later Englishmen, Henry V was the hero-king, the perfect knight claiming the rights of his ancestors, caring for his soldiers, chivalrous to his enemies, giving thanks to an approving God for his victories. His voice, in Shakespeare's play, was heard again in 1940 and 1944 putting fire into his countrymen through the mists of centuries. To the French he has seemed very different. A usually pro-English French historian recently wrote of 'his hypocritical devoutness, the duplicity of his conduct, his pretence of defending right and redressing wrongs when he sought solely to satisfy his ambition, the cruelty of his revenge'.[1] Somewhere between these two stands the real Henry; ambitious certainly; loving displays of piety – such as when he rode unsmiling to the Confessor's tomb in the triumph after Agincourt; cruel – as when he ordered the killing of the prisoners at Agincourt; willing to shed seas of blood for what he believed to be his by right, but probably sincerely believing that it was his and that God was with him. His piety was grim, but strict. He hated heresy, believing it his duty to stamp out the Lollards, but was compassionate enough to prefer converting them to burning them. He longed for the throne of France not merely for the power it would bring but because he might lead two great nations, as one, against the heathen. He lived for his ideals, but he cared little how many men died for them.

The France he attacked was weak, weary, split into warring factions. By the end of the fourteenth century little remained of the English possessions which Edward III had won. In the north there was Calais; in the south the coastal strip of Aquitaine. But success had not brought unity to France. When Henry V ascended the English throne after nearly thirty years of growling peace between the two countries, the French throne was occupied by a madman,

[1] Perroy: *The Hundred Years' War.*

Charles VI, and was alternately under the control of two princes of
the blood, the Duke of Burgundy and the Count of Armagnac,
each of whom hated the other more than he hated the English. It
was a perfect time for England to renew the war. She merely had
to choose whether Burgundy or Armagnac was the better ally.
Already, before Henry IV died, his son had been testing the
ground. Armagnac offered the restoration of the Duchy of
Aquitaine in full, but Henry preferred the Burgundian's prize,
which was no less than the Duchy of Normandy, once the English
kings' most cherished possession, lost in 1204.

It was Normandy Henry V decided to attack in 1415, having
convinced himself by reading some history that it had been
illegally seized over two hundred years before by Philip Augustus.
So he began to prepare a great expedition, and in its preparation
he showed both his own military genius and how complicated war
had now become compared with the days when a commander led
his knights into battle and let them fight as best they could. For
this expedition a mass of equipment was needed: siege towers,
scaling ladders, pontoons to make bridges, timber for ship
repairs, arrows, bowstaves, fodder for horses, food for the men –
and guns. The Agincourt campaign was the first in which guns
were extensively used for knocking down defensive walls. They
were cumbersome and treacherous to the user, but few city or
castle walls could withstand their pounding.

To all the details of this force the king gave his personal attention. Nor did he forget that an efficient army needs to be well and
promptly paid. The days of the feudal host were gone for ever.
Henry's army was professional to the core, keeping only the
trappings of feudalism in its gaily coloured shields and banners.
And beside the fighting men there went to France the king's own
household, his chaplains, his chapel choir, his heralds, his trum-
peters, his pipers, and even one 'fiddler'. To transport them a great
fleet was collected, most of it hired. To pay for it all, huge loans
were raised, on the security of taxes still to be collected, or of the
crown jewels and relics of the royal chapels. The repayment of this
loan went on well into the next reign. By the time the English had
finished paying for Agincourt the Wars of the Roses had begun.

The expedition landed in the estuary of the Seine on 11th
August, 1415. It was late in the year to begin a campaign, and it is

possible that all Henry intended this year was to take and hold a base. The first target was the port of Harfleur, which was soon invested. But it was a month before it fell, and already dysentery, the curse of armies, had begun to take its toll of Henry's force of under 10,000 fighting men. Before the walls of Harfleur some 2,000 men perished, including a number of Henry's commanders; and when at last the town was his it was clearly too late for an extensive campaign. Henry decided to make for the English fortress of Calais and with his weary army he turned north east at the beginning of October, leaving a garrison he could ill spare in the conquered Harfleur.

Before him, as before Edward III in 1346, lay the River Somme, its bridges broken by the watching French. So Henry had to march seventy miles up stream before he found a crossing place. He then struck out direct for Calais, shadowed all the time by a much larger French army. For a week neither army was sure of the other's whereabouts, though the French had now decided that the English were weak enough to be brought to battle. At last, near the little village of Agincourt, thirty miles south of Calais, the English scouts came across their foe 'filling a wide area like an innumerable company of locusts'. Reluctantly, like his great grandfather at Crécy, Henry decided he must fight.

The victory of Agincourt, like that of Crécy, was won largely through French blunders. But not wholly so. Henry's skill did not show so much in the actual conduct of the battle as in the English morale at its beginning. His army was small, exhausted by three weeks of marching, of satisfying its hunger on unripe fruit and its thirst on strong wine. Its numbers were no more than 6,000. The French had twice that. And yet Henry decided not to retreat but to advance, and his army followed him to a man.

Seeing the small force approaching them the French waited with confidence. But when they sent out a squadron of cavalry to attack the English archers it was mown down before it got near them. The main body of French knights attacked on foot but were so crowded together that their long lances were useless. They fell before the arrows. They were entangled with their own retreating cavalry. They lay in heaps on the ground unable from the weight of protective armour to rise and defend themselves against the swarming English archers who butchered them with axes, mallets,

FRANCE AT THE TREATY OF TROYES, 1420

and knives. In the words of a hero-worshipping English chronicler:
'In this deadly conflict . . . that bright shining Titan of kings so
much exposed the precious treasure of his person to every chance
of war that he thundered upon his enemies swift terrors and
intolerable attacks.' At the end of the day 7,000 Frenchmen lay
dead. The English lost a mere 500.

The importance of Agincourt was less in its immediate results –
for Henry merely continued his march to Calais and returned to
England – than in its effects on Henry's prestige. Lancastrian rule
needed success, and here was a greater success than Crécy or
Poitiers. And the French turned to recrimination and strife more
violently than before. So that when Henry landed again in 1417
with a larger force and a bolder aim, he struck fear by his very
name. He won no more pitched battles, but by methodical sieges
he won Normandy and opened the road to Paris, helped by his
Burgundian allies. In 1420, at Troyes he signed a treaty with the
French and Burgundians which marks the summit of English
success in the war. France was divided. Aquitaine, Normandy and
most of France north of the Loire was to pass at once to Henry and
his ally. On the death of the mad French king, Henry was to be
king of France. He was to marry the French princess, Catharine,
and thus found a dynasty which would unite the two kingdoms for
ever. All for which Edward III had first opened the war in 1337
had been achieved.

Yet within thirty-five years, all the English possessed in the land
of France would be the single fortress of Calais.

CHAPTER 20

The End of the 100 Years' War

1420-1453

'[THERE] shall cease all manner of dissensions, hates, rancours, enmities and wars between the said realms of France and England!' So ran a sentence in the Treaty of Troyes of 1420. Those who wrote the words could hardly have believed them. After over eighty years of warfare the hatreds were too deep. Had Henry V lived for another twenty years, he might, by superb constructive statesmanship, have built out of the ruin and bloodshed a single monarchy. But it is doubtful. And in any case the dysentery which had killed so many of his soldiers cut him down at the age of thirty-four, two years after the treaty was signed. In the midst of continuing campaigns against the French king's son, the Dauphin, who had refused to submit to the treaty, he had time for a triumphant visit to England in 1421. He was carried ashore by the barons of the Cinque Ports. His queen was crowned in Westminster Abbey. He took her on a magnificent tour of the Holy Places of England. But the splendour concealed his poverty, for though his wars had been popular he was loaded with debts, and he returned to France for his last campaign with his treasury again filled with borrowed gold.

He died in August 1422 in the castle of Vincennes to the east of Paris. His end was typical. Hearing in the chanting the word 'Jerusalem' he stopped the singing 'and said aloud, that he had fully intended, after he had wholly subdued the realm of France to his obedience, and restored it to peace, to have gone to conquer the Kingdom of Jerusalem, if it had pleased his creator to have granted him a longer life. Having said this, he allowed the priests to proceed, and shortly after, according to the prediction of his physicians, gave up the ghost.' The Crusade had long lost its power to move armies but it kept its hold on imaginations.

But before his death Henry had much to say that was more practical. His heir, intended as king of both realms, was an infant; so the regency of France, Henry left to his eldest surviving brother, John, Duke of Bedford. And he gave him sound advice – to keep at all costs the Burgundian alliance, without which the English position in France would be precarious indeed. Bedford followed the instructions capably. He was a skilful and determined soldier, and he strengthened the Burgundian alliance by marrying the Duke of Burgundy's sister. Two years after Henry's death, he defeated the Dauphin in a pitched battle at Verneuil and seemed to be surmounting the perils of the minority. For the mad Charles VI had died in the same year as Henry V and by the terms of Troyes, Henry VI reigned over both realms. But there now occurred a reversal of fortune, more sudden even than that which had followed the victories of Edward III and the Black Prince, which was to end England's domination of France for ever.

Joan of Arc was born in the village of Domrémy on the border of Champagne and Lorraine, in 1412. Her father was a peasant farmer, a simple pious man who brought up his children strictly. In the summer that Verneuil was fought, as Joan was running races with her companions in the meadows by the River Meuse, she suddenly heard a voice. As she said later: 'I was in my thirteenth year when God sent a voice to guide me.' From that time she was a changed woman. Her voices were constantly with her, but now giving her the appalling command that she was to become a soldier and go to save France. 'Go forth, and all things shall be ordered by your counsel.' For four years she was dominated by this command, as real to her as the voices of her friends, and somehow, through her utter simplicity and honesty, she succeeded in convincing the local castellan that she must be heard by the Dauphin himself. God, she believed, wanted him crowned as legitimate king of France and the English usurper overthrown. In 1429 she was allowed to lead the French soldiers trying to raise the English siege of Orleans, and such was the effect of her presence, in manly armour shining like an angel, that the English were scattered. Within three months the Dauphin was crowned Charles VII in newly taken Rheims and Paris itself was threatened.

Joan's life as a soldier was pitifully brief, for the English captured her and burned her as a heretic in the square of Rouen.

But her intervention had decisively turned the tide. The French had found again the spirit that had so long evaded them and turned in fury on the despoilers of their land. The Duke of Burgundy, whose family connection with England was broken by the death of Bedford's wife in 1430, decided the time had come to become a cautious neutral. Bedford himself died exhausted in 1435. The English Parliament lost its last shreds of warlike enthusiasm and stopped voting money for the war. The Empire of Henry V was crumbling, as had that of Henry II two centuries before. The English at home were now as weak and divided as had been the French in the days of Agincourt. Rival factions squabbled in the council of the young Henry VI. The peasantry grumbled with rebellion. Disbanded soldiers, callous from the bloodshed of foreign war, returned ready to fight for anyone and anything. The Welsh marches and the Scottish borders flared into open strife again while the young, good-natured, gentle, religious king stood listlessly by.

As in England the stage was roughly cleared for the dynastic struggle called the Wars of the Roses, the last English positions in France fell to the revived and revengeful French. In 1449 Normandy was invaded. In 1450, at Formigny, an English army was wiped out, its 'invincible' bowmen routed. In 1453 England's last great captain, Talbot, was killed at Castillon in Gascony, leading a desperate charge against the French guns; and, in the same year, as if in divine judgment, Henry VI went mad. Now only Calais was left, to be for another hundred years a memorial of the English invasions of France, not only in its splendid walls but in the money required to man them. The 100 Years' War was over, but its legacy lived on. France had suffered terribly, materially and morally, her population reduced, her countryside scorched, her only path to new greatness through the efficient tyranny of her future kings. England had escaped the invader, except on her northern and western fringes, but the war's long and costly failure made the ruin of the Lancastrian dynasty. The Lancastrians climbed to power over the body of a despotic but legitimate king. They fell in the horrors of civil war, the nemesis both of Pontefract and of Agincourt.

The wars, foreign and domestic, of the fifteenth century have given it among historians an evil reputation. In both France and England, the Black Death still struck every few years, claiming more victims than the wars. Law and justice, so painfully established by the long line of kings that France had given to England, became the toys of an unscrupulous nobility. The trade of many English cities languished as pirates sailed freely in the Channel, and Flanders, now under Burgundian rule, was an uncertain market at the mercy of a fluctuating diplomacy. The monastic life profited nothing from the criticisms of Wyclif. Few men now became monks from sheer devotion. Of those who came, many wanted merely the ease and comfort of the Church's riches. Devotion was now often near to madness, as strange bands of men and women roamed Europe flogging one another to placate God's wrath. The tombs of the great were decorated with representations of wasting corpses. The Blessed Virgin was more frantically invoked to mediate between her Son, the terrible Judge, and sinful man.

But it was a century of strange contrasts. For amid all this despair it was also superbly creative. The first onset of the Black Death in 1348 had brought a pause in church-building in England, but it was only temporary, and for many the fifteenth is the golden century of English architecture, the century too in which there was achieved a truly national style. Up to the mid-fourteenth century English architecture had been still largely dependent on French models, modified though they might be by the individual genius of English craftsmen, and French models were leading more and more to increased decoration, so that by the end of the 100 Years' War the French were building churches in a style sometimes called the 'flamboyant', when the overall design is often hidden in a complex pattern of flame-like tracery. The English never followed to this extreme, for – beginning perhaps in the chapter house of St. Paul's in London in 1332 but more decisively in the new choir of Gloucester built round the tomb of Edward II – they began to develop a style which rejected the flowing and interweaving curves beloved of the French and which boldly emphasized the right-angle. Thus the tracery of a large window, instead of breaking into curved patterns near the top, was straight and perpendicular to the ground all the way up and crossed by horizontal stone supports. The effect was grand and noble, with the beauty of simplicity rather than florid grace, and the English builders seized on it with excitement, dismantling all but the shell of the old Norman naves of their cathedrals and clothing them in this new 'perpendicular' garment, flooding them with light from the broad spacious windows which were now possible. At Canterbury, Gloucester, Winchester, Ely and many others the great Norman pillars support a structure higher and lighter than that for which they were designed. Sometimes the effect is a little monotonous, for the parts for the perpendicular windows were often mass-produced by masons and sent out to where they were required. But in those days this monotony would be alleviated by stained glass, now mostly lost, and by the bright colours of statues now broken or long since whitened.

But above all the fifteenth century is the age of the Parish Church, where the wealth of the wool-producing areas would be put to wonderful and lasting use. The great churches of Norfolk and Suffolk or of the Cotswolds, show where, at this time, England prospered. And there are the town churches, like St. Mary Redcliff in Bristol, the fairest of them all, where even the uncertainties of medieval trade left plenty of surplus wealth for building. But fifteenth-century man, building in this confident way for the centuries ahead, never forgot the shortness of human life and the judgment at its end. The great west window at Fairford in Gloucestershire depicts, as did many now gone, the terrible wrath of God on the sinful. The contrast of this century is here in the contrast of this church – the grandeur of the stonework and the aweful threat of the window.

The fifteenth century produced no poet to match Chaucer. But the writing of English prose shows the quiet development of the national language. Henry V wrote his dispatches from France in English. The Paston family in Norfolk wrote letters which give us a vivid picture of the disturbances of the civil wars. And in the midst of these wars a Warwickshire knight, Sir Thomas Malory, himself a contributor to the general disorder, wrote his collection of translations and adaptations of the old Arthurian legend. Like Bunyan, he wrote much of his work in prison. 'This was drawyn,' he ended one of his tales, 'by a knight presonar Sir Thomas Malleore, that God send hym good recover.'

But the most revolutionary and far-reaching of all this century's achievements was undoubtedly the invention of the printing press.

The first European to use a press of moveable type was John Gutenberg in Germany. England's first press was set up in the precincts of Westminster Abbey by William Caxton in 1476. He was a trader who picked up his ideas during a stay in Flanders, and he concentrated mostly on producing works in English – Malory, Chaucer, or the *Golden Legend*, a collection of lives of the saints. Works of learning in Latin and Greek came in from the Continent, and as they came the demand grew. Gone now were the days of exquisite but laborious copying of manuscripts and the slow spread of knowledge that it entailed. The importance of the invention cannot be measured, but without it that transformation of ways of life and thought and worship that is called the Reformation could hardly have happened with the speed and violence it did. The cumbersome but busy presses of Europe, together with the sharp growth in trade at the ending of the Anglo-French wars – these together held the birth of a new age.

CHAPTER 21

Henry VI and the Wars of the Roses

1422-1471

HENRY VI was nine months old when his father died. Even medieval kings were not expected to exercise authority at quite so early an age, and the royal council decided to appoint a Protector. The obvious choice was the king's uncle John, Duke of Bedford, but he was already Regent of France. Since he could hardly rule France and England at the same time, the council reluctantly decided to make his younger brother Humphrey, Duke of Gloucester, Protector. Gloucester was distinguished from his fellow nobles by being remarkably well read – he left his magnificent library to Oxford University – but they did not like him any the more for this. He was also arrogant and unscrupulous, and his ambitions reached out to the throne itself. But his authority was challenged by the Cardinal Bishop of Winchester who led the great house of Beaufort, and was the richest man in England. Already power was beginning to slip away from the throne into the hands of a few mighty magnates. Beaufort and Gloucester struggled for supremacy, and on several occasions Bedford had to rush back from France to stop their quarrels flaring into open violence.

Beaufort's success was assured when, in November 1429, Henry VI's minority came to an end, and he was crowned king of England and of France. Henry V had been the epitome of martial glory; his son was a man of peace, who never raised a hand in anger. In an age that expected its kings to be fierce as lions, gaudy as peacocks, Henry VI won affection, if not respect, by being a simple, modest, holy man. 'From his youth up,' wrote a priest who knew him well, 'he had been accustomed to wear broad-toed shoes and boots like a countryman . . . Moreover, on the principal feast days of the year, but chiefly when by custom he should wear his crown, he would put on next his skin a rough hair-shirt.' The peace-loving king had no sympathy with blustering, hot-headed Gloucester. He gave his entire confidence to Beaufort who was, at any rate in appearance, a man of peace and religion. Gloucester did not challenge the king's decision. He retired from court and left his hated rival in control.

Beaufort needed an envoy to negotiate peace with France, and in 1445 he chose for this delicate and dangerous mission the head of another proud, recently ennobled family – William de la Pole, Duke of Suffolk. The French king agreed to a truce between the two countries and offered his niece, Margaret of Anjou, as a bride for Henry VI. But in return he claimed the province of Maine, which belonged to England. Suffolk hardly dared consent to this; he knew how angry his fellow-countrymen would be if they ever discovered that he had been giving away parts of their hard-won French empire. But his prestige and his future influence depended upon the successful outcome of the negotiations, and in the end he agreed, in a secret treaty, to the abandonment of Maine. Margaret, a high-spirited sixteen-year-old, was sent over to England where her marriage was celebrated with customary magnificence.

Suffolk, on his return, became the king's chief minister, for there was no-one in England to challenge him. Bedford had died in 1435, exhausted by his efforts to maintain English rule in France. Cardinal Beaufort died in 1447. He lived just long enough to see his old enemy destroyed, for Gloucester, summoned in the king's name to attend a meeting of Parliament, was arrested as soon as he appeared. Two weeks later he was dead – probably murdered, though Suffolk insisted that he had died a natural death. The thin skin of order which lay over English life was beginning to bubble and break up. Soldiers returned from the French wars and trained in nothing but killing, were unable to find employment. They roamed the countryside in armed bands, plundering travellers and holding villages to ransom. Others took service with a great lord, wearing his livery, and acting as his private army.

As the practice of livery spread, the magnates became a law unto themselves. Many were now so rich and powerful that no man, certainly not the mild and pacific Henry VI, could control them. The Percys and Nevilles were the real rulers of northern England; the Dukes of Norfolk and Suffolk held sway over East Anglia; while the Duke of York's word was law in southern Wales. Magistrates dare not condemn, juries dare not punish, the man who wore a great lord's livery. In 1455 the Earl of Devon took an army of five thousand men to plunder the cathedral at Exeter, and later in the century the Duke of Norfolk, who claimed a castle at Caister, attacked it with siege guns and three thousand men, and battered it into surrender. A victim could appeal to the royal courts, but only an optimist would have expected justice. The king could hardly dare offend these magnates on whom he might one day have to rely for his throne. The letters of the Paston family, who were small landowners in Norfolk, describe how in 1451 Lord Moleyns came to attack and plunder their manor house. He was driven off, but when the Pastons appealed to the sheriff for justice, that official replied that 'the King hath writ to him for to show favour to the Lord Moleyns and his men'.

The smaller landowners, merchants, and lawyers who sat in the Commons were the men who suffered most from the irresponsibility of the magnates. For the lowest levels of society, the great mass of the poor, the ambitions of the barons meant employment, a temporary reprieve in the constant battle against poverty and starvation. But the middle classes found themselves forced, whether they liked it or not, into the pattern which the lords dictated. They could complain to the king, as they did in 1459, of 'robberies, ravishments, extortions, oppressions, riots, unlawful assemblies, wrongful imprisonments done unto them . . . Forasmuch as the said misdoers be so favoured and assisted by persons of great might, having towards them of their livery, expressly against your laws, such multitude of robbers, rioters and mischievous persons, which in riotous and forcible manner disturb and hinder as well your Justices of Assize as of Peace in every part of this your realm, that no execution of your law may be had, so as your said true subjects . . . suffer such wrongs without remedy'.

But Henry VI was too weak and too poor to take any effective action. While the lords of the council pocketed the revenues of the crown, the king was left with a debt of nearly half a million pounds. His income was barely sufficient for his own personal needs, and certainly could not provide for the officials on whom effective government depends.

Misgovernment at home and retreat in France were blamed on the king's chief minister, the Duke of Suffolk. He had made a bid for popularity by promising peace and good order. But peace, when it came, seemed to the belligerent English too much like national humiliation, and 'good order' was hardly the right term to describe widespread anarchy and the rule of the strongest. When one of Suffolk's cronies went down to Portsmouth in January 1450 to quieten the sailors who were demanding their pay, they fell on him and cruelly killed him, but not until they had forced him to admit that Suffolk was responsible for the surrender of Maine. This had long been suspected; now it was proved. When Parliament met, summoned in an unavailing attempt to raise money, the Commons impeached[1] Suffolk. The Duke, who had always pursued his own self-interest, had no wish to become a martyr. Slipping away to Ipswich in May 1450 he took ship for France. But his enemies were not so easily to be outwitted. One of the Paston letters describes how, as the Duke's ship was passing the coast of Kent, it was spotted by the *Nicolas of the Tower* which was lying in wait for it. When the master of the *Nicolas* 'espied the Duke's ship, he sent forth his boat to find out who they were. And the Duke himself spake to them and said he was by the King's commandment sent towards Calais. And they said he must speak with their master. And so he, with two or three of his men, went forth with them in their boat to the *Nicolas*. And when he came, the master bade him "Welcome, traitor!" . . . And in the sight of all his men he was drawn out of the great ship into the boat, and there was an axe and a block. And one of the coarsest of the crew bade him lay down his head . . . and took a rusty sword, and smote off his head with half a dozen strokes, and took away his gown of russet and his doublet of velvet mailed, and laid his body on the sands of Dover'.

[1] The Commons impeached a minister by accusing him of treason and calling on the Lords to try him.

While Suffolk was fleeing for his life, the south of England was breaking into open rebellion. Led by Jack Cade, a swaggering, hot-headed soldier back from the wars in France, the rebels marched on London. The citizens opened their gates to him, but quickly came to fear the cut-throats, tramps and rough peasants who made up the bulk of Cade's army. When he set up a court to try the Lord Treasurer, and had the old man executed, the Londoners turned against him. Cade's men were deserting in large numbers. He could not stay on in London indefinitely. When the king offered a general pardon and a promise that misgovernment would be ended, Cade ordered his followers to go back home. The pardon was worthless, of course. Cade was hunted down and killed, and the revolt accomplished nothing. It was a blind out-burst from men goaded to despair by lack of work, injustice and oppression. The yeast of violence was fermenting in English life.

For a year or two after Cade's rebellion there was an uneasy lull. Henry devoted himself to family life and to the plans he was making to found two colleges, one at Eton the other at Cambridge. The shadow of civil war seemed to be passing, particularly when, in October 1453, his queen, Margaret, bore him a son. But in that same year the last English army in France was overwhelmed at Castillon, and Calais alone survived of the empire that Edward III and Henry V had won at the sword's point. In the long run this was a blessing, for England's future greatness was to come from adventure across the seas, not from the ruinous attempt to conquer France. But fifteenth-century Englishmen, not surprisingly, knew nothing of this. Brought up in the assumption that true greatness comes from success in battle, they tasted the full bitterness of defeat. The Lancastrian dynasty which had been, under Henry V, a symbol of national glory, seemed now to be identified with national humiliation. Already there were voices urging the claims of the Duke of York, who was descended from Edward III's second son. The Lancastrians were, in origin, usurpers; why should not the house of York now assert its greater right to the throne?

The question suddenly became acute when, in August 1453, the king's mind gave way under the heavy strain to which his position subjected him. He sat for hours gazing into nothingness, unaware of his surroundings. He recognized no-one, could not walk, and

TABLE IV. *York and Lancaster*

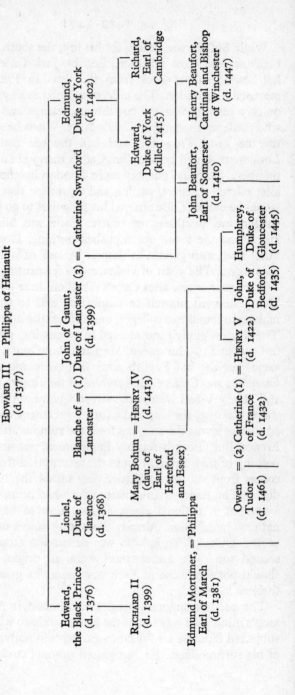

EDWARD III = Philippa of Hainault (d. 1377)

Edward, the Black Prince (d. 1376)

RICHARD II (d. 1399)

Lionel, Duke of Clarence (d. 1368)

Edmund Mortimer, = Philippa Earl of March (d. 1381)

Blanche of = (1) Duke of Lancaster

John of Gaunt, Duke of Lancaster (3) = Catherine Swynford (d. 1399)

Mary Bohun = HENRY IV (dau. of (d. 1413) Earl of Hereford and Essex)

HENRY V = Catherine (1) (d. 1422) of France (d. 1432)

Owen = (2) Tudor (d. 1461)

John, Duke of Bedford (d. 1435)

Humphrey, Duke of Gloucester (d. 1445)

John Beaufort, Earl of Somerset (d. 1410)

Henry Beaufort, Cardinal and Bishop of Winchester (d. 1447)

Edmund, Duke of York (d. 1402)

Edward, Duke of York (killed 1415)

Richard, Earl of Cambridge

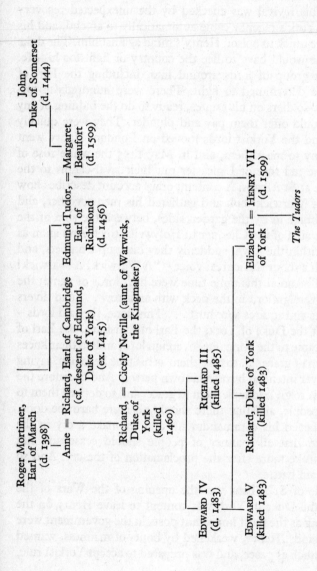

Roger Mortimer, Earl of March (d. 1398)

John, Duke of Somerset (d. 1444)

Anne = Richard, Earl of Cambridge (cf. descent of Edmund, Duke of York) (ex. 1415)

Edmund Tudor, Earl of Richmond (d. 1456) = Margaret Beaufort (d. 1509)

Richard, = Cicely Neville (aunt of Warwick, the Kingmaker), Duke of York (killed 1460)

Elizabeth of York = HENRY VII (d. 1509)

The Tudors

RICHARD III (killed 1485)

Richard, Duke of York (killed 1483)

EDWARD IV (d. 1483)

EDWARD V (killed 1483)

could speak only in half-formed incoherent phrases. The Duke of York was appointed Protector, and under his firm hand the royal administration began to work. Judges were sent out on assizes, and magnates who took the law into their own hands were imprisoned. This revival was checked by the unexpected recovery of the king. York's regency came automatically to an end, and his enemies were quick to poison Henry's mind against him. The duke knew that he would have to flee the country or fight for his life. Gathering a group of lords around him, including the Earl of Warwick, he determined to fight. There were hundreds of unemployed ex-soldiers on his estates, ready to do the bidding of any man who would offer them pay and plunder. They were quickly recruited, and the Yorkist lords moved on London. Henry went with his army to meet them, and in May 1455 the white rose of York and the red rose of Lancaster put their rival claims to the test of battle at St Albans. A contemporary account describes how 'The Earl of Warwick took and gathered his men together, and ferociously brake in by the garden sides, between the sign of the Key and the sign of the Chequer in Holywell Street. And anon as they were within the town, suddenly they blew up trumpets, and set a cry with a shout and a great voice – "A Warwick! A Warwick! A Warwick!" And at this same time were hurt lords of name; the King our sovereign lord in the neck with an arrow . . . and divers other knights and squires sore hurt . . . This done, the said lords – that is to wit the Duke of York, the Earl of Salisbury, the Earl of Warwick – came to the King our sovereign lord, and on their knees besought him of grace . . . to take them as his true liegemen, saying that they never intended hurt to his own person. And therefore the King our sovereign lord took them to grace, and so desired them to cease their people, and that there should no more harm be done. And they obeyed his commandment, and let make a cry in the King's name that all manner of people should cease and not strike any stroke more after the proclamation of the cry. And so ceased the said battle.'

The battle of St Albans was the opening of the Wars of the Roses, but the Duke of York was content to leave Henry on the throne as long as the most important posts in the government were in Yorkist hands. Henry, weakened by bouts of madness, wanted nothing so much as peace, and was prepared to accept Yorkist rule.

Not so his queen. Margaret was a woman of real courage, who never dreamed of submitting to her enemies. Her proud spirit scorned compromise, and she was determined that her young son, the Prince of Wales, should succeed to the throne of his fathers. While York kept Henry prisoner in London, she was busy on the Lancastrian estates in the Midlands, raising men and money.

By the end of 1460 she was ready. Moving north-east from Wales, she marched to attack the Duke of York, who was camped near Wakefield. She caught the Yorkists by surprise while they were out in the fields, gathering provisions. In the slaughter that followed no mercy was shown. The duke himself was killed in battle, with hundreds of his followers. The Earl of Salisbury, captured during the night, was promptly beheaded. Margaret made a triumphal progress towards London, sweeping aside the forces of the Earl of Warwick, who had rushed over from Calais to support the duke. At St Albans she was reunited with her husband, and the house of Lancaster ruled unchallenged.

Not for long, however. York was dead, his skull, circled by a paper crown, grinning out over the walls of the city from which he took his title. The hopes of his party now centred on his son Edward, the new duke. Edward had raised another army from his Welsh estates, and struck south-east to join up with the scattered forces of the Earl of Warwick. When Margaret heard that the two Yorkist leaders had combined their armies, she retreated towards the north, where Lancastrian sentiment was strong, taking with her Henry and the young prince. York and Warwick chased her. On 29 March 1461, they caught the army of the red rose at Towton Moor, not far from Tadcaster. The battle began in a blinding snowstorm, with both sides locked in savage hand-to-hand fighting. It was late in the afternoon before the Lancastrians at last gave way. York's men chased them far into the night, cutting down fugitives, and by next morning the duke was master of England. The captured Lancastrian lords were executed, and the same fate would probably have been reserved for Margaret and Henry, had they not fled towards the Scottish border. With no-one left to challenge him, the Duke of York made his leisurely way towards London. There he claimed the throne by right of his descent from Edward III, and in June 1461 he was crowned at Westminster.

The new king, Edward IV, was a good-looking nineteen-year-old, with a charm and natural ease of manner that made him very popular, particularly with women. He wore his royal dignity as though he had been born to it, but never lost the common touch. An Italian visitor described how 'if he saw a newcomer bewildered at his appearance and royal magnificence, he would give him courage to speak by laying a kindly hand on his shoulder. To plaintiffs and to those who complained of injustice, he leant a willing ear'. On the surface Edward was a pleasure-loving rake, unlikely to last long among the ruthless nobles who were waiting their opportunity to push him off the throne. But he had, like many pleasure-seekers, a knowledge of the world and an insight into human behaviour that made him a man of great strength and authority. The Wars of the Roses were faction fights among nobles who were out for nothing but their own power and advantage. The only hope for England was that one noble, more successful than the others, would destroy his rivals and so put an end to the anarchy in which they thrived. Such a man was Edward, and during his reign the restoration of royal authority was begun.

He had first to destroy his enemies. In 1463 Queen Margaret landed in the north of England and raised the banner of Lancaster again. Edward had his army ready, and as his men marched to meet this new threat they dragged along with them the recently invented cannon that battered down castle walls. Margaret was defeated, and fled to France. She had little cause for hope, but her courage never abandoned her. Describing her adventures she told how 'her husband the King, her son, and she, had for their three selves only one herring, and not one day's supply of bread. And that on a holy day she found herself at Mass without a brass farthing to offer; wherefore, in her beggary and need, she prayed a Scottish archer to lend her something, who, half loth and regretfully, drew a Scots groat from his purse and lent it to her. She also related how she was robbed and despoiled of all she had, of her royal jewels and dresses, of her plate and treasures, with which she thought to escape into Scotland. And when all this had been taken from her, she herself was seized upon, villainously reviled, run upon with a drawn sword, caught hold of by her head gear to have her neck severed'. She was saved by a Yorkist squire whom 'God caused to conceive a pity for her, so that he said

ENGLAND DURING THE WARS OF THE ROSES

"Madam, mount behind me, and my lord the Prince before, and I will save you or die, although death seems to me more likely than not".' He carried them into safety, but even then Margaret's troubles were not ended. She and her son took refuge in a forest which was a haunt of bandits. One of these wild men stumbled upon their hiding-place. A lesser woman would have given up hope. But Margaret pleaded with the man to save her life and that of her son. By a miracle the robber's heart was softened, and with his help the two royal fugitives escaped to France.

Margaret's husband, King Henry, had been captured by Yorkist troops, and was now held prisoner in the Tower of London. There was no point in putting him to death while he still had a son alive to succeed him. But to Edward the tragic figure of the mad Lancastrian was more of an embarrassment than a danger. He had greater reason to fear his powerful ally, Richard Neville, Earl of Warwick. This earl was the last of the mighty barons who plunged England into civil war for their own ambitions. Head of the great house of Neville, he was the proud owner of enormous estates, related by birth or marriage to all the leading men in England, including King Edward. He had been one of the champions of the Yorkist cause since the early days of the first battle of St Albans, and he assumed the right to advise the king and direct his policy.

He planned to marry Edward to a French princess. But the young and hot-blooded king had his own ideas. He fell in love with a youthful widow, Elizabeth Woodville, and made her his wife. He kept the marriage secret, knowing that Warwick would disapprove of such a lowly alliance. When the earl at last discovered the truth he felt bitterly humiliated. His wounded pride turned to hatred when the king lavished honours on Elizabeth Woodville's relatives, and turned to them for advice and encouragement. Peace and orderly government meant nothing to Warwick when his own ambitions were at stake. There were many hundreds of men bound to him by land or money, proud to wear his sign of the Bear and the Ragged Staff. In 1468, when all his preparations were complete, Warwick called his followers to arms and struck swiftly. Edward was taken by surprise at Northampton, and captured. This was when Warwick gained his nickname *the Kingmaker*, for the Yorkist king was a prisoner in the earl's castle at Middleham, while the Lancastrian king lay at his mercy in the Tower of London.

Success showed up Warwick's weakness, for he did not know what to do with his victory. He did not dare claim the throne himself – two kings were enough, without adding a third! All he could do was to restore Edward, after making him promise to dismiss the upstart Woodvilles and rely on high-born advisers. To drive the lesson home, the queen's father and her brother, who were Warwick's captives at Kenilworth, were executed.

Edward knew when he was beaten. He accepted all Warwick's terms, and restored the earl to favour. The two men appeared frequently together, and the breach between them was apparently healed. But Edward, although he had originally been a great magnate himself, was determined to cut down anyone who challenged his royal authority. Warwick had been a good friend to Edward the Duke: he was a dangerous enemy to Edward the King. In March 1470 the king accused the earl of treason, and Warwick only escaped by fleeing to France.

There he found the exiled Margaret of Anjou and her son, Prince Edward. Warwick had spent much of his life fighting these two, but such was his lack of any real principles that he was easily persuaded to change sides and throw in his lot with Lancaster. With troops and money provided by the French king – who loved the thought of anarchy across the Channel – Warwick landed in England in September 1470, and proclaimed Henry VI as king. A French chronicler describes how 'Five or six days after the Earl's arrival, his power was so great that he encamped within three leagues of King Edward. Notwithstanding, the King's force was greater than the Earl's, if all his men were true . . . But as the King sat at dinner, suddenly one came running in and brought news that the Marquis of Montague, the Earl's brother [who was serving with Edward's army] and certaine other were mounted on horsebacke, and had caused all their men to cry "God save King Henry!". Which message the King at first believed not, but in all haste sent other messengers forth, and armed himself, and set men also at the barriers of his lodging to defend it . . . But the messengers brought word that the report was true, and that the enemies assembled to assault the King. But God so provided for the King that he lodged hard by the sea side, neere to a place where a little ship laden with victuals that followed his armie, and two hulkes of Holland freighted with merchandise, lay at anchor. He had no other shift but to run to save himself in one of them . . . Thus fled King Edward in the yeere 1470 with two hulkes and a little bote of his own countrie, accompanied with seven or eight hundred persons, having none other apparell than that they wore in the wars, utterly unfurnished of money, and hardly knowing whither they went'.

Edward took refuge in Burgundy. The duke who ruled that state was an enemy of France. Since France had supported the Lancastrians, Burgundy was prepared to support the Yorkists. Money and men were provided, and by the spring of 1471 Edward was ready to fight for his kingdom once again. Landing in Yorkshire, he found men flocking to join him, for the Lancastrian government was as inefficient as it had always been, and hardly inspired loyalty. Edward marched rapidly south, hoping to take Warwick by surprise. But the earl was ready for him, and the two armies met at Barnet, just north of London. There in the fog of an April day, the Lancastrians were routed, and Warwick the Kingmaker, fleeing from the battlefield, was caught and killed. His death was a fitting symbol of the fall of the mighty barons who, by their overmastering pride and ambition, had destroyed their power and influence in the state.

On the very day of Barnet, Margaret and the Prince of Wales landed in England. Edward had to gather his weary troops and prepare once again to defend his kingdom. On 4 May 1471 he caught up with the queen and her soldiers at Tewkesbury. There the last army of the red rose was scattered and defeated. The Prince of Wales was killed, either during or after the battle. His mother was taken prisoner and sent to join her husband in the Tower. But she never saw Henry again. On the very night she arrived in the Tower, the last of the Lancastrian kings came to the end of his miserable existence. It was given out that he had died naturally, 'of pure displeasure and melancholy', but when his body was publicly displayed, blood welled out of its secret wounds. Margaret was ransomed by her father, and spent the eleven years of life that remained to her far from the memories of 'the bloody field of Tewkesbury', in her native Anjou. The white rose had triumphed, and Edward was now undisputed master of England.

CHAPTER 22

Edward IV and Henry VII

1471-1509

EDWARD IV reigned for twelve years after his victory at Tewkes-bury. During that time he raised the crown far above the intrigues and ambitions of the noble families who had earlier made it their pawn. After years of inefficient government England experienced the novelty of peace and good order. Judges were sent out regularly on their assizes; laws were put into operation to check the practice of livery, by which the magnates had been able to recruit private armies for themselves; and councils were set up in the north and on the Welsh border to control those remote and wild parts from which soldiers had so easily been raised. Everywhere the power of the crown was felt, pulling together again the kingdom that had been breaking up into duchies and earldoms. Many of the greatest lords were dead; other holders of proud titles were mere boys. The king was himself Duke of York, and took over the lands of the house of Lancaster. The medieval monarchy had declined because it was so poor. Edward reversed the process by building up the royal estates until he owned one-fifth of the land of England. The crown was once again the greatest of all landowners and the most powerful force in the country.

Edward made a profit from trade as well as from his royal estates. As more and more goods passed through the ports of England, the crown's income from tonnage and poundage – the import duties which Parliament granted the king for life – went up. And Edward was not above being a merchant himself. He arranged for the buying of wool and tin, shipped these to the Continent, and made a handsome profit in the process. The smaller property-owners – squires, lawyers, and merchants – who sat in the lower house of Parliament, and called themselves the Commons of England (though they were far removed, in wealth and social standing, from the common people), found their incomes rising. A strong crown meant, for them, peace and prosperity. Edward did not risk angering them by constant demands for money. He summoned only six Parliaments during his reign, and spent his last five years without one. Parliament had been too long the tool of the nobility for kings to have kind feelings towards it. Edward called the two Houses together only when he had some out-of-the-ordinary need for money. In 1474, for instance, he made a bid for popularity by declaring war against France, and called upon Parliament to vote generous supplies to maintain his own, and his kingdom's, honour. Parliament reluctantly voted a subsidy, and Edward duly invaded France. But when the French king offered him a large sum of money and an annual pension in return for peace, Edward cheerfully accepted. To have the glory of successful war and to make a profit out of it was just what he wanted.

The fact that Edward had won his throne in battle meant that he could not afford to anger his subjects. The antiquated system of taxation, which had been largely responsible for the crown's increasing poverty during the Middle Ages, needed bringing up to date. But Edward was in no position to do this. Even his moderate requests to Parliament caused the usual grumbles about over-taxation. 'I pray God,' wrote one of the Pastons in 1473, 'send you the Holy Ghost among you in the Parliament House. And rather the Devil, we say, than ye should grant any more taxes.' To avoid asking Parliament for money, Edward called on his richer subjects to make gifts to the crown. These gifts – called *Benevolences*, because they were, in theory, granted by the benevolence or good will of the giver – were really non-Parliamentary taxes, and they were most unpopular. A man could, of course, refuse to pay up, but by so doing he risked the king's displeasure, and this was something not lightly to be incurred. In the closing years of his reign, however, when Edward was not merely out of debt but actually piling up a fortune, he stopped the collection of benevo-lences. 'In which tyme of his latter days,' wrote one chronicler, 'this Realm was in quyet and prosperous estate – no feare of outwarde enemyes, no warre in hande nor none forwarde . . . the people towarde the Prince, not in a constrayned feare, but in a

wyllinge and lovynge obedyence . . . He had lefte all gatherynge
of money (which is the onelye thynge that withdraweth the heartes
of Englyshmenne from the Prince).'

By 1483 it seemed as though the Wars of the Roses were over,
and England assured of peace under a masterful king. But in that
year Edward died, leaving his throne to a boy of twelve. The dreadful prospect of a minority, leading to civil war, again opened before
the people of England. The leadership of the Lancastrian party had
passed to Henry Tudor, Earl of Richmond, descended from
Edward III through the Beauforts. He was already planning to
raise the banner of the red rose and plant it once again on English
soil. After twelve years of peace the sky was darkening, and the
leaders of the aristocracy, who had also profited by the interval of
tranquillity, saw in the charming and innocent figure of the
boy-king Edward V a last chance to assert their power. Only one
man stood in their way. That was the king's uncle and Protector,
Richard, Duke of Gloucester.

Gloucester is one of the great villains of English history,
remembered only as the sinister hunchback who, in his desire for
power, betrayed his trust, usurped the throne, and murdered
Edward V and his brother – the Princes in the Tower. Tudor
historians, who had every reason to paint a black picture of the
man who had stood in the way of their own sovereign, described
him as 'Little of stature, ill featured of limbs, crook-backed, his
left shoulder much higher than his right, hard favoured of visage
. . . malicious, wrathfull, envious'. But even if this picture of
Gloucester is true – and at this distance of time we do not know
how much was invented by his enemies – it misses the point of his
reign, which is that it gave England a breathing-space of two years
before the tide of war once again swept up her beaches. If all
medieval kings were to be judged by the number of deaths they
caused, many would have a blacker record than Richard III. If he
murdered the two princes, then the guilt must lie firmly on his
shoulders – whether crooked or not. But Edward V had, in any
case, a poor chance of survival. To be born of the blood royal in
late-medieval England was to invite an early death. 'Woe to the
land that's governed by a child,' says one of the London citizens in
Shakespeare's *Richard III*, and this might stand as epitaph to
Edward V's brief reign. The previous boy king had been Henry VI

under whose feeble hand the power of the crown had dissolved in civil war. His Protector had also been a Duke of Gloucester, whose comparative loyalty to his sovereign had been rewarded by dishonour and violent death.

Richard chose to strike for power before his enemies poisoned the young king's mind against him. He sent Edward V and his brother into the Tower of London from which they never again emerged, and in July 1483 he had himself crowned king as Richard III. He reigned firmly enough, bringing overmighty subjects to heel, and restoring the effectiveness of the courts of common law. Had he succeeded in holding the throne and passing it on to his heirs, he would be remembered today as a reviver of royal power, a worthy successor to Edward IV. But he committed the unforgivable sin of failure. His only son and heir died in April 1484, and a year later Henry Tudor, Earl of Richmond, landed at Milford Haven to claim the throne in the name of Lancaster.

The two armies met at Market Bosworth, just outside Leicester. There, on 21 August 1485, the last great battle of the Wars of the Roses took place. But the big question had already been decided. Whether Henry or Richard won, the crown would be triumphant. All that was settled on that August day was the name of its wearer. Richard fought bravely but he was surrounded by traitors. 'Knowing certainly,' in the words of a Tudor historian, 'that that day would either yield him a peaceable and quiet realm from henceforth, or else perpetually bereave him the same, [Richard] came to the field with the crown upon his head, that thereby he might either make a beginning or an end of his reign.' It turned out to be an end. With a shout of 'Treason! Treason!' Richard plunged into the thickest of the fighting, and was cut down. One of Henry's lieutenants, searching the battlefield, discovered the crown in a thornbush, where it had rolled. Picking it out, he took it to the Earl of Richmond, and placed it upon his head. Henry Tudor was king of England, and the red rose had finally won the day.

The Wars of the Roses had not wiped out the English aristocracy, but they left it leaderless. Fifty-three peers had sat in the Parliament of 1454 – the last to meet before the wars: only eighteen came to the first Parliament of Henry VII. Some nobles were in exile; many were young boys who would one day grow

up to claim their inheritance. Henry was himself the heir to many
of the greatest dignities – Duke of Lancaster, Duke of Cornwall,
Earl of Richmond. The titles survived, but not, in many cases, the
families that had been so long associated with them. A Stuart judge,
looking back on these changes over a century later, saw how many
of the great names of medieval history had vanished into oblivion.
'Time hath his revolutions,' he said. 'There must be a period and
an end to all temporal things, *Finis Rerum*, an end of names and
dignities and whatsoever is terrene . . . For where is Bohun?
Where is Mowbray? Where is Mortimer? Nay, which is more and
most of all, where is Plantagenet? They are intombed in the urns
and sepulchres of mortality.'

Henry turned for advice not to holders of ancient titles and great
estates, but to men 'raised from the dust', whose authority came
only from the fact that they served the king. Among the most
famous were Sir Thomas Lovell, descended from a Norwich
alderman; Sir Edward Poynings, the son of Jack Cade's sword-
bearer; Edmund Dudley, who came of a line of squires; and
Richard Empson, described by Bacon as 'the son of a sieve-maker'.
There were churchmen too, who had the big advantage, from the
king's point of view, that they left no legitimate heirs to succeed
to their position, and could be rewarded for service to the crown
by promotion in the Church.

This last consideration weighed heavily with Henry, who was
always delighted when he could make men serve him without
having to pay them. He was a miser, of course, but with good
reason. If poverty had caused the decline of the monarchy, then
wealth would bring about its recovery. When Henry sat up late
into the night, personally checking and initialling the accounts of
his officials, he was laying the foundations of a strong throne. By
1492 he had balanced his budget, and after that the royal administration ran at a profit. He followed the example of Edward IV,
calling Parliament only rarely, and depending for his income
mainly on import duties – tonnage and poundage – and benevo-
lences. Like Edward, too, he persuaded Parliament to vote a
subsidy for war against France, and then accepted a lump sum
from the French king in return for peace.

The income from tonnage and poundage went up as order was
restored. Merchants had cut down their activities when armies

were on the prowl, waiting to plunder their goods. But Henry enforced the king's peace, and kept the roads clear of bandits. He also encouraged trade to flow by signing commercial treaties with the seaboard states of Europe. Most famous of these was the *Magnus Intercursus* of 1496, which reopened to English merchants the valuable cloth trade with the Netherlands. Henry, again like Edward, did some very profitable trading on his own private account. He also set up a special office to deal with the crown's income from feudal obligations. The land of England was still, in theory, held by knight-service, as it had been since the days of the Conqueror. When a tenant-in-chief died, his heir had to pay a large sum of money, called a Relief, before he could take over his father's land. But if the heir was under age he was declared a royal ward, and the king took over his estates and pocketed the profits until the child grew up. This was a very valuable source of income, and Henry VII's Office of Wards, which his son turned into the Court of Wards, was as important to Tudor and Stuart governments as the Income Tax commissioners are to present-day governments. But the efficiency of the Court of Wards angered the landowners, who resented paying taxes, and saw how irrelevant feudal obligations were to the changing society in which they lived.

Commercial treaties and checking of accounts have none of the glory that goes with battles, but in the long run they are more important. Henry V had won glory at Agincourt, but the price was too high and his dynasty did not long survive him. The strength of the Tudor monarchy came from the laborious and unspectacular accountancy of its first sovereign. Henry VII was only twenty-eight when he came to the throne, but he had been trained to hardness in the school of exile. His portraits show a long, lean face and Roman nose. They also show the shrewd eyes which valued every man at his price, and were not deceived by mere appearances. Henry was more feared than loved, relentless in his determination to hold the throne and ruthless where he thought that the interests of his dynasty were at stake. Rivals were hunted down and imprisoned, like the Earl of Suffolk, or executed, like the Earl of Warwick. And if the princes in the Tower were still alive, Henry would certainly not have shrunk from killing them. There was, however, another side to his character. He was a lover of music, who never travelled without someone to play the pipe or sing to him. He was a keen sportsman, taking delight in hunting and hawking and collecting animals for his menagerie at the Tower. He spent well over £100,000 on jewellery, which was, of course, a convenient and portable form of wealth, useful for emergencies. And he had his extravagancies, spending lavishly on entertaining and ceremonial. Even the royal buckhounds were provided with costly silken collars.

Henry did not spare money where it could be used to increase the majesty of the crown. Like all upstarts, he had to make men aware of his new dignity and persuade them to respect it. For his throne was by no means secure. In a gesture of reconciliation to the Yorkists, he married Elizabeth, daughter of Edward IV, thereby uniting the red rose and the white. But his enemies were not so easily appeased. There were many Yorkist lords with estates in Ireland, and that country became a centre for hatching plots against the Tudor king. Unfortunately for the Yorkists they had no obvious leader, so severely had war thinned their ranks. They were reduced to persuading a young man called Lambert Simnel to impersonate Edward IV's nephew, the Earl of Warwick, whom they thought to be dead. Henry in fact had the young earl prisoner in the Tower, and paraded him through the streets of London to prove the hollowness of the Yorkist claims. But he could not prevent Simnel from landing in Lancashire in 1487. It looked as though the Wars of the Roses were going to break out again. But the country remained loyal to Henry. Simnel and his army got as far as Stoke, where Henry was waiting for them. In the battle that followed, the Yorkists were crushingly defeated. Simnel was taken prisoner, but Henry did not condescend to put him to death. He was sent to end his days as a scullion in the royal kitchens.

The Yorkists made one more attempt. This time they produced a young man of charm and elegance called Perkin Warbeck, and persuaded him that he was Edward V's brother, the Duke of York – one of the princes in the Tower. Warbeck was supplied with men and money by the kings of France and Scotland, who relished the prospect of a renewal of civil war in England. In 1497 he landed in the West Country, hoping to find support among the Cornishmen who had risen in revolt against Henry's taxation. But Warbeck was no leader. He was easily captured, confessed that he was an impostor, and was sent to join Warwick in the Tower. Two years later Warwick and Warbeck, the true earl and the false duke, were both executed on charges of treason. Henry could not afford to keep such dangerous rivals alive.

The rest of the reign was untroubled by Yorkist threats, and Henry concentrated on the problem of cutting down the bands of liveried retainers who acted as private soldiers for any lord who would pay them. He had no regular army, no police force, at his disposal. He had to rely on the prestige of his name and the co-operation of the property-owners whom he appointed as Justices of the Peace. Evildoers who were too powerful for the courts of common law to deal with were summoned before the king's council at Westminster. There they would be faced with the greatest men in the kingdom, sometimes including the king himself – men who feared no-one and were not to be bribed. If the person summoned refused to attend, the Justices of the Peace would be ordered to to raise soldiers and hunt him down.

There were, of course, many evildoers who got away with their crimes. Sixteenth-century governments were absurdly inefficient by our standards. But by comparison with what had gone before, Henry's reign saw a big improvement. The robber barons who had for so long terrorized the country were gradually brought to heel. The case of Sir Henry Bodrugan was typical. This Cornish land-owner had been a menace to law-abiding citizens for over thirty years by the time Henry VII ascended the throne. He had several times been summoned to appear before the court of King's Bench but had never been convicted. Sir Henry fought for the white rose at Bosworth, but quickly came to terms with the new king and was soon up to his old tricks, plundering and robbing on land and sea. He even joined up with Lambert Simnel, assuming that if the rebellion were successful he would share in the profits of victory, while if it failed, he could easily make his peace with the king. But he had misjudged his sovereign. The royal council summoned Sir Henry to appear before it. When he ignored the command, the king ordered another Cornish knight to hunt Bodrugan down and arrest him. Bodrugan took refuge in his castle, certain that no man would dare lift a finger against him. But when from his windows he caught the glint of sun on spears and armour, he knew that his carefree days of plundering were over, and fled for his life. He died in exile, and his castle and estates passed, like hundreds of others all over the country, into the hands of the king.

By the time Henry VII died, in 1509, he had made the crown rich and powerful, stronger than it had been since the days of Henry II. Law and order were being re-established, trade was flourishing, the country was at peace; and the centre of every-thing – the heart which pumped the vital blood supply to every part of the body – was the king. Henry was not a lovable figure, and he was certainly not a constitutional monarch of the sort we nowadays admire. He ruled because he was king, and because kings had a royal prerogative, a right to rule, which was denied to humbler men. In the reigns of his successors, this prerogative was to be increasingly attacked as a threat to the liberties of the property-owners, and the struggle to limit and define it was to lead to civil war. But all this was hidden in the future in 1509. The country gentlemen, merchants and lawyers who saw the restoration of royal authority under Henry VII, never questioned the limits of his prerogative, because they knew from their own bitter experience that the only alternative to a strong king was bloodshed and anarchy.

CHAPTER 23

Renaissance and Reformation

THE WARS of the Roses mark the passing of medieval England. There was no sudden break, of course. Ways of life do not change overnight, and many medieval institutions survive to this day. But forces were at work remodelling society throughout western Europe. The first half of the fifteenth century was a period of stagnation, as plague decimated the population and trade declined. Land went out of cultivation, villages were abandoned, towns decayed. In Winchester in 1430 there were nearly a thousand empty houses, and in 1446 Lincoln was said to have no more than two hundred citizens. The centres of the wool trade in East Anglia and the Netherlands continued to thrive, but even their vigorous prosperity was checked by war at home and abroad.

A declining population meant a shortage of labour, which put the peasants in a strong position. They used their scarcity value to negotiate better terms with their lords, which frequently resulted in the abolition of compulsory labour services and their replacement by money rents. In this way villeinage, which had been one of the characteristic features of the Middle Ages, gradually disappeared, and the typical peasant became much more like a tenant farmer. The end of villeinage was a slow process – as late as Elizabeth's reign a mayor of Bristol was arrested on the grounds that he was a villein, illegally absent from his lord's manor – but by the seventeenth century it had been virtually accomplished.

The upper levels of society were changing as rapidly as the lower. No medieval king had been able to ignore the feudal aristocracy. The great nobles ruled their estates like independent princes, and the roots of their power twisted deep down into English life, sapping its strength. England might have broken up into a collection of principalities, like contemporary Germany, had it not been for the fact that the greatest of the barons were closely

connected to the throne by blood and by marriage. They destroyed themselves fighting for the crown, and their wealth and
power were poured out on the battlefields of Towton, Barnet,
Tewkesbury and Bosworth.

As the stranglehold of the barons was broken, the smaller
property-owners – squires, lawyers and merchants – took over the
leadership of English life. They looked to the crown to protect
them against any baronial revival and to preserve the peace and
good order in which alone they could flourish. From this alliance
of interests between the property-owners and the crown the Tudor
monarchy at first drew its strength. In England, as in France and
Spain, the early sixteenth century was the age of kings.

The crown triumphed at the very moment when European
trade began to revive and stagnation gave way to optimism and
expansion. The new monarchs derived much of their popularity
from this fortunate coincidence. Royal authority and prosperity
went hand in hand, and the age of kings was also the age of the
wool merchant and clothier.

Art and architecture mirrored the changing scene. Henry VI
had started building the magnificent chapel at King's College,
Cambridge – one of the finest achievements of the late Middle
Ages – but as his revenues declined and disaster overtook his
armies on the Continent, the masons were paid off and the roofless
walls were left naked to wind and rain. The fall of Aquitaine in
1453 marks the end of much more than the English empire in
France. By that date John Lydgate, the leading poet of his day,
was dead, and John Dunstable, one of the great English musicians,
was nearing the end of his life. There was no-one to fill the gap left
by their deaths. The same was true of their patrons. Some of the
mightiest of the barons had been proud to patronize the arts.
Humphrey, Duke of Gloucester, had been the friend of men of
letters and had built up the finest library in England. His brother
John, Duke of Bedford, was a lover of music, and the patron of
Dunstable. They were both dead by 1453, and after that date the
barons were too obsessed by their own quarrels to have time or
money left for more civilized pursuits.

Edward IV's accession in 1471 marks the turn of the tide.
Economic stagnation gave way to growing prosperity as trade
expanded and population increased. Edward set the masons to

work in his castle at Windsor, where they built St George's Chapel – a superb example of late-Perpendicular architecture, and a triumphant assertion of the new-found majesty of the crown. By the time Henry VII came to the throne the revival was well under way. The miser-king was prepared to spend money on glorifying the monarchy. His mother, Lady Margaret Beaufort – a devout and learned woman who made many generous gifts to the university at Cambridge – persuaded her son to pay for the completion of Henry VI's chapel at King's College. What the last Lancastrian had started for the glory of God, the first Tudor finished for the glory of his dynasty. Henry VII's work is everywhere studded with heraldic emblems, unlike the sober restraint of the earlier part. This is even more true of the chapel he built at the east end of Westminster Abbey. To pass from the austere tombs of the early medieval kings into this exquisite chapel, decorated with the fine precision of a cut diamond, is to feel, almost with a shock, the splendour of Henry's achievement. From the roof, patterned with intricate delicacy like a skein of lace, the stone ribs of the fan vault curve down and are gathered into pendants carved like coronets. Everywhere the eye is caught by heraldic devices – the red dragon of Wales, the portcullis of Beaufort, the rose of Tudor – and, surmounting everything, the crown.

The day of the mailed knight charging into battle with his painted banner had passed with the invention of gunpowder, but the concern with heraldry developed into an obsession in sixteenth-century England. The new holders of property who replaced the older aristocracy, applied for coats-of-arms to proclaim and justify their rise to power. There was a scramble for titles, dignities and honours, and it focused on the king, the inexhaustible fountain from which such favours flowed. It took more than a century to satisfy the demand, and while the pressure lasted the crown became an object of veneration. Henry VIII abandoned the old royal style of 'Your Grace' in favour of the more regal 'Your Majesty', and half a century later Shakespeare's audiences were still enchanted by the symbols of kingly glory:

> '. . . the balm, the sceptre, and the ball,
> The sword, the mace, the crown imperial,
> The intertissued robe of gold and pearl.'

The end of the Middle Ages in England was signalled by the break-up of medieval systems of landholding, the decline of the feudal aristocracy, and the emergence of a new ruling class which looked to a powerful crown for support and advancement. At the same time the shape of future events was being determined by movements of thought which affected Europe as a whole. First of these, in time at least, was the Renaissance and the revival of learning. This started in Italy, where the ruins of the ancient civilizations of Greece and Rome were everywhere visible – reminders of a way of life and thought that owed nothing to medieval ideas. In the fifteenth century artists and scholars began to explore this dead world and found in it a source of life. Roman and Greek remains were excavated, their buildings studied, their statues copied. It was as though the ancient world had been reborn, which is why we call this movement the Renaissance.

Italy was soon in the throes of an artistic revival unparalleled in the splendour of its achievement, and the influence of Italy spread rapidly over the western world, including England. When Henry VII died, his son brought over a sculptor from Florence to carve a tomb worthy of the first Tudor. It stands to this day in Westminster Abbey. Around it is a fine screen of copper gilt which matches in its design the Gothic architecture of the Henry VII Chapel and owes nothing to Italy. But inside the screen is the sarcophagus on which rest the effigies of Henry and his queen, Elizabeth of York. This is very different in feeling from the Gothic screen – more like the tomb of a Roman emperor. It marks the early stages of Renaissance influence, which was to turn English art and architecture into new courses.

The Renaissance was not confined to the visual arts. Knowledge of Latin had never died out in the West, but Greek was little known. There were, however, many Greek texts surviving, and these were now avidly studied by scholars eager to liberate themselves from what they regarded as the superstition and backwardness of the Middle Ages. The greatest figure of the literary renaissance was the Dutch scholar Erasmus of Rotterdam (1466–1536). He was an enthusiast for classical learning and realized how the printing press, invented in Germany shortly before his birth, could spread the treasures of Greek and Latin literature all over Europe. He set to work to edit the various manuscripts and had his editions elegantly printed by the Venetian publisher Aldus. Erasmus also realized that Christianity had its classical texts, and he began work on these. He paid several visits to England, where he was welcomed by the leading scholars of the day – men like John Colet, Dean of St Paul's, John Fisher, Bishop of Rochester, and Sir Thomas More – who wished to strip the Catholic Church of the superstitious practices and other abuses that had grown up over the centuries, and to prepare it for the challenge of the critical Renaissance world. 'To speak of pride of life,' wrote Colet, 'how much greediness and appetite of honour and dignity is nowadays in men of the church. How run they, yea almost out of breath, from one benefice to another, from the less to the more, from the lower to the higher . . . The most part of them doth go with so stately a countenance and with so high looks that they seem not to be put in the humble bishopric of Christ, but rather in the high lordship and power of the world.' It was at More's suggestion that in 1509 Erasmus wrote one of his most famous works, *The Praise of Folly*, in which he held up to ridicule many of the dignitaries of the church. England became for a time a centre of the new learning, and Erasmus and his friends looked forward to the day when, by their exposure of pomposity and corruption, they would have shamed the Church into reforming itself. But the very effectiveness of their satire defeated their ends. By showing up the abuses of the church which they loved and wished to purify, they encouraged other men – less intelligent, perhaps; certainly less tolerant – to attack the Church itself. Erasmus went further. By publishing an edition of the Greek New Testament in 1516 he brought his sharp brain and the critical methods of his age to bear on the Bible. Until his time the Roman Catholic Church had been the undisputed authority on sacred texts, but Erasmus made it possible for laymen to study these and come to their own conclusions. By his laughter he brought the authority of the Church into ridicule: by his scholarship he gave its enemies a weapon with which to overthrow it.

The popes were in any case undermining their own prestige by living like the kings of the earth and neglecting their spiritual mission. By the beginning of the sixteenth century Rome had become the artistic capital of the western world, and the pope was the greatest of all patrons, spending money lavishly on the painters, sculptors and architects who thronged his court. The results of this enlightened patronage still survive to delight the eye and enrich the senses of the visitor to Rome. But the popes were meant to be more than patrons of the arts, and their obsession with money made the Catholic Church seem to the inhabitants of Europe more like a tax-collecting machine than a spiritual institution for the salvation of souls. Pope Julius II (1503-13), for instance, pulled down the medieval church of St Peter, which was a visible link with the early centuries of the catholic faith, and engaged Bramante to design the majestic cathedral which took its place. The shrine of saints was replaced by a monument to the glory of the papacy. To pay for this splendour agents were sent out to tour Europe and sell Indulgences. These were documents which released the purchaser from the penance which any sinner must carry out. They did not wipe out the sin itself. But the ignorant masses of Europe could hardly be expected to make this important distinction. Many of the faithful thought they were buying for-giveness of sins for a sum of money. To the German monk Martin Luther it seemed as though the popes were deliberately encourag-ing the spread of false doctrines in order to pay for their extrava-gance. He protested by nailing up on the church door at Wittenberg a list of his criticisms. Soon Germany was in revolt against the authority of Rome, and as the Reformation spread it split Europe into two armed camps. The unity which the Catholic Church had given to medieval Europe was shattered.

Luther did not intend to create a new church any more than the scholars of the Renaissance intended to create new patterns of thought. They were all looking to the past, hoping to revive in the sixteenth century the virtues of the ancient world or of the early church. But time cannot 'run back and fetch the age of gold'. Old ideas revived in a different setting produce revolutionary changes. This was true above all in the field of science, where the re-discovery of the works of Archimedes and the publication of printed editions of other Greek mathematicians was the starting-point from which Galileo developed his attack upon medieval assump-tions about the nature of the universe, and sketched in the outlines of a new interpretation. The Middle Ages had not lacked scholars who were interested in science, but they never knew the passionate interest in observation and experiment which is characteristic of the world in which we live. Galileo and the great experimenters who came after him mark the clearest and most important break with the Middle Ages, but since the scientific revolution belongs, chronologically, to the seventeenth, rather than the sixteenth, century, it will be dealt with below.[1]

While European thought and society was undergoing profound changes, an unexpected and unwished-for discovery brought to light a new continent on the far side of the Atlantic. In 1492 Christopher Columbus, searching for a seaway to the riches of China that would by-pass the extortionate Egyptians who controlled the overland route, sailed west and discovered America. A few years earlier the Portuguese navigator Bartholomew Dias, blown out into the Atlantic by a violent gale, discovered when the wind died down that an unknown sea lay before him. He, like Columbus, was searching for a new way to the east, and had been exploring the coast of Africa to see whether that great continent could, in fact, be rounded. His enterprise was rewarded for he had opened up the sea route to India that was to make the barren kingdom of Portugal one of the richest states in Europe. He called the point round which he had been blown the 'Cape of Storms'. But the king of Portugal knew better. This tip of land was a signpost to wealth and glory. He renamed it 'Cape of Good Hope'.

Into this exciting world, bursting at the seams with its own energy, the Tudor dynasty was born. England, with a mere three million inhabitants, was still one of the minor powers of Europe, far less important than the kingdom of France or the Holy Roman Empire. But in the new world that was being created, the odds were in England's favour. She was slow to follow the lead set by Spain and Portugal. John Cabot was sent out by Henry VII in 1497 to search for any 'regions or provinces of heathens and infidels . . . unknown to all Christians', and discovered Labrador. But he brought back no gold or precious stones with him; only dull fish and furs. It took a century for English merchants to realize how profitable a cargo of fish and furs could be, far outshining the glitter of gold. By the time the last Tudor died, the centre of gravity of the world had shifted. Venice stood at the heart of old Europe, midway between east and west. But her power declined as the Turks blocked the traditional trade routes, and the discovery of America

[1] See page 384.

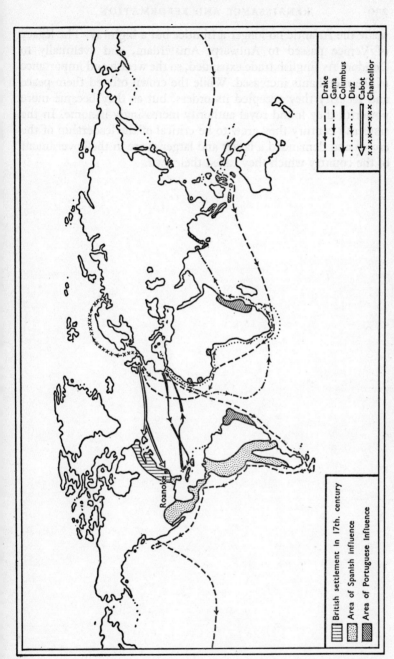

WORLD MAP OF DISCOVERIES AND COLONIZATION

made the Atlantic no longer a frontier but a highway. The legacy of Venice passed to Antwerp, Amsterdam, and eventually to London. As English trade expanded, so the wealth and importance of the merchants increased. While the crown offered them peace and security they accepted its orders, but as they became more powerful they found royal authority increasingly irksome. In the sixteenth century they grew to be critical of the leadership of the crown and demanded a larger and larger share in the government of the country which they called their own.

CHAPTER 24

Henry VIII and the Break with Rome

1509-1536

HENRY VIII, a young man not yet eighteen, came to the throne in April 1509. He was born of a Yorkist mother and a Lancastrian father. As John Skelton wrote, in his poem celebrating Henry's accession,

> 'The Rose both white and red
> In one Rose now doth grow'

and England could hope for peace. A Venetian described the king as the 'handsomest potentate I ever set eyes upon: above the usual height, with an extremely fine calf to his leg, his complexion very fair and light, with auburn hair'. He was a good musician, spoke French, Latin and Spanish fluently; was, like his father, a devout churchgoer; and had a taste for theology. He was not a pedant, locked in his study away from the world – indeed he was never so happy as when he was out hunting or playing tennis – but he was intelligent, and deserved Erasmus's description of him as 'no mean scholar'.

For the first twenty years of his reign he was content to enjoy himself and leave the business of government to Thomas Wolsey. This remarkable man, the son of an Ipswich butcher, rose, like so many able men, by carving out for himself a career in the Church. He entered royal service under Henry VII and his energy and efficiency soon distinguished him as one of the leaders of the group of councillors which advised the king. When Henry VIII came to the throne he executed his father's unpopular ministers, Empson and Dudley, on a trumped-up charge of treason, and left the way clear for the rise of Wolsey. The butcher's boy became Archbishop of York and Abbot of St Albans, and by 1518 he was also Lord Chancellor, Papal legate, and a cardinal. This meant that he was, after Henry, the most powerful man in the kingdom, the head of the king's government and, as personal representative of the pope, the head of the Church in England.

Wolsey continued Henry VII's work of restoring good order to England. As chancellor he was responsible for sending out judges on their assizes to try criminals throughout the land. He also presided over the councillors who met as judges in the Court of Star Chamber, which took its name from the pattern of gold stars decorating its ceiling. This body dealt with cases in which a great nobleman had defied the courts of common law, or had persuaded men to wear his livery. Under Wolsey Star Chamber became a famous court which showed no mercy to wrongdoers, however rich and powerful they might be. This made Wolsey popular among the poor, but there were many wealthy men who had good reason to hate the upstart chancellor and to count the days until his fall.

As head of the Church, Wolsey ought to have reformed it and set an example himself of godly and quiet living. But he was too interested in affairs of state to worry about reforms. His main concern was foreign policy, and since the young King Henry wanted glory, Wolsey planned for him a military expedition against France in 1512. This was at first a failure, but Wolsey, unsparing with the king's money and his own energy, turned disaster into victory. The French army galloped away at the Battle of the Spurs (1513) and Henry returned, poorer but happy.

Wolsey's ambition was to become pope, but to achieve this he needed the support of the Holy Roman Emperor. In 1519 a young member of the house of Hapsburg – one of the most powerful of European families – had been elected emperor as Charles V and Wolsey, in order to curry favour, supported him against France. The emperor agreed, in return, to put forward Wolsey as a candidate for the Papacy when the occasion arose. But when the moment came he conveniently forgot his promise. No doubt he thought that Wolsey was already powerful enough, and he did not wish to see the ambitious Englishman controlling the wealth and influence of the Catholic Church.

Wolsey was bitterly disappointed and, in his anger, allied with the king of France against the emperor. But he had badly

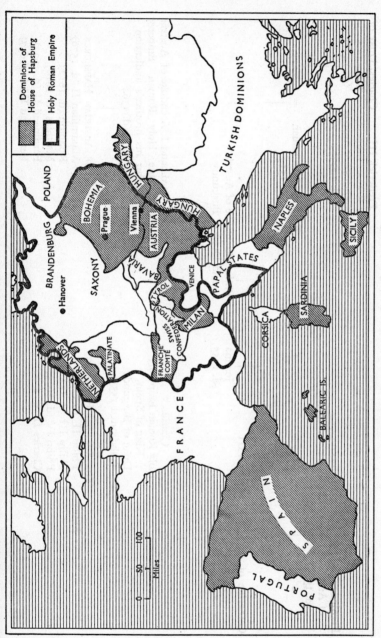

EUROPE IN MID-SIXTEENTH CENTURY

Legend:
Dominions of House of Hapsburg
Holy Roman Empire

Labels on map:
TURKISH DOMINIONS
POLAND
BRANDENBURG
Hanover
SAXONY
BOHEMIA
Prague
HUNGARY
Vienna
AUSTRIA
BAVARIA
TYROL
SWISS CONFEDERATION
VENICE
MILAN
PAPAL STATES
NAPLES
SICILY
SARDINIA
CORSICA
BALEARIC IS.
FRANCE
PALATINATE
FRANCHE COMTÉ
NETHERLANDS
SPAIN
PORTUGAL

Miles
0   50   100

TABLE V. *The Hapsburg Dynasty*

Ferdinand, King of Aragon (d. 1516) = Isabella, Queen of Castile (d. 1504)

Frederick III, Holy Roman Emperor and Archduke of Austria (d. 1493) ... Charles, Duke of Burgundy (d. 1477)

Emperor Maximilian (d. 1519) = Mary

Catherine of Aragon = HENRY VIII

Joanna (d. 1555) = Philip, Archduke of Austria and Duke of Burgundy (d. 1506)

Charles V, Holy Roman Emperor, King of Spain, Duke of Burgundy (abdicated 1555)

Ferdinand I, Archduke of Austria, became Holy Roman Emperor after his brother's abdication (d. 1564)

THE SPANISH HAPSBURGS
MARY I = Philip II (d. 1598)
Philip III (d. 1621)
Philip IV (d. 1665)
Charles II (d. 1700)

THE AUSTRIAN HAPSBURGS
Maximilian II (d. 1576)
Rudolph (d. 1612)
Matthias (d. 1619)
Ferdinand II (d. 1637)
Ferdinand III (d. 1657)

miscalculated. When the opposing armies met at Landriano in June 1529 the emperor was victorious.

The French defeat was a personal blow for Wolsey, since, at the very moment when he had made an enemy of Charles, he desperately needed his help. Henry VIII had been married for twenty years to Charles's aunt, Catherine of Aragon. The marriage had been quite happy and Catherine had borne the king a daughter, Mary, but she had failed to present him with a son. On the last occasion when a woman had come to the throne the country had been torn by civil war, and as Henry grew older he felt that the problem of who was to succeed him must be settled beyond all question. He also had genuine doubts about the validity of his marriage, since Catherine had been previously married to his brother Arthur, and special Papal permission had been necessary to set aside the law of the Church that a man may not marry his brother's widow. Now God seemed to have cursed this doubtful union by withholding a male heir, and Henry convinced himself that he had never been really married. In that case he was free to look for a wife, and his eyes had already lighted on 'the fresh and young Anne Boleyn'. His desire for her, added to his need for a son, determined him to put an end to his union with Catherine.

What one pope had done only another pope could undo. But Pope Clement VII was in the hands of Charles V, whose troops had occupied Rome, and there was little chance of the emperor agreeing to a proposal so humiliating and insulting to his own family. Henry did not at first anticipate difficulty. He was a loyal son of the Church and had been rewarded by an earlier pope with the title 'Defender of the Faith'. When his request to have his marriage annulled reached Clement VII, Landriano had not been fought and the pope met Henry's wishes to the extent of sending Cardinal Campeggio to England to hold a court in which the 'king's great matter' could be settled. The court opened at Blackfriars on the last day of May 1529. But three weeks later, on the Continent, the French armies were shattered and Charles became undisputed master of Italy. The pope could not afford to quarrel with the victor of Landriano. Campeggio was ordered to return, and the pope recalled the case to Rome, for his own consideration.

Wolsey's long rule was now nearing its close. He had served the king faithfully, but gratitude was not one of Henry's virtues. His servants were there to serve him and when they failed they must go. The king was now determined to be ruler in fact as well as in name, and he had no further use for the cardinal. Wolsey was, in any case, unpopular. He had lived regally in his London house at York Place and in the palace he had built for himself beside the Thames at Hampton. When he made a public appearance he was preceded by 'noblemen and gentlemen of his own family [i.e. household] . . . with two great crosses of silver borne before him; with also two great pillars of silver, and his pursuivant at arms with a great mace of silver gilt. Then his gentlemen ushers cried and said "On, my lords and masters, on before. Make way for my Lord's Grace"'. Such pride had angered the nobles, who never forgave Wolsey his low birth, and although there were many poorer men who had cause to remember him well, the poor could be of no use to him now. The king dismissed him from the chancellorship in October 1529 and Wolsey, to escape his master's anger, went north to visit, for the first time in fifteen years, his diocese of York. From there the king summoned him to London to face charges of treason. The cavalcade wound its way slowly south again but got no farther than Leicester, for there a greater judgment intervened and Wolsey was called to meet his God. He died, if we can believe his servant Cavendish, regretting his wasted years of royal service and reflecting that 'if I had served God as diligently as I have done the king, He would not have given me over in my grey hairs'.

Henry was now free to get his own way by bullying the pope or, if necessary, breaking with him altogether. He was in a strong position, because the Papacy was no longer the unchallenged spiritual authority it had once been. Its luxury and worldliness drove Martin Luther to make his famous protest in 1515, and from that action, small enough in itself, sprang the Reformation,[1] the movement of protest against the abuses in the Church that was to split Christian Europe into two parts – one Roman Catholic; the other called Protestant – and to bring to an end the supremacy of the pope in England, Holland and much of northern Germany and Scandinavia.

The Reformation spread rapidly through western Europe, although in countries where the ruler was Roman Catholic those who were in sympathy with it had to tread carefully. In England,

[1] See page 227.

Cambridge and London were the centres from which these new and revolutionary ideas spread throughout the whole country, and in many places they met with swift agreement. The English were not particularly interested in questions of theology but they had little love for the pope or for his English representatives. If the popes lived like kings, the bishops lived like princes. In England the Archbishops of Canterbury and York drew about £3,000 a year from their vast estates, and the seventeen bishops under them had between £1,000 and £2,500 a year to live on – this at a time when the average wage of a labourer was threepence a day. With such rewards to tempt them it is not surprising that many men made the Church a career, to get what they could out of it, as Wolsey had done. If successful, they held many posts simultaneously, and paid subordinates a small wage to do their work for them, while they spent their time at the king's court. Wolsey, who 'drew the revenues and neglected the duties of Archbishop of York, Bishop of Durham, and Abbot of St Albans',[1] was the greatest offender, but the others followed him at a distance.

Pluralism (the holding of more than one office) and non-residence were the vices of the Church at all levels, not simply among the bishops. At the other end of the scale the parish priest was poorly paid and lived like a labourer. Among this group of men there were many who were true servants of God, but the majority were no more intelligent and no more learned than the peasants they were supposed to teach and guide.

All over England could be found men who professed to serve God but were more concerned in filling their pockets with gold. The greed of the Church aroused the anger of the people. When, in 1514, the baby son of Richard Hunne, a London tailor, died, the priest demanded the linen sheet in which the baby had been wrapped at his baptism as payment for the funeral. Hunne refused to give it, was imprisoned, and later found murdered in his cell. The Bishop of London was called on to surrender his officers, since they were responsible for Hunne's death, but he refused, pleading that the citizens were so hostile to the Church 'that they will cast and condemn my clerk, though he were as innocent as Abel'.

It was this Church, rich and in some places rotten, controlled

[1] Trevelyan: *Social History* (Longmans), chapter 4.

by a distant and unloved pope, which Henry decided to fight to obtain the wife, and perhaps the son, he so badly wanted. He hoped to make the pope change his mind and annul the royal marriage, by threatening to cut down and if necessary destroy papal power in England. To make sure of the support of the middle classes he summoned the Reformation Parliament, which met in 1529 and over the next seven years passed a series of acts destroying the authority of the pope in England. The clergy were attacked first of all and accused of breaking the law by recognizing Wolsey's authority, derived as it was from a foreign ruler. The charge was preposterous but it served its purpose of reminding the clergy that they were at Henry's mercy, and he emphasized the point by fining them £100,000 for the offence. The next step was to stop the trickle of money from England to Rome, and in 1532 an act provisionally suspended the payment to the pope of Annates – the first year's income of newly appointed bishops. It might have been this threat, or simply a desire to show good will where he could, that persuaded the pope to accept Henry's nominee for the Archbishopric of Canterbury, since Warham, the previous archbishop, had just died. This most important post was given to Thomas Cranmer, a priest who had come into contact with the new ideas of the Reformation while at Cambridge, and had attracted the king's attention by speaking in favour of his marriage policy.

Clement VII did not want a break with England, but he was virtually a prisoner of the emperor, and could not risk annulling Henry's marriage, even if he had thought it right to do so. Henry therefore took the decisive step of ordering his new archbishop to marry him to Anne Boleyn. To prevent Catherine from appealing to Rome, an act was passed making the king the final judge in all cases, and declaring that 'this realm of England is an Empire' whose king is appointed by God and is not responsible 'to any foreign princes or potentates of the world'. Cranmer had then merely to reopen the king's case against Catherine, declare the marriage annulled, and recognize the new union. In June 1533 Anne Boleyn was crowned queen, and three months later she gave birth to a child. It was a girl, and she was called Elizabeth. Henry had not been given the son he longed for, but this did not encourage him to abandon his new policies. The end of Roman leadership of the Church in this country was marked by the Act of Supremacy of 1534, in which 'the King's Majesty [was] justly and rightfully [held] to be the Supreme Head of the Church of England'.

Henry's careful use of Parliament had damped down opposition. A few far-seeing men like Erasmus's friends, Thomas More – who asked only to be left at peace with his wife and family in their riverside home at Chelsea – and John Fisher, Bishop of Rochester, refused to accept the king as Supreme Head, and were executed. The reform for which they had worked and prayed had come to pass, but at a price that they could never accept. Their place in the royal councils was taken by Thomas Cromwell, son of a Putney blacksmith, who used all his cold talents in the king's service, and created an administration that ran like a well-oiled machine.

By 1536 the break with Rome was complete, but the independent Church of England was to remain Catholic in its doctrines. Henry VIII, like most educated men of the day, had been influenced by the new learning, but he only wished to change or destroy what actually stood in his way. The Act of Six Articles of 1539 told the people of England what they must believe, and there was no trace of Protestantism in it. Where matters of belief, as opposed to matters of church government, were concerned, Henry remained conservative, and shortly before his death he expressed his grief at the way in which 'that most precious jewel, the word of God, is disputed, rhymed, sung, and jangled in every Alehouse and Tavern'. Henry's desire was that the Church should stick to its established forms of service and worship, and in this, as in so many other cases, what the king willed came to pass.

The Dissolution of the Monasteries

1536-1539

CROMWELL and the king between them planned the destruction of the monasteries, the last possible stronghold of Papal power in England. The great days of the abbeys were past. They, like the papacy, had grown rich and decayed, and though they sheltered many devout men and women, the number of the good was greatly outweighed by the number of the idle and dissolute. The Act of Supremacy had declared the king to be Head of the English Church, and one of his first actions was to make Cromwell his deputy by appointing him Vicar-General. Cromwell promptly nominated commissioners to visit the monasteries and report on them. This was largely a matter of form, since the verdict had already been decided, and the men appointed for this unsavoury task were not chosen for their honesty or independence of mind. Their reports were damning, but although they painted too black a picture, they confirmed the impression of monastic decline given by the reports of ecclesiastical visitors in the century and a half since the Black Death. Occasional efforts had been made to stop the rot, and Wolsey, for instance, had suppressed twenty-one monasteries, using their wealth to endow his new colleges at Oxford and Ipswich. Henry took this as a pattern for his much more ruthless and less justified attack on the monasteries. In 1536 nearly four hundred of the smaller ones, with endowments worth less than £200 a year, were dissolved by act of Parliament on the nominal grounds that 'manifest sin, vicious, carnal and abominable living, is daily used and committed amongst' them.

The greater monasteries were, for the moment, spared, and indeed praised by the act as places 'wherein, thanks be to God, religion is right well kept and observed'. The king found it

convenient to make this assumption that an annual income of over
£200 promoted holier living, for he wished to destroy the monasteries in two stages. To have dissolved them all at one blow might
have aroused violent opposition, and in any case the transfer of
lands was an enormous task that required time unless the government departments set up to deal with it were to be choked. The
real reason for the destruction of the monasteries was their wealth.
Their total estates amounted to perhaps one-sixth of all the
cultivated land in England, and they had untold riches in plate,
jewels and robes. This was too great a temptation for the king.
He had inherited a fortune at his accession, but the campaigns in
France had eaten up his revenues and he was in urgent need of
money.

Into his empty treasury the wealth of the smaller monasteries
now poured, and over the next three years (1536–9) the larger
houses, too big to swallow in one mouthful, were bullied into
piecemeal surrender. Only in the north of England did opposition
to royal policy flare into the revolt called the Pilgrimage of Grace.
In October 1536 a riot at Louth sparked off rebellion in Lincolnshire, and this rapidly spread to Yorkshire, where a country
gentleman, Robert Aske, gathered his 'pilgrims' around him, and
called on the king to surrender Cromwell and dissolve no more
monasteries. The situation was dangerous for Henry, since he had
no standing army and needed time before forces could be raised
from the southern counties. But if the crown was unprepared, so
were the rebels. They had no clear plan of campaign, and while
trying to force Henry to change his mind they professed a genuine
loyalty to him. This reverence for their king betrayed them. When
Henry offered free pardon and a consideration of their demands,
Aske, tearing off his emblem of the five wounds of Christ, declared
that he would 'wear no badge or sign but the badge of our
sovereign lord', and persuaded his followers to return to their
homes.

Henry was never the man to waste time on keeping promises
when the authority of the crown was at stake. Now that the rebels
had disbanded, their leaders were hunted down. Aske was hanged
in chains at York, and over two hundred of his followers were
executed. By the middle of 1537 the Pilgrimage of Grace was no
more than a memory, and the old council in the north was replaced

by a new and much stronger one, to bring that wild and remote area under closer royal control.

The king and his Vicar-General were now free to complete the second stage of their plans. The surviving monasteries were called on to surrender, and the Abbot of Glastonbury, who seems to have contemplated resistance, was accused of treason and hanged in front of his own gatehouse as a reminder to those who dared oppose the royal will. In 1539 the Second Act of Dissolution, announcing that the monasteries had 'of their own free and voluntary minds, good wills, and assents, without constraint, coercion, or compulsion of any manner of person or persons' liquidated themselves, formally transferred their property to the crown. On 23 March 1540 the last great abbey, at Waltham, surrendered, and the destruction of the monasteries was accomplished.

In many ways the monasteries deserved their end. Not all were corrupt, it is true: the Carthusian houses, in particular, were models of their kind. But the majority had declined in numbers and enthusiasm, and in the new national state that Henry and Cromwell were creating there was no room for powerful institutions more or less outside royal control. The monasteries had produced no great scholar during the last century of their existence, and their libraries, so rich in treasures of the past, had not recently been added to. Almsgiving often meant little more than distributing free food to lazy hangers-on, and the duty of providing hospitality, while it meant much in the North where distances were great and inns scarce, had elsewhere swamped the monastic houses with outsiders who brought with them a very different set of values from that which was supposed to prevail within the cloister. The monasteries had decayed, and wealthy men were leaving their riches to found schools, hospitals and almshouses, rather than to swell monastic revenues. Henry chose to cut out this cancer, but all was not gain, for in doing so he destroyed many living cells. A society like that of Tudor England, dominated by men who thought only of money and power, needed a reminder of other values. If reform, rather than destruction, had been Henry's real object, the monasteries might once again have taken their place in society as spiritual centres where a holy life could be lived, remote from the bustle of the world, and where corporate prayers could be offered for the good of mankind.

The ejected monks, some ten thousand in number, were well treated. They were given pensions which were reasonably adequate and regularly paid, and many were found positions in the Church. The opportunity was taken to put into effect a scheme of Wolsey's for breaking up the vast bishoprics of Lichfield and Lincoln, which were too big to be effective. This was done by creating six new sees, of which five – Oxford, Chester, Gloucester, Bristol and Peterborough – survive to this day.

Movable property such as plate and jewels went straight into the royal coffers, and the richly ornamented shrines of saints were stripped of their treasures. The valuable libraries were broken up and dispersed, and many irreplaceable books were lost in the process. Lands were transferred to the crown, but did not remain in the king's hands for long. If Henry had kept all these estates, and been content with drawing rents from them, he would have made the crown so rich that it might have dispensed with Parliament and become as absolute as some of the continental monarchies. But royal finances were in a desperate state, and as fast as the monastic lands were transferred to the crown they were sold for ready cash. Henry managed to keep enough to increase his income by about £40,000 a year, but he sold property worth three-quarters of a million.

The biggest individual buyers were noblemen. A few were descendants of the medieval barons: the majority, however, were newly ennobled men who had risen to power and wealth by serving the crown, for Henry continued his father's policy and, as the Earl of Surrey bitterly remarked, 'would deny the noble blood around him, and employ none but mean creatures'. These big buyers were wealthy men who either had ready cash available, or could mortgage some of their actual property to add to their future estates. Officers of the royal household, and officials who had been directly involved in the land transfer, also bought heavily, and some were lucky enough to be given land by the crown as a gift or reward. The great bulk of monastic property, however, went not to the few big buyers, but to the mass of smaller men. Prominent among these were the squires or gentry whose memorials are to be seen in every parish church, and whose control of local life was strengthened by their new estates. Land, in Tudor England, meant power and prestige, for landholders had public duties thrust upon them.

When the crown wanted anything done – an inquiry into enclosures, for instance, or a survey of weights and measures – it called on the gentry, and these smaller property-owners were proud to serve at their own expense. From their number were chosen the Justices of the Peace, the most important men in the county. They met in Petty and Quarter Sessions, to deal with lawbreakers and supervise the whole business of local government within their areas. They owed their recent wealth to the king, and were staunch defenders of the new order, but in a period of poor communications they were free from close royal control, and their estates gave them a sense of independence. It pleased them to serve the crown, but only so long as the crown served their own interests. The king commanded and they obeyed; but it was upon their loyalty that the monarchy depended.

The power that land brought with it attracted buyers from outside the ranks of those who were already landowners. Rich merchants, lawyers, and doctors all bought monastic estates, and began the process of turning themselves into country gentlemen. Many an estate still bears the name of abbey, grange or priory, to betray its monastic origin, and often the house will include remains of the monks' building. Monasteries, however, are not ideal as country houses, and the new owners were usually content either to use only a part of the building and let the rest rot, or to pillage it of lead and stone to build a new house for themselves. Only the roofless walls would then remain, 'bare ruined choirs' gradually crumbling under wind and weather. Many survive to this day, beautiful in their decay, like Fountains, Rievaulx and Tintern. Others have disappeared, sharing the fate of the great shrine at Walsingham:

> Level, level with the ground
> The towers do lie,
> Which with their golden glittering tops
> Pierced once to the sky.

The monks had been good farmers, but conservative in their methods. Many of the new owners ran their estates like a business, invested their money in overseas trade, and paid the king to appoint them to some official position where they could draw large sums of money in return for very little work. There was more than a touch of ruthlessness about these men. The Tudor gentry were breaking away from the limitations which tradition and the Church had imposed upon them. They were not all Protestants, by any means, but whereas the Catholic Church had taught that the person who devoted his life to money-making was risking damnation, the newly rich of the sixteenth century came nearer to believing that prosperity was a sign of God's blessing, and that poverty was sinful. It was a convenient belief for the wealthy, but the wealth of the property-owners was gained at the expense of the poor and unemployed.

The problem of unemployment became acute in the sixteenth century. Trade was expanding but so was population, and the wealth of the merchants was gained at the expense of the lower classes. The end of the long wars at home and abroad released a large number of demobilized soldiers, but although many were absorbed by the cloth trade and new industries, many more were unemployed. Henry VII had put down the private armies in which they could otherwise have enlisted, and farmers could not afford to employ more men on their estates. Landowners were themselves in difficulties because of rising prices, and many resorted to rack-renting – that is, raising the rents they demanded from their tenants, to screw every penny out of them. If the poor tenant could not pay, the landlord could easily find someone to take his place, or he would enclose his land with a fence or hedge, and turn it over to sheep.

Not all enclosures were harmful. The medieval strip system had wasted much good land, and given no opportunity for experiment. If the lord of the manor collected the scattered strips together and enclosed them, he was doing a public service, since every peasant now farmed a single larger holding instead of several smaller ones. But enclosure for sheep-farming caused great hardship. It had obvious advantages from the lord's point of view, since one or two shepherds were all the men he needed to look after his flocks, and wool fetched a high price. For the peasants, however, it meant disaster. They could appeal to the royal courts for protection, but these were distant and expensive remedies, especially for poor, ignorant men. Many peasants were turned out on the roads to beg, steal or die, while their cottages were left, like the monasteries, to rot. 'Where forty persons had their livings,' wrote a contemporary pamphleteer, 'now one man and his shepherd hath all.'

The king's ministers tried to stop enclosure for sheep-farming. They knew that unemployed and starving men are fuel for rebellion, and they depended upon the peasants for a supply of infantry, especially archers, in case of war. The first act of Parliament against enclosures came in 1489 and was followed by another in 1515, ordering that land which had been given over to sheep should be turned back to the plough. Wolsey sent out committees in 1517 to make sure that the law was enforced. Offenders were brought before him in the court of Chancery, and his firmness in dealing with them was one of the reasons why the property-owners hated the cardinal-chancellor, and rejoiced at his fall. The government's policy did not change after Wolsey. But enclosure went on steadily and the crown was not strong enough to prevent it since it had no police, and depended for the enforcement of its policy on the country gentry – the very people who were foremost in carrying out enclosures. The marvel is that the government managed to check it at all.

The area most affected by enclosure was the midland part of England, to the north of London, and even there a great deal of land was left for the eighteenth-century landlords to fence. But about one-third of the villages in this area seem to have undergone some enclosure, and in an agricultural society, set in the unchanging routine of the seasons, any violent change has an effect out of all proportion to the numbers involved. Writers and statesmen knew from their own experience that the roads were infested with starving, desperate men, and a flood of pamphlets awakened the public conscience in a way that would have been impossible before the invention of the printing-press.

The king and his ministers could not ignore the problem of the homeless tramps. Parliament attempted to provide a remedy. Earlier legislation had shown little understanding of the real nature of the problem, but an act of 1531 drew an important distinction between those who could work, and those who, through age or illness, were unable to do so. The enfeebled were to be licensed to beg; the idle poor were to be treated with a ruthlessness typical of Tudor England, 'tied to the end of a cart naked and be beaten with whips . . . till their body be bloody', and then

returned to their native place 'to labour like as a true man oweth
to do'.

The date of this act is significant, since it comes five years before
the Dissolution of the Monasteries, and shows that the end of
monastic almsgiving, while it blocked one source of relief for
poverty, did not cause the problem. Another attempt was made in
Henry VIII's reign to deal with the problem of the poor when,
under the influence of Cromwell, a comprehensive scheme of relief
was drawn up. Only a small part of this reached the statute book,
in 1536, but it at least established the principle that every parish
should be responsible for its more unfortunate members, and
should 'succour, find, and keep all and every of the same poor
people by way of voluntary or charitable alms . . . in such wise as
none of them of very necessity shall be compelled to wander idly'.

CHAPTER 26

The Price Rise and Parliament

1539-1547

HENRY VIII's reign saw a remarkable revival in the fortunes of Parliament. His father had summoned it rarely, and Wolsey only used Parliament as a last resort when he had to find money to pay for the king's wars. This institution, which was to make possible the growth of political liberty and democratic government throughout the western world, might have died a natural death, or been revived only in moments of national emergency, like its French counterpart. It was saved and given new life by the Price Revolution and the Reformation.

Prices started rising in the sixteenth century because the amount of money in circulation increased, without any parallel increase in the amount of goods produced. There was inflation – too much money chasing too few goods. Increased production in the German silver-mines started a trickle of new coins, but the trickle swelled to a flood after 1540 when precious metals from the Spanish dominions in South America began to pour into Europe at an ever-increasing rate. Prices rocketed in Spain, and as the bullion rapidly circulated throughout Europe it brought inflation with it. In England it drove the landowners to exploit their estates by enclosing and rack-renting, but the king had an example to set and the welfare of his people to consider, and could not act in this ruthless manner. Royal income went up slowly, but rising prices sent expenditure soaring. Henry VII's good work in restoring royal finances was gradually undone, and the crown was left once more on the road to poverty and weakness. Henry VIII staved off bankruptcy by grabbing the monasteries, but by 1544 he was in such desperate financial straits that he started to debase the currency. This meant that when coins were minted a proportion of base metal was added to the gold or silver. The king made a short-term profit, for he got a larger number of coins out of the same amount of precious metal. But in the long run he suffered, because as the new coins circulated, their value dropped and inflation became yet more severe.

The crown's finances, weakened by inflation, were strained to breaking-point by war. The pope had excommunicated the unrepentant Henry in 1535, and four years later called on the Catholic princes of France and the Empire to settle their differences and combine to invade England. Henry prepared to defend himself. A navy and army were raised and held in readiness, and a chain of artillery forts (most of which, like Camber, in Sussex, survive) was constructed along the south coast. He also looked for new allies, by way of a new wife. Catherine of Aragon had died in January 1536, and four months later Anne Boleyn, who had produced a daughter, Elizabeth, instead of the longed-for male heir, was sent to the block for infidelity. The king then married Jane Seymour, and this union was crowned with success when a boy-prince, Edward, was born in October 1537. The queen, however, died in giving birth, and Henry was now free to marry again. The Protestant German princes were obvious allies, and Cromwell chose for him Anne, sister of the Duke of Cleves.

Fortunately for Henry, France and the Empire began to fall out again, and both sides bid for his support. He opted for the emperor, since he still hoped to become another Henry V by leading the English armies to triumph in France. It was a futile and expensive ambition. The campaign of 1544 resulted in the capture of Boulogne, but the total cost of the war was over two million pounds and the king had to turn to Parliament for assistance.

One of Parliament's main functions was to vote the king taxes when he ran short of money. But M.P.s knew that the taxes they voted would have to be paid by themselves, and they often lost their tempers in haggling over the amount. Wolsey had run foul of the Commons when, in 1523, he had demanded a tax of four shillings in the pound to pay for the French campaigns, and although he went down in person to hector them, he was met with a 'marvellous obstinate silence'. Wolsey could try to browbeat Parliament, but after his fall that institution became far more powerful. Henry realized that the attack upon the Church would be a tricky and dangerous operation, and must be managed by a body whose orders could not be challenged. Parliament was such a body, since it alone made statute law, against which there was, and is, no appeal. Parliament represented the nation – king, lords and commons knit into a single unit – and Henry was stating no more than the accepted truth when he told members that 'we at no time stand so highly in our estate royal as in the time of Parliament', for in that body 'we as head and you as members are conjoined'.

The Reformation Parliament, with its eight sessions spread over seven years, was vastly different from the short-lived assemblies which had preceded it. Members had time to get to know each other and to build up an idea of Parliament as something greater than themselves. They claimed, as members, privileges like freedom from arrest and freedom of speech. These were not clearly defined, but the Commons became deeply attached to their privileges, since they were evidence of the authority and greatness of the so-called 'lower' house. Henry was pleased to foster the pride of the Commons because they gave him such loyal support. So great was his power that it never occurred to him that privileges which he granted to the House might one day be used as weapons against his successors. When Henry wrote to the pope that 'discussions in the English Parliament are free and unrestricted, and the crown has no power to limit their debate or to control the votes of members' he was not so much telling a lie as leaving out part of the truth. Any member who dared oppose royal policy risked the wrath of the king, but only a few cared strongly enough to take that risk. Henry encouraged Parliament to assert its privileges because he was confident that in increasing the authority of Parliament he was adding to his own.

Cromwell was the link between the king and the two Houses. He had been a youthful member of the 1523 Parliament which had rebuffed Wolsey, and the lesson was not lost on him. 'I and others of your grace's council,' he told Henry, 'do study and employ ourselves daily upon those affairs that concern your grace's Parliament.' He oiled the wheels of government by making sure that bills were carefully drafted before being presented to either of the two Houses, and that royal officials, such as the Speaker and Privy Councillors, were well briefed. He watched over by-elections, using royal influence where he could to encourage the return of suitable members. This did not mean that Parliament was a servile body. The property-owners who sat in the Lords and Commons were men of substance, not easily to be bullied. They had a will of their own, as was shown when they rejected the first draft of one statute and held up another for five years before reluctantly letting it pass in an amended form. But these were exceptions, and in general, relations between king and Parliament were good because they shared a common interest. The first two Tudors had created a national state in which all loyalty and all authority was focused on the crown. The property-owners accepted this because it satisfied their national pride, gave them a share of the profits, and left them in peace to manage their estates.

For the efficiency of this government Cromwell was largely responsible. He created a civil service – primitive by our standards, remarkably efficient by those of the sixteenth century – out of the ramshackle royal household. Six departments, each with its own staff, watched over the royal finances, and were in turn supervised by the king's chief advisers whom Cromwell drew together in a body called the Privy Council. Co-ordinating all the activities of government was Cromwell himself, the layman-secretary who had replaced the chancellor-bishops of the medieval past, and who foreshadowed the Secretaries of State and Cabinet ministers of today.

He met the end that was frequently reserved for those who served the crown faithfully. Henry quickly tired of his unattractive wife, Anne of Cleves. He was now in love with Catherine Howard. She came from a great Catholic family, and Henry's desire for her reinforced his natural conservatism in religious matters. This decided Cromwell's fate, for he was a reformer, protestantly inclined, who had led the attack on images and relics in his Injunctions of 1536, and two years later had ordered a copy of the Bible in English to be set up in every church, with instructions that parish priests were to 'provoke, stir, and exhort every person to read the same as that which is the very lively word of God'. Cromwell fought hard to keep the king's confidence, and seemed to be succeeding when in April 1540 he was created Earl of Essex. But his enemies were by now too strong for him, and Cromwell found, like his old master Wolsey, that Tudor kings would not tolerate mighty subjects. There was no opposition party for a fallen minister to retire into. Cromwell was accused of treason and condemned without a hearing. Being of base birth he was eligible for a slow and degrading death, but in return for his services the king granted him the privilege of a swift execution. Three months after his elevation to the peerage, he was beheaded at Tyburn.

The king had no chief minister after Cromwell. As he grew older his body swelled, an ulcer in his leg gave him constant pain, and his temper became ungovernable. His fifth wife, Catherine Howard, accused of misconduct, soon followed Cromwell to the block, and the star of the reforming, Protestant section moved into the ascendant. Henry's last wife, Catherine Parr, whom he married in 1543, was said to be sympathetic to the new religion, and when Henry came to nominate a regency council for his young son, the reformers were in the majority. In his closing years the king turned increasingly towards his archbishop, Thomas Cranmer, who was a conservative reformer, recognizing the need for change, but anxious to preserve what was best in the liturgies and customs of the Church. This was very close to Henry's own attitude, and the friendship between the two men lasted until the king's death. When, in January 1547, Henry's bloated body came to the end of its strength, it was for Cranmer that he sent, and he died with his hand in the archbishop's. It was a fitting symbol, for Henry had created an independent Anglican Church, and joined it indissolubly to the crown. This alone was an astonishing achievement, but he had done more: he had enforced law and order in the remotest parts of his kingdom, and established the Tudor dynasty so firmly on the throne that it was not shaken even by the succession of a young boy and two women. Henry VIII had the Norman qualities of ruthlessness, courage, and efficiency; a disagreeable man, but a great ruler.

CHAPTER 27

Somerset and Northumberland

1547-1553

THE REFORMATION in Europe had started as a protest against abuses in the Roman Catholic Church, but as the movement expanded it developed doctrines of its own. The chief point of difference between Catholic and Protestant concerned the nature of the Mass, or Holy Communion. Catholics believed that at the moment of consecration the bread and wine were changed into the body and blood of Christ, not in any way which could be detected by the human senses, but in their real nature or substance. Since God was Himself present under the form of bread and wine, communion with Him was the most important of the Church's services, and the priest who accomplished this miracle was a man chosen by divine grace. By virtue of his holy office he was also empowered to listen to the confession of sins, impose penance, and grant absolution. For a man so chosen, marriage was out of the question since his life was dedicated to God, and any earthly ties might interfere with the task for which he had been appointed.

Protestants did not accept this lofty view of the Mass and of the priesthood. Although beliefs varied from sect to sect, most Protestants regarded the communion as a service of remembrance, a reminder of God rather than an actual contact with Him. For them, the priest was a man like any other, not a miracle-worker but an officer of the Church which existed to keep alive and spread the truths of religion. Preaching was therefore one of his most important functions, and since he held no special authority to release men from the burden of their sins, there was no need for him to listen to their confessions. The Protestant saw no reason why a priest should not be married, if he wished to be, like anyone else. He could assist men to seek salvation, but his office alone gave him

253

no supernatural powers. Neither was he the sole guardian of God's word, since Protestants held services in their native language, not in Latin, and had the Bible translated and made freely available for all to read and interpret. The more extreme Protestants, such as the followers of John Calvin, the French reformer, declared that priests were unnecessary because God, the all-powerful, had decided every man's fate for better or for worse, before he was born, and that no amount of good works could change this iron decree. This doctrine of predestination did not, however, mean that men could behave as badly as they liked as long as they were saved, for good living was a sign of salvation, and the evil liver was assumed to be damned.

At Henry VIII's death, the English Church was Catholic in its doctrines, though the influence of the reformers could be seen in such novelties as the English Bible, and the removal of images. The king was alarmed at the spread of new ideas, and in 1539 he had appeared personally before the House of Lords to argue in favour of the Statute of Six Articles, which laid down the Catholic doctrines of the Anglican Church, and declared that 'in the most blessed Sacrament of the Altar, by the strength and efficacy of Christ's mighty word, it being spoken by the priest, is present really under the form of bread and wine, the natural body and blood of our Saviour Jesu Christ'. The English Church was committed to this Catholic position for the remainder of Henry's reign, and although the penalties provided for those who did not conform were intended more as a threat than for use, there were occasional executions. Three heretics were burnt at Windsor in 1543, and only a royal pardon saved the composer John Marbeck, whose music is still one of the delights of English church services.

Henry was developing a more Protestant attitude in his closing years, but died before he could put his new ideas into effect. He left a council of regency to rule in the name of his nine-year-old son, but the council's first act was to appoint one of its own number, Edward Seymour, the king's uncle, as Protector of the realm. Seymour, now created Duke of Somerset, was the real ruler of England for the next three years. He was a proud man, greedy for money, but his tolerance in religion and his genuine desire for social justice make him one of the more attractive figures of the sixteenth century. He repealed the Statute of Six Articles, and during his protectorate no-one was tortured or executed on a charge of heresy.

As far as his own views went, he seems to have been inclined towards Protestantism. He was certainly willing to make a profit by ridding the Anglican Church of Catholic survivals. In 1545 plans had been drawn up, but not put into effect, for the dissolution of chantries, the many small foundations which existed to pray for the souls of their benefactors, and which used their funds to maintain schools, hospitals, and other charitable institutions. Somerset now carried out these plans, and the wealth of the chantries was poured into the royal treasury. The Protector made a big profit, building Somerset House out of the proceeds, and many members of the council managed to divert some of the riches into their private pockets. A few schools were allowed to survive. A few more, the so-called King Edward VI Grammar Schools, were founded. But these half-hearted attempts to spend the money usefully could not conceal the fact that most of it was used simply to make rich men richer.

The repeal of the heresy laws opened the ports to reformers, and they flocked in from Protestant centres all over Europe. Under their influence religious services were purged of Catholic traces, but there was such variety that the Anglican Church seemed in danger of breaking up into independent congregations, each with its own form of worship. The king, as head of the Church, was responsible for seeing that all his subjects worshipped in the same manner. Since Church and State were so closely linked, experiments in religion had to be checked for fear they might lead to experiments in government – i.e. rebellion. Accordingly, in 1549, an Act of Uniformity was passed, ordering that one form of service, and one only, should be permitted in English churches. This form was set out in the first prayer book, for which Cranmer was largely responsible. Based on its Catholic predecessors, it was designed to give as little offence as possible. The book was in English, a major concession to the reformers, but in those parts, such as the communion service, over which dispute was most likely to arise, Cranmer's magnificent prose was carefully vague.

Even so the book aroused much criticism. Bishop Gardiner of Winchester, leader of the Catholic party in the Church, was persuaded to accept it, and for this reason it became unacceptable to the Protestants, who attacked it as popish. Yet to many Catholics it seemed a mockery. The book was first used on Whit-Sunday, 1549, but at Sampford Courtenay, in Devon, the villagers were so furious that on the Monday they forced the priest to put on his vestments and celebrate the Latin Mass. Disturbances quickly spread until the whole of the West Country was in open rebellion, demanding the restoration of the old religion and the abolition of the new prayer book, which they compared to 'a Christmas game'. Somerset was prepared to treat the rebels leniently. 'Content yourselves, good people,' he told them. 'Do not with this rage and fury drive yourselves to the sword, your wives and children to famine and hunger.' But other members of the council did not look kindly upon disorder, and the rebels were suppressed with a heavy hand.

The Western Rebellion was shortly to be followed by a more serious one in Norfolk, but this sprang from economic, rather than religious, discontent. Prices were still rising, and Somerset made matters worse by again debasing the coinage. Property-owners had to make the most out of their estates, and the obvious solution was to enclose their land and turn it over to sheep, regardless of the fate of the peasants. But an influential group of men was reacting against the prevailing get-rich-quick attitude, and was urging the Protector to plan for the general good, or, to use their own expression, the common weal. The leaders of this group were Hugh Latimer, one of the most popular and effective preachers of the day, and John Hales. Under their influence Somerset in 1549 appointed commissions to inquire into enclosures. Hales sat on the Midland one, and its work was conscientiously done. The peasants, remembering the success of Wolsey's commissions, believed that firm action was at last to be taken to end their distress. The property-owners protested, but Somerset, himself one of the greatest, proudly told them that in spite of 'the devil, private profit, self-love, money, and such like the devil's instruments, it shall go forward'. He spoke too soon, for the enthusiasm of the peasants betrayed him. In Norfolk they rose in rebellion to break down enclosures and establish a more just society. Under the leadership of Robert Ket, a merchant and landowner, they set up a great camp on Mousehold Heath, outside Norwich. Ket and a representative council ruled this extraordinary assembly, some

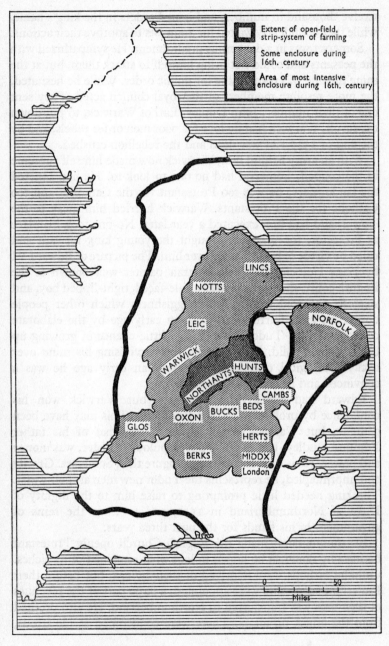

Legend:
- Extent of open-field, strip-system of farming
- Some enclosure during 16th. century
- Area of most intensive enclosure during 16th. century

LINCS

NOTTS

LEIC

NORFOLK

WARWICK

HUNTS

NORTHANTS

CAMBS

BUCKS   BEDS

GLOS   OXON

HERTS

BERKS

MIDDX

London

0   50
Miles

SIXTEENTH-CENTURY ENCLOSURES

twelve thousand in number, and issued orders in the king's name, while they confidently waited for Somerset to approve their actions.

Somerset was in a dangerous predicament. He sympathized with the peasants and could not bring himself to attack them, but at the same time he was responsible for public order. While he hesitated, the more resolute members of the royal council acted. They sent one of their number, John Dudley, Earl of Warwick, to put down the revolt. Warwick had no love for poor men or for rebels, and by the end of 1549 Ket was dead and the rebellion crushed.

With an army behind him, Warwick now made himself supreme in the council. Somerset had no one to look to. He had angered the landowners; he was too Protestant for the Catholics and too Catholic for the Protestants. Warwick hurried him away to the Tower, and had him executed a year later. No-one took his place as Protector, for Warwick brought the young king forward and ruled by virtue of his influence over him. The picture of Edward VI by Hans Holbein, the great portrait painter well known at the English court, shows the king as a pale-faced, tight-lipped boy, and suggests the cold reserve and priggishness which other people noticed in him. Surrounded from an early age by the elaborate ceremony of the Tudor court he had little chance of growing up like a normal child. He took delight in exercising his mind over tricky theological questions, and from an early age he was a convinced and intolerant Protestant.

Edward had never liked Somerset, but Warwick won his confidence by professing to be a Protestant. This may have been genuine, but Warwick's main interest, like that of his father Edmund Dudley, Henry VII's unscrupulous minister, was money and power. He is a far less attractive figure than Somerset. Greedy and unprincipled, he represents the Tudor new men at their worst. The king needed little prompting to raise him to the dignity of Duke of Northumberland in 1551, and to leave the reins of government in his hands for the next three years.

Northumberland made the English Church openly Protestant because by doing so he hoped to loot what remained of its riches. Catholic bishops were deprived of their livings, but before their Protestant successors were appointed, a large part of the revenues of their sees was transferred to Northumberland. He also profited from the attack on altars. These were condemned as idolatrous, and replaced by plain tables: the 'superfluous ornaments' in gold and silver which adorned them were handed over to the crown – and its chief minister. The tide of Protestantism was rising strongly and in 1552 Cranmer produced the second prayer book, which Parliament ordered to be used in place of the first. It was a much more Protestant book, not meant to be acceptable to Catholics. It was followed by the Forty-Two Articles, which defined the doctrines of the Church of England in uncompromisingly Protestant terms.

Northumberland was typical of the new men not only in his attitude to religion but also in his attitude towards social problems. Somerset had at least recognized his responsibility for protecting the peasants from exploitation. Northumberland had no time for such sentiment. Acts against enclosures were repealed, and for the first and last time in the sixteenth century the government came out openly in favour of the enclosing landlord. This was, in a way, a sensible policy, since economic change was bound to come about, and no institution, however powerful, could stem the tide. It was the same realism that encouraged Northumberland to attack inflation by reforming the currency in 1551. What makes him a repulsive character is not so much his policy as his indifference to human suffering. He made no attempt to protect the common people against the religious and economic forces which were breaking up the accepted pattern and the security of their exis-tence. All his sympathy was reserved for himself.

Unluckily for Northumberland's ambitions, Edward VI fell ill in January 1553. Northumberland knew that his power, and indeed his life, depended upon the king, for the heir to the throne was Edward's half-sister Mary, an intolerant Catholic. In desperation he decided to risk a gambler's throw. By working on Edward's Protestantism he persuaded the king to cut out Mary from the succession, and nominate Lady Jane Grey in her place. She was descended from Henry VII, through the female line, and had the significant advantage of being married to Northumberland's son, Guildford Dudley.

When Edward VI died 'of a tough, strong, straining cough' on 6 July 1553, Queen Jane was immediately proclaimed in London. But away in Suffolk, Mary raised her own standard at Framlingham, and although she had little to rely on except her

Tudor birth and the general hatred of Northumberland, these were sufficient. The property-owners had no wish to see the new nobility follow the example of its medieval predecessor and plunge the country into civil war. They rallied to Mary's banner and Northumberland found himself deserted, until he had no choice left but to give himself up. He was arrested and led captive to the Tower of London, to join the unfortunate Lady Jane. From there he came out, a few weeks later, to die on the scaffold, publicly declaring that he was, and had always been, a Catholic.

CHAPTER 28

Queen Mary

1553-1559

QUEEN MARY was Tudor in more than birth. She had her father's stubbornness and his courage. When Edward VI sent his councillors to persuade her to give up the Latin Mass, she had dismissed them with the contemptuous observation that 'you [should] show more favour to me for my father's sake, who made the more part of you out of nothing'. She came to the throne at the age of thirty-seven, a woman of fading charms, but the Venetian ambassador noted that her 'countenance indicates great benignity and clemency, which are not belied by her conduct'. She was, in fact, a kind-hearted, generous woman, with a love of dancing and music. It was the failure of her marriage, and the obstinate Protestantism of her subjects that made her sad and sour.

Mary, being a fervent Roman Catholic, was determined to re-establish papal power in her kingdoms. For this she needed the support of a husband, and the obvious choice, in her eyes, was Philip, son of the Emperor Charles V, the greatest Catholic prince in the world. Mary's choice was far from popular with her people. The English were proud of their independence and did not take kindly to the prospect of a foreign king, particularly one who was renowned for his persecution of heretics. Mary, however, had made up her mind, and when a Parliamentary deputation protested, she told them 'she would choose as God inspired her'.

Before the marriage could take place, there was violent opposition to overcome. Sir Thomas Wyatt, son of one of the finest poets of the sixteenth century, led a rising which broke out in Kent. It was an ill-planned, poorly organized affair, but even so the rebels fought their way into the heart of London before they were overcome. Mary, who had shown her usual courage and rallied the citizens around her, was shocked into anger by the narrowness of her escape. The leaders, and many of their followers, were executed. Lady Jane Grey and her husband, who had so far been spared by Mary's mercy, were now led out to the scaffold. They had not been implicated in the revolt, but their very existence was a threat to the throne, and no Tudor would have tolerated this. Another young woman, perhaps not quite so innocent, also came under the shadow of death, for Elizabeth, the queen's half-sister, was suspected of being in league with Mary's enemies, and was imprisoned in the Tower. Her life hung in the balance. But the lack of any clear evidence, and the fear of a popular rising in her favour, led to her release.

With her enemies defeated or dead, Mary was free to marry, and in July 1554, at a service in Winchester Cathedral, she became Philip's wife. It was an unhappy marriage. Philip was a cold man. He had little love to offer anybody, and none to spare for his doting wife. The match was useful to him politically, but otherwise he had no interest in it, and made haste to escape from England as soon as he decently could. Mary was anxious to love him, and reluctant to admit how little he cared for her. But as the months passed her affection turned to bitterness. She had longed for a child of the marriage, to cherish and to bring up in the Catholic faith as a worthy heir to the throne, but even in this her hopes were disappointed.

The revival of Catholicism in England had already been set on foot by the time of the wedding. The prayer book was abolished, bishops were ordered to restore the old faith, and leading Protestants, English and foreign, were encouraged to flee the country. Those who remained, including Latimer, Bishop Ridley of London and Archbishop Cranmer, were deprived of their sees and imprisoned in the Tower. In November 1554 the new archbishop, Reginald Pole, arrived in England, with authority to act in the pope's name. Pole, the last surviving English cardinal, and a blood-relative of Mary, had been long out of touch with English life. He and Mary shared a fanatical devotion to religion. They would never come to terms with Protestants and regarded mercy as weakness. Both were convinced that it was essential to burn heretics in order to save the souls of the rest of the nation. In 1554 the heresy laws were revived, and in that same year

Parliament swept away all the Acts passed against Rome since 1528, with the exception of those dissolving the monasteries.

The exception is significant, since it shows how independent the Commons could be. It is difficult for us, with our modern ideas of the supremacy of Parliament, to understand why sixteenth-century ones should so meekly have changed their attitude, to suit the whim of the sovereign. In fact there was a good deal of opposition from members, and where their lands were concerned, they stood firm. More than this they could not do without risking rebellion. Most men felt it a religious duty to obey the sovereign, since the Bible declared that 'the powers that be are ordained of God'. Even the bishops did their best to obey, until they were driven into opposition. The Commons were divided in their religious opinions, united only in their devotion to their own interests and the monarchy which preserved them. They were ready to join with the queen in petitioning the pope 'to call us home again into the right way, from whence we have all this long while wandered and strayed abroad' and to declare themselves 'very sorry and repentant of the schisms and disobedience committed in this realm . . . against the said See Apostolic'; but only because the same Act confirmed them in their possession of monastic lands 'without scruple of conscience . . . and clear from all dangers of the censures of the Church'.

On 30 November 1554 the king and queen and members of both houses of Parliament knelt before Cardinal Pole at Whitehall, to receive, in the name of the nation, forgiveness of their past errors and reconciliation with the Roman Church. Two months later, the first heretic was burnt at Smithfield. From then until the end of the reign, some three hundred Protestants, including sixty women, were sent to the flames. This severity had an effect quite different from that which Mary and Pole had expected. Latimer, burned at Oxford, called out to his fellow-sufferer Ridley 'We shall this day light such a candle, by God's grace, in England, as shall never be put out', and the faith of the martyrs has inspired the Church of England in a way that no act of Parliament could ever have done. There were some who, threatened with the fire, took back their opinions, but the worthlessness of these withdrawals was shown by Cranmer. He recanted twice, but when led out to make public confession, denounced his own weakness and died proclaiming his Protestant beliefs. Many less famous men and women showed an equal, or greater, firmness. In an age which was accustomed to cruelty, public anger was stirred not by the punishment, but by those who suffered. The majority of the martyrs were ordinary people, 'butchers, bakers and candlestick-makers', who had done no obvious harm. By attacking them Mary was destroying the loyalty and affection of the common people.

Mary's reign ended gloomily. Her husband became king of Spain on his father's abdication in January 1556, and showed no further interest in his wife. England got nothing from the Spanish alliance. Merchants and adventurers had taken comfort in the thought that Philip would open the Spanish dominions in South America to his English subjects, but nothing was farther from his mind. He used England as a pawn, and dragged her into war with France, in which she lost her last continental possession, Calais. It was no great loss, and the pursuit of conquest in France had for too long turned English attention from the oceans where her real opportunities lay. But to the people of England, Calais was a bright jewel in the royal crown, and with its loss went the last faint glow of Mary's glory.

Mary knew that her reign was a failure, and that her work would almost certainly be swept away by a Protestant successor. Disappointment and worry prematurely aged her, and by the time she reached her middle forties she was exhausted. Taken ill in August 1559, she lingered for several weeks, dreaming that she saw 'many little children like angels play before her, singing pleasing notes'. The end came on 17 November, and twelve hours later Cardinal Pole followed her. The Catholic reaction was over, since Mary, for all her good qualities, never understood the feelings of her people. By trying to burn out heresy in her kingdom she had lost her subjects' love, and driven Protestantism deep into the foundations of English society.

CHAPTER 29

Elizabeth I and the Succession

1559-1568

WHEN ELIZABETH I came to the throne in 1559 she was only twenty-five, and had inherited the good looks for which her father had been famous in his youth. A Venetian observer described her as 'tall and well-formed' with 'fine eyes and above all a beautiful hand, of which she makes display'. She was no classical beauty – her nose was too pronounced and her hair 'more reddish than yellow' – but she had a lively, sparkling personality that charmed all who met her, while her natural majesty commanded their respect. Her intelligence matched her features. Roger Ascham, her tutor, had done his work well, giving her a love of knowledge as well as a fluent command of Latin, Greek and modern languages. She handled her own tongue, English, with an effortless mastery, whether in repartee, for which she was famous, or in prepared speeches such as that of 1566 when she told Parliament 'I thank God I am endued with such qualities that if I were turned out of the realm in my petticoat I were able to live in any place in Christendom'.

She had her grandfather's flair for choosing advisers, and at the very outset of her reign appointed William Cecil as her Secretary. He was to become the finest administrator since Thomas Cromwell, and far more effective because he held office so much longer. Elizabeth gave him her trust and he served her loyally until his death forty years later.

The first task of the queen and her new secretary was to decide on a religious settlement. This was not easy, for the English were deeply divided among themselves, and although the fires of Smithfield had turned many away from Rome, there were others who, in a time of perpetual change, clung to the certainties of the

Catholic faith. About Elizabeth's own convictions we know little. She believed in God but was by nature tolerant, and refused, in her own words, to 'make windows into men's souls'. Cecil was inclined to a cautious Protestantism, probably reflecting in this the attitude of the governing classes, who had no wish to lose their monastic estates or their independence. Religion, then, divided Englishmen, but national pride united them, and this was the foundation upon which the queen built. She decided to create in her country a church which should be peculiarly English, and should command, like the monarchy itself, the allegiance of all sorts and conditions of men.

To do this the queen had first to restore the royal supremacy, then to establish the form of worship of the English Church. Two great statutes of 1559, the Act of Supremacy and the Act of Uniformity, accomplished this task. The first pronounced the queen to be 'Supreme Governor of this realm . . . as well in all spiritual or ecclesiastical things or causes as temporal' and required all officials of Church and State to take an oath recognizing her supremacy. The second act revived the 1552, or Protestant, prayer book, but with alterations designed to make it more acceptable to Catholics. Four years later the settlement was completed by the publication of the Thirty-Nine Articles, defining the doctrines of the Church. The Elizabethan prayer book now became the only authorized form of worship, and all the queen's subjects were commanded to attend services in their parish church on pain of a shilling fine every time they were absent. The Catholic bishops, however, appointed by Mary, could not bring themselves to accept the new settlement. All but one refused to take the oath of supremacy and were deprived of their sees. New bishops were appointed to take their place. They were headed by Matthew Parker, Archbishop of Canterbury, a man of great learning and tolerance, who carefully guided the Anglican Church through its formative years. A number of parish clergy were turned out of their livings, but on the whole the Elizabethan settlement was easily accepted, and those who found it unacceptable were not forced to become martyrs.

The Parliament that made the Elizabethan settlement was a more powerful body than that which had met thirty years earlier to cut the link with Rome. But although Parliaments met more frequently than they had done in the early days of Henry VIII, they were still only occasional assemblies. There were usually long intervals between one session and another, and members could hardly begin to work out a policy of their own, independently of the crown, even if they had wished to do so. Elizabeth summoned eleven parliaments but they sat for a total of only thirty-five months out of a reign of more than forty-four years.

Within the framework of Parliament changes were taking place. The House of Lords had lost much of its influence after the removal of the mitred abbots, and the greater part of the Elizabethan aristocracy consisted of recently ennobled families, not far removed in blood from the gentry of the lower house. The House of Commons was gradually becoming the real seat of power in Parliament. Two members were elected for every county and two for every borough. After Henry VIII incorporated Wales into the English representative system the number of county members became fixed at ninety. But during the Tudor period many new boroughs were created, thereby adding one hundred and thirty-four members to the house, just under half of them in Elizabeth's reign. This was not part of a careful plan to pack Parliament with royal nominees. The landowners, not the queen, pressed for the creation of new boroughs, although the crown actually issued the charters, and gladly collected a large fee for doing so.

In theory, the boroughs were supposed to choose their representatives from among their own inhabitants – merchants and manufacturers. In fact there were few boroughs which were not under the influence of some landed family. Towns were small places, not very rich, and were only too pleased to find a local landowner who would represent them in Parliament at his own expense. Tudor towns depended, like individuals, on friends at court. Local business men might well be honest and upright, but they would have little or no influence in the circles of government in London, where municipal privileges were to be bought, and enemies placated.

Land was the great source of power in Tudor England and governments could do little to shake its hold over Parliament. They might, like Thomas Cromwell, write to mayors and corporations urging them to elect certain named candidates; or, like Mary, advise the sheriffs to encourage the election of 'the wise, grave and

Catholic sort'; or, like Elizabeth, send letters to the great men of the realm asking them to use their influence to ensure the return of 'discreet, wise, and well-disposed' members. But these were half-hearted attempts, little more than a matter of form. Co-operation between crown and Parliament came not from packing but from common interests, and where, as in the succession question, their attitudes diverged, the queen had to fight a long, tricky engagement, not always successfully.

Elizabeth had no great love for Parliaments but she could not do without them. Mary had left her an empty treasury and a quarter of a million pounds' worth of debts. Elizabeth was by nature thrifty, and had her grandfather's accuracy in checking accounts, but even in time of peace she could only make ends meet by selling property – both her own and the Church's. She made about twenty thousand pounds a year by sales of land, but only at the cost of a steady reduction in the income from the re-mainder.

Cecil carried through a recoinage in 1561, calling in base coins and reissuing silver ones, thereby completing the work that Northumberland had started. This did not stop prices rising, since silver was still flooding in from the New World, but it re-established royal credit abroad and made it possible for Sir Thomas Gresham, the queen's agent in Antwerp, which was then the financial capital of the world, to raise money at low rates of interest. It could not, unfortunately, revive the cloth trade. Cloth was the main English export in the sixteenth century. But by the 1560's the market was reaching its limit, and as war spread throughout France and the Netherlands, sales of cloth declined. Although there were still big profits to be made out of cloth, exports never again touched the high levels they had known in the second quarter of the century. As the demand for wool slackened, the pressure for enclosures became less acute, but the council was faced with the problem of unemployed cloth-workers. It met this by drawing up in 1563 the Statute of Apprentices, which con-scripted the nation's labour-force and gave Justices of the Peace power to direct workers wherever they were most needed. Such a scheme, to operate efficiently, would have required the resources of a modern state, but it is a good example of the way in which the royal government stood for the interests of all classes, holding itself responsible for the spiritual and physical well-being of all the queen's subjects.

Elizabeth's council also had to deal with the problem of the poor. Earlier legislation had made a distinction between the enfeebled poor, who were unable to work, and the 'sturdy and idle vagabonds' who preferred to take to the roads. The enfeebled were to be looked after by their parishes, and an Act of 1563 ordered that parishioners who would not give alms of their own free will were to be summoned before the Justices, to be 'charitably and gently persuaded'. Vagabonds were to be more harshly treated. Savage laws of Edward VI's reign had laid down branding and slavery as penalties for those who roamed the roads, and although these harsh punishments were abandoned in Elizabeth's reign, whipping and exposure in the stocks were kept. But all this legislation did little more than tinker with the problem. Not until the very end of the reign did the government at last deal with poverty as a whole, and provide for a national system of poor relief, paid for by a compulsory parish rate, and administered by specially appointed overseers. This system, one of the finest achievements of a government that had a social conscience, was the only hope of the poor through the two centuries of growing indifference that followed.

The social problem occupied Parliament throughout Elizabeth's reign, but in the early days, after the religious settlement had been accomplished, it was far more concerned with the succession question. When Elizabeth came to the throne it was assumed that she would shortly marry, and the princes of Europe competed for her hand. Elizabeth encouraged them, partly out of vanity, but mainly because marriage negotiations were good diplomacy: while she kept her suitors dangling, she knew that they were building up no hostile coalitions against her. Although she was free to look for a husband at home, the history of the Northumberlands had shown her how a great family, connected to the crown by marriage, would not be satisfied until it had climbed on to the throne itself. And yet it was a member of that very family who almost persuaded her, for she lost her heart to Northumberland's son, the handsome Robert Dudley. She could not conceal her affection for him, and rumour ran riot. Unfortunately for Dudley, he was married, though living apart from Amy Robsart, his wife.

When in September 1560 the poor woman was found with her neck broken at the bottom of a staircase in Cumnor Place, Dudley was immediately suspected. Nothing could be proved against him, but public opinion would have been outraged if the queen had followed her inclinations and married him. Fortunately Elizabeth knew how to overcome her emotions when they conflicted with policy. Dudley was created Earl of Leicester, and long remained a favourite with the queen, but there was no further question of marriage.

In 1562 Elizabeth fell dangerously ill of smallpox and was not expected to recover. Her subjects were faced with the horrors of a disputed succession and bitter religious wars. Little wonder that when the queen made a miraculous recovery, they determined to put the question of the succession beyond all doubt. They petitioned Elizabeth to take a husband, but she put them off, assuring them that she had their interests at heart and could not 'with *Nunc Dimittis* end my life, without I see some foundation of your surety after my gravestone'. When the Commons raised the question again in 1566 the queen sent orders, through her privy councillors in the House, that they were to debate the matter no further.

This brought Paul Wentworth to his feet to demand 'whether the queen's command and inhibition . . . were not against the liberties and privileges of the said House?'. He and his brother Peter were a pair of fire-eaters, passionately loyal, but stubborn in their opinions and quite irrepressible. The queen's attitude was that the Commons' privilege of freedom of speech, which they claimed and were granted at the beginning of every Parliament, did not give them the right to start discussing any and every matter but only to debate freely whatever questions the crown put before them. Elizabeth told the Commons in 1571 that they 'should do well to meddle with no matters of state but such as should be propounded unto them', and the practice of her reign showed that she included the succession and royal control over the Church in the category of 'matters of state'.

She was unable, in fact, to maintain this position, for the succession, and later religion, were the burning topics of the day, and the Commons could not and would not wait for royal permission to discuss them. Elizabeth would impose a veto and then, having made her point, withdraw it. The combination of chiding and graciousness which she used so successfully is shown in the speech with which she dissolved Parliament in 1567, after it had once again discussed the succession question. 'Beware however you prove your Prince's patience as you have now done mine,' she ended. 'And now to conclude, all this notwithstanding – not meaning to make a Lent of Christmas – the most part of you may assure yourselves that you depart in your Prince's grace.'

In this way the queen preserved her freedom of action, but it was a tricky and exhausting business, and became doubly so the following year, 1568, when Mary, Queen of Scots, arrived in England. Elizabeth had been born of Henry VIII's marriage to Anne Boleyn, but the pope had never recognized this union. In Catholic eyes, Elizabeth was illegitimate, and had no real claim to the throne. The rightful ruler of England was the nearest Catholic claimant, and this was none other than the Queen of Scots, descended from Henry VII through his daughter Margaret.

Mary had been married, as a young girl, to the king of France. Towards the end of 1560, however, her husband died. Mary could have stayed on as a dowager, but she preferred to be a real queen. Sadly abandoning the delights of Paris she returned to the bleak northern kingdom that was still her own. The gaiety of the French capital was, however, to be clouded in the years that followed: 1562 saw the outbreak of the religious wars which were to ravage France for the rest of the century. It was a struggle in which the fortunes of England were bound up. For while the wars lasted, France was effectively removed from European politics, and Spain reigned supreme. Elizabeth could no longer play the two Catholic powers off against each other in order to preserve her own safety.

When Mary returned to Scotland, she already had her eye on the English throne. Probably the next best claim to her own was that of her cousin Henry Stuart, Lord Darnley, descended from Henry VII's daughter Margaret through her second marriage. He was a handsome man, and the high-spirited queen, bored by her Scottish countrymen, was delighted to serve policy and her own inclinations by marrying him in 1564. It was a disastrous step, for Darnley was an arrogant fool and Mary quickly tired of him. She was a woman of great charm, who found men as attractive as they found her. But she let her passions run away with her and never

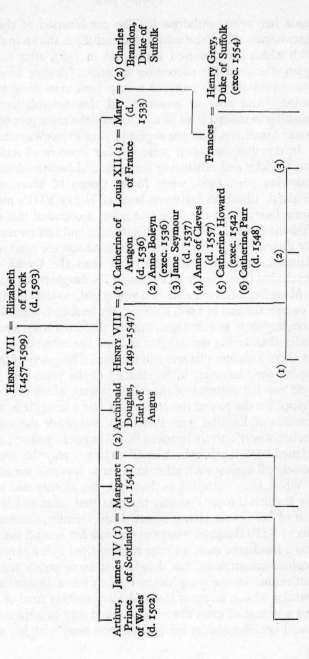

TABLE VI. *The Tudor Dynasty*

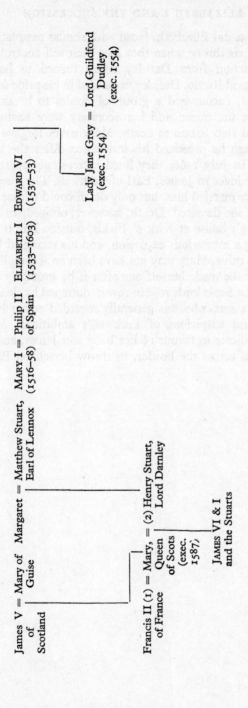

understood, as did Elizabeth, faced with similar temptations, that rulers risk their throne when they lose their self-control.

For distraction from Darnley Mary turned to her Italian secretary, David Rizzio. Darnley, wounded in his pride as much as his affections, encouraged a group of nobles to break into the palace where the queen and her secretary were having supper together, and stab Rizzio to death. Mary never forgave her husband, although he protested his innocence. After the birth of a son, James, in July 1566, they lived increasingly apart and she found a new lover in James, Earl of Bothwell. The queen would willingly have married him, but only death could release her from the husband she despised. Death, however, obliged. In February 1567 Darnley's house at Kirk o' Fields, outside Edinburgh, was blown up by a mysterious explosion, and his strangled body was found in the ruins. Mary may not have been an accomplice before the fact, but she made herself one after it by promptly marrying Bothwell. The Scots lords rose in revolt, outraged by their queen's marriage to a man who was generally regarded as her husband's murderer, and suspicious of Bothwell's ambitions. Mary was forced to abdicate in favour of her baby son James, and in May 1568 she fled across the border, to throw herself on Elizabeth's protection.

CHAPTER 30

The Armada

1568-1588

THE ARRIVAL of the Queen of Scots marks the beginning of the crisis years, in which the whole Elizabethan settlement, in Church and State, is threatened. Mary Tudor's reign had gone a long way towards destroying the friendship between England and Spain that had lasted throughout the first half of the sixteenth century, and as English seamen began to break into the Spanish monopoly of trade with the New World, relations grew worse. The 1560's also saw the early stages of rebellion in the Spanish Netherlands. Philip II had inherited these lands from his father, the Emperor Charles V, and they were the centre of the cloth industry in Europe. Philip would not let so rich a possession go, but he was determined to stamp out the Puritanism which was spreading rapidly there, as it did in so many other centres of commerce. The Dutch and Flemish inhabitants of the Netherlands resented religious persecution, and their national pride was stung by the presence of Spanish troops. The Dutch 'sea-beggars' took refuge in English harbours, from where they slipped out to prey on Spanish shipping. Philip moved more troops into the Netherlands to tighten his hold on the country, but English sympathies were with the underground rebel movement. Elizabeth could not stand by while Catholicism triumphed in Europe. When a Spanish fleet, laden with bullion for the payment of Philip's soldiers in the Netherlands, was driven into Plymouth by bad weather, Elizabeth promptly confiscated the money on the grounds that it had been borrowed from Italian bankers, and they might as well lend it to her as to Philip.

Philip was furious and ordered his ambassador in London to encourage the queen's subjects to revolt. The ambassador worked on the discontent of some of the great lords of the north, who cherished not only the old religion but the old order of things, and resented the new men like Cecil who now ruled England. They planned to marry the Queen of Scots, held by Elizabeth in honourable captivity, to Norfolk, the last surviving English duke, and force Elizabeth to recognize Mary as her successor. Norfolk was half-hearted and surrendered before trouble began. But by the end of 1569 the Northern Rising had broken out.

The prayer book was publicly trampled under foot and the sound of the Latin Mass once again echoed in Durham Cathedral. As the rebels moved south, however, they melted away, and the large army that Elizabeth had assembled was used for savage repression. Rebels who were rich enough to buy a pardon survived, but eight hundred of the poorer sort were executed. The power of the feudal nobles in the north was finally broken, and the Council of the North was free to finish the work which it had started after the Pilgrimage of Grace.

The failure of the Northern Rising was a bitter disappointment to European Catholics. It looked as though the Anglican Church was becoming in fact as well as in theory the Church of the whole nation. If English Catholics were not to slip into heresy, they would have to be given a clear lead. So in 1570 Pope Pius V, in the bull *Regnans in Excelsis*, proclaimed Elizabeth 'the pretended queen of England, the servant of wickedness . . . to have incurred the sentence of excommunication, and to be cut off from the Body of Christ. And moreover We do declare her to be deprived of her pretended title to the kingdom aforesaid'. No Catholic could now, it seemed, be a loyal subject, and although in fact many managed to reconcile their loyalty with their faith, it is not surprising that Elizabeth's government suspected all Catholics of treachery, and abandoned the tolerant attitude of its earlier days. Even Philip II appreciated this, for he wrote to his ambassador: 'this sudden and unexpected step will make matters worse and drive the Queen and her friends the more to oppress and persecute the few good Catholics remaining in England'.

The government found its suspicions confirmed when in 1571 it discovered a plot woven by Ridolfi, an Italian business man, to marry the Queen of Scots to Norfolk, and use Spanish troops to place her on the English throne. It was a poor plot, more wishful thinking than anything else, but it led to Norfolk's execution, and there were voices raised calling for Mary's death. Elizabeth would not hear of it, but all over Europe storm clouds were gathering. In 1572 smouldering discontent in the Netherlands exploded into open rebellion, while in Paris the bells rang on St Bartholomew's Day to summon all good Catholics to a massacre of the Protestants.

The Catholic Church had reeled under the shock of the Reformation, but it had not collapsed, and in 1545 a great ecclesiastical council had met at Trent, in Italy, to consider how the papacy and the Church might be restored to health. This, and the foundation of new religious orders, set off the Counter-Reformation, which stemmed the tide of Protestantism and looked as though it might reclaim all Europe for the old faith. England soon felt the effects, for in 1568 an English Catholic, William Allen, opened a college at Douai, in the Netherlands, to train priests for the conversion of England. The first of these priests landed in England in 1574, and by 1580 there were over a hundred of them. They never converted England, but they refreshed and revived the English Catholics, putting an end to Elizabeth's hopes of uniting all her subjects in one Church.

The government took strong action against what it regarded as a foreign invasion. An Act of 1571 declared that anyone publishing the bull of excommunication in England or attempting to reconcile the queen's subjects to Rome, should be 'deemed and adjudged high traitors to the queen and the realm, and . . . suffer pains of death', and 1577 saw the first Douai priest executed. The English government could hardly be blamed for its attitude. The bull of deposition had made all English Catholics potential traitors, one plot had already been uncovered, and the Spanish ambassador was doubtless hatching more. England and Spain were nominally at peace, but in fact there was cold war between them. Catholic priests were serving the pope, but in English eyes this seemed to be the same as serving the king of Spain. When more peaceful times came at the end of Elizabeth's reign, the government was prepared to accept that English Catholics could be loyal to their faith and to the crown. But had it made this assumption at the beginning, the reign might have come to a sudden and violent close.

In 1580 two Jesuits, Edmund Campion and Robert Parsons, arrived in England. They were members of the Society of Jesus, which had been founded in 1540 to fight Protestantism and other heresies. The Jesuits were the commandos of the Church, chosen for the most dangerous missions. Campion, who was a most saintly and charming person, proclaimed his intention 'to cry alarm spiritual against foul vice and proud ignorance, wherewith many my dear countrymen are abused'. The government replied, in 1581, by imposing heavy penalties on Catholics. Anyone who refused to attend his parish church was to be fined £20 a month, and a year's imprisonment awaited those found saying or hearing mass. These penal laws were no dead letter, and the campaign against Catholic priests and Jesuits was intensified. Campion went to the scaffold in December 1587, proclaiming to the last his devotion to the queen's majesty, and the total of executions mounted to about two hundred and fifty. They remain a blot on a reign that was otherwise tolerant, but the number was small compared with France and Spain, and England was not the only country where subjects were ordered to accept the form of religion drawn up by their sovereign.

By the time Campion landed in England, Elizabeth's reign was moving towards its second, and greatest, crisis. Everywhere in Europe the Protestant reformation was struggling for survival against the revived Catholic Church. Although the queen was by nature cautious, there was no middle way to follow: the defeat of Protestantism would have meant the end of Elizabethan England. Her subjects were already fighting the Spaniards at sea, to break into the rich trade with South America. John Hawkins, a Plymouth seaman, had tried peaceful commerce in the 1560's, sailing down the west coast of Africa where he picked up negro slaves and shipped them across to the Spanish American colonies to exchange for precious metals. His first voyage was so successful that the queen and Cecil were shareholders in the second, but by the time he left on his third voyage in 1567 Philip II had sent orders that on no account were foreigners, particularly heretics, to be allowed to trade with the Spanish dominions. Hawkins knew nothing of this. It was not until he was suddenly attacked while at anchor in San Juan de Ulloa in the Gulf of Mexico that he realized his danger. He managed to escape with his life, but he had to abandon his property and leave many of his comrades to the tender mercies of the Inquisition – the department of the Catholic Church which, in

Spain and elsewhere, tortured and burned heretics in order to save their souls. The incident at San Juan de Ulloa put an end to peaceful trading. The English had either to accept their exclusion from the new world, or to fight their way into it.

Hawkins, bitterly angry at the death of his companions and the loss of his property, wanted to lead the fight himself, but this honour went to his young cousin, Francis Drake, who had captained one of the ships at San Juan de Ulloa. From his own experience and from his fervent Protestantism Drake had good cause to loathe the Spaniards. His aim was revenge, not trade. In 1572 he struck at the Isthmus of Panama, the narrow neck of land where treasure from Mexico in the north and Peru in the south was concentrated to be shipped to Spain. As a convoy of bullion lumbered along, on the last stage of its journey to the town of Nombre de Dios, Drake ambushed it, captured the fabulous booty, and sailed back to England in triumph. It was piracy, of course, and it did not improve Anglo-Spanish relations. Cecil was alarmed and doubtful how far such proceedings could be justified. But Drake's assessment of the situation was, for once, sounder than Cecil's. Spain was actively engaged in the reconquest of Protestant Europe, of which England formed part, and declarations of war were meaningless formalities. When open conflict came, the safety of the kingdom depended, as always, on its seamen, and it was lucky for England that she had men of the calibre of Drake. He set off again in 1577 on a free-booting voyage that took him round the world – the first English circumnavigator. When he returned, three years later, his flagship, the *Golden Hind*, was groaning under the weight of bullion, and the queen, throwing caution to the winds, went down to Deptford and knighted him on his own quarterdeck. She knew how magnificent a leader he was, and she desperately needed a share of the spoils.

Spain, still too occupied in the Netherlands to consider direct action, built up another plot against Elizabeth, in 1583. A young English Catholic, Francis Throckmorton, was the link between the Spanish ambassador, who agreed to provide troops, and Mary, Queen of Scots, who was to be put on the throne. But Elizabeth's counter-espionage agents, under the control of Sir Francis Walsingham, ferreted out the details of the plot. Before the conspirators were ready to act, Throckmorton was arrested and executed, and the Spanish ambassador was ordered to leave the country.

Of the chief conspirators only Mary still survived. There was plenty of circumstantial evidence against her, but Elizabeth was unwilling to see a sister-monarch brought to trial. She could not, however, save Mary indefinitely, especially when Protestantism was fighting for its survival. In 1584 William of Orange, leader of the Netherlands revolt and one of the greatest champions of the Protestant cause, was assassinated, and the same fate threatened Elizabeth. The queen's life had to be preserved if Spain and the Counter-Reformation were to be checked, and all over England men joined the Bond of Association, pledging themselves, in the event of an attempted assassination of Elizabeth, to kill the person in whose name the attempt had been made. Mary was not directly mentioned, but it was a clear warning to her that she should dabble in no more plots.

The assassination of William of Orange left the Dutch rebels without a leader, and the Spanish general Parma moved irresistibly forward, occupying the southern Netherlands. By 1585 he had recaptured Antwerp, and the defeat of the rebels seemed only a matter of time. Elizabeth had already sent them supplies and encouraged volunteers to go over, but this was not enough. At last she agreed to send an English army to the Netherlands, and appointed her old favourite, Leicester, to command it. He sailed in December 1585, with seven thousand men, and was given a delirious welcome by the Dutch. Leicester, however, was no general, and his campaigns are remembered only for the engagement at Zutphen in which Philip Sidney – poet, courtier, and soldier: a typically Elizabethan combination – met his death. Although Leicester won no battles, his mere presence in the Netherlands was sufficient to give new life to the rebel cause Philip at last realized that there would be no victory for Spain until England was dealt with.

In case the Spanish king needed any reminder of this, Drake gave it him. Philip had ordered all English shipping in his ports to be confiscated. Drake set sail for the Spanish West Indies to demand compensation. There he held two cities to ransom, pillaged ships, churches and private houses, and returned home in the summer of 1586 with a fortune in his holds. As an exploit it was magnificently impudent. But it had a greater significance, for Drake had shown that while England's armies might be negligible, her navy was a force to be reckoned with. And if England was to be attacked, the invaders had no choice but to come by sea.

Philip accordingly set on foot preparations for the 'Enterprise of England', the great invasion that would bring the Protestant island to its knees. Shipyards along the Atlantic coast were a bustle of activity, and landing craft were assembled in the harbours of the Netherlands. Elizabeth and her council knew of these preparations, and made their own. But they had still to reckon with Mary, Queen of Scots, the weak point in their armour. The council were for putting her to death, but Elizabeth would never be convinced of her guilt except by the clearest proof. This was quickly provided. Walsingham got on the track of another conspiracy, in which a young man named Babington was the agent. The details were as usual: Elizabeth was to be assassinated and Mary placed on the throne with the help of Spanish troops. Walsingham managed to intercept letters that passed between Mary and Babington, and found there the evidence he needed, for they contained Mary's agreement to all the details of the plot.

The council acted swiftly. The conspirators were arrested and executed, and a special court was set up to try the Queen of Scots. She was found guilty and sentenced to death. Elizabeth was afraid what repercussions Mary's execution might have in France, and she knew that to kill a monarch was to chop at the foundations of her own throne. Even after she had reluctantly put her signature to the warrant she would not have it carried into effect. In the end it was the council, acting on its own initiative, which braved Elizabeth's fury and ordered the sentence to be carried out. Mary went to her death in the great hall of Fotheringay Castle on 8 February 1587, 'lying upon the block most quietly, and stretching out her arms [she] cried "In manus tuas, Domine" three or four times'. From her beauty and her courage at the end, has sprung the legend of the innocent queen, foully murdered. But she was far less innocent than poor Lady Jane Grey, even though she survived, through Elizabeth's mercy, so much longer. Spanish troops never, in fact, landed to proclaim Mary queen of England, but Elizabeth knew that had they done so, there would have been no mercy for her.

Elizabeth was bitterly angry when she heard the news of Mary's execution. But Philip's invasion plans were nearing their climax and she had to concentrate all her energies on defence. The Spanish plan was simple. A large fleet, or armada, would sail from Spain, sweep the Channel clear of English shipping, and convoy Parma's troops from the Netherlands. Once they landed in England the English Catholics would, so Philip had been assured, rise all over the country, the government would be overthrown, and a Spanish viceroy would rule at Whitehall in the name of King Philip. Elizabeth prepared for this threat by mustering ships and supplies, and encouraging her subjects to arm and train themselves. She never displayed herself to better advantage than at this crisis, and the speech she made to her troops at Tilbury shows why they were ready to die for her. 'I know,' she told them, 'I have the body of a weak and feeble woman, but I have the heart and stomach of a king, and of a king of England too, and think foul scorn that Parma or Spain, or any prince of Europe should dare to invade the borders of my realm; to which, rather than any dishonour shall grow by me, I myself will take up arms, I myself will be your general, judge, and rewarder of every one of your virtues in the field.'

The Armada would have sailed in 1587 but for Drake, who struck at the main Spanish port, Cadiz, and destroyed many of the ships and stores assembled there. Drake, and Lord Howard of Effingham, the English admiral, wanted to go back the following year and fight the Armada off the coast of Portugal. Bad weather and lack of supplies prevented this, however, and by July 1588 the great fleet was moving ponderously up the Channel. Watchers on the Devon and Cornwall coasts could clearly see it, 'built high like towers and castles', according to William Camden, 'rallied into the form of a crescent whose horns were at least seven miles distant'. The Spaniards, under the Duke of Medina Sidonia, kept their tight formation in spite of Howard's efforts to break it up. Both sides were equally matched. The Spaniards had about one hundred and thirty ships all told, carrying over twenty thousand soldiers and sailors. The English had about the same number, though as reinforcements continued to come in they were at an advantage. The Spanish ships were old-fashioned, with forecastles and aftercastles crammed with troops. The English vessels were long and raking, 'so fast and nimble', wrote the Spanish commander, 'they can do anything they like with them'.

As the crescent moon of the Armada moved slowly up Channel the English buzzed around it like angry wasps. But Howard was worried, for although his men pounced on a couple of Spanish ships which had straggled out of formation, he could not break up the main body. This was done by the Spaniards themselves. Looking for a suitable rendezvous with Parma they anchored off Calais on 27 July. The following night the English admiral set fire to some old ships that had been filled with inflammable materials, and let the wind carry them. The Spaniards saw the darkness of the night suddenly torn apart by blazing hulks bearing down upon them. They panicked, cut their cables, and stood out to sea. Next morning the great fleet was scattered over the waters, and the English squadrons swept down on their enemies, closing the range so that their guns could do real damage. Before the day was over most of the Spanish ships had been holed, the killed and wounded were piled on their decks and blood poured out of their scuppers. Medina Sidonia was in the thick of the battle, rallying his ships around him. By superb seamanship the Spaniards managed to form themselves into a half-moon and stood away northwards to escape from the slaughter. After two months at sea their ammunition was exhausted and food and water were running short. The English were also out of gunpowder, but they had supplies much nearer at hand. There was a lull in the battle as both sides drew apart, one to restock, the other to lick its wounds.

Although no one realized it, the battle was over. The leaky and damaged Spanish ships were blown northwards with Howard on their tail. Medina Sidonia still hoped to turn back and make a rendezvous with Parma. But the wind was against him, his enemies blocked the return route, and his fleet was so battered and short of supplies that it could no longer be considered a fighting force. The only alternative was to make for home round the north of Scotland and Ireland. It was a long and perilous route, and many a ship foundered in the stormy waters off the Irish coast. Medina Sidonia at last made port in September 1588. Other ships gradually straggled in until, by the end of the year, half the Armada had returned to its native land. The other half of that proud fleet lay at the bottom of the sea. England had been preserved, for a

time at least. Spanish pride had been humbled; the Reformation
had been saved. Protestants all over Europe hailed the defeat of the
Armada as a divine judgment, and the commemorative medal
which Elizabeth ordered to be struck records quite simply
Afflavit Deus et dissipati sunt – God blew, and they were scattered.

The defeat of the Armada did not mean the end of the war.
Before Elizabeth's reign was over, two more Spanish invasion
fleets set sail, only to be beaten back by wind and weather. The
English tried to take advantage of their supremacy at sea by
launching combined operations against the Spanish coast, but
these were expensive failures. The war petered out into stalemate,
but not until after the queen was dead did it officially come to a
close.

The years following the Armada saw the problem of Puritanism
enter a bitter phase. Puritans were those who wished the Church
to be purified – purged, that is, of all Catholic traces – and they
took as their model the sternly Protestant community which the
French reformer John Calvin had established at Geneva. The
Puritans concentrated their attack first of all on vestments. Priests
had been ordered to wear 'such seemly habits, garments, and such
square caps as were most commonly and orderly received in the
latter year of the reign of King Edward VI', but this, for Puritans,
smacked of popery. Many of them refused to obey and a number
were summoned before Archbishop Parker, and deprived of their
livings.

Vestments were a comparatively minor matter, but Parker's
action made it clear that the Church authorities, having taken up
their position, would not alter it. The Puritans came to realize that
only by challenging the authority of bishops could they hope for
a really pure Church. 'At the beginning,' commented the Dean of
York, 'it was but a cap, a surplice, and a tippet. Now it is grown
to bishops, archbishops, and cathedral churches; to the overthrow
of the established order and the Queen's authority in causes
ecclesiastical.' The question was raised in the Commons when, in
1571, a member brought forward a bill for reforming the Church.
But the queen would have none of it. She controlled the bishops,
and any criticism of them was criticism of her. The royal supremacy, she said, was a 'matter of state', not to be discussed without

her prior consent. But in trying to enforce this she came up against opposition much tougher than anything she had met over the succession question. There was a powerful Puritan group in the Commons, and the queen could not silence it. When she forbade discussion, or imprisoned offenders, members claimed that such actions were a breach of their privileges, and rather than risk a storm she would usually give way. Questions of religion brought out the stubbornness of the Commons for, as one member said: 'This cause is God's. The rest are all but terrene, yea trifles in comparison . . . Subsidies, Crowns, Kingdoms – I know not what they are in comparison of this.'

The 1570's saw the development of *Prophesyings*, Bible-study groups usually led by Puritan ministers. Elizabeth commanded Grindal, who had succeeded Parker as Archbishop of Canterbury, to suppress them, and when Grindal protested, in 1577, she suspended him from his functions and kept him in disgrace until just before his death five years later. Grindal's successor was John Whitgift, a man of strong character and great ability. He maintained strict discipline in the Church, and ministers who would not carry out the instructions laid down by the Act of Uniformity and the Thirty-Nine Articles were summoned before the court of High Commission – set up to enforce the royal supremacy – where they were deprived of their livings. This had unfortunate results, for the Puritan ministers were among the more enthusiastic and educated of the clergy and were replaced, if at all, by men of poorer quality, who helped bring the Church into disrepute, and lost the respect of their congregations. But Elizabeth and Whitgift could not ignore the Puritan challenge. The queen was head of Church and State, and the two were so closely identified that the Puritan appeal to individual conscience savoured of rebellion and anarchy.

The deprived ministers often continued to hold services in a private house, or other meeting-place. But these conventicles, as they were called, were illegal and, when discovered, were broken up by force. Other conventicles were held not by former priests, but by men who believed that every congregation was its own church, and rejected bishops on the one hand and presbyters on the other. These men were the Independents and the council was very suspicious of them, for they appeared to reject all authority.

Henry Barrow, a prominent Independent, and three of his followers were executed, and an Act of 1593 required all those who would not attend the services of the Anglican Church to go into exile or else risk a criminal's death. By these firm measures Puritanism was kept under control, but it remained alive within the Church, and many priests who outwardly accepted the prayer book showed, by their long, fervent sermons and their attack on Sunday games, where their real sympathies lay.

CHAPTER 31

The English Renaissance

NOT ALL Englishmen were Puritans. There were many who found in the services of the English Church a dignity that they thought fitting for the worship of God, and a necessary link with the Catholic past. Among these was Richard Hooker who, in his majestic work, the *Ecclesiastical Polity*, denied that scripture was the sole source of authority, and defended custom and ceremony on the grounds that 'the public duties of religion [are] best ordered when the militant Church doth resemble . . . that hidden dignity and glory wherewith the Church triumphant in heaven is beautified'. For Hooker, as for many like him, the Puritan attitude was too narrow and too desiccated, particularly in its rejection of the arts as aids to worship. 'They must,' he commented, 'have hearts very dry and tough, from whom the melody of psalms doth not sometime draw that wherein a mind religiously affected delighteth.'

Hooker could well choose music as his example, for in this, as in all the arts, late Tudor and early Stuart England saw a marvellous flowering. Three great musicians, William Byrd, Thomas Tallis, and Orlando Gibbons – the first two Catholics and the last an Anglican – led the revival in sacred music. Gibbons also wrote in a lighter vein, and from him, Dowland and Weelkes come many of the airs and madrigals still sung today. To read music or play an instrument was one of the accomplishments expected of Elizabethan ladies and gentlemen, and the songs they sang have a sparkling, spring-like quality.

Poets, like musicians, also delighted in 'the springtime, the only pretty ring time', when the world seemed young and made for love and laughter, and there was 'no enemy but winter and rough weather'. Delight in youth and love of freedom inspired a passionate devotion to England and her queen.

> Blest be the hearts that wish my sovereign well,
> Curst be the souls that think her any wrong

wrote George Peele in a poem dedicated to Elizabeth. Other poets looked back on English history to see what ages could bear comparison with their own. Michael Drayton took the battle of Agincourt for his theme, and recalled the glories of that day to inspire his fellow-countrymen:

> O when shall English men
> With such acts fill a pen?
> Or England breed again
> Such a King Harry?

Patriotism and the joys of spring were not the sole topics of Elizabethan poetry. Among the most important was religion, which is hardly surprising since it played so big a part in English life. There were Roman Catholics, like Robert Southwell who wrote a moving and beautiful poem on his vision of *The Burning Babe;* and Puritans, like Fulke Greville who knew how difficult it is for human beings to live up to the the high standards God sets them:

> O wearisome condition of humanity.
> Born under one law; to another bound.
> Vainly begot, and yet forbidden vanity;
> Created sick, commanded to be sound.

Beneath the surface glitter of Elizabethan life – 'the cloud-capped towers, the gorgeous palaces' – were squalor, disease and death. These also are faithfully reflected in Elizabethan poetry which is the mirror of its age. Thomas Nashe could be as light-hearted as any man, and showed it by writing the poem which starts 'Spring, the sweet Spring, is the year's pleasant king'. But in 1593, when plague was making one of its frequent visits to London, he wrote in a different vein.

> Rich men, trust not in wealth.
> Gold cannot buy you health.
> Physic himself must fade.
> All things to end are made.
> The plague full swift goes by.

> I am sick.
> I must die.
> *Lord have mercy on us.*

Poetry flowed over into the theatre and there produced one of the most magnificent achievements of the Elizabethan, or indeed of any, age. At the beginning of Elizabeth's reign the drama was still struggling to free itself from the conventions of the medieval morality play, but by 1574 the first actors' company had been founded, and two years later the first public theatre opened. Christopher Marlowe set the tone for the new drama. In plays like *Tamburlaine, Doctor Faustus* and *Edward II*, he showed his magnificent command of 'bragging blank verse', in which the words resounded like brass and cymbals.

> Is it not brave to be a king, Techelles,
> Usumcasane and Theridamas?
> Is it not passing brave to be a king
> And ride in triumph through Persepolis?

Marlowe was killed in a tavern brawl in 1593, and from then onwards there was nobody to challenge Shakespeare as the greatest poet and playwright of his age. In these years he wrote the cycle of history plays that fired the blood of a nation made proudly patriotic by the long struggle against Spain. The early years of James I's reign saw the first performances of the great tragedies – *Hamlet, Othello, King Lear* and *Macbeth;* and between then and his death in 1616 he wrote *The Tempest*, in more ways than one the most magical play of them all. Shakespeare's achievement may be left to speak for itself, but its very magnificence has obscured the work of other writers who, in a less gifted age, would have been suns instead of mere stars. Foremost among these were Ben Jonson, a fine poet as well as a playwright; Thomas Dekker, who paints a vivid picture of Elizabethan life in *The Shoemaker's Holiday*; and John Webster, who brought out his obsession with the horror and majesty of death in *The White Devil* and *The Duchess of Malfi*.

It was an age that set no boundary between the artist and the man of action. The poet John Donne served under the Earl of Essex in the combined operation against Cadiz in 1596; Marlowe was a secret agent; Sidney, who died fighting at Zutphen, wrote the first important critical work in English. They were typical of the many-sidedness of Elizabethan life and show its search for new ideas, its love of knowledge and experiment. A year after the Armada Richard Hakluyt published his *Principal Navigations, Voyages and Discoveries of the English Nation,* to inspire his countrymen to overseas adventures. Nearer at home William Camden was exploring England, with the help of Saxton's new maps, to record of every place 'who were the ancient inhabitants, what was the reason of the name, what are the bounds of the country, the nature of the soil, the places of greatest antiquity, and of the greatest eminence at present'.

The centres of learning were the universities of Oxford and Cambridge, enriched with new buildings and new professorships by Henry VIII and his mother. In London there were the Inns of Court. Nearly every educated Englishman had some legal training and this was particularly true of members of Parliament. The lawyers formed a powerful group in the Commons, and though they had, as a body, no definite aims, they were more than ready to defend the privileges of the House. This made it increasingly difficult for Elizabeth to control the Commons. The Puritan members persisted in their attempts to reform the English Church. When a bill for this purpose was presented in 1587 the queen ordered the Speaker to proceed no further with it. But the irrepressible Peter Wentworth leapt to his feet to demand by what right the crown could command its officials to check the Commons' freedom of speech. Wentworth and the mover of the bill were sent to the Tower, but the Commons were not easily to be silenced. In 1593 the queen was still reminding them that 'to say *yea* or *no* to bills, God forbid that any man should be restrained or afraid to answer according to his best liking, with some short declaration of his reason therein, and therein to have a free voice, which is the very true liberty of this house. Not, as some suppose, to speak there of all causes as him listeth, and to frame a form of religion or a state of government as to their idle brains shall seem meetest'.

In the last parliaments of the reign, the Commons were increasingly difficult to handle. Now that the Spanish threat had been removed they were not united to the queen's government by a common danger, and a new generation took as their starting-point claims that their predecessors had hardly dared put forward. The death of William Cecil, Lord Burghley, in 1598 marks the passing of the great privy councillors, to whom the House had listened with attention. Their successors were not always sure of a hearing. Burghley's son Robert Cecil protested in 1601 that though he had 'been a member of this house in six or seven parliaments, yet never did I see the house in so great a confusion . . . This is more fit for a grammar school than a court of Parliament'.

A new issue had arisen between the queen and her faithful Commons. Elizabeth was in dire need of money, for the price rise was still eating away the value of her revenues. Parliament, it was true, offered subsidies to help meet extra-ordinary expenditure, like war against Spain and the suppression of the Irish rebellion,[1] but these were granted only after much grumbling, and never filled the gap between income and expenditure. The subsidy was a tax on land, but it had become fixed by custom and tradition and bore little relation to the real wealth of the taxpayer. Sir Walter Raleigh admitted in 1601 that 'our estates that be £30 or £40 in the Queen's books are not the hundredth part of our wealth', but he shocked his fellow M.P.s who believed they were over-taxed and thought the crown should live off its own resources. The antiquated system of taxation needed revising, but Elizabeth did not dare risk the unpopularity that this would have brought her. Instead she tried to exploit the sources that were open to her. The Court of Wards collected feudal revenues with an efficiency that made it detested, and tonnage and poundage were made to yield more by better administration. As a last resort the queen also offered monopolies for sale.

These were licences, granted in return for heavy payments, which gave the holder the sole right to manufacture or trade in certain articles. To get back the money he had spent in buying the monopoly, the holder would put up the price of his articles, and since no one else could offer similar goods for sale, the public had to pay or go without. Monopolies benefited the crown and the monopolist, but no one else, and Parliament, representing the consumer, attacked them strongly. The queen, who could ill afford to part with so valuable a source of income, asserted that matters of trade came into the category of subjects which must not be discussed without her prior consent. The Commons, however, refused to accept this view and forced her in the end to compromise.

[1] See page 296.

CHAPTER 32

Overseas Trade and Elizabethan England

1588-1603

THE ASSUMPTION of Tudor and Stuart England was that the government should control the economic life of the nation. This was particularly true of foreign trade, which was almost entirely in the hands of companies of merchants who bought a charter from the crown and were given the sole right to trade in a certain area.

The Company of the Merchant Adventurers controlled most of the lucrative trade in cloth. The Low Countries were their chief market, but in Elizabeth's reign the Dutch revolt and religious wars encouraged a search for new outlets, particularly in Germany. For northern Europe, Danzig was a convenient port of entry, while in the south Leghorn, which had a large colony of English merchants, was the centre from which cloth was distributed throughout the Mediterranean countries.

The Merchant Adventurers concentrated on cloth because this continued to bring in big profits even after trade slackened in the second half of the sixteenth century. But they also exported many of the products of the industries which were being started or developed in Elizabethan England. This period saw the successful introduction of paper and gunpowder mills, cannon foundries and sugar refineries, and industries which had been long established, like coal-mining and salt-evaporating, grew enormously in size. The invention of drainage engines and ventilation shafts made it possible for mines to be sunk to a much greater depth, and the large sums of money needed to pay for this came from the greatly increased sales of coal. For Elizabethan England was faced with a timber shortage, as the forests were cut down for firewood and ship building. Timber soared in price, and coal burned in many a London grate that had previously known nothing but wood. One of the biggest consumers of timber was the iron industry of the Kent and Sussex Weald, which used charcoal to smelt the crude ore. Water-power was employed to operate the bellows and drive the massive hammers which beat the metal into bars. One of the centres of industrial England in Elizabethan times, unlike today, was the south, and some of the enterprises were on a large scale. By 1613 John Browne employed two hundred men in his cannon foundry at Brenchley in Kent, and the products of this industry were shipped all over Europe.

Other trading companies followed the lines that explorers mapped out. After the death of Henry VII there was a fifty-year lull in English exploration, and money and energies that might have discovered new worlds were spent on futile campaigns against France, and in exhausting religious squabbles. Mary Tudor's death marked the end of this stage. Calais was lost and with it, fortunately, went English ambitions on the Continent; while the accession of Elizabeth marked the end of constant religious upheavals. Exploring had, in fact, begun to revive under Northumberland, who gave it his blessing. The spice islands of the east, and the fabulous wealth of China were the great attraction. The Mediterranean route to these riches was, however, blocked by the Turks, while the Portuguese and Spaniards guarded the African and American approaches. The only alternative was to go round the top of the world, and in 1555 Willoughby and Chancellor set out to look for a north-east passage. Chancellor survived to enter the White Sea and visit the court of the Russian tsar, Ivan the Terrible, and his voyage led directly to the setting up of the Muscovy Company, to trade with the tsar's dominions. This was followed in 1579 by the Eastland Company, which shipped dyed and finished cloth to Scandinavia, and brought back tar and hemp and other naval stores.

One of the richest companies of all was that which traded with the eastern Mediterranean, or Levant. In exchange for cloth it imported sweet wines, olives and currants, which took up little room but sold in England for high prices. The Levant merchants were near enough to the east to know how profitable trade with that region would be. Drake had shown, by sailing round the world, that English seamen could successfully carry out long ocean voyages. All that was needed was money and determination. A group of London merchants provided these. First results were not encouraging. Out of three ships sent to the east in 1591, two failed to reach the Indian Ocean, and the third sank on the return voyage. But the lure was sufficient to overcome this setback. In 1599 a company was set up, and £30,000 contributed, 'to set forth a voyage this present year to the East Indies and other the Islands and Countries thereabouts, and there to make trade'. This was the origin of the greatest of all English trading organizations, the East India Company, which was given its charter by the queen on the last day of 1600.

There were other smaller bodies, such as the group which traded with the Guinea coast of Africa in search of slaves. There were also many individuals who refused to accept the companies' monopoly of profitable trades, and set out on their own as interlopers, to break into protected markets. Prominent among the interlopers were merchants from the provincial ports, who bitterly resented the way in which all trade was coming under the exclusive control of groups of London business men, 'as if', in the words of a west-country mayor, 'God had no sons to whom he gave benefit of the earth, but only London'. But the supremacy of London was inevitable, since only in the rich, ever-expanding capital city was sufficient money to be raised for overseas ventures.

Trade drove the English to the new world as well as the old. War with Spain made the loaded treasure ships a legitimate target for English seamen, and encouraged them to cross the Atlantic and get to know the geography of the American coastline. Hakluyt was all in favour of American exploration, and in his *Discourse of Western Planting*, published in 1584, he urged that 'this Western voyage will yield unto us all the commodities of Europe, Africa and Asia'. The first English colonizing expedition to the new world was led by Sir Humphrey Gilbert in 1583, when he took formal possession of Newfoundland in the queen's name. He was lost at sea on the return journey, but his place was taken by his half-brother Walter Raleigh, who soon became as keen an enthusiast as Hakluyt. A ship was sent out to reconnoitre the American coast, and its commander reported, on return, that the part he had explored, south of the Chesapeake Bay, in what is now North

Carolina, was ideally suited to colonization. The queen agreed that the area should be called Virginia in her honour, and this name was applied generally to the whole north American coast.

In 1585 an expedition under Grenville planted a colony on Roanoke Island in Pamlico Sound, but there was not enough to live on and when a relief ship bearing supplies at last reached the colony, it found that Drake had already taken off the survivors. In 1587 another expedition was sent out under John White, one of the earlier settlers. He successfully re-established a colony on Roanoke, and then returned to England, leaving behind him eighty-eight men, seventeen women and eleven children. A relief expedition was planned, but all shipping was needed at home to fight the Armada, and it was not until 1591 that English ships again reached Roanoke. They found plenty of evidence that the settlers had moved, but no trace of their whereabouts. The mystery of what happened to them has never been solved.

Attempts to establish other settlements, in South America, between the mouths of the Amazon and Orinoco rivers, also failed, because of the appalling climate and lack of supplies. Raleigh explored the region in 1595, hoping to find El Dorado, the fabled city of gold. But his last voyage in 1613 threatened the friendship that James I had established with Spain and Raleigh returned only to face execution. The disappointment of the Roanoke failure, and the big profits to be made from attacking Spanish shipping, put an end to colonizing attempts for the rest of the sixteenth century. In 1600 there was no permanent English settlement outside Europe. All that had been gained was a great deal of experience – in particular, the knowledge that no settlement would succeed unless it was regularly supplied from England. 'It is the sinfullest thing in the world,' wrote Bacon, 'to forsake or destitute a plantation, once in forwardness,' but swift profits were still hoped for from colonies, and it was to be many years before the truth of Bacon's other observations was generally recognized: that 'planting of countries is like planting of woods; for you must take account to lose almost twenty years' profit, and expect your recompense in the end'.

Not all colonization involved a transatlantic voyage. In Elizabeth's reign there was a determined effort to establish English settlers in Ireland. That unfortunate country was so poor that it was not really worth the expense of governing, and the Tudors might have been content with a nominal sovereignty had it not been for the Reformation. This established a Protestant church in England, but the Irish remained stubbornly addicted to Roman Catholicism. As the Spanish threat to England developed in Elizabeth's reign, it became clear that Ireland was the weakest point in the English defences, and would have to be more firmly secured.

As early as 1566 Elizabeth had sent an expedition to put down rebellion in Ulster, and after that she encouraged individuals to establish plantations in Ireland. These aroused violent opposition, for the native Irish were driven out of their holdings to make way for English settlers. Of all the attempts that were made, only Raleigh's in Munster was reasonably successful, and that was because he took over an area in which the English had just put down another rebellion so harshly that thirty thousand native inhabitants died, and Spenser described how 'out of every corner of the woods and glens they came creeping forth upon their hands, for their legs could not bear them; they looked like anatomies of death; they spake like ghosts crying out of their graves'.

Yet savage treatment failed to cow the Irish, and their spirit was kept alive by the missionary priests sent over from the Continent. The defeat of the Armada persuaded Philip to listen to Irish appeals and send troops to help them. A rebellion was planned, and ships set out, only to be turned back by storms. The Irish could not, and would not, wait. All over the country they rose in rebellion in 1598, and Elizabeth had to forget about economizing and send a full-scale expedition under her new favourite Robert Devereux, Earl of Essex. He gradually suppressed the rebellion, and the work was completed by Mountjoy. Only in 1601 did Spanish troops eventually land in Ireland, but by then it was too late. It cost Elizabeth the crippling sum of one and a quarter million pounds to pacify Ireland, but it brought that unhappy country for the first time under the effective control of the English crown.

The Irish campaign spelt ruin for Elizabeth's favourite, the Earl of Essex. This young man had captured the heart of the aging and childless queen, who made him a member of her council. The other councillors, however, were far from pleased to see this new star rising. They felt that the queen should rely on old and trusted advisers, and not let the health and safety of her kingdom depend upon a hot-headed thirty-year-old. Essex was persuaded, against his better judgment, to accept command of the army in Ireland, and once he had left the court, rumour began to do its work. Essex knew that his enemies were plotting against him, and that he would never get, in Ireland, the swift victory he needed to restore his prestige. As the reports he received from England became more and more alarming, he abandoned caution, threw up his command, and returned home.

Elizabeth's fondness for her young favourite turned swiftly to anger. She had sent him to Ireland to put down the rebellion, but the rebels were still in the field. Essex was kept under house arrest for nearly a year, and then deprived of his offices. He had spent the months of imprisonment brooding over the injustice with which he had been treated, and after his release he gathered a band of discontented gentlemen around him to plan some violent action which should restore their fortunes. There was talk of armed rebellion, and at the Globe Theatre in Southwark the plotters arranged for Shakespeare's *Richard II* to be performed – the tragic history of a monarch who lost his throne because he listened to evil advisers. The council learned what was going on and called Essex's bluff by summoning him to appear before them. His game was up, but in a last desperate throw Essex burst into the City at the head of a couple of hundred men, shouting 'For the queen! For the queen!'. No one joined them and they were overcome without fighting. Whatever the queen's private feelings, she had no mercy for overmighty subjects. Essex's fall was as swift as his rise. He was tried, condemned, and in February 1601 executed.

In these closing years of the reign the war with Spain was still dragging on. Essex had himself taken part in Drake's Portuguese expedition in 1589, and had later commanded an English army sent to support the Protestants in France. Drake and Hawkins tried to revive the glories of earlier years in 1595 by sailing for the Spanish Main – the north coast of South America – but the expedition was a failure, and neither of its leaders survived to return to England. The only successful achievement of this decade came in 1596, when a force commanded by Essex and Howard captured and burned Cadiz. But attempts to repeat the exploit the following year ended in ignominious failure.

The queen herself was an old and lonely woman. Leicester died in the year of the Armada, Walsingham in 1590, and Burghley, the oldest and closest of her advisers, in 1598. The gap in her councils was filled by his hunchback son, Robert Cecil, but there was no one to take his place in her affections. Her fondness for Essex sprang from her loneliness, and after Essex's execution she was even more isolated. Age had not destroyed her majesty, but her looks were gone. An observer in 1598 described her as 'very majestic; her face oblong, fair but wrinkled; her eyes small, yet black and pleasant; her nose a little hooked, her lips narrow and her teeth black; she had in her ears two pearls with very rich drops; her hair was of auburn colour but false; upon her head she had a small crown'.

Many pictures of the queen survive, though few of them are as revealing as this pen-portrait. Some of the best are by Nicholas Hilliard, the finest English painter of his day, particularly of miniatures. In many cases the portraits survive in their original settings, for the Elizabethans were great builders. The queen's palace at Nonsuch has disappeared, but Burghley's fine house near Stamford is still a home of the Cecil family, and Longleat, Montacute, and Hardwicke have not changed a great deal since Elizabeth's day. To see these great stone houses, so full of glass that they glitter like lanterns, standing squarely and massively in their parks, is to be reminded of the calculated splendour of Elizabethan England.

This splendour found its inspiration in the crown, and in the queen who wore it. It is easy to idolize Elizabeth, for she reigned so long that she came, like Victoria after her, to symbolize all the magnificent achievements of her age. But in one respect her reign was a failure. She was the last monarch to have sufficient authority and prestige to oppose the swelling power of the House of Commons and stand upon her rights. On the surface this is what she did. She refused to allow any change in the Church settlement, even at the cost of angering the growing minority of her subjects who were in favour of reform, and she spoke of her royal prerogative in language worthy of her mighty father. In practice, however, she was prepared to abandon a principle as long as she gained an immediate victory. She allowed the Commons to discuss 'matters of state' in spite of her prohibition, never realizing that members trained in the common law would use her concessions as precedents with which to bind her successors.

It was by these means, as the seventeenth-century philosopher Harrington observed, that the House of Commons came 'to raise that head, which since had been so formidable to their princes that they have looked pale upon those assemblies'. Elizabeth gave way because she knew that in the short run she would charm the Commons into accepting her demands. When the debate on monopolies grew particularly bitter, in November 1601, she sent for the Commons, told them she would herself cancel patents that were harmful to the public good, and assured them that 'though God hath raised me high, yet this I count the glory of my crown, that I have ruled with your loves . . . That my grants should be grievous to my people, and oppressions privileged under colour of our patents, our kingly dignity shall not suffer it. Yea, when I heard it, I could give no rest unto my thoughts until I had reformed it . . . There will never Queen sit in my seat with more zeal to my country, care for my subjects, and that will sooner with willingness venture her life for your good and safety, than myself. For it is my desire to live nor reign no longer than my life and reign shall be for your good. And though you have had and may have many princes more mighty and wise sitting in this seat, yet you never had nor shall have any that will be more careful and loving'. It was a masterly and moving speech, and she ended by charging her councillors 'that before these gentlemen go into their counties, you bring them all to kiss my hand'. By such means Elizabeth won her own way or turned defeat into triumph, 'converting her reign', as Harrington wrote, 'through the perpetual love-tricks that passed between her and her people, into a kind of romance'. But although she could play this game to perfection and win by charm what would otherwise have cost her anger and unhappiness, her successors were not so fortunate. They had all Elizabeth's difficulties and none of her magic. In the words of a modern historian, 'she made of the crown in Parliament a role which no man could have played, unless perhaps it had been her father, and trained an audience which, if sometimes barely tolerant of herself, would be charmed by no other'.[1]

[1] Sir John Neale: Article in *Tudor Studies* (Longmans), edited by R. W. Seton-Watson, p. 286.

CHAPTER 33

James I

1603-1625

QUEEN ELIZABETH died in her palace at Richmond on 24 March 1603. Just over a week later, the son of Mary, Queen of Scots, set out from Edinburgh to take possession of the English throne. The new king, James I, was not an impressive figure. His body was set on thin spindly legs, and his large rolling eyes and straggly beard, while they gave his face a kindly expression, robbed it of dignity. He had none of the natural majesty of Elizabeth, none of that hidden reserve which commands respect. He was learned and intelligent – 'the wisest fool in Christendom' – but loved to give his opinions on every subject, never realizing that he cheapened them by repetition.

Yet as he made his way from his poor northern kingdom into the promised land farther south, the nobility and gentry flocked to greet him. They had good cause, for the succession had remained uncertain almost up to Elizabeth's death, and as the translators of the Bible said, speaking from their own experience, 'it was the expectation of many . . . that upon the setting of that bright occidental star, Queen Elizabeth of most happy memory, some thick and palpable clouds of darkness would so have overshadowed this land that men should have been in doubt which way they were to walk'. The peaceful accession of James banished the shadow of civil war, and the two sons he brought with him seemed to guarantee a settled future.

James was, in his own words, 'an old, experienced king, needing no lessons'. He came to the English throne a prematurely aged thirty-nine, but he had twenty years of successful kingship behind him. His very success in Scotland led him, however, to underrate the difficulties facing him in England. For an outsider like himself

Elizabeth had been the symbol of royal wealth and princely authority. He had little idea how close she had come to bankruptcy, and how hard she had worked to keep the love of her people. James had been brought up to believe that kings were appointed by God, and had a divine right to rule their subjects. In 1610 he told members of Parliament that 'the state of monarchy is the supremest thing on earth. As to dispute what God may do is blasphemy . . . so it is seditious in subjects to dispute what a king may do in the height of his power'.

There was little in this view that Tudor monarchs would have disagreed with, but many true things are better left unsaid. In any case, supreme authority in England belonged to Parliament, for only that body could make laws against which there was no appeal. The king was, of course, an essential part of Parliament. But so were the Lords and Commons, and when James gave them long lectures on the authority of princes, he stung them into saying what they thought were their own rights and privileges. As early as 1604 James quarrelled with the Commons over a disputed election, and when they claimed the right to decide such matters he reminded them sharply that he had granted their privileges, and would if necessary take them back again. The Commons immediately protested that their privileges were their 'right and due inheritance, no less than our very lands and goods [and] cannot be withheld from us . . . but with apparent wrong to the whole state of the realm'. Both sides were right. James knew that he and his predecessors, kings of England, had always been formally asked, at the beginning of every Parliament, to grant both Houses their usual privileges. But the Commons knew that such requests had always been accepted, and being good lawyers they also knew that actions are as binding as words.

Soon after James took possession of the throne, he brought the war with Spain to a close. Now the country was no longer united in face of a common enemy. At this critical stage, when James should have gone out of his way to keep in close touch with Parliament, he cut one of the most important links. Elizabeth, whose mother came from a landed Wiltshire family, knew that the gentry who controlled the Commons were at least as important as the lords of the Upper House, especially after the dissolution of the monasteries had given them a much greater stake in the country. She kept her best councillors in the Commons, and there they sat close to the Speaker – another royal official – and worked out their tactics for debates. It was a vital link, and James snapped it. By raising Robert Cecil to the peerage in 1603 he removed his ablest adviser to the House of Lords, and left only two mediocre councillors to pilot royal policy through a suspicious Commons.

However difficult Parliament might be to deal with, James could not afford to do without it. Because of the continuing price rise the king needed more and more money, but even though he sold much of his own and the Church's land he was always in debt. Elizabeth had made ends meet by watching like a miser over every penny, but James loved spending. He started off at a disadvantage since, unlike Elizabeth, he had a family to maintain, and his wife, Anne of Denmark, had a passion for expensive clothes and jewels. But he made no attempt to match his expenditure to his income. He spent £20,000 on his coronation, and made lavish grants of money and pensions to friends and courtiers, particularly those who had come with him from Scotland. At his court, elaborate entertainments, called masques, were frequently staged. Some of them must have been beautiful, all of them were expensive. The Commons could hardly be blamed for assuming that royal extravagance was the sole reason for James's money troubles. They clung to the belief that the king should live off his own revenues, except in times of emergency, and calmly ignored the fact that while they were growing richer the king was getting relatively poorer. Even if James had been willing to swallow his pride and explain the true state of his finances he could not have done so, for the Exchequer, which handled much of his income, was hopelessly inefficient – still using medieval Latin and tally-sticks for its book-keeping, and years behind in its accounts.

Faced with a perpetual shortage of money, James and his chief minister Robert Cecil squeezed all they could out of existing sources. One method, which Elizabeth had used, was to levy 'impositions', or additional import duties on certain goods. Elizabeth's tax had aroused no comment, but James's was quickly challenged. A merchant called John Bate, who traded with Turkey, refused to pay impositions and was summoned before the court of the Exchequer in 1606. This was the first of several attempts to appeal to the law courts against royal policy. They all failed, not because the judges were corrupt, but because the king's authority could not be closely defined. Every government has, and must have, reserve powers which it can use in an emergency. English kings had always exercised these as part of their royal prerogative. What was new in James's case was that he was using his emergency powers when there was no obvious emergency. There were many Members of Parliament who assumed that a peaceful solution to all political problems could be found in the law courts. It took them years to realize that the king's actions, however unjust they might seem, were within the letter of the law. The only place in which to challenge them effectively was Parliament.

The Commons took up the question of impositions in 1610. James followed the example of Elizabeth and ordered them not to discuss matters of trade without his special permission. In the queen's reign, such prohibitions were challenged by a few fiery members such as the Wentworths, but accepted by the greater part. Time and absence of effective leadership had made members far more independent. The Commons now resolved that it was 'an ancient, general, and undoubted right of Parliament to debate freely all matters which do properly concern the subject'. This proud declaration was a challenge to the king but James chose to ignore it and allowed the debate to continue.

Religion, as well as finance, brought the king into conflict with the Commons. There were many members in the House – perhaps a majority; if not, then a powerful and active minority – who wanted to see modifications in the ritual and vestments of the Anglican Church in order to purify it and give it strength to face the European challenge of the Roman Catholic revival. At the outset of his reign James had received the Millenary Petition, supposedly signed by a thousand clergy. This was a moderate document, pleading for reforms in ceremonial but not questioning the royal supremacy or the bishops who enforced it. James would never accept a Presbyterian Church since that would mean rule by councils of elected elders, or presbyters. Had there been a clear division between religion and politics Stuart kings might conceivably have left the Church to look after itself; but in the sixteenth and seventeenth centuries religion embraced every aspect of man's life. Political, economic and social questions were all expressed in the language of religion, and Roman Catholics and

Protestants, high Anglicans and Puritans, would have agreed that
State and Church were a single society. Change in the one
inevitably meant change in the other, as James knew well when he
made his pithy observation 'No bishop, no king'. Councils of
elders, or presbyteries, bore too close a resemblance to republican
assemblies to be acceptable to Stuart sovereigns. James was
prepared to be tolerant on matters of detail, and summoned a
conference at Hampton Court in which representatives of the
Puritan clergy met the bishops. This, however, ended in failure
when a tactless Puritan member let slip the word 'presbytery'. This
stirred up all James's latent suspicions, and revived unhappy
memories of John Knox and the presbyters of the Scottish Church
constantly nagging and browbeating him. 'A presbytery,' he burst
out, 'as well agreeth with a monarchy as God and the Devil. Then
Jack and Tom and Will and Dick shall meet, and at their pleasures
censure me and my council and all our proceedings. Then Will
shall stand up and say "It must be thus!". Then Dick shall reply
and say, "Nay, marry, but we will have it thus!" . . . Stay, I pray
you, for one seven years before you demand that of me, and if you
then find me pursy and fat and my wind-pipes stuffed, I will
perhaps hearken to you.' The only positive result of the conference
was the Authorized Version of the Bible – one of the most
majestic pieces of writing in the English language. All the other
results were negative. Three hundred clergy were dismissed from
their livings for refusing to worship according to the prayer book,
and joined the ranks of the 'silenced brethren' whose cause was
taken up by Parliament.

The Commons were made more angry by James's tolerance of
Roman Catholics. The penal laws were relaxed in the early years
of the reign, but James took fright at the number of Catholics who
now came out openly to worship, and he clamped down again.
Nothing is more difficult to bear than high hopes suddenly
frustrated. A group of Catholics planned to blow up the king and
both Houses of Parliament in November 1605, and seize power in
the confusion that would follow. But one of the plotters gave the
game away in a letter, hastily and illegibly scrawled, that still
survives. 'Though there be no appearance of any stir,' he wrote, 'yet
I say they shall receive a terrible blow this Parliament, and yet
they shall not see who hurts them.' This obscure message was clear

enough to Cecil. The cellars beneath Parliament were searched, and Guy Fawkes and his associates arrested. The Catholics were driven into hiding again by public hatred and there was a deep, unreasoning suspicion of them which survived for the next two centuries and led to sudden outbursts of panic and persecution.

James, who always wore padded clothes as a protection against an assassin's dagger, was as frightened as anyone. But he was not by nature a persecutor, and soon relaxed the severe laws against the Catholics again, much to Parliament's anger. His dislike of Presbyterianism drove him to the other extreme, which was represented in the Church of England by the high-church group, generally called Arminians. These were people who were proud of their church's Catholic ancestry, and wished to preserve the ceremonies and vestments that were a visible link with earlier centuries of Christian worship. Puritans saw little difference between Anglo-Catholics and Roman Catholics, and began to suspect that within the king's court Papal agents were secretly at work. This suspicion was added to the grievances that were driving king and Parliament even farther apart.

Robert Cecil, Earl of Salisbury, worked hard to stop the split from widening. He tried to negotiate an agreement with the Commons, by which they would vote the crown a permanent addition to its income, in return for the abolition of old feudal rights, like wardship, which were a constant source of irritation. Had this 'Great Contract' come off, the crown would have regained strength, and been able to meet the Commons on equal terms, or even do without Parliament altogether. But the Commons were too suspicious and the proposal came to nothing. Cecil himself died in 1612, and the same year saw the death of Prince Henry, the king's eldest son. This young man had been widely admired and respected, and many who despised James had taken comfort from the thought that his successor would be worthy of the throne. Henry's death dashed their hopes, for the new heir was his younger brother Charles, whose acute shyness made him an unknown quantity.

James now came to depend more and more upon his favourites – the young men whose good looks were their only recommendation. First of these was a Scotsman Robert Carr, but he was replaced in 1614 by the man who was to dominate James for the rest of his life.

This was George Villiers, the son of a Leicestershire knight. Honours and riches were poured upon him, and he became successively earl, marquis, and finally duke of Buckingham – the only commoner to be created a duke in the two centuries from Henry VII's accession to the restoration of Charles II.

The English nobles were bitter at the way in which young upstarts, too many of them Scottish, came to monopolize high offices and places of profit. This was the beginning of the divorce between the crown and the House of Lords that was to remove the king's last hope of controlling Parliament. Elizabeth had kept on good terms with her nobles by letting them share in the profits of government. The royal administration was full of survivals from the medieval past, and those fortunate enough to be appointed to such offices could draw a large income from fees and gifts, while they left all the work to a deputy. These were the golden bonds that tied the nobles and the more important gentry to the crown. But by James's reign the pressure of bankruptcy was beginning to tell. There were fewer profits to be made, and the number of useless offices was cut down by ministers such as Robert Cecil and Lionel Cranfield, in a desperate attempt to make the administration pay its way. The result was much greater competition for such profitable offices as survived, and the upper classes were split between the handful who shared in the pickings, and the envious majority who were left like hungry spectators at a banquet. The court, which had in Tudor times been a magnet, attracting ambitious and talented men from all ranks of society, became in James's reign a closed shop, and the king moved in a narrow circle of friends and spongers, out of touch with the forces at work in English life.

The king's failure to give a clear lead in politics left the way open for other men. This was particularly true of the Commons where, in the absence of effective royal councillors, a number of talented speakers led the House in attacks on the government. Coke and Sandys, Phelips and Hakewill, were the driving force in the Commons during the middle years of the reign. James was not entirely blind to the danger, but his crude attempt to influence the elections of 1614 was a pathetic failure. The Addled Parliament, as it was called, lasted only two months and accomplished nothing.

Rather than suffer the indignity of quarrelling with another

Parliament, James managed without one for the next seven years. Fortunately for him he found a financial wizard in Lionel Cranfield, who entered his service in 1618. Over the next three years Cranfield pruned the king's expenditure and squeezed all he could out of every source of royal income. Half-forgotten feudal dues were demanded from holders of royal lands, forced loans were levied from the gentry, and monopolies were sold to the highest bidder. But Cranfield's efficiency led to his downfall. When Parliament at last met in 1621, Lords and Commons were united by anger and self-interest, and revived the old device of impeachment.[1] A prominent monopolist, Sir Giles Mompesson, was the first to be accused, and only escaped perpetual imprisonment by fleeing to France. Flushed with success, the Commons accused the Lord Chancellor, Francis Bacon, of bribery and corruption. Bacon's high office made him one of the most important figures in the king's government, but this did not save him. The Lords sentenced him to a heavy fine, and forbade him ever again to hold office. Finally, in 1624, Cranfield himself, now Earl of Middlesex and Lord Treasurer, was impeached. He was sentenced to 'lose all his offices which he holds in this kingdom, and shall hereafter be made incapable of any office, place, or employment in the state'.

In this dramatic fashion, the Commons called the king's ministers to account for their actions. They were not anti-royalist in intention. They wanted the king to work in harmony with them, by which they meant that he should ask for, and accept, their advice, and not simply call on them to pay for policies of which they did not approve. But James, like his Tudor predecessors, was not prepared to be a mere figurehead. The 'abuses' – like impositions and monopolies – of which the Commons complained, were the king's last line of defence. Without them he would be bankrupt, at the mercy of Parliament. Yet by clinging to them he made co-operation with Parliament impossible.

The Commons were passionate in defence of what they considered to be their liberties because they saw the power of princes daily increasing on the Continent. There the uneasy truce between the Protestant and Catholic powers was coming to an end. In every country rulers were raising armies and preparing for the struggle. Parliaments could not survive under those conditions. Only in

[1] See p. 202.

Britain, where the frontiers were guarded by the sea, could subjects criticize their ruler, refuse to pay for a standing army, and yet hope to survive.

The Thirty Years' War in Europe broke out in 1618. It was the last stage of the struggle between the Reformation and the Counter-Reformation. The fate of Protestant Europe hung in the balance, as it had done in Elizabeth's reign. Many Englishmen hoped that James would act like his great predecessor and champion the Protestant cause. James knew that war costs money and that if England intervened he would be dependent on Parliament for supplies. Yet, as a convinced Protestant, he could hardly stand aside. His family honour was also at stake. His daughter Elizabeth had married a Calvinist prince, Frederick, ruler of a German state called the Palatinate. In 1618 Frederick was offered the throne of Bohemia by the Protestant nobles of that country who had rebelled against their Catholic king. His acceptance led to war, for the deposed Catholic king, Ferdinand, was elected Holy Roman Emperor in 1619, and planned to reconquer Bohemia as a first step towards wiping out Protestantism throughout Europe. Frederick and his attractive wife spent only one brief winter in their new kingdom before the Catholic armies drove them out of it for ever.

James hoped to help his family and the Protestant cause by diplomacy rather than war. The Emperor Ferdinand was a member of the Hapsburg family, and his cousin Philip III was king of Spain. James planned to marry his son Charles to Philip's daughter. After that, he imagined, all would be plain sailing. The Spanish king, being connected by marriage with the English ruling house, would no doubt persuade his imperial cousin to call off the war against Bohemia and restore Frederick to his rightful throne. Had there been any chance of such a scheme succeeding, it would have been a good one. But every link in the chain was weak. The emperor was most unlikely to stop fighting at the request of his Spanish cousin; Philip was unlikely to ask him, and in any case would not want to see his own daughter married to a heretic.

When Parliament met in December 1621, the Commons asked the king 'to publicly avow the aiding of those of our religion in foreign parts' and expressed the hope that 'our most noble Prince may be timely and happily married to one of our own religion'.

James resented this attempt by the Commons to interfere in the affairs of the crown. His attitude was exactly that of Elizabeth when he ordered that members should not 'presume henceforth to meddle with anything concerning our government or deep matters of state'. But the Commons could no longer be checked as they had been in the queen's reign. Spain had invaded Holland. The emperor had defeated the Bohemians. Yet at this very moment when Protestantism was fighting for survival, the English king was proposing a catholic marriage for his son. It was as though Elizabeth, in 1584, had talked of marrying Philip of Spain! When they continued debating this policy James sent an angry message in which he reminded them, accurately enough, that 'your privileges were derived from the grace and permission of our ancestors and us' and warned them that they 'would enforce us, or any just king, to retrench them of their privileges'. The Commons refused to give way before this threat, and drew up a Protestation which they ordered to be entered in the journal of the House. 'The privileges of parliament,' they proclaimed, 'are the ancient and undoubted birthright and inheritance of the subjects of England; and the arduous and urgent affairs concerning the king, state, and defence of the realm and of the church of England . . . are proper subjects and matter of counsel and debate in parliament.' James sent for the journal and solemnly tore out the offending Protestation, but he could not so easily destroy the body that had passed it.

James was hamstrung by lack of money. He did not want to start a war with Spain, for although Parliament would certainly have voted money for it, parliamentary supplies always fell far short of the actual costs. In any case, war with Spain would not restore his son-in-law to the Palatinate; neither would it relieve the Bohemian Protestants. He might raise an army and send it to fight in central Europe, but military expeditions of this sort usually turned out to be expensive failures.

Since no other policy appeared possible James went ahead with negotiations for a Spanish marriage. Buckingham, impatient for success, persuaded the aging king to allow him and Charles to slip away secretly to Spain to speed matters up. It was a fantastic scheme, for the Spanish court, with its elaborate code of manners, was bound to be shocked by this unexpected attempt to cut through formalities. Such was in fact the case. Charles did his best to see the Spanish princess, even to the extent of climbing into a walled garden and dropping at her feet. But the quest had been hopeless from the beginning, and the two young men eventually took ship for England, angry and humiliated.

They returned to the sound of ringing bells and the glare of bonfires. The Spanish match had been so unpopular in England that the news of its abandonment was greeted like a victory. For the first, and last, time in their lives Charles and Buckingham were popular heroes. They quickly turned their popularity to political account by urging war against Spain. James saw no reason to change his belief that such a war would cost a fortune and accomplish nothing, but at sixty-one he was already too tired and too weak to resist the combined pleading of his son and his favourite. When Parliament met in 1624 James abandoned everything to them. Not only did he ask their advice on foreign policy – the very point on which he had quarrelled with them in 1621 – he also declared that 'if I take a resolution, upon your advice, to enter into a war, then yourselves by your own deputies shall have the disposing of the money. I will not meddle with it, but you shall appoint your own treasurers'. A grateful Commons replied by voting £300,000, which they described as 'the greatest aid which was ever granted in Parliament'. The next three years were to show that the sum was absurdly inadequate. Big wars cannot be fought on a shoestring, but Stuart parliaments were never prepared to meet the costs of their ambitious plans. For the moment, however, all was harmony, and in March 1625 James's reign closed in sunshine.

CHAPTER 34

Charles I and Parliament

1625-1629

THE NEW king, Charles I, was a short, dapper young man of twenty-five. As a child he had been weak and sickly, but he grew up to be physically strong, delighting in riding, swimming and playing tennis. The only mark of his delicate childhood was a stammer, which may well have sprung from his shyness. Forced by his birth into leading a public life, he took refuge in a chilly manner, and kept the warm, passionate side of his nature for the handful of people who knew him well.

He was a devout Anglican, described by one observer as 'punctual and regular in his devotions, so that he was never known to enter upon his recreations or sports, though never so early in the morning, before he had been at public prayers'. Charles believed, like his father, that God had called him to the throne, and he was determined to maintain the rights of the crown and of the Anglican Church. 'I cannot,' he once said, 'defend a bad, nor yield in a good cause', and although, later on, he was forced to abandon some of the prerogatives of the crown it was always with the private reservation that he would take them back again when a more favourable opportunity arose. What God had given him, only God, he believed, could take away. To Charles's subjects this was to seem like dishonesty and they despaired of coming to terms with a man who would not keep his promises. But the king was honest by his own lights. He served the cause of monarchy faithfully and truly until his death.

The new king was committed to war with Spain and still hoped to restore his brother-in-law, the Winter King, to the Palatinate, now overrun by Catholic troops. The money voted by James's last Parliament had all been spent, partly in equipping an English expeditionary force under a German mercenary soldier, Mansfeld, to fight in Europe. Charles therefore summoned Parliament and in his opening speech, after thanking God that the business in hand did not need much explaining 'for I am neither able to do it, nor doth it stand with my nature to spend much time in words', called upon members to vote more taxes for the war which they had encouraged the crown to start.

Charles confidently expected a liberal grant. He was championing the Protestant cause, and was already planning with Buckingham a combined naval and land attack on Spain that would revive the glories of Elizabeth's reign. But the Commons voted less than £150,000 and even attempted to cut the crown's regular income by voting tonnage and poundage for one year only instead of for life. They distrusted Buckingham and suspected, rightly, that however much money they voted, the favourite would waste most of it. They were also suspicious of Arminians at court. When they ordered the arrest of a clergyman called Montague for publishing a book in which he dwelt lovingly on Catholic survivals in the Anglican Church, Charles promptly made the man his chaplain. Their suspicions were increased when the king married a Catholic princess, Henrietta Maria, daughter of Henry IV of France. Charles had earlier promised Parliament not to relax the penal laws against Catholics, but in the marriage contract he agreed to do so. The news leaked out and the Commons were furious.

When Charles realized he would get no more money he dissolved Parliament. Buckingham went ahead with his plans for a combined operation against Cadiz, arguing that victory would unite the country behind the crown, and encourage the Commons to open their purse strings. There was nothing wrong with his reasoning. All that was needed was success. The expedition was, however, a shameful failure. The food and drink supplied were so bad that men died from starvation; many ropes were rotten; and some sails dated back to the Armada. When, eventually, ten thousand ragged troops were landed at Cadiz, they were so overcome by the local wine that they had to be brought back to England, leaving a Spanish treasure fleet free to anchor safely in Cadiz harbour. Charles was nearly bankrupt, and had to summon another Parliament, but he might have known that when members met they would be in a savage mood.

The king blamed failure on the Commons, who had voted nothing. But Sir John Eliot led the house in an attack upon the bad management of the war. 'Our honour is ruined,' he thundered. 'Our ships are sunk. Our men perished. Not by the sword, not by the enemy, not by chance, but . . . by those we trust.' He called on the Commons to follow the example set in James's reign by impeaching the hated favourite.

This bitter attack upon his friend brought out all the king's stubbornness. James would have bent before the storm, but Charles was not prepared to stand by and see his minister condemned for serving him. He forbade the Commons to question the actions of his servants, and when they persisted he called their bluff. 'Now that you have all things according to your wishes, and that I am so far engaged that you think there is no retreat, now you begin to set the dice and make your own game. But I pray you, be not deceived. It is not a parliamentary way, nor is it a way to deal with a king . . . Remember that Parliaments are altogether in my power for their calling, sitting, and dissolution. Therefore as I find the fruits of them good or evil, they are to continue or not to be'. When the Commons ignored this scarcely veiled threat and went ahead with the impeachment, Charles dissolved Parliament in June 1626.

Buckingham, unshaken by Parliament's hostility, was already planning another expedition. A succession of minor irritations had led to war between England and France, and Buckingham hoped to encourage the Protestants of western France to rise against their Catholic king, by occupying the island of Rhé, off La Rochelle. Money had to be found to raise troops and equip a fleet, and since Parliament had, in the king's eyes, shirked its responsibilities, he decided to use his prerogative powers. The gentry were ordered to lend the king the amount of money they would have had to pay if Parliament had granted supplies; and the troops who were raised were billeted on private householders. Some of the gentry refused to pay the loan and looked to the law courts to protect them. But the judges found for the king, and when the Lord Chief Justice dared to question the legality of the forced loan, Charles dismissed him.

The king and Buckingham hoped that the discontent aroused by their efforts to carry on the war would be forgotten in the excitement of victory. But the Rhé expedition was a failure from the beginning. Buckingham was enthusiastic, but he was no organizer. Even his mother told him that 'the kingdom will not pay your expenses, and every man groans under the burden of the times'. Buckingham led the expedition himself, and fought bravely. But the professional French troops were too good for the English collection of jailbirds and amateurs. By November 1627 Rhé had been abandoned and the survivors of the operation sailed back to Portsmouth. The king put the entire blame on Parliament. Having given his trust to Buckingham, pride and affection blinded him to his favourite's failure. 'With whatsoever success ye shall come to me,' he wrote to Buckingham, 'ye shall ever be welcome.'

The failure of the Rhé expedition left Charles even more heavily in debt, and he had to summon a third Parliament to try to get money. The days were past when a letter from the king might influence elections, or when royal councillors were given a respectful hearing in the Commons. But there were moderate men in Parliament, who thought that Eliot was too violent in his attacks on the government. Chief of these was Sir Thomas Wentworth, member for Yorkshire, who realized that the Commons, by refusing to co-operate with the king, were widening the gulf between crown and Parliament to the point where it would become unbridgeable. Wentworth wanted to close the gap by drawing up a Bill which should define the rights of the crown. Like the barons at Runnymede, the Commons would bring the king back into time-honoured and accepted ways of government. Their mood was best expressed by one member who said 'I shall be very glad to see that old decrepid law Magna Charta, which hath been kept so long and lien bedridden as it were – I shall be glad to see it walk abroad again with new vigour and lustre'.

The new Charter was the *Petition of Right*, presented to the king in 1628. It asked 'that no man be compelled to make or yield any gift, loan . . . or suchlike charge, without common consent by Act of Parliament;' and went on to condemn arbitrary imprisonment and the billeting of troops in private houses. Charles was reluctant to accept what seemed to be a limitation of his powers, but eventually he signed the Petition. Even though it made little difference in fact to the position of the king or his subjects, the Petition was an attempt at reconciliation and might have succeeded, given time and good will.

But there was little time, and no good will. After he had accepted the Petition, Charles expected the Commons to show their gratitude by voting money and making him the long delayed grant of tonnage and poundage. Money was indeed voted, but the tonnage and poundage Bill was held up while the House continued to debate its grievances. Their attack was concentrated on Arminians at Court. Eliot once more dominated the House and whipped up their fury. The more responsible members of the Commons were turning away from him in disgust, and the Lords, who joined with the Lower House in urging Charles to accept the Petition of Right, refused to co-operate any longer. Nevertheless Eliot pushed through the Remonstrance of June 1628, in which the Commons declared that by collecting tonnage and poundage the king had broken the fundamental laws of the constitution. The only fundamental law that Charles recognized was the king's right to rule. The alternative, as he saw it, was anarchy, and he sent members away to give tempers time to cool.

The London mob was so inflamed that it set on the Duke of Buckingham's doctor in the streets and tore him to pieces. They would willingly have killed the duke himself, but he was at Portsmouth, preparing yet another expedition. There he was followed by John Felton, a former army officer with a fanatical grudge against Buckingham. He joined in the throng that always filled Buckingham's house and, on an August morning in 1628, stabbed the favourite to death. The news was brought to Charles while he was at prayers. He said nothing and motioned for the service to continue. Only when it was over did he abandon himself to grief.

The three months that followed, between the assassination of Buckingham and the recall of Parliament, were a turning point in the reign, for the king was no longer prepared for compromise. He regarded Eliot and his followers in the Commons as Buckingham's real murderers, and held himself freed from the promises he had made in the Petition of Right. He no longer felt it necessary to tone down his religious policy. Montague, whom he had defended from the Commons in 1625, was made Bishop of Chichester, and Laud, the leader of the Arminians, was given the important diocese of London. Among those who had turned in disgust from Eliot was Sir Thomas Wentworth. He had been one of the chief opponents of the king until the Petition of Right gave hope of better things. Now he distrusted the Commons more than Charles, and was prepared to join the royal government. In December 1628 he was created a viscount and appointed Lord President of the Council of the North.

When Parliament reassembled in January 1629, the grant of tonnage and poundage was again held up while the Commons plunged into an angry debate about their grievances. Charles soon lost patience and ordered Parliament to be dissolved. But when the Speaker tried to put an end to debate by rising from his chair, two members held him down while they proposed three resolutions. These declared that anyone seeking to extend Arminianism, or agreeing to the payment of tonnage and poundage, was 'a capital enemy to the kingdom and commonwealth ... and a betrayer of the liberties of England'. The king's officers were knocking at the door of the House. Soldiers had been sent for to break their way in. But only after the resolutions had been carried did members at last disperse.

Charles now counter-attacked his enemies. Eliot was imprisoned in the Tower where he remained, like his Elizabethan forerunner Peter Wentworth, until his death three years later. He was a great House of Commons man, who saw that assembly as a supreme court of the nation, ready to call the king's ministers to account for their actions. Historically speaking, this was a false view, since Tudor Parliaments had been the sovereign's servant not his equal, and the Commons, in fact, represented the land-owning gentry and merchants – not the country as a whole. But institutions are living things and cannot be bound by traditions. The real justification for members' criticism of royal policy was that in their house were concentrated the wealth and power of the nation. Throughout Europe representative institutions were falling before the might of catholic monarchies: the Commons' attack on Arminianism, and their haggling over tonnage and poundage, sprang from the fear that what was happening beyond the Channel might easily come to pass in England, unless they kept watchful guard over their liberties.

For Charles, Parliament was a body which his predecessors had created to help them govern and which was now becoming a hindrance. Against the privileges of Parliament he set the rights of the crown, 'for as we will maintain our subjects in their just liberties, so we do and will expect that they yield as much submission and duty to our royal prerogative'. A more flexible ruler, recognizing that politics are a matter of give and take, would have accepted a compromise more in tune with the poverty of the crown and the increasing wealth of the Commons. But Charles saw himself as the defender of religion and liberty – religion, by preserving the Anglican Church under the supreme headship of the crown; liberty, by maintaining an ordered government without which there would be anarchy and the rule of the strongest. He saw no reason to believe that God spoke only to Puritans and members of the Commons.

Rather than risk any more stormy sessions of Parliament, Charles decided to rule through his Council, and wait for tempers to cool. The driving force behind the new administration came to be Wentworth. He had opposed royal government up to 1628 because Buckingham had made it so corrupt and inefficient. Now that the favourite was dead, however, and Charles openly committed to observing the Petition of Right, Wentworth worked to restore the prestige of the king.

He would have been more effective if only the king had trusted him. But Charles was suspicious of his former opponent and sent Wentworth first to the north, and then, as Lord Deputy, to Ireland. In his long absences from the council his close friend William Laud, who became Archbishop of Canterbury in 1633, led the campaign for thorough and efficient government. Wentworth and Laud invented a mythical figure, 'Lady Mora', to represent the inefficiency of officials and corruption at court, and in the end Lady Mora defeated them. Courtiers found it easy to wheedle pensions and profitable appointments out of Charles and his queen, and the contrast grew all the greater between the favoured circle of nobles and gentry in the court, and the much greater number of those who looked on, envious and bitter, from outside. 'The treasure of the kingdom,' wrote one Puritan observer, was 'being wasted by court caterpillars'.

CHAPTER 35

Rule without Parliament

1629-1640

THE DISCONTENT of the property-owners did not show itself during the 1630's. On the surface the country seemed, in the words of the painter Rubens, 'to announce a people rich and happy in the bosom of peace'. The struggle with France and Spain was brought to a close, and while Europe was given over to the savage fighting that marked the Thirty Years' War, England enjoyed the profits of neutrality. Even the king had money to spare, now that he did not have to keep up an army and navy, and he could afford to indulge the taste for collecting pictures, which had been with him from his youth. Charles was the greatest patron of the arts ever to occupy the throne of England, and his court became a centre to which artists flocked from all over Europe. Rubens arrived in 1629, and a few years later Van Dyck began his magnificent series of portraits of the Stuart court. In the royal palace at Whitehall the king assembled a great collection of paintings and sculpture and sent his agents throughout Europe to buy for him. When, after his death, the collection was broken up, it included four hundred pieces of sculpture and fourteen hundred paintings, many of which are to be seen today in Continental galleries.

Some of the finest work, however, survives in England, particularly the superb painted ceiling with which Rubens decorated the Banqueting House in Whitehall. The building itself was the work of Inigo Jones, the leading architect of the early seventeenth century. The Banqueting House, with its graceful columns and tall rectangular windows is, like the Queen's House which he built at Greenwich, a reminder of the elegance of Charles's court.

Architecture and painting were not the only arts that flourished during these years. From the death of the poet John Donne in 1631 until the publication of *Paradise Lost* thirty years later, English poets avoided the grand manner and spoke with a quieter voice. But their poetry is none the worse for this, and in these 'halcyon days', as Thomas Carew called them, some of the most delightful poems in the English language were written, like Robert Herrick's *Cherry Ripe* and *Gather Ye Rosebuds while Ye May*. Everything seemed to herald another Elizabethan age, with the springtime freshness of Herrick and Carew, and the intense religious feeling of Richard Crashaw and George Herbert. But the calm of the 1630's was deceptive. Civil war turned bright spring into shadowy autumn. Robert Herrick was ejected from his Devonshire parsonage in 1647 because of his devotion to the royal cause. Robert Lovelace, who served with the king's armies, was thrown into prison by his captors, though even there his courage and high spirits did not desert him and he wrote the poem which includes the proud assertion that

> Stone walls do not a prison make
> Nor iron bars a cage.

Most of the Caroline poets supported the king when war came, and suffered imprisonment, despair and poverty. Some survived to see the restoration of their fortunes with the return of the king's son in 1660. But the 'halcyon days' were gone beyond recall, and James Shirley wrote their epitaph.

> The glories of our blood and state
> Are shadows, not substantial things.
> There is no armour against fate.
> Death lays his icy hand on kings.
> Sceptre and crown
> Must tumble down
> And in the dust be equal made
> With the poor crooked scythe and spade.

The peaceful years were brought to a tragic end by the bitter quarrel over religion. Archbishop Laud, with Charles's full approval, was reviving the policy of his Elizabethan predecessor Whitgift, by imposing a standard pattern of worship on the Anglican clergy. The prayer book laid down the general outline of services, but parish priests varied the details as they felt inclined. The more

Puritan ones cut down ceremonies to the minimum and frequently moved the altar from the east end of the church into the middle of the nave, for fear that it might become an object of idol worship. Laud felt that such behaviour was an insult to God and he ordered that worship should be 'kept up in uniformity and decency and some beauty of holiness'. Those who refused to conform were hailed before the Court of High Commission, while another prerogative court, Star Chamber, dealt with anyone found distributing Puritan propaganda. By occasional savage sentences such as that of 1637, when three leading Puritan laymen were condemned to be branded, to have their ears sawn off, and to stand in the pillory, Laud hoped to curb his more outspoken critics. But he only succeeded in making martyrs of them and bringing the courts into disrepute.

Many Puritans, despairing of ever being able to worship freely in their own country, took ship for America. The first permanent settlement there had been started in Virginia in 1607. But few of the Virginian settlers were Puritans. The majority had left England because they could find no work, and they carried the Anglican Church with them to America. In 1620, however, a group of Puritan emigrants sailed from Plymouth in the *Mayflower*, and founded the first Puritan colony in New England. Altogether, in the eleven years of Charles's rule without Parliament, the number of emigrants from England was about 60,000, a third of whom went to the New England colonies. The great emigration was the Puritan reply to Laud's challenge, and although some Anglicans were relieved to see the last of these narrow-minded fanatics, others regretted the loss of so many devout, enthusiastic and capable men and women, and feared, like the Anglican poet-priest George Herbert, that

> Religion stands on tiptoe in our land
> Ready to pass to the American strand.

Not all the Puritans emigrated, of course. The large number who remained in England resisted the authority of Laud as best they could, and waited for happier times. There were many Puritans among the property-owners, and the full weight of royal government fell on them. Not since Elizabeth's day had the Council exercised so close a control over local affairs. Enclosing landlords were heavily fined, and the statutes which provided for the relief of the poor and the training of apprentices were put into effect. Workhouses were built, highways and lighthouses were constructed, and orders were issued to stop London straggling farther and farther into the countryside. The crown demonstrated once again that it stood for the interests of the nation as a whole rather than for any particular group. By doing so it angered the property-owners who wanted to be left alone to run local affairs, convinced that what suited them was best for England. The supervision of the royal council which Wentworth called 'that public and common protection which good kings afford their good people', they called tyranny.

Their convictions were reinforced by the methods Charles used to raise money for his government. He continued to collect tonnage and poundage, although Parliament had still not granted it, and he fined landowners for breaking half-forgotten medieval laws. Such devices brought in a good deal of money, and could not be challenged since they were within the letter of the law. But efficiency in collecting money, accompanied by inefficiency in spending it, is a classical cause of revolt. And always it was the property-owners – men who, in the normal course of affairs, went to the law courts only as magistrates – who had to pay or go to prison. Edward Hyde, who was one of them, commented that the 'burden lighted most upon persons of quality and honour, who thought themselves above ordinary oppressions, and were therefore likely to remember it with more sharpness'.

Most notorious of all Charles's expedients was Ship Money. The king had no regular navy, but by old custom the seaport towns could be called on to provide ships, or the equivalent in money, when they were needed. Charles ordered them to do so in 1634, on the grounds that pirates were making the seas unsafe for English shipping. This was no mere excuse. In the first Parliament of the reign one member complained that 'pirates come into our sea and take our ships at our doors' and raiders from North Africa – the dreaded Barbary Corsairs – sacked Baltimore, on the Irish coast, in 1631. In 1635 Charles demanded more Ship Money, and this time called on the inland counties to contribute, since 'that charge of defence which concerneth all men ought to be supported by all'. The money was, in fact, used to build a fleet. But when Charles repeated his demand in 1636 it seemed obvious to the property-owners that he was imposing another permanent tax on them, while denying them the right, or the opportunity, to vote it in Parliament. One of their number, John Hampden, who had a large estate in Buckinghamshire, refused to pay, and looked to the courts to protect him. But the Ship Money Case finally showed that the Common Law courts could not act as umpires between the king and his people. Hampden's plea was dismissed on the now familiar grounds that the king had, and must have, emergency powers, and that he alone could decide when to use them. Even so, five of the twelve judges voted for Hampden, and the narrowness of the majority showed on how slender a foundation of legality royal policy was poised. As for the property-owners, they turned from the law courts in disgust, and looked for safety to their own strength and unity.

Already the leaders of the opposition were meeting regularly. For instance, the company which had been founded to promote a Puritan settlement on Providence Island, in the Caribbean, had Lords Warwick, Saye, and Brooke among its shareholders, as well as John Hampden. These men met frequently in London, to discuss business with their solicitor, Oliver St John – a Puritan lawyer, who had defended Hampden in the Ship Money Case – and their secretary, John Pym. At such meetings those who opposed royal policy came to know each other, and to work out their tactics. They were united by their loathing of Laud's Arminian policy and by their suspicion of Catholics at court. The Thirty Years' War was still in progress, and the Protestant Dutch were fighting for their lives and their religion against the Spaniards. Yet Charles had agreed, in return for cash payments, to supply English ships for the transport of Spanish troops to the Netherlands, and his wife, Henrietta Maria, was surrounding herself with a group of influential Roman Catholic converts. The Puritan property-owners wanted the king to lead England into battle against Roman Catholicism. They knew as well as he did that he would then be at the mercy of Parliament, which alone could provide the money needed to fight a war. But this, after all, was what they wanted.

Because the king believed in monarchy, he kept out of war on the Continent. But he blundered into one at home. Laud was working in the 1630's to bring the Scottish Church under his control. On the face of it this seemed the obvious policy, since Charles was king of both countries and there was no reason why the Presbyterians should flourish in the north when they were being brought to heel in the south. But Laud took no account of the deep-rooted Puritanism of the Scots. James I, who was much more of a politician than his son, had recognized that Laud was a born meddler. 'The plain truth is,' he said, 'that I keep Laud back from all place of rule and authority because I find he hath a restless spirit, and cannot see when matters are well, but loves to toss and change.' This was exactly what Laud did when he prepared a new prayer book for the Scottish Church. Charles ordered that it should be used from July 1637. But when the Dean of St Giles's Cathedral, Edinburgh, used the new service, a riot broke out. 'The Mass is entered among us!' cried one woman. Another flung her stool at the bishop in the pulpit, and the magistrates had to be called in to clear the church. The revolt spread like an epidemic until the whole of Scotland was up in arms. Thousands flocked to sign the National Covenant, binding themselves to defend the Presbyterian system of worship. A general assembly of the Scottish Church was summoned. Charles tried to come to terms by abandoning the new prayer book. But the assembly turned its attack on the Scottish bishops. This was a point on which Charles would not give way, for bishops were the support of his throne. He ordered the assembly to dissolve. When it refused, he prepared to use force.

Years of peace had left England unprepared for war. 'In the Exchequer,' wrote one of Wentworth's correspondents in 1638, 'there is found but two hundred pounds ... The King's magazines are totally unfurnished of arms and all sorts of ammunition, and commanders we have none.' The Scots, on the other hand, had many good soldiers, since the poverty of their country encouraged young men to serve for pay in one of the Continental armies. Many now came home to enlist under Alexander Leslie, a veteran of the Thirty Years' War. But this first *Bishops' War*, as it was called, ended without a shot being fired. Charles ran out of money before the armies met, and agreed, in June 1639, to leave all matters in dispute to be settled by a new Scottish Parliament and general assembly of the Scottish Church.

When the Parliament and assembly met, they declared the

abolition of bishops in Scotland, and ordered every Scot to sign
the Covenant. Charles was faced with the overthrow of his
authority in his northern kingdom. In his dilemma he recalled
Wentworth from Ireland, created him Earl of Strafford, and asked
for his advice. Strafford and Laud urged Charles to fight and to
summon the English Parliament to meet the costs of war. When
Parliament met, they argued, petty bickerings would be submerged by patriotic anger. In any case Strafford saw no reason
to fear Parliament. 'The people,' he had recently written, 'are
in great quietness and, if I be not much mistaken, well satisfied
if not delighted with his Majesty's gracious government and
protection.'

Strafford was gravely mistaken. When Parliament met in April
1640, it was not prepared to co-operate. The Commons were
dominated by John Pym, who led the attack on the king's government. A westcountryman, born four years before the Armada, he
had grown up hating Spain and believing that England's mission
was to defend the Protestant cause. After leaving Oxford he studied
law in the Middle Temple, and then became secretary of the
Providence Island Company. This post brought him friends among
the Puritan nobility and business men, and when Parliament met
he had his programme ready. He was not a republican, but wanted
to cut away the prerogative rights of the crown, and force the king
to work in harmony with Parliament. He was, in fact, Eliot's heir
and successor. But where Eliot had been fiery and uncontrollable,
Pym was sober and self-disciplined. With ruthless determination
this bull-necked, broad-shouldered man welded the critics of
Charles I into a steel-hard opposition.

When Charles realized that he would get no money but simply
lay himself open to attack, he dissolved the Short Parliament, in
May 1640, less than a week after it had met. The Scots were still
in arms, and he appointed Strafford commander-in-chief of the
royal forces. Strafford did all that one man could do to turn a
rabble into an army, but it was an impossible task. The property-
owners, upon whom the king depended for troops and money,
looked on the Scottish invaders as friends come to liberate them
from royal tyranny. Strafford reported 'our horse all cowardly.
The country from Berwick to York in the power of the Scots. An
universal affright in all. A general disaffection to the king's service.

None sensible of his dishonour'. Charles, in desperation, agreed to
an armistice, by which the Scottish troops were to occupy the
northern counties of England and be paid £860 a day for their
pains until such time as a peace treaty was signed.

CHAPTER 36

Civil War

1640-1649

THE KING had to summon Parliament, for he could not possibly find sufficient money himself to pay the Scottish army of occupation. He relied on Strafford to defend the royal cause against its Parliamentary critics, but Strafford was so unpopular – he was known as Black Tom the Tyrant – that his life might be in danger if he came to London. Charles promised him, on the word of a king, that he should not be harmed, and Strafford set out 'with more danger beset', he wrote to a friend, 'than ever man went with out of Yorkshire. Yet my heart is good and I find nothing cold within me'.

By the time Strafford reached London, Parliament was already sitting. Pym had roused the anger of the Commons by reciting a long list of grievances against the crown. In this way he prepared for his attack upon the king's chief minister. He knew that he was matched with a dangerous opponent, for if Pym did not destroy Strafford, Strafford would certainly destroy Pym. When he learned that Strafford planned to accuse him of treason, on the grounds that he was in league with the king's Scottish enemies, Pym acted swiftly. On the day after Strafford arrived in London he made his way to the House of Lords, only to find the doors barred against him. The Commons had impeached the hated minister and called on the Lords to try him for treason. Before Strafford could open his mouth, he was ordered off to prison.

While Westminster Hall was being prepared for Strafford's trial, the Commons attacked the king's other ministers. In early December, Laud was impeached and imprisoned in the Tower. Later that month two other leading members of the king's council fled to France. Just at the moment when Charles desperately needed men to advise him, he was being stripped of them.

Early in 1641 Strafford's trial opened and Pym, who led the prosecution, tried to prove the charge of treason by showing that Strafford had ruled tyrannically in Ireland and had built up an army there with which to subdue England. But these charges could not be proved, and even if they were true they did not amount to treason. After three weeks it became clear even to Pym that the Lords, while willing to get rid of Strafford, would not condemn him on such flimsy evidence. He therefore abandoned the impeachment and introduced a bill of attainder. This simply declared Strafford guilty of treason, without attempting to prove it, and sentenced him to death. The bill passed the Commons by a large majority. When it reached the Lords, about half the peers were deliberately absent. Of those who came, twenty-six voted for Strafford's death, nineteen against.

If was left to the king to seal Strafford's fate by giving his assent to the bill of attainder. He had promised his minister that he should not be harmed. But from the Tower, Strafford wrote to his master: 'To set your Majesty's conscience at liberty, I do most humbly beseech your Majesty (for preventing of evils which may happen by your refusal) to pass the bill.' While the mob surged around the royal palace at Whitehall, howling for Strafford's blood, Charles turned the question over and over in his mind. Then, with tears in his eyes, he gave his assent. On 11 May Strafford went to his execution on Tower Hill, looking up as he passed to the window of Laud's cell, where the archbishop held his hand raised in blessing.[1] One of the vast crowd which had assembled round the scaffold described how, at the news of Strafford's death, 'many that came up to town on purpose to see the execution, rode in triumph back, waving their hats, and with all expressions of joy, through every town they went, crying "His head is off! His head is off!"'.

Pym had destroyed the chief agent of thorough and efficient royal government. He now went on to destroy the prerogative powers of the crown, by which Charles had been able to rule

[1] Laud was kept prisoner in the Tower until his execution in January 1645.

without Parliament. To make sure that his plan could be carried on without interruption, he had pushed through a bill declaring that Parliament was not to be dissolved without its own consent, and the king had assented to it at the very moment when his thoughts were concentrated on Strafford's fate. Now, in the summer months of 1641, all the long-standing grievances like tonnage and poundage and ship money, which the king had used to finance his policy, were declared illegal. Other acts swept away the prerogative courts – Star Chamber, the Councils of the North and of Wales, and the Court of High Commission. Charles, deprived of ministers and of support, agreed to all these bills even though they meant the destruction of the ideal of monarchy for which he stood. In future the crown was to be closely tied to Parliament, with only the ordinary law courts to enforce its will.

As summer drew to its close the king went north to Scotland, hoping to find a few friendly faces in the land of his birth. His cause, which had seemed so low, was already reviving. There were many who felt that Parliament had done all that was needed, and in the country as a whole there was anger at the heavy taxes which Parliament had voted in order to pay the Scottish army. In towns and villages through which Charles passed the inhabitants flocked to greet him, and when reports of this triumphant progress reached London, Pym knew that he must act quickly. The king was still a force to be reckoned with, and given time might swing the people behind him and take his revenge. Pym had to keep tempers near boiling-point so that the attack on the crown could be continued until the king was powerless.

Pym, however, was losing his hold on the Commons. The moderates, who felt that reform had gone far enough, were beginning to organize themselves under one of their members, Edward Hyde. They were particularly suspicious of Pym's proposal to abolish bishops and establish a Presbyterian system in England. They had supported Pym and the Puritans in the attack on Charles's government because they felt the crown was becoming too powerful. But now that the prerogative courts had been swept away, the king appeared as the defender of the Anglican Church which they wished to see preserved. For almost the first time in the seventeenth century, religion and politics, which had seemed to be different aspects of the same cause, were splitting apart. And Pym, unintentionally, was the reason for this. By dealing first with the political grievances against the king, and leaving the attack on the bishops to a later stage, he had given his more moderate followers time to collect their senses and realize that a Presbyterian Parliament would be no more acceptable to them than an Arminian monarchy.

While both sides were jockeying for position in October 1641, news suddenly came that rebellion had broken out in Ireland. In that unhappy country Strafford had ruled strongly and enforced order, but once he left, the system broke down. The Irish Catholics, who could hardly be worse off, rose up against their Protestant masters, and refugees were soon flooding into English ports, bringing with them tales of bloody massacres. It was November, the month of the Gunpowder Plot, and panic fear of Popish plots was mounting rapidly.

An army was needed to put down the rebels. But the commander of the army was the king, and Pym knew that troops raised to put down rebellion in Ireland might easily be used to suppress another nearer home. Already in April there had been rumours of an army plot to save Strafford and arrest the leaders of the Commons. For his own safety, and as he saw it for the good of the kingdom, Pym had to persuade Parliament to take away the king's control of the army. But this would be a violent break with tradition. So far everything that Parliament had done might be interpreted as turning the government back into paths from which it had strayed. But no Parliament had ever claimed control of the army. Pym decided that the only way in which he could carry the House with him would be once again to whip up anger against the king by reciting, in one long list, all the complaints which the Commons had ever made against the Crown. Nothing was omitted in the two hundred clauses eventually put together and aptly called the *Grand Remonstrance* – the great complaint of the property-owners against the king. But Pym went beyond the political grievances into the second stage of his programme – the attack upon the Anglican Church. The Grand Remonstrance demanded that bishops should be deprived of their seats in the House of Lords, and that 'a general synod of the most grave, pious, learned and judicious divines of this island, assisted with some from foreign parts' should be invited to purify the corrupted Church of England. The king was

also called on to choose as ministers only those men in whom
Parliament had confidence.

The debate on the Grand Remonstrance showed how deeply
the Commons were divided. Edward Hyde led the royalists and
moderates who opposed the bill on the grounds that it would serve
no purpose but to inflame tempers. Pym led the Puritan extremists
(who included the member for Cambridge, Oliver Cromwell) in
demanding that the Remonstrance should be passed. Speech
followed speech throughout the long winter afternoon and, as
night fell, candles were lit. At one o'clock in the morning a
division was called: 148 voted against the Remonstrance, 159 in its
favour. Pym had won by eleven votes. His victory was immediately
challenged by the royalists. Members sprang to their feet, shouting
and reaching for their swords. 'I thought,' wrote one of them, 'we,
like Joab's and Abner's young men, had catched at each other's
locks and sheathed our swords in each other's bowels, had not the
sagacity and great calmness of Mr Hampden, by a short speech,
prevented it.' It was past two o'clock before the House finally
emptied. Pym could breathe freely, but his victory had been a
narrow one, and Cromwell later confessed 'that if the remonstrance
had been rejected, he would have sold all he had the next morning,
and never have seen England more'.

In the month that followed the extremists went ahead with their
plans and introduced a Militia Bill, giving Parliament control of all
army appointments. Meanwhile the king was preparing his
counter-attack. To give the impression that he was working for a
reconciliation with the leaders of the Commons he offered Pym
an important post in the royal government as Chancellor of the
Exchequer. Pym, as Charles expected, refused. The king promptly
appointed one of the moderates to this post, bidding for the support of all those members of the Commons who distrusted Pym
and feared that he would not be content until he had stripped the
king of the last rags of royal authority.

At the same time as he worked, at Hyde's suggestion, to win
over the moderates, Charles was also listening to the queen, who
advised him to take some strong action against the leaders of the
Commons. He decided to carry out Strafford's plan of impeaching
the extremist leaders, on the grounds that they had committed
treason by trying to overthrow royal government. Had Charles

acted swiftly and secretly, Pym, Hampden and the three other accused members would have been in his power, and the history of England might well have taken a different course. But news of his intentions leaked out. When, on 4 January 1642, Charles made his way, with a guard of soldiers, to the House of Commons, the five members were no longer there. John Rushworth, one of the clerks of the House, has left us a description of the scene. Members rose and took off their hats as Charles came in – the first king of England ever to enter the House of Commons. 'By your leave, Mr Speaker,' he said, 'I must borrow your chair a little,' and stepped on to the dais from which he could scan all the faces. When he realized his enemies had escaped, he turned to Speaker Lenthall and asked him where they were. 'To which the Speaker, falling on his knees, thus answered: "May it please your Majesty, I have neither eyes to see, nor tongue to speak in this place, but as the House is pleased to direct me, whose servant I am here".' Charles knew he was defeated. 'Well,' he said, 'since I see all the birds are flown, I do expect from you that you shall send them unto me as soon as they return hither,' and he made his way out again, leaving the House in an uproar. A week later the five members returned to the House in triumph, but by that time the king had already left London.

Civil war was now certain, not simply because any reconciliation between the king and the extremist leaders of the Commons was out of the question, but also because Charles now had a party. A year before he was so unpopular that few men of influence would have dreamed of fighting for him. But Pym had driven all those who loved the Anglican Church, and who thought that political reform had gone far enough, into the king's camp. Charles could eventually count on most of the peers, as well as a third of the Commons.

Support for the king came mainly from the north and the west country. Parliament held East Anglia and the south, including London. Many of the towns, even in royalist areas, declared for Parliament. So also did the fleet, on which Charles had spent so much. Parliamentary ships controlled the sea and stopped supplies reaching him from Henrietta Maria, who had taken refuge in her native country, France. But the king's chances were good, particularly if the war was a short one. His supporters included some of the richest men in England, who put their private fortunes at his

disposal, and he found a brilliant cavalry leader in his nephew
Rupert, son of his sister Elizabeth and her husband, Frederick of
Bohemia – the Winter King. Only if the war went on a long time
would the king get poorer while Parliament, controlling London
and the ports, would grow steadily richer. But few could foresee,
when Charles raised his standard at Nottingham in August 1642,
that four years of harsh fighting lay ahead.

Charles hoped to end the war by a swift thrust south across the
Midlands to capture London. Had he moved quickly this daring
plan might have succeeded. But the royal army was held up by the
Parliamentary forces under the Earl of Essex, the son of Elizabeth's
unfortunate favourite, and had to fight its way through in the first
big battle of the war, at Edgehill. Essex retreated and left the road
to London open, but as the king's troops dawdled south, the
trained bands – London's amateur soldiers – joined up with
Essex's retreating army, and made ready to defend the capital.
Charles was not prepared to take London by storm. Street fighting
would have needed more men than he had available, and he wanted
at this early stage of the war, to avoid bloodshed where he could.
His armies reached the pleasant village of Turnham Green, but
there turned back and retired to the royal capital, Oxford.

The king still had the initiative, and in 1643 he and Rupert
planned another attack on London. From the north and from the
west, royal armies were to close like nutcrackers on the stubborn
capital. But once more the plan failed, for behind the royal lines
were parliamentary towns, which could not be taken. West-
countrymen were reluctant to go far out of their own counties
while roundhead troops occupied Gloucester and Plymouth, and
the northerners were held back by the obstinate resistance of Hull.
When the king abandoned the pincer movement and turned to
attack Gloucester, the Earl of Essex and the London trained bands
marched west to relieve the besieged city. The cavaliers met them
at Newbury in a battle that raged all day long. Neither side was the
victor, but Charles's men were short of ammunition, and the siege
of Gloucester was abandoned.

It was clear to Pym and his supporters in Parliament that unless
they found help from outside, they would never be able to finish
the war. Charles had ordered Ormonde, his lieutenant in Ireland,
to come to terms with the Roman Catholic rebels there, so that the

THE CIVIL WAR, 1642–50

troops used in putting down the revolt might be sent to join him in England. To meet this threat Pym opened negotiations with the Scots. These led, in September 1643, to the signing of the Solemn League and Covenant, by which Parliament promised, in return for the assistance of a Scottish army, to abolish bishops in England and to establish a Presbyterian Church. It was Pym's last service to Parliament, for he died before the year was out.

By this final effort Pym had swung the scales in favour of his own side. In January 1644 the veteran Leslie once again led a Scottish army across the border, and joined Fairfax and Cromwell near York. Rupert forced the combined armies to battle at Marston Moor. There, for the first time, the two great cavalry leaders, Rupert and Cromwell, were face to face. The roundhead right wing was forced to retreat, but on the left Cromwell led the charge against Rupert's men, and by savage fighting, routed them. 'God made them,' he wrote later, 'as stubble to our swords.' Unlike the cavaliers, who could never hold back when they were in pursuit of the enemy, Cromwell's troops were well trained. While the cavalier cavalry fled, Cromwell reformed his brigades and led them to support the right wing. The move was decisive. By nightfall the cavaliers had been swept from the field, and the whole of northern England lay at Parliament's mercy.

The king's cause was not yet lost, for in the west his men had triumphed and forced Essex's army to surrender. Cromwell was convinced that if the war was to be fought to a finish, more ruthless men would be needed at the top. Essex and Manchester could hardly be dismissed, but Cromwell persuaded Parliament to pass a 'Self-Denying Ordinance', by which all its members, including the lords, gave up their commissions. It was decided to create a new army, thoroughly trained, regularly paid and well equipped. The commander of the *New Model*, as it was called, was Sir Thomas Fairfax, a Yorkshire knight. His second in command was the Lieutenant-General – Cromwell.

The big test of the New Model came in summer 1645, when it met the main royal army at Naseby. Rupert's cavalry charged magnificently through their opponents' wing and chased them until the sounds of battle grew dim. Meanwhile Cromwell, on the other wing, cut through the cavaliers opposite him and wheeled his disciplined troops in to attack the centre. The royalist infantry, caught between two fires, fought bravely, but the day was lost.

Charles's cause never recovered after Naseby. Fairfax and Cromwell defeated the surviving royal army in the west at Langport, then went on to mop up the pockets of resistance that survived, mainly in country houses. Many of these surrendered rather than meet the fate of Basing House, seat of the Marquis of Winchester. There Cromwell brought cannon to batter down the thick walls, and through the gaps the roundhead besiegers poured in a furious onslaught. In less than an hour the great house was theirs. They stripped it of its magnificent treasures of furniture, pictures and plate, and even pulled the clothes off seventy-year-old Inigo Jones, leaving him nothing but a blanket. When the house was little more than an empty shell they set fire to it. The destruction of Basing House marked the end of cavalier England.

In May 1646 Charles gave himself up to the Scottish army at Newark. He hoped to come to some agreement with his fellow-countrymen, but the Scots insisted on the abolition of bishops and the setting-up of a Presbyterian Church in England. Charles was prepared to accept Presbyterianism for a trial period of three years, but it went against his conscience to offer more than that. Negotiations lingered on throughout 1646, but in the end the Scots despaired of ever coming to terms, and handed the king over to the English. He was brought to Holmby House, in Northamptonshire, and kept in honourable imprisonment there, while the Commons debated what to do with him.

Although Parliament had won the war, it was in danger of losing the peace. Puritans had been united against the king, but victory had opened a gap between the two wings of the reforming party. On the one side were the Presbyterians, who wanted to replace the hated and intolerant Anglican Church by an equally intolerant Presbyterian Church, governed not by bishops but by elected elders – 'presbyters'. On the other side were the Independents, who thought that every congregation should work out its own form of worship, and who dreaded a persecuting Presbyterian Church as much as the Anglican one they had been fighting against. In Parliament the Presbyterians had an overwhelming majority, but in the country as a whole, and particularly in the army, the Independents were very powerful. At the moment of victory Parliament found itself challenged by the army, and to prevent more violent changes, the leaders of the Commons hastily opened negotiations with the king.

By May 1647 Charles and his old opponents were near to agreement. A Presbyterian Church was to be established in England for a trial period of three years, and Parliament was, for a time, to control the army and navy. The problem was, would the soldiers accept these terms? They might have done if treated generously, but Parliament tried to pay them off with more or less worthless notes. The soldiers were stung to anger by this shabby treatment, and held meetings to protest against it. They met to discuss grievances, but as the discussions continued, they began to work out proposals of their own for settling the state of the kingdom.

The leaders of Parliament, frightened of the army – this monster they had created but could not control – decided to bring the king back to London, so that a settlement could be agreed on as quickly as possible, But they were too late. The greatest of the Independents was Cromwell, the army leader. In June he sent an officer called Joyce to take possession of the king at Holmby and bring him to the army headquarters at Newmarket. The trump card was now in the hands of the officers.

The army formed what was, in effect, its own Parliament. It was called the Grand Council, and included representatives of officers and men. It claimed the right to speak for the people of England, since it was, in its own words, not 'a mere mercenary army, hired to serve any arbitrary power of a state, but called forth . . . to the defence of our own and the people's just rights and liberties'. Speaking for the people, it demanded that the Long Parliament should dissolve itself, and that religious toleration should be allowed for all Protestants. When Parliament ignored this challenge and went ahead with its plans for demobilizing the army, Fairfax and his troops promptly marched on London and occupied the city in August 1647.

The army was bound to win, since it held the power of the sword. But it was not united. The officers, led by Cromwell – who, although only second in command, had more influence than Fairfax – wanted to preserve the traditional pattern of English government, but make it work by having frequent elections and by giving Parliament control over the king's ministers. Some of the officers, however, and many of the men, wanted sweeping changes. These people called themselves Levellers, and claimed to represent the common people of England. They saw no need for either a king or a House of Lords. Their solution to the problem of how England should be governed was that every man, regardless of his rank or wealth, should have the right to vote. Like the peasants in the revolt of 1381 they wanted an end of class distinction, a recognition that all men have the same needs. 'The poorest he that is in England,' said one of their number, 'hath a life to live, as the greatest he.'

Cromwell was no Leveller. He described himself as 'by birth a gentleman, living neither in any considerable height, not yet in obscurity', and he had not fought to see class distinctions overthrown. For him the proposals of the Levellers meant anarchy, and when the soldiers, led by the irrepressible John Lilburne, refused to return to their units, he put down the mutiny by force. For the moment at least the Levellers were quelled. The soldiers, who had done most of the fighting, gained little for their pains. 'We were ruled before by King, Lords, and Commons,' wrote one; 'now by a General, Court Martial, and Commons. And we pray you, what is the difference?'

While his enemies squabbled among themselves, Charles, afraid that the soldiers might kill him, decided on flight. On the night of 11 November 1647 he slipped through the soldiers who were guarding him at Hampton Court, and rode south as fast as he could. Three days later he presented himself before the governor of Carisbrooke Castle in the Isle of Wight, and demanded protection. The astonished governor allowed the king to take up residence in the castle, since he had no orders to the contrary.

From the comparative safety of Carisbrooke, Charles opened negotiations with the Scots and with royalist groups throughout England. On the day after Christmas 1647 he signed the *Engagement* with the Scots, in which they promised an army to help him regain his throne, on condition that once he was restored he would put down the Independents and establish a Presbyterian Church for at least three years. For Charles, this meant temporarily abandoning the bishops, but even Presbyterianism seemed better than the chaos of Independent congregations without any central control. And by accepting these terms he could hope to be reconciled with Parliament.

As royalist hopes rose in the early months of 1648, revolts broke out all over the country. But they were premature. When eventually a Scottish army crossed the border in July 1648, Cromwell had crushed the revolts and was ready for it. In August he pounced on the Scots near Preston, and in three days of savage fighting smashed them. It was a decisive victory, for the king now had no-one to support him. Even before Cromwell had set out to put down the risings, the army leaders had sworn to 'call Charles Stuart, that man of blood, to an account for that blood he had shed, and mischief he had done'.

Parliament was still negotiating with the king, hoping to save what was left of the old pattern of government, when, on 1 December 1648, the army once again took Charles prisoner. Cromwell was determined that the split between Parliament and the army, which had led to a renewal of civil war, should be ended once and for all. Early in December he sent one of his officers, Colonel Pride, to purge the House of Commons of its Presbyterian members. Forty-five were arrested; another ninety-six were forbidden to enter. In the end only about seventy members, most of them Independents, assembled in the Commons. Although they claimed the full authority of Parliament, they were given the contemptuous nickname of *The Rump*.

Acting on Cromwell's order the Rump set up a court to try the king. Only about half the hundred and fifty men named as judges were present when the court opened in Westminster Hall on 20 January 1649. It was a unique event in English history – the only occasion on which a king has been publicly tried by his subjects. The president of the court was John Bradshaw, an obscure lawyer who acted throughout with a grave dignity that matched the king's. Charles himself, grey-haired and looking older than his forty-eight years, never showed to better advantage. He refused to accept that any court had the right to try an anointed king, and would not condescend to reply to the charge that 'being admitted King of England, and therein trusted with a limited power to govern by and according to the laws of the land' he had 'out of a wicked design to erect . . . an unlimited and tyrannical power . . . traitorously and maliciously levied war against the present Parliament and the people therein represented'. Charles maintained that the court's authority rested only on force, and if he, as king, accepted that might was right, then 'I do not know what subject . . . can be sure of his life or anything that he calls his own . . . I do plead for the liberties of the people of England'.

Since the king refused to offer any defence, the court proceeded to sentence him, declaring 'that he, the said Charles Stuart, as a tyrant, traitor, murderer, and public enemy to the good people of this nation, shall be put to death by severing of his head from his body'. Only after sentence had been passed was Charles ready to defend his actions. But Bradshaw ordered the guards to remove their prisoner. 'I am not suffered to speak!' exclaimed the king. 'Expect what justice other people will have!'

Fifty-nine judges were persuaded to sign the death warrant. By their orders a scaffold was erected outside the king's own Banqueting House in Whitehall. Below it, on the afternoon of 30 January 1649, an enormous crowd watched and waited in silence. In a short speech Charles summed up the principles of government on which he had based his rule. 'For the people . . . truly I desire their liberty and freedom as much as anybody . . . but I must tell you that their liberty and freedom consist in having of government – those laws by which their life and their goods may be most their own. It is not for having a share in government . . . that is nothing pertaining to them. A subject and a sovereign are clean different things.'

When Bishop Juxon, his confessor, asked him to say something about his religious beliefs, he affirmed that 'I die a Christian according to the profession of the Church of England as I found it left me by my father'. A few minutes later the crowd below saw the glint of the axe as the executioner swung it above his head, 'at the instant whereof', reports an eye-witness, 'there was such a groan by the thousands then present, as I never heard before, and desire I may never hear again'.

By the courage and dignity of his last days the king had gone far to wipe out the memory of his earlier mistakes and to make sure that the crown and church for which he gave his life would one day be restored. Even the poet Marvell, a great admirer of Cromwell, could not restrain his admiration for so noble an ending:

He nothing common did or mean
Upon that memorable scene,
But with his keener eye
The axe's edge did try

Nor called the Gods with vulgar spite
To vindicate his helpless right,
But bowed his comely head
Down, as upon a bed.

CHAPTER 37

The Interregnum

1649-1660

AFTER CHARLES'S execution the Rump abolished the monarchy and the House of Lords, and declared England a republic. One of the first tasks of the new state was to restore order in Ireland, where the royal commander, the Earl of Ormonde, having come to terms with the rebels, had proclaimed Charles II as king. In the late summer of 1649 Cromwell was sent with an army to bring the Irish Catholics to heel. He was still burning with indignation at the massacre of Protestants during the rebellion of 1641, and planned to take his revenge. Cromwell was a tolerant man by the standards of his day, but his tolerance did not extend to Roman Catholics whom he, in common with his fellow-Puritans, regarded as dangerous beasts. When the inhabitants of Drogheda refused to surrender, Cromwell took the place by storm and, in his own words, 'put to the sword the whole number of the defendants. I do not think thirty of the whole number escaped with their lives. I am persuaded that this is a righteous judgment of God upon those barbarous wretches'. From Drogheda he moved south along the coast and, a month later, captured Wexford and slaughtered the garrison there. Only his recall to England prevented him from completing the conquest of Ireland.

Cromwell was summoned back by Parliament to deal with trouble in the north, where the Scots had proclaimed Charles II as king of Scotland. The new king was no fonder of Presbyterianism than his father had been, but he was prepared to compromise if it would save his throne. With obvious reluctance he signed the Covenant, and in June 1650 he landed in Scotland.

Cromwell appealed to the Scots to see the error of their ways and abandon the young king. When they refused, he led his army into Scotland. But the wily Leslie, who still commanded the Scottish troops, skilfully avoided a pitched battle. By September he had hemmed the English army in near Dunbar, and seemed to have Cromwell at his mercy. Had he stuck to his commanding position in the hills he might have won the day. But the impatient Scots, hoping to cut the English off from their only escape route by sea, made their way down to the coast. Cromwell charged, caught them unprepared, and routed them.

Although the Scots had lost a battle, they had not yet lost the war. Charles II, with another army, slipped past Cromwell and marched south into England. But Cromwell caught up with him at Worcester, and there, on 3 September 1651, put an end to royal hopes. The battle, as Cromwell reported to Parliament, 'became an absolute victory – and so full an one as proved a total defeat and ruin of the enemy's army ... It is ... a crowning mercy'. Charles II managed to escape with a price on his head. Disguised, and in constant danger, he made his way to the south coast, where he found a ship to take him to France. Nine years were to pass before he saw England again.

The republic was now secure at home and could concentrate on establishing its prestige abroad. Many English merchants were jealous of their prosperous Dutch rivals. As a result of their complaints the Rump passed the Navigation Act of 1651, which ordered that only English ships were to carry most of the goods imported into England. The Rump also claimed that Dutch ships should recognize English supremacy in the Channel by dipping their flags in salute to English vessels. These disputes were brought to a head when the ambassadors sent by the Republic to Holland were greeted with shouts of 'King-murderers!', and given an icy reception by the Dutch government. By 1652 war had broken out between the two countries.

For the first time England had a permanent navy. This 'new model' fleet had at its head Robert Blake, the first great English seaman of the seventeenth century. He had already driven the royalist ships, under Rupert, off the seas. Now he led his fleet into action against the Dutch. By hard fighting he drove the enemy ships into harbour and set up a strict blockade of the coast. The Dutch, who lived by trade, saw starvation ahead of them, and grass was growing in the shipyards and streets of Amsterdam. The

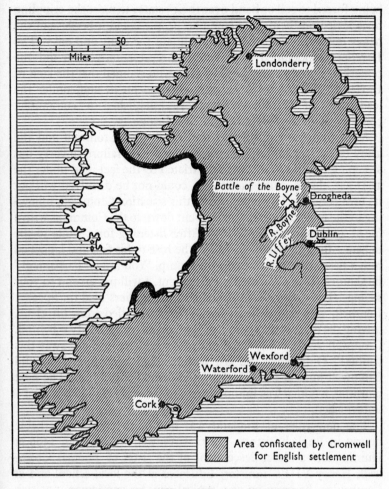

Area confiscated by Cromwell
for English settlement

IRELAND IN THE TIME OF CROMWELL

Dutch admiral Martin Tromp tried to break the blockade in July 1653, but his ships were sunk and he himself killed. Early in 1654 the Dutch sued for peace, and by the Treaty of Westminster recognized English supremacy at sea.

Long before the war was over, the rule of the Rump had come to an end. The so-called Parliament really represented nobody, and had enemies on all sides. The royalists hated it because they were being forced to sell or hand over their estates to meet the crippling fines levied on them. The common people hated it because of the heavy taxes they had to pay to maintain the army and navy. The Levellers condemned it as being unrepresentative. So did the remarkable group called the Diggers, who claimed that the land of England belonged to those who laboured on it, and, under the leadership of Gerard Winstanley, established a communist community on St George's Hill, Weybridge.

Most important of all was the hostility of Cromwell and the army officers, who despised the Rump for its failure to carry out sweeping reforms. They were infuriated by the fact that, under the 1641 act, the so-called Parliament could not be dissolved without its own consent. To put an end to this situation Cromwell, following in the footsteps of Charles I, went down to the Commons with a file of soldiers on 20 April 1653. After listening for a while to the debate – for he was still an M.P. – he rose to his feet and launched into a passionate attack upon the Rump. 'You are no Parliament,' he shouted. 'I say you are no Parliament. I will put an end to your sitting.' The doors were opened and the soldiers filed in. Speaker Lenthall, who had defied Charles I, was hustled from his chair, leaving the mace – the symbol of Parliamentary authority – behind. Cromwell saw it and ordered one of his soldiers to 'Take away this bauble!'. Only when the last member had been forced out did Cromwell himself leave, locking the doors behind him. The next morning, a notice was found pinned to them: 'This House to let – unfurnished.'

The new ruler of England was one of the most remarkable figures in English history. Oliver Cromwell was born in 1599 at Huntingdon, a direct descendant of the sister of Thomas Cromwell, Henry VIII's minister. Educated at the local school and at Cambridge, he grew up as a typical country gentleman, not rich but proud, and, in politics and religion alike, an Independent. A cavalier described him as he appeared in the early days of the Long Parliament, wearing 'a plain cloth suit, which seemed to have been made by an ill country tailor . . . His stature was of a good size, his sword stuck close to his side, his countenance swollen and reddish, his voice sharp and untunable, and his eloquence full of fervour'. He fought the king because he believed in religious toleration and parliamentary rule. But the years which followed the expulsion of the Rump showed him that these two beliefs could not, in practice, exist together. Cromwell was genuine in his desire to transfer power from the army to the Commons, but he could not stand by and see the tolerance for which he had fought destroyed. While he depended on the army for his authority, he could be little more than a tyrant. And yet, if he were to demobilize it, he would be at the mercy of men more bigoted, more self-interested, than himself.

Cromwell had driven out the Rump; he now summoned a Parliament of persons chosen by the Army Council for their godliness. But when this assembly – often called the Barebones Parliament, after the name of one of its members – met, it began reforming with such enthusiasm that Cromwell could not hold it back. It looked as though they would pull England to pieces so that they could rebuild it. But although they had confidence in their own ability to produce a perfect system of government and administration out of their own heads, Cromwell had not. With his encouragement, the more moderate members of the House met early one morning, before the rest arrived, and voted for the dissolution of Parliament. Once again Cromwell was left in sole charge of the government of England.

A new constitution was drawn up by the Army Council. England was to be a Commonwealth, ruled by a Lord Protector advised by a Council of State, with money voted by a single House of Parliament, and there was to be freedom of worship for all except Roman Catholics and Anglicans. In December 1653 Cromwell was solemnly installed as Lord Protector at a ceremony in Westminster Abbey, and in April of the following year he and his family moved into the royal palace at Whitehall.

For about nine months, before the first Parliament of the Commonwealth was summoned, Cromwell showed how good a ruler he could be – reforming the law courts and universities, improving the electoral system, establishing a Puritan Church, and leaving Anglicans and Roman Catholics alone as long as they did not attempt to worship publicly. Scotland was united to England, and ordered to send representatives to the new Parliament, and under the enlightened rule of General Monck peace and prosperity were restored to that country. Only in Ireland did Cromwell show the worst side of his nature. There the Roman Catholic faith was prohibited, and about half the land of Ireland was taken away from its native owners and given to English settlers. Thousands of Irish men and women went into exile rather than face slavery or starvation. Those who remained cursed the name of Cromwell, and handed down their hatred of England to generations of their children.

The Lord Protector built up an efficient civil service, and found good men to serve him. Monck was an admirable governor of Scotland, Blake made the English navy the finest in the world; and Cromwell's secretary, John Thurloe, kept the administration functioning smoothly. Foreign affairs were in the hands of the Lord Protector's Latin Secretary, John Milton – one of the greatest English poets. He was already working on the first draft of *Paradise Lost* when Cromwell came to power, but much of his time and energy had been spent on prose works like the *Areopagitica*, published in 1644, in which he attacked the censorship of books and called for 'liberty to know, to utter, and to argue freely according to conscience'.

When, in September 1654, the first Parliament of the Protectorate met, it proved to be as unco-operative as any Stuart Parliament. Already the House had grievances to complain of, particularly the heavy taxation which was needed to maintain so large an army and navy. Cromwell, like Charles I, had been goaded into violent action by his need for money. When a merchant called Cony refused to pay duties on silk because they had been imposed by the Protector alone, and not by Parliament, Cromwell had him imprisoned. And when Parliament refused to vote supplies until it had criticized the Protector's government, Cromwell dissolved it.

There was widespread discontent in the country as a whole. Members had hardly returned to their homes when, in March 1655, a royalist rising broke out in the west. Cromwell crushed it, and used the excuse to squeeze more money out of the royalists. To guard against further troubles he divided England into eleven districts, each under control of a Major-General. These officers were mostly high-minded and efficient men, but by prying into the private lives of individuals, suppressing Sunday games, and closing theatres and public houses, they made the rule of the Protector gloomy and oppressive to the majority of his subjects.

Only the success of Cromwell's foreign policy lightened the gloom. Brought up when the memories of Elizabeth's reign, growing more glorious with every year that passed, provided a bitter contrast to the powerlessness of James I's England, Cromwell had come to hate the Roman Catholics and their traditional maintainer, Spain, and to long for a revival of England's greatness. By the time he came to power, Spain's finest days were past, but by attacking her Cromwell could at least recall the exploits of Hawkins and Drake. In 1655 a naval squadron, fresh from its successes in the war against Holland, set out for the West Indies and the Spanish Main. An attack upon the island of Santo Domingo was a failure, but Jamaica was occupied, and by 1656 Blake was blockading the coast of Spain. He won his last victory when, in the best Elizabethan tradition, he attacked and destroyed a Spanish treasure fleet at Santa Cruz, and captured booty worth a quarter of a million pounds. He was on his way back to England to present it personally to Cromwell, when death put an end to his glory.

Unfortunately for the Lord Protector, his victories cost far more than he ever made from them. In spite of heavy taxes, forced loans, and sales of land, the Commonwealth government was running heavily into debt. Though the exploits of Blake made Englishmen proud of him and of themselves, the war against Spain was really a waste of energy and money. The only concrete gain came in June 1658 when the English, fighting with the Catholic French against the Spaniards in the Netherlands, distinguished themselves by their bravery at the Battle of the Dunes, and were given Dunkirk as their share of the spoils.

Cromwell, in his need for money, summoned the second Protectorate Parliament in September 1656, and posted soldiers at the doors to keep out a hundred of the less co-operative members. Those who were allowed in voted £400,000 in return for the removal of the Major-Generals. Cromwell was an aging man, and a recent attempt on his life had reminded Parliament that he would not live for ever. But when he died, who was to succeed him, and how was anarchy to be prevented? The obvious solution was to recognize that Cromwell was, in fact, a 'king' and offer him the crown, so that his son could rule after him. The Commons made the formal offer in March 1657, and Cromwell hesitated. He saw the advantages of becoming king. But he knew that by accepting the crown he would anger the army officers, who had not fought against one king merely to replace him with another. In the end,

Cromwell declined the offer of the crown, but he was given the right to nominate his successor.

When Parliament met again in January 1658, Cromwell had taken another step towards the old constitution by choosing an Upper House. After all his experiments in government, he was coming back to the old pattern of King, Lords and Commons, since this alone had the authority of many centuries behind it. The Lower House was, however, unwilling to accept the new 'lords'. Ignoring Cromwell's demands for money, it insisted on debating whether the members of the Upper House had any right to be there at all. Furious and impatient, Cromwell dismissed this Parliament after it had sat only fifteen days. When members protested he told them proudly, 'Let God judge between you and me!'.

The government was, by this time, two million pounds in debt, and without the help of Parliament there was no obvious means of raising so vast a sum. Cromwell reluctantly came to accept the fact that he would have to summon yet another Parliament, although he knew that when it met it would be merciless in its criticism of him. By the irony of history, the man who did more than anyone else to ensure the victory of the Commons in the civil war, and whose statue stands today outside Parliament, had come to share the feelings of James I, who said of the Commons: 'At their meetings nothing is heard but cries, shouts and confusion. I am surprised that my ancestors should ever have permitted such an institution to come into existence. I am a stranger, and found it here when I arrived, so that I am obliged to put up with what I cannot get rid of'.

But the Lord Protector never met Parliament again. Exhausted by his long struggles, he died in the royal palace at Whitehall on 3 September 1658, the anniversary of the Battle of Worcester. He was buried in pomp, and lay among kings in Westminster Abbey. But two years later his body was dug up to be hanged on the gallows at Tyburn, and nobody is now certain where his bones rest.

Richard Cromwell succeeded his father as Lord Protector. But this mild-mannered country gentleman had little ambition to rule. His father had stayed in power because he was the army's greatest commander, but Richard was no soldier. He shared the opinions of his first, and only, Parliament, that the army should obey the civil power. The generals, however – Fleetwood and Lambert – had no respect for either Parliament or the new Protector. By the middle of 1659 they had forced Richard to retire into private life, and to restore the fortunes of the 'good old cause' for which they had fought, they recalled the Rump – that remnant of the Long Parliament which survived after Pride's Purge, and which symbolized republican government.

When the Rump reassembled, its members showed that they had lost none of their old spirit. They issued orders to the army and so irritated the officers that in October 1659 Lambert expelled the Rump once again.

This time, however, Parliament had a powerful ally. The finest army in Britain was that commanded by General Monck in Scotland, and he had already informed Speaker Lenthall that 'obedience is my great principle; and I have always, and ever shall, reverence the Parliament's resolutions in civil things, as infallible and sacred'. While Monck waited in Scotland, England was plunged into anarchy. Without a Parliament or a Lord Protector, there was no authority, and the soldiers, unpaid and hungry, were raising money at the sword's point. In these dark hours the thoughts of many Englishmen turned back nostalgically to the years before the revolution, when King, Lords and Commons had ruled a peaceful and prosperous country. They longed for such days to return.

Fleetwood tried to end disorder by persuading Lenthall to assemble the Rump yet again. But by the time it met, Monck was already marching south. In February 1660 he arrived in London. At his command the Rump reluctantly opened its doors to the members whom Colonel Pride had expelled. Then at last, on 16 March, the Long Parliament, which had sat for twenty years, declared itself dissolved.

On the other side of the Channel Charles II was waiting, hardly daring to hope that his exile might be coming to an end. But the elections for a new Parliament, held in March, made sure that the king would return. Everywhere royalists were elected, for it seemed that the only alternative to restoring the king was rule by brute force. The important question to be decided was on what terms the king should come back. Charles, on Monck's advice, published at

Breda a declaration in which he promised that, in order to heal
'those wounds which have so many years together been kept bleed-
ing' he would pardon all that was past, allow his subjects to worship
in peace, and leave everything to be decided 'in a free Parliament,
by which, upon the word of a king, we will be advised'.

The Declaration of Breda was welcomed by the new Parliament
when it met in April, and commissioners were appointed to go over
to Holland and invite the king to return to his own country.
Charles landed at Dover on 25 May 1660. Four days later he
celebrated his thirtieth birthday by arriving in London, where, in
the words of the diarist John Evelyn, who saw it all: 'the ways were
strewed with flowers, the bells ringing, the streets hung with
tapestry, fountains running with wine . . . And all this was done
without one drop of blood shed, and by that very army which
rebelled against him'.

CHAPTER 38

Charles II

1660-1685

'CHARLES STUART, a long dark man, above two yards high' –
this was the description of the king of England given in the
advertisement for his capture published after the Battle of
Worcester. Charles learned a lot from the dangers and the years of
exile through which he passed. He was at ease in any type of
society, distrusted all men and delighted in the company of women.
Bishop Burnet, who knew him well, describes how 'he had the art
of making all people grow fond of him at first, by a softness in his
whole way of conversation, as he was certainly the best bred man
of his age'. But although he was all things to all men, Charles had a
mind of his own. On the surface he was light-hearted and cynical.
Beneath it he was hard-working and relentless in his determination
that he and his family should never again be forced from the
throne.

His restoration had been possible because Presbyterians and
Anglicans, Republicans and Royalists, had dropped their differences
and called back the king, rather than risk anarchy or another
military dictatorship. But the differences remained, and the effects
of the past twenty years could not be wiped out in a moment.
Parliament was restored in 1660 as well as the king, and since the
acts to which Charles I had given his assent remained in force,
Star Chamber and Ship Money were gone for good. The restored
king was to be dependent on Parliament for money and on the
common law courts for punishing offenders.

One of the first problems to be dealt with was that of providing
the king with an income. Royal lands and customs duties would
bring in about £500,000 a year, but it was reckoned that Charles
would need another £700,000 if his government was to pay its way.

The Commons for the first time voted the king a regular income, but since they would have to do the paying they were careful not to be too generous. In fact for the first twelve years of his reign Charles's income fell far below the estimate, and he was constantly in debt.

1660 saw the restoration not only of king and Parliament, but also of the Anglican Church. The Presbyterians hoped that in return for their help in bringing back the king, the Church of England would be reformed in such a way that they could accept it. Charles was in favour of toleration, and summoned a conference to the Savoy Palace, at which he hoped Presbyterians and Anglicans would be able to come to terms. But the conference was a failure, and although the prayer book was revised there were no concessions to the Presbyterians. The Parliament which was elected in 1661 was dominated by the triumphant cavaliers, out for revenge on their old enemies. All parish priests were ordered not merely to use the revised prayer book but also to take an oath that they fully accepted everything it said. Over a thousand gave up their livings rather than conform. Further acts of Parliament harried the Nonconformists by forbidding them to hold services of their own. The Church of England had finally abandoned the pretence that it was the Church of all the English people. Roman Catholics on the one hand, and Nonconformists on the other, were driven out of the Church and were forbidden to teach, to attend the universities, or to take any part in town government. Nonconformists found holding services of their own were arrested, particularly those who belonged to new sects, like the Quakers, of whom over a thousand were in prison in 1662. The persecution of harmless men and women whose only offence was that they could not accept the Anglican prayer book was a shameful business. But we owe to it one of the most moving works in English literature – *Pilgrim's Progress*, which the nonconformist John Bunyan wrote during his years of imprisonment in Bedford gaol.

The great days of Puritanism as a political force were over. In the first half of the seventeenth century the Puritans, in their hatred of tyranny and their assertion that the individual conscience must be the final judge in spiritual matters, had seemed to be the defenders of English liberties. More than this, they had been an apparently irresistible force, the flood-tide of the age, sweeping away the feeble breakwaters that James and Charles constructed. But the critical years from 1640 to 1660 had shown up the falseness of this view. The first two Stuarts represented more than themselves. They stood for order and government, the control of Church and State by institutions which had survived the test of time. They asserted that the alternatives to strong royal government were tyranny or anarchy; that an intolerant Anglican Church would be replaced only by another form of intolerance. The Interregnum had shown how right they were. The anarchy of the Diggers and Levellers and the absolutism of the Lord Protector were the two poles between which the revolutionary movement swung. And the religious toleration which Cromwell had to defend against his Parliaments was narrowly limited and hardly worthy of the name.

The property-owners had been Puritan in their sympathies during Charles I's reign because they resented the arbitrary taxation of an Arminian monarchy, and saw in the administration of the royal council a threat to their own domination of local life. But the Interregnum taught them how easily extremist revolutionaries take over when the barriers built up by time and custom are swept away. After 1660 the property-owners accepted the restored monarchy as a guarantee of the stability of the social order upon which their power and position were based, especially as Charles II had neither the intention nor the means of continuing that close supervision of local life by the royal council which had marked his father's reign. They accepted, also, the Church of England, which abandoned its attempt to impose an Arminian pattern of worship upon all Englishmen and by its insistence on obedience – 'the powers that be are ordained of God' – gave its blessing not only to the restored monarchy but to the whole social order.

The roles of the early seventeenth century were reversed after the Restoration. Parliament was now the ardent supporter of the Anglican Church for which Charles I had died. The king was the advocate of toleration. Religion was still a vital force but it was no longer the controlling passion of which all activities, including politics, were merely an aspect. On the Continent the Thirty Years' War had ended in 1648 with one Catholic power, France, fighting and defeating another, Spain. Catholics and Protestants, since they could not destroy each other, were forced to live together, and the desire for national glory came to replace religious intolerance as the driving force in international politics. In England, too, religion gradually became an instrument of the social system which it had at one time dominated. Fear of Roman Catholics survived, particularly as they were associated in the popular imagination with the despotic Catholic monarchies of Spain and France. Nonconformists were also persecuted, and thousands died from imprisonment and ill-treatment in Charles II's reign. But in both cases the motives were increasingly political. The property-owners in Parliament, now firmly allied to the Anglican Church, were determined to prevent any change in the social system, coming either from Catholic absolutists or Nonconformist republicans. And as they grew more secure in their position, they persecuted less. By the end of the century Nonconformists and Roman Catholics were allowed to worship as they wished, although the controlling positions in society were still reserved for Anglicans.

The Church of England preached the divine right of kings to rule, and the duty of subjects to obey. These doctrines were very acceptable to Charles II who believed, like his father, that kings are appointed by God to control the destinies of their peoples. But the fact that the Church of England was now so warmly supported by Parliament made it less agreeable to the king. Confronted with an Anglican House of Commons protesting its loyalty and yet making demands on him which he found unacceptable, his sympathies moved gradually towards the Church of Rome, which seemed to provide the only sure defence of royal authority.

Charles, who had promised toleration in the Declaration of Breda, tried to bring it about by suspending the operation of the penal laws in December 1662. But when Parliament reassembled early in 1663 it forced him to abandon his attempt. In spite of selling Dunkirk to the French, he was already in debt, and his marriage to Catherine, daughter of the king of Portugal, meant that he now had a queen and a larger court to maintain. He needed money, too, for the navy, since English merchants were already fighting their Dutch rivals off the coast of Africa, and war seemed certain. The diarist Samuel Pepys, who worked in the Navy Office, wrote that in India the Dutch were 'showing scorn to all the English . . . saying that they will do what they list, and be masters of all the world there; and have so proclaimed themselves sovereigns of all the south seas'.

Jealousy over trade led to open war with Holland in 1664. The English fleet was commanded jointly by James, Duke of York, the king's brother, and General Monck – created Duke of Albemarle for his great work in bringing about the Restoration. At first everything went well, and in 1665 the Dutch were defeated and their admiral, Opdam, killed in a three-day battle off Lowestoft. But the strain of war, which even Cromwell had found too much for his finances, quickly exhausted the king's treasury. Parliamentary grants were, as usual, inadequate, and the royal administration was full of corrupt officials who kept for themselves money that should have been used in building or equipping ships. By the beginning of 1667 both sides were negotiating for peace, and Charles ordered the fleet to be laid up, to save the expense of keeping it at sea. But he acted too soon. In June of that year, the Dutch sailed up the river Medway, burnt several English warships where they lay at anchor, and towed away the flagship, the *Royal Charles*.

The honeymoon period, when the king and his subjects competed only in paying compliments to each other, was over. There was widespread anger about the humiliation of the Medway – Pepys called it 'as dreadful a spectacle as ever England saw, and a dishonour never to be wiped out'. Parliament was openly critical of the king, and preparing to attack his chief minister, the Earl of Clarendon. Clarendon had served the crown loyally ever since, as plain Edward Hyde, he had led the Moderates against Pym in the Long Parliament. He had been by the side of Charles II during his years of exile and after the Restoration the king, who had no practical experience of English politics, appointed him as Lord Chancellor and relied on him to lead the royal government. Clarendon was mainly responsible for the mildness of the Restoration settlement. As an old parliamentarian, deeply attached to this institution, he made sure that king and Parliament were restored on more or less equal terms – although the tide of royalism was flowing so strongly that he might well have been able to give Charles II all the powers that his father had ever had. He was a hard-working, methodical administrator, not above making money out of his high office, but comparatively honest by the standards of the day. However, he had made many enemies. The Nonconformists blamed him, unfairly, for the severe laws against them –

the *Clarendon Code*, as they were called. Politicians commented
enviously on the marriage of his daughter Anne to the Duke of
York, the heir to the throne, and on the great house he was
building for himself near Piccadilly. Even Charles was tired of the
pompous old man, and probably not sorry to use him as a scapegoat. In August 1667 he dismissed him from the Chancellorship,
and later that year Clarendon fled to France to escape impeachment. He spent the rest of his life in exile, working on his *History
of the Great Rebellion*, which is one of the finest pieces of historical
writing in the English language.

The Dutch war was at last ended by the Peace of Breda, in
July 1667. All that England gained from it was the New Netherlands – the Dutch colony in America which divided the English
settlements in the north from those farther south. Now the gap
was closed, and the old Dutch capital, New Amsterdam, was
renamed, in honour of the king's brother, New York.

The Dutch were not the only enemies England had been fighting.
In the closing stages of the war the Great Plague struck at London.
It was the last violent outbreak of the epidemics from which
England had been suffering since the Black Death, and it spread
rapidly among a population that cared little about sanitation and
personal cleanliness.

Among the narrow streets and rat-infested alleys of London the
Plague claimed at its height a thousand victims a day. Doctors,
such as they were, could do little. At night, carts were wheeled
through the streets to the melancholy cry of 'Bring out your dead!',
and on the doors of houses where the Plague had struck red
crosses were painted, with the inscription *Lord have mercy on us*.
The king and his court, and all those who could afford to do so, left
the stricken capital. Only Albemarle stayed on at his post, to keep
order.

Those who believed the Plague was sent by God to punish a
pleasure-loving nation seemed to find proof of this in another
calamity. In the first week of September 1666, a fire which broke
out at a baker's shop in Pudding Lane, near the place where the
Monument now stands, was caught by a strong wind and for three
days and three nights burned its way remorselessly through the
city. Pepys describes the 'poor people staying in their houses . . .
till the very fire touched them and then running into boats, or

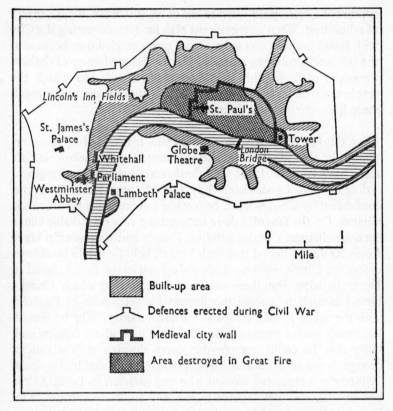

LONDON AT THE TIME OF THE GREAT FIRE

clambering from one pair of stairs by the waterside to another', and at night he watched the fire spread 'in corners and upon steeples, and between churches and houses as far as we could see up the hill of the City in a most horrid malicious bloody flame . . . The churches, houses and all on fire and flaming at once. And a horrid noise the flames made, and the cracking of houses at their ruin'. Charles went down to the City to help fight the fire, and ordered houses to be blown up to make a gap across which the flames could not pass. But when at last the Great Fire burnt itself out, most of the City, including St Paul's Cathedral, lay in ruins. Rebuilding quickly started, however, and the king ordered that all new buildings should be in brick or stone instead of inflammable wood. He

appointed Christopher Wren as one of his surveyors, to take charge
of rebuilding. Wren's magnificent plan for reconstructing the City
with broad avenues and squares was never carried out, because of
the cost and conflicting interests. But he designed many of the new
churches, including his masterpiece, St Paul's, in which the
severe classical style of Inigo Jones gave way to something much
more high-spirited and dramatic.

After the fall of Clarendon, Charles was his own chief minister,
though he took advice from the ill-assorted group whose initials
form the word *CABAL* – Clifford and Ashley, Buckingham,
Arlington and Lauderdale. Only two of these were taken into
confidence by Charles when he worked out his plans for a French
alliance. On the face of it there was nothing very remarkable about
such an alliance. Charles admired France and its powerful king,
Louis XIV, and hoped that with French help he would be able to
defeat the Dutch republic. This was agreed in the treaty signed at
Dover in 1670. But there was a secret clause in which Charles
bound himself to restore the Roman Catholic faith in England
with the aid of French troops and French money. Why he should
have made such a promise, when he cared little about religion and
knew that he could not possibly carry through such a violent
change, is not at all clear. He was certainly influenced by his sister
'Minette' – a charming woman who was married to Louis XIV's
brother. Charles was devoted to her, and since she came over to
Dover in 1670 to sign the treaty, it may well have been her
pleading that persuaded Charles to accept the secret clause.

In March 1672 war was again declared against Holland. Two
days before it, Charles made some show of carrying out his secret
agreement by issuing his second Declaration of Indulgence,
suspending the penal laws against Roman Catholics and Nonconformists. It was a gamble that depended on victory. Unfortunately for Charles the war went badly. The Dutch admiral De
Ruyter kept the English fleet at bay, and the invading French
armies were held up when the Dutch, led by Charles's nephew, the
young prince William of Orange, cut the dykes and flooded great
areas.

Charles postponed calling Parliament as long as he could afford
to do without one, but by February 1673 he could wait no longer.

The Commons were on the warpath. Eliot and Pym were no longer alive to lead them, but the same forces were at work – fear of Roman Catholics, distrust of absolutism, hatred of France, anger at corruption and waste of money. The division was growing between those who supported the king and his 'Court', and those who stood for the 'Country', by which they meant Protestantism and Parliamentary control. Charles recognized the danger and cancelled the Declaration of Indulgence in March 1673. But Parliament went on to pass the Test Act, by which all holders of public office were compelled to take the sacraments of the Church of England. This was a political measure aimed at the king's brother James, Duke of York, who had been converted to Rome. James, the Lord Admiral, threw up his post rather than conform. So did Clifford, the Lord Treasurer.

Clifford was succeeded by Sir Thomas Osborne, a Yorkshire landowner, who was created Earl of Danby. Over the next five years Danby reversed Charles's policy of friendship with France. He knew that Parliament, which had already appointed auditors to examine the king's accounts after the failure of the second Dutch war, would never accept a Roman Catholic foreign policy. He revived the Court party in the House of Commons by bringing the war with Holland to an end, and carefully distributing pensions and offices of profit among M.P.s. The Cavalier Parliament, elected in 1661, was still sitting, although by-elections had brought many new faces into it. Danby was content to keep this Long Parliament in being, since it gave him time to get to know members and to bind them to the crown. The closed circle of the court was deliberately expanded and the golden bonds between crown and Commons, which had snapped in James I's reign, were carefully reforged. Danby, accepting the fact that the Commons were divided, gave the king's supporters not only the major share of the profits of government but also a policy of which they could approve. Instead of fighting the Dutch, he allied with them, and his policy was crowned by the marriage of James's daughter Mary to William of Orange. In these years of peace trade flourished, the revenue from customs and other taxes went up, and Charles found, to his astonishment, that his income was at last beginning to equal his expenditure.

Danby's policy was threatened from two sides. On the one hand

Charles kept up negotiations with Louis XIV; on the other, the Country party in the Commons was being organized by Anthony Ashley Cooper, Earl of Shaftesbury, who wanted closer control by Parliament over royal policy, and the exclusion of the Catholic James from succession to the throne. Shaftesbury, the son of a Dorset country gentleman, was educated at Oxford and Lincoln's Inn and elected to Parliament at the age of nineteen. During the civil war he supported first the crown then Parliament, and trimmed his sails so carefully that he managed to be a member of Cromwell's Council of State and yet be acceptable to the restored Charles II. For a time he was Chancellor of the Exchequer and a member of the Cabal, but when news of the secret clause of the Treaty of Dover leaked out, he went over to the opposition. High ideals and personal ambition were mixed together in this ruthless scheming nobleman. The poet John Dryden described him brilliantly:

> For close designs and crooked counsels fit,
> Sagacious, bold and turbulent of wit,
> Restless, unfixed in principles and place,
> In power unpleased, impatient of disgrace.
>
> In friendship false, implacable in hate,
> Resolved to ruin, or to rule, the state.

Shaftesbury's opportunity came when, in September 1678, two fanatical and fantastic characters called Israel Tonge and Titus Oates, revealed to the horrified royal council the details of a popish plot to kill the king and bring over foreign armies to impose Catholicism on England. Such a revelation brought to the surface all the fear and hatred of Roman Catholics that lay, scarcely concealed, in English life. Fear turned to panic when Sir Edmund Berry Godfrey, a magistrate to whom Oates had originally made his revelation, disappeared for five days, and was then found murdered. Godfrey's murder was widely accepted as proof of everything that Oates had said, and although this arch-liar had invented most of the details of the plot, there was a kernel of truth in the fact that the king was a secret catholic, pledged to convert his subjects with the aid of French troops. This was not generally known. But suspicion is a good breeding ground for rumour. Since nothing was certain, everything – however un-likely – was believed.

As panic mounted, Shaftesbury accused Danby of secret negotiations with France. The Lord Treasurer had, in fact, written to Louis XIV at Charles's command, asking for money so that the king need not summon Parliament. It was against Danby's principles, but he was Charles's servant, not his master. Louis refused to pay. He distrusted Danby, whose Protestant foreign policy was a danger to France, and in the end he sent money not to the king but to Shaftesbury. The earl used it to win over more followers in the Commons. He also bought a following among the London mob and roused their tempers with propaganda put out from his headquarters – the Green Ribbon Club.

To save Danby, Charles dissolved the Cavalier Parliament, after it had sat for sixteen years. But Shaftesbury's followers were triumphant in the election which followed. When the new Parliament met in March 1679 it was in as ugly a mood as the Long Parliament had been in 1640. Danby was impeached and sent to the Tower (where he stayed in comparative safety and comfort until the crisis was over). Shaftesbury then introduced a bill to exclude James, Duke of York, from the succession to the throne. The Commons were divided and tempers ran high. Shaftesbury's followers – the Country party, or *Whigs*, as they came to be called – were in the majority. But their opponents – the Court party, or *Tories* – kept their heads and refused to panic. The king was willing to limit James's power in advance, but he would not agree to cut him out of the succession altogether. To allow Parliament to appoint kings would have gone against everything the Stuarts stood for. Rather than accept such an ultimatum Charles decided to do without money. 'I shall find means to pay the Fleet,' he said. 'It will be difficult and uncomfortable for me, but I will submit to anything rather than endure the House of Commons any longer.'

Before Parliament could meet again the king fell seriously ill. Sympathy for him began to check the tide which was still running in Shaftesbury's favour, and although panic was at its height and innocent men were being condemned to death, fever pitch could not be kept up for ever. A new Parliament eventually assembled in October 1680, and Shaftesbury again sprang to the attack, with another bill to exclude James from the succession.

Charles still refused to consider such a revolutionary proposal. He was prepared to fight rather than see the succession altered, and this very fact told in his favour. The civil war had been a savage business, accomplishing little; few people were prepared to risk another. The Whigs could not count on the fiery Puritanism which had made their predecessors so dangerous in 1640. They were, in any case, divided. One group, led by Shaftesbury, wanted to make the king's illegitimate son, the Protestant Duke of Monmouth, heir to the throne. The other thought the succession should pass to James's Protestant daughter Mary and her husband, William of Orange. The Exclusion Bill passed the Commons, but after a tense debate in the Lords it was thrown out by thirty-three votes. Charles sensed that the tide was turning, and dissolved Parliament in January 1681. He summoned another one to meet in March at Oxford, the old royalist capital, away from the pressure of the London mob.

When the Whig lords rode into Oxford with their armed retainers, they were confident of victory. But Charles had brought his lifeguards with him – the small regular army that he had kept in being after the Restoration so that he would never be, like his father, entirely at the mercy of the mob. In his opening speech the king offered to agree to a regency in James's name after his death. When Shaftesbury rejected this and insisted that Monmouth should be named as the king's heir, Charles cut him short: 'My lord, let there be no self-delusion. I will never yield, and I will not be intimidated . . . I have reason and law in my favour. Well-minded people are on my side; and there is the church which will remain united to me.' Shaftesbury felt sure Charles would have to give way in the end because of his need for money. But the king had a trump card. Louis XIV had no wish to see Monmouth or William of Orange on the English throne, and was ready to pay Charles a small pension if he could prevent this. While the Whigs were preparing to celebrate their victory, Charles suddenly dissolved Parliament. It was a masterly stroke, for it caught the Whig lords off balance. They had brought armed men with them to Oxford, but they knew that the country did not want another war. Before they could collect their senses, Charles was out of their grasp, on the road to London. Since they would not fight, they had no choice but to abandon the struggle and go home. Charles had triumphed. And yet in the long-run he had failed. By forcing the English to accept his Catholic brother as their future king he made sure that his family would eventually be swept from the throne.

After the Oxford Parliament, Charles ruled alone until his death four years later. A royalist reaction set in, and the king was more popular than at any time since the Restoration. Shaftesbury fled to Holland, where he died in 1683. In that year also, two of his closest supporters, Lord Russell and Algernon Sidney, were executed after the failure of their plan to assassinate Charles and James at the Rye House near Hoddesdon on their way back from Newmarket.

In these closing years of the reign the king strengthened his hold over England in a way that no Stuart had ever attempted before. All that was needed to control the counties was the appointment of Tories as magistrates in place of Whigs. The boroughs were a more difficult proposition. Many of them had long been centres of opposition to the crown, and since they elected the majority of M.P.s they had great influence over central as well as local government. All boroughs, however, derived their special rights from the charters which the crown had originally issued to them, though they added to these rights by custom and tradition over the years. Many borough corporations were now summoned by the judges to show by what authority they were exceeding their privileges in this way. If (as was usually the case) they could produce no authority, then their charters were confiscated. Even the capital city, London itself, had its charter taken away from it after a legal action in 1683. The charters were restored, at a price. But only after they had been revised in such a way as to give the crown a right of veto in the election of borough councillors. It seemed as though, after years of struggling with Parliament and the towns from which it drew its main strength, the Stuarts had at last discovered a way to control it.

Charles spent his last years quietly, riding to Newmarket to watch the races there, of which he was extremely fond, or walking in the lovely park he had created between his two palaces of Whitehall and St James. He had made London a much gayer place to live in, and led the reaction against the sombre seriousness of Cromwell's day. No sooner had the king been restored than the theatres reopened and poets, playwrights, and musicians came into their own. Dryden was foremost among the poets and was also a popular dramatist. He and Wycherley set the fashion for the highly polished comedy of manners which was to find its supreme exponent, after Charles's death, in William Congreve. In music the great figure was Henry Purcell (1659–95), who joined the choir of the Chapel Royal in 1669. He could not have done so had he been born a few years earlier, for under the Commonwealth Church music was frowned on as papist and ungodly. It came back with the king, and Pepys records in his diary for 1660 'To Whitehall chapel where . . . I heard very good musique; the first time that I ever remember to have heard the organs and singing-men in surplices in my life'.

Purcell, in his brief life, enriched the Anglican Church with music of a quality that it had not heard since the days of Byrd and Tallis. Indeed late-Stuart England was another Elizabethan period for the arts – in a lighter vein, perhaps, and under the influence of French fashions, but bubbling over with a sparkling vivacity. The king himself led the way, appointing Dryden as his Poet Laureate, paying frequent visits to the theatre, and sending young composers over to study in France. He had no great love for the arts, but he knew how they could be used to add lustre to his throne, and he enjoyed them because they brought him into close touch with some of the wittiest men and women of his day. Beautiful women and witty men held a privileged position at his court and were permitted liberties denied to those who had no talent to recommend them. When the poet Earl of Rochester wrote his famous mock-epitaph of Charles

> Here lies a great and mighty King
> Whose promise none relies on.
> He never said a foolish thing
> Nor ever did a wise one.

the king dismissed it with a laugh. 'Quite right,' he said. 'Quite right. For my words are my own, but my actions are my ministers'.'

In February 1685 came the sudden illness which led to Charles's death. Although his life was drawing towards its end, he refused to accept the sacraments of the Church of England. But James sent for Father Huddleston, a Roman Catholic priest who had looked after Charles in his flight from Worcester, and Huddleston received the king into the Roman Catholic Church. Charles lingered for some time after that, apologizing, with typical humour, for 'taking such an unconscionable time about dying'. But when the morning of 16 February came, James was king of England.

CHAPTER 39

James II and William III

1685-1702

THE NEW King James was, like his father, stubborn and high-principled, but unlike Charles I he was a convinced Roman Catholic – a member of that small and much-hated minority. He made the conversion of England the main aim of his life, admitting that if he had 'agreed to live quietly and treat his religion as a private matter . . . he could have been one of the most powerful kings ever to reign in England . . . but having been called by Almighty God to rule these kingdoms, he would think of nothing but the propagation of the catholic religion'.

James's reign opened well. The attack upon the boroughs had been carefully carried out, and when the first Parliament of the reign was elected, it had an overwhelming Tory majority. Before it met, Titus Oates, the fabricator of the Popish Plot, was brought to justice. At the height of the panic in 1678 Parliament had granted him a pension of £1,200 a year and apartments in White-hall Palace. Now he was found guilty of perjury, sentenced to be flogged, imprisoned for life, and publicly exhibited in the pillory every year. This savage treatment was designed to kill him, but he survived until the next reign, when the Whigs released him and restored his pension.

The Londoners who came to watch Oates's punishment showed their sympathy with this strange creature who represented their hatred of Roman Catholics. And later in 1685 the West Country demonstrated its Protestantism by supporting the Duke of Monmouth, who landed at Lyme Regis in June, and proclaimed himself king. The rebellion was easily put down by the royal forces under the command of the old Earl of Feversham and his deputy,

John Churchill. Monmouth's troops were cut to pieces when they tried to attack across the marshes of Sedgemoor, and the duke himself was captured and executed. His followers were given no mercy. James's Lord Chief Justice, Jeffreys, moved round the West Country in his 'Bloody Assize', showing obvious pleasure in sentencing about 150 men to death and another 800 to transportation as slaves to Barbados.

James was alarmed by the support which Monmouth had found, and used it as an excuse to expand the royal army. About 15,000 men camped on Hounslow Heath, just outside London – a reminder to citizens of what they might expect if they dared oppose their monarch. Many of the officers appointed by James were Roman Catholics. The Test Act made their appointment illegal, but James claimed the right to 'dispense' with the law in certain cases. As dispensation was used more and more frequently, it became clear that the king was ignoring the law where it did not suit him. This strained the loyalty of the Commons to breaking-point. In France, Louis XIV had started persecuting the Protestant Huguenots and refugees were pouring into England. Members of Parliament were alive to their own danger, and refused James's demand that they should repeal the Test Act. James therefore dissolved Parliament.

Without Parliament to trouble him, the king could go ahead with his plans for making England Catholic. One Roman Catholic was made Lord Lieutenant of Ireland; another was put in charge of the navy. When the Anglicans protested, James set up a new court to exercise his supremacy over the Church. It was suspiciously like the Court of High Commission which the Long Parliament had abolished in 1641. The new court was used for an attack on Oxford and Cambridge, which were compelled to admit Roman Catholics as undergraduates and fellows of colleges. Meanwhile, town councils and city companies were under strong pressure to add Roman Catholics to their number.

These measures aroused such opposition that James was frightened. He had expected a large number of conversions to Catholicism, but the vast majority of the population remained obstinately Protestant. In a search for allies he issued in 1687 a Declaration of Indulgence, suspending all the penal laws, not simply against Catholics but also against Nonconformists. By doing

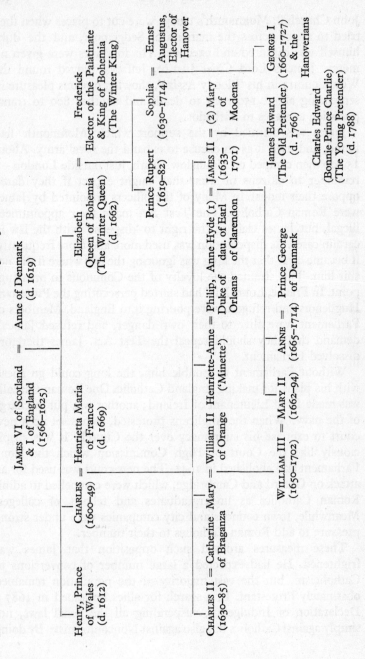

TABLE VII. *The Stuart Dynasty*

JAMES VI of Scotland & I of England (1566–1625) = Anne of Denmark (d. 1619)

Henry, Prince of Wales (d. 1612)

Elizabeth Queen of Bohemia (The Winter Queen) (d. 1662) = Frederick Elector of the Palatinate & King of Bohemia (The Winter King)

Charles (1600–49) = Henrietta Maria of France (d. 1669)

Sophia (1630–1714) = Ernst Augustus, Elector of Hanover

Prince Rupert (1619–82)

GEORGE I (1660–1727) & the Hanoverians

JAMES II (1633–1701) = (2) Mary of Modena

JAMES II = Anne Hyde (1) dau. of Earl of Clarendon

James Edward (The Old Pretender) (d. 1766)

Charles Edward (Bonnie Prince Charlie) (The Young Pretender) (d. 1788)

CHARLES II (1630–85) = Catherine of Braganza

Mary = William II of Orange

Henriette-Anne ('Minette') = Philip, Duke of Orleans

ANNE (1665–1714) = Prince George of Denmark

WILLIAM III (1650–1702) = MARY II (1662–94)

this he hoped to win the support of an influential section of the population.

The king's claim to dispense with the law in individual cases had been opposed by Parliament. Now he had expanded this into the right to suspend laws altogether when he did not approve of them. As the volume of criticism and anger swelled, James issued a second Declaration to reinforce the first. This time he ordered it to be read in every church in the kingdom. But when the appointed Sunday came, there were only seven churches in London where the priest could be persuaded to read the Declaration.

The bishops, who had up to this moment supported the king, would do so no longer. The Archbishop of Canterbury and six other bishops petitioned James to withdraw the Declaration. The king promptly had them arrested for libel. They were tried in Westminster Hall, where Strafford and Charles I had once stood. But such was the effect of James's policy that the bishops were now heroes. One man who was present in the hall describes the excitement when the jury returned the verdict *Not Guilty*. 'There was continued shoutings for half an hour, so that no business could be done . . . And at night was mighty rejoicing, in ringing of bells, discharging of guns, lighting of candles, and bonfires in several places . . . a joyful deliverance to the Church of England.'

Before the trial opened, an event had taken place which changed the whole situation. James's second wife, Mary of Modena, gave birth to a son. There was no hope left now for those who had been prepared to put up with a Catholic king because he would, in the not too distant future, be succeeded by his Protestant daughter Mary. All over the country the opponents of James united. He had angered the Anglicans by his support of Catholicism, and Non-conformists by his crude attempt to bribe them with the Declaration of Indulgence. Most important of all, the property-owners – nobles, country gentry and merchants – resented the way in which the royal council was challenging their control of local life by securing the appointments of Roman Catholics as Lords-Lieu-tenant, magistrates and town councillors. Seven representatives of this dominating section of English society met in secret and sent an invitation to William of Orange to bring an army to England and save the country from the Catholic menace. The signatories included the suspended Bishop of London; leading Whigs like Henry Sidney, brother of Algernon who had been executed for his part in the Rye House plot; and the old Tory Danby, who had been responsible for William's marriage to James's daughter Mary.

William had one overriding ambition – to defeat Louis XIV, whose aggressive foreign policy was a threat to the very existence of Holland. The English fleet might easily swing the scales against France in this struggle. It was this prospect that decided William, and in October 1688 he sailed. The 'protestant wind' blew him down Channel, past the English fleet which was waiting for him on the east coast. On 5 November, while England was celebrating an earlier deliverance from a Catholic threat, he landed in Devon, at Torbay.

There was no general rising in William's favour. The majority of Englishmen dreaded the thought of war, and waited to see what James would do. As William moved slowly towards London, the royal army was faced with the choice of retreating in front of him or spilling the first blood. Rather than fight they retreated. And as they retreated their numbers melted away, until there was nothing between William and the capital. James had joined his troops at Salisbury, but he was sick at heart, and when John Churchill, his best commander, went over to William, he made his way back to London. His daughter Anne had already deserted him, and fearing to meet his father's fate James tried to slip away to France on 11 December. Much to William's embarrassment he was captured by some fishermen and brought back again. But he was given every encouragement to make a second attempt, and this time he succeeded. On 23 December he took boat from Rochester, and two days later landed in France.

Once James had gone, elections were held so that Parliament could meet and decide the fate of the nation. Technically speaking the assembly that met in February 1689 was not a Parliament, since the king had never summoned it, but the Convention, as it was called, had as much real power as any legitimate Parliament. It was not a revolutionary body. Many of the members had been elected by Tory borough councils and were reluctant to accept the fact that James had gone. They wanted to make William regent for the absent king, and when he refused this they tried to preserve the principle of hereditary descent by making Mary queen in her own right. But William had the last word. Unless he was crowned king and his wife queen, he threatened to take himself and his army back to Holland, and leave the ungrateful English to solve their problems alone. This threat was sufficient. The Convention hastily made a formal offer of the throne to William and Mary.

William III was a thin-faced, long-nosed man, aged thirty-nine. Like his grandfather, Charles I, he was cold and aloof, not easy to know or to love,and he had constantly to struggle against ill-health. But he was an excellent judge of men, and knew exactly what he wanted. His aloofness was softened by the charm of his twenty-seven-year-old wife. The fact that Mary was James's daughter and an Anglican reconciled many Tories to the new rulers, and William was strengthened by his wife's obvious devotion to him.

The 'Glorious Revolution' of 1688, carried through without spilling one drop of blood, was the work of Anglicans and Non-conformists, Whigs and Tories. They had united against James's tyranny, and while they welcomed the new king and queen, they hastily drew up a list of limitations on the crown, to protect them-selves against any future attacks on their liberties. The *Bill of Rights*, as this list was called, marks the point at which the property-owners in Parliament, who had been growing in strength through-out the seventeenth century, turned the scales against the crown. The power, which James had claimed, to dispense with and sus-pend laws, was declared illegal. So was the court he had set up to rule the Church. So also was a standing army without Parliament's permission. The bill laid down that Roman Catholics should, in future, be barred from the English throne, and to make sure that no king would ever again attempt to tell the Commons what they might or might not discuss, it was declared 'that the freedom of speech . . . in Parliament ought not to be impeached or questioned in any court or place out of Parliament'.

The Church of England, which had been tied so closely to the Stuart monarchy and had preached the duty of subjects to obey their divinely-appointed ruler, was shaken by the Revolution. Six bishops, including the Archbishop of Canterbury and four more of the famous Seven who had been tried by James II, gave up their livings rather than take the oath of allegiance to William and Mary. They were followed by about four hundred of the clergy, and formed the group known as the Non-Jurors. The Nonconformists, many of whom helped William, expected some reward for their loyalty. By the Toleration Act they were permitted to hold their own services, but the Anglican gentry who controlled Parliament were not prepared to relax the laws forbidding Nonconformists to take part in public affairs. Roman Catholics were still officially denied freedom of worship, though in fact they were not persecuted after 1689. But they remained, like the Nonconformists, banned from public life.

The Revolution was welcomed in the Scottish lowlands, where Presbyterians had bitterly opposed James's revival of Roman Catholicism, and William was offered the Scottish crown. But the highland clans, many of whose chiefs were Catholic and loyal to the Stuart cause, were not easily won over to the new rulers. They routed William's troops at Killiecrankie, in 1689, and the king ordered the building of Fort William as a base from which the wild northern region could gradually be brought under control. His agent in Scotland, looking for some opportunity to demonstrate the power of his master's government, ordered the chieftains to take the oath of allegiance to William and Mary. All did so on time except MacDonald of Glencoe, who arrived late. He was singled out for punishment. Royal troops were billeted on the MacDonald clan, and at given signal suddenly turned on their hosts and massacred them.

Acts of brutality like the Massacre of Glencoe prevented the growth of friendship between England and Scotland. So did the failure of the Darien scheme in 1699, when English commercial jealousy, and William's desire to avoid offending Spain, forced the Scots to abandon a trading colony they had established, at enormous expense, on the Isthmus of Panama. Tempers flared up, and three English seamen were arrested in Leith on a trumped-up charge, and executed. William realized that the only way in which to put an end to these disputes would be by uniting the two countries, but he died before he could bring this to pass. Not until 1707 were all the difficulties overcome. The Act of Union of that year welded the two nations together. Under its provisions Scottish M.P.s were to sit in the Parliament at Westminster, and Scotsmen were allowed to share the trading privileges that England had acquired. Scotland kept her own code of law and her own Presbyterian Church, but the frontier between the two countries lost any real significance. The hostility of many centuries very slowly gave way to co-operation and friendship.

Ireland had, like Scotland, been united with England by Cromwell, but at the Restoration the union was broken and a Protestant Irish Parliament once again ruled over the Roman Catholic majority. The confiscations which had taken place under Cromwell were confirmed, and the English remained in possession of most of the land. James brought hope to the Irish by appointing a Roman Catholic as Lord Lieutenant, and allowing freedom of worship. The result was that while England welcomed William III, Ireland continued to recognize James II, except for the Protestant minority in Ulster. James landed in Ireland in March 1689, hoping to win over the whole country so that he could then use it as a base for the reconquest of England. But Londonderry stubbornly refused to surrender, and defied James's besieging forces for over three months. Meanwhile William had sent an army into Ireland, and landed there himself in June 1690. A month later he met James's forces near Drogheda, and put them to flight in the Battle of the Boyne. James gave up hope and returned to France. By 1691 Ireland had been subdued. Many Irish Catholics despaired of finding happiness in the land of their birth, and took service with the armies of the Catholic king of France. Those who remained were subjected to ruthless penal laws that made them once again no better than slaves in their own country.

When Ireland was settled, William turned back to the great struggle in which he had been engaged before the invitation from England reached him. The Thirty Years' War, which ended in 1648, had seen the decline of Spain and the rise of France as the greatest power in Europe. Now, under her King Louis XIV, France was at the summit of her pride and ambition, pushing out her frontiers towards the Rhine. This brought French troops into the Spanish Netherlands – present-day Belgium – and within striking distance of Holland. William was determined to check their advance, and the struggle raged round the fortress towns south of Brussels. English troops were fighting side by side with those of Holland, Spain and the Holy Roman Empire, in a Grand Alliance against France. There were no big battles, but every year William was with his troops, hammering at the forts which guarded the road into France. His only major success came in 1695 when the fortress of Namur surrendered – the first big blow to French prestige. But the allied armies saved Holland from invasion, and forced the French to terms at the Treaty of Ryswick in 1697. Louis had to recognize William as king of England, and promise to withdraw his support of James.

The war at sea was more exciting. The French aim was to knock out England by invasion. The English fleet, increased in size and efficiency by James II, was ready to defend the English coasts and to blockade France. The first engagement, fought off Beachy Head in June 1690, was indecisive, and the English admiral was dismissed for holding back his ships. But in 1691 the French assembled an invasion army at Cape La Hogue, where James II joined it. The commander of the English fleet was Edward Russell, one of the peers who had signed the invitation to William. When French warships came out to sweep the Channel clear, so that the troop transports could cross, Russell sent fifteen to the bottom in a battle that lasted for several days, and so crippled the rest that England was free from danger of invasion for the rest of the war. The French, recognizing this, played the much more profitable game of pouncing on English merchant ships. Jean Bart, the most successful of the French captains, became almost as much of a legend in his own country as Drake had been to England a century earlier.

Eight years of war cost more than Stuart kings could ever have laid their hands on. This, rather than any statute, tied William to the Commons. The government could not raise enough in taxation and had to borrow on a large scale. Rich merchants would have been hesitant about lending money to the king alone, since kings had a poor record in paying back debts. But they were prepared to lend when Parliament guaranteed repayment. This led, in 1694, to the foundation of the Bank of England, which raised money and lent it to the government (with Parliament's approval) at a handsome rate of interest. More and more business men put their capital into the Bank, and this made them keen supporters of the Glorious Revolution. They knew that if James returned, they would never see their money again. In this way the merchants, who were among the richest men in the kingdom, were at last persuaded to put their money at the service of the State. Loans from the Bank of England paid for the campaign which led to the capture of Namur, and by the time peace was signed the government had piled up a large national debt, on which it paid yearly interest.

By the end of William's reign the amount of money paid out in interest alone was equal to Charles II's entire annual income. Only the Commons could finance this scale of spending. They voted the king's income for a year at a time, and took over responsibility for financing the war. Following the example set after the second Dutch War, they appointed commissioners in 1691 to examine the government's accounts, and made sure that the large sums of money voted were not being wasted. Stuart kings had found their Parliaments unwilling to vote more than a mere fraction of the cost of their wars. But now that William was committed to a Nationalist, Protestant foreign policy of which Parliament approved, the Commons were prepared to vote money on a scale larger than anything known before.

The king was still very powerful, of course. He appointed and dismissed ministers as he wished, and had the right, which he exercised, to refuse his assent to any bill of which he disapproved. If there had been no war he might have been as independent as Charles II. But the overriding need for money forced him to co-operate with Parliament. He had no alternative, if he was to defeat France. He could not, in any case, rely on the almost religious devotion to the crown which the Stuarts had encouraged. The Anglican Tories accepted him, but only reluctantly. They kept their enthusiasm for Mary, and after her death in 1695 waited impatiently for Anne to come to the throne. The Whigs were more enthusiastic supporters of William, but this was not much comfort to the king since the Whigs were believers in Parliamentary supremacy. Their attitude was most clearly expressed by the philosopher John Locke, formerly secretary to the Earl of Shaftesbury. He dismissed divine right as nonsense, and held that kings ruled because their subjects wished them to do so. If they ruled badly, the terms of the agreement were broken, and their subjects had a right to get rid of them.

When, in 1700, Anne's only surviving child died, there was the dismal prospect of an uncertain succession. Anne would succeed William, but who would succeed Anne? Parliament determined to settle this question before squabbles could break out over it. There were several descendants of Charles I to whom the crown might have been offered, but they were mostly Roman Catholics. The most satisfactory Protestant claimant was Sophia, wife of a German prince, the Elector of Hanover. She was descended from James I through his daughter Elizabeth, the Winter Queen. By the *Act of Settlement* of 1701 Parliament decreed that the throne of England was to pass, on Anne's death, to Sophia and her descendants. This act, as well as deciding the succession, also placed further restrictions on the monarch. In this way Parliament completed the revolution of 1688. Future sovereigns were to be members of the Church of England. They were not to dismiss judges, except at Parliament's request; neither were they to pardon any minister whom the Commons had impeached. They were not even to leave the country without Parliament's approval.

William resented these new limitations, but he could do nothing about them, for the uneasy peace concluded at Ryswick was coming to an end. In 1700 the king of Spain died, leaving no children. He named as heir to the great possessions of the Spanish crown the grandson of Louis XIV. William might have been willing to agree to this had not Louis immediately moved troops into the Spanish Netherlands and made it clear that he intended to treat them as his own. Faced with this new attempt to dominate Europe, William re-formed the Grand Alliance against France.

The War of the Spanish Succession was about to begin, and the English succession was also at stake since, on the death of the exiled James II, Louis recognized his son James III as lawful king of England. William prepared to join his armies, but he was not to see the end of his life's work. In February 1702 his horse stumbled on a molehill and threw him, while he was riding at Hampton Court. He only broke his collar-bone, but the strain of ill-health and long struggles against the English Parliament and the French king had weakened him. By 8 March he was dead, and Anne – daughter of James II and granddaughter of Clarendon – became queen of England.

CHAPTER 40

Queen Anne

1702-1714

ANNE, THE LAST of the Stuart sovereigns, was a stout, rather dull woman, proud of her descent, revelling in the fact that she was, in her own phrase, 'entirely English'. She felt guilty about the way in which she had treated her father, but was comforted by the reflection that the Anglican Church, to which she was devoted, had triumphed. In politics she was no mere figurehead, but the real ruler, making her own choice between the groups of politicians who squabbled for her favours. For the greater part of her reign she turned for advice to her intimate friend Sarah, wife of John Churchill.

Sarah's husband was the finest soldier of his age. He was the obvious person to command the allied armies in the Netherlands, and Anne showed her approval by creating him Duke of Marlborough. For the next eight years Marlborough guided the fortunes of England on the Continent, while his friend Sidney Godolphin, whom Anne made Lord Treasurer, looked after affairs at home.

Marlborough, Godolphin and Anne were all committed to William III's policy of fighting the French on land. To prevent the Spanish empire from passing to France, they proclaimed Charles, son of the Holy Roman Emperor, as king of Spain. Marlborough's plan was to drive the French out of the Netherlands, and to lead his armies along the road to Paris. He was handicapped in this by the Dutch, who were far more concerned with their own safety, and wanted to keep the allied armies stationed more or less permanently on the Dutch frontier.

While Marlborough was spending his energies trying to persuade the Dutch to let him attack, the French were invading the Empire and moving on Vienna. Marlborough was in a dilemma. If he went south-east to meet this new threat he would leave Holland defenceless behind him. But if he stayed in the Netherlands he would leave the Emperor, his most important ally, at the mercy of France. In the end he decided to take the risk of challenging the French on their chosen ground. Leaving the Netherlands in the spring of 1704, he marched his army swiftly east, and by June had reached Vienna. Two months later he encountered the French troops – the finest soldiers in the world – near the little village of Blenheim. There, on 13 August, he was triumphantly successful, capturing four-fifths of the enemy's troops and routing the rest. As night fell, he scribbled a note to Sarah: 'I have not time to say more, but to beg you will give my duty to the queen, and let her know her army has had a glorious victory. Monsieur Tallard [commander of the French forces] and two other generals are in my coach, and I am following the rest'. This was the first time since Agincourt that a British army, fighting on the Continent, had gained such a resounding success. The Empire was saved, and French prestige was shaken.

Two years later, at Ramillies, Marlborough defeated the main French army in the Netherlands, and occupied Brussels and Antwerp. But in the south the war was going badly. Although Rooke had captured Gibraltar in 1704, the allied armies in Spain made little headway in their attempt to drive Louis XIV's grandson Philip off the throne and replace him by the Archduke Charles. Spanish national pride was aroused by this attempt to force an Austrian ruler on them, and Louis, although he wanted peace, would not abandon his grandson. The war might have been decided in the north, especially after Marlborough's third victory at Oudenarde, in 1708. But the road into France was stubbornly defended, and Louis bankrupted himself in order to raise new armies. Marlborough was actually on French soil when he fought his last great battle at Malplaquet in 1709. He cleared the enemy from the field, but 17,000 of his men lay dead and he could go no farther.

At home in England, enthusiasm for the war waned as the cost mounted. The main tax was one on land, and this struck heavily at the gentry, the smaller landowners. They opposed the policy of sending huge armies to fight on the Continent, as this cost so much

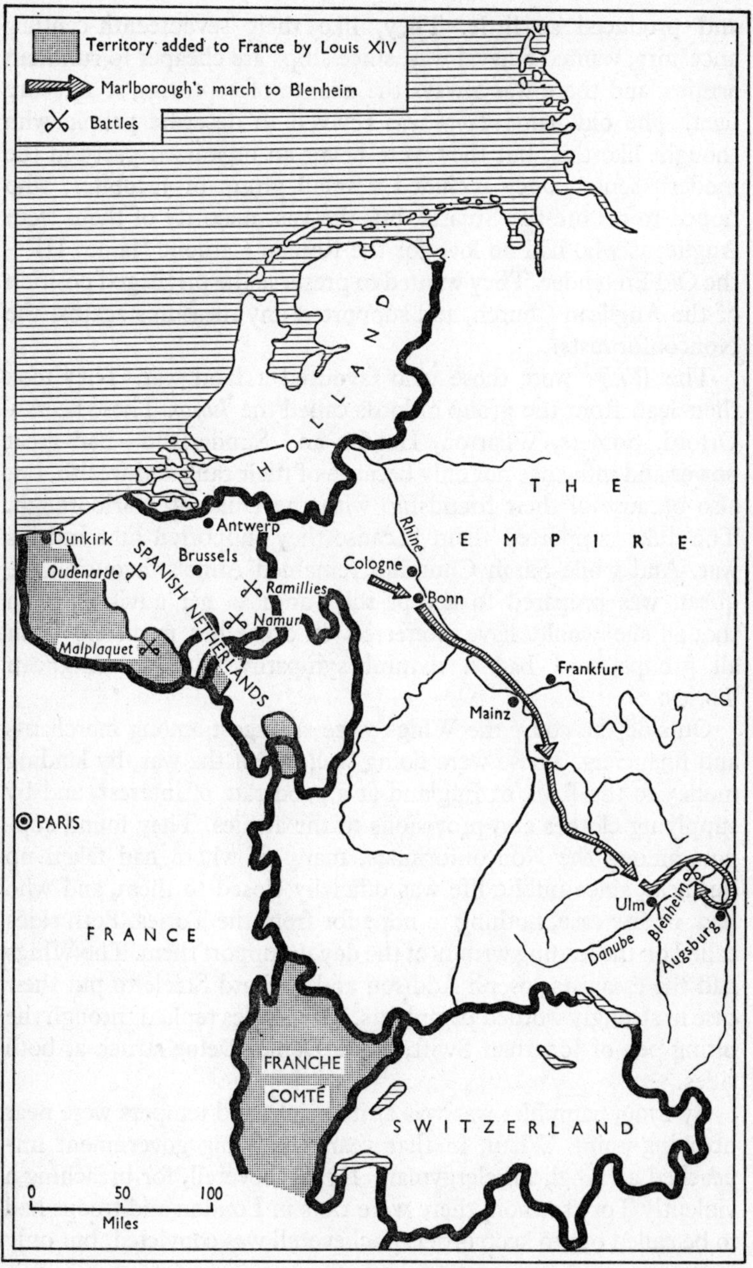
Territory added to France by Louis XIV
Marlborough's march to Blenheim
Battles
HOLLAND
THE EMPIRE
Antwerp
Dunkirk
Brussels
Oudenarde
SPANISH NETHERLANDS
Ramillies
Namur
Malplaquet
Rhine
Cologne
Bonn
Frankfurt
Mainz
PARIS
Ulm
Blenheim
Danube
Augsburg
FRANCE
FRANCHE COMTÉ
SWITZERLAND
0
50
100
Miles

MARLBOROUGH'S CAMPAIGNS

and produced so little. They, like their seventeenth-century ancestors, wanted a naval war, since ships are cheaper to run than armies, and there was always the chance of capturing a treasure fleet. The old name *Tory* was revived to describe people who thought like this, but they were never an organized party in the modern sense. They included a small group of Jacobites, who hoped to restore the Stuarts, but the vast majority of them were Anglicans who had no love for the Roman Catholic 'James III' – the Old Pretender. They wanted to preserve the privileged position of the Anglican Church, and supported any measures against the Nonconformists.

The *Whigs* were those who favoured a land war. They took their lead from the group of lords called the *Junto*. These peers – Orford, Somers, Wharton, Halifax and Sunderland – had great power and influence not only because of their rank and wealth, but also because of their friendship with the Duke of Marlborough. The duke supported them because they supported him and his war. And while Sarah Churchill remained Anne's favourite, the queen was prepared to accept the Junto as her advisers, even though she would have preferred to draw her ministers from all groups, and had a natural sympathy with the Anglican Tories.

Outside the court the Whigs were strongest among merchants and financiers. These were doing well out of the war, by lending money to the Bank of England at a good rate of interest, and by supplying clothes and provisions to the armies. They found support among the Nonconformists, many of whom had taken up business, since public life was officially closed to them, and who had, in any case, nothing to hope for from the Tories. Both sides called on the leading writers of the day to support them. The Whigs had the essayists Joseph Addison and Richard Steele to put their case in strongly worded pamphlets. The Tories replied through the biting pen of Jonathan Swift, while Daniel Defoe struck at both sides.

By 1709, pamphlet war was at its height and tempers were near breaking-point. When, in that year, the Whig government impeached an Anglican clergyman, Dr Sacheverell, for preaching a violently Tory sermon, there were riots in London and troops had to be called out to keep order. Sacheverell was convicted, but only by a small majority of votes. The Tories greeted this as a victory, and their spirits soared.

Anne was turning away from the Whigs. The Sacheverell case brought out all her Anglican sympathies and she was also tiring, at last, of Sarah Churchill. Her new favourite was Abigail Masham. And Mrs Masham supported a moderate Tory called Robert Harley. With great skill Harley and Mrs Masham won the queen over to their policy of negotiating peace with France. Godolphin was dismissed in August 1710 and a general election was held. 'Never so much money spent, nor so foolishly,' wrote Defoe. 'Never so much drunkenness, ravings, feuds, raging of parties, at least not in my time, have been seen in this nation . . . We strive not like men, but like devils, like furies. We fight not as if we would kill one another only, but as if we would tear one another's souls out of our bodies. We fight with all the addition of personal envy, revenge, hellish rage, irreconcilable implacable malice.'

The Tories swept the polls but unfortunately for Harley the new Parliament was dominated not by the Moderates but by the Extremists, who demanded far-reaching changes in the administration, and looked for leadership to one of the Secretaries of State, Henry St John. Harley, appointed Lord Treasurer and raised to the peerage as Earl of Oxford, was the nominal head of the ministry and had the queen's confidence. But St John, created Viscount Bolingbroke, was in charge of the negotiations for peace with France.

Public opinion against Marlborough and the Whigs was whipped up by Swift in his most famous pamphlet *The Conduct of the Allies*. 'We have been fighting for the ruin of the public interest and the advancement of a private,' he wrote. 'We have been fighting to raise the wealth and grandeur of a particular family [i.e. Marlborough's], to enrich usurers and stockjobbers, and to cultivate the pernicious design of a faction by destroying the landed interest. The nation begins to think these blessings are not worth fighting for any longer and therefore desires a peace.' The Tory campaign was successful. On the last day of 1711 the fall of the Whigs was signalled by Anne's dismissal of Marlborough. The letter she wrote to the greatest captain of her age was curt and offensive, and the duke tossed it into the fire. He spent the rest of Anne's reign in voluntary exile, before returning to the enormous palace which Sir

John Vanbrugh had built for him at Woodstock, outside Oxford. The new English commander was instructed by Bolingbroke not to advance with his Dutch and German allies against Paris. Nothing must be done to upset the prospects of peace. The allies were understandably furious, particularly the German princes whose territory was now open to invasion by French troops. Among these princes, who blamed their troubles on Bolingbroke, was George, Elector of Hanover, heir to the English throne.

Peace was concluded at Utrecht in 1713. Louis XIV's grandson Philip was accepted as king of Spain and of Spanish America. The Archduke Charles, who had by now become emperor, was given the Netherlands and the Spanish possessions in Italy. Louis XIV agreed to withdraw all support from the Stuarts and to recognize Anne and her Hanoverian successors. England was given more concrete advantages in the shape of Gibraltar and Minorca – the keys of the Mediterranean – and Nova Scotia and Newfoundland in the New World. She was also promised trading privileges with the Spanish empire, including the valuable contract, known as the Asiento, for supplying slaves to the Spanish American colonies.

The Tory peace was popular. But soon after it was signed, Anne fell ill, and the problem of the succession loomed up again. Bolingbroke and Oxford were not Jacobites, but they suspected, rightly, that the Elector of Hanover, the heir to the throne, would not forgive them for holding back the British armies in 1712. They were, like most English politicians, in secret touch with the Old Pretender. If they could persuade James to turn Protestant, they would almost certainly be able to ignore the Act of Settlement and restore the Stuarts to the throne. But James, although the crown was within his grasp, refused to abandon his faith.

Oxford and Bolingbroke were by now open enemies. Bolingbroke wanted some positive policy which would keep the Tories in power – either the restoration of James, or a negotiated agreement with George of Hanover. But Oxford was unable and unwilling to make up his mind. He let things drift, and turned to drink for consolation. Bolingbroke knew that his only hope of staying in power was to take Oxford's place as Lord Treasurer before Anne died. He would then be able to use the last weeks of Anne's life to build up his power by lavish distribution of government money and offices. But death frustrated his plans. On 27 July 1714, after an appalling scene in the queen's bedchamber, when the two rivals shouted insults at each other, Anne dismissed Oxford. On the 30th she gave the white staff of the Lord Treasurer not to Bolingbroke but to the Duke of Shrewsbury. Two days later she was dead. 'The Earl of Oxford,' wrote Bolingbroke in his diary, 'was removed on Tuesday. The Queen died on Sunday. What a world is this, and how does fortune banter us . . .'

With Anne, died the Stuart monarchy. She had been not merely queen, but queen by divine right, and had continued practices – like touching for the King's Evil[1] – that derived from the days when monarchs had been part-priests, part-gods. No-one could pretend that the Hanoverians who followed her ruled for any other reason than that Parliament had invited them to do so. The property-owners, who had seen in the early Tudors a guarantee of their own security, had grown wealthy through buying-up land and trading overseas, had adopted a rugged Protestantism which suited their natural independence and suspicion of authority, and had claimed the right to rule the country in which they had so big a stake. On the Continent, the seventeenth century was the age of absolute monarchies: but in England the Stuarts, however absolute they would have liked to be, were crippled by poverty, weakened by their love of Anglo or Roman Catholicism.

The overthrow of the Stuart monarchy was not all gain. It had stood for the nation as a whole, caring (however inadequately) for the poor and unemployed, checking the greed of enclosing landlords. The 'Glorious Revolution' did not bring about democracy, but the rule of the property-owners who dominated Parliament. Yet without it England might never have become a world power. The Stuart monarchs, though they often inspired respect and devotion, failed to win the whole-hearted support of their richer subjects. As a result England cut a poor figure in European politics. Cromwell had shown how powerful an English ruler could be when he had the wealth of the country fully behind him. But only when Parliament took over the responsibility for making policy and

---

[1] The King's Evil, or Scrofula, which the sovereign was popularly supposed to be able to cure by touching the diseased person. Anne was the last English monarch to continue this practice.

paying for it did the transformation of Britain into a world power begin.

The end of the Stuarts coincided with the decline of fanaticism and of religious intolerance. The sixteenth and seventeenth centuries were dominated by religious passion, but the eighteenth century was the Age of Reason. This came about partly as a result of exhaustion after a hundred and fifty years of religious wars. But it was also due, in part, to the developments in man's knowledge of the world in which he lived – changes in attitude so fundamental that they amounted to a scientific revolution. One of the characteristics of the world of today is its obsession with the physical sciences, its love of observation and experiment. This had not been true of the Middle Ages, when men had ignored the lead of a few exceptional thinkers, like Grosseteste and Roger Bacon, and had been content to accept Aristotle's picture of a universe in which the changeless sun, stars and planets revolved in fixed circles round the stationary earth. Not all the Greek thinkers had shared these views. There were some who had believed that the earth was itself a planet and revolved either round the sun or around some unknown centre of the universe. In the late fifteenth and early sixteenth centuries their works, which had been lost sight of in the Middle Ages, were made available once again by Renaissance scholars. Printing encouraged their dissemination throughout Europe, and newly invented techniques like wood-cutting and copper-engraving made possible the accurate reproduction of scientific illustrations.

Among the first to challenge the accepted explanation of the universe was the Pole Nicholas Copernicus (1473–1543). He was not an observer or experimenter but a scholar looking for a more satisfactory explanation of the movement of heavenly bodies. He found it in the writings of the followers of the Greek philosopher Pythagoras. 'Occasioned by this,' he wrote, 'I decided to try whether, on the assumption of some motion of the earth, better explanations of the revolutions of the heavenly spheres might not be found.' In his book *On the Revolution of the Celestial Spheres* published in 1543 he put forward his view that the sun was the centre of the universe and that the earth and other planets moved in circles round it, spinning on their own axes as they did so. As an explanation it was not much more satisfactory than the one it replaced, but it made a decisive break with the medieval, Aristotelian interpretation.

Copernicus was a theorist, but little progress could be made until more facts became available. They were provided by the Danish astronomer Tycho Brahe (1546–1601) who, from his island off Copenhagen, watched the heavens and recorded all that he saw. Brahe was, however, no mathematician, and although he provided the data he could not interpret it. This was left to his literary legatee Johannes Kepler (1571–1630), a shy scholar who had been appointed imperial mathematician at the court of the Holy Roman Emperor at Prague. Kepler's long study of Brahe's observations, led to his discovery that the planets move round the sun in ellipses, not circles, and that there is a mathematical relationship between the time they take for each revolution and their distance from the sun.

Englishmen had so far taken no great part in the scientific revolution, but the Scotsman John Napier (1550–1617) published in 1614 the first tables of logarithms, which he had worked out. This device cut out a great deal of the drudgery involved in complicated calculations, and Kepler used Napier's logarithms in his later works. Advances in mathematics were essential since the book of the universe, as Galileo said, 'cannot be understood unless one first learns to understand the language and to know the letters in which it is written. It is written in the language of mathematics, and the letters are triangles, circles and other geometrical figures, without which it is humanly impossible to understand a single word. Without these one wanders about in a dark labyrinth'.

Galileo (1564–1642), one of the greatest figures in the scientific revolution, was himself responsible for extending mathematics into the realm of movement. He realized that motion is a natural, not an exceptional, state, and in a series of experiments he worked out the relationship between the distance travelled by an object and the time taken. He created, in fact, the modern study of mechanics and dynamics, and in his *Dialogue on the Two Chief Systems of the World* he described a universe in perpetual motion. Unlike Copernicus he based his beliefs on observation, for he invented the telescope and used it to scan the heavens from his villa at Fiesole, outside Florence. Milton, who visited him there in 1638, has left us a picture, in *Paradise Lost*, of the old man watching the moon:

> whose orb
> Thro' optic glass the Tuscan artist views
> At evening from the top of Fesole,
> Or in Valdarno, to descry new lands,
> Rivers, or mountains, in her spotty globe.

Galileo was typical of the new spirit in his insistence upon observation, experiment, and calculation. One of the leading exponents of this method was James I's Lord Chancellor, Francis Bacon. He was not himself a practising scientist, but in such books as the *Novum Organum*, published in 1620, he rejected medieval assumptions and urged experiment and research. By putting his superb prose and the authority of his high office at the service of the new philosophy he defended its followers from the charge of atheism and encouraged English experimenters to come together and exchange information. For England was at last becoming one of the centres of research. In 1600 William Gilbert (1546–1603) who was physician to Queen Elizabeth, published his book *On the Magnet, and Magnetic Bodies, and that great Magnet the Earth*, in which he described the experiments he had carried out and the deductions he had made about the properties of magnets. Another royal physician, William Harvey (1578–1657), who attended Charles I and was present at the battle of Edgehill, watched the heart movements of living animals and came to the conclusion that the blood circulates through the body. He published this important discovery, without which the development of medicine and surgery would have been impossible, in 1628.

Observation, experiment, and measurement were epitomized in the work of Robert Hooke (1635–1703) and Robert Boyle (1627–91). In his *Micrographia* Hooke described the minute examination of living objects which he had carried out with a microscope. He also collaborated with Boyle to produce an efficient air-pump with which the properties of the atmosphere could be studied. They discovered the law, to which Boyle's name has been given, that the volume of air varies according to the pressure exerted on it, and their work was the foundation of the study of gases and of pressure which was eventually to make possible the steam-engine – even though Pepys 'laughed mightily' at the philosophers, as he records in his Diary for 1663, 'for spending time only in weighing of air'. Boyle also laid the foundations for the modern study of chemistry by rejecting Aristotle's concept of four basic elements – fire, earth, air and water – and substituting his own definition of elements as 'certain primitive and simple or perfectly unmingling bodies which, not being made of any other bodies, or of one another, are the ingredients of which all those called perfectly mixed bodies are immediately compounded and into which they are ultimately resolved'.

Boyle was a member of the club which began meeting in London in the 1640's, and fulfilled Bacon's vision of an academy where scientists should share in discussion and experiment. Another member described how 'we barred all discourses of Divinity, of State affairs, and of News . . . confining ourselves to Philosophical Inquiries and such as related thereunto, as Physick, Anatomy, Geometry, Astronomy, Navigation, Staticks, Magnetics, Chymicks Mechanicks and Natural Experiments. We there discoursed on the circulation of the Blood, the Valves in the Veins, the Copernican Hypothesis, the Nature of Comets and new Stars . . . the Improvement of Telescopes and grinding of Glasses for that purpose, the weight of air . . . the Descent of Heavenly Bodies, and the Degrees of Acceleration therein, with others of a like nature'.

Civil war broke up these meetings in London, but after the Restoration this group formed itself into the Royal Society, which still carries out its original purpose of encouraging scientists to exchange information about the work they are doing. Charles II, who built a laboratory of his own and had an interest in ship-building and the principles of navigation which Burnet described as 'exact rather more than became a prince', gave the Society his patronage and presented it with a mace.

Greatest of all members of the Royal Society, and indeed one of the greatest Englishmen of all time, was Sir Isaac Newton (1642–1727). A native of Lincolnshire, he studied at Trinity College, Cambridge. It was while on a forced holiday from there, when all students were sent home for fear that the Plague, then ravaging London, might spread to the universities, that he turned his mind to the problem of gravitation. Copernicus, Kepler and Galileo had done much to destroy the Aristotelian system, but they had not replaced it. Each had sketched in a part of the new scheme. Kepler had shown that the planets moved in mathematically determined ellipses. Galileo had worked out the dynamics of falling bodies. It was left to Newton to take the work of his predecessors and, by his own genius, complete the new picture of the universe. He combined Kepler's laws and Galileo's observations into a single theory of gravitation, stating that all particles attract all other particles with a force (gravity) which varies according to their masses and to the distance between them and can be mathematically determined. The entire solar system was explained by this law, and the force that makes an apple drop to the ground was shown to follow the same rules as the force which swings the planets in their courses.

This was only part of Newton's achievement. His researches into the nature of light, and his development of the differential calculus, were outstanding advances in themselves. But his fame rests mainly on the theory of gravity which he expounded in his *Principia Mathematica*, published in 1687. It was as though the secret of the universe had been lying hidden, waiting for a man of genius to discover it; as though, in the words of the poet Alexander Pope

> Nature and Nature's Laws lay hid in night.
> God said 'Let Newton be!' And all was light.

Although Newton did more than anybody else to give man a truer picture of the universe in which he lived, and was to dominate European thought for the next two centuries, he was himself aware of how much remained to be done. 'I do not know,' he wrote shortly before his death, 'what I may appear to the world, but to myself I seem to have been only like a boy playing on the sea shore and diverting myself in now and then finding a smoother pebble or a prettier shell than ordinary, while the great ocean of truth lay all undiscovered before me.' His humility and moderation were in sharp contrast to the religious intolerance which had characterized the sixteenth and early seventeenth centuries. The advance of knowledge was a triumph for human reason, and as its influence spread, reason was exalted at the expense of the emotions. This helps to explain the decline of religious feeling and the acceptance of toleration in the early eighteenth century. Evidence of God came to be looked for not in the angry individualism that had marked the

years of Reformation and Counter-Reformation but in the pattern
and harmony of the universe. In this well-ordered system the
hostilities of human beings seemed futile and irrelevant. Toleration
grew as fear declined. Sorcery, for instance, so real and so terrible
to men and women of the earlier period, was ridiculed, and after
1712 executions of supposed witches came to an end in England.
The passions let loose by religious conflict and the struggle for
political liberties went out with the Stuarts. The eighteenth-
century's judgment on its immediate predecessor was best
expressed by Pope:

> For forms of government let fools contest;
> Whate'er is best administered is best.
> For modes of faith let graceless zealots fight;
> He can't be wrong whose life is in the right.

TABLE VIII. *The Hanoverian Kings of England*

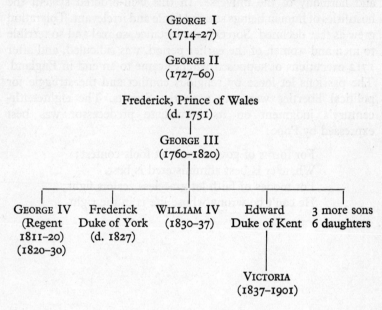

GEORGE I
(1714–27)

GEORGE II
(1727–60)

Frederick, Prince of Wales
(d. 1751)

GEORGE III
(1760–1820)

GEORGE IV   Frederick   WILLIAM IV   Edward   3 more sons
(Regent   Duke of York   (1830–37)   Duke of Kent   6 daughters
1811–20)   (d. 1827)
(1820–30)

VICTORIA
(1837–1901)

PART THREE

TO THE CLOSE OF THE
SECOND WORLD WAR

CHAPTER 41

The Hanoverian Succession and Sir Robert Walpole

1714-1742

GEORGE or James: which was to be king? When Queen Anne died the people of the United Kingdom had to choose between them. George the Elector of Hanover was an unknown German prince who had only once visited Britain. His claim to the throne was the Act of Settlement of 1701. James Stuart, the son of James II, was also a stranger. His life so far had been spent as an exile at the Court of France. He was known to be a brave and honourable young man, however, and if blood counted for more than an Act of Parliament he was the rightful heir. But James was a Catholic, and George a Protestant; and this was the factor which tipped the balance against the Stuart claimant. The Tory leaders, who would have liked to seat him on the throne of the United Kingdom, hesitated at the crucial moment, fearful of provoking another civil war by proclaiming a papist as king. While their resolution faltered their opponents the Whigs stepped in and declared the succession of George. They sent word to Hanover to bid him hurry over and occupy the throne.

The Elector did not make haste, but on a foggy day at the end of September he sailed up the Thames to Greenwich. There, next day, he set foot in his new kingdom for the second time in his life, accompanied by a crowd of German friends and advisers. George I of Britain and Ireland proved to be a thickset man of fifty-four who could not speak or understand a word of English. He was slow-thinking and obstinate; not an attractive monarch, by any means. Nevertheless, there is no doubt that many of his new subjects were glad to see him. At least the ones who mattered were. The Whigs and the great landowners, the London bankers and the merchants in the provinces: people like these did not want a Catholic and a Stuart as their king. They feared that such a monarch would try to bring England back to her old obedience to the pope, and interfere with the religious freedom which the 'Glorious Revolution' had established. Even more, perhaps, they feared for their property and for the political power which the revolution had brought them. They echoed the slogan of the wealthy wool-merchants of York-shire: 'Liberty, Property and no Pretender'.

Not everyone agreed with them. The Highlanders of Scotland for example, who hated the Act of Union, and the Fellows of Oxford University who clung to their belief in the divine right of the Stuarts: these people would have preferred James. To judge by the anti-Hanoverian riots which flared up in London and Man-chester in the autumn, many of the common people would have welcomed him as well. The Whigs did not consult them when they made their bid for power, of course; but Englishmen and Scotsmen soon had a chance to choose for themselves, in 1715.

For in that year James Stuart, prompted by the exiles who surrounded him in France and ignoring the advice of Bolingbroke, who had seen the waxing power of George and the Whigs and fled from England, decided to make a bid for the English throne. He was assured that he could count on the swords of the Highlanders to aid him. In the north of England, Tory squires awaited the word to rise. In the west they planned to raise the Stuart banner at Bath. Jacobite hopes ran high in fact; but bad luck dogged the adventure from the start. Louis XIV of France, the great protector of the Stuart cause, died when his help was needed most. The King of Sweden, besieged in his castle of Stralsund, could not send the army he had promised. Spies and informers told the Whig government all the Jacobite plans, and the plotters in the west of England were already under arrest when the Earl of Ormonde made two vain landings in Devon. Bad weather and his own indecisiveness delayed James's voyage. When he landed in Scotland, in December 1715, the Scottish rising led by the Earl of Mar and the rebellion of Thomas Forster in the north of England had already been suppressed by Hanoverian troops. Within two months James was back again in France, and the '15 was over.

Thus Jacobitism was relegated to the Highlands and Oxford, the homes of lost causes, and England and Scotland kept the king whom many, perhaps most of their people wanted: an unexciting, uninterfering monarch, who, in the words of Lady Mary Wortley Montagu, the wife of one of his ministers, 'would have been so well contented to have remained in his little town of Hanover, that if the ambition of those about him had not been greater than his own, we should never have seen him in England'. Except where the affairs of Hanover or his own income were concerned, George I left the work of government to his ministers. He took care over their appointment, choosing Germans and Whigs, and he discussed affairs with them; but he left the administration of the United Kingdom in their hands. He had nothing to do with Parliament, for he hated the institution. In Hanover his merest wish was law but in England, as he well knew, he owed his crown to Parliament, and he depended upon its consent for his income, for permission to raise taxes or to start wars, even for leave to revisit his home. George left the management of Parliament to his Whig ministers and his son George II, who succeeded him in 1727, did the same. The younger Hanoverian described his subjects as 'king-killers and republicans', and had little to do with them. And so, during the reigns of the first two Hanoverians, the power of the government passed into the hands of the Whig ministers of the crown, and their hardest task became not to deal with the king their master but with the members of Parliament who criticized their policies and coveted their places. Foreign observers and English lawyers praised the system by which England was governed: a system of 'checks and balances' which prevented either the king or Parliament from wielding absolute power. As the eighteenth century went on, however, the balance tipped ever more surely in the favour of Parliament. The ministers of the crown discovered that the crown's support was of little value to them unless they could count on the support of a majority in Parliament as well. Parliament represented the nation's will; and anyone who had an opinion to express or coveted power, or wanted to make himself a reputation tried to gain election to a seat in the House of Commons.

Except in a very few cases the candidates of the eighteenth century did not have to concern themselves winning the favour of thousands of voters by good deeds and fair promises. The great majority of the constituencies had less than a thousand voters each. They were boroughs which had gained the right to be represented in Parliament by the grant of a Royal Charter, perhaps in the reign of Queen Elizabeth or back in medieval times. The charters made many different sorts of rules as to who in the boroughs should have the right to vote. In some it was restricted to the mayor and corporation, in others to the owners of certain buildings or plots of land. In a 'potwalloper' borough every man could vote who could prove that he cooked his own meal each evening over his own fire. There were other qualifications too. The principle behind them was to make sure that the voters were responsible, property-owning people who could be relied upon to think and vote with independent minds. In fact, however, almost every borough came under the influence of some local landowner who owned the houses or appointed the mayor or had some other hold over the voters. The candidate's chief task was to enlist the influence of this man, for once the landowner had promised his support the election was as good as won. A famous example of such a borough was Old Sarum, near Salisbury, which had once been a residence of Norman kings and still returned two members to Parliament. An American who visited Old Sarum in the eighteenth century could not find the electors however. He discovered only a grassy mound on which sheep were grazing, and a single family living near by and 'supplying the curious who visit there with wine, punch and tea'. The electors were seven local farmers, and they took instructions from the Pitt family. One of England's most famous statesmen of the eighteenth century, the elder William Pitt, represented the farmers of Old Sarum.

There were many other boroughs like it, all in the pocket of a local family; but there were some, equally famous, like Preston or Westminster, where over two thousand voters had to be won over by a certain amount of speechmaking and a good deal of free beer and entertainment. Winning these 'open boroughs' was a more difficult matter, and so was victory in the county constituencies, which also boasted many people qualified to vote and returned two members each. Even in the small boroughs the voters demanded their refreshment and any election, unless it had been clearly decided by a bargain between the candidates and the patron before polling day, was likely to be a lively and expensive affair. The electors, suitably refreshed by the candidates' generosity, mounted a platform or 'hustings' and declared their choice to a clerk in the hearing of everyone around. Hired bullies might be standing about to clear a path for voters of their own side and block the way of others. It was a noisy and a violent scene, and the winners might be chaired around the town and back to another feast to celebrate their victory. By the end of the day they were likely to be bruised, exhausted and poorer men. No wonder they preferred a private arrangement and a straightforward election for a pocket borough.

For all the expense of elections and the exertion of private influence, few people demanded a change in the electoral system during the first half of the eighteenth century. From time to time members of Parliament protested at corruption and dishonesty but not, in general, if they were likely to profit from it themselves. The king's ministers in particular were the last to wish for change. Their chief concern was to try to manipulate the elections in order to obtain a majority of supporters in the House of Commons. The worst examples of bribery occurred in fact once Parliament had been elected, for then the ministers went to work with promises of lucrative government posts or contracts to provision the armed forces, or commissions in the army and navy or places in the Church for sons and brothers. The loudest accusations of corruption were raised by men who despised this traffic in public office and honours, or could not hope to gain from it themselves.

But influence, whether private or exerted by the crown, was seldom strong enough to pass an unpopular bill or save a discredited government. The opinion of England's ruling classes could generally make itself felt in Parliament, and this is why no move was made to alter the existing system. The elections returned the right sort of people: sensible men of property, the type who made the revolution of 1688-9; and the curious manner of their election did not prevent these men from doing their duty, as they saw it to be, conscientiously and well. It was only when the new

morality of evangelical Christianity made its impact at the end of
the century, when new and powerful social groups arose who were
not represented in Parliament, and when crown and politicians
began to fall out among themselves that serious demands were
made for the reform of Parliament.

Many years passed before anything like that happened, however. The reign of George I was quiet and uneventful, that of
George II full of wars, but wars which, after initial reverses, went
well for England. During these years the main debate was over
who should run the government and make use of all the power
and profit which it gave to the king's ministers. In this atmosphere
the old quarrels between Whigs and Tories were forgotten. The
party names were retained, but in practice they meant only the
great difference between men who knew the ministers and gained
by their friendship and patronage, and those who despised the
Hanoverians and the Whigs and had no influential connexions.
The Tories, excluded from the golden circle, had nothing but
their high principles; the Whigs had the profits.

The chief concerns of the Whigs were to make sure that the
Hanoverian succession and, by extension, their own power were
secure from any threat at home or abroad; and to make money,
not only for the king, his German courtiers and themselves, but
in order to pay off the huge debt which the government had
incurred by its borrowings to finance the wars with France and
Spain. The first aim, that of security, was achieved by a startling
move in foreign policy. The foreign secretary, James Stanhope,
concluded an alliance with the Duke of Orleans, the new regent
of France, who was as anxious for his own position as the Whigs
were for that of George I. Holland joined the alliance. Austria
joined, broke with her allies and then joined them again. Spain
was constantly hostile. The Anglo-French alliance proved strong
enough however to keep the peace between England and Europe
for twenty years, and deprived the Jacobites of the Continental
support vital to a renewed attempt to displace the Hanoverians.

Whig diplomacy played for safety and achieved success; but
Whig finance was adventurous, and almost ruined them. In 1710 a
company closely connected with the Whigs had been formed to
build up a flourishing trade in the South Seas. With the Asiento
treaty of 1713 the South Sea Company seemed likely to do well.

By 1720 the directors had grown so confident of success that they undertook to pay off the whole of the 'national debt' owed by the government to its creditors, within a matter of years. Inspired by the Company's confidence in itself, people rushed to buy shares in it for themselves and the price of shares rose quickly from £100 to £1,000 each. The craze for investment spread. New companies were formed to trade in all manner of commodities, and their shares proved just as popular. Suddenly however the great 'South Sea Bubble' burst. Suspicious shareholders discovered that the South Sea Company and the others had nothing like the trade they claimed; indeed members of the government had been bribed to declare that the company was flourishing when it was not. In the panic which followed as investors rushed to sell their overpriced shares many people were ruined without a hope of getting their money back. It seemed at first that the king and the government would be ruined also by their implication in the affair; but they were saved by a Whig minister who came forward with a plan for the Bank of England and the East India Company to take over most of the shares and repay some of the investors. The plan was adopted and the scandal of the government's part in the affair was glossed over. The minister who had saved the situation shortly became the head of the government. He held the reputation of the court and his colleagues in his hand, and they could not refuse him. Indeed they had no wish to, for the minister had clearly proved himself the ablest of the Whigs.

The man of the moment was Sir Robert Walpole, a hard-drinking, hard-swearing Norfolk squire. He was a country gentleman first and foremost but he was also a very shrewd man of business, as he showed not only by his solution of the South Sea catastrophe but also by selling his own share in the venture at a profit long before the panic began. Although Walpole always opened the letters from his Norfolk gamekeeper before any State dispatches, he kept such a grip on England's affairs that he was not dismissed from managing them for twenty years. From 1722 until 1742 he held the balance between crown and Parliament in his own hand. He got on well with George I, who liked his coarse company and trusted his ability; and when the first George died, Walpole established himself as the friend and adviser of the second – or at least of his wife, Queen Caroline, who exercised great influence over her husband's mind. With politicians, on the other hand, Walpole played the game of politics as a master. Men who were loyal to him could hope for honours and rewards, but if they crossed him Walpole set out to ruin them, by driving them from office and branding them as Jacobites. He had few illusions about the men he was dealing with; with rare exceptions, he maintained that every one of them had his price. From Walpole's dealings and the memoirs of his gossiping son Horace we gain the impression that all the politicians of the time were grasping and self-seeking men. Not all of them were, of course, but there were enough to keep Walpole in power.

No man can hold the position that he did, or keep it by Walpole's methods, without making enemies. Walpole had many. He was frequently accused of acting as 'sole' or 'prime' minister and ignoring the wishes of anyone but himself. But he owed his long term of power not least to the fact that he served his king and country well, and the great majority of his countrymen approved of his management of their affairs. When he ran up against strong opposition, as he did, for instance, in 1733, when he tried to bring in a scheme for checking and taxing English imports of wine and tobacco, he gave up the scheme rather than resign, and, incidentally, allowed a national industry, smuggling to and from France, to continue unchecked. The great feature of Walpole's policy, as shown by this example, was that he did nothing to interfere with the liberty or threaten the property of his countrymen. He realized moreover that the way to prosperity lay not in schemes of foreign trade but in keeping taxes low and encouraging farming and industry; and the best way of doing this was to avoid the expense and uncertainty of war. So far as he could Walpole kept out of the diplomatic intrigues which every few years brought the rulers of Europe to the brink of war and more often than not pushed them over the edge. 'Madam,' he told the queen with pride, in 1733, 'there are fifty thousand men slain this year in Europe, and not one Englishman.' While Walpole ruled England this country ceased to decide the future of European dynasties by the victories of its armies; but it also avoided the shame and expense of defeat, and farmers and merchants prospered.

As the quiet years went by however English merchants began to remember the rich promise of foreign trade which the South

Sea Company had once held out. Secure in the mounting prosperity of their counting-houses, they thought perhaps the time had come for a more adventurous foreign policy. In comfortable country houses the squire and the nobleman read in their newspapers how Spanish sailors and coastguards insulted English seamen, refusing them free passage in the Indies and suppressing their trade. Over his sherry, which came from Spain, or his pipe, which like as not was filled with tobacco from French or Spanish colonies, the squire grew angry at the insults to national pride and like the merchant demanded a more positive and warlike policy from the government to defend the nation's interests. In 1738 this opposition to Walpole's peaceful policies came to a head, when a certain Captain Jenkins was brought to the bar of the House of Commons. He claimed that as his ship was coming home past the Spanish port of Havana, Spanish coastguards had come aboard and roughly searched her for contraband. Committing 'his soul to God and his cause to his country' the gallant captain had resisted; but he had been bound to the mast and a Spanish officer had torn off his ear. He produced the organ in a bottle. Now some people said that Jenkins had never lost his ear, as the removal of his wig would have proved; but Walpole's opponents and many more Englishmen demanded war with Spain. Walpole worked hard to avoid one, but England was greedy for revenge and Spanish trade, and war was declared in 1739. In 1740 a dispute over the succession to the throne of Austria provoked a war in Europe, and England soon joined in this dispute on the side of the young Austrian queen, Maria Theresa, against her French and German enemies.

Walpole had no heart for these wars in Europe and the Indies which he was called upon to wage. He used men and money sparingly, and without success. In 1742, after repeated demands for his resignation and an election which for all the means of influence lavishly bestowed on it went very badly for the government, he admitted that the time for his leadership was past. George II was sorry to lose the man who had made his throne secure; but he too had to admit that in this new age of English history, when Parliament and public opinion demanded that a minister should go, then the king could not resist their will for long. The balance of the constitution had tilted firmly the other way.

CHAPTER 42

Hanoverian England

1742-1756

THE WAR of Jenkins's ear was a war with Spain over trade in the West Indies: the war of the Austrian Succession was a European affair. The two conflicts were linked however by the fact that England took the opposite side to Spain in the European war. Since 1733 moreover the young king of France, Louis XV, had linked his fortune with that of his uncle, Philip V of Spain, by a 'Family Compact': so England's war with Spain became a war with France as well and the Anglo-French alliance came to an end. The third of England's adversaries was Frederick, King of Prussia. So far as George II was concerned he was by far the most dangerous, for his armies, on the move against Austria, threatened the safety of Hanover. George demanded that England's war effort should be directed against him, and against the French army which was allied with him. In 1743 he led an army into battle himself, the last English king to do so, and defeated the French at Dettingen on the River Main.

The Whigs agreed that the European war was the more important. France, after all, was England's traditional enemy, the great Catholic power which had supported the cause of the Stuarts and still gave shelter and covert assistance to the Jacobites. A war with France however could no more be confined to Europe than a war with Spain could be confined to the West Indies; for the rivalry of England and France spread all over the known surface of the globe. There were French colonies in the West Indies as well as Spanish and English, and English merchants coveted their trade as much as that of Spain. On the mainland of North America too, where a line of English colonies now stretched from Georgia, founded in 1733 as a new home for debtors and criminals from the Fleet prison, up to New England and Hudson's Bay, England

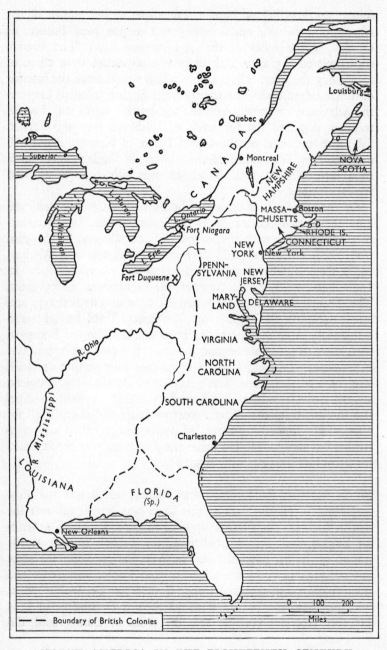

Louisburg

Quebec

L. Superior

Montreal

NOVA
SCOTIA

CANADA

NEW
HAMPSHIRE

L. Huron

L. Ontario

Fort Niagara

MASSA-
CHUSETTS

Boston

L. Michigan

L. Erie

RHODE IS.
CONNECTICUT

NEW
YORK

New York

Fort Duquesne

PENN-
SYLVANIA

NEW
JERSEY

R. Ohio

MARY-
LAND

DELAWARE

VIRGINIA

NORTH
CAROLINA

SOUTH CAROLINA

Charleston

LOUISIANA

FLORIDA
(Sp.)

Mississippi

New Orleans

0   100   200

Miles

— — Boundary of British Colonies

NORTH AMERICA IN THE EIGHTEENTH CENTURY

sensed the hostility of France. Louisiana, at the mouth of the
Mississippi, was a French colony and so was New France, or
Canada, in the valley of the St Lawrence River. The French
contemplated a plan to link these two territories by a chain of
forts along the Ohio valley; a plan which would make the interior
of the continent theirs, and imprison the English colonists between
the Alleghany mountains and the sea. Farther north still, French
trappers disputed the fur trade of Hudson's Bay and French
fishermen intruded on the Grand Banks of Newfoundland. All
over the New World, in fact, the interests of England and France
came into collision, and neither side was loth to go to war and
try conclusions.

On the other side of the globe the East India Company enjoyed
a monopoly of English trade in the Indian Ocean. Its merchant-
men sailed home with rich cargoes of raw silk and cotton yarn
from the Company's ports at Bombay, Calcutta and Madras,
coffee from Mokha on the Persian Gulf and tea from China. In
India, however, just as in America, the French were also present.
The French India Company had its base at Pondicherry, and
strove to capture the English company's trade. Until the eighteenth
century the Mogul emperors of India had not allowed European
merchants to penetrate beyond the coast, but now the empire was
breaking up and local viceroys or nawabs were setting up small
kingdoms of their own. The governor of Pondicherry, Dupleix,
sought their friendship. He aimed with their support to expel
the English from the eastern coast of India and claim it all for
France. He formed regiments of native troops called sepoys to
further his design. He too made the European war the occasion
for a trial of strength with England.

So the war between England and France, which was the most
important of all the wars at this time, was fought all over the
world. In India the French captured Madras. In North America
an English fleet seized Louisburg, the French fortress at the
mouth of the St. Lawrence. In the West Indies, Admiral Hawke
cut the lines of communication between France and Spain and
their colonies and captured a huge French convoy. In Europe, as
we have seen, the French were defeated at Dettingen. In 1745
however George's younger son, the Duke of Cumberland, did

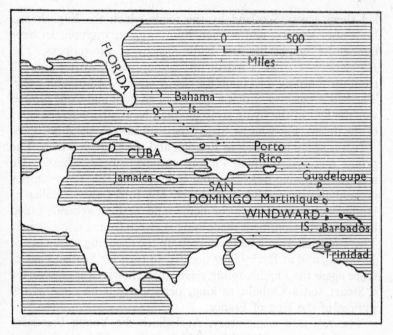

THE WEST INDIES

not equal his father's success when he himself fought at the battle of Fontenoy, in Flanders. His army was broken and put to flight, and the defeat had a sequel which brought the war to the British Isles themselves.

Walpole had warned that if England went to war with France the Jacobites would make another attempt to seize the throne. In 1744 stormy weather and the vigilance of the English fleet had frustrated a French invasion plan, but the defeat at Fontenoy put fresh heart into the Jacobite exiles. The Stuart heir was now young Charles Edward, the son of James the Old Pretender. 'Bonnie Prince Charlie' was handsome and gallant, a fit leader for a movement which kept young on romantic memories and vague hopes for a brighter future. He was too impatient to wait any longer, but sailed for Scotland with only two ships and landed at Loch Moidart with only seven companions. The first man he met advised him to go home. 'I am come home,' the Young Pretender replied, and sure enough the Highlanders rose to follow him. He led them across Scotland by the roads which the English had built after the '15, and entered Edinburgh in triumph. In September he fought his first battle nearby at Prestonpans. The Highlanders crossed a marsh just as day was breaking and fell from the morning mist upon the sleepy sentries of Sir John Cope. The battle was over within a quarter of an hour and Cope himself was the first of the flying army to reach Newcastle with the news of the defeat. For Charles Stuart the road into England lay open.

It was still a long way to London and the English crown. The prince marched south to Preston and then to Manchester. He received a rousing welcome from common folk, but few promises of help from powerful landowners. His forces grew smaller as Highlanders turned back for home, and English generals called back from the Continent shadowed his march from a safe distance. There was not even a battle to keep up the drooping spirits of the Jacobites, and at Derby they decided to turn for Scotland again. Once again the English ruling classes had shown their distaste for a Stuart and a Catholic as king, particularly if he came as the puppet of the king of France.

The rest is a tragic story. At Falkirk the Young Pretender checked the army of English and Hanoverians which now pursued him, but at Culloden, in April 1746, the fierce charge of his Highlanders faltered and died away before trained artillery fire and point-blank volleys from the muskets of infantrymen. The Jacobite force dispersed over the Highlands, and the Duke of Cumberland compensated himself for his failure at Fontenoy by a shameful campaign of terror and revenge. Charles himself, with a price of £30,000 on his head, escaped to the Western Isles and thence to France. The Whig government now broke up the clans and forbade the wearing of the tartan. Old Scotland disappeared in a haze of burning homes and lamentations, and with it went the last of the Stuart hopes.

The final defeat of the Jacobites was about the only definite result of the war of the Austrian Succession. The war came to an end in 1748, but few of the quarrels which had caused it were settled. The young queen of Austria kept her disputed throne. Spain agreed to allow more English ships to trade unhindered in her colonies. The French handed back Madras, in return for

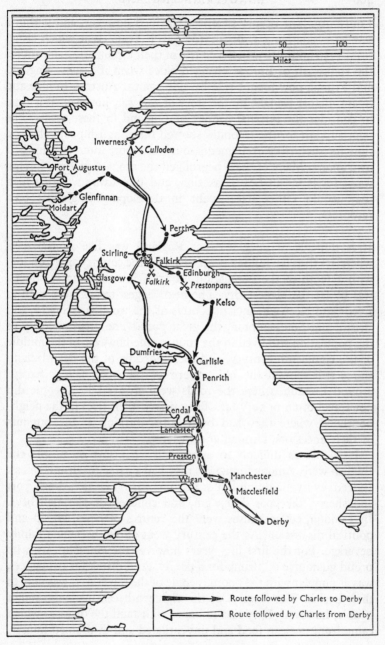

THE FORTY-FIVE

Louisburg. The deeper rivalries remained however, and within a few years another war began, the Seven Years' War which lasted from 1756 until 1763. In the course of their diplomatic manoeuvres the statesmen of Europe changed sides when it began: England and Prussia now fought side by side against Austria, France and Spain. Before we take up the story of this war, however, it is time to consider the internal history of England in these years. The poor support for the Jacobites showed that English people had no time for such risky excitements, but were more interested in their own affairs. Many of them begrudged the money spent on foreign wars, for it meant heavy taxation, and took away wealth which they would rather have spent in developing England's own resources.

It is difficult to imagine what England was like in the days when less than ten million people lived in the country and London, with a tenth of the population crowded into its narrow streets, was by far the biggest city. The next biggest towns were such as Leeds and Norwich, ancient centres of the woollen industry, and Bristol and Southampton, the great ports. The great majority of the population still lived in the countryside however in the middle of the eighteenth century, and the landscape of the flat Midland shires still showed the old pattern of the open fields. Except around London, where the roads were always busy, people did not travel often or very far. They passed their lives in the neighbourhood where they had been born, working at the pursuits of their ancestors, farming and weaving.

It is just as difficult to appreciate what sort of people the English were. Among foreigners they had a name for drunkenness. Indeed, everyone drank liquor of some sort. The rich drank port and sherry, the poor drank gin, and children drank small beer. In London, coffee-houses were the centres of news, gossip and political discussion. As the century went on tea became a family beverage. For the first fifty years however the gin-shop, with its proud guarantee of 'drunk for a penny, dead drunk for twopence', was as popular with the poorer people of the towns as it was fatal to their health. The English of the eighteenth century were tough people, however. They had to be, to withstand the diseases which came from unclean food and unventilated and ill-drained houses, and the surgical operations performed without anaesthetic on infected or fractured limbs. They did not treat each other gently, or expect gentle treatment in return. As a Victorian historian said of slightly earlier times, 'Masters well born and bred were in the habit of beating their servants. Pedagogues knew no way of imparting knowledge but by beating their pupils. Husbands of decent station were not ashamed to beat their wives'.[1]

Callousness and drunkenness were the least pleasant of English characteristics. They were really a protective covering which people put on against the harshness and uncertainty of their uncomfortable lives. Englishmen had a reputation for hard work and practical skill as well, however, and by their efforts they gradually made their lives less hard. The occupations in which they exercised their skill and energy were principally, as we have seen, farming and weaving. The Midlands and the southern counties were the great farming areas. Weaving, except in the west of England, was the occupation of the valleys and hill-sides of the north. The Yorkshire woollen industry was old-established, and on the other side of the Pennines the 'Manchester trade' in linen and fustian had also been well known for years. The wool came from the backs of English sheep, but flax for linen was imported from Ireland and cotton for fustians from India, Cyprus and the Levant. In Derbyshire and Nottinghamshire the weavers worked in silk brought home by the East India Company. There were silk workers in London too, at Spitalfields. The silk-weaving was sometimes done in workshops, but in most of the industries the weavers worked at home. Each Friday they took their week's work – a piece of cloth some two by forty feet – to the draper's warehouse. Here they were paid, and collected new supplies of raw material. This 'domestic system' of industry, like the open fields in agriculture, had centuries of tradition behind it.

Since Tudor times there had been coal-mines in the north of England, and iron foundries in the western Midlands and the forests of the Weald. The mines did not go very deep however and there was not much demand for coal except as household fuel. The ironmasters used charcoal for their smelting: that is why their forges stood among the wooded areas of England. In 1709 however a Quaker ironmaster of Shropshire, Abraham Darby,

[1] Thomas Babington Macaulay: *History of England*.

devised a method for smelting pig-iron with coke, in a tall furnace
lined with sand. He kept the discovery to himself for many years,
but when it finally got about coal became much more important
as a raw material for industry. Another invention was made in
mining itself in the early years of the century, which was to prove
as important as coke-smelting. It was the construction by Thomas
Newcomen of a pump for clearing water from mines, which
worked by steam and atmospheric pressure. Newcomen's 'atmospheric pump' was soon used in coal-mines in many parts of the
country but its great importance lay in its use of steam power,
which was to change all the old industries in the next century or so.

These two inventions, right at the beginning of the eighteenth
century, set the pattern of experiment and change which English
manufacturers followed throughout its course. In 1733 John Kay,
a Lancashire weaver, devised a mechanical 'flying shuttle' which
wove much faster than the traditional method of working by hand.
In the same year a farmer, Jethro Tull of Berkshire, applied
mechanical principles to the ancient work of seed-sowing, by
performing the task with a horse-drawn drill. Sir Robert Walpole's
brother-in-law Lord Townshend experimented with a new and
scientific rotation of crops on his Norfolk farm, introducing on a
large scale the cultivation of the turnip. Robert Bakewell of
Leicestershire experimented with new breeds of cattle, sheep and
horses. Men like these had plenty to occupy their minds apart
from politics and the events of distant wars.

A man who was a landowner however was probably a Justice of
the Peace for his neighbourhood as well. He had to take an interest
in the public affairs of his county, whether he engaged in national
politics and stood for Parliament or owned a borough or not. The
government depended on the Justices to keep law and order
throughout the country. There was no police force, except for the
'Bow Street Runners' who pursued the vain task of keeping the
peace in London's teeming and ill-lit streets. In the countryside
the gamekeeper and the parish officials were the Justice's only
assistants. The law set out to help him by imposing sentences of
death, flogging and imprisonment for some of the smallest
offences, such as stealing a loaf or poaching a rabbit. Since there
were so few officers to prevent law-breaking, the principle
adopted was to terrify would-be offenders by the penalty for crime,

and so deter them from engaging in it. To judge from the tales of lawlessness which fill the newspapers and novels of the time the principle did not work.

The Justice of the Peace had other tasks: to fix the wages of labourers in his neighbourhood and to administer the Poor Law were two of them. He had plenty of leisure to perform these tasks however, and to find time for country pursuits and long visits to London or the waters of Bath. The English aristocracy of the eighteenth century were a wealthy and leisured class of men and women. They lived a free and comfortable life, whether in London or at home in the country. 'The man who is tired of London,' said the great literary figure of the eighteenth century, Dr Samuel Johnson, 'is tired of life.' In London there were theatres and clubs, gaming- and coffee-houses, and parties and political discussions at the great houses of Whig nobles. In the graceful, well-built country houses, on the other hand, there were cool and spacious libraries for the scholar and well-planned parks outside, stocked with game for the man who preferred to go shooting. The English aristocrat was free to travel all over Europe, and did. Unlike the noblemen of France however he did not spend all of his time at pleasure or at the royal court. He governed his country in Parliament, and his county as a Justice of the Peace; and he did the job fairly and well enough to put off criticism for many years. Even when criticism came, at the end of the century, it did not take the form of hatred and revenge which marked the French revolution against the aristocracy.

England in the eighteenth century was a country of contrasts. There was a great difference between the lives of the rich and those of the poor, between life in London and life in the country, and there were beginning to be great differences between old ways of industry and agriculture and new ones. There were people of great culture, who enjoyed books and music and decorated their houses with the fine paintings and furniture which distinguished the century; and there were others who never went to school, could not read or write, and were hard pressed to find their next meal. There were lawless and cruel people in England; but there were law-abiding, charitable men and women too. One of the greatest contrasts was between the religious life of the past and the present, for in the eighteenth century Englishmen no longer fought each other over their religious beliefs. The squire and his villagers were church-going people, and the merchant and his apprentices perhaps frequented the chapel or meeting-house of a Nonconformist sect. The laws still held which prevented Roman Catholics and dissenters from becoming Members of Parliament, Justices of the Peace, lawyers, officers in the army or navy, or students or fellows of the universities. Few people became excited about their religious beliefs however, and in practice there was a great deal of toleration for dissenters and papists.

Later in the century this peaceful atmosphere was shattered just as the old ways of industry and agriculture were broken up. An Anglican clergyman from Oxford, John Wesley by name and a 'Methodist' by nickname for his stern self-discipline in religious matters, took on himself the mission of 'redeeming the time'; he aimed to cure his countrymen of their religious apathy and of gambling, drinking and cruelty as well. Between 1739 and his death in 1791 Wesley toured England on horseback, preaching his particular gospel. 'I look upon all the world as my parish,' he declared, but he chose especially to visit the places where there were neither churches nor meeting-houses: Cornwall in the west, and the steel-making and textile areas of the Midlands were two such areas. He was not always welcome there, but he was a courageous man and his striking manner and quiet, moving sermons had a great emotional effect on many of his hearers. In the end the Church of England broke with him, for it could not tolerate his wanderings and the style and effect of his preaching; and some of his fellow-Methodists drew apart because they resented his masterful ways and disagreed with his belief that anyone could be saved who was prepared to make the effort. So Methodism brought further schism to English Christianity; but it also brought back enthusiasm and caused many people to live less brutal lives. It was another aspect of the determined efforts which English people made to improve the conditions of their lives: efforts which made up the busy background to the wars and politics of the Hanoverian years.

CHAPTER 43

The Foundation of the British Empire; George III

1756-1775

LONG BEFORE the Seven Years' War began English and French soldiers were fighting again in India and America. In 1755 an English expedition set out to capture Fort Duquesne, the key to the Ohio valley; but it was ambushed and massacred by the French and their Red Indian allies. On the other side of the globe the Frenchman Dupleix, although he had been forced by his government to hand back Madras to the East India Company, still seemed likely to fulfil his ambition of bringing the eastern coast of India under French control. He was checked at the crucial time however by two Company soldiers, Robert Clive and Stringer Lawrence. Clive had entered the Company's service as a clerk. He was a man of neurotic and unstable character, whose family and neighbours had not been sorry to see him off to seek his fortune in India; but his type of reckless courage now proved a match for the ambition of Dupleix. Along with Lawrence he fought and frustrated the French design, and Dupleix was summoned home by his government in disgrace.

A new threat now appeared to British power in India. The nawab of Bengal, Suraj-ud-Daula, resolved to expel the Company himself and attacked Calcutta in 1756. The governor fled and the city was taken. The Europeans who were left behind, about 150 in all, were imprisoned throughout a stifling, sub-tropical night in a small room with two barred windows. Only twenty-three of them survived their imprisonment in the 'black hole' of Calcutta. When the news of these events reached Madras, Clive was sent to re-capture the city. He had only a small force of British and Indian

soldiers at his disposal, but within six months he had retaken
Calcutta, and one year after the atrocity of the 'black hole' his
small army faced the hordes of Suraj-ud-Daula at Plassey, in
Bengal. Daring, the defection of the nawab's lieutenant and a storm
which soaked his powder combined to give Clive victory. Suraj-
ud-Daula fled and Meer Jafeer, the prince who had deserted him,
became the new, pro-British ruler of Bengal.

When the Seven Years' War began there was more fighting in
India against the French. The English government was more
concerned with the war in Europe however, which started badly.
The chief minister, the Duke of Newcastle, who had succeeded his
brother Henry Pelham as Walpole's heir in 1754, was a man of
Walpole's stamp. He had devoted great efforts to keeping the peace
and he was in any case a man whose talents were more fitted to the
management of elections than to the conduct of war. He shared in
the national disgrace when a French fleet captured the Mediterranean naval base of Minorca; and though he found a scapegoat in
Admiral Byng, whose ships had made only a half-hearted attempt
to raise the siege and who was now court-martialled and executed
for cowardice, it was Newcastle who bore the brunt of criticism
for the defeat.

The loudest critic of the government was now brought in to join
it. He was William Pitt, once member for Old Sarum and until a
year before the Paymaster-General of the Forces. Pitt was like
Walpole in a way that Newcastle was not. Like Walpole he was able
to sum up and express the public opinion of his time. Public
opinion was all for war with France now, and Pitt was the man to
lead the fight. He was a gaunt and restless figure, a man with a
fiery mind and scorching tongue. He could terrify individuals and
encourage them by turns, and dominated the House of Commons
by his presence and his oratory. Pitt has often been described as the
'Great Commoner', and said himself that he had been 'called by
my Sovereign and by the Voice of the People' to lead the government: but the voice which sounded loudest in his ears, apart from
the promptings of his own arrogance, was the voice of the City of
London. Pitt was the friend of London merchants deeply interested
in capturing French colonies and French trade, and this aspect of
the war was always the centre of his strategy. Nevertheless he
despatched an army to Europe in 1757 to assist England's German

allies against the French and the Austrians, and throughout the war he mounted raids on the French coast designed to distract and weaken the French effort elsewhere. A British fleet was set to blockade the ports of France and keep the French men-of-war, which were superior to British ships in sail and guns, at home. This manoeuvre left other British warships free to attack the West Indian islands and the fortresses of Canada.

Pitt wrote to the governors of the American colonies to instruct them to use 'your utmost Endeavours and Influence with the Council and Assembly of your Province' to raise an army to help in a projected invasion of Canada; the British government would pay for everything. At the same time a fleet was sent to the mouth of the St Lawrence and in 1758 recaptured Louisburg. Farther south however the English generals made heavy going of their journeys across a terrain of mountains, rivers and woods beset by hostile Indians. Fort Duquesne was taken, and proudly renamed Fort Pitt, but a second army was defeated at Ticonderoga. Next year three armies were on the move in America; two advanced on Canada from the south again while the other, with the fleet, sailed down the St Lawrence and laid siege to Quebec. For over two months this northern force was held at bay by steep cliffs, floating batteries and gallant French defence. By September, Quebec was a smoking ruin and the surrounding countryside a wilderness; but still the fortress held out and the British general, James Wolfe, lay sick with fever, unable to rouse himself for another major effort. At last, on the night of 12–13 September, he made his final attempt. Five thousand men were rowed with muffled oars past the French batteries to the cliffs behind the town. They scrambled up and overpowered the sentries. At break of day Wolfe and his men looked across the Plains of Abraham towards Quebec; and after a day's fierce fighting the French were defeated. Wolfe was struck down in the moment of victory, but within a few days the fortress of Quebec was in British hands.

The fall of Quebec was the signal for London bells to ring until Horace Walpole declared they must be threadbare; but there were more victories to celebrate in 1759. Guadeloupe, the richest of the French sugar islands, had been taken at the beginning of the year. In August, England's German allies defeated their enemies at Minden. Fresh troops were sent to assist Clive in raising the siege of

Madras and capturing French ports in India; and in November Admiral Hawke broke up the French fleet which was sailing to win control of the Channel for a French invasion of England. This victory alone would have made 1759 a wonderful year for Pitt and his country; but what else had the war achieved in return for the immense expenditure of men and money involved? The global struggle was resulting, as Pitt and his city merchants had intended, in 'the total stagnation and extirpation of French trade upon the seas'. The territorial conquests however had brought as many problems as they had victories. In 1760 Quebec was barely saved from French reconquest, and even after final victory had been won in Canada with the surrender of Montreal, England had to find a way to pay for the war and maintain the American empire. The Seven Years' War was followed in America by twenty years of friction between England and the colonists which ended in England losing the whole of the continent south of Canada. In India too imperialism brought its problems. The East India Company won itself an empire there, but found it hard to govern it well. Indian politics pulsated with intrigue and Company officials were accused of injustices and extortions which outweighed the atrocity of the black hole of Calcutta in many minds. In 1760 however these imperial problems lay in the future; for the moment victory was enough and Pitt was famous.

In 1760 George II died: 'the best king, the best master, and the best friend that subject ever had', in the opinion of the Duke of Newcastle. Like his father however George had never cared much for his English subjects and their Parliament, and the English cared little for their second German king. His grandson George, on the other hand, who now succeeded him as George III, was the first of the Hanoverians to be clearly an Englishman. He had been brought up in England and soon declared that he wanted nothing to do with Hanover – 'that horrid Electorate', as he called it, 'which has for so long preyed upon the vitals of this poor country'. He also declared his intention of bringing to an end the 'bloody and expensive' war with France. Pitt altered these words before they reached the public's ear to 'expensive but necessary'; but many English people were glad to hear the news nevertheless. George started his reign as a popular

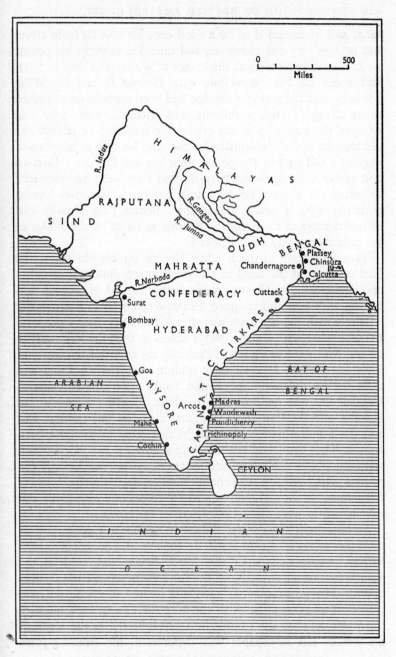

INDIA IN THE EIGHTEENTH CENTURY

king, and he intended to be a good one. He was far from clever
but he was very conscientious, and intended to serve his people
well. His father Frederick, the Prince of Wales, who died in 1751,
had spent his life quarrelling with George II and his Whig
advisers, and the younger George had been brought up to regard
them all as 'proud, ambitious and deceitful men' who had
usurped the authority of the crown. He intended to restore the
old balance of the constitution by choosing his own ministers and
playing a full part in the government himself. But the politicians
had grown used to power by now, and they were not prepared
to watch the balance tip back to a position where they shared
authority with a brash young king. Before long George had
offended most of them and he became as hated by the Whigs as
his grandfather had been beloved.

Trouble started at once, when George set his old tutor, the
Earl of Bute, at the head of the government. Bute was haughty
and unpopular; within two years both Pitt and Newcastle had
broken with him and resigned. Pitt who could never share power
willingly with another man, was offended most by Bute's proposal
to make peace with France. Nevertheless in 1763 the war came to
an end with a treaty signed in Paris. By the terms of the treaty of
Paris the French kept all their trading 'factories' in India and
their fishing rights on the Grand Banks were also recognized.
Guadeloupe was handed back to them. England kept Canada
however and the East India Company's empire was assured. Pitt
and the London merchants thought that more might have been
gained. They launched against Bute a political campaign which
soon brought him to resign, and for the next few years George had
to work with ministers who could claim a majority in the House of
Commons. He showed himself ready to co-operate with them, but
the politicians were always suspicious of the crown.

An affair now arose which did credit neither to George nor his
ministers nor Parliament itself. It concerned a journalist, John
Wilkes, whose newspaper the *North Briton* was used as the
mouthpiece for Pitt's attack on Bute and the peace of Paris. Wilkes
described the government as 'a weak, disjointed, incapable set', and
professed to sympathize with the king for having to work with
them. He relished the trouble into which he fell as the result of
his words. His newspaper was suppressed, his printing-press

closed down and he himself arrested; but the Lord Chief Justice dismissed his case on the ground that he was a Member of Parliament and therefore privileged to criticize the government, and Wilkes successfully sued the government for damage to his property. The government retaliated by declaring the judgment incorrect and expelling him from the House for uttering 'a false, scandalous and seditious libel'. Pitt had abandoned his assistant by now and Wilkes fled to France. Since he was not present to answer the charge of libel he was declared an outlaw. In 1768 however he returned to England and stood for election to Parliament once more. In the City of London he came bottom of the poll but in the popular county constituency of Middlesex he was elected to shouts of 'Wilkes and Liberty'. Now he went to serve his prison sentence of two years for libel, and his friends kept him in splendid style at the King's Bench prison while Virginian planters supplied him with tobacco. The government however, although it was now composed of a group of Whigs, pursued the vendetta. Wilkes was expelled from the Commons again, but returned once more for Middlesex. Rejected once more by the decision of Parliament, he won another election, and then a third, all within three months. On the last occasion however the Commons agreed that his opponent 'ought to have been returned', and Wilkes was still denied a place. He left prison in 1770, and in 1774 became Lord Mayor of London. At length, in 1775, he was re-elected to Parliament and allowed to take his seat, and became a most respected and responsible citizen; but by now the damage had been done. 'That devil Wilkes', as George III described him, had become in the public eye the champion of free speech and the right of Englishmen to choose their representatives. The king and Parliament appeared, by contrast, tyrannical and oppressive.

Since the time of the Civil War the English Parliament had never been so proud of its position and sure of its authority as it was in the years when it took on John Wilkes. The members prohibited publication of their debates for public scrutiny and one of them, Edmund Burke, the Member for Bristol, rebuked the citizens who had elected him for presuming to instruct him how to vote in debate. Members of Parliament, Burke maintained, were chosen for their good sense and knowledge of public affairs and once elected must be allowed to follow their own judgment. They were representatives of the country's best talents, not delegates sent up to repeat the local prejudices of the people. The plain fact was that Parliament had no more the intention of taking the peoples' advice than it had of tolerating the king's interference. As noblemen, country gentlemen and substantial merchants the Members of Parliament regarded themselves as naturally the best rulers of England. They were literally an 'aristocracy': a government formed by the best people. It had taken them many years to achieve such power in their long contest with the crown and they had no intention of sharing it now with George III, the electors of Bristol or anyone else.

It was just at this point, when Parliament's pride and power were at their height, that the Wilkes affair provoked the first loud demands for its reform. These demands found support among Londoners and Northcountrymen, among Nonconformists sick of the corruption of public life and among their 'evangelical' counterparts within the Church of England. People like these made a ready audience for the angry words of Major John Cartwright, who addressed them in a pamphlet in 1776. 'Whether, indeed, the house of commons be in a great measure filled with idle schoolboys, insignificant coxcombs, led-captains and toad-eaters, profligates, gamblers, bankrupts, beggars, contractors, commissaries, public plunderers, ministerial dependants, hirelings, and wretches, that would sell their country, or deny their God for a guinea, let everyone judge for himself,' wrote Cartwright. 'Trust not, I say, in princes nor in ministers; but trust in YOURSELVES, and in representatives chosen by YOURSELVES alone!' These were the words of an extreme and radical reformer; but they made their impact against the background of the Wilkes affair, and in the next few years a further blow was dealt to the power of the king and the aristocracy. This next assault came from the American colonies for which the wars of recent years had been, in great measure, fought.

CHAPTER 44

The American Revolution

1775-1783

WHEN THE Seven Years' War ended, the English colonies in America were flourishing. The merchants of Boston and New York had done well out of provisioning the English armies, and they had managed to keep up their strictly illegal trade with the French West Indies as well. They did not regard the war between England and France as any concern of theirs. They had grown so used to managing their own affairs in the last fifty years, with very little interference from royal governors, that they were ceasing to think of themselves as English subjects at all, but rather as New Englanders and free men. Even the old Navigation Laws, which restricted their trade in so many ways, tended to be forgotten because they were not strictly enforced. That was why the illegal trade with the French West Indian islands was doing so well. There were more recent laws, passed in Walpole's time, which prohibited the colonists from making hats or iron or woollen goods which might compete with English industries. These were more of a nuisance to the New Englanders; but they could usually be avoided as well. Royal customs officers could usually be bribed to turn a blind eye to all sorts of illegal activities; and since the royal governors of the colonies depended on the colonial assemblies to grant their salaries, they were usually the last people to want to interfere with trade and upset influential merchants. The New Englanders were in fact a law unto themselves.

The planters of the south felt the weight of English influence rather more heavily. English merchants made sure that they observed the trade laws and sent the whole of their tobacco crop to England each year. In its way this regulation was an advantage to the planters, because they could be sure of selling everything they grew. In the last few years however they had fallen heavily into debt with English merchants, and they were growing restless for the sort of freedom the New Englanders enjoyed. Farther to the west, beyond New England and the Virginian plantations, the settlers who had already begun to cross the Alleghany mountains and make their way into the Shenandoah valley were more independent-minded than any of the colonists. In the free, tough life of the frontier they had completely forgotten that they were the subjects of an island three thousand miles away. It is clear that in 1763 a great many English-speaking Americans regarded themselves as free men; or else they were determined to become so in the very near future. And yet it was just at this moment that the English government chose to step in heavily and remind them that they were the subjects of George III and his Parliament. A royal proclamation of 1763 prohibited any further emigration to the west. In 1764 the government put a new tax on sugar imported from the West Indies and announced its intention of catching the smugglers who would certainly try to break this law just as they had broken earlier ones. Special courts were to be set up to try people who broke the trade laws; and customs officers were given powers to enter and search American homes for contraband. The government could not have chosen a worse moment to interfere like this. The Americans were naturally infuriated and England was asking for trouble. What possessed the government to act as it did?

So far as the proclamation against emigration was concerned the English intention was to prevent another war breaking out in America, this time between the colonists and the Indians. For in 1763 a confederacy of Indian tribes led by the chieftain Pontiac had attacked the western borders of Virginia, capturing forts, burning homesteads and murdering settler families. The Indians resented the westward advance of these pioneers; if they had to put up with the white man at all they preferred the French, who came only to trade with them and build forts, not to take away their land. Eventually English redcoats restored peace in Virginia, but the government was determined to prevent another outbreak. The proclamation was intended to keep the peace between Indians and colonists until a general plan for westward emigration had been worked out.

From the English point of view it was a sensible answer to a threatening situation; but naturally the settlers did not approve of it. The other regulations were sensible to English minds as well. After all, the theory of the time was that colonies were established for such profits as they afforded and not for the benefit of the colonists themselves. In 1763 the colonists in America were clearly doing well for themselves while English money and English soldiers defended them from the French and the Indians. The government intended to divert some of that wealth into the English treasury. They argued that the Americans should help to pay for the bloody and expensive war which had helped to make them prosperous; and since the Indian threat still made it necessary to keep an army in America, the Americans should share the cost of that operation too. This was not an unreasonable argument. We can appreciate the point of view of either side; but the Americans and the English, and George III in particular, could not or would not understand each other's position, and this deep misunderstanding eventually led to an American revolution against the crown.

In 1765 the English government, which consisted at the time of a group of Whigs led by George Grenville, imposed another new tax on the American colonies: a stamp tax to be paid on newspapers, legal documents and commercial receipts. The stamp duty would not ruin the Americans, and it was imposed specifically for the purpose of 'defending, protecting and securing' the colonies. But the new tax offended powerful groups of people – merchants, lawyers, and newspaper editors. The last group in particular were in a position to whip up a great deal of excitement over the stamp tax, and they did, to such an extent that on the day it went into operation stamps were burned in the streets of New England, while shops closed, church bells tolled and flags hung at half mast. English people were amazed at the commotion; they had paid stamp duty for years without complaint. But an American lawyer found a legal argument to justify this resistance to the will of Parliament: since the colonies were not represented in Parliament, he argued, Parliament had no right to tax them. 'No taxation without representation' became the popular slogan; but the American agitators did not want to elect members of Parliament any more than they wanted to pay taxes. They wanted England to stop interfering in American affairs.

A few men in England realized what was at stake. Pitt was one, and he urged the Whigs to repeal the Stamp Act rather than run the risk of losing the colonies altogether. In 1766 the stamp duty was taken off; but in the very next year another Whig government with Pitt, now Earl of Chatham, at its head put new taxes on all sorts of commodities including paper, paint and tea. And so the excitement mounted for the next three years. Excisemen were tarred and feathered and the revenue ship 'Liberty' was set alight as she lay at anchor off Rhode Island. An incident which occurred in Boston on a wintry day in 1770 showed how tense the feeling between soldiers and citizens had become. A group of people began to throw snowballs at soldiers on guard. A soldier went down and his comrades opened fire. Five people were killed, and the newspapers told America about the 'Boston Massacre'.

At this point however a new government came to power in England. Lord North was its chief minister and its members called themselves the 'King's Friends', to show that they were different from the Whigs. The Whigs attacked this ministry as fiercely as they had attacked the government of Lord Bute, calling it a corrupt instrument of a tyrannical king. Lord North, who was an easy-going man at the best of times, had far too many enemies at home to want to make any more for himself on the other side of the Atlantic. He repealed all the taxes except the one on tea.

Lord North wanted to please everyone, for the sake of a quiet life, and that was the trouble. Within a few years he had stirred up more excitement and discontent than had existed before. In 1773 he allowed the East India Company, which was powerfully represented in Parliament, a monopoly of the export of tea to America. The tea was to be admitted at a reduced duty which would make it much cheaper than smuggled Dutch tea, but the Americans did not appreciate the favour. So far as they were concerned this was a blow to their own trade, and seemed another attempt to use the colonies merely for the convenience of English interests. They refused to drink what Parliament prescribed for them. When the tea arrived at Charleston no-one would buy it. At Boston, local men thinly disguised as Indians boarded the

Company's ships and consigned their cargoes to the bottom of the harbour.

As a result of this action the harbour was officially closed to trade. The town was placed under martial law and a soldier, General Gage, became the governor. The Bostonians' right to manage their own affairs was taken from them. They said that the English Parliament had taken away the last of their liberties, and the rest of the colonists agreed with them. In 1774 a Continental Congress met at Philadelphia 'to consult upon the present unhappy state of the colonies'. At this congress, for the first time perhaps in American history, planters from Virginia and merchants from New England met and talked with each other. Hard frontiersmen from the backwoods of Pennsylvania encountered easy-living slave-owners from Carolina. The upshot of their conference was a decision to stop importing English goods and to stop sending American goods to England until the government altered its policies. The planters were not entirely content with the decision, but as we have seen, many Virginians were deeply in debt to English merchants and they were not reluctant to make the break. In any case, matters were passing beyond the control of cautious men and into the hands of agitators and 'patriots' like Samuel Adams, the Boston journalist. Adams was clear in his own mind that the only satisfactory solution to American problems was complete independence from English authority. In England too the moderate counsels of Chatham and Lord North had given way to the fierce determination of George III to tax the colonies. 'The die is cast,' said the king, 'the Colonies must either submit or triumph.'

And so, while the king sent out reinforcements on the six weeks' journey across the Atlantic, the New Englanders collected guns, powder and shot and stored them in quiet country towns and lonely farms. Early in 1775 Governor Gage learned that there was a cache of arms at Concord, twenty miles inland. Intent on preventing fighting rather than starting it, he sent troops to confiscate the arsenal. News of his plan travelled swiftly however, and patriots barred the way at Lexington. A few shots dispersed them, but by the time the soldiers reached Concord the arms had gone. As they made for Boston their red coats became the targets for every gun in New England, and they suffered heavy losses before they got home. The American revolution had begun.

Another Congress met and decided to form an army, with George Washington, a Virginian planter who had fought for the crown against the French and Indians, as commander in chief. Another General, Benedict Arnold, was sent to raise Canada in support. Even while these decisions were being made more fighting had begun. A force of New Englanders occupied a ridge across the bay from Boston, and the townspeople watched on a hot summer day as Brigadier Howe, with troops fresh from England, set out to dislodge them. He led his men up the steep slopes of the hill as though they were going into battle on the plains of Europe. Ragged volleys tore into them as they struggled on, perspiring in close-fitting uniforms and carrying full equipment. A third of the force had fallen before the ridge was cleared, and the enemy were not pursued.

From now on Boston was virtually in a stage of siege and in 1776 Howe evacuated the town and set up his base at New York, after expelling Washington's troops. He did not set out to crush the rebel resistance by a determined campaign however, for he liked the Americans, and he disliked the idea of fighting in the North American winter. In any case, he hoped that some settlement of their grievances might soon be achieved. But there was little hope of that. In 1776 Congress made its famous 'Declaration of Independence', rejecting the authority of the king of England and his Parliament forever, and justifying the revolution:

'We hold these truths to be self-evident, that all men are created equal; that they are endowed by their Creator with certain in-alienable rights; that among these are Life, Liberty and the Pursuit of Happiness. That to secure these rights governments are instituted among men, deriving their just powers from the consent of the governed; that whenever any form of government becomes destructive of these ends, it is the right of the people to alter or abolish it, and to institute a new government . . . .'

Proud and revolutionary words, though the doctrine of equality sounds strange on the lips of the slave-owner, Thomas Jefferson, who phrased it. Behind the fine words, moreover, lay some harsh realities. Washington was finding it hard to train his volunteer army, or to keep it in the field once autumn began and the harvest

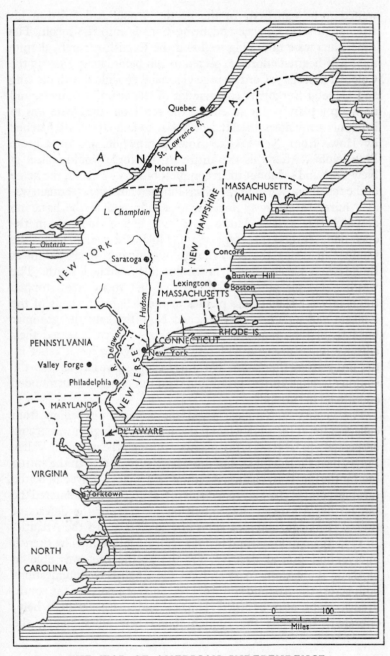

THE WAR OF AMERICAN INDEPENDENCE

waited to be gathered. In the north, Arnold had failed in his attempt to seize Quebec and bring Canada into the revolt. The Americans were not doing well and the English generals, despite their half-hearted efforts, expected to win before long. In 1777 the Colonial Secretary, Lord George Germain, consulted with the king and General Burgoyne, commander of the army in Canada, and drew up a plan to put an end to the rebellion. Burgoyne was to bring his army down the Hudson valley to join a force despatched by Howe from New York. Howe meanwhile was to capture Philadelphia. After this the entire British force would collect at New York and set about the reconquest of New England, the home of the rebellion. When the plan was finished however, Germain was in a hurry to get away for the weekend; and in the haste no despatch was sent to Howe to inform him of his part in the operation, beyond the capture of Philadelphia. He spent the summer in taking the city, though Washington delayed him at Brandywine Creek. Burgoyne meanwhile marched south. The weather was pleasant, and the officers and their wives stopped frequently for champagne picnics in the delightful woods of the Hudson valley. When they reached New England the grimmer business of the campaign began. American forces checked their advance and Burgoyne withdrew to Saratoga to await relief by the army from the south. No army came however, and as the summer weather turned to autumn rain, Burgoyne was surrounded and forced to surrender.

The victory at Saratoga saved the American rebellion from collapse; for at the time when it occurred Washington was trying desperately to keep his army together through the winter at Valley Forge, near Philadelphia, and must have surrendered in the spring but for the northern victory. As it was that victory proved to be the turning-point of the war. As a result of Saratoga, France entered the war on the American side, intent on revenge for the defeats of twenty years ago, and sent ships and soldiers across the Atlantic. In 1779 Spain followed and in 1781 Holland joined in. The French intervention proved decisive, for the hostile fleet was able to blockade the eastern coast and cut the English communications both across the Atlantic and from the northern ports to the south. French ships also besieged Jamaica and, with Spanish help, Gibraltar. In India the French found new allies among the chieftains of the Mahratta Confederacy, and made another attempt to overthrow English power on that side of the globe. The American war became a world war, and even touched the coasts of the British Isles when John Paul Jones, a privateer who took up the American cause, used the French port of Brest as a base for raids on the shores of Scotland and northern England. The one Englishman who might have been able to carry on such a war was Chatham, but he died in 1778. In any case he had always urged peace with the Americans. 'If I were an American,' said he, 'as I am an Englishman, while a foreign troop was landed in my country I never would lay down my arms – never – never – never!' Words like these were little consolation to Lord North, who would also have liked to put a stop to the war with the Americans, but was driven on by the king's determination to win. In 1780 another campaign began in America, based on the southern colonies where many American planters had remained loyal to George III. At first it went well, and General Cornwallis seized Savannah and Charleston and inflicted a defeat on Washington. By the autumn of 1781 however Washington had forced him back to the port of Yorktown, in Virginia. French ships closed the seaward approaches and Cornwallis, after a vain attempt to fight his way through the besieging army, was forced to surrender. For the second time in a few years an English general gave up his sword to a Yankee rebel.

'Oh God! It is the end!' exclaimed Lord North when he heard the news of Yorktown. In the last year his government had completely lost its grip on affairs, not only in America but at home as well. They had been quite unable to quell anti-papist riots which flared up in London in 1780, and the king himself had intervened to restore order. In Ireland another revolution against the English Parliament threatened. In this atmosphere of crisis the government's parliamentary critics combined to defeat it and to demand peace in America. George III contemplated abdication. Lord North resigned. Another group of Whigs succeeded him and immediately began negotiations for peace. Their hand was strengthened by Admiral Rodney's victory over the French fleet in the West Indies, and the raising of the siege of Gibraltar. India too held out under the energetic Governor-General Warren Hastings. The Americans too were ready to make peace, and the war came to an end. By a treaty signed in 1783 at the palace of

Versailles, so near the city where twenty years before another peace had won Canada for England, George III recognized the independence of the thirteen former colonies.

The American Revolution was one of the most important events in the history of the modern world. It brought into existence a great new nation, and a government which claimed to represent the will of a people rather than the wishes of a king. This idea of representative government was a revolutionary thought for the French soldiers to take back with them to Europe, the old continent where kings still purported to rule as the representatives of God on earth. More important still was the second American argument: that revolution is justified in order to alter a form of government which has become unpopular. The Americans had shown how to do this in practice. None of these lessons of revolution had been wasted on the French, and we shall see how they affected the history of France and Europe in the years to come.

The American arguments echoed in England too, where Wilkes had already made the king and Parliament seem tyrants to English freedom. The Whigs, many of whom had sympathized with the Americans in their opposition to George III, blamed him for everything that had gone wrong. They maintained that he was the true tyrant in England, and Lord North the incompetent tool of tyranny who had started the American war and then lost it. The people were less certain who was to blame. They noted that one of the leading figures in the government which signed the peace of 1783 was none other than Lord North, back in power as the ally of the Whigs. The amiable peer was now the king's enemy rather than his friend. This cynical conclusion to all the bitter criticisms which the Whigs had hurled at North for years, and all the incompetence which North had shown in dealing with the American problem, suggested that the aristocratic politicians who ruled England were more interested in seizing power for themselves than they were in serving their king and country well. Many people sympathized with George for having such poor material from which to choose his own and England's servants. While the Whigs claimed that 'the king's influence has increased, is increasing, and ought to be diminished', the greater demand for the reform of Parliament itself gathered strength.

CHAPTER 45

The Industrial Revolution; William Pitt

1783-1792

WHOEVER was to blame for it, the loss of the American colonies turned out to be nothing like the disaster it was feared to be. The French gained little by their intervention and their government was bankrupt as a result of it. England on the other hand soon recovered from the financial loss. Trade with India and Europe increased and within a few years English ships were crossing the Atlantic to Georgia and Carolina again, and American vessels were bringing tons of raw cotton to Liverpool. As the years went by it became apparent that the northern colonies had been more trouble than they were worth. Indeed a Scots professor named Adam Smith had pointed this out soon after the war began, in a book called *The Wealth of Nations*. 'No doubt,' wrote Smith, 'to the undiscerning eye of giddy ambition they seem a dazzling object to fight for,' but he was sure that the endless wars in which the colonies involved the parent country, and the clumsy and inefficient system of the Navigation Laws were not bringing any profits worth the effort. The money and the energy involved would be far better employed in developing England's own resources.

English people had been doing this for years of course. We have already seen them at work at their experiments and their enterprises in the reigns of Queen Anne and the first two Georges. In the reign of George III there were more inventions and the war in America provided an incentive to English industries with its demands for uniforms and guns. The long cannons which John Roebuck cast, for instance, at his foundry at Carron, near Glasgow, became famous as 'carronades'. But it was after 1783 that the merchants and the manufacturers, the bankers and the farmers, took Adam Smith's advice to heart and employed their skill and capital in developing the new inventions and increasing the nation's production. They did so now less in the hope of foreign trade than in order to feed and clothe the population at home, which was increasing rapidly. In these years at the end of the eighteenth century the speed of industrial development became so fast, and resulted in so many changes in old English ways of life, that historians have coined the phrase 'the Industrial Revolution' to describe what happened. This revolution was ultimately far more important in English history than the American revolution, and it was the chief reason why this country recovered so quickly from the loss of her former colonies.

The new inventions are the most interesting aspect of the Industrial Revolution, at least in its early stages. During the reign of George III there were three famous inventions in the textile industry: James Hargreaves's Spinning Jenny, Richard Arkwright's Spinning Frame, and Edmund Cartwright's Power Loom. These machines, the last two of which were adapted to be driven by water power, made the work of spinning and weaving almost completely mechanical. They worked much faster and more efficiently than the domestic spinners and weavers could, or than they wanted to at first. The Lancashire weavers broke up Hargreaves's first machines and drove him away from his home near Blackburn. In time however they realized that the Jenny could be used to help increase their own wages, and by 1790 it was widely used. In the iron industry Darby's method of smelting was eagerly developed in these years, and big structures were made of the new pig-iron, like the bridge which John Wilkinson, the Birmingham iron-master, threw across the Severn in 1779. Between 1782 and 1784 Henry Cort developed the 'puddling' process for removing the last impurities from coke-smelted iron, so that it could be used both for small and essential goods like horseshoes, nails and tools and also for wheels and machine-parts.

The most important of all the inventions however was the steam engine which James Watt of Glasgow devised and patented. Watt took his idea from Newcomen's atmospheric pump, but he made the engine much more efficient and adapted its principle to many different machines. Steam power was eventually used to drive the bellows of the blast furnace, to power corn-mills and giant hammers for beating iron, to stamp coins and bore cannon and, later still, to drive the power-loom. Watt refused to believe that steam locomotion was possible however, and stopped the experiments of his assistant, William Murdock, along these lines. Murdock eventually became famous as the inventor of gas-lighting, but it was Richard Trevithick, a Cornish mining engineer, who first devised an efficient locomotive, and took his friends out in it on Christmas Eve, 1801. Perhaps 'efficient' is too strong a word for Trevithick's steam carriage however, for the engine caught fire while the inventor and his friends were celebrating the adventure in a local inn.

These inventions, and particularly the steam engine, were the basis of the Industrial Revolution. They substituted the efficiency of water- and steam-power for the traditional methods of work by hand, and gave rise to three great modern industries – cotton, iron and coal. Coal was essential to the blast furnace and the steam engine. Coal mines were primitive places however, where the danger of collapse, flooding and explosions was always present. Conditions in the mines changed very slowly, whereas the foundry at Coalbrookdale and the Soho factory at Birmingham where Watt and Murdock worked became famous showpieces of contemporary enterprise. In the cotton industry the machines produced a fundamental change. Drapers and manufacturers became impatient with the slow, old-fashioned methods of the hand-spinners and the hand-loom weavers, and began to install the water frame and the power loom in mills of their own, where spinners and weavers had to come and work for them. This was a rough break with the old domestic industry, in which the weavers did the work at home. Some of them resisted the change to the factory system for many years, and their losing battle with the power loom was still going on when George III's reign ended in 1820. In the woollen, silk and lace industries, which had still older traditions of work at home behind them, the spinners and weavers held out even longer.

Among conditions which had to change immediately were the old English methods of transport. The roads were quite unfit to bear the new business of the country. Dusty and pitted in summer, and

covered with mud and water once autumn began, they were dangerous enough for the traveller on horseback or the stage-coach, let
alone the loaded pack-pony and the lumbering goods waggon.
During the eighteenth century one government after another had
tried to encourage people to improve the surface of the roads in
their neighbourhood, by authorizing them to set up toll-gates at
either end of an improved stretch and charge travellers a fee for
passing over it. These 'Turnpike Trusts' made great improvements
in some areas, but not everywhere, to judge by the remarks of
Arthur Young, a man who travelled widely in the later years of the
century. He had some harsh things to say about Lancashire roads
for instance. 'Let me most seriously caution all travellers,' he wrote,
'who may accidentally purpose to travel this horrible country, to
avoid it as they would the devil; for a thousand to one but they
break their necks.' It is not surprising that Northcountrymen
preferred other methods of transport for their goods. Cheshire
farmers, for example, had long made a habit of sending their cheese
to London by boat, along the rivers to Hull and then by sea, or even
around by Liverpool. In 1759 the Duke of Bridgewater decided to
send the coal mined on his estates at Worsley to Manchester by
water – a distance of nine miles or so. He hired an uneducated
engineer named James Brindley to build him an artificial waterway,
and the 'Duke's Canal' was opened to his coal barges in 1761. The
barges travelled slowly enough, but they were faster than the pack-
horses used in the past, and much more coal could be carried. The
canal proved efficient and inexpensive and the price of coal in
Manchester was halved. Intelligent businessmen in other parts of
the country were quick to appreciate the value of this new, safe and
cheap way of transporting bulky goods. Josiah Wedgwood, the
Staffordshire pottery manufacturer, realized its advantages for
carrying his fragile wares. He was one of the men responsible for
covering the Midlands with a network of canals by the end of the
century. The 'canal mania' took such a hold that the problem of
improving the roads was not seriously studied until the turn of the
century. Before that, blind John Metcalfe had resurfaced some two
hundred miles of road, but the great period of roadmaking began
during the Napoleonic wars with the work of Thomas Telford and
John Macadam.

As travellers like Arthur Young moved around the country they noticed that changes were taking place in the fields to match those elsewhere. The ancient landscape of the open fields was giving way to a chequered pattern of small farms enclosed by fences or haw-thorn hedges. This enclosure movement, which completed the change begun by Tudor farmers, was the work of landowners who were anxious to try out the new ideas in agriculture and stock breeding which men like Tull and Townshend had introduced in earlier years. It was impossible to plant new crops scientifically or to breed cattle or sheep selectively under the old system of land ownership whereby a man's holding was scattered over two or three great unfenced fields, while the rotation of crops was decided by a jury whose history went back to Anglo-Saxon times, and animals roamed freely together over the wastes and common lands. The 'improving' farmer wanted all his land and all his stock together in one place; and if possible he wanted to put the wastes and commons under the plough as well. Since Tudor times however, when the government had tried to put a stop to enclosures because of the unemployment and hardship they caused in the countryside, it had become necessary to obtain the permission of Parliament before breaking up the open fields. The improving farmer or landowner had to persuade the other major landowners of the neighbourhood to fall in with his scheme, and then present a petition to Parliament 'for dividing, allotting and enclosing the open and common fields, meadows, pastures and wastelands' of the parish. Once the petition came before the House of Commons it was unlikely to be refused. The Members of Parliament were landowners themselves, and had no wish to frustrate the ambitions of these enterprising members of their class. They gave their assent, ignoring counter-petitions, and the enclosure bills became law. Commissioners were appointed to draw up a new map of the parish, redistributing the land in compact blocks proportionate in value – not necessarily in size – to the scattered holdings of the past. It was then up to each individual to enclose his new land within six months, or forfeit it to his neighbours.

The redistribution was seldom done fairly. Small farmers often ended with less land than before and sometimes, if they could not produce documentary proof of their rights, they got no land at all. The poorest villagers, who had relied on grazing their cattle on the commons and wastes, had nowhere to put them now. A good many people were left without land, rights or homes in the newly enclosed village; the squire took the lion's share of everything. Against this evidence of hardship we must put the fact that the yield of English farming immediately increased, and it is clear that the improvements in agriculture which followed enclosure were essential to the task of feeding England's growing population. But there is no doubt that a great deal of injustice was done when the open fields were enclosed, and the changes produced at least as much anger and unhappiness as the machines and the mills did elsewhere. The agricultural revolution and the industrial revolution between them had effects both good and bad, and historians have disputed the balance of happiness and misery ever since. In the long run these changes made England a country better fed, better housed and better clothed than it had been before, and everyone shared in the improved standards of living. At first however the changes caused a painful break with old ways for many people; and the benefits were not shared equally.

The inventors of the eighteenth century are every bit as important in English history as the politicians; in fact they did more than the politicians to create the country we live in. Nevertheless it is interesting to see how the politicians coped with all the changes of the times, and the growing challenge to their power. One of these statesmen is particularly interesting, because he became Prime Minister in 1783 when he was only twenty-four years old. The young man whom George III chose in that year to lead his government was William Pitt, old Chatham's second son. He was a tall, pale and clever young man, very cold and reserved of manner. It must have been exciting to be Prime Minister at the age of twenty-four, but Pitt showed no sign of it. He was confident that he could rule his country. His self-confidence convinced the English people that he must be the right man for the job, and he stayed at the head of affairs, except for one short break, for the next twenty-two years. He did so because he was determined to stay there, because the king wanted him there, and because English people had faith in him. He was another Walpole in fact, but much more respectable in every way.

The young Prime Minister needed all his confidence and all the support he could find in his early years of power, for he faced complicated problems and determined political opponents. The most troublesome of these was Charles Fox, a Whig leader whose father had been one of Chatham's greatest rivals. Fox was a very different man from Pitt – thickset and swarthy in appearance, witty and sociable in company. He was a gambler and a man of the world, with a host of friends which included George, the Prince of Wales. Fox was always in debt, and he had sunk deep in the corruption of politics. He was certainly not respectable, and the king detested him. Pitt regarded him with slightly nervous admiration, and Fox felt much the same toward Pitt; but he wanted to take Pitt's place if he could. At one time it looked as though he might succeed in his ambition. In 1788 George III fell a victim to the mental illness which was to cloud the last thirty-odd years of his life, and Fox insisted that the Prince of Wales should become Regent. That would mean the end of Pitt and the beginning of Fox, and Pitt appreciated the threat. He played for time until the king saved him by making a temporary recovery. After that other factors intervened and Fox's challenge was never dangerous again.

Apart from dealing with his political enemies in Parliament, Pitt had to deal with the demand that Parliament itself should be reformed. He had to reorganize the government's finances after the expense of the American war. Manufacturers expected him to do something to encourage industry; and his old friend William Wilberforce urged him to abolish the slave trade, which still packed hundreds of Africans into the stinking holds of old ships and carried them to bondage in America. It was only in 1772 that slavery was declared illegal in England itself. In America Pitt had to solve the problem of Canada, where French, English and Scottish settlers jostled irritably against each other and 'United Empire Loyalists' who did not want to live in the United States emigrated across the frontier and demanded a home. In India he had to take responsibility for the empire which his father and Clive had gained for England and which Warren Hastings had defended against the renewed French threat. There was enough to do to keep the most imperturbable young man busy.

Pitt tackled all these problems at one time or another. In 1784 he increased the government's control over Indian affairs by appointing commissioners to oversee the East India Company's administration of its empire. In 1785 he proposed to abolish many of the rotten boroughs. In 1786 he took various steps to set the government's finances in order, and simplified the system of taxation. In the same year he concluded a commercial treaty with France to allow French wine and oils into England at low duty, in return for similar favours to English textiles, hardware and pottery, entering France. This was a move toward 'Free Trade': the system of free import and export which Adam Smith had recommended in the *Wealth of Nations*. In 1788 Pitt proposed the abolition of the slave trade in a fine speech before Parliament; gave permission to Admiral Phillip to make a convict settlement on the coast of Australia, which Captain James Cook had explored and charted some years before; and gave way to a Whig demand that Warren Hastings should be impeached before Parliament for cruelty and extortion in governing the Company's territories.

Pitt often gave way if the opposition to his schemes was loud and substantial, and his surrenders reveal a different aspect of his career. When the Commons refused to give up their rotten boroughs, for example, he dropped the projected reform. He gave up the abolition of the slave trade when powerful London and Liverpool merchants opposed it, and he did not pursue his scheme to extend the idea of 'free trade' to English relations with the colony of Ireland, because English textile manufacturers feared that Irish linen would compete with their own products, if it was allowed cheaply into this country. Like Walpole before him Pitt preferred to yield to rather than oppose determined and influential opposition. This is yet another reason why he stayed in power as long as Walpole had done. After the incompetent governments of recent years he seemed a good prime minister however. He seemed to have a grasp of the changing times, which was in itself an achievement. His solution of the financial problem certainly worked well until another war upset his arrangements; and his work on the Canadian question, which he answered by dividing the greater part of Canada into two provinces, one English-speaking and one French, each with its own representative assembly, lasted for half a century and kept Canada within the Empire. The impeachment of Warren Hastings seemed unnecessary to Pitt, but he yielded to majority opinion when the Commons decided to proceed with it. Although Edmund Burke impeached Hastings with tremendous crimes 'in the name of the English nation whose ancient honour he has sullied . . . [and] . . . in the name of the Indian peoples whose rights he has trodden underfoot', the trial altered nothing in India. Hastings was acquitted after seven years, and the English rulers of the sub-continent continued to make colossal fortunes out there, governing neither more nor less justly than before.

CHAPTER 46

Britain and the French Revolution

1792-1805

BY 1792 WILLIAM PITT had good reason to be pleased with himself and with his country. He was the most popular prime minister since his father's day; and England was prosperous, completely recovered from the American war. It was particularly encouraging to compare the state of this country with that of others – with France for example, where the government had never recovered from the expense of the American war, and where industries were developing much more slowly than they were in England. In 1792 a revolution was in progress in France, but it was a political revolution, directed against the king, Louis XVI, and the aristocracy. Within a year, this French revolution was to involve England in another war with her old enemy across the Channel. What provoked that war, and what had made French history so different from English?

Since the reign of Louis XIV, Englishmen had always believed that the chief cause of the incessant wars with France was the pride and greed of the Bourbon kings of France. These monarchs threatened constantly to engulf the whole of western Europe in the tide of their territorial ambitions, and most of America and India as well. If there had been a parliament in France, or if the French aristocracy had tried to check the power and the ambition of their kings, then the wars might not have occurred – or so Englishmen argued when they forgot for the moment the deep commercial rivalry which underlay the Anglo-French hostility. It was a fact however that the French Parliament or Estates-General had not been summoned since 1614, and the French aristocracy, so far from opposing the will of their kings, spent their lives dancing attendance on them at the palace of Versailles, and enjoying the

reflected glory of the royal sun. In France the king's power was
absolute. As Louis XIV put it: *'L'état? C'est moi!'*. And so the
Bourbons pursued their ambitions, and noblemen and important
merchants who shared the desire for foreign empires and foreign
trade supported them. The aristocracy, in return for their loyal
acquiescence, paid no taxes. Nor were they called upon to do the
work of local government in their neighbourhoods, as English
squires were. The work of governing France, both at the centre and
in the provinces, was done by servants of the king. As for the taxes,
they were paid by merchants, in the form of innumerable tolls for
the movement of their goods around the country, and by the
peasants, who paid a great proportion of their income in a variety
of taxes which fell even on their salt. The peasants also supported
the Church and the Lord of the Manor by their work and their
wealth. They provided the bulk of the armed forces and the forced
labour which built and repaired French roads. Two thousand of
them each year went as chained criminals to man the French
galleys in the Mediterranean. They could never hope to rise above
their servile station, just as the merchants could not hope to join
the ranks of the aristocracy, as their counterparts in England often
did. There were exceptions to all these rules, but in general the
state of France in the eighteenth century was a mixture of feudalism and absolute monarchy, based on a system of taxation which
never yielded enough to meet the demands of the government,
either for wars or for the prodigal existence of the court. The War
of American Independence struck a final blow at this shaky and
obsolete structure. The cost of the war broke the government, and
the ideas of liberty, equality and representative government undermined the social and political system of the *ancien régime*. It was
the misfortune of Louis XVI, a monarch very like the first two
Hanoverians in character, to inherit the catastrophe which had
long been forecast by French thinkers and politicians. In 1789 his
government had to admit that it was bankrupt of money and ideas
for getting any, and the Estates-General were summoned, after a
lapse of almost two centuries, to help the king solve his problems.
It was a fatal move, for the men of the commons or Third Estate
used their opportunity not to save the old régime but to put an end
to it. Within a year of their first meeting they had established a
representative government. In Paris meanwhile a hungry mob

directed by political agitators had stormed the Bastille, the political prison of the old régime. In the countryside, peasants began to burn the châteaux of their feudal lords.

These early incidents in the French Revolution made welcome news to many people in England. Charles Fox declared that the storming of the Bastille was the greatest and best event that had happened in the history of the world; like many people he hoped that France might in the future share the benefits of constitutional government which England had enjoyed for more than a century. Edmund Burke on the other hand, for whom anything old was sacred by definition, lamented that 'the glory of Europe is gone for ever' – a curious comment on the fall of a despotic government by a man who had for years attacked the mild influence of George III as tyrannical. 'He pities the plumage but forgets the dying bird,' remarked Tom Paine, a writer whose sympathies were with the people of France. Paine's reaction to the French revolution was to repeat the demand for reform of England's parliamentary system, to give this country a representative government. Many people shared his views, and working men formed societies to obtain political rights, while a young Whig nobleman, Charles Grey, formed a society known as the 'Friends of the People' to help them.

By 1792 however the situation in France had altered. In the hands of determined Paris politicians the revolution had taken another turn, and Louis XVI was a prisoner in his own country. His nobles had deserted him and gone into exile, and the armies sent from Austria and Prussia to rescue him were held at bay in Flanders by volunteer armies of Frenchmen. The extermination of 'enemies of the people' had begun in France, and reached a dreadful climax in January 1793 with the execution of the king himself. These sinister events seemed to England's rulers to confirm Burke's views that the revolution across the Channel threatened all established government. Fox proposed an alliance with the revolutionaries, but Pitt maintained that they had broken 'the public law of Europe'.

The killing of the king and the threat of the French armies to overrun the Low Countries were the events which brought England to war with France. Hostilities began in the spring of 1793, when the French ambassador was sent home from England, and the revolutionary government was the first to declare war. Pitt fought the war as his father might have done, and in a manner approved of by the City. He sent subsidies to the other European powers to enable them to carry on the Continental war, but few English soldiers followed English guineas across the Channel, and their efforts did not trouble the French. The bulk of the British army went to the West Indies to damage French trade and protect English colonies. They enjoyed some early victories and captured a few islands, but soon yellow fever proved a deadlier enemy than either the French or rebellious negro slaves, and in the event eighty thousand men were killed or rendered unfit for further service by its ravages.

By 1797 the revolutionary armies in Europe were carrying all before them. They had captured Holland and defeated Austria, Prussia and Spain. In northern Italy a young general named Napoleon Bonaparte was employing military tactics as new as the ideas of the French republic, and equally fatal to his Austrian opponents. His soldiers charged in flying columns which broke and scattered the traditional lines of infantry who opposed them. Farther west, a French attempt to invade Ireland had been thwarted only by bad weather, and a project to invade England, the only opponent who remained in action against them, was checked by the action of English ships which destroyed the French invasion fleets. The only English victories had occurred at sea and in 1797 it seemed for a time that these efforts would be sabotaged by a mutiny among the sailors who manned the fleets at Spithead and the Nore. Ashore in England things were going badly. The war had destroyed the delicate balance of government finances which Pitt had created in the peacetime years, and even the Bank of England could not pay its creditors. In an attempt to meet the cost of the war Pitt had introduced a tax on income–an unheard-of imposition on free Englishmen. There were taxes on manufactures, on windows, bricks, hats and the powder for wigs. The country grumbled. In Ireland the promise of French help inspired a rebellion in 1798 which was savagely repressed by English troops and Protestant Irish yeomanry.

The war was not going well for Pitt, and his attempt to settle the Irish grievance was no more successful than his efforts to beat the French. He took away Ireland's Parliament and united it with England's, intending to complete the transaction by giving Irish

Catholics the right to sit at Westminster. At this suggestion however George III crossed his Prime Minister's wishes for the first and only time. He regarded 'Catholic Emancipation' as a threat to the Protestant liberties of England which he had sworn at his coronation to protect. Pitt resigned. The Irish lost their Parliament and got nothing in return, and George's obstinacy lit the fuse of a century of explosive hatred and violence.

These years at the end of the eighteenth century were years of trial for England, and Pitt chose a critical time to give up his responsibility for leading the nation. The nation endured however. One of England's greatest seamen, Horatio Nelson, led the English Mediterranean fleet to victory over the French at the battle of the Nile, and three years later played a leading part in the defeat of the 'Armed Neutrality' of the Baltic States at Copenhagen. At home, English farming and industry proved strong enough to withstand the strain of war and even to profit from the absence of competition from foreign wheat and textiles. The industrial revolution continued, and at the turn of the century Thomas Telford was hard at work building a new canal to link the Thames and Severn. When he reflected on the state of his country it was not to mourn defeats and rebellions, or even to celebrate victories, but to 'think of such a mass of population, industrious, intelligent and energetic, in continual exertion'. 'I do not believe,' said Telford, 'that any part of the world, of like dimensions, ever exceeded Great Britain as it now is, in regard to the projection of wealth and the practice of the useful arts.' To read this, one would hardly believe that this country was at war and it is clear that all the fighting of the last few years had no more broken England than it had broken the French republic. After almost ten years of conflict, however, both sides were ready to pause for a moment, and in 1802 Pitt's successor Lord Addington signed the Treaty of Amiens with Napoleon Bonaparte.

The Peace of Amiens lasted for little more than a year. By the spring of 1803 England and France were again at the point of war. England was the first to declare renewed hostilities, stung by Napoleon's demand that she should surrender the naval base of Malta to its ancient guardians, the knights of St John. Behind this quarrel however lay the deeper rivalry of the two countries which had always existed, and which Napoleon took up where the Bourbons had left it. France would never accept the English claim to rule the seas of the world and enjoy the trade of three continents. England, on the other hand, would never allow the French to dominate western Europe, whether as a monarchy or a republic. The revolutionary struggle disappeared beneath the old commercial and political hostility. Napoleon, who was now the master of his country, was soon to become 'Emperor of the French', and take his crown from the hands of the pope, who had been brought to consecrate him, to set it on his head himself. He was a determined and ambitious man, as this action makes clear, and he aimed to extend his empire over the whole of Europe. He regarded the peoples of eastern Europe, the Germans, the Russians and the Slavs, as barbarians to be civilized by France. Eventually, he aimed to rule and civilize the whole of the east, from Egypt to India, and the west from the Mississippi to the Pacific.

But every move towards the accomplishment of this great design was blocked by England. An English army and an English fleet had prevented the conquest of Egypt in 1798. Now English ships blockaded the coast of Europe, and English money supported one new coalition after another of the European powers whom Napoleon had once defeated, but who were encouraged by England to take him on again. This widespread and constant resistance to his ambitions infuriated Napoleon. 'All the ills and curses which can afflict mankind,' he said, 'come from London.' He nourished a deep hatred for the English aristocracy and their bland assumption of their country's superiority over the rest of the world. He despised the merchants and the manufacturers as 'a nation of shopkeepers'. He felt sure that the common people were waiting for a chance to revolt against them all. And so he decided to invade England, to destroy his enemies at home, and to put an end to their world-wide resistance to his plans. As soon as the peace of Amiens ended he began to assemble an invasion force on the coasts of France: one hundred thousand men and two thousand flat-bottomed boats to carry them across the Channel. Napoleon was so confident of success that his generals were hard put to stop him making the attempt on the first dark night that occurred. They realized the difficulties of the enterprise: the treacherous coastal currents, the variations of wind and tide, the size of the force to be transported and the certainty that unless their own warships could gain control of the narrow seas the English fleet would blow their transports out of the water. Napoleon was persuaded to wait at least until the Channel had been cleared of English men of war.

His plans were well known in England, where Pitt had become Prime Minister again on the day that Napoleon became Emperor of the French. Pitt organized the country's defences, building towers along the southern coast and digging military canals across the low coastal lands. All over southern England volunteers were trained in the use of arms by veteran soldiers. These enthusiastic preparations gave the lie to Napoleon's belief that English people would welcome him as a liberator; but no amount of patriotic fervour could conceal the fact that England's defence depended on her fleet.

The fleet maintained a ceaseless patrol in the Channel, blockading Boulogne and Brest. In the Mediterranean, Nelson kept watch off Toulon. In March 1805 however, rough weather forced him to stand off from the coastal waters, and the French admiral Villeneuve slipped out to sea. He collected the allied Spanish fleet which lay at Cadiz and set course across the Atlantic for Martinique. His plan was to meet the French Atlantic fleet there, to inflict what damage he could on the British West Indian islands, if possible to decoy the English squadrons away from the coasts of Europe, and then to double back and clear the Channel of its remaining defenders. The French Atlantic fleet failed to break out of Brest, however, and only Nelson followed Villeneuve in belated pursuit. The Frenchman turned back for Europe. Nelson realized that he would not catch him, but sent on a fast brig which brought news to the Channel fleet of the French and Spanish approach. When Villeneuve reached Cape Finisterre, Admiral Calder was waiting for him. The Frenchman declined battle after his long voyage, and put into land to refit.

These naval delays exasperated Napoleon. He called off the invasion plan, and turned his great army to the east where a new coalition of Prussian, Austrian and Russian armies awaited him. Villeneuve had no further mission to perform, so he decided to go back to Toulon. When he emerged from Cadiz harbour on the morning of 21 October 1805, Nelson was waiting for him off Cape Trafalgar, with twenty-seven ships against thirty-three. The enemy had the edge in numbers, and superior sail- and gun-power; but the English fleet sailed in to attack them, forming two columns as they did so, aimed at breaking the enemy line and throwing the French and Spanish ships into confusion. They moved very slowly at first, for the offshore breeze was light, and at one point Nelson's flagship *Victory* came under fire from two or three opponents without being able to reply. The fleet pressed on however, obedient to the famous signal: 'England expects that every man will do his duty'. Just before midday they engaged the enemy in a close and devastating battle. Within four hours nineteen of the French and Spanish ships were taken or destroyed. The rest made for Cadiz and were not pursued.

Although Napoleon had already abandoned his invasion scheme before the battle was fought, Trafalgar ended the war at sea. It was a famous victory, and English people celebrated it with bells and bonfires, although their excitement was shot through with sorrow at the news of Nelson's death on his quarter-deck at the height of the battle. He was remembered as a hero by seaman and landsman alike. In three great naval victories he had maintained English naval supremacy, and he left to the navy a tradition of attention to duty, and resourcefulness.

CHAPTER 47

Britain and Napoleon

1805-1815

AFTER Nelson, Pitt was the national hero. London merchants toasted him as 'the Saviour of Europe'. Pitt himself took a different view. 'Europe is not to be saved by any single man,' he said. 'England has saved herself by her exertions, and will, as I trust, save Europe by her example.' Indeed, it was true that Pitt's own strategy had done very little to check Napoleon's conquest of the Continent. England's victories had all been at sea, and at the end of 1805 yet another of Pitt's European coalitions began to collapse, when Napoleon defeated the Austrian and Russian armies at Austerlitz. Napoleon was invincible, and Pitt became depressed and exhausted by his efforts to defeat him. In 1806 he died. He was not remembered as a failure however, for he was the symbol of English resistance, 'the pilot who weathered the storm'. He had rallied England to her sick and ailing king and revived a new Tory party, dedicated to the monarchy and the old constitution. On the other hand, this show of unity had been achieved at the expense of ignoring the demands for political reform, and suppressing the freedom of speech and criticism of which Pitt had once been so proud. The government had prohibited any public meetings, unless licensed by a magistrate, censored newspapers and suppressed political debating societies. 'Agitators' were prosecuted, and even the ancient liberty of Habeas Corpus was suspended to give the authorities power to arrest and imprison a suspected person without producing evidence of crime. Resistance to Napoleon, in fact, was coupled with resistance to any sort of criticism or change at home, and this conservatism would cause new threats to the king and the power of the aristocracy in the future.

446

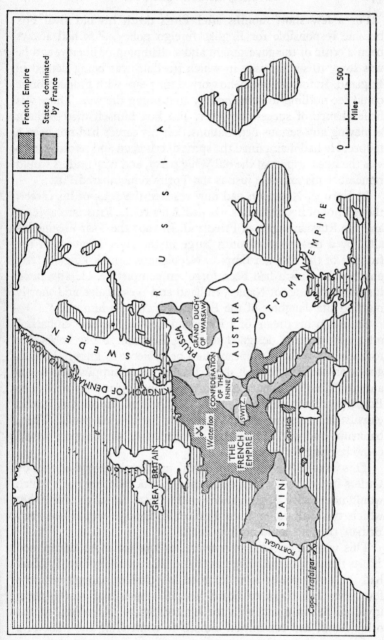

NAPOLEON'S EUROPE

French Empire

States dominated
by France

0   500
Miles

For a few short months after Pitt's death his old rival Fox became responsible for English foreign policy. Fox had always been a critic of the government and a champion of liberty, and he was sorry to see the way in which freedom was being denied in England. In foreign policy he worked for peace with France, for he could see nothing to be gained by continuing the war. There was little chance of success however, and Fox himself died without achieving any serious negotiations. Yet his career had not been a failure. He had maintained the spirit of criticism and reform which was the finest aspect of the old Whig party, and new leaders would remember his example just as the Tories remembered Pitt.

In Europe, Napoleon had now reached the peak of his career, though not of his ambitions. He had defeated the Prussians at Jena, and the Russians again at Friedland. In 1807 the Tsar became his ally, by a treaty signed on a barge in the river Niemen, at the frontier of the Russian Empire. Napoleon was now king of Italy and republicanism had been forgotten completely. He appointed his brothers kings of Naples, Holland and Westphalia, and shortly married the daughter of the Emperor of Austria himself.

Secure in his dream of a European Empire, he now embarked on a new scheme designed to bring England to her knees. He forbade any of his European allies or subjects to import English goods or harbour English ships. France would supply their needs and continue to export certain goods to England as well. The Emperor reasoned that England, robbed of customers, would exhaust her reserves of gold in paying for French goods. Then, bankrupt and out of business, the nation of shopkeepers would come begging for peace.

This was the 'Continental System', and England replied to it by Orders in Council, which threatened to blockade any ports which would not receive English goods, and to seize the cargo of any ship which travelled to or from France. If Europe would not 'buy British' then it should not buy at all.

This was a new kind of warfare, calling for more disciplined efforts than any of the belligerent nations had made before. England had the naval power to make good her threats, though within a few years her claim to board neutral vessels and search them involved her in a war with the United States. Napoleon, on the other hand, had committed himself to controlling the trade of a continent, an impossible task in his time. His efforts to enforce the system provoked his allies into rebellion against him; but not before French industries had taken profit from the scheme, and English had suffered from the dislocation of their trade. The economic war brought the Napoleonic struggle nearer home than even the threat of invasion had done. It caused high prices and unemployment, and the fact that some manufacturers found ways through the system, or new markets in South America, did not make life easier for people who were out of work or could not afford the high cost of a loaf of English bread. Perhaps Fox's ideas of peace would have been more popular in the country, by 1811 or 1812, than they had been in 1806. As it was the new threat to trade only increased the determination of the Tory government to defeat Napoleon, and this time they went straight to the mainland of Europe in order to do so.

The first country to rebel against the Continental System was Portugal, which had ancient trading ties with England. The second was Spain, stung by Napoleon's decision to dismiss her Bourbon king and put his brother Joseph in his place. The Bourbon kings of Spain were not good rulers; but their proud and religious subjects preferred them to the upstart Bonapartes. In 1808 they rose in rebellion against Joseph, and against the French troops who were using their country as a base for the attacks on Portugal. England sent an army to support the Portuguese resistance, but it faced an overwhelming task. Before it lay a rugged and unfriendly country occupied by armies of Frenchmen which never numbered less than two hundred thousand men. To the rear lay only the sea. At Vimiero a French army was defeated, and Portugal was freed from Napoleon; but the army was allowed to return to France, and even went in English ships. Joseph Bonaparte was driven from Madrid by Spanish guerrillas, but this success served only to bring Napoleon himself to Spain, and the English forces under Sir John Moore were driven back to Corunna on the coast, where Moore himself was killed in defending this last foothold. By 1809 English forces held little more than the Lisbon peninsula, on the edge of Portugal. Napoleon returned east to meet yet another Austrian army which had been raised to oppose him, and defeated it at Wagram. An English expedition to Walcheren, off the Low Countries, ended in miserable failure.

At this stage however the tide of French victories turned. Sir Arthur Wellesley, the general who had distinguished himself in India in the Mahratta wars and defeated the French at Vimiero, returned to the Iberian peninsula and won a further victory at Talavera. Wellesley was later to become Duke of Wellington, and it is by this name that he is better known to history. The 'Iron Duke' was a stern and unimaginative man who held the frank opinion that the soldiers he commanded were 'the scum of the earth, recruited for drink'. His discipline was accordingly severe; but in battle his imperturbable calm gave confidence to his men. 'His long nose among us on the morning of a battle,' wrote one of his officers, 'was worth ten thousand men.' In 1809 the Duke advanced from Portugal into Spain and confronted the overwhelming French forces. In battle their flying columns of infantry and horse at last met their match in the hollow squares of red-coated British infantry. No charge could break through these stolid, well-disciplined formations, which drew closer together as comrades fell. The British counter-attacked, won victories and captured fortresses. When autumn came Wellington retreated, devastating the countryside to starve his enemies of supplies, and halting finally behind the impregnable fortifications which he built across the Lisbon peninsula. Throughout 1810 and 1811 the French held him within the frontiers of Portugal, but Wellington advanced once more in 1812. His lack of numbers and his natural caution prolonged the Iberian campaign, but this slow warfare of attrition blunted Napoleon's taste for the Peninsular war.

In 1812 the Emperor withdrew his best troops from Spain, and marched east to counter another rebellion against the Continental System, led this time by the Tsar of Russia. In the next two years the armies of France, stretching their resources to the limit by a war on two fronts against implacable enemies, tasted misery and defeat. The *Grande Armée* crossed the Niemen and fought one terrible battle at Borodino before it reached Moscow only to find that the Russians had deserted the city. There was no enemy to fight and nothing to do but retreat. As the French trudged back through the deepening winter, Cossack horsemen emerged from the snow to harass and destroy them, and barely a thirtieth part of the great army returned across the Niemen. Napoleon, racing ahead of the remnants of his shattered army, raised another one in France, and came back in 1813 to confront the renewed coalition of Russians, Prussians and Austrians at the 'Battle of the Nations' at Leipzig. Here, for the first time, he was defeated. In Spain, meanwhile, the French fought a war of mutual savagery with the Spanish guerrillas, and Wellington at length began to advance. In the spring of 1814 he broke through the French, forced them into their final retreat, and crossed the frontier towards Toulouse. Farther north the Tsar rode into Paris at the end of March. Napoleon was forced to admit defeat and put his signature to an act of abdication. He was exiled to the island of Elba and a Bourbon prince was restored to the throne of France as Louis XVIII. Wellington and the statesmen of the victorious allied powers foregathered at Vienna, in an atmosphere of relief and gaiety, to celebrate victory and divide its spoils.

As things turned out however a stroke of the pen was not sufficient to remove Napoleon from history. In 1815 he escaped from Elba and returned to France. A huge volunteer army joined him and Louis XVIII fled. In the ballrooms of Vienna the music faltered and died at the news of his escape and Wellington hurried westward to lead another coalition of armies, pledged to remain in the field until 'the scourge of Europe' had been finally defeated. In the Austrian Netherlands, Napoleon faced two commanders and two armies who had come to meet him: Wellington, with English, Dutch and German troops, guarded Brussels, while a Prussian army under Marshal Blücher lay farther to the east. Napoleon resolved to meet and beat them singly, and on 16 June 1815 threw back the Prussians at Ligny while one of his marshals, Ney, held off the English who attempted to assist them. Napoleon, thinking he had finished the Prussians, now turned to face Wellington. The next battle would decide the fate of Brussels, and of Europe.

On the morning of 18 June, after a night of pouring rain, watery sunshine revealed the two armies confronting each other across a narrow plain. Wellington's forces were drawn up on a low hill before the village of Waterloo. Napoleon, who despite the experiences of Spain had no great opinion of Wellington or his troops, expected confidently to dislodge them and eat his supper in Brussels. He disregarded reports that some Prussians were returning from the east, and waited almost until midday before sending his main columns forward in furious charges against the British squares. There were terrible losses on either side in the battle of Waterloo, for both were determined that this conflict, for good or ill, should be their last. The British troops were not, by their own account, well supported by their allies, and though the red-coated formations held, they were in desperate straits when Blücher and a large Prussian force appeared, about half past four in the afternoon, on the hills to the east. The Prussian guns hammered the weary French, and the Emperor's Old Guard failed with a last charge against the British centre. The French turned to retreat, and the retreat became flight as Prussian cavalry hunted down the broken enemy.

Even phlegmatic Wellington admitted that Waterloo was 'the nearest run thing you ever saw'. He ended the day with supper in Brussels however, while Napoleon ended his life a few years later as a sick and unhappy exile on the island of St Helena. To the last that great and imaginative man, in his own words 'a fragment of rock launched through space' which had shaken Europe by its impact, spoke and wrote in terms of what might have been, and maintained that England had been 'the most powerful, the most constant and the most generous' of his foes.

The battles of Waterloo and Trafalgar brought an end to the long contest between England and France. There was no doubt that England had won. France lost all her territorial gains in Europe, and the revolutionary republics and the Napoleonic kingdoms beyond the Meuse, the Rhine and the Pyrenees were erased from the new map which the statesmen drew when the Congress of Vienna reassembled. England, on the other hand, gained colonies: Malta in the Mediterranean, the Cape of Good Hope, Mauritius and Ceylon in the Indian Ocean, and Trinidad, St Lucia and Tobago in the West Indies. In the course of the war English ships had established their mastery of the seas of the world, and the trade of three continents lay ready for English merchants to exploit it. At home, the war had given the final impetus to the industrial revolution, and England stood equipped to supply Europe and the world with textiles, iron goods and machines. England was a world power, and France scarcely a European one. Yet France had still her part to play in history. Her people were restless under the rule of the restored Bourbons. They often remembered the revolutionary slogans of liberty and equality, and the glories of the Napoleonic empire. In the next fifty years they twice expelled their kings and finally, after an attempt to create a second republic, gave their loyalty to an adventurer, Louis Napoleon, whose only claim to it was his name and his relationship to his dead uncle, the great Emperor himself. The peoples of other European countries took their example from France, and themselves rebelled in the name of national freedom and constitutional government against the rulers whom the Vienna powers had set over them. The nineteenth century was to be a century of revolutions in fact, both political and industrial; and France shared with England the responsibility for creating them. As a modern historian has put it, 'French ideas and English techniques helped to transform the nineteenth-century world'.[1]

[1] Asa Briggs: *The Age of Improvement.*

CHAPTER 48

Toryism: Reactionary and Enlightened

1815-1827

WHAT EFFECTS had over twenty years of war had on English peoples' lives? If we were to answer this question from the evidence of the novels of Jane Austen, which were written at this time, then we should conclude that the effects were hardly noticeable. The Napoleonic struggle is scarcely ever mentioned in her pages and the characters pursue their interesting lives without any interruption from the great events that are taking place elsewhere. The novels probably reflect the truth as accurately as they describe human nature. The pleasant, cultured life of the aristocracy was not upset by the war, except that they could no longer travel abroad. Heavy taxation and rising prices at home did not impair their comfortable standards of living. The war came no nearer home than it threatened to in the days when Napoleon contemplated the invasion of England.

The strain of the long conflict had its effect however, both on English minds, in the form of revolutionary ideas and Tory distaste for them, and on English ways of life. Jane Austen's is not the complete picture of English society, even in the countryside. For during the war the enclosure of the fields and commons was virtually completed and numbers of labourers and small-holders were left without land. They depended on the farmers' slender wages, made up by payments from the Poor Law fund, to meet the rising cost of living and feed their families. For people like these the war years meant a violent change from old ways and a good deal of misery, even though the war itself was not directly responsible for it. Jane Austen does not mention them. Nor does she mention Manchester. In the north of England, where the majority of England's population was now to be found, the war meant change and progress. The progress was hindered by the Continental System, which deprived the textile industry of its markets, and interrupted by the war with the United States, which deprived Lancashire of cotton. But it had reached a speed by now at which it could not be halted. The war meant more steam engines, more blast furnaces and more power looms; more factories and mills. It also meant for the people who lived in the new towns and worked in the mills and factories twelve, fourteen or sixteen hours work a day, for wages which lagged behind the rising cost of bread and meat. The town labourers' new houses had been built in a hurry, back to back, without proper ventilation or drainage and sometimes without floors or windows. The biggest windows were in the mills, designed to let in every hour of daylight for the increasing work which the machines and their masters demanded.

Not everyone lived and worked in these harsh conditions. The unskilled labourer was the real victim, the weaver who had given up the losing battle with the power loom for example. Or the orphan boy or girl, to take another. There was plenty of work in England for young hands to do, and children were brought from orphanages all over the country to do it. Often too the young workers were the children of the labourers themselves. In the mills they could skip among the machinery to tie up loose threads of yarn or clean the moving parts. Elsewhere, in the coalmines, they sat for twelve hours or more a day in darkness, opening and shutting doors. But that was work for small children. Bigger boys and girls could haul trucks of coal by ropes slung around their bodies or their foreheads. Small children, on the other hand, were the best suited to work as chimney sweeps, crawling among chimney flues in private houses. They were less likely to get stuck.

Once again these are the worst examples of social conditions. But even if the children's jobs were more congenial than the ones described and their masters well-meaning and considerate men, it was impossible to keep them at work for over twelve hours a day without stern discipline. In many occupations, we may be certain, the children were harshly treated and poorly fed, and every day risked injury, disease and even death. The story of their employment casts a dark and shameful shadow across the years of the Napoleonic war and the years afterwards which are sometimes remembered as 'Regency England', an age of pleasure and extravagant fashions; or as the romantic years, when Constable and Turner were painting and Wordsworth, Keats and Shelley wrote poetry of beauty, love and childhood. In one of her novels, *Emma*, Jane Austen wrote that 'One half of the world cannot understand the pleasures of the other'. With fuller knowledge of the time, we may add that one half did not know about the other's hardships either.

So the sailors from Trafalgar, and after them the soldiers from Waterloo, came home to a country where prosperity and misery lived side by side. They found jobs hard to get, for the end of the war struck a telling blow at the growing English industries. There were no more government contracts for guns and uniforms, and the war-torn European countries who had been customers of England in the past could not afford to bring back their custom yet. The result of this falling-off in the demand for English goods was a fall in war-time prices, but the slump caused lower wages and unemployment as well. Where jobs were available the demobilized soldiers had to compete for them with impoverished weavers and with Irish immigrants who came flooding into England from a country where there was neither land enough nor industry to support the growing population. The Irish were willing to live anywhere and work for the lowest wages, and their willingness forced down the wages of Englishmen as well. The law however forbade any combined attempts on the part of working men to raise their wages. As long ago as 1799, Pitt's government had forbidden such 'combinations'. So to poverty was added helplessness to change it for the better.

Soon hunger was added as well. The government introduced a law to prohibit the import of foreign corn until the price in England had reached the level of eighty shillings a quarter: that is to say, about a shilling a loaf, or the total of some country labourers' weekly wage, without the charity which the Poor Law added. The Corn Law was designed to protect farmers from a sudden fall in prices when imports of foreign wheat were resumed after the war, though as it turned out it did not do that efficiently. Taken together with new taxes on tea, sugar, beer, tobacco and soap which were levied to replace the income tax which was abolished, it forced the cost of living to a height where men without steady wages or employment were threatened with starvation and deprived of even the smaller comforts of existence.

These details of England's condition when the war ended make the ruling classes seem a selfish and callous caste, intent on protecting their own income and standards of living even at the expense of their poorer countrymen. The Prince of Wales, indeed, who was now Regent in his sick father's place, was a man both selfish and callous, consuming his life in pleasure and a sordid and public quarrel with his wife. The members of the Tory government, led by Lord Liverpool, were more conscientious men according to their lights; but the fact was that they faced economic difficulties and social problems beyond their experience or understanding, and their only solution was to protect the propertied classes of society, whose needs and demands at least they understood. For this reason they introduced the Corn Law, abolished the income tax and gave permission to complete enclosures; but so far as industry, low wages and unemployment were concerned, they had no answer. So they took the advice of writers of the time on economic matters, and left well alone. The economists assured them that prices and wages were decided by inexorable laws of supply and demand whose operation no government could affect. They added the gloomy but comforting assurance that it was part of nature's law to keep the poor on the edge of starvation and, if their numbers became too great for their wages to support them, to carry off the surplus by hunger or disease.

There were some men in Parliament however who pressed the government to attack the social problems of the time. In general they received little support, but sometimes a determined man achieved results. In 1819, for example, after being rejected once in 1815 by the House of Lords, a bill was forced through Parliament to limit the hours of children in the mills and forbid their labour altogether, under the age of nine. This bill was largely the work of mill-owners themselves. The problem now however was to enforce it. The government shrank from compulsion and left the task to local magistrates. These country gentlemen did not press the matter, and the law was easily evaded. The majority of manufacturers maintained that child labour and long hours were essential to the recovery of the cotton industry and the magistrates, like the government, treated their views with uneasy respect. They realized that the manufacturers were intelligent and determined men, whose opposition to the government would be dangerous if once aroused.

The manufacturers were on the same side as the magistrates and the government however when it came to dealing with the lesser orders of society and their threats to public peace. They were scared of crime, and even more of revolution. There was plenty of lawlessness in post-war England, for poverty and hunger breed crime as well as other diseases. Some men went no farther than poaching and petty theft, but others staged violent strikes in contravention of the Combination Laws. During the war, in 1811 and 1812, weavers in Nottinghamshire organized in groups under a mysterious leader, Ned Ludd, had taken to smashing the weaving machines which they blamed for putting down their wages. In the post-war years there was more machine-breaking. There were political demonstrations too, aimed at forcing the government into action over social problems, or even at reforming Parliament itself; and there were more sinister agitators still who aimed at provoking rebellion. Where crime was concerned the government met the challenge to law and order by increasing the penalties for it until over two hundred offences were punishable by death. Strikers and machine-breakers were arrested and imprisoned, or transported to the penal colonies in Australia, and so were poachers and other small offenders. To suppress political agitators the government, and principally Lord Sidmouth, the Home Secretary, adopted the methods which Pitt had used, censoring newspapers and free speech and suspending Habeas Corpus once again.

Few among the agitators were revolutionaries, however. 'Equality' and 'democracy' meant little to them compared with the need for work and food. The Manchester weavers, for instance, who set out to march to London and tell the Prince Regent about their hardships, took with them only blankets to sleep in, but they were arrested and some of them were imprisoned without trial. Some of the agitators, on the other hand, had violence in mind. Jeremiah Brandreth and the 'Derbyshire Rebels' planned to seize Nottingham Castle. Other demonstrators had vague political aims like those of the Spa Fields rioters in London, who wore 'caps of liberty' like those seen in France in the revolutionary years.

Whatever their intentions Lord Sidmouth and the magistrates regarded all the demonstrators as would-be revolutionaries. They used spies to ascertain their movements and provoke them to break the law, and soldiers to disperse their meetings and marches and arrest their leaders. The penalties proposed for agitators were so harsh that many juries refused to convict the wretched prisoners who came before them.

The grim story of discontent, misunderstanding and oppression which is the history of these post-war years reaches its climax on an August day in 1819, when a crowd of over sixty thousand men, women and children assembled in St Peter's Fields at Manchester to hear a well-known orator, Henry Hunt, speak about the need for a change in the policy of the government, and particularly the need for reform of Parliament to give representation to the manufacturing north. From the windows of an inn near by the local magistrates watched anxiously as the great concourse assembled in an orderly and obviously well-organized manner. They took alarm at the numbers and the evidence of organization and, fearing they knew not what sort of rising, ordered cavalrymen to arrest the speaker and break up the meeting. The mounted soldiers moved into the crowd but they were brought to a halt and separated from each other by the press of people. They drew their sabres and laid about them. Reinforcements charged to join them and a dreadful panic ensued as the crowd scattered to escape them. Six people were killed and four hundred injured as the meeting broke up in disorder.

This victory of soldiers over unarmed people became known, ironically, as 'Peterloo'. It shocked many people in England, squires, manufacturers, reformers and Tories alike. The government however congratulated the magistrates in the Prince Regent's name on 'their prompt, decisive and efficient measures for the preservation of the public tranquillity'. They passed new laws to suppress public meetings and seditious speech.

This final act of fear and callousness marked the lowest point in the régime of oppression however. Next year there was a wild plot to murder the whole cabinet as it sat at dinner. The plot failed and the cabinet lived, but better times began. Hunger and unemployment, the causes of discontent, became less urgent as English trade began to recover its prosperity. The new markets in South America began to pay dividends, and old ones in Europe were regained. Private houses and public buildings began to go up in great numbers at home. There were more jobs, better wages; and 'peace, cheerfulness and industry' returned to the manufacturing areas. Against this happier background Lord Liverpool and his cabinet took up more constructive and less terrifying policies. The more sensible and more humanitarian characteristics of Englishmen began to show through the mask of tyranny which England's rulers had worn throughout the post-war years.

The nature of the government began to change in several ways during the 1820's. For one thing the governors themselves were different men. In 1820 the Prince Regent succeeded his father as King George IV; but this was not really an important change. George proved no more or less the ruler of his country in the next ten years than he had in the last ten. His quarrel with Caroline, his wife, had now turned into a scandalous lawsuit and English people, after first examining the evidence with some interest, became bored with both their new monarch and his queen. The really important changes were among the ministers. Lord Sidmouth was replaced as Home Secretary by Robert Peel, the son of a Lancashire mill-owner. Another young man, George Canning, took the place of Lord Castlereagh, the Foreign Secretary who had represented England at the second Congress of Vienna, and whose name had become linked with the régime of oppression both abroad and at home.

These new brooms began to perform their proverbial task. Peel's achievement was to abolish the death sentence for over a hundred crimes and to create the Metropolitan Police, a force of three thousand constables, armed with staves, who soon made their impression on the criminals of London. The provincial cities followed London's example and created police forces of their own. Indeed they had to do so in order to deal with the exodus of criminals to the provinces which was the result of the 'Bobbies' ' efficiency in the capital. And so a new body of officers was found to keep the peace in England, and sabre-rattling cavalrymen were required less often to charge their own countrymen.

Canning pursued a new foreign policy, which Castlereagh had already begun in part. He drew away from the rulers of Europe and their attempts to suppress the ambitions of their subjects to rule themselves, and used the English fleet and English diplomatic influence to support the Spanish colonies in South America in their revolt against the parent country, and to protect Portugal against the threat of Spanish invasion. Not only did this policy gain England a reputation as the friend of liberty and the protector of the rights of small nations, but it was good for trade as well. The new states of South America were as grateful for English exports as they were for English diplomatic help.

In eastern Europe, Canning sent a fleet to the help of the Greeks, who were in rebellion against their Turkish overlords. There was nothing particularly to be gained from this move, but it was forced upon the Foreign Secretary by English public opinion, which drew its knowledge of Greek affairs from the study of Homer, and concluded that the rebels must be heroes in the mould of Ulysses and Achilles. Volunteers like the poet, Lord Byron, went to fight in Greece, and Canning had to give in to the mood of the moment, and add government support. His other motive was to prevent Russia, who had also intervened, from getting all the credit for the affair and extending her influence towards the Mediterranean. Distrust of Russia was to be as marked a feature of British foreign policy in the nineteenth century as support for the aspirations of subject peoples.

So the 'Enlightened Tories', as historians have come to call them, began to show that their ideas could move with the times. As yet they had not tackled social questions however. They had not touched the worst conditions in the new towns, or set the children in the factories free. Nor had they faced the problem of poverty in the countryside, which was costing the nation £7 million a year in poor relief. Their knowledge of these problems was still imperfect, and they were still reluctant to interfere. They still left it to the conscience of individuals to tackle the problems, and relied on Christian charity to do the work which they were not ready to begin.

There were religious and conscientious people who were ready to take action; women like Elizabeth Fry, the Quaker, who devoted herself to work among prisoners, and men like young Robert Ashley, later to become Earl of Shaftesbury, who had already resolved to spend his life in getting the children out of the factories. There were other humanitarians like Robert Owen, the mill-owner in Lanark, who right back in the war years had built good houses and schools for his workpeople and paid them good wages for reasonable hours. There were also determined men like Francis Place, a London tailor, who forced through Parliament by his skill and persistence the repeal of the Combination Laws.

Conscience and resolution were at work in England in the 1820's, and by the end of the decade Home Secretary Peel had begun to make inquiries into social conditions. But the Tory Parliament had yet to make a positive effort to improve the condition of England, and some of the would-be reformers were becoming impatient at the delay. Among these critics of the government was William Cobbett, a farmer and journalist who toured England at the end of the 1820's and described the poverty which enclosures and the high price of bread had caused. Cobbett had reached the conclusion that there would be no improvement until Parliament itself had been reformed. He blamed the aristocracy for causing the distress by selfish legislation, and demanded a change in the character of the government. 'There is,' wrote Cobbett, 'in the men calling themselves English country gentlemen something superlatively base. They are, I sincerely believe, the most cruel, the most unfeeling, the most brutally insolent. I know; I can prove; I can safely take my oath that they are the most base of all creatures that God ever suffered to take human shape.' Evidently, for all the tribulations of the post-war years, free speech was not yet dead in England.

CHAPTER 49

The Reform of Parliament

1827-1832

THE REFORM of Parliament now became the great issue of English politics. Not everyone shared Cobbett's distaste for the aristocracy or his taste for strong language; but more and more people shared his view that England's form of government should be changed. A philosopher, Jeremy Bentham, had put the argument in a different way some years before. He represented human life as a sum, in which pleasures were the plus qualities, and pains the minuses. If the sum had a positive answer, then a man was happy; if a negative, then he was miserable. The government's duty, Bentham went on to argue, was to create the greatest possible amount of happiness for the greatest possible number of people. Clearly, the government was not doing this at the beginning of the nineteenth century. The power of the aristocracy had outlasted their usefulness to the country. It was time that their undisputed authority was brought to an end, and a more useful form of government put in its place.

Bentham's arguments and Cobbett's complaints were echoed by manufacturers. These men were now prosperous and influential in the country and they realized that they had played as important a part in the history of the last fifty years as the aristocracy had done. Birmingham and Manchester were as important in English life as London, and far more important than Old Sarum. Yet that old mound still sent its representatives to the House of Commons, and so did many other rotten boroughs, while Manchester and Birmingham were unrepresented. The English electoral system still made it a principle, as the politician and historian Macaulay said, 'to invest a hundred drunken pot-wallopers in one place, or the owner of a ruined hovel in another, with powers which are withheld from cities renowned to the farthest ends of the earth, for the marvels of their wealth and their industry'. It was a situation which the manufacturers would not endure. They realized that their occupations and their wealth had made them into a new class: a middle class, as different in position and outlook from the gentry of the countryside as they were from the working men whom they employed. They determined to make their different viewpoint heard in Parliament, by altering the old electoral system and giving members and votes to the industrial cities. It was time, they thought, that Parliament ceased to protect the interests of farmers and landowners alone, and encouraged industry as well. The manufacturers also wanted to put an end to the Corn Laws and the taxes on imports and exports of manufactured goods. 'Free Trade' was their objective, and they argued that it would bring prosperity to every class of the community.

Even within the unreformed Parliament there were men who shared the conviction that the electoral system should be changed. The Whigs had little use for a system of voting which had kept them out of power for fifty years. They hoped that a new electorate would put its confidence in them, rather than the Tories; and they realized that the impatience of the middle class would end in the threat of revolution, unless its demands were met in time. So the Whig leaders, Lord Grey and Lord John Russell, allied themselves with the manufacturers and the radical reformers in demanding electoral reform.

And in the Tory government itself there were men who appreciated the middle-class point of view. Peel, after all, was himself a manufacturer's son, and Canning's foreign policy was aimed at encouraging English commercial interests. Another of the enlightened Tories, William Huskisson, was busy reducing the taxes on manufactured goods and scaling down the price level at which foreign corn might be imported. But still the Tories jibbed at the reform of Parliament. In 1827 the Duke of Wellington became Prime Minister, and he was the man least likely to alter any old institution. It became clear that while the Tories remained in power Parliament would never reform itself.

At this juncture English politics were upset by events in Ireland. In many respects Ireland was a forgotten country at the beginning of the nineteenth century. No industrial revolution had taken place

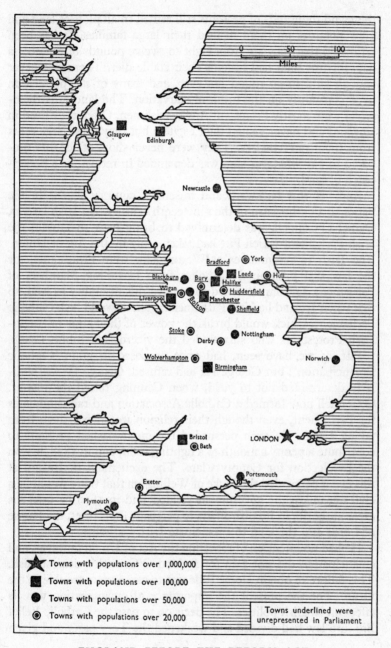

ENGLAND BEFORE THE REFORM ACT

there and thousands of peasants still rented small plots of land and grew potatoes on them to feed their large families. It has been estimated that they ate from eight to twelve pounds of potatoes a day, for this food had become their staple diet. There was never enough land to go round however, and many of the population lived constantly on the brink of starvation. The landlords themselves were mostly Protestant Anglo-Irishmen. Often they lived in England and never visited their estates; but they drew large rents from them nevertheless. They were never short of tenants prepared to pay whatever sum was demanded in return for a potato-patch of land.

And yet this backward and miserable country shared in the nationalist enthusiasm of the nineteenth century. An Irish lawyer, Daniel O'Connell, was determined to bring back to Dublin the Irish Parliament which Pitt had taken away by the Act of Union. The Irish representatives at Westminster were Protestants, for the law still prohibited Catholics from becoming Members of Parliament. O'Connell aimed to remove this disability as well, so that when Ireland had her Parliament again it would be a Catholic Parliament, which would break the power of the clique of Anglo-Irish Protestants who surrounded the viceroy at Dublin Castle.

Pitt, as we have seen, had once proposed to grant 'Catholic Emancipation': but George III had refused. George IV was similarly determined not to yield, when Canning raised the matter. O'Connell now formed a Catholic Association and ran candidates for Parliament, even though their religion would bar them from taking a seat. He even persuaded the impoverished peasants to contribute a penny a month to a fighting fund, and in 1828 he won the by-election for County Clare. The excitement in Ireland at this event persuaded the Duke of Wellington that there would be a civil war unless the government yielded, and in 1829 he used his great authority in English affairs to persuade the Tories, the House of Lords and the king to emancipate Irish Catholics.

He had no intention of repealing the Act of Union however, and emancipation did not gain for Ireland O'Connell's dearest wish. This failure to obtain Home Rule was to cause more trouble in the future. For the present the importance of emancipation was its effect on English politics. The decision to pass the Catholic Relief Bill into law had divided and weakened the Tory party and given the Whigs the first glimpse of the path to power. In 1830, upon the death of George IV, a general election was held at which the reform of Parliament was the greatest issue involved. Even the unreformed electorate reflected the public demand for political change, and the Tories came back to office with only a slender majority over the Whigs. It proved too slender to cover up the divisions within the party, and Wellington was soon forced to resign by the defection of his own Tory supporters.

Amid great excitement, Lord Grey became the first Prime Minister of the reign of William IV, and the first Whig Prime Minister for almost half a century. The excitement over reform at home reflected a similar commotion all over Europe. In July the French king Charles X had been overthrown by politicians who demanded a constitutional monarchy. There had been risings in Belgium, Germany, Italy and Poland, all aimed at national independence and constitutional government. In England itself radicals talked in terms of a revolution, if changes were not made. The Whigs were ready to make them however, and before the year was out a committee of four had been appointed to plan a reform of the electoral system 'of such a scope and description as to satisfy all reasonable demands'.

On 1 March 1831 Russell introduced the Great Reform Bill in the House of Commons. The Bill proposed to abolish the rotten boroughs and halve the representation of many others. The vacant places in Parliament were to be given to Manchester, Birmingham and other big towns, and to the county constituences. So far as voting was concerned, the Whigs had no intention of giving power to the uncouth and violent masses of the people. They aimed only to enfranchise respectable and intelligent men 'who are most interested in preserving tranquillity, and who know best how to preserve it'. The new voters were to be responsible, middle-class people whose qualification was the amount they paid in rates or rents. In the county constituencies, substantial tenant-farmers were to join the ancient freeholders as voters.

So the Reform Bill did not aim to make England a modern democratic state, but merely to give the middle class a share of political power. It was not intended to be a revolutionary measure but a compromise by which the aristocracy would retain a great deal of their old authority. After all, the Whigs were aristocrats themselves, and they had no intention of surrendering political power now that they had just obtained it. They did not even propose to put an end to the open ballot and the means of influence and intimidation to which it gave rise.

Nevertheless the Reform Bill seemed an act of treason to the Tories. They regarded all demands for changes in the constitution as unreasonable by definition. It was not only that they feared the loss of their rotten boroughs, though naturally this threat had much to do with hardening their resistance. They also feared that the new electoral system would hand over the government of England at best to 'as many tyrants as there are shopkeepers' and at worst to radical politicians and the mob. Regarding themselves as the natural rulers of England, they were determined to prevent demagogues and republicans from usurping their power.

The Tories resisted the Reform Bill at every step. At its first reading, it was carried by one vote; at the second it was defeated. The Whigs resigned and there was another election. They won it, and used their increased majority to pass a second Bill through the House of Commons. This time the Tory House of Lords turned it down. The Whigs put forward a third Bill and demanded that the King should create enough new Whig peers to make sure of a majority for it. The King declined to create as many as they wanted. Grey resigned, and William IV called on Wellington to form another government. The Duke began to work out a plan for a less sweeping reform bill of his own.

All these events took place against a background of mounting excitement in the country. There was no doubt that the middle class, and working people too, were determined to have 'the Bill, the whole Bill, and nothing but the Bill'. When the Lords first rejected it there were demonstrations all over the country. At Bristol a mob sacked the Mansion House, attacked the Tory Member of Parliament and burned down the Bishop's Palace. When Wellington took over the government he had to put iron shutters over the windows of his London house to protect them from the missiles of the crowd. Respectable citizens refused to pay their taxes, and rich men withdrew their savings from the Bank of England in an effort to break the government's finances and 'stop the Duke'. The Tories, the Lords and the King, in fact, had come nearer to provoking a revolution than Tom Paine and the radicals had ever done. At length their leaders realized this. Wellington resigned and William and the Lords gave in. Grey and the Whigs came back, and the Bill became law in June 1832.

When the Great Reform Bill had been passed however, and when the ancient boroughs had lost their representation; when the manufacturing towns had gained their seats and the middle class their votes it transpired that, as the Whigs had intended, the power of the aristocracy had not been destroyed. Out of the next half-dozen Prime Ministers of England only one was not a nobleman; and he was Sir Robert Peel, who had been a leader of opposition to the Bill. On the other hand, the very next election produced a Parliament which contained William Cobbett, Robert Ashley and, for good measure, Jim Gully, a champion prizefighter, as well. The Duke was heard to say that he had never seen 'so many shocking bad hats in my life'. The new, radical members of Parliament demanded more reforms to follow the first one, and in the next three years they achieved their aim. So the Great Reform Bill did mark a change in England's form of government, and in the government's attitude to social problems. In both respects 1832 was the first year of modern English history.

These events have been described in detail because they were so important. There was at least one other however which occurred in 1830 and which also marked an epoch in English history. On 18 September of that year, before he resigned for the first time, the Duke of Wellington opened a railway from Liverpool to Manchester. It was chiefly intended for freight, but there was to be a regular passenger service along it as well. The trains were to be drawn all the way by steam locomotives. A competition had been held to choose the most efficient, and it had been won by the Rocket, an engine designed by George Stephenson, a mining engineer from north-eastern England. The Rocket was not the first, but it has become the most famous of locomotives; not least because it had no brakes, and knocked down and killed William Huskisson, though it rushed him to hospital at a speed of forty miles an hour.

The railways met with opposition just as the Reform Bill did; but equally they marked the beginning of a new age. They replaced canals and even roads as methods of transport for industry, and completed the first stage of the industrial revolution. In time they linked the manufacturing north to the agricultural south, and lessened the ignorance and suspicion of each other which these two areas had previously exhibited, and which lay behind the conflict over the Reform Bill. A few years after the first passenger railway had been opened a traveller from the south of England went from Manchester to Liverpool along it. He set down his impressions of the journey in his diary, and he was ready to admit that this aspect of progress, at least, was well worth the effort spent on it. 'Nothing can be more comfortable,' Charles Greville wrote, 'than the vehicle in which I was put, a sort of chariot with two places, and there was nothing disagreeable about it but the occasional breaths of stinking air which it is impossible to exclude altogether. The first sensation is a slight degree of nervousness and a feeling of being run away with, but a sense of security soon supervenes, and the velocity is delightful.'

CHAPTER 50

The Whigs and Reform

1832-1838

CHILD LABOUR, poverty, ignorance and disease: these were the threats to the 'greatest happiness of the greatest number' which the reformers set out to remove. In doing so they came up against many of the difficulties which earlier reformers had encountered. Parliament was now on their side, but there were still vested interests opposed to ending child labour or pulling down old houses. Religious bodies opposed the plan to create a new state system of education and working people as well as employers resisted the proposal to shorten their hours.

At least Parliament could examine the conditions for itself. In the next few years commissions of inquiry were appointed to look into everything about which reformers complained. It was a determined and sensible step towards making improvements and when the commissions reported their evidence was usually quite enough to spur the government into action. When Ashley obtained an inquiry into child labour in the mills, the stories which the commissioners brought back produced reform immediately. By an Act of Parliament of 1833 the labour of children under nine was prohibited throughout the textile industry, except in silk mills (here a vested interest intervened). Children of older years were limited to nine or twelve hours a day, depending on their ages. The most important feature of the act however was the appointment of inspectors to make sure that it was observed. Clearly the 'liberty-undermining Whigs', as their opponents called them, had made up their minds that where unhappiness and injustice were concerned, they would not hesitate to interfere with the freedom of industry. The new Factory Act, unlike the old one of 1819, was enforced.

When a commission explored education it found itself in a maze of private enterprises which left a great proportion of English people unlettered and untaught. There were public schools and grammar schools, dame schools and Sunday schools. There were Church of England schools, founded by a clergyman, Andrew Bell, 'for the education of the poor in the Principles of the Established Church', and Nonconformist schools which had originated with Joseph Lancaster, a Quaker. Some of England's school teachers were graduates of universities, while others were themselves barely able to read and write. In Bell's schools the teacher instructed older pupils in tomorrow's lessons and then these 'monitors' repeated what they had learned to younger children. The monitorial system was typical of 'education on the cheap'. Many people were still not convinced that education was necessary for the lower orders of society, and it is to the credit of the Church and the chapels that they had charity and sense enough to undertake the task at all. They were jealous of each other however, and both resented the suggestion that state schools should be erected. In the end, the reforming Parliament was content to make a grant of £20,000 to the voluntary societies, a small sum by comparison with the £50,000 granted in the same year for the renovation of the royal stables.

In the countryside Cobbett's England was still the same. In the autumn of 1830, after a bad harvest, labourers had become desperate at the want of work and food, and pulled down hedges, burned hayricks and smashed machines. The mysterious 'Captain Swing' had terrorized the farmers just as Ned Ludd had done the manufacturers twenty years before. The first action of Grey's Whig government had been to suppress this 'Labourers' Revolt' with all the brutality and severity which the ruling class had learned from its experience of popular disturbances since the days of the Luddites. But Grey was the first to contribute to a fund for the relief of distress, and the reformed Parliament appointed a commission, with a man named Edwin Chadwick as its secretary, to find out what could be done about poverty in the countryside and in the towns.

Chadwick was a bureaucrat, however. His chief concern was not with helping poor men, but with stopping the drain on the Poor Law funds. Indeed, he considered that charity was the cause of the trouble, for it encouraged labourers to be idle in the knowledge that they could always make up their wages by the parish dole. The Poor Law Commissioners persuaded Parliament to substitute 'indoor relief' for this kind of 'outdoor relief'; that is, to build 'workhouses' and rule that anyone who wanted help must come and live in them. Chadwick studied to make conditions in the workhouses no better than 'the situation of the independent labourer of the lowest class'. The food was accordingly scanty, the work dull, and families were separated from each other. Singing, whistling, even talking in some houses, were forbidden. If a man stepped outside the door he was regarded as 'discharged'. The doctrine of the Poor Law reformers was harsh; they believed that idleness was the cause of poverty, and that the way to prosperity was hard work. This was half true, of course; but Robert Owen had already demonstrated at New Lanark that people worked better in a freer and more comfortable environment; while Cobbett indignantly asked: 'What is a pauper? Only a very poor man.' He was not satisfied with the reform. Indeed, he was getting on no better with the Whigs than he had with the Tories. In the rural troubles of 1830 he had been arrested and tried as an agitator, but had defended himself with such vigour that in the end the authorities were glad to acquit him.

So much for the countryside. The reformers had encountered there the worst effects of the agricultural revolution, and their task of relief was far from easy. In the towns, on the other hand, they had to deal with the worst effects of the industrial revolution: half a century of careless planning, haphazard building and neglect. In the early 1830's epidemics of cholera swept through English towns with effects only less horrifying than those of the earlier plagues. The reforming government acted at once however. They sent doctors to Russia, where the epidemics had originated, to find out how that country was dealing with the problem. They encouraged towns to set up Boards of Health, and begin to tackle insanitary conditions.

This was the reformers' characteristic answer to the problems of the towns: to encourage them, like the paupers, to help themselves. In 1835 an Act of Parliament created in every borough a Municipal Corporation, with a mayor to be elected by aldermen, and councillors to be elected by the ratepayers. Great towns which

were not already boroughs could petition Parliament for the right
to become so and elect their own corporations. The new corporations were charged with the task of making whatever improvements
seemed necessary in their towns. The amount of improvement
effected thus depended on the town itself. In Manchester, for
example, 'improvement commissioners' had been at work for
years and they were already proud of their gas-works before 1835.
In 1838 the city became a borough and continued the work.
Cleaning up Manchester was a Herculean labour however; just
as Tories said that it would take 'a monastic institution' to
'Christianize' the city.

The Municipal Corporation, like others of its kind, and like
factory inspectors, the managers of voluntary schools, workhouse
governors and officers of health, faced great and challenging tasks
in nineteenth-century England. Just as their ancestors had done in
the previous century however, English people now showed that
they were ready to make an effort to improve the conditions of
their lives and put right old mistakes. The age of reform had only
just begun in the 1830's; and the first reforms were often half-
measures or less. Nevertheless they were reforms, and they marked
the determination of government and people to do all that lay in
their power to tackle problems as far as they understood them.

Reform did not end with social conditions. One group of radicals
was determined to reform the established Church. In 1833 an
Ecclesiastical Commission maintained that too much of the nation's
wealth was going into the pockets of deans and chapters and clergymen who never visited their benefice. Eventually Parliament
decided that 'pluralism' should stop: one clergyman, one parish
was to be the rule. The funds of deans and chapters would be used
in future to build more churches in the industrial towns. The old
system of tithes would be finally replaced by cash-rents, fixed by
the commissioners.

The Church was the last stronghold of old beliefs and Tory
principles and the changes were hotly opposed. The canons of
Manchester, for example, regarded the attempt to take away their
revenues as 'most unrighteous, unjust and sacrilegious'. 'If
Manufacturers like yourself,' wrote one of the canons to one of
the reformers, 'who have brought large bodies of operatives into

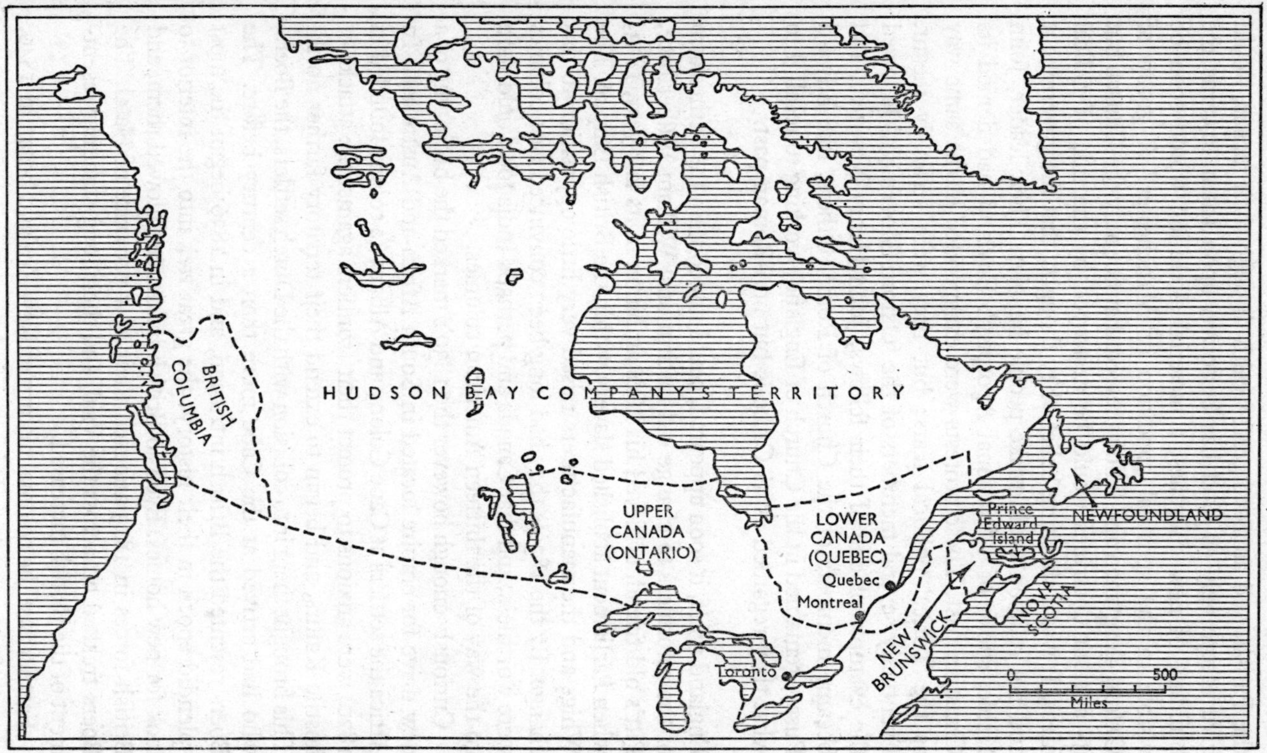

HUDSON BAY COMPANY'S TERRITORY

BRITISH COLUMBIA

UPPER CANADA (ONTARIO)

LOWER CANADA (QUEBEC)

Toronto

Montreal

Quebec

NEW BRUNSWICK

NOVA SCOTIA

Prince Edward Island

CAPE BRETON

NEWFOUNDLAND

500

0

Miles

CANADA BEFORE FEDERATION

the Parish, and amassed great wealth through their means, would give accordingly as God has bestowed upon them towards the building of new churches, a material alteration would soon be visible in the spiritual condition of Manchester.' A group of Oxford clergymen and fellows feared that not only the Church but its ancient doctrines would be destroyed by the tide of radical ideas. It was a shocking belief, they thought, that the government and not religion could make people happier. Their leader, John Keble, spoke of a 'National Apostasy'. England had denied its Christian past. These protests were exaggerated in the same way as the Tories' political fears; but they were seriously meant. Eventually several members of the 'Oxford Movement' followed the example of one of their fellows, John Henry Newman, and became members of the Church of Rome. Others, like Edward Pusey, remained in the Church of England, working to recall it to what they regarded as its Catholic but non-Roman past.

England itself, it soon appeared, could not contain the enthusiasm of the reformers to change old institutions. William Wilberforce, Pitt's old friend, achieved his life's ambition in its last year, 1833, when Parliament abolished slavery within the British Empire. The Whigs and the manufacturers raised very little opposition to this change. By the 1830's they had long been convinced that colonies were worthless, and that Canada and perhaps India too would soon go the way of the thirteen American colonies.

Curiously enough however the 1830's marked the beginning of a new drive for empire located in South Africa and Australasia. In Africa the settlers at Cape Colony and Albany (a colony founded in 1820) were anxious to protect their frontiers against the attacks of hostile Kaffirs, and began to extend their territory farther north. This brought them into collision with the Dutch settlers, the Boers, who had arrived at the Cape more than a century before. The Boers resented the British intrusion, and in 1836 began the most splendid epoch in their history: the great trek into the interior to look for new homes. Even so British influence followed them, and British forces in 1843 annexed their new province of Natal. The Boers trekked on across the Vaal, and their long-standing resentment of the British increased.

Farther east the colonial history of New Zealand began in 1840,

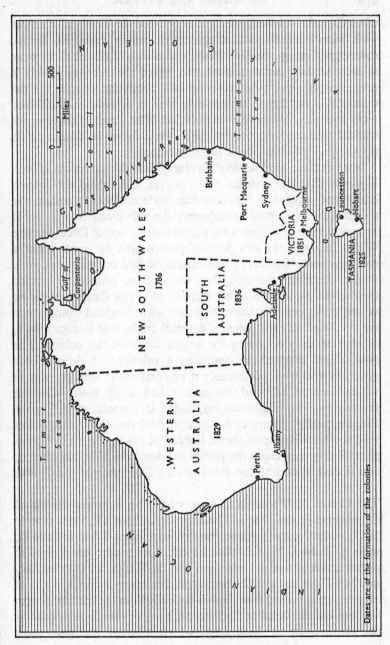

AUSTRALIA IN 1851

Dates are of the formation of the colonies

when Captain Hobson landed and negotiated the Treaty of Waitingi with Maori chieftains: an agreement which admitted British sovereignty but guaranteed Maori ownership of the land. In years to come trading companies came to regard the treaty as merely 'a praiseworthy device for amusing and pacifying savages for the moment'. They began to take over land in a number of dubious ways and the Maoris in turn rebelled. The English government worked constantly to protect the natives, however, admitting its responsibility for justice in the new colony.

In 1837 there were settlers' revolts against the governors of both Upper and Lower Canada. Many people in England shook their heads and prepared for Canadian independence whether the government attempted to suppress the rebellions or not. As it turned out the rebellions were suppressed by armed force; but the Whigs followed the new idea of government by sending out a commissioner, 'Radical Jack' Durham, to find out what had gone wrong. Durham reported that the settlers wanted to govern themselves; he suggested that Upper and Lower Canada should be united and given a Parliament of their own. England would retain the responsibility for defence, external trade, and foreign affairs, as well as for developing the empty lands of the colony. The government adopted his solution; a solution which was both generous and wise, particularly if we compare it with the way in which George III and Parliament had dealt with American grievances. The Canadians responded by remaining within the Empire, partly perhaps because they feared that the United States would otherwise engulf them. Instead of taking the risk of complete liberty they chose the partial freedom which Britain offered; and it developed into the freedom of a Dominion of the Crown.

The Crown itself seemed in danger of being forgotten among all the changes of the 1830's. The reign of William IV, from 1830 to 1837, was an age of reform, but the king himself had little to do with it. Indeed, he did what he could to restore the Tories to power and frustrate the reformers and the Whigs. In 1837 he died, not hated but not greatly respected. His niece Victoria, a girl of nineteen, was roused from bed in the early hours of the morning to become Queen: head of Parliament, head of the Church, head of the Empire. In the long reign which followed she gave these hallowed titles a new meaning and restored the crown to the affection and adulation of most English people. As a constitutional monarch Victoria became more popular than any English monarch had been for centuries. Already, in 1837, she was beginning to cast her own particular spell. 'She never ceases to be Queen,' wrote Greville, 'but is always the most obliging, unaffected Queen in the world.' In 1838 huge and cheerful crowds attended Victoria's coronation, and foreign observers, as they watched, were bound to admit that 'nothing could be seen like it in any other country'. In their continued respect for the Crown, just as in their reform of Parliament, their industrial achievements, their colonial policies and their work towards the greatest happiness of the greatest number at home, English people were setting an example of peaceful progress to the world.

When English people had to deal with foreigners they found it hard to conceal their feeling of superiority. No-one was worse at doing so than Henry Temple, Viscount Palmerston, the handsome, witty and outspoken Irish peer who was responsible for England's foreign policy for most of the period between 1830 and 1865. Palmerston made no secret of the fact that he regarded England after the Great Reform Act as the most civilized and best-governed country in the world. He was ready to offer criticism and advice to other powers whenever he thought the occasion demanded it. He always expected the worst from Russia and Austria, two empires whose rulers' power was absolute; and he regarded the French as a nuisance because of 'their vanity, which prompts them to be the first nation in the world'. Palmerston lost no chance to reduce the power of these three states. He continued the policy of Canning by giving encouragement to small states in their struggle for independence. In the 1830's England watched over the creation of an independent Belgian state, which Palmerston hoped would act as a check to the old ambition of France to dominate western Europe. In the 1840's he tried to thwart the French attempt to secure possession of the Spanish throne by marrying a French prince to a Spanish princess. Palmerston was full of sympathy for the Polish attempt to gain freedom from Russia, and for the Italian revolt of 1830 against Austria; but he could not use the chief English diplomatic weapon, the fleet, to intervene in these affairs.

Of all the reactionary powers in Europe at this time the Turks were the most cruel and oppressive, particularly towards their Christian subjects, the Slavs of the Balkans. The Sultans themselves took little part in governing their great empire, but passed luxurious lives in their palaces by the Bosphorus. Their emirs and pashas and their tax-gatherers were the effective tyrants, for their lives depended on meeting the royal demands for wealth. As we have seen, the Greeks, with English, Russian and French assistance, had won their freedom from this tyranny. The other Slav peoples were beginning to share the desire for liberty, while the Pasha of Egypt, Mehemet Ali, had ambitions to rule the whole Ottoman Empire himself, or at least to be master of Egypt and Syria. Palmerston did not support the rebels within the Turkish Empire however. He feared that if that empire collapsed then a huge Russian one would take its place. So he pursued a policy towards the 'Eastern Question' of trying to maintain the Ottoman Empire while making its system of government less brutal and inefficient. An English ambassador, Stratford Canning, spent many years in Constantinople trying to persuade the Turkish government to mend its ways, and Palmerston was even ready to work with Russia to prevent Mehemet Ali from seizing power for himself. He took care that the Russians should not gain by the intervention, however. By an international agreement – the Straits Convention – the powers agreed that the Bosphorus and the Black Sea should be closed to the fleet of any nation but the Turks. This treaty was to reveal its importance in the future.

Farther east Palmerston used British ships to protect and extend British interests. In 1840, when the Emperor of China refused to import more opium from British India and Burma, British gunboats and soldiers persuaded him to alter his decision in a war which lasted two years and ended in the acquisition of Hong Kong. The 'Opium War' is as good an example of Palmerston's attitude to other nations as any. It is little wonder that the Chinese, like the Russians, the Austrians and the French, resented Britain's attitude of superiority. Many foreign statesmen hoped for the downfall of '*ce terrible milord*'. He had his critics in England too, for even his colleagues were alarmed at his readiness to go to the brink of war to prove his point. The majority of his countrymen however regarded Palmerston as the living symbol of British superiority to other nations. They thoroughly approved of a policy which not only advanced trade and national interests but also championed the cause of liberty and representative government. In later years Palmerston was hotly attacked in Parliament for taking high-handed action against Greece and risking war with France in order to support the dubious claims of a Portuguese financier, who claimed British citizenship, for damages against the Greek government. He cleared himself in the public eye however by a speech in which he claimed that the object of his diplomacy had always been to ensure that 'a British subject, in whatever land he may be, shall feel confident that the watchful eye and strong arm of England will protect him against injustice and wrong'. After all, this was only doing in foreign affairs what the government had begun to do both in the colonies and at home.

CHAPTER 51

The Chartists and Sir Robert Peel

1838-1851

'THE HUNGRY FORTIES': this sinister phrase comes with a shock after the history of the previous years, which had been so full of achievement and promise. Nevertheless the years from 1837 to 1848 were hungry years for many people. Bad harvests were partly to blame, but so was a slump in industry. British industry seemed to have developed a certain rhythm, in which periods of prosperity and full employment alternated with years of depression when employers had to cut their losses, reduce wages and dismiss many of their workmen. Such a depression occurred in many industries from 1837 to 1842, and again from 1847 to 1848, and the bad harvests of these years made its effects worse.

The government, for all its good intentions, seemed powerless to affect these economic trends. The only consolation it could offer was the workhouse; and we have seen what life within those walls was like. In the north of England unemployed weavers stormed the 'Poor Law Bastilles' in these years, demanding a return to the old system of outdoor relief. The Whigs and the reformers grew discouraged by the failure of their efforts to improve conditions. They could not even balance the budget however, let alone bring back prosperity. For the time being, at least, no further reforms were attempted. 'Try to do no good, and you won't get into any scrapes,' was the opinion of Lord Melbourne, who had succeeded Grey as Whig Prime Minister.

So working men were left once again to help themselves if they could. In some occupations they tried to form Trades Unions, to bargain for higher wages and protect their jobs. Back in 1834 Robert Owen had tried to form a 'Grand National Trades Union' of all industries. His great project had failed however, and individual unions also found the going hard. The authorities and the employers frowned on them – in 1834 six labourers from Tolpuddle, in Dorset, were found guilty of 'administering illegal oaths' when they tried to form a farmworkers' union, and sentenced to transportation. The workmen in industry themselves did not co-operate willingly. Union funds were slender, and treasurers sometimes made off with them. A host of difficulties stood in the way of organized labour. Nevertheless this was the period when the foundations of the Trade Union movement were laid.

Various groups of radicals and working-class leaders in London, Birmingham and the north thought the Trades Unions a poor weapon. They reasoned that the best way of helping themselves was to get the vote, as the middle class had done in 1832. This was the idea behind the 'People's Charter' which was drawn up in 1838. The Charter put forward the demand for a vote for every adult male; for a secret ballot and an election every year; for the abolition of the property qualification for membership of Parliament; and for payment of members. These changes, the Chartists hoped, would result in bringing working men to Westminster, where they could look after their own interests. The Chartists believed that change could only come through Parliament; but they had lost faith in the Whigs and the middle class as reformers.

They found many excited supporters. At mass meetings in provincial towns and rallies held by flickering torchlight on northern moors thousands of people put their signatures to the Charter. An Irishman, Feargus O'Connor, published a Chartist newspaper, the *Northern Star*, and a Chartist Convention met, first in London and then in Birmingham. Its representatives brought the Charter before Parliament, in 1839.

Neither Whigs nor Tories, squires nor manufacturers had any sympathy with Chartism however. The petition to Parliament to consider the Charter received only forty-six votes and the Chartist demonstrations served only to revive the old fears of 'sedition' and rebellion. Soldiers were despatched to keep order in provincial towns where the Chartists had made sinister threats of a 'national holiday' or general strike, or even a 'sacred day' of revolution, if the Charter was rejected. But in the event there was no 'national holiday', for the government's precautions were well taken. Nor was there a rising, except in Newport, Monmouth-shire, where twenty-four men were killed in an affray with the militia. When matters reached the point of direct action the Chartist leaders hesitated, and after the failure of 1839 the movement broke up into separate units, some of which planned violence, but others of which went no farther than discussion and agitation. In 1842 however and again in 1848, both years of depression and hunger, the Charter came before Parliament again.

The middle class had its own answer to the depression: the introduction of free trade. The reformed Parliament had neither abolished the Corn Laws nor taken the taxes off manufactured goods and imports of raw materials. The 'Manchester School' of manufacturers maintained that these were the causes of distress. If the Corn Laws were repealed, they argued, bread would be more plentiful and cheaper. Wages, however small, would go farther when it came to buying food; and people would have more to spend on clothes and household goods as well. If the demand for these things increased, then factories and mills would soon be working full time again to meet it. There would be a job for everyone, and people would buy more bread as well as more of everything else they needed. The removal of taxes on manufac-tures would help, but cheap bread was the first essential. The manufacturers did not stress the other conclusion to the argument: that they would not have to pay higher wages if prices fell. They concentrated on attacking the Corn Laws, and in 1839 formed the Anti-Corn Law League to put forward their demand. The League, unlike the Trades Unions, had copious funds. Unlike the Chartists, its members were respectable. John Bright and Richard Cobden, the north-country businessmen who were its leaders, were eloquent and influential men. The League campaigned all over the country, and in Parliament as well, where Cobden sat as Member for Stockport.

The Chartists did not like the League. They distrusted it as a selfish instrument of their employers. They had no votes however, so their opposition counted for little. The Tory squires did not like it for its political programme; and they had influence. In 1841 in fact the Tories won a general election against the disillusioned Whigs and came back to power determined to maintain the Corn

Laws. Sir Robert Peel, that tall fair-haired northcountryman whose icy manner and vaguely Lancastrian accent jarred on the Tories of the countryside, was now Prime Minister. He had a second chance to prove his ability in tackling hunger and discontent. His first measure had nothing to do with the Corn Laws or wages however. It was directed at conditions in the coal mines, which had been described in the report of a commission of inquiry, published in 1840.

The commission's report is among the most terrible documents in English history, recording as it does the labour of little children underground for twelve hours or more a day. The commissioners found 'a beautiful girl, only six years old, carrying half a hundredweight of coals, and regularly making with this load fourteen long and toilsome journeys a day'. Another little girl, of eight, told the commissioners: 'I go at four and sometimes half past three in the morning, and come out at five and half past. I never go to sleep. Sometimes I sing when I've a light, but not in the dark; I dare not sing then.'

Even after Parliament had heard the commissioners' report there was still some opposition to making changes in the mines, but Peel did not listen to it. He may have seemed 'an iceberg' to his ministerial colleagues, but he showed that his attitude to social problems was now more enlightened and determined than that of the Whigs. Melbourne had done nothing about the report, but Peel acted on it. The Mines Act of 1842 prohibited the work of women and children in the mines, and once again appointed inspectors to enforce the law. In 1844 another Factory Act limited the hours of children to six and a half each a day, and those of women to twelve. While trade was bad however Parliament could not be brought to agree to a ten-hour day for every man and woman in industry. The ten-hour day which was Ashley's great objective did not become law until 1847.

The Factory and Mines Acts were great reforms; but what had Peel done about hunger and free trade? Cobden was on his feet in Parliament continually to put his case, and gradually Peel was convinced by his logic. Year by year his budgets reduced the taxes on trade and brought down the prices English people had to pay for the necessities of life. To offset the budget deficit Peel reintroduced the income-tax. Finally, in 1846, he repealed the Corn

Laws. 1845 had been another year of bad harvests, particularly so in Ireland, where steady rain rotted the potato crop in the ground. Peel's move towards free trade in corn and cheaper bread was intended to help Ireland first. 'Rotten potatoes have done it', maintained Wellington. 'They have put Peel in his damned fright!' He used his authority to rally the Tory party behind repeal, but the Tory squires were sure that Peel had betrayed them. The repeal of the Corn Laws revealed more clearly even than the Reform Act had done that their domination of English politics was at an end. They took revenge on Peel by voting against him on a trivial motion and forcing his resignation. He was never in power again, and died in 1850, but he had made his mark as an outstandingly intelligent, conscientious and courageous politician, ready to examine difficult problems and put the solutions into effect regardless of opposition and unpopularity. His character and his career did credit to the age in which he lived. In the long run however cheap corn did not save Ireland from poverty. The peasants remained as they always had been on the brink of starvation, and more and more of them each year emigrated to America. There they blamed the rule of the English Parliament for all the woes of Ireland, even though it had just tried to help them. The 'Fenian Brotherhood' raised funds and made plans for rebellion, and talked of eventual freedom from the 'Saxon yoke'. In 1848 there was a rebellion in Ireland and it was suppressed by brutal methods which added more resentment to the mounting score.

In England, 1848 was the year of the third Chartist petition, which was launched at a monster rally in Hyde Park and carried so many signatures that it had to be taken to Westminster in a fleet of hansom cabs. When it arrived it was rejected as before however. In the next few years the Chartist agitation died away. Chartism had always been a political movement based on hunger, and hunger was on the decrease for almost twenty years after 1848. From then on business recovered and factories returned to work. Farming too, despite the gloomy predictions of the Tories, entered a golden age of productivity. The Manchester School claimed all these improvements as triumphs for free trade; but there were probably other reasons behind the recovery, connected with currency and movements in international trade.

Whatever the causes of recovery, there is no doubt that the

1840's ended better than they began. A German writer, Freidrich Engels, who visited England at the beginning of the period, was so enraged by the poverty and affluence which he saw existing side by side that he forecast a revolution. 'The war of the poor against the rich,' wrote Engels, 'will be the most bloodthirsty the world has ever seen.' But there was no revolution in England and during the 1850's every class of the population shared in the mounting prosperity of the country; though of course the shares were not equal.

The nearest thing to the 'proletarian' or working-class revolution which Engels predicted occurred in France in 1848, when workers and middle class both rebelled against the last of the Bourbons, Louis Philippe. There were revolutions in Austria, Hungary, Italy and Germany too: all aimed at breaking the power of the Austrian Empire, and securing representative governments. These risings came very near to success before they were suppressed with the usual brutality. In Hungary Russian troops had to be called in to restore the Austrian government. Throughout these years of revolution Palmerston was in his element, criticizing the old governments of France, Austria and Russia and giving encouragement and advice to the rebels. When the revolutions failed England became a refuge for exiles. Louis Kossuth, the Hungarian patriot, was a guest at Palmerston's own home.

By comparison with European events, the third Chartist demonstration was nothing and Ireland was easily forgotten. The revolutions served only to confirm how different England was from Europe. 'In the midst of the roar of the revolutionary waters that are deluging the whole earth,' wrote Greville, 'it is grand to see how we stand erect and unscathed. It is the finest tribute that ever has been paid to our constitution, the greatest test that ever has been applied to it.' England remained at peace, and returned to prosperity.

The German Prince Albert of Saxe-Coburg-Gotha, who married Queen Victoria in 1840, was so impressed by the material achievements of his new countrymen that he suggested that they might compare these publicly with those of the rest of the world. He was one of the promoters of a scheme for a 'Great Exhibition of the Works and Industries of All Nations' which took place in 1851. On a cool spring morning in that year the Queen drove through London to Hyde Park to open it. The Exhibition was housed in the Crystal Palace, a huge iron structure covered by nine hundred thousand square feet of glass. On show inside were manufactured goods and raw materials, machines, furniture and sculpture gathered from every corner of the Empire and the world. Six million people came to visit this great monument of the Victorian age. For many of them, we may guess, the greatest thrill was the journey by rail, whether they came in the covered coaches of the First and Second Class, or in the open and weather-beaten trucks of the Third. Some came from the south-west along the broad-gauge line which Isambard Kingdom Brunel had built; others came on the narrower gauge of the north, but all lines led to London.

The railways which now covered England, like the Crystal Palace itself, marked the end of the age of iron and steam, the first phase of the industrial revolution. They were the clearest evidence that the last fifty years or more had been years of progress. Whether the England of 1851 was compared with Europe or with the England of ten, twenty or a hundred years before, the evidence of progress could not be denied. The Victorians were proud of these achievements, material, social and political. They firmly believed that there were still better times to come. In the *History of England* which he wrote at this time, Thomas Babington Macaulay concluded that 'the history of our country during the last hundred and sixty years is eminently the history of physical, of moral and of intellectual improvement'; and he forecast a future age when 'numerous comforts and luxuries which are now unknown, or confined to a few, may be within the reach of every diligent and thrifty working man'.

CHAPTER 52

Palmerston; the Crimean War; Victorian England

1851-1865

THE GREAT EXHIBITION was designed to show what years of peace and hard work could achieve. The Prince Consort hoped that it would set an example to the nations of the world, and convince them that wars and revolutions were a waste of time and energy. Within three years however England and the other European powers were engaged in an expensive and slow-moving war which proved to be one of the most pointless ever fought.

The war began over a religious dispute in the Middle East: who had the right to look after the Holy Manger and the Church of the Nativity at Bethlehem – the monks of the Roman Catholic Church or those of the Eastern Orthodox? The decision lay with the Turkish Sultan, for Bethlehem, like the rest of Palestine, lay within the Ottoman Empire. The affair became an international trial of strength however, for it was Louis Napoleon, now the second Emperor of the French, who had revived the western claim, which had lapsed for many years; while the patron of the eastern church was the Tsar Nicholas of Russia. When the Sultan decided in favour of the Latin monks the Tsar refused to surrender the right and put forward a further claim to protect all the Christian subjects of the Sultan, from Palestine to the Danube. Napoleon prompted the Sultan to refuse. Since both the Tsar and the Emperor were determined not to yield, it seemed likely that war would begin at any moment.

Palmerston was not in charge of foreign affairs at the time but he was a member of Lord Aberdeen's cabinet, which had to decide whether to intervene. In practice England had intervened already,

489

since Stratford Canning had been instrumental in persuading the Sultan to resist the Tsar's demands to interfere in his affairs. It was still uncertain, however, whether England would go to war over these distant squabbles, particularly if she had to work with the unstable and ambitious Emperor of France.

In the end, the universal suspicion of Russia decided the issue. Everyone in western Europe suspected that behind his pious professions the Tsar was searching for an excuse to destroy the Turkish Empire and extend his own to the warm-water port of Constantinople and the shores of the Mediterranean. 'Men dwelling amidst the snows of Russia,' said a contemporary English writer, describing the war, 'are driven by their very nature to grow covetous when they hear of happier lands where all the year round there are roses and long sunny days.'[1] English people still thought of the Russians as the first Napoleon had done, as untrustworthy and dangerous barbarians. And so, when Russian troops invaded the outlying provinces of the Turkish Empire and Russian ships entered the Black Sea in defiance of the Straits Convention and destroyed the Turkish fleet, England combined her forces with those of France to go to the aid of Turkey. Napoleon III had a vague and ambitious scheme in mind to attack Russia through Poland and liberate the Poles from their Russian masters on the way, but England insisted on a more limited objective. It was decided to attack the Russian naval base at Sevastopol, in the Crimea; and a combined English and French fleet, made up of both sail and steamships, set out with an army on board.

The Crimea was a hilly country, cut across by rivers and steep ravines; the roads were poor or non-existent. It was a land much easier to defend than to invade. The climate, moreover, produced extremes of heat and cold; and the allied armies were prepared for neither. Their smart uniforms proved too hot and too tight in the summer and too thin in the winter. But this disadvantage was only one of many. The truth was that the expedition was hastily and badly planned. The British army, which had not seen action since Waterloo, went out without sufficient food, ammunition, medical supplies or even tents. The men were badly

[1] Alexander Kinglake: *History of the Invasion of the Crimea.*

trained for living off the country. The officers had only the vaguest idea of the geography of the war zone. The commander-in-chief, Lord Raglan, was another veteran of Waterloo who sometimes embarrassed his allies by referring to the enemy as 'the French'. With all these military handicaps however the army decided to disembark some distance to the north of Sevastopol and approach it by land rather than mount a naval attack.

The allies took two years to capture Sevastopol. Huge losses were sustained in the dreadful battles of the Alma, Inkerman and Balaclava; and the Crimean winters accounted for many more. The battle of Balaclava was in its way the climax of this war of mistakes, for it saw the most fatal and courageous blunder of all in the charge of the six hundred men of the Light Brigade straight at the Russian guns. The charge of the Light Brigade which Lord Tennyson's poem made famous in military history, was set in motion by the misunderstanding and stubbornness of England's well-born commanders in the field.

In England the decision to fight the Russians had been twice as popular as the Great Exhibition. Only the Manchester School, intent on international peace and free trade, regarded the war as an unjustified and expensive adventure. John Bright called it 'a crime', and Cobden was disgusted to see people 'of all classes – and especially those called middle and respectable, in a frenzy of patriotic belligerence'. No-one listened to these comments at the time; but when the war began to go badly and William Russell, the correspondent of *The Times*, sent back reports of the state of the army and the conduct of the campaign, there was a storm of indignation against the commanders and the government. Aberdeen resigned and Palmerston was called to power. Another result of the *Times* despatches, which was more important so far as the soldiers were concerned, was the departure of Florence Nightingale for the military hospital at Scutari, to bring comfort to the wounded and terror to the officers and orderlies.

As soon as Palmerston took over the government, in February 1855, frustration in the Crimea turned into victory. Sevastopol fell within a few months. The chief reasons for this success were the steady bombardment of the city by allied guns and the final gallant assault by the French; but Palmerston was the victor in English eyes. He wanted to go on fighting, but the other powers were more than ready for peace and the Crimean war ended with the Treaty of Paris in 1856. The Russians promised to keep out of the Black Sea and the Turkish Empire; the Turks to reform their government. Neither side made any lasting attempt to keep these promises however and the 'Eastern Question' continued to vex international relations. The most important result of the war, so far as England was concerned, might have been the reform of the army; but although the commission of inquiry which had been set up as the result of Russell's reports expressed the hope 'that every British army may in future display the valour which this noble army has displayed, and that none hereafter be exposed to such sufferings', nothing was done. The soldiers were still flogged for breaches of discipline, and their officers still gained the right to lead them by purchasing their commissions. The Crimean war did not change the army; and the calamities which it produced did not lessen the aggressive self-confidence which had led English people to demand war in the first place. In 1857 Palmerston ordered the bombardment of Canton as a reprisal against the Chinese for boarding a smuggling vessel which flew the British ensign, and won a general election on the strength of doing so.

In 1857 British soldiers were in action again, this time in India. Although a hundred years had passed since the battle of Plassey and the establishment of the Indian Empire, fighting in the subcontinent had never ceased. British troops and loyal sepoys had fought on the scorched plains of central India against the Mahrattas, the Gurkhas and the Sikhs, and in the humid jungle of the Irrawaddy against the kings of Burma. By 1857 the territories which the East India Company shared with the Crown reached across the subcontinent from Peshawar to Rangoon. Along with these conquests went a steady process of 'westernization' which undermined the ancient caste system of Hindu society and the power of the Indian princes. Reforming governors, particularly Lord Bentinck and Lord Dalhousie, set out to bring the civilization of which England was so proud to India. They built roads, canals and harbours and opened coal and iron mines. Education in English was introduced and barbarous religious practices which derived from India's past were suppressed. Dalhousie was so anxious to extend British rule in Indian interests that he developed the policy of annexing to the Crown independent states whose rulers seemed corrupt or inefficient, or lacked direct heirs to succeed them. In 1856 he left for England, and all his achievements were left to depend on the loyalty of the Indians to their British masters and the force of forty thousand British troops. In 1857 the Indian garrisons of central India mutinied and murdered their British officers.

The Indian Mutiny was the last attempt of disinherited princes and disgruntled priests to regain the power they had lost. They had used religious prejudice to foment the mutiny and now installed the old Mogul prince, Bahadur Shah, in the ancient capital of Delhi. Throughout the next few months British authority hung in the balance, while Indian rebels executed frightful atrocities in the cities which they captured. Outside central India however the princes and the people did not rise, and in a month or two reinforcements from Calcutta and the Punjab recaptured the rebel cities. The mutiny was soon over, though British commanders took a harsh revenge on the rebels and mutually bitter memories left a cloud over the relations of the two races in years to come. The British government now took a step long overdue by transferring political power completely from the Company to the Crown. The policy of westernization continued, and no further resistance to British power occurred until the nationalist movement of the twentieth century associated with the name of Mahatma Gandhi.

In England the years after 1851 were uneventful – one reason perhaps why the Crimean War provoked such excitement in the country. The years of upheaval and rapid change in home affairs were over and a calm prevailed which had not existed since the eighteenth century. But there was no mistaking the great material changes which had taken place since then. The sight of new agricultural machinery in the fields and the flaring passage of trains across the countryside were both reminders of the progress of the last half-century, while over the towns a constant pall of smoke bore witness to the growth of industry. A second phase of the industrial revolution was beginning now, based on Henry Bessemer's process which made possible the mass production of steel and Michael Faraday's earlier discoveries of electrical power. Britain was due to be left behind by both Germany and the United States in this phase of industrial growth, but the social effects of change were less severe than they had been previously. In some factories wretched conditions still prevailed but wages and living standards were constantly improving. Moreover, Lancashire people could now get away to Blackpool at the week-end: the fare from Manchester was one and sixpence return – a shilling for ladies. For people of the middle class these mid-Victorian years were a great age of prosperity and solid comfort. It was an age of big families, over-furnished rooms and regular Sunday church-going. The Queen and her husband set the pattern of family life in their homes at Windsor Castle, Osborne and Balmoral, ruling their own large family religiously and strictly.

Against this background of progress and hard work the sharp political struggles of earlier years were not repeated. Palmerston was Prime Minister from 1855, and he was not the man to press for reforms. Nor was the Tory leader, Lord Derby, a scholarly man and a great debater, but much happier at his country house among his friends and his books than in Parliament. In these years the old party divisions of Whig and Tory were dying out. The Whigs were now under the control of the Manchester School, who preferred to call themselves 'Liberals' to signify their belief in free trade. Tory, on the other hand, was giving way to 'Conservative' as a party name.

The great questions of the time were not those raised by politicians but those provoked by writers. In 1859 Charles Darwin published the *Origin of Species*, a long and scientific treatise which hinted at a shocking theory: that man and all the other species of life had evolved from a common source – that there were similarities in fact between human beings and apes! As Darwin put it in a later work: 'Man, with all his noble qualities, still bears in his bodily frame the indelible stamp of his lowly origin'. The theory of evolution seemed to be not only a challenge to the biblical story of creation but an insult to all the achievements of the Victorian age. In the hands of scientists and churchmen the argument became a bitter battle of words which damaged the cause of religion and of science for a century.

Other books received a better welcome. *Self Help*, by Samuel Smiles, insisted that there was nothing which a man could not achieve if he lived soberly and thriftily and worked hard. The theory that only the idle and the wicked did not prosper was very popular, though curiously enough it was very similar to Darwin's theory that in life's jungle only the fittest could survive. The essay *On Liberty* by John Stuart Mill insisted that the individual must be left as free as possible to find happiness in his own way. These books contain the gist of Victorian beliefs: the freedom of the individual is sacred, and carries with it the responsibility to make one's own way through life. Charles Dickens's novels, on the other hand, with their wealth of sympathy for the unwanted and the cruelly treated, reminded the Victorians that individual selfishness could cause great suffering, particularly to the young; and Mill himself insisted that 'it would be a great misunderstanding of this doctrine, to suppose that it is one of selfish indifference, which pretends that human beings have no business with each other's conduct in life, and that they should not concern themselves about the well-doing or well-being of one another, unless their own interest is involved. Instead of any diminution, there is need of a great increase of disinterested exertion to promote the good of others.'

Victorian liberalism, at its best, was a compound of respect for the individual and concern on the part of society to make his life worth living; and the fact that England's ruling classes, in their better moments, pursued this dual aim of government, distinguishes the history of Victorian England from that of other countries and gives it its claim to greatness. Another writer of the time, however, Karl Marx, a German who wrote in England, maintained that the prosperity such as England's rulers enjoyed was based on exploitation and injustice. Marxist ideas were destined to exercise a revolutionary influence on the European mind; but England continued to follow the path of Mill, and the example it gave to the world was not a bad one.

While the people of England were working and reading and getting and spending, great events were taking place in the world outside. The Italians were making a final successful bid for independence and unity, which English diplomacy supported. The United States were torn by civil war. In this conflict between the Southern slave-owners and the industrial North, England was tempted to intervene; but the question was: on which side to fight? Should this country support freedom or property? In the end England settled for making battleships for the South. It was a characteristic contribution to world events by the 'workshop of the world'. In politics however England had less influence. When Otto von Bismarck, the Minister-President of Prussia, began his programme for the unification of Germany under Prussian domination by taking Schleswig-Holstein from Denmark, Palmerston was powerless to intervene.

The rise of Germany as an ambitious industrial state was to provide a challenge to England's position as the 'workshop of the world' in years to come, and so was the development of the United States. But nothing had happened yet to shake English peoples' confidence in their world position. It was difficult to believe that anything was wrong while trade and agriculture were booming and Palmerston was still Prime Minister. In 1865 he was in his eighty-first year, still vigorous and still the master of his country. 'Die, my dear Doctor?' he said to his physician. 'That is the last thing I shall do.' These were his last words, however, or so we are told; and upon Palmerston's death his country entered a new age of economic change and political debate, while Europe shortly entered a new era of power politics in which England had to manoeuvre skilfully to find a place.

CHAPTER 53

Gladstone and Liberalism

1865-1874

IN THE QUIET YEARS when Palmerston ruled England, elections and football matches provided the people's excitement. The Football Association was formed in 1863, and tried to draw up a single code of rules for the game which hundreds now played and watched on Saturday afternoons. For elections however there were no rules. There was still no secret ballot and election day was sometimes rowdy and bibulous on a bigger scale than before. The candidates still competed for the voters' favour with food and drink and entertainment. Charles Dickens described the scene in *Pickwick Papers*.

The working class, for the most part, did not pay enough in rates or rent to qualify for the vote. Their part in election day was still confined to adding to the general riot and excitement. By now however less and less of them made up the 'impulsive, unreflecting, violent' mob which England's rulers had always feared. With full employment, rising wages and higher living standards most of the working class were hard-working, sensible people. In Lancashire they showed their qualities during the American Civil War, when supplies of raw cotton were cut off for two or three years and many mills had to close. There were no riots and demonstrations during the cotton famine and the Liberal leaders were impressed by the steady behaviour of the cotton operatives. When the famine was over however these people along with radical leaders all over the country took up the Chartists' old demand for a vote for every man. The demand had never been forgotten, but the politicians had not pressed it in recent years. Palmerston had not favoured the idea and that had been sufficient to suppress it. But now a new industrial depression increased the determination of the common people to make their voices heard in Parliament; and two rival political leaders began to look for the opportunity to give them what they asked.

The first of these was the new leader of the Whigs and Liberals, William Gladstone; the second Benjamin Disraeli, who led the Tories or Conservatives in the House of Commons. Gladstone was a stern and serious-minded man who had started his political career as a Tory but changed his party. For the last few years of Palmerston's administration he had been Chancellor of the Exchequer. During his career his conscience had driven him to accept the need for one great reform after another; and when he had convinced himself that a reform was right and necessary he regarded anyone who opposed him as frivolous and wicked. Both his opponents and his colleagues were sometimes exasperated by his sudden conversions, and his righteous and rather obscure way of expressing them. 'I do not object to Gladstone's always having the ace of trumps up his sleeve,' said Henry Labouchere, 'but only to his pretence that God has put it there.' The ace which Gladstone now produced was the idea of giving the vote to the working class. He believed that it was a political right; or as he put it, 'that every man who is not presumably incapacitated by some consideration of personal unfitness or of political danger, is morally entitled to come within the pale of the constitution'.

Disraeli was the opposite of Gladstone in character. While the Liberal leader was tall and rugged in appearance the Conservative was stooping and sallow. He was Jewish by birth though he had been baptized as a Christian at an early age. He dressed colourfully in purple waistcoats, dark blue coats with light blue trousers and black stockings with red stripes. He wore gloves and rings and carefully arranged his hair in a drooping curl over his forehead. In short he was flashy in appearance; but his thoughts and his feelings lay hidden behind an inscrutable expression. His mysterious air, his clothes and his race led many English people to distrust him, and we may well ask how such a man had succeeded in becoming leader of the party of Church and tradition, whose members suspected everything which was new or un-English.

The answer is that he had done so by the force and attraction of his ideas. He had been a novelist in his earlier years and in his novels denounced the dreadful conditions of the 'hungry forties'. He did not blame the Corn Laws for them however. On the contrary, he held the manufacturers responsible for creating the hunger, the poverty and the slums. The middle class, said Disraeli, were 'a miserable minority', who had seized power 'in the specious name of the people' and used it for their own selfish ends, causing misery for the people as a result. 'The proper leaders of the people,' he wrote, 'are the gentlemen of England. If they are not the leaders of the people, I do not see why there should be gentlemen.' His words put heart into the Tories in the years when the Corn Laws were repealed and the middle class was triumphant. Disraeli convinced them that there was still a place for them in English politics if only they would show themselves determined to build better houses and to eliminate hunger and poverty. He was convinced that the working class, if they had the chance, would vote for the Tories, their best friends and natural leaders. So he too wanted to give the working man the vote.

Not surprisingly, Disraeli and Gladstone did not get on together. Their characters grated on each other. Disraeli thought Gladstone 'a sophistical rhetorician, intoxicated with the exuberance of his own verbosity'. Disraeli, said Gladstone, 'set his teeth on edge'. And then there was political rivalry. They shared the same ambition for power and the same concern for the future of their country. And so for ten years they sparred with each other across the House of Commons and succeeded each other in power. The new political parties gathered around them and the whole country took sides for one or the other. Their political debates were followed more keenly than football matches were then or are now; and from 1865–7 the question was: who would give the common man the vote?

Gladstone and Russell, the Liberal leaders, were the first to propose a new reform of the electoral system, but their own supporters defeated them in Parliament. When the Conservatives succeeded them Disraeli met the same opposition among his supporters. He himself did not intend to give the vote to everyone, but only to people who had earned the privilege by showing evidence of 'virtue, prudence, intelligence and frugality'. He suggested that responsible householders in town and country should be enfranchised. To make sure that their votes did not swamp those of the middle class, Disraeli proposed that university graduates, doctors, lawyers or those who held shares in government funds or paid a lot of income tax, should have two votes each. Gladstone had no time for this 'fancy franchise'. So far as he was concerned the vote was a right not a privilege, and the principle should be one man, one vote. Disraeli was stung by his criticism and finally gave one vote to every householder in the towns and most of the tenant farmers in the villages. More Parliamentary seats were redistributed to increase the representation of the great towns and London.

The second great Reform Act in English history, which passed through Parliament in 1867, was another big step towards making this country a democracy. But it was a step in the dark: no-one was quite sure how the new electorate would behave or what demands it would make on the politicians. The politicians received their first lesson in these mysteries of democracy in the general election of 1868. The Conservatives who had introduced the reform were defeated, while even Gladstone, who had made up Disraeli's mind for him, was rejected by the weavers of South Lancashire.

He found another seat however, for influence could still be used in some constituencies, and he became Prime Minister. When the news reached him he was felling trees at his country house. He always had plenty of energy; and as Prime Minister he needed it. For the problems which faced him now were many and various, and far from easy to solve. First of all he had to face the constant challenge of Disraeli, frustrated and angry at the electors' refusal to fulfil their part of his bargain with them. Then Gladstone had to keep his own party together and try to please the aristocratic Whigs, the free traders and the radical social reformers at the same time. He had to steer a course through complicated foreign affairs, while at home he was expected to save money and reduce taxes. As it happened however none of these problems seemed as important to Gladstone as a new one which had taken possession of his mind. When he received the message in the woods he leaned on his axe and said, after a pause, 'My mission is to pacify Ireland'.

Gladstone had chosen the most difficult problem of all. The Irish question, as we have seen, was a tangle of religious grievances, hunger and the demand for an Irish Parliament. It was a problem which grew more tangled with every bad harvest and every suppressed rebellion. The peasants desperately wanted land for themselves, just a few acres to support their families. The Fenians wanted political freedom, and they were resorting to every kind of violence in order to get it. They had begun a campaign of terrorism against unpopular landlords in Ireland, while their fellows in America had tried to provoke a war between England and the United States in 1866 by making a raid across the Canadian frontier. In Manchester in 1867 Fenians had raided a police van to rescue two men who had been arrested, and killed a policeman in the struggle. These acts of violence were more than enough to turn away any English sympathies for the cause of 'Home Rule'.

In any case, Gladstone did not have Home Rule in mind as the solution for Ireland's problems. He decided to deal with the religious grievance and the land question first. In 1869 the Anglican Church of Ireland was disestablished; that is to say, its bishops lost their places in the House of Lords and, much more important, the Irish ceased to pay tithes to a Church to which four out of five of them did not belong. Most of the Church revenues were diverted to helping people in need. The Irish Land Act of 1870 guaranteed the peasants compensation if their landlords evicted them for any reason except not paying the rent. The government undertook to lend them money to buy the land for themselves, if the landlord was willing to sell. But that was the root of the trouble of course. Most landlords did not want to sell. The best of them wanted to enclose the land and carry out an agricultural revolution like the one which had taken place in England. The worst of them wanted to continue to live off the rents, and after the Land Act put them up still further, confident that they could always find tenants among Ireland's overcrowded population. Gladstone's measures did not alter this situation. The fact was that Ireland could never support its people unless the fields were enclosed; and that would cause more misery in the short run. So the peasants continued to emigrate, the Fenians to terrorize the landlords, and Gladstone and the Liberals turned their attention back to England, hoping that people there would be more grateful for their efforts to help them.

As we have seen, many of the Liberals had not approved of giving working people the vote. Now that they had it however, these politicians had to make the best of it and look after the new voters' interests. 'We must educate our masters,' one Liberal minister ruefully remarked, and it was to education that the Liberals turned first. In 1870 the government undertook to build schools wherever the voluntary societies had not provided them. The Liberal intention was to try to make sure that people could read and understand enough at least to know what politics were about. To ensure that they would vote according to their own mind and not under the influence of employers, landlords, thugs or anyone else, the Liberals introduced the secret ballot at last in 1872. In a further bid to meet the demands and protect the rights of the working class the government declared that Trade Unions were completely legal, with power to protect their funds and withhold their labour. But what they gave with one hand the Liberals took away with the other, for the strikers were forbidden to picket the factory gates in order to discourage other people from going to work. This was typical of Liberal thought. They wanted to help people to help themselves, by teaching them to read and write, and by giving them the vote and the right to strike; but they were determined to prevent them from interfering with the liberty of others. It was a reasonable and in many ways an admirable purpose for a government to pursue: but it cost the Liberals votes in the long run.

The Liberals wanted to do their job well – not only conscientiously but economically and efficiently. Gladstone always reduced taxes where he could, and cut down government spending. His government reformed the civil service and the army, trying to ensure that men earned their places in both by merit and not by purchase and influence. These measures were expected to appeal to hard-headed and thrifty middle-class people, but once again they made the Liberals many enemies.

The fact was that the Liberals were interfering with too many privileges and prejudices. They had upset many Englishmen by introducing the secret ballot, which was described as 'a mask to an honest face'. They had offended Church people by disestablishing the Church of Ireland, and Nonconformists by promising to go on supporting schools where Church doctrines and the Catechism were taught. They had annoyed employers by making Trades Unions legal, and Trades Unions by forbidding picketing, without which no strike could hope to succeed. They had offended civil servants by reorganizing the civil service on efficient but revolutionary lines, and gentlemen who wanted to be army officers by forbidding them to purchase their commissions. And Gladstone had infuriated every English patriot who remembered Palmerston by paying over £3,000,000 to the United States as compensation for damages which a Confederate ship, the *Alabama*, had inflicted upon Northern shipping during the Civil War. The *Alabama* had been built in a British shipyard and Gladstone accepted responsibility for her exploits. Once again his action was scrupulously just; but it was a cruel blow to English pride.

Of all the Liberal measures however perhaps the most unpopular was the Licensing Act of 1872. The Act not only forbade landlords to put salt in their customers' beer but also closed down a number of public houses and limited the hours of opening in others. Now the Englishman's right to drink what he liked where he liked at whatever time he chose to do so was one of his most precious liberties. His readiness to pursue happiness in this way had been proverbial for over a century. Such freedom meant drunkenness of course; and drunkenness often meant poverty, cruelty and crime. There is no doubt that many people, mostly Nonconformist and middle class, approved of the Licensing Act. Many others did not however. The question of freedom was the great issue to them. A much-respected bishop declared that he would rather see 'England free than England sober'.

So when, in 1874, the Liberals faced the people at a general election, they encountered a great deal of resentment. Although every one of their reforms was justified and most of them proved invaluable in their long-term effects they had interfered with liberty and upset privilege and prejudice too quickly and too much for the people of their time. The government's actions over the last six years had brought to the surface the latent tensions of Victorian liberalism: the conflicts between the freedom of the individual and the claims of society to protect the rights of others; between idealistic radicalism and an instinctive conservative reaction against change; the clash of class interests; and the collision between patriotism and international justice. Despite a good deal of middle-class support and the secret ballot, the Liberals were rejected by the electorate. Gladstone became the victim of his own good intentions; though he himself maintained that 'I was borne down by a torrent of gin and beer'.

CHAPTER 54

Disraeli and Conservatism

1874-1886

SO NOW it was Disraeli's turn. After the excitements and the upsets of the Liberal years the Conservatives were expected to call a halt to radical legislation. 'Conservatism', after all, means the belief that the old and established ways of doing things are best and the fear that any sort of change is likely to turn out for the worse. That at least is what it meant in the nineteenth century; but Disraeli, as we have seen, had rather different ideas. He was a reformer, and under his leadership the Conservatives became reformers too.

The times had changes since Disraeli wrote his angry novels of the 'hungry forties'. People of the working class received higher wages now and worked shorter hours. They had political rights, which Disraeli had given them, and their children had the chance of schooling, which was the gift of the Liberals. They had learned how to help themselves by joining Trades Unions and Co-operative Societies. Their lives had changed in many ways in the last thirty years; and Disraeli himself had changed as well. He was older now and less indignant. He suffered painfully from gout, which often laid him up. But he was still a social reformer. He found younger men to carry out the work and they found plenty still to do.

The Conservatives passed a new Factory Act which established a fifty-six-hour week or ten-hour day (with six on Saturday) in every factory. They made it possible for Ashley (now Lord Shaftesbury) to complete his life's work by prohibiting the employment of boys and girls as chimney sweeps. They made a regulation – the Plimsoll Line – for the safety of merchant seamen. Most important of all perhaps for the future of working men in general, they made picketing legal, provided that it was 'peaceful', and thus began the age of strikes.

Conservatives do not like to use the powers of the state to compel people to do anything; but they passed laws at this time to encourage local authorities to pull down the worst of the slums and build more spacious dwellings for the 'artisans'. They asked for better drains and unpolluted rivers. They prohibited the sale of unclean and adulterated food. These latter measures the Liberals termed scornfully 'a policy of sewage': but they were measures of a practical kind which contributed to the improvement of English life.

'The policy of sewage' did not turn England into a healthy country overnight. The Victorians were only just beginning to realize the connexion between dirt, drains and disease. The hospitals had only just begun to practise antiseptic surgery, developed by Joseph Lister in 1866, and private houses with their imperfect drains and water-closets, their piles of dusty furniture and windows which were never opened, were still the breeding-ground for germs. Germs indeed were no respecters of class or social position. The drains at Windsor Castle probably helped to cause the Prince Consort's early death in 1860 and both the Queen and the Prince of Wales suffered serious attacks of typhoid fever. Like everyone else, the royal physicians did not realize at once the cause of these ailments; but it did not need much medical science to make people realize that the houses of the poor ought to be rebuilt on better lines.

It is not surprising, in view of all the Conservative reforms, to learn that one working-class Member of Parliament claimed that 'the Conservatives have done more for us in five years than the Liberals did in fifty'. It was not true of course, for many of these laws were only putting into words what had been going on for many years. It was true however that they had encouraged the local authorities to set about improvements with a will. The Mayors and Corporations of Birmingham and Manchester, for example, took the government at its word and began the endless task of clearing up their great, grim cities. Birmingham, in the proud words of Joseph Chamberlain the mayor, was 'parked, paved, assized, marketed, Gas and Watered, and improved – all in three years'.

In Manchester we can still see the first fruits of the Corporation's energy in the magnificent Town Hall; and here and in London and all over the country we can see the great memorials to Prince Albert which are also the memorials of municipal pride and enterprise.

The Queen was particularly pleased with these memorials. She still mourned her husband, and welcomed sympathy. Disraeli gave her plenty of it. His great power and influence in these years was largely based on the Queen's affection for him. 'Everyone likes flattery,' he said, 'and when you come to royalty you should lay it on with a trowel.' He wrote to Victoria twice a day and consulted her over everything. He gave her a new title: 'Empress of India', and the Queen made him Earl of Beaconsfield. Gladstone on the other hand she did not like. He addressed her, she complained, 'like a public meeting', and Victoria was not amused.

The titles and the flattery were not pointless gifts however. In Disraeli's scheme of things there was a very important place for the monarch at the head of a united nation and a great Empire. He meant to build the Empire into a great British nation beyond the seas, and he spoke with pride and hope of 'those distant sympathies which may become the source of incalculable strength and happiness to this land'. As time went on Disraeli became more and more interested in imperial ideas and plans. He encouraged the British government in India to adopt a 'forward policy' and push the north-west frontier into Afghanistan. He showed that his ideas for the future of India were practical by rushing to purchase a large block of shares in the Suez Canal, which a French engineer, de Lesseps, had completed in 1869. The canal route cut short the voyage to India by a month, and made a closer economic link with the eastern colonies; though the great clipper ships with tea from China and Australian wool still used the trade winds to bring them home around the Cape of Good Hope.

Britain however was not the only power to take a new interest in imperialism and the Middle East. France owned a majority of the Suez shares and shared an interest in Egypt, while the Russians were on the move again in eastern Europe and Asia. They pushed out feelers towards Afghanistan and northern India; but their main interest lay as ever in the affairs of eastern Europe. The Turks had not fulfilled their promises to be better rulers. They were still harsh and grasping when they dealt with the Christian Slavs of the Balkans. When the tax-collectors came to Bosnia in 1875 the people chased them out. The Serbs and Bulgars joined them in revolt and the Turks suppressed the rising with terrible massacres and atrocities. The Tsar declared war on the Sultan in the name of the persecuted Slavs, and by the spring of 1878 his victorious armies were within easy reach of Constantinople.

So once again the Eastern Question disturbed the peace of Europe. English people had not perhaps appreciated the importance of the Suez Canal shares or Disraeli's 'forward policy'; but since the days of Palmerston they had been taught to suspect the Russians, and now they were ready once again to put a stop to their ambitions. The queen herself told Disraeli that 'she feels she cannot remain the Sovereign of a country that is letting itself down to kiss the feet of the great barbarians'. A music-hall song caught the people's mood:

> 'We don't want to fight, but by jingo if we do,
> We've got the guns, we've got the men, we've got
> the money too,
> We've stopped the Bear before, and while Britons shall
> be true,
> The Russians shall not have Constantinople.'

Disraeli sent the fleet to the Dardanelles. Along with Austria he demanded that the Russians should make peace with the Turks. They did so by the treaty of San Stefano, which secured independence for several Balkan states, among which Bulgaria was to be administered and assisted by Russian envoys and Russian troops. The terms of the treaty revived British suspicions of Russian aims. Disraeli now assembled more ships and troops in the Mediterranean area and threatened war again unless the terms of peace were revised by an international congress. In the end the Bear yielded to the Lion and a new treaty was arranged by Britain, Austria, Germany and Russia at the Congress of Berlin. As a result of the Congress some of the Balkan States gained their independence, but Russian influence was reduced to the northern part of the Balkans. The Turks made another promise to treat Christians better, and Disraeli came home with the island of Cyprus in his pocket; or as he put it, 'peace with honour'.

The Congress of Berlin seemed a triumph for European diplomacy. It marked a return to the Vienna system of avoiding wars by conferences among the great powers, and it was followed by thirty years of peace among them in the Near East. But the only people interested in settling quarrels by peaceful discussions are those who have something to lose by a war: in this case Russia, Turkey, Britain, Austria and Germany. The Balkan states had nothing to lose by war, and everything to gain. For them, wars were the only way to freedom, and for the next thirty years they were always trying to start new ones. It took the great powers all their time to avoid a major outbreak, and in their efforts to do so they became so involved in Balkan affairs that in the end the Russians had to fight the Austrians and the Germans to settle the ambitions of all three.

This lay in the future. At the time the most interesting feature of the Congress of Berlin was that it was held in Berlin and that the Chancellor of Germany, Otto von Bismarck, presided as the 'honest broker'. Until then he had been better known as the 'Iron Chancellor' whose acts of violence and aggression, culminating in the defeat of France by Prussia in 1871, had created the German Empire from a mass of separate states. Bismarck's nationalism had until now had nothing to do with protecting small states against aggression, and secret treaties were more in his line than international congresses. His ambitions and his methods boded ill for the peace of Europe in the same way as the troubles in the Balkans. In 1878 however he wanted peace in order to consolidate his new state of Germany. So he worked with the other powers even though the Balkan affair affected him, as it did Britain, only indirectly.

The Balkan affair had its curious aspects from the British point of view as well. Some people found it difficult to understand why this country was prepared to go to the point of war to save the Turks from the just retribution for their crimes. Gladstone thought it a sin to befriend them and went up and down the country saying so. He found some listeners too, though there were also many loud voices to praise Disraeli for defying the Russians and showing what Britain was made of once again. Just when Disraeli's popularity was at its height however the 'forward policy' began to go wrong. In Africa, British forces had annexed the Boer republic of the Transvaal, which was barely able to defend itself, in order to protect white South Africa from the war-like Zulus: a giant race of native warriors who had sworn before their ruler, Cetewayo, to wash their spears in the white man's blood. The Zulus overwhelmed and massacred a British force however at Isandhlwana in Bechuanaland. Farther east, in Afghanistan, a British military mission to Kabul was murdered by rebel tribesmen in the year 1879. These sensational and degrading failures of British arms outweighed Disraeli's own success at Berlin when he went before the country at the general election of 1879.

Foreign affairs were also beginning to affect England in another way, less likely to make newspaper headlines but more permanent in its effects. The 'enemy' here was foreign wheat, imported from the corn lands of Europe and the prairies of America in huge quantities, at prices with which English farmers could not compete. The year 1879 in fact was a black year for English farming in many ways, for quite apart from the foreign challenge the home harvest was ruined by rain, and the wet weather caused disease among sheep and cattle. Hard times came back to the countryside and at the same time a new depression hit the towns. Gladstone began to find ready listeners when he accused the government of wasting money abroad while English farmers, manufacturers and workmen faced renewed hardship at home. He won the election, and Disraeli's first and only ministry was over. Disraeli died in 1881, and one of the most interesting and inscrutable figures in English history passes from our story. He was un-English to the end, in his looks and his ways; but his policies touched the roots of English traditions and national pride, and he created the modern Conservative party.

And now it was Gladstone again, and Gladstone without his greatest rival. There were many other men however, much younger than himself, to plague the 'grand old man's' later years. There was Joseph Chamberlain, now a radical Liberal Member of Parliament, demanding further practical reforms on the lines which the Conservatives had laid down. On the other side of the House of

Commons Randolph Churchill, a 'Tory democrat', took every opportunity to tease and criticize Gladstone. He demanded the same social reforms as Chamberlain. An atheist, Charles Bradlaugh, horrified Gladstone by refusing to take the oath on the Bible required of every new Member of Parliament, while Charles Stuart Parnell, the leader of the Irish party, developed among his supporters a technique of 'filibustering', or speaking one after another at great length, so that Parliament could not find time to discuss anything except Irish grievances. In 1880 Gladstone faced more opponents and more problems than ever before. Once again he chose the Irish question as the one to be tackled. He tried to make up for the failure of the first Irish Land Act of 1870 by another passed in 1881, which set up special courts to fix fair rents and reasonable terms of tenancy. Irish landlords who belonged to the Conservative party did not thank him for doing so. The Irish political leaders ignored the courts altogether. They had taken matters into their own hands by now. They decided what they thought was a fair rent and refused to allow the tenant to pay more. If the landlord would not agree the 'Irish Land League' and the Fenians prevented the peasants from having any dealings with him. He was boycotted – the word is derived from the name of an Irish landowner who suffered from this treatment. The League and the Fenians maimed the landlord's cattle or sniped at him from behind hedges. Sometimes they came by night and dug his grave before his door.

Parnell himself encouraged resistance to the Land Act, and appeared no better than a Fenian to English eyes. At the height of the troubles he was arrested and gaoled, and only released when he undertook to put an end to the violence. Neither he nor anyone else could control it however. The Secretary of State for Ireland and his Under-Secretary were murdered in broad daylight in Phoenix Park, in Dublin. Parnell was horrified, and Gladstone became convinced that nothing short of home rule would pacify the Irish. In 1886 he proposed to give Ireland her own Parliament again. The English Parliament rejected his suggestion by thirty votes. Although the Irish party voted for it, many of the Liberals, led by Chamberlain, joined the Conservatives in voting against it. So Ireland remained unpacified, and Gladstone resigned from office.

His second term of power had not been a happy one. While he was concentrating on the problems of Ireland the depression in English agriculture had continued. Most people in the countryside thought that it was 'all up with farming'. The Liberals, true to their doctrine of free trade, would not bring back the Corn Law to meet the challenge of foreign wheat and many English farmers gave up growing it. Only once did the Liberals intervene in the affairs of the countryside, and that was in 1884, when country householders were given the vote. This proved to be the final blow to the influence of landowners on elections; but it was a poor exchange for low wages and lost jobs. The Liberals seemed to have no better answer to English problems than they had to Irish. At the election of 1885 they promised more social reform, but the controversy over Ireland prevented them from taking any steps to fulfil their pledge.

So far as many people were concerned Gladstone's greatest failure had once again occurred in foreign affairs. He had inherited the forward policy, which he did not like, and he brought it no further success. Although the Zulus were finally defeated at Ulundi the Boers began to make trouble on their own account. They defeated British forces at Majuba Hill in 1881 and restored the Transvaal's independence. There was little that Gladstone could do to influence these events and in any case he approved of Boer independence. A greater failure occurred in North Africa, where England and France had taken financial and political control of Egypt as a result of their interest in the Suez Canal. An English force under General Gordon took on the task of quelling an Arab revolt in the Sudan. Once they had broken up the rebels, Gladstone's government ordered them to return to Egypt; but Gordon stayed on in the Sudan to put right the injustice and cruelty he found there. Within a year the Arabs had risen again and he was besieged in Khartoum. The government at home was slow to send troops to support him and his defences finally collapsed in 1882 with relief forces less than two days' journey away. Gordon was killed and Gladstone was blamed. This too went against him in the reckoning and many people were glad to see him go in 1886. English politics had not seen the last of him and it would be wrong to think that everyone considered him a failure. The fact was however, as Disraeli's ministry had shown as clearly as Gladstone's, that English politics at home, in Ireland and in foreign affairs had now become so complicated and uncertain that no-one could hope to master them completely. In many ways the future of England had passed beyond English control. Gladstone and Disraeli took the blame for all the disappointments of English people. Gladstone's great achievement was to maintain his principles and carry out his reforms in the face of all these unsettling and unfavourable factors.

TABLE IX.   *The Family of Queen Victoria*

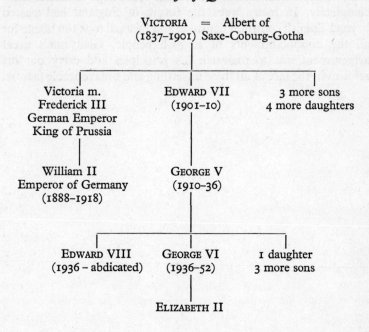

VICTORIA = Albert of
(1837–1901) Saxe-Coburg-Gotha

Victoria m.
Frederick III
German Emperor
King of Prussia

EDWARD VII
(1901–10)

3 more sons
4 more daughters

William II
Emperor of Germany
(1888–1918)

GEORGE V
(1910–36)

EDWARD VIII
(1936 – abdicated)

GEORGE VI
(1936–52)

1 daughter
3 more sons

ELIZABETH II

CHAPTER 55

Imperialism; the Last Years of Victorian England
1886-1901

BY THE LATER years of the nineteenth century the history of England has become a complicated and shifting story. It is not really the history of England any more. Although this country pursued a policy of isolation in foreign affairs, avoiding alliances and entanglements with other nations, she could not cut herself off from her colonial responsibilities or break free from the network of imports and exports which had made her the centre of the world's commerce. England was a part of the world which steamships and the telegraph made smaller every day; and English history has to be seen against this background. The background itself was changing all the time. New nations like the United States and Germany were becoming world powers. They had less and less need of British coal and iron or British manufactured goods, for they had used British machinery to build up their own industries, and now they competed with Britain for customers in Europe, America and every known part of the globe.

Even if we could ignore this international background we could not speak of British history as though it were a simple tale. For there was always Ireland, the exception, 'John Bull's other island', backward and embittered. Ireland was still ruled by the British Parliament, and the Protestants of Ulster wanted to keep that close link; but in the south the patriots, the priests and the peasants wanted a Parliament of their own to rule a land that was theirs alone.

And in England, the home country, we cannot talk of 'the nation' as though there was only one, undivided people who shared the same beliefs, the same prejudices and the same standards of living without any exceptions or divisions. There was still a huge gulf between the rich and influential world of the ruling classes and the world of the farm labourer, the mechanic and the factory workers. The middle class, with ideas and ambitions of their own, did little to bridge this gulf. They disliked the idea of government by the majority of the people as deeply as they resented the continuing power of the landed aristocracy. There was a great conflict of class interests in late Victorian England; and along with it went a fierce clash of ideas and opinions. Some people looked forward to the day when every man and woman would have the vote and the House of Lords would be abolished; others believed that democracy would mean national ruin. They were sure that Britain could only prosper and maintain her place in the changing world under the continued rule of the men of wealth, intelligence and experience who had made her great. Some people welcomed the efforts of the state which Gladstone and the Liberals had begun to provide education and security for the masses of the people; while others maintained that such favours sapped the independence and vitality of the race. They forecast that the government's increasing interference in the lives of its subjects would destroy liberty and undermine initiative, producing eventually a nation of listless slaves serving a tyrannical government.

In all this confusion of ideas and events it is not surprising that English people looked to the old Queen as the one fixed point. Victoria had become the symbol of British tradition and the guarantee of enduring greatness. In 1887 she entered the fiftieth year of her long reign and it was celebrated as a year of jubilee. The celebrations began when the Queen, accompanied by the cavalcade of European princes who were her sons, sons-in-law and grandsons, went in procession to Westminster Abbey. They continued with a review of the army and the Grand Fleet and a conference of representatives from all the colonies. There were bonfires all over England and squire, parson and villagers sat down together to a feast in the open air. Everyone celebrated Victoria's Golden Jubilee, for the nation was proud of her. She had come to the throne as a young and inexperienced woman, and ruled for over half the fifty years as a lonely widow; but she had held her own among wise and ambitious statesmen. Through all the great technical, political and social changes of the times Queen Victoria remained unchanged: proud and gracious, stubborn and devoted to her people. That was why her people loved and respected her. But there were some exceptions even to this rule. The Queen herself noticed that as she passed through the crowds to Westminster there were some people, 'Socialists and low, bad Irish', who booed and jeered at her.

The Queen's ministers had to steer a course through all the changes and all the disagreements of the time. As we have seen in the case of Gladstone and Disraeli, it was far from an easy task. Conservatives and Liberals in turn learned the hard lesson of democratic politics: that you cannot please all the people all the time. At one election, in 1885, the Liberals had gained a majority; in 1886 they lost it. In 1892 the Conservative majority disappeared at another election; but in 1895 they regained it. These unpredictable changes in power were partly due to the eighty-odd representatives of Irish seats who swung their support from one party to the other in the hope of getting home rule from them or in revenge for not obtaining it; but they were also due to sudden changes in public opinion, which was just as confused about the times as its rulers were and chose first one party and then another to solve the many problems.

In Parliament the names of the parties reflect this confusion. There were Liberals and Conservatives: but there were still members who preferred the old-fashioned names of Whig and Tory. The Conservatives began to call themselves Unionists to demonstrate their support for the union of England and Ireland and their determination not to give home rule; but there were Liberal Unionists led by Chamberlain as well. There were Liberal Radicals and Conservative Radicals; and there were always the Irish. Amid this chaos of party names, leaders appeared and disappeared overnight. Randolph Churchill, who seemed certain to succeed Disraeli as leader of his party, suddenly resigned and disappeared from the Unionist government in 1886. In 1890 Charles Parnell, the Irishman who dominated Parliament though he hated it, was suddenly forced to give up his position when he became involved in the scandal of a divorce case. Only Gladstone went on, and became Prime Minister again in 1892 at the age of eighty-three. He too resigned however after another attempt to pacify Ireland. Apart from the great reforms which he supported, the old man had made a special contribution to English political life. He believed that conscience, justice and religious beliefs – the principles that should govern everyone's private life – should govern public affairs as well. He never cheated or wilfully misled, and he treated men, classes and nations with scrupulous fairness and respect. In the violent quarrels between men and nations which began at the end of the century his example was badly missed.

The Unionist leaders who remained throughout most of this period at the head of affairs were Lord Salisbury and Joseph Chamberlain. Their chief interest lay in the consolidation and extension of the Empire, and Salisbury, whose particular skill lay in dealing with foreign statesmen, used his diplomacy to smooth the way for Britain to gain more colonies without resorting to war against foreign powers. Indeed, very few people believed that there would ever be a war again between civilized peoples. The world, they thought, had passed beyond the age of fighting to the age of conferences and international co-operation.

The British government in particular took pride in the level of civilization which its country had achieved. For them, 'Imperialism' meant the opportunity to extend the benefits of civilization and religion across the globe. They inherited Disraeli's dream of a great British nation extending across the world and bringing both machines and morals to the benighted peoples of other continents. But there were hard facts behind imperialism as well. Britain was losing European markets to Germany and American ones to the United States. New colonies meant new markets, protected by the Union Jack and British arms from foreign competition. There would be new sources of raw materials; and the natives of Africa and Asia might be expected in return for the blessings of civilization to provide cheap and willing labour without strikes or demands for political rights. All these motives lay behind the imperial policy of the Unionist government, and as they pursued this policy the Unionists put other problems in the background. They left the building of schools and houses to local authorities: County Councils and Urban and Rural District Councils were created to share the work with Municipal Corporations. They promised Ireland 'twenty years of resolute government', which proved to

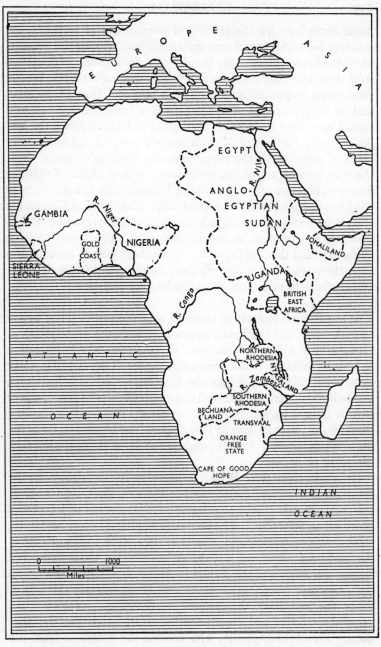

EUROPE

ASIA

EGYPT

R. Nile

ANGLO-
EGYPTIAN
SUDAN

GAMBIA

R. Niger

GOLD
COAST

NIGERIA

SIERRA
LEONE

SOMALILAND

UGANDA

BRITISH
EAST
AFRICA

R. Congo

ATLANTIC

OCEAN

NORTHERN
RHODESIA

NYASALAND

R. Zambesi

SOUTHERN
RHODESIA

BECHUANA-
LAND

TRANSVAAL

ORANGE
FREE
STATE

CAPE OF GOOD
HOPE

INDIAN

OCEAN

0   1000
Miles

**BRITISH AFRICA AT THE END OF THE NINETEENTH
CENTURY AND THE BOER REPUBLICS**

mean stern laws for the arrest and punishment of agitators, but schemes for railways and new industries and help for the peasants as well. The Unionists set out to give their country 'dominion over palm and pine', and we will follow their adventures; but we must never forget that many Liberals opposed them all the time, and in 1893 proposed once again to give Ireland home rule and would have done so, but that the House of Lords rejected the bill. And outside Parliament, though many people shared the excitement of imperialism, there were others with more domestic aims: the men who organized the great London dock strike of 1889 for example, or those who founded the Independent Labour Party in 1893 to put up working-class candidates at elections. Although the story moves away from English shores, England remains a restless country, full of rival ambitions and ideas. The home scene is confused; and this, perhaps, is why so many people were glad to turn their attention to the Empire, where problems were more straightforward and tasks were challenging and clear.

The imperialists looked for trade all over the world. They hoped to make new and profitable agreements with the government of Canada and with the provinces of Australia which formed a federation within the Commonwealth in 1901. They hoped to make even better use of India than the East India Company had done, and to build up new commercial links with China and Japan, where British traders backed by British gunboats had been demanding concessions since the days of Palmerston. The highest hopes of the imperialists however were centred on the development of the dark continent of Africa.

Of course there were British interests in Africa already. In the south there was Cape Colony and in the west the Gold Coast. In the north, Britain shared responsibility for the affairs of Egypt and guarded the Suez Canal. The boundaries of these British territories were always advancing and usually at the cost of war: war against the Sudanese rebels, against the Ashanti of the Gold Coast and against the Zulus and the Kaffirs to the north of Cape Colony and the Transvaal. But the great interior of Africa was still untouched. Since the middle of the century, travellers and explorers had mapped its rivers and chronicled its wealth: men like the missionary David Livingstone, who crossed the continent from the mouth of the Congo to the Zambesi and renamed the great cascade which the natives called 'the smoke that sounds' as Victoria Falls; or John Speke, who discovered and named Lake Victoria Nyanza, the source of the Blue Nile. Now traders of every nation wanted to follow in their steps. All the European nations were interested in Africa; not only Britain but Germany, Belgium and France as well, and to a lesser extent Spain, Italy and Portugal. It took the best efforts of Bismarck and Lord Salisbury to prevent these rival imperial ambitions from leading to the brink of war; eventually they marked out 'spheres of influence' for each country, and Britain took parts of western, southern and eastern Africa, the territories which now make up Nigeria, Ghana, Bechuanaland, Rhodesia, Nyasaland, Kenya and Uganda as hers.

The trading companies moved in: the British East Africa Company, the Niger Company and, greatest and most enterprising of all, the British South Africa Company founded by Cecil Rhodes, who became Prime Minister of Cape Colony at the end of the eighties. Rhodes was the most ambitious of all the imperialists. In his petition to the government for a royal charter for his company he set out his beliefs: that the extension of British influence in southern Africa 'would be advantageous to the commercial and other interests of your Majesty's subjects', and, equally important, 'that the condition of the natives inhabiting the said territories will be materially improved and their civilization advanced'. Rhodes dreamed of taking British trade and civilization all the way from Cape Town to Cairo. It was a tremendous journey, bristling with difficulties at every step. There were huge physical obstacles in the way: great mountains, forests and rivers. There were warlike and resolute tribes to be subdued and placated: the Kaffirs, the Matabele and the Sudanese. And right across the beginning of the route there lay the stubborn republic of the Boers.

There was a heritage of distrust between British and Boers. Old Boer farmers remembered the Great Trek which they had made as children. Cape Colonists called to mind the more recent shame of Majuba Hill. Behind these hostile memories lay a complete difference in ways of life. The Boers were farmers, the British were traders. The British hoped to civilize the natives, but the Boers took a different attitude towards them. 'In their own estimation,' said Livingstone of the Boers, 'they are the chosen people of God, and all the coloured race are "black property" or "creatures" – heathen given to them for an inheritance.' This difference of feeling towards the people of Africa was another cause of suspicion and dislike between British settlers and Boers.

And now, in the 1880's, a new cause of hostility was found. Gold was discovered in the Transvaal, and British prospectors, backed by the Company, rushed to mine it. The Boers were not interested in the gold for they were not businessmen; but they were determined to resist the new British advance into their republic. The President of the Transvaal, Paul Kruger, imposed heavy taxes on the 'Uitlanders' or outsiders, and heavy charges on their railways. He denied them political rights. The Uitlanders appealed to the Company for protection, and the ambitions of Rhodes came face to face with Kruger's stubbornness. Dynamite, in other words, met solid rock. The explosion followed quickly.

In the last days of 1895 the Company's manager, Dr. Jameson, took 470 men and eight machine guns, and set out to capture Johannesburg, the capital of the Transvaal. On the fourth day of the 180-mile journey the Boers surrounded and arrested them. The plan had been a hopeless risk from the start; but Rhodes had supported it and, so many people said in England, Chamberlain as well. So far as many English people were concerned the Jameson raid was just the sort of adventure which made imperialism exciting. The raiders became heroes and so did Rhodes, though he had to resign as Prime Minister of the Cape. Loud public opinion demanded that the Unionist government should support the Uitlanders and the Company; and on the other side the German Kaiser William sent a telegram to Kruger to congratulate him on 'maintaining the independence of your country against attacks from without'. In the event three years of truce followed, while British forces fought more wars against the Ashanti and the Matabele and Sir Herbert Kitchener destroyed the power of the Sudanese Arabs at the battle of Omdurman. But through these years the Uitlanders kept up their demands for full political rights in the Transvaal and lighter taxation; while the Boers imported guns from Germany. It became clear to everyone, as it had been clear to Kruger, Rhodes and Jameson all along, that either the

Transvaal must expel the British, or the British conquer the Transvaal.

In the event the Boers declared war, in October 1899, and when the Boer War began they held many advantages. They were skilled horsemen and they knew the country they were defending. The country itself, the broad grassland of the veldt, was surrounded on three sides by mountain ranges. The Boers however decided to attack and drive out the intruders. By the end of the year they had laid siege to three British bases: Mafeking and Kimberley in the west and Ladysmith on the borders of Natal in the east. The Boers planned to overrun the whole of Natal and capture the port of Durban. They were not overawed by the might and reputation of the enemy they had taken on, and when the first British relief columns advanced from Cape Town towards the besieged towns they were defeated, three of them in the same week, at Magersfontein, Stormberg and Colenso.

This 'black week' of British defeats occurred at the end of 1899, and the first days of the new century brought the bleak news to England. Germany and most other European countries made it clear that they sympathized with the Boers, though they were not prepared to go to the length of war to support them. England stood alone, and her isolation at the moment was not splendid. The Queen however declared her confidence that her country would prevail, and in the new year a new commander, Lord Roberts, led his forces deep into Boer country, taking the risk of ambush and the loss of his supplies, and raising the siege of Kimberley. He defeated the Boer Commandant Cronje at Paardeberg while other forces relieved Mafeking and Ladysmith. In October he captured Pretoria, and Kruger fled into exile. By the end of 1900 defeat had turned into victory and the war seemed nearly over. There were still many Liberals and radicals at home who maintained that the war had been unjust and unnecessary from the beginning; but they were not popular. The mass of public opinion was bursting with confidence and pride and its spirits were lowered only by an announcement from Windsor in January 1901 that 'the Queen's health is not what it was'. At the end of the month, in the sixty-fourth year of her reign, Victoria died, and no news of South African victories could compensate for the national sense of loss. In an uneasy and changing world the one fixed point had gone.

CHAPTER 56

Unionists and Trades Unionists;
Liberals and Labour; Lloyd George

1901-1914

THE VICTORIAN AGE had been a great age for England. For
almost a century this country had stood at the pinnacle of world
power, and her internal history had been a record of peaceful
progress and achievement. English people thought that they had
set an example to the world. But the future was less certain.
Although England had worked hard for her great position, her
industries were not expanding quickly any more, and other
nations were challenging her supremacy. The Germans were the
great inventors now and they coveted England's world trade. The
French on the other hand coveted many of her colonies. The
Americans were bidding for the commerce of the Pacific and South
America. The Japanese were building cotton mills and ships of
their own.

Among less important nations moreover there were many
critics of England. The Boers and the Irish, the Indians and the
Chinese had all felt the touch of British imperialism. They were not
convinced that it brought them unmixed blessings. Above all,
perhaps, along with the Germans, the French and the rest they
resented the Englishman's sense of superiority: his calm conviction
that whatever his country did was right and just and for the best.

'There is nothing so bad or so good that you will not find
Englishmen doing it; but you will never find an Englishman in the
wrong. He does everything on principle. He fights you on patriotic
principles; he robs you on business principles; he enslaves you on
imperial principles.'

524

This verdict on English history, written by an Irishman, George Bernard Shaw, was harsh and meant to shock. It reminds us that there was another opinion of English achievements; and that England stood alone in the world when the twentieth century began.

At first however it seemed that the British government could cope with their country's changing position. The Unionists brought the Boer war to an end, though it took them another year and the use of concentration camps to do it. The peace of Vereeniging concluded in 1902, was marked by greater generosity towards the Boers. From then on an appearance of unity between the two white races was established, and in 1910 the Union of South Africa entered the Commonwealth. The Unionist government, conscious of England's lonely world position, tried to draw tighter the bonds of friendship which linked England to the other Commonwealth countries: Canada, Australia and New Zealand. They secured new allies: Japan in the east, as a guardian of British trading interests there, and France in the west. The French alliance was called an *entente cordiale*: it was not a promise of military support but only an expression of friendship and good will. It served however to bring to an end many years of suspicion and disagreement about Egypt and the Sudan. At home, Arthur Balfour, who became the Unionist leader when Lord Salisbury died, introduced another great Education Act which was the beginning of secondary schooling for everyone in this country. It could not be said that the Unionists were failing entirely to meet the challenge of the times; but many people said that they were failing in particular and important ways. The Unionists could not make up their minds whether to help the farmers by returning to a policy of protection against foreign imports, or whether to stick to free trade. They continued to govern Ireland resolutely, and refused home rule. They refused to give women the vote. The Trades Unions disliked them because they would not remove a new Trade Union grievance: the decision of a judge, in 1901, that the Taff Vale Railway Company, in South Wales, could claim damages for the loss of receipts caused by a strike of their workmen. The Liberals condemned the concentration camps in South Africa as 'methods of barbarism', used to win a war that had never been justified. And so, although they had won a huge majority in the election of

1900, held at the height of their success in the Boer War, the Unionists went down in a landslide at the election of 1906, amid angry criticism.

The Liberal government which came into office in 1906 remained in power under two Prime Ministers, Sir Henry Campbell-Bannerman and Herbert Asquith, until 1915. It was, until the 1960's at least, the last Liberal ministry to govern England. It left behind it a splendid record of social achievements. This government was responsible for introducing Old Age Pensions and National Insurance against unemployment and ill health. It made cruelty to children a criminal offence. It established Labour Exchanges, and it provided school meals and medical examinations. In many different ways it laid the foundation of the modern 'Welfare State' in which the government takes responsibility for ensuring the health and happiness of the people.

And yet the Liberals made their enemies. They won the support and respect of a new political party, the Labour party, which had been founded in 1900 to represent directly the interests of the working class and won along with supporting groups, fifty-three seats at the 1906 election; but they deeply offended the old political party, the Conservatives or Unionists, who were stung by their election defeat and the accusations of barbarous conduct towards Boers and Chinese and indifference to English and Irish problems which had brought it about. The Conservatives were not happy to see power passing from the hands of old-established social classes to Trades Unions and Socialists. For that was what they thought was happening when, for instance, the Liberals passed a law which reversed the Taff Vale judgment and declared that Trades Unions were not liable for damages caused by strikes. The Trade Disputes Act of 1906 marked the beginning of a period of rapid growth in the numbers and confidence of the British Labour movement. The Conservatives were determined to halt this shift of power, and as soon as the catastrophic election of 1906 was over Balfour predicted that 'whether in office or in opposition, the Unionist party will continue to control the destinies of the British Empire'.

How did he propose to do it? The answer is, by using the huge Conservative majority in the House of Lords to thwart and delay Liberal bills which passed through the House of Commons. The Lords did not hold up the social measures which have already been described, but they vetoed others which were dear to Liberal hearts. They were clearly determined to fight; and the Liberal leaders, convinced that the electors had given them their full approval, set out to defeat their noble opponents.

The man most determined to do so was the Chancellor of the Exchequer, a fierce and subtle Welshman named David Lloyd George. He chose as his weapon the budget of 1909, which he termed, proudly and pointedly, 'the People's Budget'. The People's Budget proposed to pay for Old Age Pensions by a super-tax on high incomes and a new and heavy tax on landed estates. Death duties, introduced by the Liberals in 1894, were to be increased. The landowning Lords rejected the budget at once as the most 'socialistic' proposal yet; and Lloyd George cried: 'We have got them at last.'

For it was a constitutional principle that the Lords should never interfere with bills concerned with taxation. In rejecting the budget they were overstepping their constitutional powers. Lloyd George declared that they were using their privileged political position to defy the will of the people, as expressed at the last election. 'Should five hundred men,' he asked, 'ordinary men, chosen accidentally from among the unemployed, override the judgment – the deliberate judgment – of millions of people who are engaged in the industry which makes the wealth of this country?' The Liberals backed up their argument by going before the people at another general election early in 1910. For several reasons, not all of them connected with the constitutional question, their majority was greatly reduced; but it was clear that there was very little support for the House of Lords. So the Liberals returned to the fight with a Parliament Bill, which proposed to reduce the power of the peers so that they could not hold up bills which had passed the Commons for more than three sessions of Parliament – that is, for about two years. The Lords were to lose the power to veto 'money bills' entirely.

The Conservative Lords prepared to reject the Parliament Bill, and a year of tension followed. While the crisis was approaching its height Edward VII died. A conference between the party leaders failed to produce an agreement, and the new monarch, George V, was called on to solve the problem as soon as he came to the throne. He undertook to create enough peers to pass the bill, provided the

Liberals won another election. They won it. Finally the Lords gave way without any new peers being created. The People's Budget and the Parliament Bill became law. It was the biggest change in the constitution since 1832; but it no more marked the end of the power of the aristocracy than the first reform of Parliament had done. In the armed services, the civil service and local government the aristocracy still kept its established place in a democratic state.

So far as the general public were concerned, the constitutional struggle had become boring long before it was concluded. They grew tired of elections and political harangues. The crisis had taught them one lesson however: if you want something badly enough, then violence is the way to get it. The sad habit of using angry words and violent actions spread and during the sweltering summer of 1911, when the temperature for days on end stood at 90°, there were strikes on the railways and in the docks. Next year there was a strike in the coal industry. During these years the 'Women's Social and Political Union' was campaigning for a vote for women. Suffragettes chained themselves to the railings of Buckingham Palace and when they were arrested refused to eat anything until they were released. They set fire to pillar boxes and public buildings, cut telephone wires and attacked the British museum, showing that women were as adept at violence as men and therefore, presumably, as worthy of a vote.

This wave of violence which swept through England probably had its fundamental causes back in the quiet years of the Victorian age, when respectability stifled every sort of excitement and pushed violence and wayward behaviour beneath the surface of polite society. The fact was however that the aptitude for violent words and threats of violent action was now spreading all over Europe. In 1908 Austria and Russia seemed likely to go to war over the Austrian annexation of Bosnia. In 1912 the Slav state of Serbia joined with Greece, Bulgaria and Montenegro in an attack on Turkey. These crises had their roots back in the time of the Congress of Berlin. In those days the German Bismarck had worked to keep the peace, but the Kaiser William II was less discreet. He promised his help to Austria should a war begin, and he drew closer to Turkey. In 1906 and again in 1911 he clashed with France over the control of Morocco. With England he kept on friendlier terms. He was, after all, Queen Victoria's grandson and Edward VII's nephew. We have already heard him congratulating the Boers however and it was an open secret that Germany had supplied them with guns. It was equally well known that Germany was building a great fleet to rival that of England. Neither the Kaiser's letter in an English newspaper assuring this country of his friendship nor his visits to the English court did anything to lessen the naval and commercial rivalry and the growing hostility between the two nations, while the development of the German army and the strengthening of the Austro-German alliance seemed increasingly to threaten the peace of Europe.

The peace was kept however; partly by international conferences and patient negotiations in which Sir Edward Grey, the British Foreign Secretary, played a leading part; and partly because the rival powers were not yet ready for a trial of strength. If Austria fought Russia, for instance, then she would probably make an enemy of France as well, for France and Russia had been allies since 1893. If Austria were attacked, on the other hand, then Germany would almost certainly come to her assistance. It was this knowledge of having to take on two opponents at once which discouraged Austria and Russia from declaring open war in the Balkans. Britain alone stood outside these military alliances, and this apparent neutrality made it possible for Grey to play the role of peacemaker. As the challenge from Germany increased however Britain moved steadily closer to France, and in 1907 the *Entente Cordiale* became a Triple Entente with the settlement of differences between Britain and Russia. Despite Grey's determination to leave his country's hands untied Britain was now virtually a member of the second of Europe's 'armed camps'.

For the rival systems of alliances were arming all the time. They hoped by their preparations to deter the other side from provoking a war against them; but they meant to be ready for war should it come. Germany and Britain spent vast sums on new warships each year in a race to keep on level terms. The two governments talked constantly about disarmament and 'naval holidays'; but they continued to arm themselves. In 1912 there were 'military conversations' between British and French chiefs of staff. We may be sure that similar conversations were going on farther east. Slowly, in fact, the two systems of alliances and ententes which were meant to keep the peace by a balance of power were turning into instruments of war. Behind the visits of royal families and ministers, the international conferences and protestations of good will, there lurked the shadows of battleships and guns.

It was the same in English life. The country went about its business and its pleasure in these years, and though many people were out of work many others purchased motor-cars (a German invention) and went to the seaside for their holidays in the splendid summers of the time. But every now and then the popular newspapers would appear with a story of a scandal in high places or a threat of violence by Trades Unions or an international crisis. Under the peaceful surface of society dark and restless forces were at work, threatening from time to time to break out into frightening reality.

Such forces had been at work in Ireland for many years, and now they played their part in creating further tension. After the election of 1910 the Liberals depended on the votes of eighty-four Irish members to keep their majority in the House of Commons. The Irish demanded home rule as the price of their support. In 1912 therefore Asquith introduced a third bill to give Ireland her own Parliament and responsibility for most of her own affairs. The Unionists opposed it fiercely and the House of Lords rejected it at once; but under the new rules of the Parliament Act home rule would become effective in any case at the end of two years, in the summer of 1914. At last it seemed the Irish question would be solved; but it was not to be so. The Protestants of Ulster did not want an Irish Parliament, for they feared that it would pass under the control of Catholics and probably into the hands of Sinn Fein as well. 'Sinn Fein' was the name of the political party which aimed to make Ireland completely free of the English Crown. The Ulstermen prepared to resist the passage of the Home Rule Bill and the Conservative leader in England, Bonar Law, who had just succeeded Balfour, declared that he could imagine 'no length of resistance to which Ulster will go, which I shall not be ready to support'. So, once again, determined men ignored the authority of Parliament and issued an invitation to violence and even civil war. A private army, the Ulster Volunteers, was formed; and on the other side the Irish Volunteers prepared for action. Both sides made plans to bring guns into Ireland; but the authorities missed the Ulster gun-runners, while they stopped and arrested the Irish Volunteers who tried to do the same. Officers of the British Army in Ireland, who would be responsible for maintaining order in the country, declared that they would rather be dismissed than intervene against the Ulstermen. The War Office assured them that they would not be ordered to fight. As the summer of 1914 approached, Ireland seemed doomed to a civil war, in which the British army would not intervene.

CHAPTER 57

Britain and the First World War

1914-1918

AS THINGS TURNED OUT there was no civil war in Ireland in the summer of 1914. The Irish question was swallowed up and forgotten, at least for the present, in the catastrophe of a European war.

The incident which finally shattered the uneasy peace of the last few years and set the two machines of war in motion was the assassination of the Crown Prince of Austria, the Archduke Franz Ferdinand, on 28 June. The Archduke was visiting the Bosnian town of Serajevo, near the borders of Serbia, and his car was moving slowly through the streets when a student leapt on the running-board and shot him and his wife at point-blank range. The Serajevo assassination, which had been planned by a Serbian terrorist organization, provoked a crisis between Austria and Serbia. The Austrian government waited for a month however, until they had obtained Germany's promise of support, before they protested to the Serbian government. The Serbs proved willing to apologize and negotiate, but the Austrians rejected their offer, declared war, and moved their army forward to besiege Belgrade.

Russia encouraged the Serbs to resist the invasion and mobilized for war with Austria. Germany declared war on Russia. The German High Command realized that the next step would be war with Russia's western ally France, and seized the initiative by declaring war first. They put into operation a plan for the invasion of France which had been designed almost ten years before by a general named von Schlieffen. In the first days of August two massive armies began a pincer movement through Belgium and Lorraine towards Paris. If the Schlieffen plan succeeded the Germans expected to be in Paris within six weeks, victorious and able to concentrate their major effort on the eastern front. An obstacle to their design appeared immediately however when the King of the neutral Belgians refused them passage through his country, and prepared to resist the German war machine.

What part did England play in these critical decisions and events? She played at first the peacemaker – the part which Sir Edward Grey had always chosen. He tried to arrange another conference to discuss the Austrian grievances against the Serbs. It was much too late for that, however. Too many ambitions were at stake, too many armies on the march for peace to be a possibility in 1914. The real choice before England was not between war and peace: but between supporting France, her Entente ally, and Belgium, whose neutrality this country had guaranteed for almost a century, and standing aside to allow Germany to dominate western Europe, and German warships to patrol the North Sea. English history and English strategic interests dictated the same choice: to support the Belgians' fight for freedom and prevent the conquest of Europe by a single power. As Bernard Shaw had said, Englishmen did everything on principle, and these were the principles which had governed their foreign policy since the days of Palmerston and Pitt. On 4 August Sir Edward Grey received a negative reply to his demand that the Germans should not enter Belgium, and announced to Parliament the government's reluctant decision to declare war on Germany.

It was difficult at first for English people to realize what had happened. They had been so intent on their own problems for the last few years that they had not considered the possibility of a war. It was hard to believe that the world of shadows had broken its bounds and become the world of reality. What was the war about? they asked. Why were they fighting the Germans? What would war be like, after a hundred years of peace? Many of them were sad to see the conclusion to which all the achievements of the nineteenth century had come. 'The lamps are going out all over Europe', said Grey 'We shall not see them lit again in our lifetime.' But this was from an old man's point of view. Younger people did not stop to consider the deeper implications. For them the war was a novel and exciting challenge after the frustrating years of respectability and peace. They rushed to volunteer for the army and said they would be home for Christmas.

And so, while the Germans swept on through Belgium, the British Expeditionary Force crossed the Channel, and in the late summer of 1914 their drab khaki uniforms followed the blue and red of the French infantry and the black and gold of their artillerymen across the plains of Picardy and Champagne. Here, on the borders of France and Belgium, the first battles of the western front were fought. In this first shock of war, more than three hundred thousand Frenchmen were killed or made prisoner, and the British Expeditionary Force was saved only by retreating from its position at Mons.

Meanwhile the Germans pressed on, well up to the schedule of the Schlieffen plan, and paused in the autumn on the banks of the River Marne, just fifteen miles short of Paris. By a tremendous effort the Allies regrouped and held them there, and the Germans retired to the River Aisne. They made a last effort at a speedy victory by racing to seize the Channel ports and sever the chain of supplies and men between England and France. A British force stopped them at Ypres, and the Germans retreated to dig themselves into the soil of occupied France. By the end of the year the western front extended over four hundred miles, from the Alps almost to Ostend. From trenches a few hundred yards apart the enemies faced each other and contemplated their next move. For the next three years the front did not move for more than twenty miles in either direction, and millions of lives were lost in keeping it where it was. Four years of war were to prove that the side which attacked trenches, barbed wire and machine guns would always suffer colossal losses. The Schlieffen plan had failed however, and the Germans were now forced to divide their strength between two fronts, in the west against France and England and in the east against the Russians. But that was not the worst feature of their position. The British fleet closed the North Sea to them, and the French the Mediterranean. The Italians, who had been the allies of Germany and Austria in the pre-war years, now declared their support for the powers of the Triple Entente. Turkey joined Germany, so that Russia was deprived of a link with her western allies and could not receive vital war supplies; but Germany itself

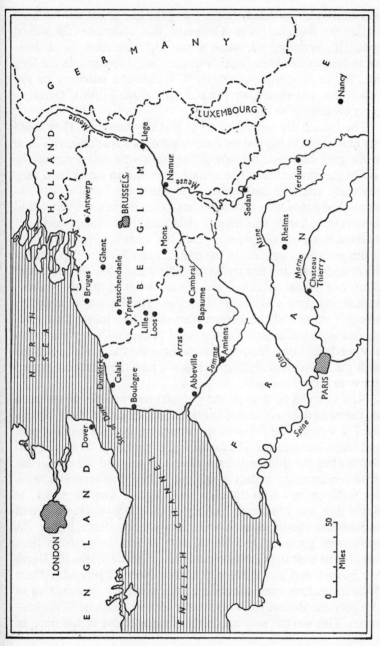

THE WESTERN FRONT, 1914–18

was entirely surrounded, except along the line of the railway from Berlin to Baghdad. For Germany this stalemate threatened eventual starvation: starvation of raw materials from the colonies for industries and the essentials of war, and starvation, in the long run, of the necessities of life itself. Unless the stalemate on the two fronts was ended, or the naval blockade broken, Germany must eventually be forced to yield.

The French did not see things in this way however. They could not look ahead to the distant future, but only across no-man's land at the grey coats and helmets of the Huns who still occupied the soil of the motherland. The French plan was to attack, and keep attacking, until the last German was either dead or back in Germany. For Englishmen, on the other hand, it was more difficult to feel the same hatred for Germans. England and Germany had been rivals in many ways in pre-war years but friends, almost relations, in others. The 'Tommies' in the trenches could not stir up feelings of bitter hatred in a few weeks. At Christmas 1914 some of them came out of the trenches and shook hands with the 'Fritzes', exchanging good wishes and cigarettes. The British commanders however supported the French plan of attack. In 1915 they advanced again and ninety-five thousand British soldiers were lost in one battle at Loos. Despite this catastrophe the Allies continued with the strategy of 'killing Germans', and the Germans settled down to killing them.

New weapons such as poison gas, and new vehicles of war such as the aeroplane could not break the deadlock. In 1915 Britain tried to increase the pressure on the eastern front by sending men and ships to force the Dardanelles and take help to Russia and Serbia; but the ships withdrew after a month and the men, even when reinforced by gallant troops from the Commonwealth, were not sufficient to storm the cliffs of Gallipoli. Another attack, at Suvla Bay, was reinforced too late to be effective. One hundred and twenty thousand men were lost on this front before the attack was given up and Serbia and Russia were left to their fate. In the west the German fleet tried to break out into the North Sea in 1916 and met the British Grand Fleet off Jutland. After a day's inconclusive manoeuvring in the mist they were content to slip past the British ships and back to their base at Wilhelmshaven. This was the only major naval engagement of the war; an ignominious anticlimax to the frantic shipbuilding and naval armament in which Britain and Germany had engaged for the last ten years. The war was not to be won or lost at sea, but on the icy plains of eastern Europe and in the mud, the trenches and the barbed wire of the western front.

At home in England few people appreciated the horrors of the European front as yet. The newspapers sustained their patriotic feelings with stories of German atrocities and visions of angels hovering over the Expeditionary Force on its retreat from Mons. From time to time huge German Zeppelins appeared over England and caused great alarm; but otherwise the war in Europe made little impact on British life. There was no food-rationing before 1918 and no systematic direction of industry or labour before the end of 1915, when Lloyd George set out to organize the war effort necessary to sustain the gigantic consumption of ammunitions in France. The war was consuming men too, but until May 1916 there was no systematic call-up of civilians. Lord Kitchener's poster with its stern demand 'Your country needs you' was sufficient to send a host of volunteers to France. So many of these soldiers were going to their deaths; their countrymen, with growing awareness of the facts of war, were proud of them.

In Ireland however there were men who did not share these patriotic feelings. These were the leaders of Sinn Fein. They hoped that Germany would help them to gain independence from England; and when help was not forthcoming they took matters in their own hands. On Easter Monday 1916 over a thousand of them seized the Post Office and other buildings in Dublin, and held them for a week until English soldiers forced them to surrender. Very few Dubliners supported the rebels however and the Easter Rising was a complete failure. But England was bitterly angry at the treason of the Sinn Feiners, and their leaders were executed. This action made the rebels martyrs in many Irish eyes, and gave yet another cause for hatred to the brooding spirit of Irish nationalism.

To return from the British Isles to the front line in France is to go back to a landscape of desolation. The farms and the villages had been shattered by gunfire and the flat countryside was bare of foliage. Only the red poppy bloomed in the muddy fields of

Flanders. The soldiers made their temporary homes in half-covered dug-outs in the sodden ground, and waited under the constant fire of heavy guns and solitary snipers for the order to go over the top in a frantic charge through rifle and machine-gun fire towards an enemy trench or salient, less than a hundred yards away. By 1916 many soldiers were tired of the war with its endless risk and bloodshed; but loyalty to their comrades and strict discipline kept them in constant readiness for action, and there were always more recruits.

The war of killing Germans, Frenchmen and Englishmen went on without a halt. In the summer of 1916 the Germans launched a tremendous onslaught against the French fortress of Verdun. The British commander, Sir Douglas Haig, relieved his allies by a counter-attack across the River Somme. Sixty thousand men were killed on the first day of this battle; and though the Germans called off their attack on Verdun after two months the allies gained no more than six miles of territory at any place on the front.

In 1917 the pressure of the war began to tell and the first cracks appeared in the opposing sides. The Russian war effort collapsed in the Bolshevik revolution which the Germans encouraged. The Italians were routed by the Austrians at the battle of Caporetto. Serbia surrendered. Several units of the French army, driven beyond endurance in another reckless assault, mutinied; and even British confidence was shaken when another four hundred thousand men were killed or drowned in a fruitless attack across the waterlogged plain of Flanders against Passchendaele ridge. Germany too was strained to the limit of its resources by these huge attacks, and by the unceasing blockade of the Baltic. Even so German submarines slipped out to hit back at British merchant vessels and troopships, and threatened at one time to starve England herself into surrender. In this, the third and most desperate year of the war, British forces had only one victory to record: in Palestine, where General Allenby, supported by desert tribesmen under Lawrence of Arabia, rolled up the Turkish forces and captured Jerusalem. In the west, Britain and her allies held on, inspired by the fighting leadership of Lloyd George, who had become Prime Minister of a coalition government in 1916; and even gained a new ally when the United States became exasperated with U-boat attacks on her shipping and entered the war against Germany.

Although the situation was bad for the western allies it was now critical for Germany. The Austrian Empire, for all its military successes, was collapsing like the Russian, and Turkey was in retreat. Germany would soon be alone, and unless German forces could break the deadlock on the western front before the first American troops reached Europe the starved and exhausted nation would have to surrender. And so at the beginning of 1918 a new German commander in the west, von Ludendorff, launched a tremendous offensive aimed at separating the British forces in Flanders from the French and seizing the Channel ports. Within a week the Germans advanced forty miles until a British stand at Ypres and Béthune once again thwarted their drive for the coast. The attack changed direction, and by the beginning of May the Germans stood within fifty miles of Paris. Here they hesitated again however, just as they had done in 1914, and after a last great assault around Reims began to withdraw. They were demoralized by the new strength of the American troops they encountered, and by the tanks which were now brought into the war for the first time on a large scale. Throughout the spring, the French and the British, the Americans and the tanks continued to drive the Germans back. There were many stops and starts and more tremendous losses before they pushed across the Somme, and then the Aisne, and finally, in October and the first days of November, drove their adversaries out of France.

'With death in my heart,' wrote Ludendorff afterwards, 'I saw that our hopes were falling like dead leaves in the autumn.' His great effort in the west was spent. From Italy came news that the Austrians were in retreat. Turkey surrendered unconditionally. In Germany the fleet refused to sail on a last desperate mission against England, and the civilian population of Berlin rose in rebellion and chased the Kaiser into exile. The German commander had no choice but to surrender. An armistice was arranged between the rival powers, and on 11 November 1918 firing ceased on the western front.

The dreadful military contest which might with a little good will have been avoided was over. Three and a half million men were dead on the German side; the western allies and Russia had lost five and a quarter. A whole generation of young men had passed away, and with them had disappeared the four great empires of Germany, Austria, Russia and Turkey. At first however these great events did not preoccupy men's minds. The first emotion was one of overwhelming relief that the brutality and suffering of the last four years was over; and the victorious powers were determined that such a catastrophe should never happen again.

CHAPTER 58

Irish Independence; the General Strike; The Economic Crisis

1918-1931

GREAT WARS create as many problems as they solve, however. In western Europe the gigantic struggle of the last four years had left destruction, hunger and disease as its legacy. Eastern and central Europe seemed likely to pass under the control of Communist governments supported by the Red Army of Bolshevik Russia. So far as England herself was concerned, the war had destroyed her international trade and upset her industries. Like every other country involved she had lost thousands of her young men, and in the winter of 1918 an epidemic of influenza swept through the undernourished population and claimed more lives. It was difficult for English people in the post-war years to summon up the easy optimism of the Victorian age. Nevertheless they were determined to enjoy themselves, and they were full of hope for a future in which both the war and the social discontent of the immediate pre-war years might be forgotten. At the general election of 1918 Lloyd George became Prime Minister again at the head of a coalition government and promised 'to make Britain a fit country for heroes to live in'. The new age began with an Act of Parliament to give political rights to every man over twenty-one, except criminals, lunatics and peers of the realm, and to every woman over thirty. Women were in the majority now, and the politicians would have been unwise not to recognize the fact.

Britain could not confine her attention merely to her own future. Along with the other victorious powers this country had to try to solve the problems of Europe. Everyone hoped that the last war had been the 'war to end war', but no-one believed that lasting peace was possible until 'German militarism' had been destroyed. The German representatives at the peace conference were obliged to sign an admission of their country's responsibility for provoking the war, and the new German republic was forbidden to keep a great army or navy in the future. Germany was deprived of her colonies and lost European territory in the west and in the east. The Austrian Empire was completely broken up and the new republics of Austria, Hungary, Czechoslovakia and Yugo-Slavia took its place. Finally the defeated belligerents were required to pay for the damage the war had caused. The sum of German reparations was not fixed until 1921, when German industry showed signs of recovering; and Germany was told to pay £6,600 million. Nothing like this sum was ever paid in fact. The reparations were scaled down and finally abandoned, and the United States loaned huge sums to the new republic; but German politicians in years to come were able to find ample evidence of injustice and vindictiveness in the 'Diktat of Versailles'.

Poland and Finland were other new republics created by the peacemakers of 1919. The new nations were created after plebiscites held to test the wishes of the majority of their inhabitants. The idea of self-determination belonged to Woodrow Wilson, the idealist President of the United States who hoped to 'make the world safe for democracy'. He was the moving spirit behind the League of Nations, the international organization set up to promote co-operation between peoples and solve international disputes by discussion and arbitration. But even while Wilson's high-minded proposals were under discussion allied troops were fighting the Bolsheviks in eastern Europe, and Russia was not invited to join the League for many years.

Lloyd George led the British delegation to the peace conference. He occupied an uneasy position between Wilson and Georges Clemenceau, the French Premier who was responsible for the punishment of Germany. Lloyd George would have preferred a more lenient policy towards defeated Germany, designed to build up the new republic into a bulwark against the advance of Bolshevism; but the electors of 1918 had sent him to Paris with cries of 'Hang the Kaiser' and 'Squeeze Germany until the pips squeak' echoing in his ears, and he ended by supporting Clemenceau's vindictive proposals. On the other hand Britain was bound to feel uneasy when Wilson advocated the rights of subject peoples to rule themselves, while this country still ruled Ireland and India against the wishes of at least a great proportion of their people. In the end none of the peacemakers were quite happy about what they had done. Although they had tried to act with greater justice and realism than the statesmen of 1815, they were conscious of German and Russian resentment, and the weakness of the new nations they had created. And as it turned out their settlement lasted for only a fraction of the time that the reactionary peace of Vienna had done.

Among the representatives of small nations who went to Paris to put forward their claim to rule themselves were Irishmen. At the election of 1918 Sinn Fein had won over seventy Irish consti- tuencies, and they were determined to gain their independence now. They refused to sit in the English Parliament and set up their own assembly – Dail Eireann – instead; but they sent their leaders to Paris in the hope of getting international and particu- larly American support there. They gained nothing from the conference however, and they did not expect to get much from England's coalition government, which contained a number of Unionists. So the Sinn Feiners, not unwillingly, turned once more to violent methods of gaining their political ends. They formed an Irish Republican Army, whose character is summed up in the police description of its handsome and popular leader, Michael Collins: 'a dangerous man. Care should be taken that he does not fire first'. The English government formed a special force, known from its distinctive uniform as the 'Black and Tans', to assist the police in suppressing the I.R.A. The Tans in their turn were described by an English general as 'a pretty tough lot'. For the next two years, from 1919 to 1921, Ireland was terrorized by these rival armies. In the countryside the Black and Tans were ambushed and attacked in broad daylight. In the towns of Dublin and Cork they imposed a nightly curfew, and hunted I.R.A. gunmen through the darkness with searchlights and machine-guns. Over the two violent years honours and dishonours were about even; and shocked public opinion both in Ireland and in England demanded a settlement. Finally, in 1921, Lloyd George concluded an 'Anglo-Irish Treaty' with Sinn Fein. By its terms, Ireland

was divided: the six counties of Ulster in the north obtained a
Parliament of their own, but remained a part of the United
Kingdom; southern Ireland became the Irish Free State, responsible for its own affairs but still within the Commonwealth like
Canada, Australia or South Africa. Thus, after two years of
rebellion, the Irish nationalists gained what they had wanted for a
century. But it was not enough now for the extreme Sinn Feiners,
who demanded a united Ireland, completely free from any connexion with England. There were more years of fighting between
these extremists and the forces of the Irish Free State, and Michael
Collins was killed by Irishmen before the question was settled. In
1930 Eamonn de Valera became Prime Minister, and in the next
few years completely severed the links which joined southern
Ireland to England.

So it was that for three years after the First World War ended,
British soldiers remained under arms. They fought in Ireland and
they stayed on active service in Russia, joining the other powers
in a vain attempt to support the counter-revolution of the White
Russians against the Red. They fought in Iraq, to establish the
new state there, and in the Sudan, against a new tribal leader
known as the 'Mad Mullah'. In India, in 1919, British soldiers
massacred Indian nationalists at Amritsar. By 1921 most of this
fighting was over, but in that year soldiers were out in England
and Wales, pointing their guns at strikers and colliery pitheads.
These are sad events to record, but they were part of the precautions taken by the government against the possibility of a general
strike. Since 1918 there had been strikes on the railways and in
the coal industry, and even a threatened strike among policemen.
The strikes reflected the workers' disappointment that the post-
war years had not lived up to their promise. Wages were not rising
and hours were still long. The fact was that Britain had not
recovered her foreign trade, and everyone suffered in consequence.
There was no demand for British coal in impoverished Europe and
the United States and Japan had taken over Britain's place as the
world's supplier of textiles, steel and ships. The miners and the
railwaymen believed that British industry could be made to work
more efficiently; and government commissions appointed to
look into their grievances agreed with them. One commission

recommended 'nationalization', or public ownership of the mines; another suggested amalgamation of the railways. In 1921 the government followed the railway commission's advice, and created four great railway groups: the G.W.R., L.M.S., L.N.E.R. and S.R. In the coal industry however they allowed private ownership to continue, though they introduced a seven-hour day by law. The coalition was trying to satisfy both sides, but made friends neither among the miners nor the coal-owners. The strike of 1921 collapsed however when the other Trades Unions would not support the miners' continuing fight.

In 1922 the coalition itself broke up, and the three English political parties returned to the struggle for power, producing their respective policies for the country's economic recovery. The Liberals as always insisted on free trade; the Conservatives favoured protecting English industries against competition. The Labour Party took nationalization as its policy. At three general elections, from 1922 to 1924, the parties took their policies before the public; and first a Conservative government, then the first Labour government of Britain, then the Conservatives again, took office. The Liberal Party had become fiercely divided during the war, when Lloyd George replaced Asquith as Prime Minister. They never regained their old unity or their old appeal to the public. Middle-class people tended to vote Conservative now, and working-class people Labour. There was no place for the Liberals in this keen class division. Nevertheless the first Labour government depended entirely on Liberal support, and this effectively prevented it from carrying through its nationalizing policy.

The leader of the Conservatives after 1925 was a phlegmatic, pipe-smoking Midlands businessman named Stanley Baldwin. His refusal to become excited over affairs at home or abroad won many peoples' confidence. The Labour cabinet on the other hand was rather a shock. Its leader, Ramsay MacDonald, was moderate enough in his views, but he was a Scots clerk, and among his ministers were an engine-driver, a foundry labourer and a mill-hand – a representative group of the industrial revolution, but quite a change from the landowners and business men who had ruled England for so long! Some people feared that Britain would become a Bolshevik state before long, and this fear brought down the Labour government within a year. There was really very little connexion between British socialism, which had its roots in the ideas of men like Robert Owen and in Christian beliefs, and the communism of Karl Marx and the Russian leader Lenin, with its doctrine of revolution. Similarly British Conservatives and Liberals might bear a passing resemblance to the grasping capitalists of communist theory; but they were also the heirs of Grey and Peel, Gladstone and Disraeli, dedicated by the history of their parties to social reform as well as free enterprise. On either side of the party division however there were men who seemed to their opponents to fit into the categories of communist and capitalist, and the parties viewed each other with suspicion.

The old suspicion and hostility which existed between the miners and the coal-owners broke out into open conflict in 1925 and 1926. Bad times had returned to the pits after a period of recovery, and the miners feared that the Conservative government would support a move by their employers to lower their wages and lengthen their hours. The miners were determined to have 'not a penny off the pay, not an hour on the day', and in 1926 they decided to strike again. This time the other Trades Unions supported them, and in the spring of 1926 the General Strike which had been expected for so many years occurred. On the morning of 4 May the great cities and ports of Britain were silent. There were no trains or buses. The docks were idle. Newspapers were not delivered, because they had not been printed the night before. The strike was solid, and the country at a standstill.

Strikes like this, only much less well organized, had been the prelude to the Russian Revolution and to rebellion and bloodshed in other European countries. Some Communist observers thought that the General Strike might be the beginning of the 'proletarian revolution' in Britain; but within a fortnight the strike was over and everyone except the miners was back at work. There were several reasons for this undistinguished collapse. The first was the government's attitude: 'Is England to be governed by Parliament and the Cabinet,' as one member put it, 'or by a handful of Trade Union leaders?' The government was out to break the strike, and the man most determined to do so was the Home Secretary, Winston Churchill. The government called out soldiers and took emergency powers to seize land and buildings for food stores and military bases. They called for volunteers to help run the country's essential services, and found them, in great numbers, among professional people of the middle class and under-graduates. These volunteers drove buses and trains and carried food supplies in lorries or private cars. They unloaded ships and acted as special constables. They were the second reason for the strike's collapse. The third was a week of perfect spring weather, which made the General Strike a holiday for many people, and took the hostile edge from their feelings. There were acts of violence on both sides in the strike, particularly where the special constables were involved, and there was deep hostility in places like the East End of London and the Clyde, where strikers faced armed troops. But there was never anything like a revolution. Most of the Trade Union leaders were peaceable men, and their wish to avoid a conflict was the final reason why the strike collapsed. When it became clear that the country was keeping going and that the government would not yield to the miners' demand for security, the Trade Union leaders sent their members back to work. Only the miners stayed out, for another seven months, until hunger drove them back. The General Strike settled nothing, and it left some bitter memories, but the nine days made it clear that Britain, with its strong and constitutionally-minded middle class, was not the sort of country where revolutions occurred.

But social tension was not the only characteristic of the 1920's. It was also a decade of noisy parties and extravagant fashions. Women used their superior numbers to set the tone of life in many ways, and every one of them over twenty-one gained the vote in 1928. The twenties were also a time of material achievement: years when Britain began to catch up with Europe and the United States in the development of the motor-car and the aeroplane, and the country became electrically powered. The British Broad-casting Corporation began to play its part in instructing and amusing the nation; and for the inquiring mind there were many new things to learn. Science began a second revolution to equal or surpass that of Newton's making when Sir Ernest Rutherford described his experiments to split the atom and Albert Einstein enunciated the theory of relativity which altered the scientist's whole Newtonian concept of the universe. Biologists and psychologists probed deeply into human nature and its origins. So too did novelists and poets. T. S. Eliot and D. H. Lawrence drew diverse inspirations from the post-war years, but both attacked the mechanical civilization which threatened to engulf individuality and frustrate or pervert the true feelings of men and women. For less sensitive minds than these however the growth of industry which was resumed at the end of the twenties was the surest sign that humanity was gathering strength again after the catastrophe of the war and its bitter aftermath. Britain could no longer hope to play the leading part in the industrial revolution, but British people were recovering their confidence in their country. In politics a second Labour government succeeded the Conservatives in 1929. The memory of 1926 decided the election, but social tension was less by now. It seemed that some of the bright hopes of 1918 might come true.

The same wilful optimism occurred everywhere in Europe. Industries recovered from the post-war depression and nations showed their willingness to work together. In 1926 Germany settled her differences with France and was admitted to the League of Nations. In 1928, statesmen of many nations signed a pact to 'outlaw' war. The power behind these political agreements and the economic recovery which made them possible was not Britain however, but the United States. Although the U.S.A. was not a member of the League, American statesmen worked for international co-operation and along with American businessmen loaned dollars to Germany and the rest of Europe to set these countries on their feet. The United States bought European products and sold to Europe. America, in short, took Britain's place at the centre of a great system of imports and exports, loans and purchases, which stretched across the Atlantic and round the world. American industries throve as British industries had done in the nineteenth century, and Britain occupied an uneasy, intermediate position, half in and half out of the system, borrowing money from the United States and lending to Europe in order to enable European countries to buy British goods again. British people were not altogether happy about the way things were going, but it was hard to resist the feeling of confidence which emanated from Wall Street, the New York centre of American finance, and spread through the banks and business-houses of the world.

In the summer of 1929 however a sudden doubt seized Wall Street. Americans wondered if they would ever see profits for all the money they had invested. They rushed to sell their shares, and despite the efforts of the United States government and bankers the great edifice of lending and borrowing and buying and selling collapsed. Every country which had dealt with America felt the draught of fear. They could not sell their products or buy those of other countries. They could not repay their creditors or find work for their factories to do. Although Britain was now playing a much smaller part in the world's economy than she had done before the war, she felt the effect of the Wall Street Crash as keenly as any country. Her industries and her shipping lines lost their customers, her banks could not get back their European loans nor the government pay its American debts. British industries collapsed again and by 1931 three million men, one-fifth of the total labour force, had been thrown out of work. In these critical circumstances Ramsay MacDonald sank his political differences with the Liberals and the Conservatives and became the head of a 'National' government. The Labour Party said he had betrayed them, but at a general election the country gave the new government a 'doctor's mandate': instructions to find out what had gone wrong, and permission to take any steps thought necessary for national recovery.

CHAPTER 59

Britain and the Dictators

1931-1940

IN THE 'economic blizzard' which swept over the world after the Wall Street Crash, nations gave up their attempts to co-operate with each other and concentrated on helping themselves out of their own difficulties. The United States made no more efforts to give assistance to Europe, and the countries of Europe gave up free trade with each other and returned to protection, keeping out the products of other countries by high tariff barriers and encouraging their people to buy only from their own manufacturers and farmers. Soviet Russia, like every other country, concentrated on building up her own economy, and the threat of communist revolutions in Europe grew less; but a new threat to democracy appeared in the form of dictatorships. The democratic governments which had been set up after the war took most of the blame for the economic disasters of 1929-31, and many countries turned to follow the example of Italy, which had been governed by one party – the Fascists – and one man – Benito Mussolini – since 1922. The people of Germany, after barely a dozen years of governing themselves by democratic means, surrendered power to the Nazi Party and its leader, Adolf Hitler. And as a final sign that the age of peace and international co-operation was over, Japan began the invasion of northern China, and the League of Nations failed to check this act of aggression. The member nations and the United States, which were called on to help, would not undertake the risk and the expense of intervention in Far Eastern affairs.

England followed the same path as other nations, returning to protection after a century of free trade and ceasing to concern herself with foreign affairs. This country did not pass under a dictatorship, because the successive Prime Ministers, Ramsay MacDonald and Stanley Baldwin, were not the sort of men who make dictators; but the 'doctor's mandate' gave them almost unlimited power had they chosen to use it, and there was only a very small Labour opposition in Parliament to question the National government's decisions.

The government set out to cure the nation's economic ills by keeping out foreign competition and by encouraging home industries. They made it easy for business to borrow from banks at low rates of interest. They set up marketing boards for the sale of farm products, so that farmers could be sure of a fixed price. They tried to make new trading agreements with the Commonwealth countries, which would provide markets for English manufactures and for the agricultural produce of the Empire; but neither English farmers nor Empire manufacturers were keen on the terms proposed, and 'Imperial preference' was not a great success. In fact the government's prescriptions came second to the patient's own efforts in restoring the nation's health. Some of the great industries, among which steel and shipbuilding are examples, cut their losses and increased their efficiency by amalgamating small companies into bigger combines. Smaller industries set out to sell more to people at home; clothes and motor-cars, radios and cosmetics are examples of this increase in 'consumer goods'. One way and another, Britain regained a good deal of her prosperity in the 1930's. Before the reign of George V ended in 1936, over two million houses were being built each year, stretching in ribbons beside the roads of southern England. Along the roads sped thousands of private motor-cars; and on the corners stood department stores and cinemas. These were all signs that the standard of living was rising again for everyone – for everyone, that is, who had a bank account or a steady income.

For those who had neither the thirties were less affluent times. Now and then the people of southern England were shocked by the sight of groups of Welsh miners shuffling and singing along the kerbs of provincial towns, or the two hundred 'Hunger Marchers' making their way from Jarrow to London, in 1936. These unhappy spectacles were a deliberate and grim reminder that there were 'distressed areas' in Britain, where jobs were almost impossible to find. In South Wales and industrial Lancashire, and on the Tyne and Clyde, the reorganization of the big industries had closed down mills, factories, mines and shipyards. Unemployed men lived on the 'dole', a payment by the state based on the 'means test' – a calculation of the family's income, its savings and the value of its belongings. The dole was often more than older men had been paid each week before the war, but that was little consolation to the younger generation who could scarcely earn sufficient to support their families.

There were two nations in England again in the 1930's, but the government knew that the 'special areas' existed, and tried to provide new jobs, as well as unemployment relief. Private individuals and religious and charitable organizations like the Society of Friends were also anxious and able to help. King Edward VIII, who succeeded the conscientious and much-respected George V in 1936, promised the South Wales miners that 'something must be done about this'. But recovery was a slow process in the distressed areas, and the problem of unemployment had not been solved when the Second World War began.

Edward VIII reigned only for a short time before abdicating in order to marry an American divorcee whom English people would not accept as their Queen Consort. His brother succeeded him as George VI. The abdication and the coronation caused considerable excitement at the time; but they were unimportant when compared with the movement for Indian independence which Mahatma Gandhi was leading, or with the bitter struggles for political power which were going on in Europe. Violence had returned to Europe in the person of Mussolini, who had long ago declared that he 'did not believe in perpetual peace'. In 1935 his tanks and dive-bombers defeated the medieval cavalry of the Emperor of Abyssinia (now Ethiopia), and added his country as a new province to the African Empire which Mussolini dreamed of creating. In 1936 Hitler's troops marched into the German territories across the Rhine which the peace treaty of 1919 had declared 'demilitarized'. The League of Nations was alarmed at these actions but proved powerless to prevent them. The member nations who might have intervened to stop Hitler and Mussolini – England and France – chose not to do so, and the dictators celebrated their successes by an agreement which they called the Berlin–Rome Axis. They soon intervened together in the civil war which divided Spain between the communist supporters of the five-year-old Spanish republic and the Fascist forces of the army, supported by the Catholic Church and the landowners. In this small-scale but savage war between the forces of 'right' and 'left' the Axis powers sent soldiers, guns and aeroplanes to help the rebel General Franco, while Russia gave aid and instruction to the republicans. England remained aloof however, though British citizens fought on either side, and the Spanish nationalist forces sank English ships in the Mediterranean.

Why did England choose to keep out of these conflicts? There are several possible answers to this question. The Baldwin government was preoccupied with home problems, for one, and shrank from the possibility of another great European war which would add to the horrors and economic chaos of the last. For another, the government tended to prefer the dictators to the threat of communist domination in Europe. One of the most important reasons for non-intervention however was that the people who wanted to stop the dictators could not agree on the best way of doing so. The Labour Party maintained that England should support the League of Nations and 'collective security'. Many of its members followed the lead of the veteran socialist George Lansbury in demanding that Britain should take the lead in complete disarmament. Anthony Eden, one of the National government's experts in foreign affairs, favoured the traditional foreign policy of a 'grand alliance' of European states to preserve the balance of power against the dictators. Neither of these policies proved feasible however; the first because Britain, along with the other European powers, had lost faith in the League of Nations as a political instrument, and made a start on rearmament in 1935; the second because there was no-one for Britain to ally herself with. The United States were not interested, France, herself on the brink of political chaos, was not trusted and Soviet Russia, so far as many members of the National government were concerned, was out of the question. Negotiations went on with all these powers, but the effective policy which Britain pursued towards the dictators was different again.

It was the policy of Neville Chamberlain, who succeeded Baldwin as Prime Minister in 1937. Chamberlain believed in direct negotiation with the dictators, to make them say what they wanted and then to try to meet the more reasonable of their demands. Chamberlain was a businessman, and he thought it was possible to make business-like deals in foreign affairs as well. Like many of his friends moreover he did not believe that Hitler and Mussolini were essentially lawless men. The Chamberlain group admired the way in which Hitler had put his country on its feet again after the post-war collapse. He had given Germans their self-respect once more. When he occupied the Rhineland, they felt that he was taking no more than his due. They regretted the harsh penalties of the peace treaties, and they listened with approval to Hitler's bitter verbal attacks on Communism.

The men who pursued the policy of 'appeasement' towards Hitler chose to ignore the other side of the coin. They did not take notice of his venomous attacks on the Jewish race, or the brutality of his storm-troopers towards them and his political opponents. They applauded the brilliant German organization of the 1936 Olympic Games, but ignored the equally efficient organization of concentration camps and political purges; and they woefully misjudged Hitler's other achievements. It was true that he had rebuilt German industry – but on a diet of rearmament. It was true that he instilled pride in his Nazi followers – but it was the arrogant pride of the 'Herrenvolk', a master-race destined to rule the world. Hitler was not content with getting back the territories lost at the peace conference; he intended to conquer the whole of eastern Europe, as 'living-space' for the master-race. The pride and energy of Germany were being perverted to serve the ambitions of Hitler, and his schemes of power threatened the freedom and even the existence of millions of people; but Chamberlain and the small group of men who shared power with him hoped to negotiate with the Führer and keep the peace.

Early in 1938 German troops occupied Austria without opposition and added the country in which Hitler had been born to his 'Third Reich'. A few weeks later Hitler began the violent propaganda attack which was the certain prelude to another act of aggression and conquest. This time the threatened area was the Sudetenland: the salient of Czechoslovakia which protruded between Germany and Austria and contained over three million

German-speaking people. Hitler made the alleged sufferings of this minority the pretext for his attack on Czechoslovakia; but in reality he coveted the Sudetenland for its strategic importance in his eastward drive and the great Skoda armaments works which lay within its boundaries.

Czechoslovakia, almost alone among the new states of Europe created in 1919, had remained a democracy since its foundation. It was a country equipped with industry and resources to maintain itself, and it had a military alliance with France to help in its defence. The Czechs prepared to resist Hitler's demands, and the French to support them. Chamberlain regarded the crisis as 'a quarrel in a faraway country between people of whom we know nothing', but he realized that a war was likely, and that Britain could not stay out of a conflict between France and Germany. Intent on appeasing Hitler and preventing war, he flew to Munich to meet the Führer. Daladier, the Prime Minister of France, joined in their discussions, and Mussolini was brought in to make up numbers on the Axis side. The Czechs were not consulted, but as a result of the Munich conference they were ordered by the western powers to give up the Sudetenland in return for a promise from Hitler that this would be the last of his territorial demands.

Deprived of support, the Czechs submitted; Chamberlain came home to a tremendous welcome as the man who had achieved 'peace for our time'. Hitler waited until the spring of 1939 and then sent the German army and their sinister companions, the Gestapo, to take over the whole of defenceless Czechoslovakia. So far as he was concerned the lesson of Munich was that neither France nor Britain would fight to stop him. 'My enemies are worms,' he said, 'I saw them at Munich.' He prepared for the next step in conquest: the invasion of Poland. He concluded a ten-year pact of non-aggression with Russia, and a 'pact of steel' with Mussolini. At this late stage however the worm turned. The British government promised its support to Poland and two of Hitler's next likely victims, Roumania and Greece. These promises did not stop Hitler. At dawn on 1 September 1939 his bombers and panzer divisions raced across the frontier of Poland, catching the Polish Air Force on the ground, destroying Warsaw by bombing, and crushing the valiant resistance of Polish lancers and infantry.

On 3 September however Britain declared war on Germany and France did the same.

And so, twenty-one years after the 'war to end all wars', Britain was at war again. This time however there was little doubt that war was necessary and justified: it was a straightforward test of the strength of freedom to prevail against aggression, and freedom was ill-prepared to meet the threat. For seven months however, while Poland fell to attacks by Germans from the west and Russians from the east, and while Germans invaded Denmark and Norway, the war did not touch British people personally. During this pause Britain counted her resources, and hurried to make up for years of half-hearted preparation for a war which she had hoped might never come. By the spring of 1940 a small force of British troops and aeroplanes was in France, ready to resist the German attack which was sure to materialize. More troops went to Trondheim and Narvik fiord in an attempt to support Norwegian resistance. At home it became clear that the government of appeasement would not suffice for the great struggle ahead, and on 10 May Chamberlain was succeeded as Prime Minister by Winston Churchill, the strong man of the General Strike whose truculence had kept him out of office since.

Churchill and his new War Cabinet, which included Chamberlain, the Labour leader Clement Attlee and Ernest Bevin, one of the Prime Minister's opponents of 1926, needed all their determination and fighting spirit when they came to power. For on 10 May German armies crossed the frontiers of Belgium and the Netherlands as the northern claw of another great pincer attack at the heart of France. To the south another army group moved into Luxembourg. The French High Command, drawing on the bitter experience of the last great war, when attack had almost always meant defeat, had prepared a strategy of defence. They had built a great fortification, the Maginot Line, which stretched from south of the Ardennes to the border of neutral Switzerland, and their best troops defended it; another army, with British support, moved north to the Belgian frontier to meet the northern pincer arm. But the Maginot Line was never tested, for the German panzers raced through the unguarded Ardennes and with their first advance cut a gap of fifty miles between the Line and the allied armies in the north. It soon appeared that there were no reserves to fill this gap, and the German armour raced on across France. Within a week they were through the Somme valley and threatening Boulogne. In the north, German bombers devastated Holland and Belgium, and German armies pressed across the Flanders plain.

The Allies could not recover from this initial breakdown of their defensive plan. By the end of May, when the King of the Belgians surrendered his country to the Germans, the remnants of the allied armies of the north were trapped between the pincer claws on a front between Calais and Ostend. Churchill gloomily foretold 'the greatest military disaster in our history'. And then, as if by a miracle – and indeed the reasons for it have never been completely explained – the German tanks halted when they were only fifteen miles from the port of Dunkirk. For forty-eight hours they left a gap between their two advancing armies, and the Allies poured through it and reached the coast. In the nine days between 26 May and 4 June, 338,226 men – British, French, Belgian and Polish, were rescued under fire from Dunkirk beach, by a fleet which included every sort of vessel from warships to pleasure craft and yachts to Thames fire-fighting tenders. The courage and resource of every man involved could not conceal the defeat nor the loss of equipment, guns and planes, but the miracle of Dunkirk steeled the British resolve to fight on until Hitler had been defeated.

For a free people, peace with Nazi Germany was impossible; and English people realized this as they stood by, for the moment helpless, while France surrendered and Hitler became master of western Europe. The Prime Minister rejected the Führer's offer of negotiation, and rallied the nation to forget for the moment the divisions between class and party which had marked the last ten years or more of English history.

'Let us therefore brace ourselves to our duties,' said Churchill, 'and so bear ourselves that, if the British Empire and its Commonwealth last for a thousand years, men will still say, "This was their finest hour".'

CHAPTER 60

Britain and the Second World War

1940-1945

'AS ENGLAND in spite of her hopeless military position has so far shown herself unwilling to come to any compromise, I have decided to begin preparations for and, if necessary, to carry out the invasion of England.'

Such was the Führer's communiqué to his forces on 16 July 1940. From now on throughout the summer the German war effort was directed at mounting 'Operation Sea-lion' – the invasion of England – in the autumn. Hitler, like Philip of Spain and Napoleon before him, assembled men and invasion craft in the ports of France and the Low Countries. Like those other would-be conquerors, he had to cope with the problems of coastal current, moon and tide, and the certain knowledge that the English fleet was waiting to stop him. In Hitler's war there was a new factor however – air-power – and Hitler possessed it. The Luftwaffe, victors of Warsaw, Oslo, Rotterdam and Brussels, outnumbered the Royal Air Force by at least two to one. To them was given the task of wiping out England's air and sea defences, and clearing the way across the Channel for Operation Sea-lion.

The Luftwaffe began by testing their opponent's strength in dog-fights over the Channel. Then, in mid-August, they began to raid airfields, ports and radar stations in southern England. From the start however they encountered fierce resistance. Fighter Command alone among England's defences had not been neglected in the appeasement years. As soon as Germany began to re-arm in 1934 the Royal Air Force had set out to keep pace with her. They had not succeeded, but since 1938 they had made a tremendous effort to catch up, and England alone among the countries subjected to the German 'blitzkrieg' could hope to defend herself in the air. In the event the Hurricane and the Spitfire, manned by young pilots of reckless courage and guided into battle from the ground by radar instruments which plotted the approach of the massed German formations across the Channel, proved a match for the hitherto invincible Messerschmitt. The British fighters were always outnumbered, but they shot down over six hundred German planes during August for the loss of about two hundred and sixty of their own. The Luftwaffe chief, Hermann Goering, stepped up his attacks until the weight of numbers was sometimes ten to one, and in September the Royal Air Force began to lose planes and pilots more quickly than Britain could afford. At this point however Goering, misled by overestimation of the damage inflicted upon the R.A.F. and stung by the damage done to his proud force, and Hitler, enraged by the retaliation of British bombers which raided Berlin at the height of the attack on Britain itself, altered their plans. The German air attack was switched from the airfields to London, in an effort to shatter England's will to resist. Although London suffered, this respite allowed Fighter Command to recover, and on 15 September the R.A.F. joined with the Luftwaffe in the decisive battle of the summer, and won it. Within the next few days Hitler decided 'to postpone Operation Sea-lion indefinitely', and the invasion fleet dispersed. Churchill was the first to say that through the summer this country had owed its safety to the 'few' – the pilots of Fighter Command and the ground staff and planners who kept them in the air.

Now it was the turn of the whole nation to reveal its powers of resistance, as Hitler turned to long-term methods of forcing England to surrender. From the autumn of 1940 to the summer of 1941 the Luftwaffe mounted the 'blitz': a nightly succession of heavy bomber raids on London, the great provincial towns of Birmingham and Manchester, the ports of Bristol, Southampton, Liverpool and Hull, and centres of war manufacture such as Coventry. While this was going on, German long-range bombers, U-boats and surface raiders moved from their bases in France and Italy and Norway to strike at convoys of food and supplies from the United States, the Commonwealth and the Middle East. By December 1940, while the toll of blitz casualties mounted at home, 450,000 tons of allied shipping were being destroyed each month. England was ill-equipped to meet the new threat from the air, for she could make no effective reply to night bombers. At sea however British aeroplanes and ships combined to track and sink the *Bismarck*, reputedly the most powerful ship afloat, and in time more British bombers struck back at German cities. Nevertheless the winter months of 1940-1 were a time of hard endurance for English people, and their armed forces fought against tremendous odds.

As soon as the invasion threat had passed, Churchill sent men and guns to Egypt. There was another danger here, that the Italian forces who had already driven British troops out of Somaliland and Libya might capture the Suez Canal. Elsewhere in the Mediterranean, Italy had launched attacks against Greece and Crete. There were friends and vital interests to be defended in this part of the world; and there was a chance, as Churchill saw it, to strike a blow at the weaker of the Axis powers. By the end of 1940 British and Commonwealth forces under the command of General Wavell had driven the Italians back to Libya. But the Germans too had realized the importance of the Mediterranean war, and in 1941 they reinforced the Italians to make sure of the conquest of Greece and Crete and sent crack forces under General Rommel to North Africa. Rommel immediately forced Wavell to retreat and recaptured everything the British and Commonwealth forces had gained except the port of Tobruk, which was vital to Axis supplies.

Supplies were the key to the war in the desert. Without the certain flow of food, ammunition and petrol, either side was doomed to surrender. First Wavell and then Rommel were able to advance from their bases at Alexandria and Tripoli respectively until they reached the limit of their supply lines – five hundred miles or so. Then the advance wavered, the enemy counter-attacked, and the advancing army turned in headlong retreat to save its supply lines from destruction. In the last months of 1941 it was Rommel's turn to retreat again before the counter-attack of a new Commonwealth commander, Auchinleck. When Auchinleck's advance had reached its limit Rommel turned again, and the second British advance became a retreat. In all this fighting, Tobruk was the vital target, for if the Axis powers captured it they would have an advance base for attacks into the heart of Egypt.

While the war in the desert swung backward and forward, and while Britain withstood the blitz and the threat to her merchant shipping, the war against the Axis powers became a world war. In the summer of 1941 Hitler launched an attack on Russia, ignoring his promise of non-aggression and pursuing his idea of the conquest of eastern Europe. His armies advanced to Leningrad, Moscow and Stalingrad before winter and the Russians held them at bay. Farther east, in the last months of 1941 Japan attacked the British colonies of Malaya and Burma. Without a declaration of war, Japanese aircraft attacked the great American naval base at Pearl Harbour, in the Hawaiian Islands, and crippled the battle fleet which lay at anchor there. Three days later more Japanese aircraft attacked and sank the British *Prince of Wales* and *Repulse* in the Gulf of Siam. Within a few months, Japanese soldiers had captured the Philippines and the Marshall Islands, both American possessions, and Singapore, the centre of British power in the Far East. Burma fell next, and British and Commonwealth prisoners of war were set to build the railway which could carry their conquerors to the frontiers of India.

Japan became the new ally of the Axis; but Britain gained new allies from these conflicts in the United States and Soviet Russia. The President of the United States, Franklin Roosevelt, had already begun to supply Britain with food and arms under the scheme of 'Lend-Lease', and the Atlantic Charter which he and Churchill had signed in 1941 showed that America shared the aims for which Britain fought. Now the whole of America's industrial power was added, along with the huge manpower of Russia as well. The forces of democracy, imperialism and communism combined in an unexpected alliance against the 'New Order' of the swastika, the fascist symbol and the rising sun. A year of crucial battles between these great alliances followed. In 1942 the United States fleet checked the Japanese advance at the battles of the Coral Sea and Midway Island. In the spring of 1943 the Russian retreat turned into an advance at the battle of Stalingrad. In the west, long-range bombers from either side of the Atlantic began to get the measure of the U-boats, and released Britain from the threat of starvation. British-based bombers stepped up attacks on the industrial centres of Germany.

Perhaps the supreme British and Commonwealth effort was

made in North Africa however. Here, by the summer of 1942, the position was critical. Rommel had taken Tobruk, and used his new base to mount an attack which drove his opponents back to within sixty miles of Alexandria. His supplies were still uncertain however, for allied aircraft and submarines, based on the island of Malta, played havoc with tankers and cargo vessels on the short journey from southern Italy to Tripoli and Tobruk. When a series of tremendous air attacks had failed to put Malta out of the war, and Hitler refused to go through with plans for an airborne invasion of the island, Rommel was forced, through lack of petrol and ammunition, to call a halt to his drive for the Suez Canal. He stopped on the line of El Alamein, in western Egypt, and here new British commanders, Alexander and Montgomery, 'hit him for six', as the latter officer was wont to say. They counter-attacked with overwhelming air-power, artillery, tanks and infantry and after two weeks of all-out attack, Australian infantry and British tanks broke through Rommel's line. Threatened with the loss of his supply lines, Rommel did what every desert commander had had to do in turn; he made a headlong retreat toward his base at Tripoli. In twenty days Montgomery chased him eight hundred miles into Tunisia; but there the British forces had to wait for reinforcements, and it was not until May 1943 that Montgomery from the south-east and the American general Eisenhower attacking from Algeria and Morocco, broke through 'the desert fox's' final resistance. They drove between the Axis forces and the sea at Tunis and captured three hundred thousand of the enemy.

The victory in the desert was in Churchill's phrase 'the end of the beginning' of the Second World War; but the total achievement of the allied powers by the middle of 1943 marked the beginning of the end for the Axis. Japan retreated from island to island in the Pacific and a British army re-entered Burma. German soldiers withdrew from Russia with terrible losses. Italy was on the verge of revolt against the leader who had failed her. For the allies, the question now was how to co-ordinate their attacks for the final defeat of the enemy; and the question was debated by Churchill, Roosevelt and Stalin and their representatives at meetings in Canada, Casablanca and Teheran. Stalin had long demanded a 'second front' in western Europe to relieve him from

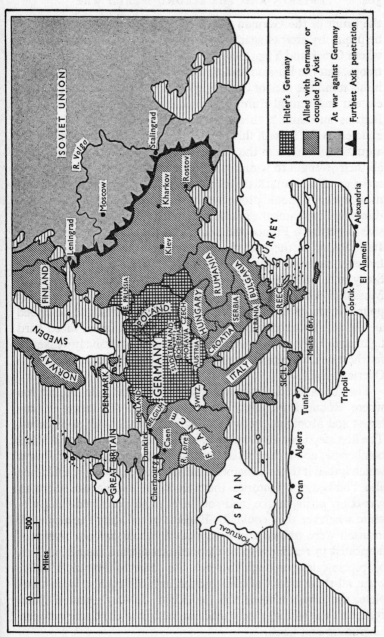

HITLER'S EUROPE, 1942

the brunt of the German attack. Churchill was now prepared to help him by attacks against crumbling Italy and in the Balkans, where Greek and Yugo-Slav partisans were still resisting German troops. But the Russian leader, who was perhaps already maturing in his mind the idea of extending communist government all over eastern and central Europe, wanted his allies to keep out of the Balkans and launch their attack against France. Roosevelt was inclined to fall in with this plan. The Americans were anxious for a quick conclusion to the war in Europe, so that they could turn all their strength to winning back the Pacific. They were ready to make an all-out attack through western Europe against Germany itself, even if it should prove expensive. Out of these agreements and disagreements came the final allied strategy: to launch a great offensive in northern France and another in the south. An invasion in Italy was to be the prelude to operations 'Overlord' and 'Anvil' however, and this began in July 1943 with the allied conquest of Sicily and went on with landings in Italy. The government of Mussolini collapsed, and free Italy joined the allies; but Germany poured in troops to defend the area which Churchill had described as 'the soft underbelly of the Axis'. The allied forces faced hard fighting in Italy, and the armies there were progressively weakened for their task, as troops were drawn away to prepare for Operation Overlord itself.

The Allies faced the prospect of stiff resistance in France too where Rommel prepared to meet his old opponents Eisenhower and Montgomery by building an 'Atlantic wall' of defences. The first step towards Overlord was to weaken this wall, and allied bombers set about the precise demolition of the canals and railways which linked it to the armaments factories of Germany itself. They also bombed the factories themselves, weakening the German war-effort at its source, and sought out and destroyed the Luftwaffe wherever they could. In England meanwhile the armies of invasion were trained and equipped. A whole harbour was prefabricated in readiness to be shipped across the Channel, and an oil pipeline long enough to reach the shore of France. Finally, when all these works of construction and destruction were complete, the invasion itself was launched. 'D-day' was 6 June 1944, and the landings were made in the bay of the Seine between Cherbourg and Caen.

The Germans were as ready as the British had been in 1940 to fight on the beaches, though their loyalty to the Führer was shaken now, and a plot to blow him up had come near to succeeding early in 1944. There was a fierce struggle before the allies broke through their defences, crossed the Seine and entered Paris in August. At the same time they learned of the fall of Rome; and in September they pressed on to enter Brussels. The people of these cities greeted their liberators with unrestrained joy. For them, years of oppression and secret resistance were over. For the people of southern England too the conquest of western Europe meant an end to the new threat of rockets launched from along the coast of Europe which had bombarded Londoners in a last attempt to break their morale. Even now however the path to final victory was not open. As autumn turned to winter the German commander von Runstedt made a strong and dangerous counter-attack through the Ardennes: the last great German effort of the war. At first he achieved great success, but his attack had no lasting effect and after Christmas the allies resumed their advance.

The Ardennes counter-offensive had exhausted the strength of the German armies in the west. In March 1945 the British and the Americans crossed the Rhine and entered a ruined country. Germany had been devastated by their bombing and Hitler himself, from his bunker refuge in Berlin, ordered the destruction of German industries to be completed. He was determined that if the victory could not be his, then his enemies would gain nothing for their efforts. So this was the end of the 'Thousand Year Reich' which Hitler had promised to build. The conclusion to all his schemes, to all the efforts of the German people, and the sacrifice of millions of lives in the concentration camps and gas-chambers was this: destruction of Germany itself. The final act was Hitler's suicide in the bunker, as the Russians fought their way into Berlin.

For the Russians were the first to reach Berlin, in May 1945, while the Americans wheeled away to southern Germany and Austria, and Montgomery received the German army's surrender in a tent on Lüneburg Heath in the north. The Russian advance to Berlin and the river Elbe was to be the cause of many post-war problems, for unlike its western allies the Red Army did not withdraw once the fighting had ended, and Germany was divided between the rival power-blocs of Communist Europe and the

West. For the moment however all that seemed to matter was that the war in Europe was over. The American commanders were impatient to transfer the full power of the allied war effort to the eastern hemisphere, where the war in Burma and the Pacific still proceeded slowly and expensively. English people were similarly anxious for the whole war to be brought to an end. For four long years they had withstood bombing and gone on short rations, sharing the common anxiety of the war along with more personal worries over relatives and friends killed or reported missing or prisoners of war. In this atmosphere of tension and impatience on both sides of the Atlantic the conditions of peace in Europe seemed of secondary importance, and the decision was taken to end the war in the Pacific by dropping first one and then another atomic bomb on the mainland of Japan. The atom bomb brought the war to an end, but killed 80,000 people in one explosion, and cast a dark shadow over the war's conclusion and the lives of the world's peoples in years to come.

In the second world war of the twentieth century Britain had once again saved herself and helped to save Europe. This war had demonstrated once again that Britain could never separate herself from the affairs of Europe. European problems were her problems and the freedom of Europe was linked with her own. In the post-war world moreover Britain had other responsibilities, as the ally of the United States, the leader of the Commonwealth and Empire and a member nation of the United Nations Organization. The problems of the world were Britain's problems now; and still she had her own. The new Labour government which was elected in 1945 set out to find a way back to economic recovery and full employment. They also intended to remove the social inequalities of the inter-war years and to complete the construction of the Welfare State. There were great tasks and fierce political conflicts ahead in 1945; but as they faced them English people could remember how their ancestors had met the different challenges of their times. They could draw examples and encouragement from over a thousand years of national history.

TABLE X

THE GROWTH OF THE BRITISH COMMONWEALTH IN THE 18TH AND 19TH CENTURIES

CANADA			1763
INDIA			1784
INDIAN OCEAN	Seychelles Islands		1814
	Mauritius		1814
WEST INDIES	Virgin Islands		1713
	Trinidad		1802
	Tobago		1815
WEST AFRICA	Sierra Leone		1807
	Gambia		1814
	Gold Coast		1850
	Nigeria	1861 (Lagos)	1900
	Kenya		1890
	Zanzibar		1890
	Uganda		1893
	Tanganyika		1922
SOUTH AFRICA	Cape Colony		1814
	Natal		1843
	Basutoland		1868
	Bechuanaland		1885
	Swaziland		1903
	Union of South Africa		1910
CENTRAL AFRICA	Rhodesia		1889
	Nyasaland		1891
MEDITERRANEAN	Gibraltar		1713
	Malta		1814
	Cyprus		1878
FAR EAST	Singapore		1814
	Straits Settlements		1824
	Hong Kong		1842
	Brunei		1888
	North Borneo		1888
	Sarawak		1888
	Malay States		1896
PACIFIC	Fiji		1874
	Solomon Islands		1893
	Tonga		1900
AUSTRALIA	New South Wales		1786
	Tasmania		1825
	Western Australia		1829
	South Australia		1836
	Victoria		1851
NEW ZEALAND			1840

TABLE XI

LIST OF PRIME MINISTERS
SINCE THE GREAT REFORM ACT

1832 Lord Grey	1886 William Gladstone
1834 Lord Melbourne	Lord Salisbury
Sir Robert Peel	1892 William Gladstone
1835 Lord Melbourne	1894 Lord Rosebery
1841 Sir Robert Peel	1895 Lord Salisbury
1846 Lord John Russell	1902 Arthur Balfour
1852 Lord Derby	1905 Sir Henry Campbell-Bannerman
Lord Aberdeen	1908 Herbert Asquith
1855 Lord Palmerston	1916 David Lloyd George
1858 Lord Derby	1922 Andrew Bonar Law
1859 Lord Palmerston	1923 Stanley Baldwin
1865 Lord Russell	1924 James Ramsay MacDonald
1866 Lord Derby	Stanley Baldwin
1868 Benjamin Disraeli	1929 James Ramsay MacDonald
William Gladstone	1935 Stanley Baldwin
1874 Benjamin Disraeli	1937 Neville Chamberlain
1880 William Gladstone	1940 Winston Churchill
1885 Lord Salisbury	1945 Clement Attlee

TABLE XII

Kings and Queens of England from Alfred

871–901	Alfred		1422–61	Henry VI
901–25	Edward the Elder		1461–83	Edward IV
925–40	Athelstan		1483	Edward V
940–6	Edmund		1483–5	Richard III
946–55	Edred		1485–	
955–9	Edwy		1509	Henry VII
958–75	Edgar		1509–47	Henry VIII
975–8	Edward the Martyr		1547–53	Edward VI
978–	Ethelred II, the		1553–8	Mary
1016	Unready		1558–	
1016	Edmund Ironside		1603	Elizabeth I
1016–35	Canute		1603–25	James I
1035–40	Harold Harefoot		1625–49	Charles I
1040–2	Hardicanute		1649–60	
1042–66	Edward the		in exile	Charles II
	Confessor		1660–85	
1066	Harold Godwinson		1685–8	James II
1066–87	William the		1689–94	William III and
	Conqueror			Mary II
1087–	William II (Rufus)		1694–	
1100			1702	William III (alone)
1100–35	Henry I		1702–14	Anne
1135–54	Stephen		1714–27	George I
1154–89	Henry II		1727–60	George II
1189–99	Richard I		1760–	
1199–			1820	George III
1216	John		1820–30	George IV
1216–72	Henry III		1830–7	William IV
1272–			1837–	
1307	Edward I		1901	Victoria
1307–27	Edward II		1901–10	Edward VII
1327–77	Edward III		1910–36	George V
1377–99	Richard II		1936	Edward VIII
1399–			1936–52	George VI
1413	Henry IV		1952–	Elizabeth II
1413–22	Henry V			

General Bibliography

The Oxford History of England, 14 vols. (one not yet published)
  all with very good bibliographies
The Pelican History of England, 7 vols.
WINSTON CHURCHILL. *A History of the English-speaking Peoples,*
  4 vols.
They Saw It Happen. A series of eye-witness accounts of famous
  events, 4 vols.

55 B.C.-A.D. 1485	W. O. Hassall.
1485–1688	C. R. N. Routh
1689–1897	T. Charles Edwards and B. Richardson
1897–1940	Asa Briggs.

G. M. TREVELYAN. *English Social History.*
'Teach Yourself History' series being published under the
  general editorship of A. L. Rowse.
The Oxford History of English Art: in course of publication.

Bibliography to Part One

A. L. POOLE, ed. *Medieval England,* 2 vols. 1958
M. W. BERESFORD and J. K. S. ST JOSEPH. *Medieval England.* An
  aerial survey. 1958.
W. STUBBS. *Constitutional History of England.* 1891.
G. BARRACLOUGH, ed. *Social Life in Early England.* 1960.
H. CAM. *England before Elizabeth.* 1952.
V. GORDON CHILDE. *The Prehistoric Communities of the British
  Isles.*
JACQUETTA *and* CHRISTOPHER HAWKES. *Prehistoric Britain.* 1937.
  (Pelican 1943.)
R. J. C. ATKINSON. *Stonehenge.* 1956. (Pelican 1960.)
Anglo-Saxon Chronicle. Trans. N. Garmonsway. 1954.

BEDE. *A History of the English Church and People. Trans.* L. Shaley-Rice. 1955.

P. HUNTER BLAIR. *Introduction to Anglo-Saxon England.* 1956.

R. H. HODGKIN. *History of the Anglo-Saxons.* 1939.

C. PLUMMER. *The Life and Times of Alfred the Great.* 1902.

G. O. SAYLES. *The Medieval Foundations of England.* 1948.

D. KNOWLES. *The Monastic Order in England.* 1940. *The Religious Orders in England.* Vol. I, 1948 Vol. II, 1955.

G. W. S. BARROW. *Feudal Britain.* 1956.

F. BARLOW. *The Feudal Kingdom of England.* 1954.

F. M. POWICKE. *The Life of Ailred of Rievaulx by Walter Daniel.* 1950.

H. E. BUTLER. *The Chronicle of Jocelyn de Brakelond.* 1949.

H. S. BENNETT. *Life on the English Manor.* 1937.

C. PETIT-DUTAILLIS. *Studies Supplementary to Stubbs' Constitutional History.* 1930.

F. M. POWICKE. *Stephen Langton.*

A. F. POLLARD. *The Evolution of Parliament.* 1926.

V. H. H. GREEN. *The Later Plantagenets.* 1955.

JUSSERAND. *English Wayfaring Life in the Fourteenth Century.* 1950.

A. MURE MACKENZIE. *The Kingdom of Scotland.* 1947.

J. E. MORRIS. *The Welsh Wars of Edward I.* 1901.

T. F. TOUT. *The Place of Edward II in English History.* Revised H. Johnstone. 1931.

J. H. RAMSAY. *The Genesis of Lancaster.* 1892.

E. PERROY. *The Hundred Years' War.* 1951.

N. COGHILL. *The Poet Chaucer.* 1949.

Bibliography to Part Two

G. R. ELTON. *England under the Tudors.* 1955. (Very good bibliography.)

CHRISTOPHER MORRIS. *The Tudors.* 1955.

J. E. NEALE. *Queen Elizabeth.* 1938.

J. C. NEALE. *Elizabeth I and her Parliaments*, 2 vols. 1953.

WALLACE NOTESTEIN. *The Winning of the Initiative by the House of Commons*. 1924. (A brilliant short pamphlet.)

WALLACE NOTESTEIN. *The English People on the Eve of Colonization*. 1954.

WILLIAM HALLER. *The Rise of Puritanism*. 1938.

J. P. KENYON. *The Stuarts*. 1958.

C. V. WEDGWOOD. *Strafford*. 1938.

C. V. WEDGWOOD. *The King's Peace*. 1955.

C. V. WEDGWOOD. *The King's War*. 1958.

SIR CHARLES FIRTH. *Oliver Cromwell and the Rule of the Puritans in England*. 1900.

MAURICE ASHLEY. *The Greatness of Oliver Cromwell*. 1957.

ARTHUR BRYANT. *King Charles II*. 1932.

G. M. TREVELYAN. *The English Revolution, 1688–9*. 1938.

C. M. TREVELYAN. *England in the Reign of Queen Anne*, 3 vols. (i) Blenheim. 1930. (ii) Ramillies. 1932. (iii) The Peace and the Protestant Succession. 1934.

CHRISTOPHER MORRIS. *Political Thought in England, Tyndale–Hooker*. 1953.

G. P. GOOCH. *Political Thought in England, Bacon–Halifax*. 1915.

H. LASKI. *Political Thought in England, Locke–Bentham*. 1920.

C. V. WEDGWOOD. *Seventeenth Century English Literature*. 1950

R. H. TAWNEY. *Religion and the Rise of Capitalism*. 1926.

SIR JOHN CLAPHAM. *A Concise Economic History of Britain, from the earliest times to c. 1750*. 1949.

D. M. TURNER. *The Book of Scientific Discovery*. 1933.

H. BUTTERFIELD. *The Origins of Modern Science*. 1949.

C. SINGER. *A Short History of Science*. 1941.

R. R. SELLMAN. *A Student's Atlas of Modern History*. 1952.

E. K. WATERHOUSE. *Painting in Britain, 1530–1790*. 1953.

JOHN SUMMERSON. *Architecture in Britain, 1530–1830*. 1953.

(Both the above volumes are in the Pelican 'History of Art' series.)

Bibliography to Part Three

J. H. PLUMB. *Sir Robert Walpole*. 1956.

SIR L. B. NAMIER. *England in the Age of the American Revolution*. 1930.

J. STEVEN WATSON. *The Reign of George III*. 1960.

T. S. ASHTON. *The Industrial Revolution*. 1950.

C. R. FAY. *Great Britain from Adam Smith to the Present Day*. 1950.

J. L. *and* B. HAMMOND. *The Village Labourer*. 1948.

J. L. *and* B. HAMMOND. *The Town Labourer*. 1950.

ASA BRIGGS. *The Age of Improvement*. 1959.

E. L. WOODWARD. *The Age of Reform*. 1938.

G. M. YOUNG. *Victorian England: portrait of an age*. 2nd edition. 1953.

LYTTON STRACHEY. *Queen Victoria*. 2nd edition. 1948.

P. GUEDALLA. *Palmerston*. 1937.

W. F. MONYPENNY *and* G. E. BUCKLE. *Life of Disraeli*, 4 vols. 1910–18.

J. MORLEY. *Life of Gladstone*. 1903.

P. MAGNUS. *Gladstone*. 1954.

J. L. HAMMOND *and* M. R. D. FOOT. *Gladstone and Liberalism*. 1952.

SIR R. C. K. ENSOR. *England, 1870–1914*. 1936.

G. M. TREVELYAN. *British History in the Nineteenth Century and after (1789–1919)*. 1937.

E. HALEVY. *History of the English People*, 6 vols. New edition 1949–52.

G. D. H. COLE. *A History of the Labour Party from 1914*. 1948.

A. J. P. TAYLOR. *The Struggle for Mastery in Europe, 1848–1918*. 1954.

C. FALLS. *The First World War*. 1960.

SIR H. NICHOLSON. *George V*. 1952.

C. L. MOWAT. *Britain between the Wars*. 1955.

SIR W. S. CHURCHILL. *The Second World War*, 6 vols. 1948–54.

INDEX

Index

Printed in Great Britain by
Taylor Garnett Evans & Co. Ltd.,
Watford, Herts.